W9-CKF-338

THE NATURE COMPANIONS

SHARKS AND WHALES

THE NATURE COMPANIONS

SHARKS AND WHALES

SHARKS

TIMOTHY C. TRICAS, KEVIN DEACON,
PETER LAST, JOHN E. MCCOSKER,
TERENCE I. WALKER, LEIGHTON TAYLOR

WHALES

MARK CARWARDINE, ERICH HOYT,
R. EWAN FORDYCE, PETER GILL

CONSULTANT EDITORS

LEIGHTON TAYLOR (SHARKS)
MARK CARWARDINE AND ERICH HOYT (WHALES)

Published by Fog City Press
814 Montgomery Street
San Francisco, CA 94133 USA

Chief Executive Officer: John Owen
President: Terry Newell
Publisher: Lynn Humphries
Managing Editor: Janine Flew
Art Director: Kylie Mulquin
Editorial Coordinator: Tracey Gibson
Editorial Assistant: Kiren Thandi
Production Manager: Caroline Webber
Production Coordinator: James Blackman
Sales Manager: Emily Jahn
Vice President International Sales: Stuart Laurence
European Sales Director: Vanessa Mori

Project Editors: Helen Bateman, Elizabeth Connolly,
Kathy Gerrard, Bronwyn Sweeney
Copy Editor: Lynn Cole
Editorial Assistants: Edan Corkill, Miriam Coupe,
Vesna Radojcic, Shona Ritchie
Project Designers: Clive Collins, Lena Lowe,
Kylie Mulquin, Mark Thacker
Picture Research: Annette Crueger

A catalog record for this book is available from
the Library of Congress, Washington, D.C.

ISBN 1 877019 03 8

Color reproduction by Colourscan Co Pte Ltd
Printed by Kyodo Printing Co (S'pore) Pte Ltd
Printed in Singapore

10 9 8 7 6 5 4 3 2

A Weldon Owen Production

One touch of nature makes the whole world kin.

Troilus and Cressida,
WILLIAM SHAKESPEARE (1564–1616), English playwright

Contents

Introduction

Over the past few decades, there has been a significant change in people's perceptions of sharks and whales. Environmental groups, marine biologists, amateur and professional divers and whale watchers have all played their part in increasing our understanding of these mighty creatures.

Sharks are not the demon-like beasts of movies and cartoons, but interesting, powerful fish that have survived from Earth's earliest history to dominate a vital niche in the oceans of our planet. Whales, once regarded as monsters of the deep that wreaked havoc on whaling ships, are now understood to be intelligent mammals with sophisticated communication systems and complex family structures.

But despite this improved understanding, there is still work to be done. The senseless slaughter of sharks and whales continues, and ignorance and fear at times override commonsense and respect. The more people take the time to observe and learn about these creatures, the better our understanding of the contribution their kind makes to us, to ocean ecosystems, and to the other species that depend on them.

Sharks and Whales is a detailed reference source that will enlighten and inspire. This book presents the current thinking on the ecology, biology, and behavior of sharks and whales and their relatives. It also takes you on a journey to some of the most beautiful locations around the world where it is possible to encounter and marvel at many species of sharks and rays, whales, dolphins, and porpoises.

If there is magic on this planet, it is contained in water ... Its substance reaches everywhere; it touches the past and prepares the future; it moves under the poles and wanders thinly in the heights of air. It can assume forms of exquisite perfection in a snowflake, or strip the living to a single shining bone cast upon the sea.

The Immense Journey,
LOREN EISELEY (1907–77), American anthropologist and writer

SHARKS *and* RAYS

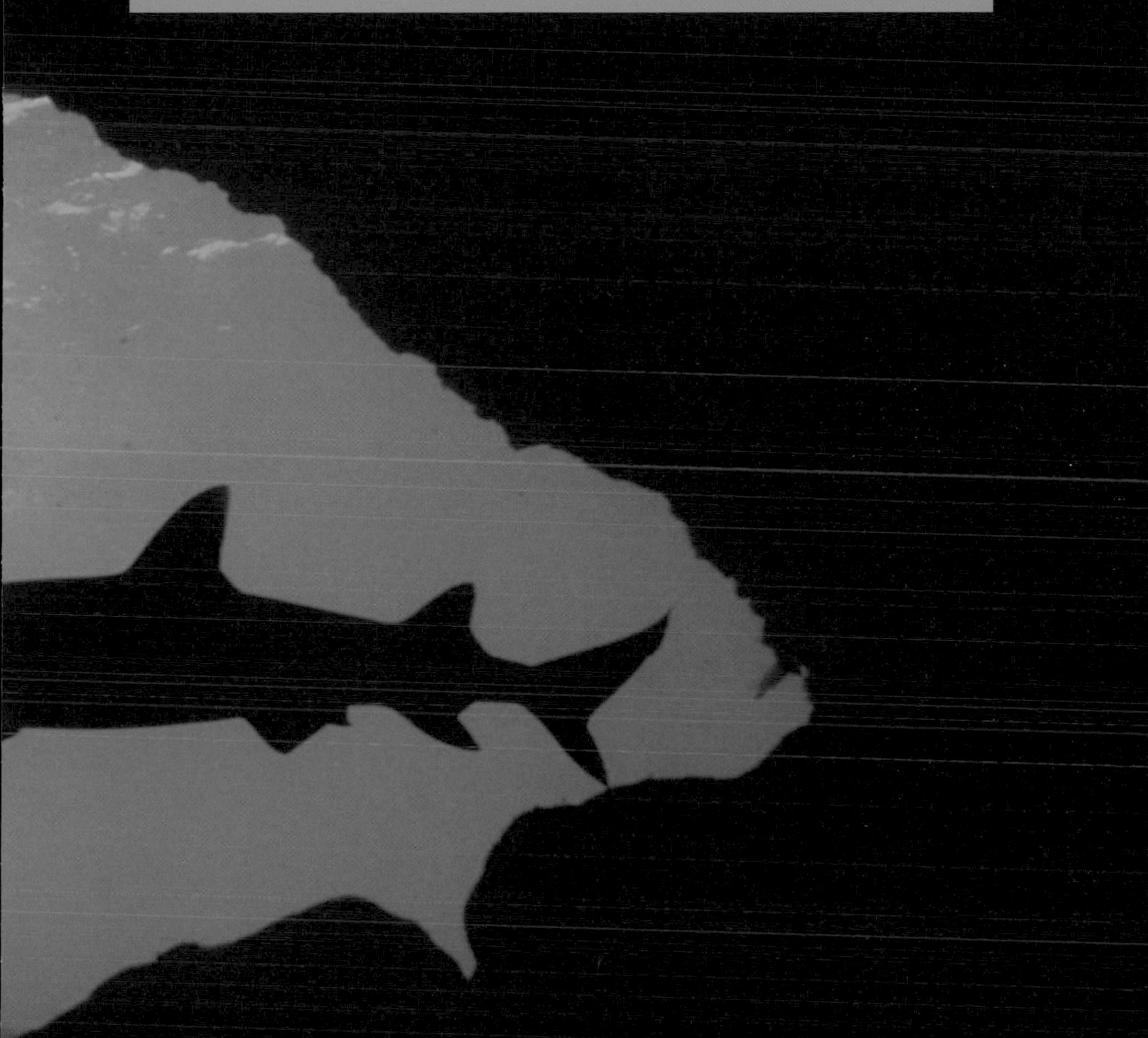

… A dark
Illimitable ocean without bound,
Without dimension, where length, breadth, and highth
And time and place are lost.

Paradise Lost,
MILTON (1608–74), English poet

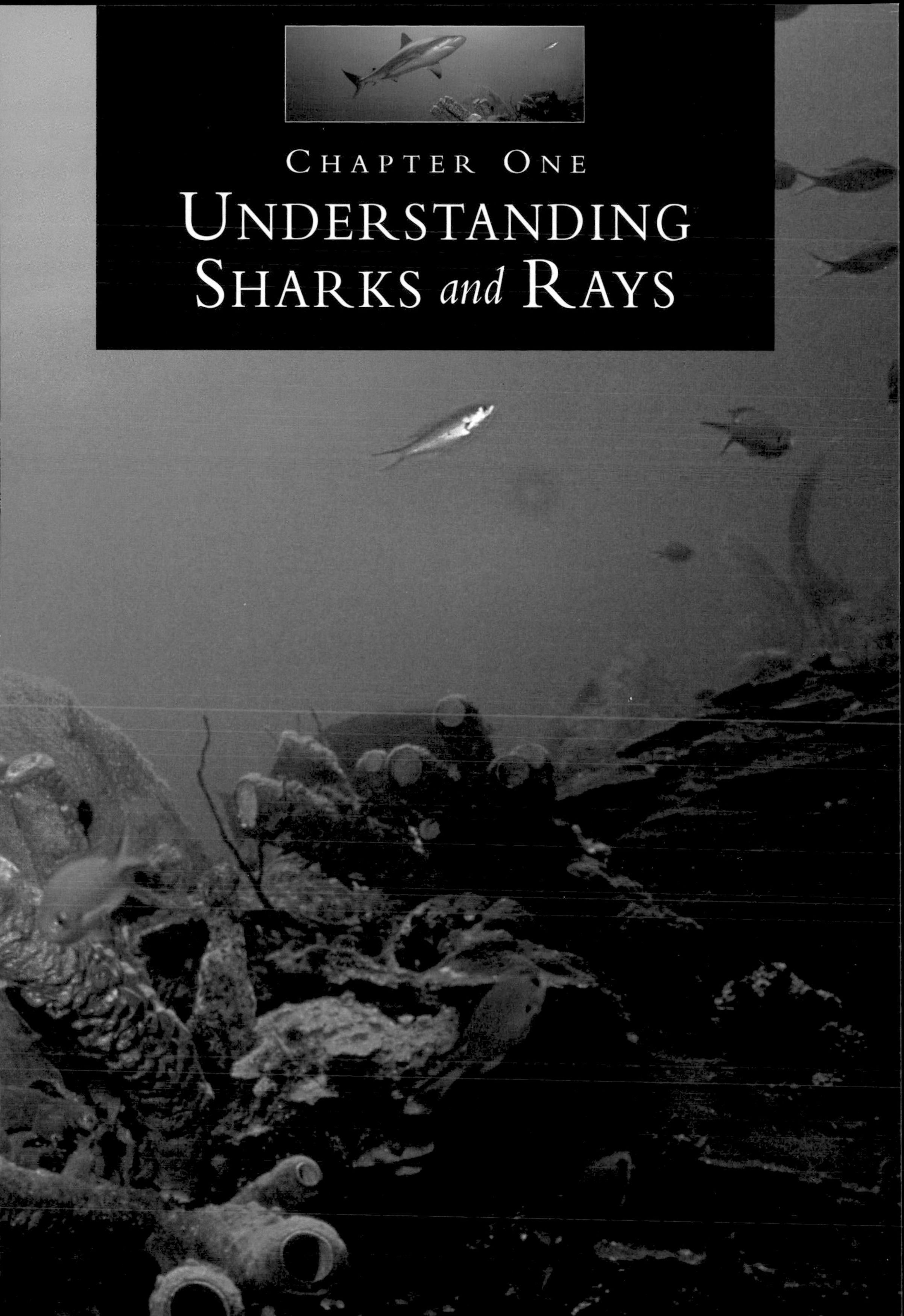

CHAPTER ONE

UNDERSTANDING SHARKS *and* RAYS

THE FASCINATING WORLD *of* SHARKS *and* RAYS

Sharks and rays touch the lives of nearly all organisms that live in their seemingly inhospitable marine environment.

From the perspective of a land-dwelling human, the world's oceans represent an intimidating, hostile, enigmatic environment. Our terrestrial habitats are dwarfed by the oceans, which cover more than three times as much surface area.

The seas are a diverse three-dimensional environment, ranging from the warm, sunlit shallows of tropical reefs to near-freezing waters of abyssal trenches. Laden with salty minerals that sting our eyes and make the water undrinkable, the oceans are quite unlike our clear, gaseous atmosphere. They are often clouded by silt or microscopic plankton, which can reduce visibility to only a few feet. So it is not surprising that humans find it an inhospitable habitat.

WATERY WORLD

Suspended in this alien world are the fishes, the most successful group of vertebrates in Earth's history. Estimates put their numbers at more than 25,000 living species, and for many, there is a rich fossil record from which we can trace their evolution.

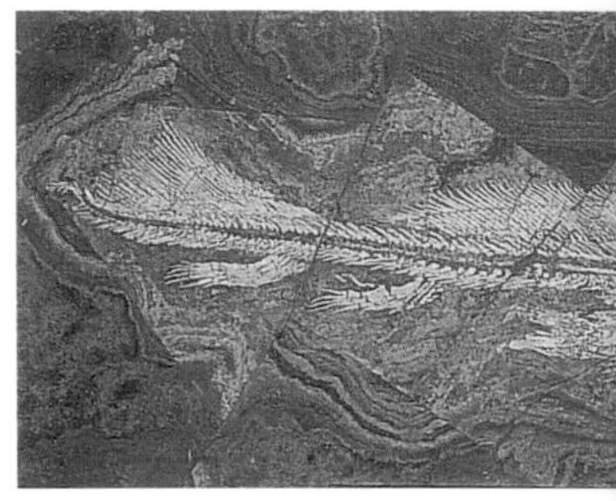

Within the group is a wide array of relatively recently evolved bony fishes that inhabit nearly every aquatic environment on Earth. For example, herbivorous parrotfishes and surgeonfishes harvest microscopic algae on tropical coral reefs, while large tunas and billfishes cruise the open oceans where they feed on small fishes and squid.

But the lives of each of these species are touched by a unique group of boneless fishes known as the sharks and rays, which can compete directly with them for food resources, or in many cases prey directly upon them.

The elasmobranch fishes consist of about 800 species of living shark, ray, and skate. Unlike the skeletons of their bony cousins, the body frames of elasmobranchs are composed primarily of cartilage, a light and flexible support material. Most of their fossil

LITTLE CHANGED *A fossil ray (above)* (Cyclobatis longicaudatus) *from the Cretaceous, and an early Permian shark fossil (left)* (Orthacanthus senckenbergianus)*, share features with descendants such as the whale shark (below left).*

record comes from a few calcified body parts, such as teeth, spines, or vertebrae. Occasionally, whole fossilized skeletons, formed under fortuitous geological conditions, provide a glimpse of their evolution between ancestor and modern form. Today, paleontologists believe the direct descendants of modern sharks date back more than 400 million years.

Design Elegance

Their long evolutionary history and lack of bone can give the false impression that sharks and rays are primitive animals. On the contrary, the elasmobranch fishes, thought to have descended from bony ancestors, show remarkable adaptations for a successful life in nearly all marine communities. Most living species have a protrusible upper jaw and specialized dentition that make them very proficient predators. The sensory system is extremely well developed, and the brain is large.

The reproductive system and behaviors are often highly specialized, and in many ways are more similar to birds and mammals than to the other fishes. These characteristics have made the sharks and rays successful organisms in a diversity of marine habitats.

The Rays

Closely related to sharks, rays (also known as batoids) fill many ecological niches. They are thought to be a sister group of the sawsharks, and are represented by more than 450 species. Some batoids, such as guitarfishes, skates, and electric rays, have well-developed dorsal and caudal fins, and strong tails. Others, such as the stingrays, eagle rays, and devilrays, have greatly reduced tails that usually have only a rudimentary caudal fin, if any. These fishes range in size from small bottom-dwelling stingarees that may be only the size of a human hand, to the massive manta rays that swim in the open ocean and are more than 20 feet (6 m) in wingspan.

They are found in nearly all marine habitats and are also common in many estuaries, freshwater rivers, and lakes. While most skates and rays eat invertebrates that live in soft sediments, some butterfly rays feed only on small fishes, and many mantas feed primarily on plankton. Much remains to be learned about the behavior and biology of these most remarkable fishes.

SHARKS AND HUMANS

Even in today's world most people are under the impression that sharks live in a secretive environment far removed from our daily lives. In reality, humans and sharks have major interactions with sometimes dire consequences for these fishes. In the early part of this century, sharks and rays supported small regional fisheries in many parts of the world. However, the recent human population explosion and improved fishing technologies have resulted in the massive harvesting of sharks and rays around the world. In addition to their food value, there is now a major international market for fins, especially those of the shortfin mako shark pictured above, which are used to make shark fin soup. There is a smaller market for cartilaginous shark skeletons used in health-food remedies. While many shark stocks have recently suffered a serious decline in numbers, some countries are starting to regulate shark harvests in the hope of maintaining a sustainable shark fishery. Individual, national, and international cooperation are necessary to ensure the shark's survival.

WHAT IS a SHARK?

Sharks share most of the general features of the other fishes, but are distinguished by some unique characteristics.

Sharks comprise only about 1 percent of all living fishes, and share nearly all the major features of their finned relatives. Like all fishes, sharks use gills to extract oxygen from the water in which they live. The body of most species is designed for hydrodynamic efficiency and usually has three types of unpaired fins (dorsal, anal and caudal) and two sets of paired fins (pelvic and pectoral).

Swimming is achieved by side-to-side undulations of the tail, which creates forward propulsion. The vertebral column, or backbone, is composed of a series of individual vertebrae held together by connective tissue, cartilage and surrounding tissues. Sharks also share with other fishes nearly all the same general features of their internal anatomy, including circulatory, digestive, reproductive and nervous systems.

But there are a number of features that separate the elasmobranchs from the other fishes. Externally, all of the shark's five to seven gill slits are visible, while the gills of most other fishes are protected by a bony plate known as a gill cover or operculum. The shark's fins are thick and relatively stiff, and lack the delicate bony spines that are found in the fins of most bony fishes. The shark's skin has a layer of tiny, but tough, dermal denticles, as opposed to the much larger flattened scales in most other fishes.

ALL RELATED
While the silvertip shark (above) in Papua New Guinea looks very different from the Pacific angelshark (left) in California, and the hammerhead shark (top of opposite page), they all share many distinctive characteristics.

THE SKELETON

Internally, the body is supported by a cartilaginous skeletal frame, complete with a protective cartilage skull, while most other fishes have a hard, more dense skeleton made of true bone. Sharks do not have an internal swim bladder to help achieve neutral buoyancy but instead rely upon their low-density cartilage, liver oils, and hydrodynamic planing to keep from sinking. Some of the most notable

NO MISTAKE *A great hammerhead shark is one of the easiest to identify.*

differences in the anatomy of sharks and most bony fishes are found in the construction of the jaw, the method of its suspension from the head, and the organization of the teeth.

The upper jaw of the shark bears a full set of teeth, and is derived directly from the palatoquadrate cartilages that form during development from the upper mandibular arch. In the more recently derived bony fishes, this structure also supports the upper jaw, but the major tooth-bearing elements develop from special bones derived from the skin.

Similarly, the lower jaw in sharks, known as Meckel's cartilage, is formed from the lower portion of the mandibular arch during development and also bears a full set of teeth in the adult. This structure is greatly reduced in bony fishes, and forms the joint in the corner of the jaw. The teeth develop from other specialized dermal bones.

In most living sharks and rays, the upper jaw is seated on the underside of the skull where it is loosely attached by ligaments and connective tissue. It is suspended from the skull by the hyoid cartilage, which attaches near the back corner of the jaw. This arrangement permits the upper jaw to be thrust out from the skull during feeding, and this is an important means by which many sharks are able to take large, powerful bites from relatively large prey.

Groupings

Like all living organisms, sharks are classified by the characteristics they share—sharks with more shared characteristics are thought to be more closely related. The differences that can separate major groups of sharks are usually apparent to casual observers. For example, hammerhead sharks are easily distinguished from all other sharks by the broad lateral extensions of the head that give them their name. However, among the different species of hammerheads, characteristics as subtle as the number of lobes on the leading edge, or the presence of a central notch on the head may be a key feature. Other detailed differences of their internal anatomy or their skeleton are usually used by scientists to identify species.

ARISTOTLE'S EARLY OBSERVATIONS OF SHARKS AND RAYS

The first critical look at shark biology in the Western world was by Aristotle (right) in his work entitled *Historia Animalium*, which appeared in 350 BC. Aristotle was a great observer and logician, and made many insightful observations on their anatomy, reproduction and behavior. For example, he recognized that sharks differed from other fishes in the construction of their uncovered and exposed gill slits. He wrote: "And of those fish that are provided with gills, some have coverings for this organ, whereas all the selachians [sharks and rays] have the organ unprotected by a cover."

He also understood the differences in the swimming mode of the sharks and rays: "Of the shark-kind some have no fins, such as those that are flat and long-tailed, as the ray and the stingray, but these fishes swim actually by the undulatory motion of their flat bodies."

And he formally recognized the sexual difference between male and female sharks: "Again, in cartilaginous fishes the male, in some species, differs from the female in the fact that he is furnished with two appendages hanging down from about the exit of the residuum, and that the female is not so furnished; and this distinction between the sexes is observed in all the species of the sharks and dogfish."

What Is a Ray?

The ray lives in an almost two-dimensional body yet continues to thrive in a three-dimensional world.

Rays and skates, known collectively as batoid elasmobranchs, are closely allied with the sharks. This remarkable group is represented globally by nearly 500 species and accounts for more than half of all living elasmobranch fishes. They are widespread in almost all bottom-dwelling communities of the oceans, inhabit offshore pelagic environments, and also extend into many inland freshwater habitats.

Batoids made a relatively recent appearance in evolutionary history, appearing some 200 million years after the first sharks. The first rays, relatives of present-day guitarfishes, are thought to have been derived from flattened sharks around the time of the dinosaurs.

Living rays and skates have some important features that separate them from the sharks. The main body is highly flattened, both on the top and bottom. Unlike most sharks, which have short and stout pectoral fins that extend from the body below and behind the head, the pectoral fins of the batoids are attached at the back of the skull, and are greatly enlarged to form a body disc. The tail of most rays is usually reduced in size and not used for swimming. Instead, locomotion comes from the undulation of the tips of the pectoral fins.

The majority of species either lack dorsal and caudal fins on the tail, or have small ones. The eyes, positioned on the top of the body rather than on the sides, provide a good view of the bottom around the animal, the distant horizon, and the waters above, but batoids are blind to their lower surface. Objects, such as prey items, under the animal are detected and located by a well-developed olfactory system in front of the mouth, and lateral line and electroreceptor systems that span much of the body's underside.

Breathing Equipment

Another major difference is the positioning of the gill slits. In batoids they are located on the bottom surface of the body, whereas in sharks they are found along the sides. Like several bottom-dwelling sharks, the batoids have well-developed spiracles behind the eyes, and these serve to take in water for breathing when

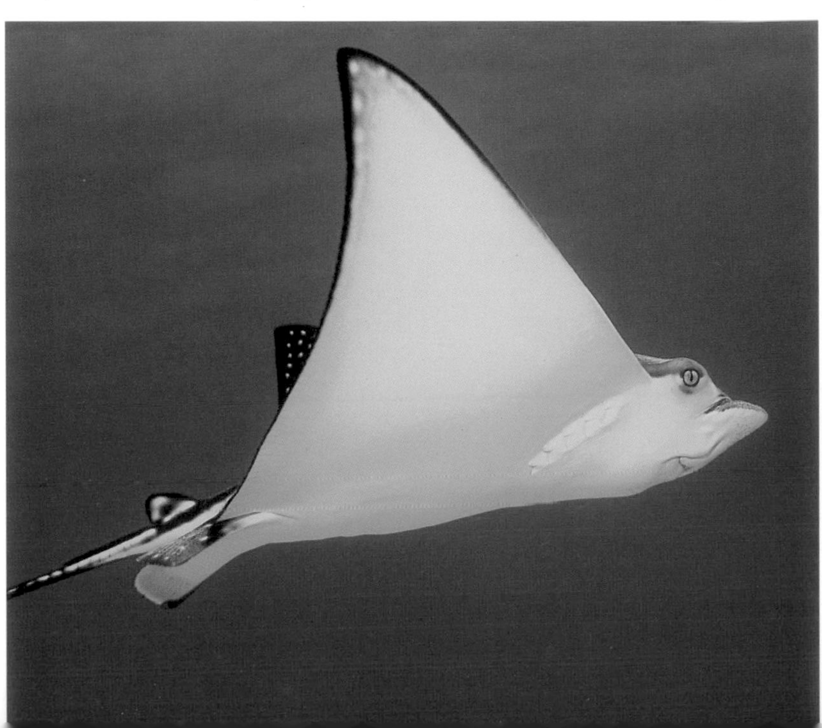

SOCIABLE ANIMALS
The spotted eagle ray (right) and the thornback skate (above) both belong to groups that engage in complex social behaviors. The whole family has a well-developed sensory system.

DESIGNED FOR A HABITAT *The large pelagic manta ray (left) sails through the open ocean, while the southern fiddler ray (below), a guitarfish, lives on the bottom.*

the ray is at rest on the bottom or the mouth is being used for feeding.

Many batoids, such as whiptail stingrays, stingarees, eagle rays, some devilrays, and others, have sharp spines on the tail. These venomous weapons are used defensively against large shark predators and also during social interactions among their own species.

Rays and skates show a wide range of body forms and sizes. Skates are characterized by a round or diamond-shaped body with a small muscular tail that bears two small dorsal fins, and a tiny caudal fin. They are common inhabitants of deep waters around the world but also occur in near-shore areas.

Skates have weak electrogenic organs along both sides of the tail, that may be used in social interactions in the wild. Electric rays usually have a rounded disc, well-developed dorsal and tail fins, and modified muscles in the pectoral fins that in some species can produce electric discharges of hundreds of volts for capture of prey and defense. Whiptail stingrays and stingarees are common inhabitants of inshore reef areas, and are major predators of small invertebrates in the soft bottom sediments, and also small fishes. Eagle and cownose rays actively swim near the bottom or up in the water column around reefs or open coastal waters, and have broad dental plates used to crush hard-shelled mollusks, such as snails and bivalves.

The large pelagic mantas and other devilrays inhabit waters of the open ocean and are distinguished by the presence of cephalic fins on either side of the mouth, which are used to channel water into the mouth while the manta feeds on plankton or small fishes.

The body shape of some batoids seems to be midway between that of a shark and ray. A good example is the guitarfishes, which have a flattened ray-like head and a muscular shark-like tail with well-developed dorsal and tail fins. A remarkable convergence can be seen between the batoid sawfishes (Pristidae) and the sawsharks (Pristiophoridae) in which the body shape is much like that of the guitarfishes, with the addition of an elongated rostrum in the shape of a toothed sword that is used to capture prey.

Sizable Brains

The rays have the largest of the elasmobranch brains, and are highly complex animals that use their exquisite sensory systems for intricate social behaviors. For example, researchers have recently shown that male stingrays in wild populations use their electroreception system to find buried mates.

Other species form large schools that can be seen making long migrations along the coastline. Divers often encounter large aggregations of rays or skates engaged in social interaction or mating activity near the bottom. These animals are easy to watch and can usually be followed for an extended period of time. From simple observations, much can be learned about the behavior of these remarkable creatures.

RELATIVES *of* SHARKS *and* RAYS

The closest living relatives of the sharks and rays are the chimaeras, thought to be descended from the same direct evolutionary lineage.

Sharks and rays are members of the taxonomic class known as Chondrichthyes, and are separated from most other living fishes by having a cartilaginous skeleton. They have a long evolutionary history dating back more than 400 million years. During this long time period, they have coexisted with many different forms of fishes, many of which are still living today.

Also within the class Chondrichthyes are the chimaeras, sometimes referred to as ratfish, elephantfish, or ghostsharks, which are the closest living relatives of the sharks and rays. There are approximately 35 species of chimaera worldwide and all are marine creatures. Recent work by paleontologists has shown that the chimaeras first appeared about 340 million years ago during the Devonian period, when they are thought have split off from the early sharks. Some of the extinct species that lived during this time looked much like their living descendants, reinforcing the long history of these fishes.

The body plan of living chimaeras is quite different from that of the sharks or rays. The head is large, with prominent eyes, and the mouth is located on the ventral surface. The skin of the body is smooth and without scales, and a network of electrosensory pores and lateral line canals is evident on the head and body. Most species have elongate bodies that taper to a small and sometimes whip-like tail.

CLOSE RELATIVES *Ratfish (above) occur mainly in deep offshore waters. They have compressed, cartilaginous bodies and rodent-like teeth.*

The first dorsal fin is movable and positioned above the pectoral fins, while the second dorsal is smaller and fixed. There is a long, sharp spine on the leading edge of the first dorsal fin that often bears a venom gland for defense. These fishes swim either by rapid movements of their pectoral fins, or by slow lateral movements of their tails. They are found in cold-water habitats on deep continental shelves and slopes but some species frequent cold shallow waters in the higher latitudes.

THE BASIC DIFFERENCES

Like sharks and rays, the chimaera skeleton is formed of cartilage with only slight calcification in some parts. They have a spiral valve intestine and possess no swim bladder. The palatoquadrate cartilage that forms the upper jaw is fused to the bottom of the skull, and does not move during feeding as in most sharks and rays. This type of jaw suspension, termed "holocephaly" or "holostyly," is a major reason for their separation from the elasmobranch fishes, and the source for their scientific name "holocephalans."

In addition, the four gill arches on each side of the head are shielded by a gill cover with a single opening behind it. The ratfish gill apparatus is located below the skull, as opposed to behind and to the side in the sharks, and there is no spiracle. Water for breathing is taken in through the large nostrils rather than the mouth. The teeth are usually arranged into grinding plates that are beak-like or knobby, compared to the numerous, small, cutting teeth found in many sharks.

LONGNOSE CHIMAERAS *The snout of the spookfish (left) is used for sensory perception. The two elephantfishes (below) belong to the same genus. Note the mucus canals and sensory pores on the head (top picture) and the distinctive plownose (lower picture).*

These are used by most species of ratfish for feeding on small fishes, hard-shelled invertebrates, or cephalopods.

Like the elasmobranchs, all male chimaeras have pelvic claspers, which are used during mating for sperm transfer from the male to the female. However, male holocephalans also have a secondary clasper located on the head known as a frontal or head clasper. This auxiliary structure is used by males to grasp the rear portion of the female's pectoral fin while the pelvic clasper is inserted into her cloaca. This sexual difference may explain why most male chimaeras are smaller than the females. A set of prepelvic claspers is also found in the male chimaera, but its function is still enigmatic. Female chimaeras lay large, tough, flask- or tadpole-shaped egg cases on the ocean bottom where the young later hatch.

THE LIVING CHIMAERAS

There are three families of living chimaeras distributed in tropical and temperate seas of the world. The shortnose chimaeras, also called ratfishes or ghostsharks, (family Chimaeridae) consist of the two genera *Hydrolagus* and *Chimaera*, and about 21 species distributed widely across the Pacific and Atlantic oceans. These have a large head, a short, usually round snout, and a body that tapers to a thin, pointed tail, often with a filament extending beyond. The ratfishes occur in deep offshore waters but sometimes move into shallow waters along the coastline.

The plownose chimaeras, also known as elephantfishes, (family Callorhynchidae) occur in the southern hemisphere, mainly off the coasts of Africa, South America, New Zealand, and Australia. This family has one genus (*Callorhynchus*) and four species, which occur in shallow to deep waters. The plownose chimaeras are easily recognized by their elongate snout, which is down-turned directly in front of the mouth. They have a small tail with an elongate upper lobe, like that seen in many sharks.

The longnose chimaeras, also known as the spookfishes (family Rhinochimaeridae), are named for the long, straight, and pointed extension of the snout. There are three genera (*Rhinochimaera*, *Harriotta*, and *Neoharriotta*) and about six species. They occur in deep waters of continental slopes and the bottom of most oceans of the world.

The Oceans—Their Habitat

The lives of the sharks and rays are shaped by the nature of the diverse habitats in which they occur.

In many ways, the ocean realms in which sharks and rays live are stable, predictable, and forgiving. The daily fluctuation in temperature is usually low because of the water's good heat retention, and mass movement of water is constant due to slow wind-driven currents or coastal upwellings.

Atmospheric storms cause destructive physical disturbances, but these are usually limited to the upper few yards of the water column, and can be avoided by short vertical migrations. The photoperiod of shallow-water species is set by the movements of the Sun and phases of the Moon. Many deep-dwelling species live in constant darkness while others are surrounded periodically by low levels of light.

Despite the ocean's many amenable features, it also imposes some unique challenges. Unlike the Earth's gaseous atmosphere, water presents a very dense environment and calls for an efficient power engine and hydrodynamic design to produce rapid movements during swimming. The high salt content of the oceans constantly removes water from the soft body tissues, and requires efficient water barriers and physiological mechanisms to replace it.

Compared to air, the oceans have a relatively low oxygen content, so ingenious oxygen-extraction factories have evolved in the gills. Relatively low visibility in the marine environment has resulted in many specializations of the eye, and the evolution of specialized sensory organs.

Different Habitats

Many habitats are recognized in the world's oceans, with distinct boundaries for the different species of shark and ray. On a horizontal scale, habitats can be distinguished as coastal and open water. In the higher latitudes, intertidal and coastal-reef habitats are composed largely of rock and rubble substrates, on which grow vast beds of macroalgae that present habitats for small fish prey and invertebrates.

Vast stands of kelp forests stretch along the shores of many temperate coastlines, where they provide a good habitat for food items and shelter. In tropical regions, living corals and coraline algae build calcium carbonate reefs that support a high density of invertebrate and fish organisms. Between these reef areas of most seas are found stretches of beaches that support a rich variety of sand-dwelling

HOME GROUNDS *The megamouth shark (above) inhabits the mesopelagic zone to great depths and is rarely seen. The whitetip reef shark (right), on the other hand, is easily sighted in the coral environment that suits its way of life.*

worms, mollusks, crustaceans, and small fishes.

Also adjacent to many temperate and tropical reef areas are sea-grass beds, which may cover the sandy bottom. These harbor a rich diversity of organisms. The productive waters of back bays and inland estuaries provide rich food resources for sharks and rays, and also important habitats for mating, pupping, and nursery grounds for their young.

TAKING COVER *A juvenile lemon shark (above) is a common sight in shallow mangrove swamps, especially those near tropical reefs. The Pacific electric ray (below) seeks the cover of a kelp forest for its foraging expeditions.*

Continental Shelves

The coastal regions of major landmasses and islands are usually surrounded by a shallow submarine shelf made primarily of sediments and rocky outcroppings. These can extend many miles seaward and hundreds of feet deep. These regions are usually inhabited by large populations of numerous species of shark, ray, and skate. At its most seaward extent, the shelf usually breaks to a descending slope, which on the upper reaches attracts large elasmobranch populations that decline in numbers with increasing depth.

Pelagic waters differ from other marine habitats by being separate from the bottom and therefore have little habitat diversity. The epipelagic zone, which begins near shore and extends out to the open oceans, ranges from the surface to about 330 feet (100 m) deep.

This zone receives abundant sunlight, which in near-shore areas with nutrient upwellings supports a rich supply of phytoplankton, zooplankton, and small planktivorous fishes. Many species of shark and ray take advantage of these highly productive waters for their food resources. In the nutrient-poor epipelagic waters far out to sea, only a few species of shark and perhaps only one ray are found.

Going Deeper

Below the productive surface waters is the mesopelagic zone, where daytime light levels fade into darkness and cannot support phytoplankton populations. This extends down to about 3,300 feet (1,000 m) and is characterized by a decline in oxygen and nutrient levels, and water temperature, which makes this a relatively inhospitable environment. As a result, many of the invertebrates and small fishes that inhabit this region make daily migrations (usually at night) up into the epipelagic zone to feed. This includes many species of small sharks and a few pelagic rays that prey on small fishes, crustaceans, and cephalopods near the surface.

And Deeper

The bathypelagic zone extends from below the mesopelagic to the ocean floor. This habitat is populated by relatively few organisms adapted for a slow, dark, cold life. Although many species of shark are collected at depths below 3,300 feet (1,000 m), few could live exclusively in this area because of lack of food. More deep-water sharks and skates are found near the bottom, especially below the mesopelagic zone. Here sharks feed on bottom dwellers and mesopelagic fishes that venture close to the bottom. There is also a considerable invertebrate community, which provides food for many species of skate.

WHERE *in the* WORLD?

Sharks and rays are found in nearly all geographic regions of the world, and there are few boundaries that can restrict their movements.

A human's view of the Earth differs considerably from that of a shark or ray. Marine organisms are free to roam at will, restricted only by the availability of resources, such as food, shelter, mating grounds, and nursery habitats.

The polar regions of the world are characterized by cold waters, relatively long annual periods of darkness, and seasonal productivity. The ice-capped Arctic regions are further limited by weak surface currents that do not promote high biological productivity. As a result of seasonal productivity, year-round food chains that can support sharks and their prey are meager.

Only a few species of shark are found in polar waters, and usually this represents an extreme of their range. Best known examples of polar sharks are the sleeper sharks of the genus *Somniosus*. The Greenland shark, *S. microcephalus*, extends its range into shallow Arctic waters to about 80 degrees north in the cold winter months, but retreats to deeper waters in the summer.

Similarly, the Pacific sleeper, *S. pacificus*, extends its northerly range into the Bering Sea. The primary batoid elasmobranchs that occur in polar regions of the world are the skates, which are usually found on the outer region of continental shelves down to abyssal depths.

FOOD ABUNDANCE

As one moves away from the polar regions of the Earth, there is a dramatic increase in primary productivity and complexity of the marine food webs. The subpolar and temperate coastal regions of the Earth are rich in inorganic nutrients where spring and summer light levels produce large phytoplankton blooms. This extra light triggers a seasonal explosion of zooplankton and the small bony fishes that feed upon them.

Basking sharks take direct advantage of this seasonal productivity and make migrations into higher latitudes near almost all large islands and continents during summer months. Here, a basking shark may filter a half million gallons (2 million L) of water per hour to collect large numbers of the abundant zooplankton, such as larval crustaceans, small copepods, and fishes and fish eggs.

Blue and mako sharks make seasonal migrations to higher latitudes to feed upon small zooplanktivores and large species, such as mackerel and small tuna. Other species, such as the porbeagle and thresher sharks, may also leave their normal epipelagic habitat to come to inshore waters during the summer to feed on the abundance of small fishes.

Similar trophic links to the distribution of sharks and rays are seen in coastal areas of

CHOICE OF HABITAT *Pacific cownose rays (above) schooling in a quiet lagoon on the Galápagos Islands. A southern stingray (right) prefers tropical shallows, such as around the Cayman Islands.*

REEF DWELLERS *Hornsharks (left) dwell in temperate, rocky, reef habitats, such as those of California's islands and the Galápagos. An ornate wobbegong (below), Great Barrier Reef, Australia.*

temperate seas. In coastal temperate habitats, a high amount of photosynthetic energy is captured during the summer by both populations of phytoplankton and also by large expanses of macroalgae that grow on the bottom.

Numerous species of hornsharks, catsharks, houndsharks, and small requiem sharks are prominent members of temperate rocky reef habitats around the world, where they feed heavily upon herbivorous invertebrates and smaller fishes. Because of their relatively small size, most of these species do not make long seasonal migrations to other areas, and can be observed year-round.

Temperate Zones

Many species of stingray and bat ray are found in shallow temperate regions where they feed mainly on large bottom-dwelling mollusks and crustaceans. Larger shark species, such as many requiem sharks, are regular inhabitants of these areas and feed upon larger predatory fishes including other small sharks and rays.

The distribution of sharks and rays in the warm waters of the tropics is often related to the features of a particular region. For example, many large sharks, such as the whitetip reef, gray reef, and blacktip reef sharks, live almost exclusively on coral reefs of the Indo-Pacific. Among these sharks one may see eagle rays swimming up in the water column, or whiptail stingrays feeding on invertebrates on the sandy bottom.

Usually found on the coral bottom are wobbegongs, catsharks, or nurse sharks, which coexist with round stingrays, torpedo rays, or guitarfishes. Up off the bottom are the whale sharks and mantas, which feed upon plankton and small fishes in nearshore waters or lagoons. Other species, such as many hound and weasel sharks, bat rays, and some whiptail stingrays, congregate near river mouths and on continental shelves in tropical regions.

Unlike many species that are associated with a particular area, most pelagic sharks and rays are circumglobal in distribution. This includes the epipelagic blue, oceanic whitetip, thresher, and mako sharks; the mesopelagic crocodile sharks; and the bathypelagic cookiecutter and pygmy sharks. Similarly, pelagic rays, such as the manta ray, are also widely distributed in oceanic waters of the world.

... all at last returns to the sea—to Oceanus, the ocean river, like the ever-flowing stream of time, the beginning and the end.

The Sea Around Us,
RACHEL CARSON (1907–64), American writer and biologist

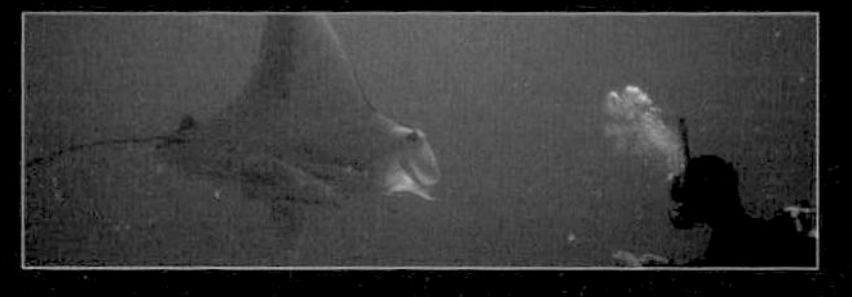

Chapter Two
Our Relationship *with* Sharks *and* Rays

Shark Fishing

Although some traditional cultures have shown respect and even reverence for sharks and rays, humans have, for the most part, considered them as creatures to be at the least exploited, or at the most exterminated.

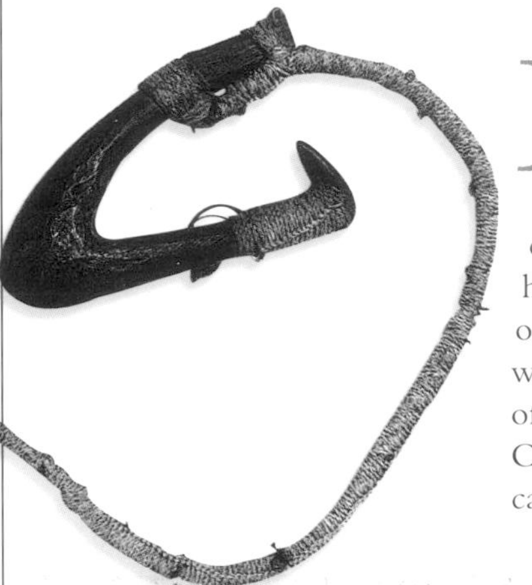

Even cultures with great respect for sharks have fished for them. It is likely that humans have caught sharks since prehistoric times. Ancient graves of the Chumash people of what is now the coastal area of Santa Barbara County in California contain nasal cartilages of mako sharks. The purpose for which these cartilages were used is unknown, but they were probably associated with rituals of some sort.

Cultures of Melanesia, Micronesia, and Polynesia have long traditions of shark fishing. The hooks they crafted especially for shark fishing can be large and elaborate. They used shark skin in drum heads, shark teeth in weapons and tools, and shark flesh for food as well as for ritual purposes.

THERE'S ALWAYS A CATCH

A wooden hook with rope attached (above left), used by islanders in the South Pacific to catch sharks. Shark teeth are embedded in these swords (right) from Wuvulu Island, Bismarck Archipelago. The pile of shark carcasses (below) was discarded after a sportfishing tournament.

WHO IS THE MORE FEARSOME PREDATOR?

From 1990 through 1996, sharks attacked 344 people worldwide and killed 44, an average "take" of about 6 humans per year. Although there are remote areas of the world where a shark attack might go unreported, death by shark is sensational enough to come to wide attention, so we have some confidence in this estimate.

According to the United Nations Fishery and Agriculture Organization (UN/FAO), humans landed at least 633,600 metric tonnes of sharks in a single year, 1991. Most fishery biologists believe that this is only a fraction of the real catch. Many countries do not report their catch to UN/FAO, and unlanded bycatch is not included. In any case, even if this number is low, humans catch many sharks every year. If the average shark caught is estimated to weigh 110 pounds (50 kg), the UN/FAO figure indicates that humans killed at least 12 million sharks in 1991 alone. And we have every reason to believe that shark fishing has increased in the past five years.

For every human killed by a shark, two million sharks are killed by humans. In other words, 12,000,000 sharks are killed by humans per year compared to 6 humans killed by sharks. If we express these statistics as the score of a sports competition, it is obvious that sharks are losing disastrously. And so, in fact, are we humans, because by fishing at this rate we are jeopardizing world populations of top predators that are essential to the health of marine communities.

COSTLY DELICACY *Sharks are often taken by the unscrupulous for their fins (right) alone, which command high prices for shark fin soup. But the cost to the shark is its life. How can society tolerate such greed and waste?*

Exploitation

Modern fisheries continue to exploit a wide diversity of sharks, from small (spiny dogfish) to large (giant whale sharks), from coastal to pelagic, and from tropical to temperate seas. There is strong evidence that all shark fisheries are over-exploiting their resources. Because of their small litter size and slow rate of reproduction, sharks are particularly vulnerable to overfishing.

A wide selection of shark products (see pp. 32–3) is sold in modern marketplaces. These include fins and flesh for food, liver oil as a source for pharmaceuticals and vitamins, hides for leather, skin for abrasive sheets and for surgical skin implants, teeth and skeletal parts for jewelry, and blood components and cartilage for health-food supplements (reputed to diminish the risk of cancer). Demand for these products has varied over time, in part because of technological and cultural changes.

Fisheries

Since the mid-1980s, demand for shark products has greatly increased. As swordfish and tuna catches have fallen, fishers have, increasingly, turned to sharks. Because of demand for shark meat and for the fins used in shark fin soup, many species of sharks have come under heavy harvesting pressure in North American waters. Historically, with a few regional exceptions, there have been few commercial shark fisheries in these waters.

A significant harpoon fishery for whale sharks is now underway in the western Pacific. Scientists have plans to see whether the whale sharks of Ningaloo Reef, Western Australia, may travel to the area of this extensive fishery.

Information on the international shark trade is limited, but it is estimated that world trade of shark products exceeds $240 million. True numbers are unknown because many foreign markets do not reveal catch or trade statistics.

Protecting Species

Recently, the United States published plans to protect 39 species of shark. This Fishery Management Plan aims to reduce commercial and recreational fishing of sharks through quotas and licensing requirements. The plan also bans the practice of stripping the fins from sharks and dumping the maimed sharks back into the ocean.

Major environmental groups are also becoming increasingly concerned about overfishing of sharks and other species. In the United States, the Ocean Wildlife Campaign was launched recently as a collaborative effort involving the National Audubon Society, the National Coalition for Marine Conservation, the World Wildlife Fund, and other interested organizations. The effort is intended to increase public understanding of giant ocean fishes (sharks, tunas, and billfish) and to facilitate management measures that are appropriate.

Conservation of sharks is gaining support in many quarters. Some species, including great white sharks (*Carcharodon carcharias*), are protected in California and in Australia. Perhaps in the twenty-first century, the exploitation of the twentieth century will turn toward the reverence held for sharks by coastal cultures of long ago.

THE USE *of* SHARKS *and* RAYS

Sharks and rays are a valuable resource, but their harvesting will have to be carefully monitored and regulated if they are to be used and yet conserved.

The use of sharks and rays for meat and other products predates recorded history. Every part of these creatures has been used by humans for some purpose. As a result, their conservation is a serious problem (see pp. 38–9). In a traditional fishery in northern Australia, Aborigines continue to catch sharks and rays to prepare *buunhdhaarr*, in which the liver and flesh are boiled separately, then minced and mixed for food. They also use the stinging spines of stingrays as tips for spears.

ARTIFACTS

Shark teeth have traditionally been used in many cultures for making functional and ceremonial objects. The Maoris of New Zealand used the teeth of the broadnose sevengill shark (*Notorynchus cepedianus*) to make war weapons, and prized the teeth of the mako shark (*Isurus oxyrinchus*) as ear ornaments. Inuit people made knives from the teeth of the Greenland sleeper shark (*Somniosus microcephalus*). Today, the teeth and jaws of this shark are widely used in local curio trades, and are eagerly sought after by trophy hunters.

When Europeans first settled Australia in 1788, as well as eating shark meat, they began to extract oil from shark livers for lighting and medicinal purposes. This practice continued through the first half of the nineteenth century. Later, between 1875 and the early 1920s, sharks were used as fertilizer for Tasmanian orchards. Today, in other regions, sharks and rays are still processed into fertilizer and fishmeal to

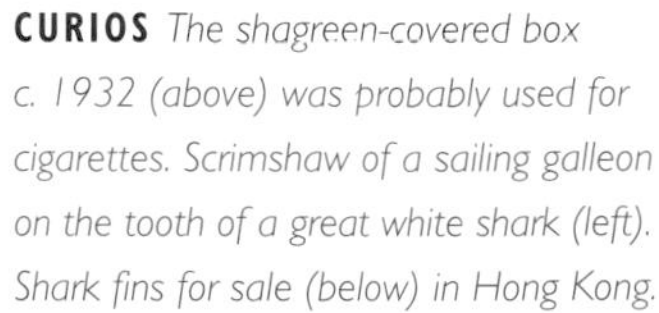

CURIOS *The shagreen-covered box c. 1932 (above) was probably used for cigarettes. Scrimshaw of a sailing galleon on the tooth of a great white shark (left). Shark fins for sale (below) in Hong Kong.*

feed domestic animals.

During the 1930s and 1940s, shark liver was in demand as a source of vitamin A, but this market collapsed during the 1950s when synthetic vitamin A became available. Recently, there has been a demand for squalene oil, extracted from the livers of several species of shark, particularly deep-sea dogfishes. Rapid development of fisheries was triggered by demand for the soupfin shark (*Galeorhinus galeus*) in several parts of the world. Considered an aphrodisiac in parts of Asia, shark fin soup has been regarded as a delicacy by the Chinese for more than 2,000 years—it became an essential part of formal banquets during the Ming Dynasty (1368–1644). The fins of many species of shark and ray are currently among the world's most expensive fishery products, with Hong Kong the acknowledged world capital for shark fin cuisine.

LIVER OIL

The oil (or lipid) content of shark liver varies from nil to more than 90 percent, depending on the species and the maturity of the shark. The lipid contains vitamin A and squalene. Vitamin A is essential for the formation of visual pigments within the retinal cells of the eye; people lacking this vitamin are likely to suffer from night blindness. Squalene, which is synthesized by sharks, has many commercial applications. It is used as a fine, high-grade machine oil in high-technology industries; as a skin rejuvenator in the cosmetics industry; and for pharmaceutical products requiring a non-oily base. Oils rich in squalene are low in cholesterol. They may also be rich in the polyunsaturated fatty acids that act as anticoagulants and keep the blood moving freely.

Varied Uses

Because it is embedded with enamel-tipped scales, the skin of sharks and rays is quite rough. Dried but untanned skin, called shagreen, is often used like fine sandpaper for polishing wood. In Sumatra, the stretched shagreen of the cowtail stingray (*Pastinachus sephen*) is used for the skins of drums and tambourines, and in Japan, it was used to bind the hilts of swords to provide a non-slip grip. During the seventeenth century, European artisans began imitating the Oriental practice of binding books with shagreen and also used it to cover personal articles, such as jewelry boxes, spectacle cases and silverware cases.

Today, boroso leather, made from the shagreen of small sharks by lightly polishing the scales to a high gloss, is expensive and in demand in specialty markets. Shark leather, made by chemically removing the enamel tips, has higher tensile strength than leather made from cattle hides.

Although it is traditionally consumed dried, salted, and smoked by coastal communities around the world, shark meat today forms a significant part of the fresh fish trade. Marketing campaigns have been introduced to overcome consumer resistance to shark meat for human consumption, and shark has often been sold under market names designed to disguise its true identity. For example, piked dogfish (*Squalus acanthias*) has been marketed in the United States as grayfish. Various shark organs are eaten in some areas, too. In the Solomon Islands, for example, all tissue other than the intestine is consumed. Elsewhere, consumption of intestine, stomach, heart, and even the skin is common. The rough scales are first removed, then the skin is prepared for the table by bleaching.

Interest in sharks and rays for medicinal purposes is also growing rapidly. In the United States, shark corneas have been transplanted to humans. Many scientists believe that extracts from shark cartilage suppress the development of tumors and now use these extracts in the treatment of cancer. Chondroiten, derived from cartilage, is used as artificial skin for burn victims, and extracts of shark bile have been found effective for treating acne. Anticoagulant bloodclotting agents have also been extracted and may be beneficial in the treatment of some cases of cardiac arrest.

THE EYE OF THE SHARK *In the US, shark corneas are proving successful as transplants for human eyes.*

Decline *in* Shark *and* Ray Populations

Fishing practices, habitat modification, and programs designed to reduce the risk of shark attack to bathers have all contributed to the decline in shark and ray populations.

All around the world, shark and ray populations are falling as harvesting continues by traditional, artisanal (which includes small-scale commercial and subsistence fishers), and industrial fishing. Game fishers, divers, and other recreational fishers also play a significant part in the harvesting process. This raises serious ethical questions about the conservation of sharks and rays (see pp. 38–9).

RAYS *Spotted eagle rays (above) with their white markings and whip-like tails. A large manta ray (below) caught in the Sea of Cortez, Mexico.*

Industrial Fisheries

Reported landings of cartilaginous fishes currently exceeds 700,000 tons a year. A small part of this consists of chimaeras, with the rest fairly evenly divided between sharks in one category and skates and rays in another. Although cartilaginous fishes comprise less than 1 percent of the world's fish catch, commercial fishing is having a major impact on shark and ray populations.

The catch has been rising steadily since the 1920s, but several fisheries began much earlier than that. One fishery off the west coast of Ireland caught basking sharks (*Cetorhinus maximus*) for some 60 years from 1770 until the species became scarce. As stocks subsequently became re-established, the fishery renewed its activities during the 1940s, but the catch had peaked and then declined to a low level again by the end of the 1950s.

A similar pattern occurred in the Norwegian fishery for porbeagle sharks (*Lamna nasus*), where the catch peaked in the 1940s and 1960s but declined to a low level by the mid-1980s.

Demand for shark liver oil during the 1930s and 1940s stimulated rapid growth of fisheries for the soupfin shark (*Galeorhinus galeus*) on the continental shelves off California, New Zealand, southern Australia, South Africa, the east coast of South America in southern Brazil, Uruguay, and northern Argentina. While profits fell during the 1950s because of a drop in demand for liver oil, the fishery had already collapsed in California during the 1940s because of a decline in the population of mature females.

In southern Australia and New Zealand, where this species was persistently targeted for the production of shark meat, catches have fallen steadily. More recently, similar trends have occurred for the piked dogfish (*Squalus acanthias*) taken in trawl fisheries off North America and in the eastern Atlantic, and for some of the larger species of shark taken off the east coast of the United States.

In addition to such specialized fisheries, trawl and tuna fisheries operating over wide areas take significant numbers of cartilaginous fishes as

HUNTERS AND HUNTED *A diver inspects the carcass of a scalloped hammerhead shark (left) caught in an illegally set net. Anglers A. Dean and B. Rogers with a great white shark (below) caught in Australian waters. One-time attack victims Rod Fox and Henri Bource look on.*

bycatch. Much of this accidental catch from bottom trawling on the continental shelves and continental slopes of the world is not adequately reported, or is discarded dead at sea. The widespread practice of removing the fins (finning) and discarding the rest of the carcasses, often while the animal is still alive, raises huge ethical questions.

Inshore Fisheries

Many of the world's unregulated artisanal and recreational fisheries for bottom-living sharks and pelagic sharks have large numbers of small fishing boats in coastal waters. This results in the overfishing of many species of shark and ray in these waters. The effects of this vary considerably among species, because many of the species harvested are distributed widely inshore and offshore, and the boats are restricted to a much smaller range, generally only a few miles from shore. The falling catch rates in these areas probably reflect falling numbers of sharks in the local area rather than a major decline in overall population.

Traditional fisheries are wide and varied but, like the artisanal and recreational fisheries, have been confined to inshore and coastal waters. Catches have been small compared with those from the industrial and artisanal fisheries and for most species have had negligible impact on populations of sharks and rays.

Habitat Modification

The stock of juvenile soupfin sharks in Port Phillip Bay, Australia, has been depleted over the years, probably permanently. As a result of intensive fishing of juveniles, the catch from the bay increased threefold between 1942 and 1944, and then fell rapidly until the early 1950s, when small sharks of the species became protected by the introduction of a legal minimum length. At this time, the western region of Port Phillip Bay, known as the Geelong Arm, was identified as an important nursery area for the soupfin shark. Given the high movement rates of adult sharks, it is surprising that this inshore area has not been replenished. It now seems likely that the reduced use of this formerly important nursery by soupfin sharks is a result of habitat modification in the now highly industrialized area of the Geelong Arm.

Shark-attack Strategy

The trend of initial decline in catch rates followed by stable numbers is a common one for most species detected in shark-fishing programs designed to reduce the risk of attack. These are in place at such centers as KwaZulu-Natal, South Africa, and in Queensland and New South Wales, Australia. Some of the trends seem to be caused by a fall in local numbers rather than by stock depletion. This theory is supported by the general pattern where catch rates are higher when fishing begins at a new site than at neighboring sites that have been fished for long periods.

OCEANS *under* THREAT

Pollution of the oceans occurs worldwide, and whether deliberate or not, it has devastating and far-reaching effects on the marine environment.

Dumping chemical, animal, and plant waste products into the oceans must be closely monitored. The shipping and oil industries must be tightly controlled to minimize their impact on marine ecosystems. And rapidly developing aquaculture practices—the cultivation of marine plants and animals for human consumption—must be regulated.

POLLUTION

Physical disturbances and pollutants can affect whole ecosystems. Some of the more obvious pollutants are sewage effluent, plastics, chemicals, and pesticides. Extra amounts of the nutrients nitrogen, phosphorus, and silicon can find their way into the marine environment, causing an increase in phytoplankton and other plant growth. An abundance of nutrients often promotes or contributes to

algal blooms (some of which are toxic), leading to clogged rivers, channels and bays, or overgrowth of corals and reefs.

Some pollutants, such as heavy metals and organic chemicals—for example, PCBs (polychlorinated biphenyls)—take a long time to break down. When these materials persist in the environment, they can adversely affect aquatic organisms and ecosystems in general. Some are absorbed from the sea water into the tissues of organisms that feed on polluted materials. Individual organisms can accumulate some of these pollutants to concentrations much higher than background levels ("bioaccumulation"). When these organisms are in turn eaten, the concentration of pollutants increases again, and so on, up the food chain ("bioamplification").

The heavy metal mercury is one pollutant that reaches high levels in sharks and rays. Mercury accumulates naturally in these organisms in the course of feeding, but when its background levels are further elevated from human sources, concentrations can become markedly increased. Very low levels of some organic pollutants ("environmental estrogens") can suppress the number of male fish produced.

OIL AND SHIPPING

More than two million tons of oil escape into the marine environment each year, and only about 15 percent of this comes from natural seepage. The remainder comes from discharges by tankers and other shipping, discharges from storage facilities and refineries, and accidental events

POLLUTION *Underwater sewer outlets (above) and industries, such as this paper mill (left) in New Brunswick, Canada, pollute the oceans mercilessly.*

CLEAN-UP *An oil spill in Prince William Sound, Alaska, is a nightmare to rectify.*

such as oil spills and ruptured pipelines. Recent wars resulted in major oil contamination in the Middle East.

Although less of a problem in open waters, hydrocarbons and other toxicants in oil can contaminate fish flesh either through direct contact or via the food chain. Impact from oil spills is most likely through damage to vulnerable coastal sea grass, mangrove, salt marsh, coral reef, rocky reef, and polar habitats. Nurseries and shallow waters where sharks and rays gather are prone to harm from oil spills.

Dredging harbors and shipping channels can stir up mud and silt that may settle in sensitive coastal ecosystems. Replenishing sand on beaches for recreational purposes can have similar localized effects.

Spread of Marine Organisms

Biological invasion of marine areas by foreign organisms is a major threat to the natural communities of plants and animals. Organisms that become attached to the hulls of ships and to oil rigs are transported with them. Ships draw sea water into ballast tanks and floodable holds for stability. This water is later discharged while the ship is underway or in various ports. Water taken aboard may contain planktonic organisms and sediments. In this way, plankton groups are spread over long distances. Surveys show that all major taxonomic groups are being introduced to new areas in this way.

These transported organisms occur at all levels of the food chain, but some of the species that keep the system in balance may be missing. Without these natural controls, certain species may proliferate to levels that swamp the new site and replace indigenous species.

Many of the inshore and coastal waters receiving ballast water are already disturbed by the effects of urbanization around ports. This makes them particularly vulnerable to invasions that further alter community structure and function. Invasion by exotic species is a very serious threat to marine habitats, and the ecological impacts cannot be fully predicted by knowing the biology of the introduced organisms and ecology in their original habitat. Inshore areas used by sharks and rays as nurseries are particularly sensitive.

FARMING COASTAL WATERS

As catches from wild fishery stocks decline, one way to supply an increasing demand for fish is by aquaculture. But such operations have many drawbacks. Aquaculture requires pollution-free waters but its practice alters and pollutes mangroves, marshlands, and other inshore habitats. Some species, such as shrimp, are farmed in such huge numbers that disease is a constant threat. When a site becomes contaminated, the industry tends to move on to a fresh location, devastating whole stretches of mangrove coastline. Escape of cultured exotic species and genetically altered strains is another worrying factor.

The most rewarding targets for aquaculture are high-value species such as prawns, shrimp, scallops, abalone, oysters, pearl oysters, salmon, and tuna. So far, there is no interest in farming sharks and rays. Their relatively low value and the small number of young produced by individuals make them poor prospects.

SHOULD *the* FISHING *be* REDUCED?

Sharks are valued as a food resource and for other products by many communities, but there are signs that current usage levels are not sustainable.

Declining catch rates from many of the world's fisheries indicate that if we continue to harvest the oceans as we are now doing, populations of many species will continue to collapse. Sharks and rays tend to be longer-lived than other types of fish, and produce fewer offspring.

After the early stages of life, when all animals are most vulnerable, sharks and rays tend to have low natural mortality. Harvesting populations of such long-lived animals that produce only small numbers of young requires special care. It is usually safer to harvest short-lived animals that produce large numbers of young.

THREATENED SPECIES *The sand tiger shark (above) and the great white shark (below) now have protected status in certain parts of the world.*

SUSTAINABILITY

Only a small proportion of the shark and ray populations can be taken sustainably each year. In southern Australia, it is estimated that with gummy sharks (*Mustelus antarcticus*), about 5 to 6 percent of the population can be taken each year without threat to the population. That means no more than 5 to 6 percent of the combined weight of all the gummy sharks in the population before fishing began. This species has a maximum lifespan of about 16 years.

For the soupfin shark (*Galeorhinus galeus*), which is known to have individuals older than 50 years, no more than about 2 to 3 percent of the population can be taken sustainably. Continued harvesting of these species at greater than the above rates will inevitably lead to collapse of their stocks. Abundant species, such as the gummy shark, can continue to be harvested sustainably at present levels of fishing. But for some other species, fishing must be stopped, or markedly reduced. For example, populations of the great white

WHAT IS SUSTAINABLE FISHING?

The low natural mortality rate and well-developed young of sharks and rays provide for remarkably stable populations compared with many short-lived bony fishes where the populations can vary greatly from year to year. In a fishery where the population size and the catch remain fairly constant over time, the population is said to be in equilibrium and harvested sustainably. Here, there is a rough balance between the number of fish recruited to the population from reproduction each year, and the number dying from natural causes and from fishing.

Fishing can be sustainable at many levels. Low levels result in small sustainable catches, and the population remains large. High levels can result in a similarly small sustainable catch, but the population becomes smaller, and the fishers have to work much harder to take the catch. The highest sustainable catches are obtained somewhere in between low and high levels of fishing. If the level of fishing is very high, such that total mortality is too high for recruitment to keep up, the population will continue to decline until it is either uneconomic to continue fishing, or the population collapses.

Mullet (left) netted by professional fishermen.

(*Carcharodon carcharias*) have been severely reduced in most regions where it occurs. As a relatively long-lived, top-level predator, producing very few young in a lifetime, it cannot replace losses quickly. In most areas, fishing for this species needs to cease immediately if the populations are to be allowed to build up again.

THREATENED SPECIES

Several species of shark that gather in coastal waters to feed or breed are regarded as vulnerable. Notably, large, maturing or mature great whites are easily caught when feeding around seal-breeding colonies. The decline in abundance of the great white has led to its being protected in South Africa and several states of the United States and Australia. The sand tiger shark (*Carcharias taurus*), vulnerable to spearfishing, is protected in New South Wales, Australia.

Dogfishes and chimaeras inhabiting the continental slopes are taken as bycatch in several bottom trawl fisheries. Much of the catch of these species is either discarded dead, or not recorded. Like many of the bony fishes studied from these deeper and colder waters, the dogfishes are likely to be particularly long-lived and to have relatively few young. Given the limited areas occupied by these species, and the intensity of fishing, some of the species of dogfish and chimaera are at risk of severe depletion in some regions.

Some of the most "at risk" species of shark and ray are those occurring in freshwater habitats. These species are more vulnerable than those inhabiting marine waters, first because the amount of fresh water in rivers and lakes is small compared with the amount of sea water on Earth. Second, tropical rivers and lakes where freshwater species occur are mostly in developing countries with large and expanding human populations. Such areas are much more vulnerable to exploitation than marine waters.

At least three species of "river shark" are now extremely rare. The Ganges shark (*Glyphis gangeticus*) is known only from the Ganges-Hooghly River system of the Indian subcontinent, although it is possible that more than one species of *Glyphis* occurs in the region of New Guinea, northern Australia and Borneo. The giant freshwater whipray (*Himantura chaophraya*) is considered endangered throughout its range and, as a result of fishing and river-habitat changes, it is critically endangered in Thailand. Sawfishes (family Pristidae), which to varying degrees occur in fresh and estuarine waters, seem to be much less common today than they were 50 to 60 years ago.

VANISHING ACT *The sawfish (right), a type of ray, is now becoming much less common.*

The Nature *of* Shark Attack

Sharks are beautiful; they are graceful; their biology and behavior are complex and fascinating. But the fact remains: some of them have bitten and killed people.

From a statistical point of view, shark attack is a very rare event. On average between 1990–6, 50 attacks per year were recorded worldwide, and fewer than 15 percent of these were fatal. To a victim, however, small statistical probability becomes total certainty. Interestingly, some survivors of even severe attacks have expressed philosophical attitudes. At least one Australian survivor, Rodney Fox, has made a career of helping people appreciate and understand the value of living sharks. Other survivors have continued their enjoyment of ocean sports and activities, declaring themselves guests in the sea, and assigning no hint of blame to the sharks.

Knowledge and good judgment are the best protection against shark attack. Good judgment means understanding the behavior of the kind of large shark that has been implicated in attack. In some cases, judgment may dictate that one avoids swimming or diving in an area known to abound with sharks.

NATURAL BEHAVIOR *Tiger sharks in Hawaiian waters often take the green sea turtle (above) for food and may attack humans by mistake. Since surviving a shark attack in 1963, Australian Rodney Fox (right) has made it his mission to work for their welfare.*

Why Do Sharks Attack Humans?

Most shark attacks on humans are prompted by two basic situations. First, there are those attacks related to threat and aggression. This kind of attack has been likened to a watchdog biting a mail carrier who enters a yard the dog is protecting. Second, there are attacks related to feeding, in which the shark approaches the victim as a meal.

Attacks in the first group can be subdivided into provoked attacks and unprovoked attacks. Provoked attacks involve the very poor judgment of divers who may, for example, pull the tail of a whitetip reef shark as it rests in an underwater cave, or attempt to hand-feed it. In the same way, any fisher who is bitten by a landed shark is considered to have provoked the "attack."

Unprovoked attacks are those in which victims blunder into the behavioral sphere of a shark and seem to threaten it with harm. For example, a surfer or windsurfer may speed into an area where a reef shark is swimming. If the surfer falls from the board near the shark, the shark will lash out to meet the perceived "threat."

Attacks motivated by feeding are most frequently

associated with large species, such as the tropical tiger shark and the temperate great white shark. It is these attacks that can result in fatalities. Tropical tiger sharks have a diverse diet but are known to feed on large sea turtles. It is probably good judgment to avoid swimming in areas where sea turtles abound. Tiger sharks are also known to feed on floating carcasses of whales. Off Maui, Hawaii, in 1995, the body of a male humpback whale killed in courtship activities attracted at least five large tiger sharks. This would have been an area to avoid!

At smaller sizes, great white sharks feed on fishes. As they mature to a larger size they change their diet to seals and sea lions. It would be advisable to avoid swimming in areas of seal rookeries.

Even smaller species of shark may be confused by stimuli that are associated with prey behavior, for example, flashing of shiny surfaces such as jewelry, bleeding, and distressed swimming motions.

Shark Bite

Any injury from a shark should be considered a significant medical problem. Such injuries can range from slight abrasions to deep punctures, tissue damage or loss, and severe bleeding. In many coastal areas influenced by human activity, puncture or abrasion of the skin can result in severe infection. In some tropical areas, serious bacterial invasions are almost certain.

Abrasions from rough shark skin can result in many tiny cuts caused by the sharp streamlining edges of the denticles on the skin of the shark. Tissue damage from shark teeth is a far more serious matter, and medical attention should always be sought. First-aid measures include staunching the bleeding by pressure and covering the wound with cloth or rubber.

Medical treatment of shark bites involves treatment for shock; careful cleaning, debriding, and closure of the injury; treatment of broken bones crushed by the shark's jaws; removal of any tooth fragments; antibiotic regimens to fight infection; and the restoration of fluids.

Some people have survived very serious shark attacks because of the initial control of blood loss. When Rodney Fox was severely bitten by a great white shark in Australia, his rubber wetsuit undoubtedly helped control the loss of blood. Joe Thompson, a surfer attacked in Hawaii by a tiger shark, lost one hand in the attack but managed to control blood loss with the other.

First Aid

The Natal Sharks Board of South Africa reports a decrease in fatal injuries through the development of a treatment procedure and the widespread availability of a specially designed first-aid kit, known as the Shark Attack Pack. The key to treatment lies in stabilizing the victim before transfer to hospital.

RARITY OF ATTACK

Risk of human death by shark attack is far down the list compared to other causes of death. Below are selected statistics for Hawaii, an area where shark attack is likely to be higher than many other places, yet where disease and accident rates are "near-normal." In Hawaii, millions of people engage in ocean activity, fatal shark attacks have occurred, and both great white sharks and tiger sharks (shown above) have been implicated in attacks.

Selected Causes of Death in Hawaii, 1996

Cause	Deaths
Total deaths, all causes	7,206
Heart disease	2,178
Cancer	1,713
HIV	145
Motor vehicles	124
Falls	58
Homicide and legal intervention	44
Poisoning	40
Drowning	40
Shark attack	0

(Two non-fatal attacks were recorded in Hawaii in 1996)

LUCKY ESCAPE *Surfer Rick Grunzinski shows the chunk bitten from his board during a shark attack off Hawaii.*

The Reality of Shark Attack

Although the chance of being attacked by a shark is statistically small, to each observer entering their watery world, it is a very real possibility.

For peace of mind when diving, it helps to have an intellectual understanding of shark behavior and the low probability of attack. It also helps to appreciate that you are entering a world that is wild, natural, and not totally predictable. Knowing that sharks share the same waters with you yet, one hopes, keep their distance, adds to the thrill of any ocean experience.

IN TROUBLE *Snorkelers (left) should swim in groups so they have less chance of being attacked by a shark. A hammerhead (below right) hopelessly entangled in a mesh beach net in Queensland, Australia.*

Knowing the Odds

Any gambler, whether card player or swimmer, likes to know the odds. To estimate the chance of an event, a statistician needs to know at least two numbers: the observed number of "hits" (in this case, shark attacks) and the number of opportunities, that is, how many people were in the water where dangerous sharks occur. Thanks to the International Shark Attack File and the biologists who maintain it, there is fairly good information on the first figure, although the estimate might be slightly low because not all attacks are reported.

Estimating total human exposure is more difficult. It is less than the world population because not everyone enters the ocean. One thing is certain: as human populations continue to increase, and as more people enter the sea for their livelihood and recreation, more people are exposed to attack.

There is also a third important figure to estimate: how many sharks of the kinds implicated in human attack are there in the sea? We don't know but, given increased fishing catches, there is little doubt that there are fewer than there were a decade ago.

In the panel at left are statistics for the seven-year period 1990–6 for selected coastal areas with significant human activity in the sea. Note that death from a great white shark and a nip on the hand from a small reef shark are both considered to be shark attacks in this summary.

SHARK ATTACK NUMBERS

Area	average number attacks/year	average number fatal attacks/year
World	50	6
Australia	6	1
New Zealand	1	0
Brazil	5	<1
South Africa	4	<0.5
Hong Kong	1	1
Japan	1	<0.5
Florida, USA	15	0
California, USA	3	<0.2
Hawaii, USA	3	<0.5
Other Areas	10	<3

Better Chances

Regardless of the estimated chances of shark attack in an area, humans can attempt to influence them, individually and collectively. Of course, individuals can greatly change the odds in their favor by staying out of the water—but

MISTAKEN IDENTITY *From a shark's viewpoint, a surfer on a board looks like a turtle or a seal.*

that's no fun. In the panel at the right, there are some suggestions for swimming safely with sharks and rays.

Group Action

Groups of people have acted collectively to reduce the likelihood of shark attack. The best known of these measures is the netting of beaches to separate the activities of people and sharks, and in many cases to catch and remove sharks from the entire area. Netting of beaches is practiced most notably in Australia and South Africa.

In South Africa, as early as 1904, the Durban City Council ordered the installation of a semicircular enclosure, about 320 feet (100 m) in diameter, to protect swimmers. By 1928, the successful barrier had deteriorated and was removed. Few attacks were recorded in the next 20 years, but between 1945 and 1951, Durban recorded 21 attacks, 7 of them fatal. Desperate city authorities adopted an Australian system first used in 1937 when large-meshed gill nets were anchored seaward of the breaker zone at many Sydney beaches. The nets trapped large sharks and greatly reduced the incidence of shark attack. In 1952, 7 gill nets, each 400 feet (130 m) long, were stretched along the Durban beachfront. In the first year, 552 sharks were caught in these nets and they were judged successful in reducing serious injuries from shark attack on local beaches.

Cluster of Attacks

A series of shark attacks at seaside resorts without nets south of Durban between December 1957 (since known as Black December) and Easter 1958 claimed the lives of 5 people in 107 days. After trying such ad hoc methods as depth-charging and the hasty construction of temporary barriers, authorities decided to expand Durban's netting operations. Soon after, the government established the Natal Anti-Shark Measures Board, now called the Natal Sharks Board, and charged it with "the duty of approving, controlling and initiating measures for safeguarding bathers against shark attacks." By March 1966, 15 beaches had protective nets, maintained either by commercial fishers or municipal employees. In 1974, the Sharks Board assumed the servicing and maintenance of net installations, and since 1982, it is solely responsible for all shark netting in the province.

Barrier netting has not been used in the United States because the practice also catches and kills significant numbers of sharks. Changed attitudes now argue against such wholesale "fishing."

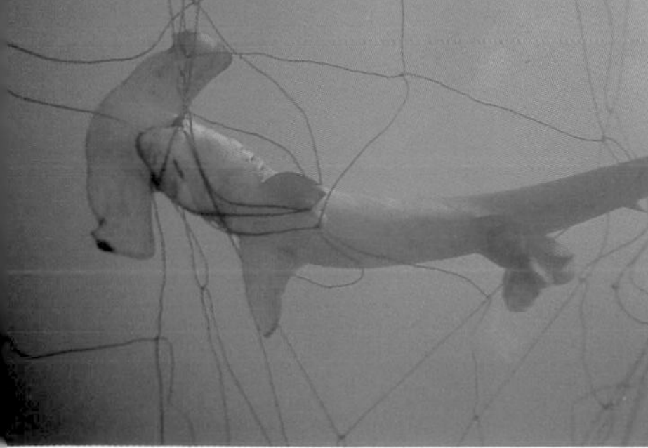

AVOIDING ATTACK

- When visiting a new area, seek local advice
- Be cautious, especially when spearfishing
- Don't swim at dawn, dusk, or at night, when sharks are most active
- Avoid swimming near flooding rivers or in murky or polluted waters
- Avoid swimming with an open wound or while menstruating; sharks are attracted by blood and other body fluids
- Don't wear shiny jewelry; reflections can resemble the sheen of fish scales
- Swim in groups, not alone
- Just because porpoises are in an area does not indicate that sharks are absent; both are predators, often feeding on the same prey

If you are attacked, report the incident to the International Shark Attack File.

LIVING SAFELY *with* SHARKS *and* RAYS

It seems that people's attitudes toward sharks are changing. Twenty years ago, sharks were widely feared and assigned little value.

Today, people may still be apprehensive, but they are beginning to view sharks as interesting, even beautiful creatures, that deserve their place in the ocean. More than one shark attack survivor has said, in essence, "I regret the attack, but it wasn't the shark's fault. The sea is the shark's home, and I am only a visitor there."

KEEPING SHARKS AWAY FROM PEOPLE

Around the world, people have attempted to lessen the chance of shark attack by controlling sharks in two ways: physically excluding them from places of human activity, and killing and removing them from such areas. Both methods have their own sets of problems. Physically excluding sharks usually involves stretching long nets across the mouths of bays with swimming beaches. This is the method of choice in Australia and South Africa, but netting is labor intensive, nets need repair and even reinstallation after storms, and sharks that become entangled in them must be removed.

In South Africa, the Natal Sharks Board provides protection against shark attack at some 60 beaches. It services more than 25 miles (40 km) of netting, spread at intervals along 200 miles (325 km) of coastline in KwaZulu-Natal.

Beach-netting is also maintained in Australia. There, as in South Africa, nets occasionally entrap other kinds of marine animals, including whales. Recently, authorities in Queensland have begun trials with acoustic signals to warn away baleen whales that may become entangled in shark nets.

DEVICES *The US Navy Shark Chasers (above) were widely used during WWII. In an anti-shark bag (below) the navy diver is safe from the nearby tiger shark.*

Fishing programs to reduce shark numbers, in attempts to reduce the threat of shark attack, were in notable use in Hawaii in the 1950s, '60s and early '70s. Such fishing programs are ecologically questionable, expensive, and probably doomed to failure. Extermination of any species, especially a top predator, is inadvisable at best, and probably not practically possible.

PROTECTING AND REPELLING

The best kind of repellent against shark attack is to avoid attracting or confusing sharks. Always avoid murky water, areas filled with prey, waters polluted by a dead or bleeding animal, and waters over drop-offs.

Choice of activity can make a difference, too. An analysis of shark attacks indicates that scuba divers are attacked more rarely than swimmers and snorkelers on the surface. In the few recorded attacks, the scuba divers have either been at the surface rather than at depth, or have been associated with unusual activity that may have excited the shark. For example, in an attack on a scuba diver in July 1995, off Monterey, California, at a midwater depth of 40 feet (12 m), the diver was driving a submarine scooter with a battery-powered electric motor. It has been suggested that the electrical activity of the motor may have confused or even attracted the shark.

COSTLY SECURITY
Swimmers frolic safely in the surf (right) at a net-enclosed inner-harbor Australian beach. A great white (below) strikes at the motorized cage of an abalone diver.

The quest for a chemical repellent was ambitiously pursued by the United States Navy and cooperating biologists during and after World War II in order to protect downed fliers and ship-accident victims awaiting rescue from the sea. Various substances were tested. A chemical preparation named "Shark Chaser" was routinely attached to life jackets. It consisted of a copper-based chemical packaged in combination with a brightly colored dye. Behavioral tests with sharks indicated that the repellent was ineffective, but it may have comforted many a survivor by its visual effect.

A physical barrier was also developed by the United States Navy to protect crash survivors from sharks. The Johnson Shark Bag was essentially a surface flotation device with a long, closed tube extending downward. The survivor filled the sleeping-bag-sized tube with water and climbed into it. The tube retained any blood or other olfactory cues. Studies showed that the bag was effective, except that sharks would still approach and investigate if stimulated by bait in the water around it.

Safety First

Although scuba divers are rarely attacked, some divers wear protective suits or carry protective devices (see p. 58) if they are exposed to sharks in the course of their work. Steel mesh suits and gloves are worn by divers filming sharks in feeding situations, and by guide-divers who feed sharks for diving shark-watchers.

Photographers and researchers also use stainless-steel and aluminum cages to protect themselves from large species. Australian abalone divers have adapted cages into mobile bottom-vehicles for protection from sharks while prying abalone from the bottom. Pole spears with explosive heads have been used to kill sharks as they approach divers. But interest in repellents and defensive devices seemed to be higher in the past decade than now.

Recently, the Natal Sharks Board of South Africa has developed a battery-powered electrical repellent called a POD (Protective Oceanic Device) (see p. 59). This is intended to protect against attack from the three species considered "most dangerous" in the Natal region, the great white, tiger, and bull sharks.

Most scientific divers and scientists are cynical about the promise of repellents. As one diving scientist has said, "The best repellent for shark attack is dry desert sand. Lie down in it and you will be safe."

SHARKS *and* RAYS *behind* GLASS

Zoos and aquariums in the past were often categorized as simple menageries, merely catering to the curious observer.

If you satisfy people's curiosity, you have the opportunity to educate them about the animals they are viewing. Millions of school children around the world visit public zoos and aquariums annually. Most of these children are simply curious. Their exposure to live, display animals, such as sharks and rays, will help them to develop not only a better understanding of wild animals but also, with supporting educational programs, a strong conservation ethic.

ANIMALS IN CAPTIVITY

Most zoos and aquariums now have education, conservation, and research programs. In fact, much of what we know about sharks and rays has come directly from public aquariums. They also assist indirectly, by allowing fisheries and other research organizations the use of their facilities and space to house their research animals.

The downside to keeping animals in captivity is often their lack of ability to adjust to the artificial environment. This can be due to inadequate or inappropriate management, or poor selection of the species to be kept. Great white sharks (*Carcharodon carcharias*), for example, have been displayed at several aquariums around the world with little success. A great deal of research is needed on the quality of the food provided for great whites and the design of a facility that can house them successfully. Fortunately, inappropriate management is becoming less of a problem as we become more aware of the needs of captive animals, and because of government regulation of zoological institutions.

When sharks and rays are kept in aquariums, it is always a balancing act to keep the animals at a healthy weight. Most sharks and rays, when well maintained in a low-stress environment, grow larger than their wild counterparts. In most species of animal, one finds a physical difference between the wild and the captive creature. In captivity, the problem is often trying to keep an animal's weight down, whereas in the wild it is quite often the opposite. This is because in captivity an animal has more food available, and needs to expend less energy to catch its prey. After a few weeks in captivity, the sand tiger (*Carcharias taurus*), for example, which is often collected in a very lean state, can dramatically increase in weight. Most sand tigers will

VICARIOUS DANGER *Part of the aquarium experience in many places is to see divers actually feeding sharks.*

feed the day they are brought into a captive environment, which is a good indicator of their ability to adapt.

Sharks in Aquariums

Most species of shark can be kept in aquariums, and with adequate husbandry they will prosper, reproducing as regularly as they would in the wild. In fact, with a few notable exceptions, sharks and rays in aquariums live longer than those in the wild. Whale sharks (*Rhincodon typus*) and basking sharks (*Cetorhinus maximus*) both feed on large quantities of plankton and are difficult to hold for any period of time because this food is difficult and expensive to supply. Being very large, these animals also require gigantic aquariums to give them adequate space for a healthy lifestyle. The king of sea beasts, the great white shark, is also difficult to display for reasons of size. Some smaller sharks, such as angelsharks (Squatinidae), need a deep, sandy or muddy bottom so that they can bury themselves.

Most sharks in aquariums are housed in multi-species exhibits, so they need to be able to survive within a mixed community. There may be as many as 20 different species of shark within one communal exhibit, as well as an assortment of rays and bony fish. If the correct species are housed together, the end result can be a spectacular exhibit with little or no aggression among its inhabitants. The ability of most sharks to live together makes them one of the most suitable large aquatic animals for display. Their ferocious reputation adds to the mystique surrounding them, and makes them the most popular of all the aquarium animals.

Rays in Aquariums

Rays are one of the most intriguing of all the animals that aquariums display. They do not usually have obvious fins, their mouth generally faces the ground, and they have a reputation of being dangerous to humans. They are also one of the hardiest marine creatures kept in aquariums. All of which makes them particularly desirable as display animals.

Of all the rays, there are only a few that present any problems in captivity. Devilrays (Mobulidae) are by far the most difficult to display. They need a constant supply of plankton and a very large aquarium because of their size. Torpedo rays (Torpedinidae) and shorttailed electric rays (Hypnidae) can be a handful for aquarium keepers, as they can deliver an electric shock capable of stunning a human. These animals are not often kept in aquariums for that reason. The main environmental requirement for most rays is a soft, deep substrate in which to bury themselves.

As with sharks, rays that are given the right conditions in aquariums will reproduce and prosper just as well as they would in the wild.

TUNNEL VISION *Displays are often set up so that sharks pass within a few feet of viewers walking through a tunnel, as at Sydney Aquarium (above); divers in the tank at feeding time (below).*

Getting Involved *in* Shark Conservation

The oceans of the world need our help. The human race is harming the habitats of marine creatures and it is up to us to stop the damage.

Knowledge and awareness are the keys to living in harmony with the diversity of life on Earth. As we learn more about sharks, we begin to appreciate their important ecological roles and to understand the consequences of our predation on them and of our disturbance, and destruction of their habitats.

Faced with drastically changed environments or catastrophically reduced population sizes, many species may change and evolve, become rare, or even go extinct. The changes humans continue to make, through the effects of our technology and our sheer numbers, gravely affect many habitats and species, including most sharks and rays.

Overfishing of sharks, especially those caught as bycatch, is of growing international concern. Few shark fisheries have any kind of enforced management controls in place. Combined with the longevity and low reproductive rates of sharks, overfishing is certain to result in rapid declines in populations.

Biologists and conservation groups recommend immediate measures to reduce fishing to sustainable levels, to stop wasteful fishing practices, and to protect fragile habitats, such as inshore breeding grounds.

People Power

Humans have the power to change the world. Of course, so do many other species. Birds transport seeds to newly created islands and forests are born. Corals and algae build reefs and islands. But the power humans possess is in many ways unique. We can make changes by accident or by design. We can try to understand the consequences of our acts or we can act in ignorance and carelessness.

Like every species, Homo sapiens interacts with and depends upon the multitude of other species with which we share the land and ocean. But unlike other species, our power to change is greatly magnified by our technology and by our overwhelming

GOOD AND BAD MANAGEMENT
Responsible control of Australia's Great Barrier Reef Marine Park (above) means that it will survive in good order for future generations to enjoy. Poor local government practices result in rubbish on beaches (below). Cleaning up after oil spills (below right) is a recurring problem.

numbers. Many of the changes we have made and continue to make are careless or heedless of consequences, motivated by greed and selfishness. Every environmental change we make, oil spills, silting of reefs, forest clear-cutting, even flushing a toilet, eventually affects the seas.

Each of us can choose to act in ways that do not harm the ocean. We can act in ways that cause the least disturbance to the species around us, realizing that every action will still have some effect. We can assure that, for example, the flushed toilet goes to an environmentally sound treatment plant; that land-grading for our house lots does not send mud into coastal waters.

One of the best ways to help is to see that our children and our fellows recognize the power we have to change the environment, but we risk our credibility if we oversimplify or preach stridently. Sharks and rays and all other creatures are in jeopardy unless we truly understand how nature works and modify our acts to have minimal consequences.

The Public Forum

We can act individually, and in concert. Consider joining one of the societies or conservation groups. Work toward having effective marine park areas and no-take zones declared. Subscribe to natural history and diving magazines and add your vote to campaigns they orchestrate for the protection of the environment. Work with the public aquarium in your area to learn about local and global marine issues and ways to act. The Internet and the World Wide Web are also great tools for learning and for sharing your observations and ideas for solving problems.

If you dive regularly, record shark sightings to help to add to our knowledge about various species. Make notes while your memories are fresh and send them off with photos, if possible, to magazines, or groups such as the American Elasmobranch Society. An important contribution you can make is to report any unusual objects or dramatic changes in numbers of marine creatures in areas you visit regularly. Such changes may indicate a problem that can be fixed by prompt local action.

Your every act affects the natural world in some way. Strive to know what these effects may be and work to make them helpful to land and sea. Live so that your effect on the world enhances its diversity and wonder.

GREENPEACE: A FORCE TO BE RECKONED WITH

An international action group, Greenpeace has been a visible force for change in the way we treat our environment for the past 25 years. Formed by a group of Americans and Canadians, it has since attracted a growing band of activists and supporters worldwide. It accepts no government or corporate funding, financing its campaigns solely from donations and member support. Some of its abiding concerns are the ecology of the oceans, and how to prevent them from becoming a barren dumping ground for waste. It is often Greenpeace that blows the whistle on dubious activities taking place unobserved far out to sea.

Greenpeace works in a non-violent way by studying problems and suggesting viable solutions, by lobbying governments and businesses to change bad practices, such as drift-net fishing, and by making people aware of irresponsible activities, such as unsustainable levels of fishing and the dumping of toxic pollutants. Sometimes, Greenpeace intervenes directly. Pictured above, supporters protest about whaling activities in Icelandic waters. Contact a Greenpeace office in your nearest major city to find out how to offer your support.

When once [the ocean deep] has been seen, it will remain forever the most vivid memory in life, solely because of its cosmic chill and isolation, the eternal and absolute darkness and the indescribable beauty of its inhabitants.

Half Mile Down,
CHARLES WILLIAM BEEBE (1877–1962), American scientist

CHAPTER THREE

IN *the* FIELD

PLANNING *a* FIELD TRIP VACATION

Careful planning is essential to ensure that your encounters with sharks and rays are safe, environmentally sound, exciting, and memorable—for all the right reasons.

Sharks and rays can be found in all the world's oceans, but because they occur in smaller numbers than other species of fish, they can sometimes be hard to locate. In some areas, access to sharks and rays may be fairly easily gained, and little planning is required. Caribbean reef sharks in the Bahamas or stingrays at Grand Cayman, for example, can be found there all year round, and day trips provided by local dive centers or dive resorts will virtually guarantee sightings. If you are fortunate enough to live near an ocean environment that sharks or rays inhabit, perhaps all you need do to see them is to don mask, fins, and snorkel, and wade in off the local beach.

Many species are not only unique to certain countries, but they may congregate in an area for only limited seasons. The whale sharks at Ningaloo Reef in Western Australia are an excellent example of this—they congregate there only during late March, April and May. To meet up with them may involve traveling long distances, and proper timing of your trip is critical.

Some sharks and rays are found in remote locations. For example, to see the silvertip sharks in Papua New Guinea or the sharks and rays in the Galápagos Islands, you may have to take a trip on a live-aboard dive boat for 7 to 10 days to reach the area.

When planning your trip, contact a dive-travel specialist experienced in dive-vacation packages. Some vacation

ERODED BY TIME *The Natural Arch near Darwin Island in the Galápagos. A great white shark (above) glides past.*

I must go down to the seas again, to the lonely sea and the sky.

Sea Fever,
John Masefield
(1878–1976), British poet

packages provide encounters with just one species, but because some of the congregations are seasonal, you may be able to combine several in the one trip. For example, if you were to take a trip to Australia during March or April, it would be possible to see gray nurse sharks in New South Wales and great white sharks in South Australia when the weather is favorable, before pursuing sightings of whale sharks at Ningaloo Reef from March to May.

Field Guides and Books

The best way to find out what options are available for shark and ray encounters is to study reference books and a well-respected field guide dedicated to this subject. The Field Guide section in this book (see p. 108) provides an introduction to 64 species of shark and 20 species of ray. The appearance, behavior, and habitat of each species is discussed. *Encounters with Sharks and Rays* (see p. 200) features 19 sites worldwide where you are likely to view specific sharks and rays.

BIODIVERSITY *Tropical coral reefs (above) and temperate zone kelp forests (left) are famously diverse communities. In both, sharks and rays are dominant predators.*

Surfing the Net

Another good source of information is the Internet. Many operators, dive-travel agencies, and divers with experience of shark and ray sightings communicate on the Net. Be aware that some of the information may not be accurate, and further research will be necessary to maximize your chances of an encounter. Animal behavior can vary, weather can be unreliable and even the best dive operator can experience problems that affect the normal operation of the tour. Nevertheless, the Internet is a good place to get ideas, information, and many contacts that can be checked out directly with the dive operators on the Internet.

Getting Closer

A good dive-travel agency will take the time to determine your expectations and level of experience before helping you plan a trip to your chosen destination.

Choose your dive-travel agency carefully. Try to ensure that the consultants are reputable and experienced, as well as environmentally responsible.

Dive Operators

Enthusiasts who want to encounter sharks and rays will find they need the services of a dive operator to organize air and scuba equipment, a dive boat, accommodation, and shark cages or other specialized equipment or support. These dive operators also know the best dive sites, the species and behavior of sharks and rays in their area, and other marine life of interest to the dive traveler. Operators who are skilled in the field soon make a name for themselves that becomes respected worldwide.

Dive-travel Agents

Dive operators are represented worldwide by specialist dive-travel agents. These consult directly with dive travelers wishing to plan a vacation or excursion that can include encounters with marine life. Dive-travel agents have first-hand experience of the area you wish to visit. They also have video promotional tapes, brochures and photographic material that provide information about the destination, the dive operator, and any special features of the area.

It is very important to make your expectations known to your consultant. A good dive-travel consultant will always try to ensure your expectations are met. If it is important to you, always ask about weather patterns and seasons. If you don't, your consultant may assume this is not an issue for you. Some shark and ray enthusiasts are unconcerned that it is cyclone season in a particular area if that is the best time for them to see sharks and rays.

Once you have agreed on the trip you want, the dive-travel agency will put together a package that will include all flights; transfers; accommodation; and a diving package that includes boats, divemaster services, scuba cylinders and weights. If you do not have your own diving equipment, check if it is cheaper to take a hire package from your local dive center or to hire at your chosen location.

If your trip involves a live-aboard dive boat, meals will be included. This is rarely the case if you are staying at a shore-based resort.

SCUBA SCHOOL *Last-minute briefing (right) from the divemaster. A dive vessel at Roach Island, off the north-east coast of Australia.*

Dive Centers

Today's dive center provides a much wider range of service than just scuba training and gear sales. The modern dive center offers specialized training; scuba equipment sales, hire and service; and underwater photographic equipment and photography training. Most important, it offers group trips guided by an experienced tour leader/divemaster. Many dive centers have a travel consultant on the staff who will understand your needs and expectations. The dive operators also have trained and experienced staff at the dive destinations who can provide information to clients through their local dive centers.

UNLIMITED GEAR *is available from dive centers such as this (left). Live-aboard dive boats, like the* Telita *(below), offer divers every comfort.*

Group Travel

There are many advantages to participating in a group diving vacation. The solo dive traveler cannot take advantage of the experience of a tour leader who has local knowledge of the area, and the ability to smooth out occasional difficulties during the trip. Dive-tour leaders are often qualified divemasters or instructors who have an intimate knowledge of unique marine life and shark or ray behavior. They are skilled in helping group members improve their diving skills during the trip. Group trips are also very social, and new divers will soon feel welcomed into the group.

Live-aboard versus Shore-based Diving

At many locations that are known as "hot spots" for sharks and rays, there is a choice of staying at a shore-based resort or participating in a 7 to 10 day trip on a live-aboard dive boat.

The main advantage of shore-based facilities is a greater variety of other interests that may suit non-diving partners and children. Also, there is usually the option of a shorter stay and fewer dives, which makes a budget vacation possible.

Live-aboards, however, provide the best value for money. Your trip aboard will include unlimited diving, all meals and refreshments, a greater range of dive sites, and much more opportunity to meet special creatures—such as sharks and rays. Going diving on a live-aboard trip is much simpler and more comfortable. The vessel is often at the dive site for many hours, so divers can choose their own dive times. Equipment is carried on board, and showers and food are readily available. Live-aboard dive groups are smaller and more intimate.

Keep in mind that the quality and performance of the various dive operators can often differ greatly. Ask for recommendations from your dive center or dive-travel agency, or from friends who have already experienced enjoyable trips. In the highly competitive world of the diving industry, if one deal is cheaper than another, be wary. There is always a very good reason for it.

ENCOUNTERS *with* SHARKS *and* RAYS

For the most part, sharks and rays do not pose a threat to humans. They are not aggressive animals—they are usually prepared to live and let live.

Having swum among sharks for generations, indigenous people of Polynesia and Melanesia are well aware of their behavior. Yet they do not live in fear of them, and shark attacks among these people are very rare. They have a spiritual relationship with these sea creatures and will not kill them. In some cases, they believe that sharks are the reincarnated souls of their deceased family members.

Most other cultures do not share this attitude toward sharks and rays, being, at the very least, wary of these creatures. Indeed, if you are snorkeling or diving in areas where you are likely to encounter sharks and rays, you should be especially careful. There are a number of precautions you should take, and guidelines to follow.

KNOWING THE QUARRY *People of Papua New Guinea (right) are on good terms with sharks. The silvertip shark (below) is territorial and not to be trifled with. This giant black stingray (far right) was seen in Queensland, Australia, and the zebra shark (top right) in the Red Sea.*

GUIDELINES FOR SHARK AND RAY ENCOUNTERS

- Never panic. Most approaches by sharks and rays are motivated by simple curiosity. Do not assume that you are in trouble.
- Maintain eye contact. If you want to retreat, do it in a slow, controlled manner.
- Don't be afraid to move toward these creatures. Move slowly so as not to intimidate them. They are wary of other large predators, and they will often swim away rapidly. The exception to this is a reef shark defending its territory. Do not approach any reef shark that is swimming with an exaggerated side-to-side motion with its back hunched, and its pectoral fins down. Instead, calmly and quickly leave the area.
- Avoid periods of low light (dawn or dusk) and low visibility. At these times, a shark could mistake you for its natural prey.
- On the surface, avoid excess splashing. To a shark, you will appear to be a disabled animal and you will attract the wrong kind of interest. Underwater, swim with slow, deliberate strokes so that you will appear to be another healthy predator, and sharks will be wary.
- Avoid areas where people are spearfishing. A struggling fish transmits distress signals that sharks are able to pick up from miles away.
- If baits are used to attract sharks into the area, pay careful attention to the ocean current and make certain you are always up-current of the bait. Any object in the odor corridor carried along by the current will attract sharks.
- Make sure the dive boat is up-current and not far away.
- Beware of any small, light-colored object that contrasts with your equipment, especially if it is hanging loosely. Sharks can mistake white fins, gloves, a white underwater slate, or torch for a piece of bait.
- Diving in a group can be safer. When you are finished, leave the site as a group because sharks will become bolder as numbers reduce.
- Never touch, surround or try to contain a shark or ray. They must always be allowed plenty of room to retreat, or they may panic and rush you in a frantic attempt to escape.
- If a shark becomes overly curious and approaches too close for comfort, a hard punch on the nose will usually cause it to retreat rapidly. Some divers carry a shark billy (any short, blunt rod) for just this purpose.

Always remember, although they are not aggressive, there is no such thing as a harmless shark or ray. Each can and will defend itself if threatened, and this is the natural response.

Protective Equipment

Over the years there have been many attempts to provide effective protection for those professionals who must work with sharks and rays.

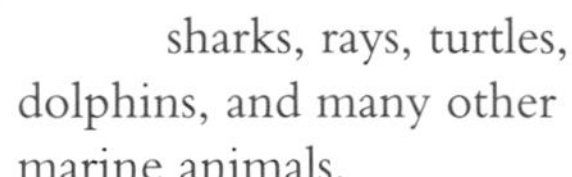

During the past 60 years, many strategies designed to protect swimmers and divers from sharks have been developed and tested (see pp. 44–5). Until very recently, all have failed.

Protecting the Professional

During the Second World War, the United States Navy put its faith in a chemical shark repellent. The sharks swam right through it. They also kept swimming through other repellents, such as air bubble curtains, sound wave barriers and dyes. Mesh netting has been installed at a number of beaches to create a safety barrier for bathers. But, unfortunately, these nets kill a great number of harmless sharks, rays, turtles, dolphins, and many other marine animals.

Divers developed a number of strange, and unsuccessful, devices. Dressing a diver as a black-and-white sea snake was one unusual strategy put to the test—until it was realized that some sharks eat sea snakes. Weapons with a detonating device were developed to shoot any aggressive shark. But, since most shark-attack victims never see the shark coming, these weapons were directed at sharks that were mostly harmless. A hypodermic gas device called a "shark dart" was also developed. This killed the shark, after first inflating it and rendering it harmless. However, because the dart had to be fired into the shark's stomach, it was effective only on sharks swimming by rather than ones that were attacking.

A very effective device—a stainless-steel suit of chain-mail—was finally developed by Australian underwater photographers and shark

TESTING TIMES *Developing the protective stainless-steel chain-mail suit involved close contact (above) and trying to get a shark to bite it (left).*

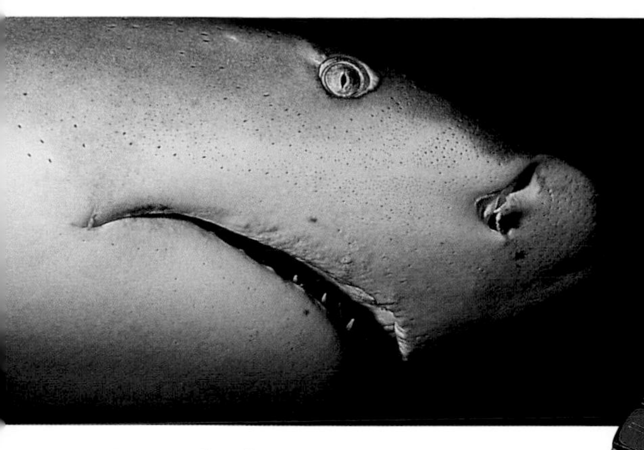

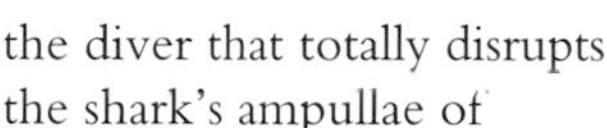

PROTECTIVE DEVICE *The POD (below) disrupts signals picked up by a shark's natural detectors, the ampullae of Lorenzini, situated along its face.*

experts, Ron and Valerie Taylor. This suit has become standard equipment for film makers, dive guides, and scientists who work with sharks. However, it does have some disadvantages, and must be used only by experienced specialists trained in its use. It can restrict movement, and its weight prevents it from being discarded easily in an emergency. It is also possible that a very large shark could crush or tear the garment.

A recent major breakthrough, however, promises to provide the ultimate protection from accidental shark attack for all divers, snorkelers, and water sport enthusiasts. It is a device called the shark POD (or Protective Oceanic Device). It has been rigorously tested by the South African Natal Sharks Board and by Ron and Valerie Taylor.

The shark POD is a compact accessory that fits onto a diver's scuba cylinder. It is connected to a wire that runs from the POD to a small plate attached to the diver's fin. A switch is provided to enable the diver to turn it on before entering the water, and a warning light reveals that the unit is on and working. The unit can be switched off in the water should the diver want to get closer to sharks or rays. A red light display indicates the remaining battery life, giving the diver time to surface and replenish both battery and air supply.

The POD repels sharks at close quarters by creating an electrical force field around the diver that totally disrupts the shark's ampullae of Lorenzini. These are the natural electrical detectors situated along a shark's face that it uses to detect minute electronic signals emitted by potential prey. This disruption cannot be tolerated by sharks.

Tests have shown that the shark POD is very effective, does not injure sharks or rays and has no effect on other marine life, as these creatures do not have ampullae of Lorenzini.

The Natal Sharks Board is currently developing a version that can provide a complete screen for a beach or bathing area. Once this has been perfected, the meshing of our beaches against sharks would become unnecessary. This would relieve the community of a major annual expense, and much innocent marine life would be spared.

SHARK PARTNERS

Both Australian-born, Ron (b. 1934) and Valerie (b. 1935) Taylor originally shared a common interest in spearfishing, at which they both excelled, and underwater photography. Working independently and together, they have notched up a list of extraordinary films and TV documentaries, including *Playing with Sharks, Shark Hunters, Blue Water, White Death,* and *Inner Space*. The Taylors' focus of interest has altered over the years to one of committed conservation of all marine creatures, no matter how fearsome. They now work tirelessly for better understanding of the denizens of the deep, especially the much-maligned and misunderstood shark. Valerie and her husband pioneered the use of a protective mesh diving suit made of stainless steel, which made possible photographic work among sharks without the photographer being confined to a shark cage. More recently, the Taylors have been helping to test the POD.

Underwater Photography

Capturing encounters with sharks and rays on film can be a thrilling and satisfying exercise for many dive travelers.

Fortunately for both the amateur and professional photographer, great advances in technology mean that successful underwater photography is now possible.

Camera Equipment

The complete beginner might choose a disposable camera in a waterproof housing. This is an inexpensive system that calls for no technical knowledge of photography. Such cameras produce a good result, particularly in shallow, clear, sunlit, tropical waters.

More serious photographers prefer amphibious 35 mm cameras with interchangeable lenses, underwater strobe lighting, variable focus, and exposure control. Such features allow a much wider range of photographic composition and the means to deal with low light levels or limited visibility.

Advanced or professional photographers should consider combining a current model auto focus 35 mm SLR (single lens reflex) land camera with one of the many excellent waterproof camera housings that are now available. These systems provide a very wide choice of lens options that allow photography of small, medium, or very large sharks and rays. Auto focus, auto exposure, and motor drive film transport features are invaluable for action shots of fast-moving subjects.

RECORDING THE COLORS *of sea stars and coral in Hawaii (above); and a special amphibious camera (above left).*

Type of Film

Sharks and rays are often encountered near the water surface where light levels are good, so any slide or print film with a medium sensitivity rating of ISO 50 or 100 is suitable. In deeper water, below 30 feet (10 m), the photographer can use a strobe (flash unit) to provide extra light and restore natural colors. Films with sensitivity ratings of ISO 200 are often used for fast-action subjects photographed in available light situations. Choose a film that favors the blacks, whites, and subtle shades of color common among shark and ray species.

Technical Considerations

Photographing sharks and rays frequently involves the use of available natural light, so it is very important to be aware of the position of the

FINGERTIP CONTROL *Strobe units and cameras are securely mounted on a bracket for maximum flexibility.*

LIGHTING THE WAY *Two divers (left) prepare to dive in a low-light area. Snapping a shot of a shark (below).*

Sun. To ensure that details of the shark or ray are revealed, try to position yourself so that the Sun is always coming at an angle over your shoulders. Avoid photography around midday when the Sun is directly above you.

When a strobe is used to provide light, the angle of the Sun in relation to the subject is not so critical, but beware of suspended matter in the water that may be emphasized by the strobe light and spoil the image. This effect is termed "backscatter" and it can be avoided by using low power settings on the strobe and longer strobe arms. Some common sources of back-scatter in shark photography are chum—a mixture of products used to attract sharks; particles of shark bait used for feeding sharks once they arrive; and plankton—a natural food source of whale sharks and manta rays. Also a problem are the small bubbles constantly created by the movement of shark cages, the dive boat, or the wake from other snorkelers' fins.

To ensure clear, sharp images underwater, avoid shooting until you are less than a few yards from the subject. If the subject is a very large shark or ray, you will need a 15 mm or 20 mm wide-angle lens to capture the whole creature. Lenses of the 60 mm, 35 mm or 28 mm variety are useful for portrait shots of the face, details of the body, or for complete images of smaller species.

Because many sharks and rays are dark in color, the camera's light meter may be less accurate than normal and may tend to give an over-exposed image. You can compensate for the dark color by overriding the camera's automatic exposure functions and setting them manually.

Practical Considerations

A dive buddy willing to act as a rear guard can be very valuable—particularly when the photographer is pre-occupied with composing pictures of one shark while other sharks are about. Since chum is often used to attract sharks, and baits are provided to over-come their natural caution, the sharks will often become very excited and curious. It is not unusual for several sharks to approach at once. A second set of human eyes is useful at this point.

Photographers may sometimes find it necessary to extend their camera and upper body through the windows of shark cages to obtain a good angle. The shark you can see is not a problem, but another shark approaching from the side could be. Once again, a vigilant companion is vital.

The diver needs to exercise care whenever making a close approach to any large shark or ray, even if it is a harmless species. A whale shark, for example, can break bones or knock a diver unconscious with its tail. Be particularly careful always to leave space for a shark or ray to retreat and remember that they all have some method of defense, such as biting, ramming, or a powerful tail slap.

UNDERWATER FILMING

Words seem inadequate when you describe diving with sharks and rays to others, but underwater videos convey all the wonder and excitement.

WATERTIGHT HOUSINGS *(above) are specially designed to make video equipment feel lighter under the water.*

The variety of compact video camcorders and well-designed watertight housings on the market today makes it possible for anyone to capture all the underwater action and drama of shark and ray encounters.

CAMERA EQUIPMENT

Video cameras, or camcorders, are the world's most user-friendly cameras. They are effective in low light, fully automatic, and simple to operate. Not only do they provide more than one hour of continuous recording time, but the results can be viewed almost at once. This means that any missing or poorly recorded images can sometimes be re-shot before you leave the site.

A compact model is the best choice of camcorder and the most popular format is Video 8 or High 8. The size of these compact camcorders makes them ideal for use in an underwater housing.

The best watertight housings are made of aluminum and feature magnetic switches, water alarm, interchangeable lens optics, and many controls. Basic acrylic housings are also available and are sometimes cheaper. Although they have certain limitations, if you are on a restricted budget, it is still possible to get good underwater images with cameras in these housings.

TECHNICAL CONSIDERATIONS

To capture good images of sharks and rays you will need a housing with wide-angle lens optics to encompass large species, and a zoom control that enables you to use a telephoto option to capture small or shy species.

Filters are also available to offset the excessive blue of tropical water or the predominant green cast of temperate water. They work well, but should not be used in shallow water less than 10 feet (3 m) deep, as the filter color will dominate and distort the natural color.

Because video camcorders respond even in very low light, underwater lighting will not be necessary. There will be a lack of bright colors at greater depths, but few sharks

UP CLOSE *It is possible to video the most intimate life happenings of reef creatures and the fascinating reef itself.*

and rays are colorful. The added feature of movement and action will compensate for any lack of color, but the enthusiast keen on recording faithful color could consider adding underwater lighting to shoot more colorful species. Although flash and strobe units do not disturb marine life, stronger lighting may. Check with local operators to see if any lighting restrictions apply in a particular area.

Practical Considerations

Since the camcorders are automatic, most problems are caused by the operator. To ensure quality footage, the camera must be held steady to prevent wobble. Keep the action in the center of the viewfinder so that the automatic focus does not need to hunt for focus, and shoot in sequences of wide shots, medium shots, and close-ups.

Beware of air bubbles on the lens—these bubbles are created by snorkelers' fins, scuba exhaust, dive-boat propellers, shark-cage movement, and breaking waves. The bubbles cling to the camcorder lens port and become very pronounced once the image is reviewed on the television screen. Wipe your hand regularly over the port to remove them.

Editing

Do as the professionals do and plan a "shot list" of everything you think you will need to make an interesting and cohesive short story. Shoot everything on the shot list, including any unexpected encounters, before you return home. Finally, edit the useful shots into an action-packed short story by dubbing across from your camcorder to your home video cassette recorder.

THE HUGE MANTA RAY *(below), with long, gray remoras attached, presents an exciting scene. A photographer's buddy must keep a vigilant watch (right).*

BOATING *and* FISHING

Many sharks and rays are killed each year because of ignorance or lack of understanding on the part of boating and fishing enthusiasts.

Today, the waterways and oceans off our coasts are busy with a continual stream of traffic consisting of ships, powercraft, yachts, and jet-skis. These craft all take a toll on the many species of sharks and rays that spend much of their time on the surface—some of which may already be close to being classified as endangered species. It is not uncommon to see whale sharks, the largest and most gentle of all sharks, displaying the scars of encounters with watercraft. Some have had an entire fin torn off by a propeller blade.

Today's conservation-minded boaters and sailors should keep a careful watch for any creatures just beneath the surface so that the injuries to marine animals can be reduced. People on watch should wear polarized sunglasses that allow a much improved view through any glare on the water surface.

UNINTENDED CATCH

It is not unusual for fishing enthusiasts to find they have accidentally caught a shark or ray. The correct management of the problem can go a long way toward preventing the death of an innocent creature.

Take great care—it is very important to avoid injuring

ACCIDENTAL DAMAGE *The whitetip reef shark (above) may have escaped being caught, but a hook remains lodged in its jaw. The whale shark (below) has probably had its dorsal fin and tail tip amputated by a boat propeller.*

UNNATURAL HAZARDS
A discarded fishing net snares some angelsharks and Port Jackson sharks (left). This shark's mouth (below) was damaged by a hook and line.

yourself. Bring the creature as close as possible, but not so close that you are at risk from its teeth or barbs. Do not use a gaff or any instrument that will injure the animal. Cut the line as close to the hook as safety permits. Avoid the temptation to remove the hook. To do so is hazardous to you, and the creature will struggle so much that it will probably be injured, or die later from the stress.

Consider fishing with hooks made of regular, rather than stainless, steel. Such hooks will rust away reasonably quickly if they are left in the mouth of the fish. A shark or ray that is encumbered by a hook and attached wire leader could become tangled in the wire and either suffocate, or starve slowly to death.

APPROACHING SHARKS OR RAYS WITH BOATS

An informed skipper can contribute greatly toward a worthwhile shark or ray encounter that is safe for all involved. The boat operator should be aware of certain procedures.

- Never drive the vessel directly toward the creature.
- Steer a parallel course. Move approximately 100 yards (90 m) ahead, then turn across the animal's course and drop the divers in its probable path.
- If the passengers are non-divers, stop the vessel in the animal's path and turn off the motor.
- When divers or snorkelers are in the water, have a lookout on watch at all times and be ready for an urgent pick-up.

Protected Species and Protected Areas

Ignorance is no excuse. It is the responsibility of fishing enthusiasts to make themselves aware of which shark and ray species are protected, and of restrictions to fishing areas. They should also know about prohibited fishing practices.

Sharks, rays, and other forms of marine life are now under a great deal of pressure from overfishing, loss of habitat due to development, diminishing fish stocks, accidental by-catch, and pollution of all kinds, so our acts of conservation are vital.

There is, one knows not what sweet mystery about this sea, whose gently awful stirrings seem to speak of some hidden soul beneath.

Moby Dick,
HERMAN MELVILLE (1819–91), American novelist

Chapter Four

Sharks

IDENTIFYING *and* CLASSIFYING SHARKS

To recognize a shark, you need a good understanding of its external features, and sometimes a quick eye and a keen memory.

Classification and description of the 350 or so species of living shark is based on the science of taxonomy, in which the morphological characteristics are used to group closely related species. Early modern taxonomists, such as Carolus Linnaeus (1707–78), did not fully understand evolutionary relationships among organisms and often used superficial features to form these groups.

ANATOMY OF A SHARK *The diagram below shows the key external characteristics of a typical shark. The pygmy or dwarf shark (above) reaches a maximum size of 10 inches (25 cm).*

Modern shark taxonomists use shared characteristics that have appeared in species throughout evolutionary history, such as the way the upper jaw is attached to the skull, how the skeletal structures are arranged, and the shape of the teeth. Since such features cannot be readily observed in living animals, the keys we have for the identification of most organisms are still based largely on external features that can be observed or measured with relative ease. These are not necessarily important evolutionary markers.

THROUGH THE AGES

The basic body plan of sharks has been conserved for hundreds of millions of years. The features of extinct fossil sharks, such as *Cladoselache*, are found today among living species, such as the whale shark, *Rhincodon typus*, which can be more than 43 feet (13 m) in length, and also the unrelated spined pygmy shark, *Squaliolus laticaudus*, which reaches only about 10 inches (25 cm). The identification of different shark species usually involves information on relative sizes of the animals, placement and shape of fins, and detailed anatomical features, such as tooth shape.

Sharks can be separated into the higher taxonomic level of order by observation of basic anatomical features. For example, the angelsharks (Squatiniformes), sawsharks (Pristiophoriformes), and dogfish sharks (Squaliformes) can be identified by their lack of an anal fin. Once this feature is known, it is relatively easy to differentiate among the three orders by the shape of the body and head. Some other important identifying features at the order level are the number of gill slits, the presence or absence of dorsal fin spines, the position of the

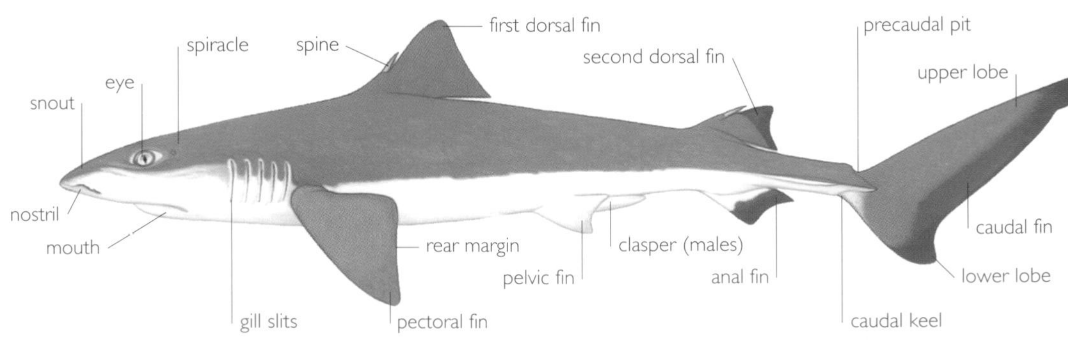

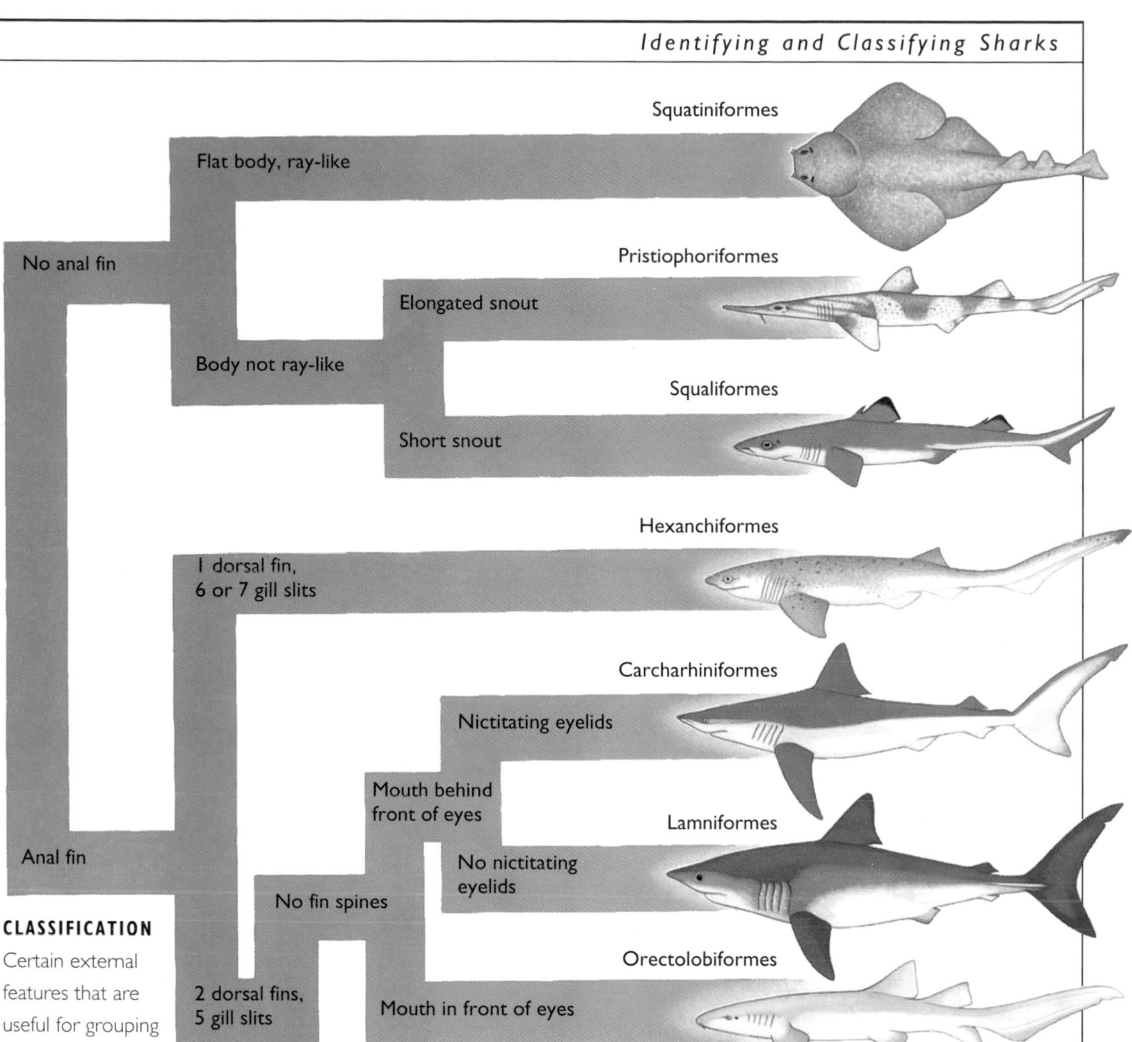

CLASSIFICATION
Certain external features that are useful for grouping sharks (right) evolved in them as time passed.

mouth, and the presence or absence of a nictitating eyelid.

To identify species, shark taxonomists have developed a list of external features and standard measurements. These include descriptive features such as the presence or absence of spiracles, dorsal fin spines, an anal fin, a lower lobe on the caudal fin, an interdorsal ridge, caudal keels, and nictitating membranes. Total body length, interdorsal distance, head length and width, fin length and height, or size and number of teeth, must also be measured or counted. Collectively, these features usually provide the investigator with enough information to make a positive identification.

Unfamiliar Sharks

To identify an unfamiliar species of adult shark, first examine the basic features, body size, location of fins, and shape of head. If, for example, the shark is greater than about 16 feet (5 m) in total length, the list of potential species shrinks to only a handful that includes the whale, basking, great white, tiger, sleeper, thresher, megamouth, and great hammerhead sharks. While a few species are very small, less than 1 foot (30 cm), most adult sharks range from about 3–10 feet (1–3 m). In these cases, shape of body, color pattern, and fin placement may confirm the species.

While scientists using preserved specimens can spend weeks making a tedious examination of the external features, internal anatomy, and teeth, divers may encounter a shark on a reef for only a few seconds. When trying to identify an unknown species, a good knowledge of distribution, habits, and ecology may help to narrow the field. For example, if a 6½ foot (2 m) requiem shark was observed in the waters off Hawaii, the choice can be narrowed to about a dozen possibilities. If it was observed in blue oceanic water, the candidates could be further reduced by about half.

THE EVOLUTION *and* RADIATION *of* SHARKS

Sharks have dominated the oceans for more than 400 million years, yet the sharks of today still look much like their ancestors.

The sharks, rays and chimaeras are all "cartilaginous fish," members of the taxonomic class Chondrichthyes. As the name implies, the skeletons have no true bone but are composed of cartilage, a soft, firm tissue with little, if any, calcification (similar to tissue supporting our nose and ears).

TWO MAJOR GROUPS

Living cartilaginous fishes fall into two groups. The Elasmobranchii (sharks and rays) are characterized by five to seven external gill slits on each side of the head, placoid skin scales known as denticles, teeth that are replaced regularly, and an upper jaw that is not firmly attached to the skull as it is in mammals, birds, reptiles, and amphibians. The chimaeras, or ratfishes (Holocephalii), differ from sharks in that the gills are covered by a flap with only one opening. They also lack scales and have plate-like teeth for eating hard-shelled invertebrates. The upper jaw is firmly attached to the skull.

As a result of the lack of a hard skeleton, fossils of complete sharks (and ratfishes) are rare, and paleontologists must rely instead on finds of fossilized teeth, small dermal scales, and calcified vertebrae to piece together their evolutionary history.

Sharks appeared in the fossil record more than 400 million years ago in the Silurian and Devonian Periods. At this time, the early insects had appeared in primitive plant forests. Early amphibians had emerged from their aquatic habitat to invade terrestrial environments, but the dinosaurs would not arrive for nearly 200 million years. Similarly, the oceans were teeming with small planktonic life and the marine benthos was rich with widely varied forms of shelled invertebrate animals. This seemingly primitive era marked the beginning of the Age of Fishes, when many diverse groups of jawless and jawed fishes evolved to inhabit the wide marine oceans and fresh waters of the planet. Prominent among these were the ancestors of today's sharks.

EVOLVING FEATURES

The best known shark ancestors of the Devonian Period were members of the genus *Cladoselache*, which shared many of the features of modern sharks. Cladodonts had five external gill slits, two well-developed dorsal fins with spines, pectoral and pelvic fins, and a powerful symmetrical tail. The upper

DENTAL RECORDS *A fossil tooth (above) extinct* Carcharodon megalodon *shown b a tooth of the great white shark. The fossil hybodont (below),* Hybodus hauffianus.

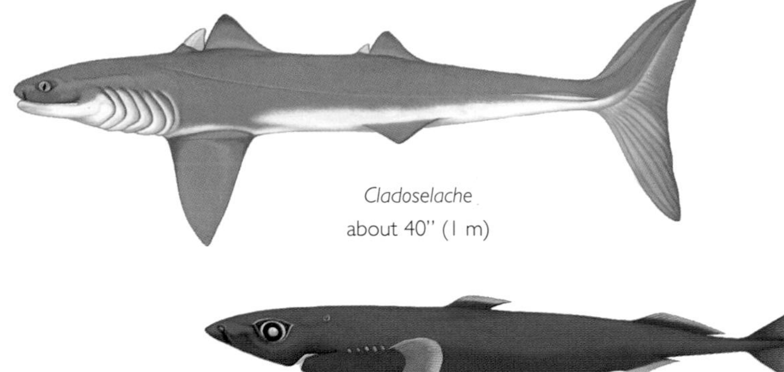

Cladoselache
about 40" (1 m)

THE SHAPE OF SHARKS
Long before the dinosaurs ruled the world, sharks had already evolved their basic powerful, streamlined body shape, and little modification has occurred since the Devonian Period.

Spined pygmy shark
about 10" (25 cm)

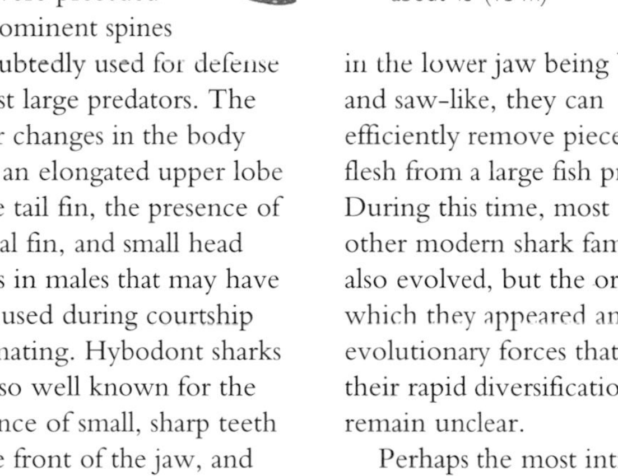

Whale shark
about 43' (13 m)

jaw was loosely attached to the skull, and the lower jaw was large, with many sharp teeth, each equipped with a single prominent central point and smaller lateral cusps (*clado* = branched, *dont* = tooth). These features made *Cladoselache* a swift predator, well adapted for feeding on fast-swimming fishes. This is verified by impressions of large fish prey found in the stomachs of fossilized sharks. Fossils of later species show that, over time, the teeth underwent a wide range of changes in size and number of cusps per tooth, which probably reflected the expansion of the shark's feeding habits in different ecological niches.

About 150 million years later in the Triassic and Jurassic Periods, when dinosaurs ruled the terrestrial reaches of the Earth, the hybodont sharks (*hybo* = hump) were the dominant fish predators in the oceans. Like its *Cladoselache* ancestor, *Hybodus* had two dorsal fins that were preceded by prominent spines undoubtedly used for defense against large predators. The major changes in the body were an elongated upper lobe of the tail fin, the presence of an anal fin, and small head spines in males that may have been used during courtship and mating. Hybodont sharks are also well known for the presence of small, sharp teeth in the front of the jaw, and broader-based teeth at the back, much as occurs in the unrelated hornsharks (Heterodontiformes). The broad teeth of some hybodont species supported many small cusps for grasping soft-bodied prey; those of others were smooth and flat and used for crushing hard-shelled invertebrates.

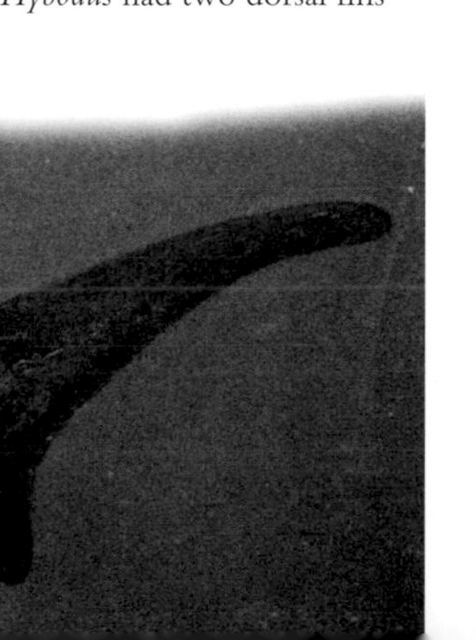

Diversification

The expansion of the hybodont sharks was quickly followed by the appearance of most modern forms. The sixgill and sevengill sharks (cowsharks) were among the earliest to appear in the fossil record and are distinguished by the presence of a single dorsal fin rather than two. With their upper jaw bearing sharp, pointed teeth and those in the lower jaw being broad and saw-like, they can efficiently remove pieces of flesh from a large fish prey. During this time, most of the other modern shark families also evolved, but the order in which they appeared and the evolutionary forces that drove their rapid diversification remain unclear.

Perhaps the most intriguing fossil shark of all is *Carcharodon megalodon*, the largest shark ever to have lived and a close relative of the living great white shark, *Carcharodon carcharias*. Fossil teeth of *C. megalodon* are routinely found from excavations dating back 3 to 25 million years. Reconstructions of the jaw indicate that this shark reached total lengths of at least 45 feet (15 m) and had a mouth gape of about 6½ feet (2 m). Using data on the great white, we can assume that a large megalodon weighed more than 25 tons (25,000 kg). This mammoth carnivore probably fed on large marine animals, such as marine mammals, other sharks, and dead whales, as does its living relative.

The Body Form *and* Function *of* Sharks

The shark's body is beautifully attuned to life in an unforgiving watery world. It provides the ultimate biological example of hydrodynamic efficiency and power.

Many features of the shark's body have evolved in response to the physical constraints of its dense aquatic environment. The internal skeleton of sharks and rays is composed of cartilage, an elastic tissue much higher in water content than bone. A skeleton of cartilage allows a high degree of body flexibility, provides protection and support for organs, and reduces total body mass. Skeletal parts that experience physical stress, such as vertebrae, jaws, and parts of the skull, are often stiffened by secondary calcification rather than by heavier bone. It is unlikely that large, modern sharks would be capable of such quick, agile movement had they evolved bony skeletons.

Blue shark, a graceful swimmer

Mako, a powerful swimmer

Angelshark, a sluggish bottom dweller

Biological Torpedoes

A species that swims actively in the water column, such as the blue shark, usually has a fusiform (cigar-shaped) body. The diameter of the body is greatest at about a third of the way back from the snout, and tapers off toward the tail. This shape lets water flow smoothly over the body as the shark swims and reduces turbulence along the skin.

Swimming power and stability are provided by the shark's well-developed fins. In most sharks, the tail, or caudal fin, creates forward thrust by wide side-to-side movements that produce an undulation of the body. Special helically wound connective tissue fibers under the skin transfer much of the body's power directly to the tail. The unpaired dorsal and anal fins keep the body from rolling to either side during forward motion. The pectoral and pelvic fins, paired and displaced off the body midline, are used for lift and control of movements.

The fastest sharks, such as the mako, are perhaps the

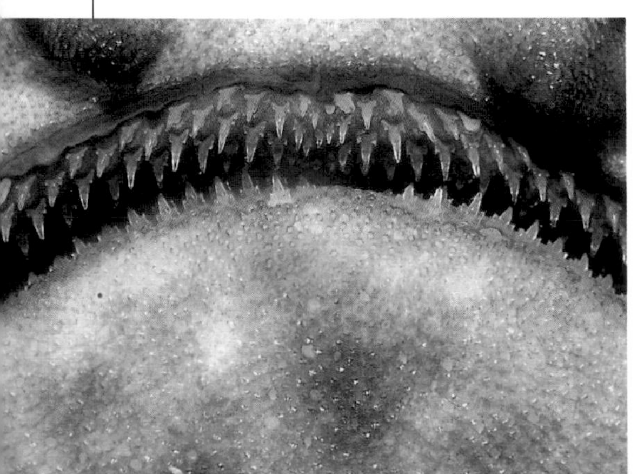

CONVEYOR BELT *The teeth of the swellshark (left) are arranged in rows and are constantly replaced by new ones produced at the back. The body shapes of sharks (above) have become adapted to their differing lifestyles.*

BODY SHAPE *The bottom-dwelling angelshark (left) disappears on the ocean floor.*

ultimate biological example of hydrodynamic efficiency and power. The snout and head are fused into a missile-like nose cone, and the stream-lined body is stout, and massive. Thrust is derived almost exclusively from quick lateral motions of the symmetrical tail with only minimal flexing of the body. The pectoral fins are short with a small surface area to reduce drag. Their stiffness helps the fish to maneuver at high speed. The claspers of males are retracted into special grooves behind the pelvic fins. Well-developed lateral keels on the caudal peduncle act as horizontal stabilizers. These swift, biological torpedoes are capable of bursts of speed of 22 miles per hour (36 km/h).

Bottom Dwellers

In contrast to species that are constantly on the move, some are adapted for a life near the sea bottom. One extreme example is the angelshark, which has a flattened, ray-like body and spends much of the day buried in the sandy bottom waiting to ambush passing fish prey. Sawsharks have a broad, flat-tened surface under the head that helps to detect and capture benthic inverte-brates. They retain the powerful tail for long-distance move-ment across their marine habitat.

The outer skin is composed of many tiny placoid scales, known as denticles, which are usually about $\frac{1}{32}$ inch (less than 1 mm) wide. These are formed in the dermal layer of the skin. The surface of the denticles consists of hard enamel that covers a dentine layer and pulp cavity. The enamel crowns have multiple sharp ridges that reduce drag during swimming as well as protect-ing the animal from injury.

The jaw is beneath the skull so the opening of the mouth is usually behind the snout on the underside of the head. In large, predatory sharks, the jaw is highly adapted for grasping or cutting prey. The upper jaw (palatoquadrate cartilage) is loosely suspended under the skull by ligaments and connective tissue. The lower jaw (Meckel's cartilage) is connected to the upper jaw at the corners of the mouth and is covered by massive muscles used for biting. This entire mechanism is suspended from the skull by the hyoid cartilage.

The attachment of rela-tively small muscles between the jaw, skull, and adjacent cartilages results in a powerful, highly protrusible mechanism that can be decoupled from the skull and thrown forward from the head during a bite. This enables predators, such as great whites and reef sharks, to bite off parts of prey that are too large to swallow whole.

The Teeth

The teeth, formed from skin tissue, are arranged in ordered rows on both jaws. An enamel crown forms the primary cutting edge of the tooth, which in many species has additional lateral cusps or serrations. New rows of teeth form along the rear margins of the jaws, migrating forward as they become enlarged. This constant supply of sharp teeth emerges from the gums to replace those that are dulled or lost during use.

JAW ATTACHMENT

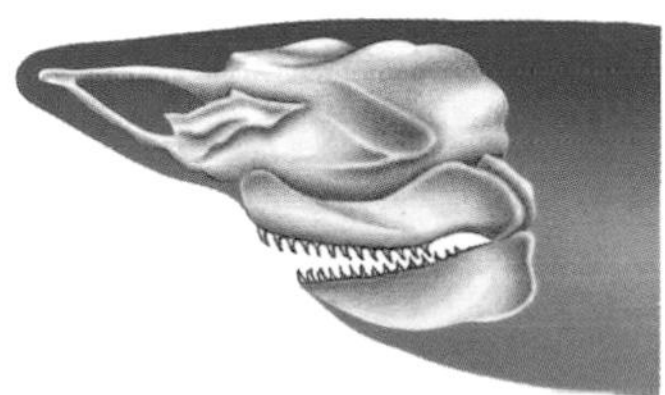

Like ancestral form, the jaw is normally positioned below the skull.

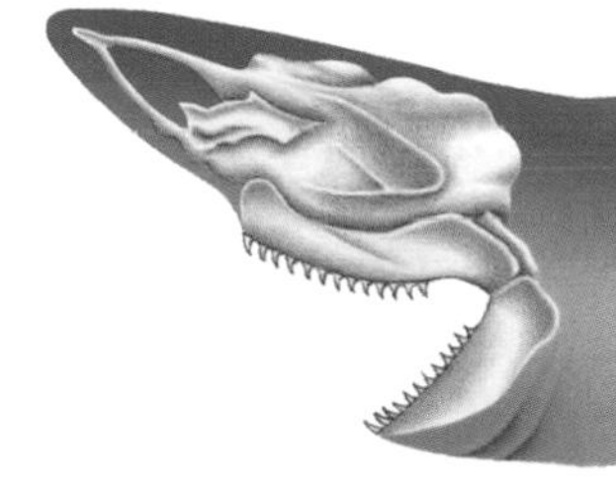

Like ancestral form, upper jaw remains close to skull as mouth opens.

Modern shark's upper jaw can detach from skull.

The Internal Environment *of* Sharks

Beneath the denticled skin of the shark lies a well-organized and coordinated biological factory that is designed for maximum efficiency.

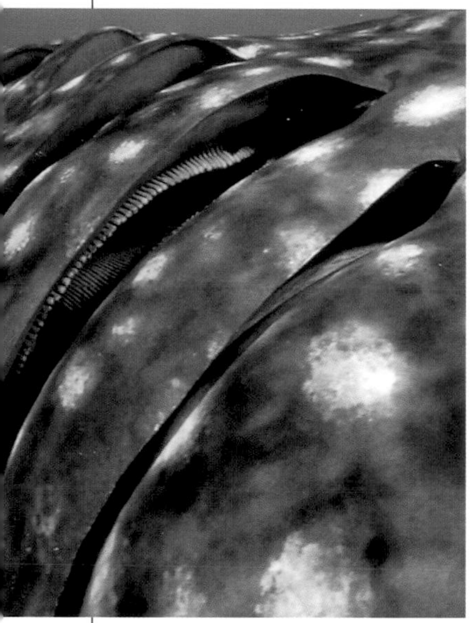

RESPIRATION *The gill slits of a whale shark (above). The illustration (below) shows the heart, gill arches and direction of water flow. Water enters the mouth (and spiracles), passes over the gills and out the gill slits. Diagram (right) shows detail of water flowing counter to blood.*

As well as being a superb hydrodynamic vehicle, a shark's body also controls many biological processes. Its internal organs share many features that are common in other fishes, but also show a number of specializations unique to vertebrates.

Respiration

Sharks and rays extract oxygen from the water to metabolize their food. The gills are found on five to seven vertical arches that form the walls of the external gill slits. In a separate chamber beneath the gills, the heart pumps oxygen-depleted blood to capillary beds in the arches. Water is pumped into the mouth and out across the gills counter to the direction of blood flow. This exchange system greatly enhances the rate and efficiency of oxygen diffusion into the blood. In fast-swimming species, water flows into the open mouth as the animal swims. In bottom-dwelling species, such as sawsharks and spiny dogfish, there are well-developed spiracles that serve as auxiliary water inlets when the animal is resting or using the mouth to feed.

Digestion

When prey is captured in the mouth, it is usually swallowed whole or cut into large pieces.

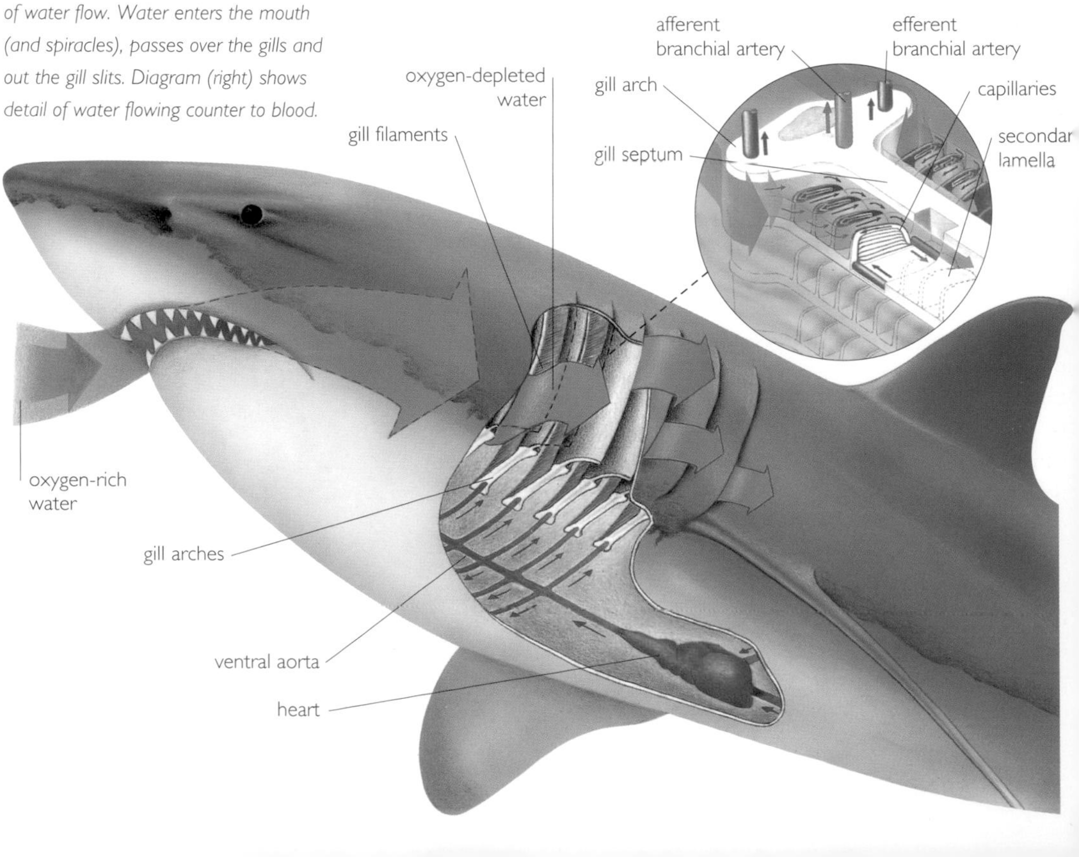

afferent branchial artery
efferent branchial artery
gill arch
capillaries
oxygen-depleted water
gill filaments
gill septum
secondar lamella
oxygen-rich water
gill arches
ventral aorta
heart

THE SPINAL COLUMN *(below) runs the length of the body. The section (right) shows stacked vertebral centra, and (far right) a cross-section stained to show concentric rings that may mark age in years.*

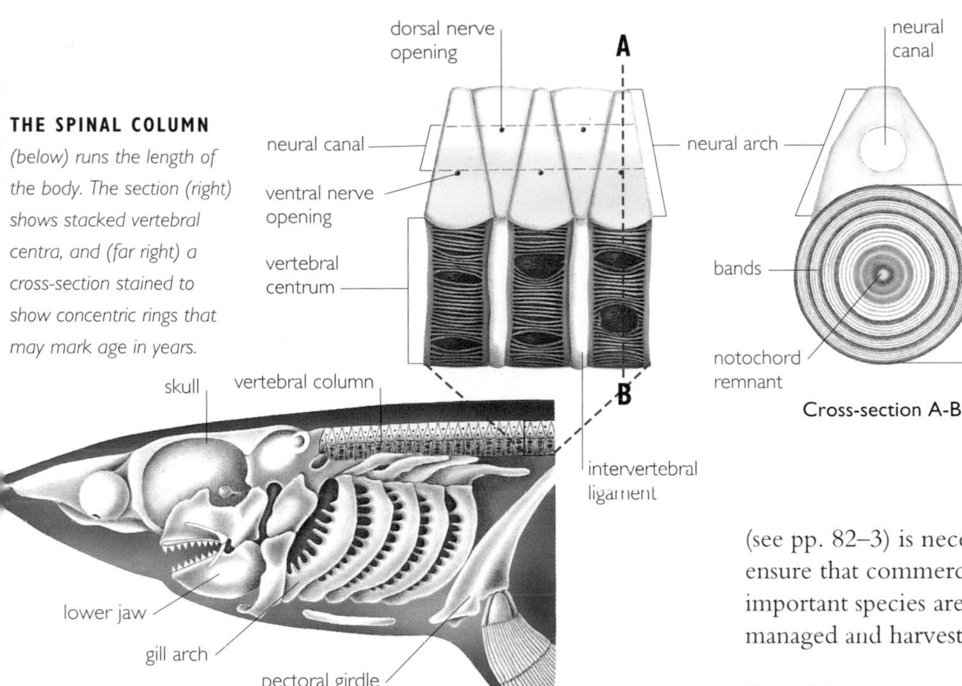

The stomach produces strong acid and digestive enzyme secretions that, eventually, emulsify the food to a thin, soup-like consistency. Large bones and other indigestible material in the stomach are blocked from entering the intestine by a very small pyloric opening and regurgitated later. The absorptive surface area of the intestine is greatly increased by internal coils that are wound like a spiral staircase (spiral valve intestine) or, in some species, like a long, rolled up sheet of paper (scroll valve intestine).

Water Balance

The concentration of minerals in the body tissues of sharks is maintained by remarkable physiological processes. In marine fishes, the concentration of salt is about three times greater in the water than in the body, so there is a constant tendency for dehydration by loss of water across the gills. Sharks greatly reduce this loss by retaining urea, derived from the digestion of protein. They also produce an organic compound, TMAO (trimethylamine oxide), which helps to maintain osmotic balance. When excess sodium chloride enters the body after the animal swallows sea water or ingests prey, it is removed by secretions from a specialized organ called the rectal gland.

Growth

Lack of bony body parts in sharks and rays makes it hard to estimate age and growth rate of individual species. The vertebrae, which are partly calcified, can be stained to reveal concentric rings much like those seen in tree trunks, but we do not know if each ring represents a single year's growth. Additional research is necessary to confirm the meaning of each ring.

Tagging and recapture methods are another means of determining growth rates. Some species, such as the sandbar and dusky sharks, grow very slowly and may not reach sexual maturity for 15 years or more. Other smaller species, such as the sharpnose shark, reach maturity in three to four years. Information on growth rates and reproduction (see pp. 82–3) is necessary to ensure that commercially important species are reliably managed and harvested.

The Muscles

Most body muscle consists of white muscle fibers with relatively poor vascularization. These are an excellent source of power for brief bursts of speed. Normal swimming activity is produced by contractions of relatively small bands of highly vascularized red muscle along the sides of the body. Red muscle can be used almost indefinitely for sustained swimming.

The fast-swimming lamnid sharks (great white, mako, and porbeagle) have developed a counter-current vascular system ("rete mirable") in the red body muscle and viscera. Heat that would be lost in blood leaving the muscle is retained locally by warming the cooler, oxygen-rich blood as it enters. In this way, the muscle maintains a temperature 9 to 15 degrees Fahrenheit (5–8° C) above that of the surrounding water and produces more power when burning oxygen. This provides faster cruising and bursts of speed useful for following large prey, such as tuna and mackerel, and also when diving to deep, cold waters in search of prey.

VISION, SMELL, TASTE, *and* TOUCH

Sharks have at least eight well-developed sensory systems and a large brain, which makes it rather illogical to think of them as primitive.

Even today, sharks are often presented as sluggish, instinctive, and uncalculating predators that possess poorly developed sensory systems and rudimentary brains. This view stems from their long fossil history, and the assumption that they are less advanced than the more recently evolved vertebrates. Nothing could be further from the truth.

VISION

The location of the shark's eyes on the sides of the head provides it with an excellent field of vision, in almost all directions. The eyeball is elliptical with a clear central cornea, and the globe wall is made of a white fibrous sclera. The amount of light entering the eye is regulated by a well-developed iris, which contracts and expands to change the size of the opening, called the pupil.

A clear, nearly spherical lens behind the pupil can be moved to focus images on the retina which lines the inner surface at the back of the eye. Within the retina are photoreceptors, called cones. These provide color vision and good detail in daylight.

Images seen during twilight and at night are mediated primarily by rod photoreceptors. Compared to cones, the rods provide relatively poor detail, but they

THE SENSES OF THE SHARK *The diagrams (below) show the components of the various sensory systems and their location on the body. For an explanation of how they function, see the text on this and the following three pages.*

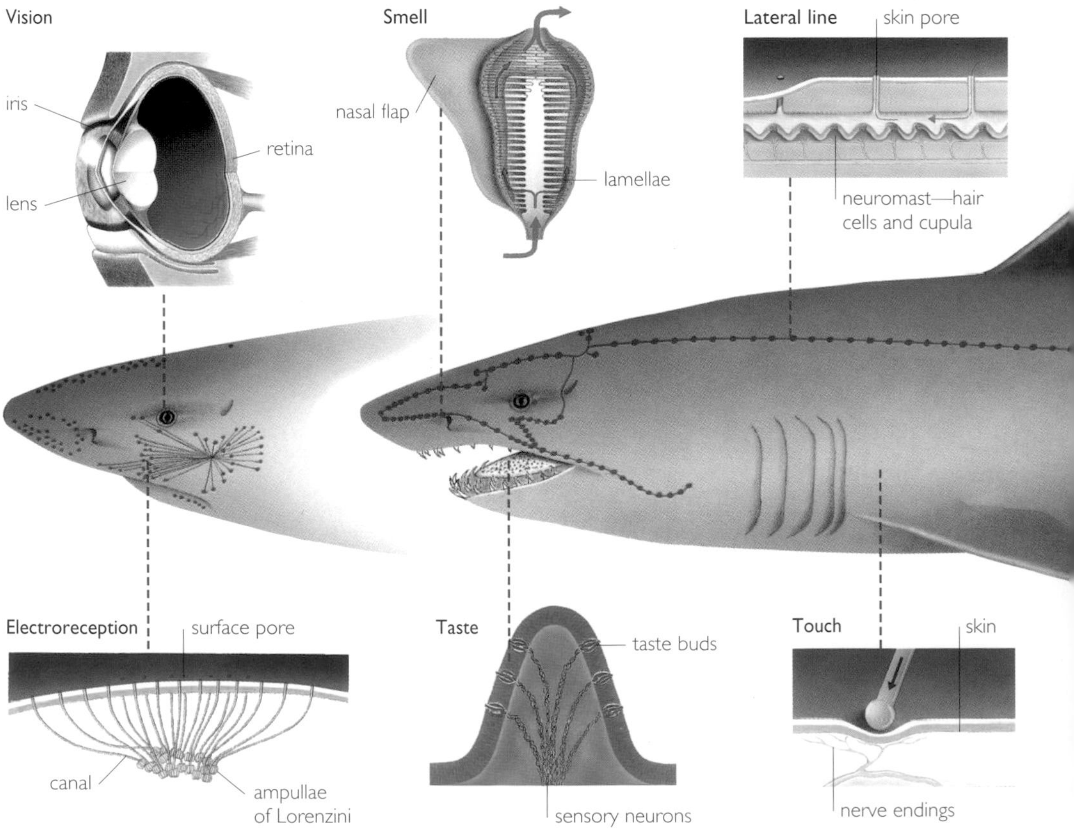

are highly sensitive in low-light conditions and excellent discriminators between light and dark objects.

Another such adaptation to low-light conditions is the tapetum lucidum, which is located behind the retina. This structure is a layer of minute mirror-like crystal plates that functions as a biological photomultiplier, reflecting any light that passes through the retina back again onto the photoreceptors. Sharks and rays feed during the periods of dusk, night, and dawn, so this is an especially useful adaptation for them.

THE SHARK BRAIN

Contrary to popular belief, the relative size of the brain in sharks and rays rivals that of some birds and mammals. Like the brains of all vertebrate animals, the shark brain consists of hundreds of thousands of specialized cells known as neurons. Neurons receive electrical impulses from the various sensory systems of the body, process information in different regions of the brain, and send control commands to the muscles of the body.

The hindbrain processes information from many sensory systems, controls movements of the head and jaw, and is also a relay station between the higher brain centers and the spinal cord. The cerebellum coordinates body movements and may even be capable of motor learning. The tectum receives and integrates visual, electrosensory, lateral line, and other sensory information (see main text and pp. 78–9).

Below the midbrain is the diencephalon, which regulates the production of hormones, controls behaviors and activity patterns, and acts as a relay station for information passing to the forebrain. Finally, the forebrain, which is especially well developed in stingrays and mantas, receives information from the olfactory, electrosensory, and lateral line systems (see also pp. 78–9). Much work remains to be done to determine how the forebrain controls the behavior of sharks and rays.

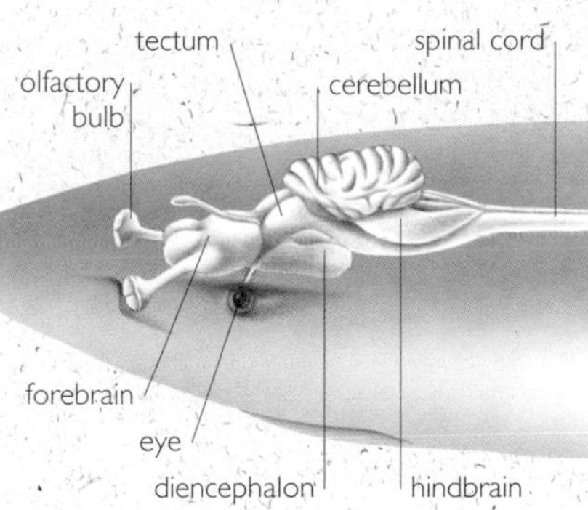

SMELL

The sense organs for smell are found within the two olfactory sacs under the snout. Each sac is covered by a flap of skin that channels water into the chamber and across the sensory lamellae. Water, along with any dissolved molecules or suspended particles, flows through the series of small valleys between the lamellae, which are lined with olfactory receptor cells.

Molecules such as amino acids, the building blocks of proteins, bind to the surface of the receptor cells and evoke neural discharges that are carried to the brain for processing. Researchers have reported a neural response to solutions of glycine, and also behavioral responses to fish extracts at concentrations of about 1 part per 10 billion parts of water.

TASTE

Like the olfactory system, the sense of taste is specialized to detect biological compounds. There are taste receptor cells on small taste buds that cover small bumps inside the mouth. They are best stimulated by direct contact with items such as food. The shark normally uses this sense to decide whether the food item it has captured is palatable.

SUPERSENSITIVE *With its elaborate nostrils, the hornshark (above) is able to detect minute amounts of chemicals.*

TOUCH

Tactile sense in elasmobranchs is mediated by a network of nerve endings beneath the surface of the skin. Free nerve endings are simple, unspecialized touch receptors near the skin surface. They discharge impulses briefly when the overlying skin is depressed by as little as 0.0008 inch (20 µm). In Wunderer corpuscles, a more defined organization is seen, with the nerve endings tightly coiled into small capsules lying deeper in the skin layer. These structures respond both to direct touch and to the fin or body bending.

Finally, the Poloumordwinoff endings are thought to be stretch receptors for muscle fibers of the fins of rays, providing information on muscle length and contraction rate.

BALANCE, HEARING, LATERAL LINE, *and the* ELECTROSENSE

Signals relayed through a system of amazingly sophisticated sensory organs keep the shark fully informed about what is going on within and around it.

Sharks and rays have exquisite sensory organs for balance (vestibular system), hearing (auditory system), and detecting prey (lateral line and electrosensory systems). In all these sensory systems are hair cells—small receptors that excite sensory neurons when a physical force is applied to them. The hair cell is ubiquitous among vertebrates, including the organs of balance and hearing within our own ears.

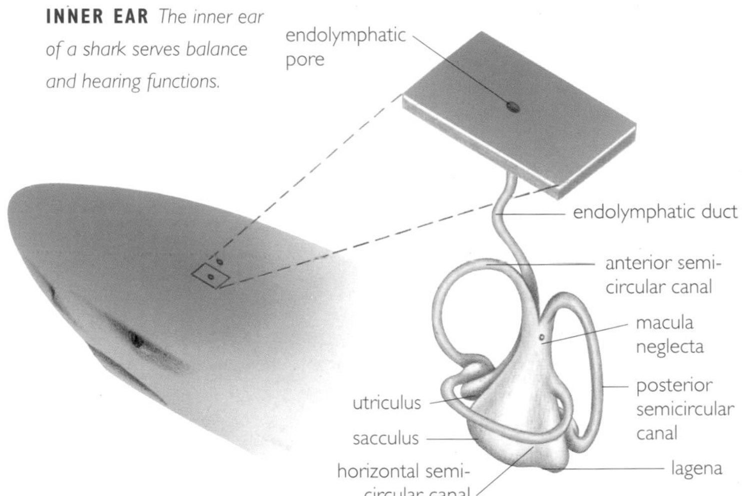

INNER EAR *The inner ear of a shark serves balance and hearing functions.*

THE VESTIBULAR SYSTEM

The vestibular system is a complex of fine membranous organs designed to maintain the shark's orientation, balance, and control of body movements. Inside each ear are three fluid-filled semicircular canals, at right angles to each other and firmly embedded in the otic capsules of the skull. As the shark turns its body, or moves its head from side to side during swimming, the fluid in the canals that are within the plane of rotation presses against a vane of hair cells, and stimulates nerve impulses to the brain.

Attached directly below the semicircular canals are the three otolith organs. The hair cells of each of these organs are arranged in a carpet-like layer known as the maculae, suspended vertically (the sacculus and lagena) or horizontally (the utricle) within the inner ear.

A conglomeration of hard calcium granules, known as otoconia, rests on each macula and, depending on the orientation of the body, will produce a shearing tug on the hair cells due to the force of gravity. Signals from these organs let the brain know about the position of the body relative to gravity and also tell it in which direction the body is moving.

HEARING

Although sharks and rays lack any external evidence of well-developed ears, their hearing is very acute. In field studies, many sharks are regularly attracted to sounds like those made by struggling fish played through underwater speakers. Recent work suggests that the macula neglecta

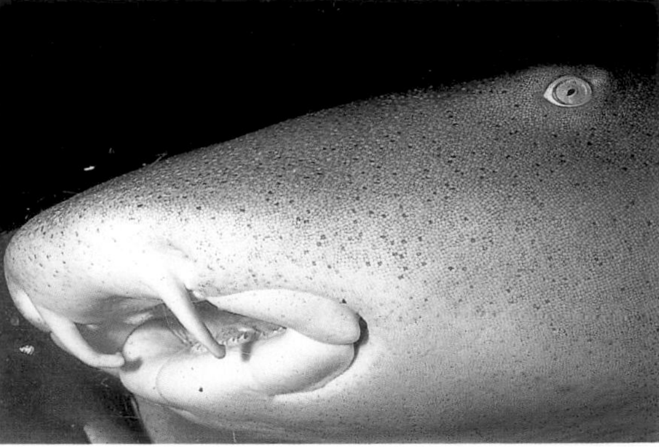

SENSORS *Along the lateral line, which runs down the shark's head and sides, are special hair-cell receptors that provide the animal with an amazing fund of information. Ampullae of Lorenzini are visible on the nurse shark (right).*

HYPERSENSITIVE *The whale shark (right) uses its extraordinary electrosense to locate the fish on which it preys.*

is probably the organ of hearing. These tiny, paired hair-cell organs, located near the top of the skull above the semicircular canals, lack otoconia. It is currently proposed that sound-pressure waves traveling through the water, such as those produced by the movements of fishes or unusual acoustic disturbances on a reef, are channeled down tiny cartilaginous tubes in the top of the skull where they enter the inner ear to stimulate the macula neglecta.

Lateral Line

The lateral line of sharks and rays is an important means for detecting water movements made by prey and potential predators. Sensory hair cells are arranged in tiny clusters less than 1/50 inch (0.5 mm) long, known as neuromasts (see p. 76). On the surface of the skin there are superficial neuromasts, often referred to as pit organs, that detect water movements (velocity) relative to the surface of the body. These organs are distributed across the shark's body, and are especially well positioned along the tail of the stingray for detecting an approach from the rear by a foraging hammerhead or bull shark.

The lateral line canal neuromasts are also found within an extensive network of small, water-filled canals immediately below the surface of the skin on the head and sides of the body. Neuromasts among the skin pores are stimulated by water movements within the canal that result from differences in pressures at the pores. This makes them sensitive to water acceleration. Much of the canal system on the head lacks surface pores altogether, which means that these neuromasts are relatively insensitive to water disturbances on the skin. Laboratory research indicates that, when stimulated, the unpored lateral line system in the stingray probably functions as a specialized touch receptor for use when handling prey.

Electrosensory System

The electrosense is perhaps the most intriguing and mysterious sensory system of the elasmobranch fishes. This sense is used to detect and locate prey, and in stingrays also to locate mates during the reproductive season.

Each of the electrosensory organs, known as ampullae of Lorenzini (see p. 76), consists of a small chamber (the ampulla) lined with hair cells, and attached to an insulated tube filled with a conductive jelly. Many ampullae are grouped, like small grapes, in three to five clusters on each side of the head and lower jaw. From these, the tubes radiate to pores at separate locations on the skin, so that these small "biological cables" can sample voltage potentials at different locations.

The weak bioelectric stimuli produced by prey originate primarily from their biological membranes, and appear to the shark or ray as a weak electrical aura around them, even when the prey is buried in the sand. Sharks and rays use the electrosensory system to detect voltage gradients as low as 5 nanovolts/cm, or 5 billionths of a volt measured across a distance of only about ½ inch (1 cm). The strength of the bioelectric fields produced by small organisms falls off rapidly with distance from the source, so the effective range of the electrosense is usually less than 1 foot (20–30 cm).

The Shark's Lair

Each species of shark is exquisitely adapted for life in one of the many vast realms of the world's oceans.

Sharks inhabit almost every marine ecosystem on Earth. Nearly all coastal regions of the world have large populations of small, bottom-dwelling sharks that are almost always an important component of the local marine ecosystem. Temperate latitudes are usually dominated by small requiem sharks, hornsharks, catsharks, houndsharks, spiny dogfish sharks, and sometimes angelsharks. These species frequent rocky algae-laden reefs, muddy bottoms of bays, and open sandy habitats. Their major food source is a rich abundance of small fishes, and a selection of bottom-dwelling invertebrates, such as crabs, shrimp, and mollusks.

The most common sharks associated with the bottom on tropical reefs include the collared carpetsharks, catsharks, nurse sharks, zebra sharks, and wobbegongs, although not all may be present on any single reef. Like their counterparts in temperate zones, most small tropical reef sharks feed heavily on bottom-dwelling invertebrates and small fishes.

Large Sharks

The larger sharks are also commonly found near coastal areas, but differ from most smaller sharks by swimming constantly over large ranges. In temperate latitudes, these include the large sevengill sharks, which are common visitors to shallow waters along the shoreline and the deeper continental shelves.

Great white sharks are seasonal visitors to many temperate coastal waters near rookeries and haul-out sites for seals and sea lions. Other large species, such as sand tigers and many requiem sharks, frequent coastal areas adjacent to their normal distribution ranges above the continental shelves.

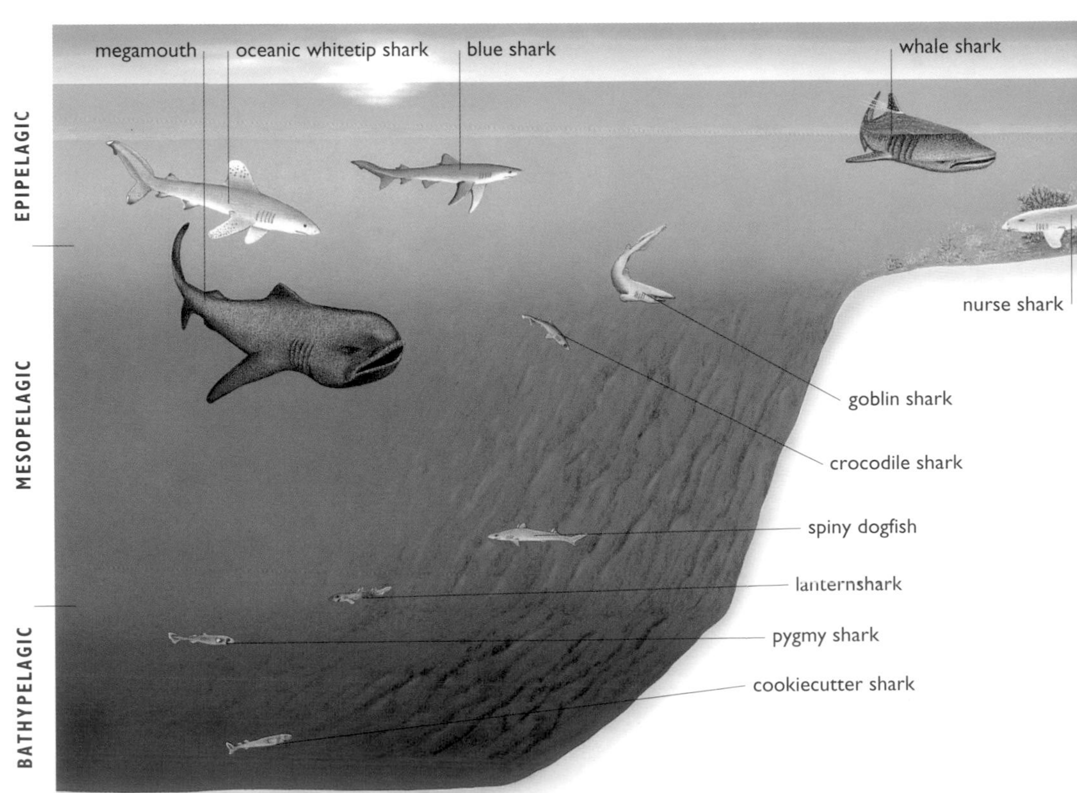

TO EACH HIS OWN *The bull shark (left) scours sandy bottoms, while the whitetip reef shark (far left) feeds at night and rests during the day in quiet places such as mangrove bays (below) and reef caves.*

In tropical reef habitats we find relatively large, mobile species of requiem sharks, including many well-known species, such as the gray reef, Queensland, whitetip reef and silvertip sharks of the Indo-Pacific, the Caribbean reef shark, and lemon sharks. The largest members of circum-global tropical reef sharks include the tiger shark, great hammerhead, and bull shark.

Finding Food

Many species live in the open ocean. Blue sharks are quite common in temperate pelagic waters both near and far from land. Other oceanic visitors to coastal areas are the mako, salmon, and porbeagle sharks, which often follow coastal migrations of their fish prey. In tropical oceans, blue sharks avoid the warm surface temperatures and swim at greater depths where the water is cooler. Mako sharks are commonly found among tuna schools in tropical seas. The most common open-ocean requiem shark is the oceanic whitetip, which feeds on fishes and cephalopods.

There are three families of very large sharks that are known to filter feed on small oceanic plankton. The most commonly encountered planktivore in temperate waters is the basking shark, which has extremely long gill slits and reaches a length of about 30 feet (10 m). These sharks feed on tiny zooplankton in coastal areas with a rich upwelling of nutrients.

Another planktivore found in tropical and subtropical coastal seas is the whale shark, which reaches a length of 39 feet (12 m). The diet of the recently discovered megamouth shark (see p. 130) probably includes plankton, small crustaceans, copepods, and jellyfish.

TERRITORIAL WATERS *Different ocean realms (left) are favored by various species of shark for a variety of reasons, including availability of food. As well as the preferred locality, coastal, reef, or open ocean, three depth levels are differentiated. (Sharks are not illustrated to size.)*

The Wonders of the Deep

The least-known realms of the shark are the deep mesopelagic waters of the open ocean, the slopes of continental shelves, and the abyss of deep oceans. The large and sluggish bramble sharks range from shallow shelf waters to the upper continental slopes. Velvet dogfish and gulper sharks are regularly collected at bottom depths of 2 miles (3,500 m).

The world's smallest sharks, including pygmy sharks and lanternsharks, inhabit the mesopelagic and bathypelagic regions. They show special adaptations to their gloomy environment, such as well-developed luminescent photophores that are probably used for visual communication in these dark depths.

Many of the most unusual species, such as goblin sharks and roughsharks, are found on continental shelves and on their upper slopes.

Shark Reproduction

The reproductive strategies of sharks, which in many ways are more like those of birds and mammals than other fishes, serve to enhance the survival of their relatively few precious offspring.

Females of most fishes eject thousands (or millions) of small eggs to be fertilized outside the body by males. Female sharks, on the other hand, produce a relatively few large eggs that are fertilized inside the body by males. The gestation period, inside the female, may be as long as almost two years. So in many ways, a shark's reproductive system is more like that of mammals (including our own) and birds than that of other fishes.

The Journey Begins

Before or during the mating season, sperm is produced by male sharks within their testes, paired organs found in the body cavity just below the backbone. Mature sperm are transported down a series of small ducts and, in some species, assembled into packets known as spermatophores. Sperm is then stored in the collecting ducts or specialized sperm sacs near the cloaca.

Mating in sharks is facilitated by the clasper organs of males, which develop from medial folds of the pelvic fins. During courtship a single clasper is rotated, inserted into the female's cloaca, and then flared. In many species it is anchored by spines or hooks. Sperm is then forced through the folds of the clasper into the female.

On the female side, small germ cells within the ovaries grow and develop into large, yolked eggs up to 1½ inches (4 cm) in diameter. After ovulation, the eggs pass through the ostium and enter the reproductive tract. They are usually fertilized one by one in the shell gland, and are encased in either a horny protective shell in egg-laying species (such as swellsharks and hornsharks), or a thin membranous covering in livebearers (such as requiem and hammerhead sharks). The fertilized egg

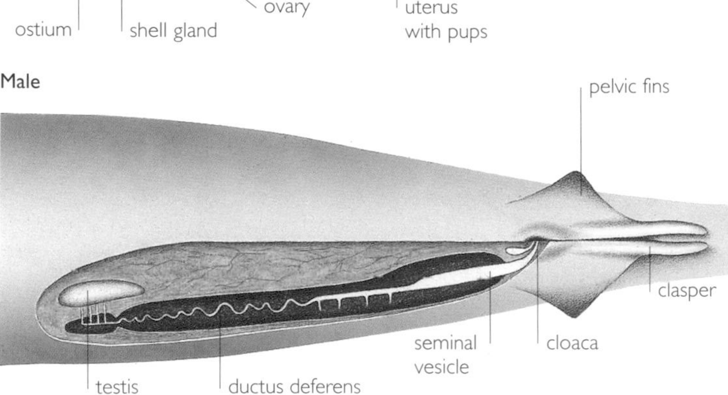

THE NEXT GENERATION *The diagram (left) shows the bottom view of male and female reproductive organs of a typical shark. In the two egg cases (right) the almost fully developed embryos of the lesser spotted dogfish are clearly visible.*

BIRTHDAYS *The pup of a lemon shark emerges from its mother's uterus (right); and a whitespotted bambooshark hatches from its egg case (left).*

then descends the oviduct and passes to the uterus, where the embryo develops. Nutrients pass from the egg yolk by means of the yolk stalk.

MOTHERCARE

Egg-laying, or oviparous, species deposit their eggs on the bottom substrate where the embryos develop, receiving nourishment entirely from the egg yolk. The egg case of hornsharks is soft when first laid, and a female often picks it up in her mouth and deposits it in a crevice so that when it hardens, it becomes wedged. Catsharks have purse-like egg cases with long tendrils that twist around objects on the bottom. In zebra, bamboo, and epaulette sharks, there are sticky filaments instead of tendrils.

The majority of sharks are viviparous, livebearers, and the embryo develops entirely within the uterus. Most species show a placental viviparity in which the embryo is nourished entirely by the yolk but is not released by the mother until fully developed. In others, the embryo remains in the mother's uterus even after the yolk sac has been fully absorbed. In the tiger shark, the uterus provides additional nutrient-rich secretions that are thought to be absorbed directly by the embryo. Embryonic sand tiger sharks receive supplemental nutrition through sibling cannibalism. The first-born consumes its siblings, then continues to feed upon hundreds of unfertilized eggs produced by the mother.

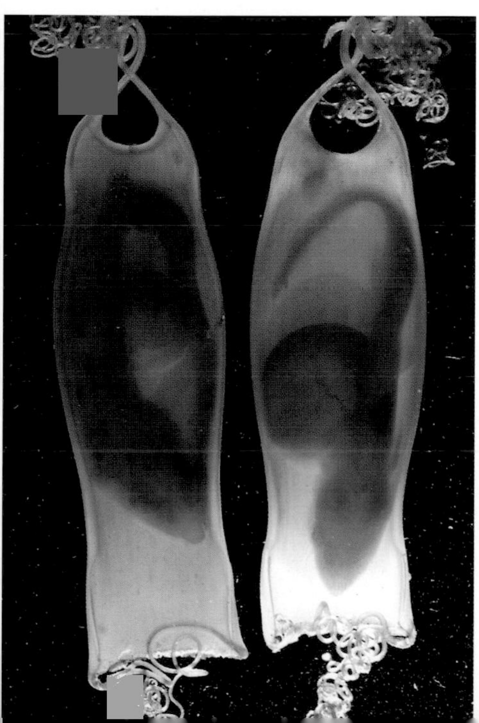

In species with placental viviparity, the spent yolk sac forms a connection with the uterine wall and absorbs nutrients from the mother. These are passed to the embryo via the yolk stalk umbilicus. In other species, the yolk stalk shows leaf-like elaborations that absorb nutrients directly from the surrounding rich uterine fluid.

Sharks and rays do not guard eggs or newborn young. The young are small versions of their parents, active swimmers, and begin to feed almost immediately.

THE MATING GAME

Most oviparous sharks mate for a brief period each year and lay eggs that hatch 3 to 15 months later. The reproductive cycle for viviparous sharks is often limited by the gestation period. Small species may mate annually and give birth to live young from a few months to about a year later.

For example, sharpnose sharks, which reach a maximum size of about 40 inches (1 m), carry 1 to 7 young for 10 to 12 months. At the other extreme is the spiny dogfish shark, which takes nearly 2 years for up to 20 young to develop to a viable size.

Larger sharks, such as the blue shark, may have litters of more than 100 pups after a gestation period of 9 to 12 months. In the other large requiem sharks, such as the blacktip, the gestation period is 10 to 12 months, and they are thought to give birth only in alternate years, but this is by no means certain.

Shark Behavior

Most sharks have a diversity of often complex behaviors related to feeding, mating, and social interactions that we still don't fully understand.

Although inhospitable to humans, the ocean realm has very few boundaries that can contain the movements of sharks. Scientist divers are able to spend only a few hours at a time in the water, and are limited in their movements to relatively short distances and shallow depths. In contrast, the streamlined bodies of large sharks are designed to carry them over great distances each day, and they are also capable of rapid, deep dives. As a result of the shark's wide-ranging journeys in the ocean, information on their behavior is usually limited to brief snapshots of their daily lives.

Activity patterns are often closely tied in with a shark's daily feeding. The blue shark, whitetip reef shark, catsharks and many other species feed primarily at night, but only a few species are known to feed mainly during daylight hours. These include the bonnethead shark, which takes crabs, shrimp, and small fishes in bays and along sandy beaches. Lemon sharks are especially active around dusk and dawn, but these are only the times of major activity. Like most predators, sharks feed whenever there is an opportunity.

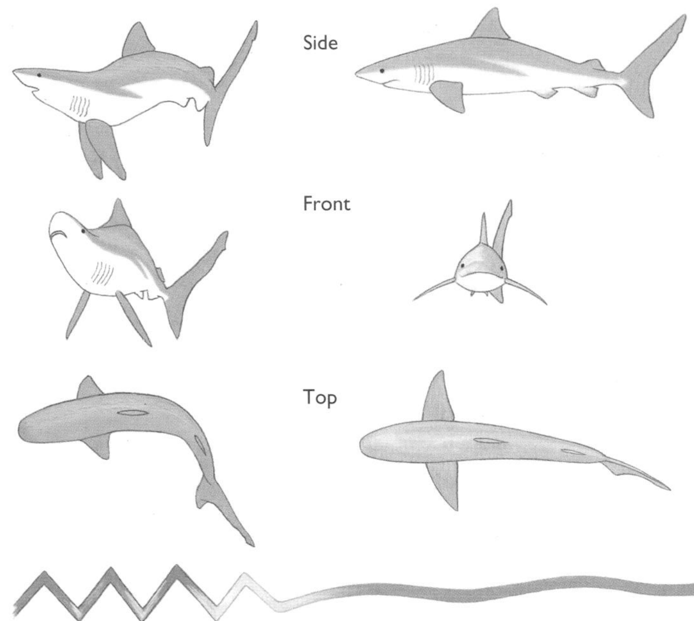

SIGN LANGUAGE *The agonistic display (above) of the gray reef shark. Hammerheads (below) schooling with Pacific creole fishes, Galapagos Islands.*

Safety in Numbers

Sharks are known to occur both as solitary individuals and

in various groupings. For example, tropical reef species, such as blacktip reef, gray reef and lemon sharks, are often observed by divers as solitary individuals in search of food. At other times, these same species are seen swimming together in small groups, apparently engaged in hunting or social activities.

Research in the Sea of Cortez has identified a large population of scalloped hammerhead sharks that forms schools on seamounts during the day, then moves off at night to feed on fishes and squid. Some species, such as the pelagic blue shark and bottom-dwelling bonnethead sharks, often form large, single-sex schools or schools of similar-sized individuals. There may be biological reasons for these aggregations, including the avoidance of larger predators, habitats that have preferred food items, and optional birthing grounds for females, to name only a few.

Pecking Order

Many social interactions are observed within schools or groups of sharks. While feeding on whale carcasses, large white sharks will often aggressively chase away or even severely bite smaller individuals of the same species, and will ultimately do most of the feeding. Dominance hierarchies between species over food are also common, such as the interaction between reef whitetip sharks (low dominance), gray reef (middle dominance), and silvertip (high dominance). Similar hierarchies also clearly exist for many species in non-feeding situations. For example, male bonnethead sharks will display a threat posture known as a "hunch" toward others in the group, and physically bump and bite females or smaller males.

Perhaps the most spectacular and well-documented of the shark's social behavior is the agonistic (ready for combat) display demonstrated by the gray reef shark of tropical Pacific reefs. When approached by a diver at rapid speed or cornered against the reef, the shark will exhibit a threat display in which it arches its back, depresses the pectoral fins, and moves in an exaggerated swimming motion. This is a graded behavioral display in which the intensity of the display increases with the level of the shark's agitation.

If a shark in an intense display is further pressed, it will probably attack the source of the threat. Because the agonistic display of the gray reef shark occurs in non-feeding contexts, it may be a form of territorial defense, but it seems to be unrelated to defense of any specific site, so it may represent some defense of personal space or be anti-predator behavior.

Courtship

All species of shark yet studied engage in some form of complex social reproductive behavior because the male must copulate to fertilize the female's eggs. In many species, a male closely follows a female during the mating season with its nose near the female's vent, which is probably a way of obtaining chemical information about her reproductive condition. During courtship, a male may aggressively bite the back, flanks, and fins of the female, inflicting severe wounds, but this seems to stimulate her willingness to copulate.

COURTSHIP AND MATING *A diver observes a group of Port Jackson sharks mating (below). It is hard to gather data for species living in some remote habitats.*

Near the end of courtship, the male usually grasps the female's pectoral fin in his mouth, flexes a single clasper and rolls on his side to insert the clasper into the female's cloaca. In most large reef species, the pair will rest together for a few minutes on the bottom during sperm transfer, but some large species continue to swim while they copulate.

In smaller species, such as catsharks, which are more flexible, a male will often coil its body around the female during copulation without biting her fins. While nearly all of our information on shark mating comes from reef-dwelling species, almost nothing is known about the sex lives of the large pelagics because of their inaccessible environment and wide range.

FOOD *and* FEEDING

Each species of shark occupies a specific feeding niche within its habitat, and provides an important link in the flow of energy through the Earth's oceans.

Contrary to popular myths, sharks are not scavengers of the deep, feeding indiscriminately on garbage or anything that crosses their path. They are carnivores occupying nearly all feeding levels of all marine food webs. Most small sharks associated with reef systems or bays are major predators of large invertebrates, such as crabs, shrimp, worms, squid, and small bony fishes. Snails and sea urchins, which are primary grazers on fields of benthic algae, are also important prey for hornsharks and some other small species.

The diet of the wide-ranging requiem sharks of reef habitats includes larger bony fishes, squid, cuttlefish, and octopus. Large tiger sharks, usually found in the deeper regions of tropical reef systems, consume a wide variety of vertebrates,

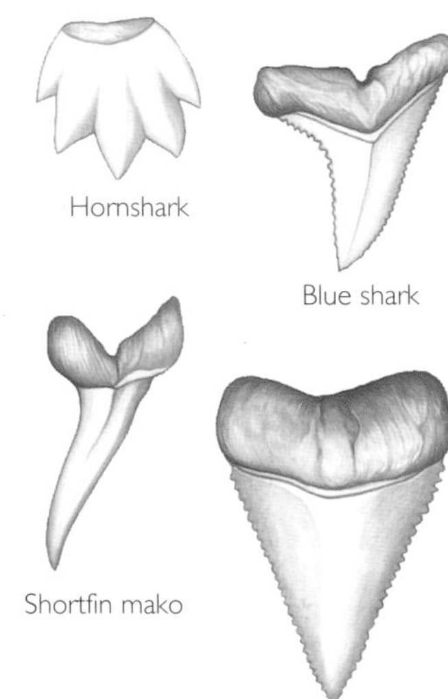

including large fishes, turtles and sea birds. Even large marine mammals, such as seals, sea lions, and dolphins, are preyed on by adult great whites and other large sharks.

HUNTING STRATEGIES

Each species of shark usually hunts in a certain way. Many small reef sharks, such as hornsharks and smooth-hounds, are benthic foragers that move over wide areas of the reef or open sand bottom in search of invertebrates. Other benthic species, such as the wobbegongs and angel-sharks, are ambush predators. Their bodies are camouflaged by cryptic colors and patterns that match their background. They lie concealed on the bottom until an unsuspecting small fish or crustacean comes close enough for a strike.

Many ambush predators also use trickery. For example, the wobbegong mimics benthic algae, and the nurse shark rolls its pectoral fins under the body to mimic a small reef crevice. Both of these strategies are designed to lure unsuspecting small reef fishes into what looks like a safe shelter. Other sharks are pursuit predators that actively chase down their fleeing prey. Blacktip reef sharks move in groups over coral reef flats during the day in search of surgeonfishes and mullet. Gray reef sharks cruise the edges of coral reefs at dawn and dusk, pursuing prey fishes.

Hammerhead sharks commonly roam the sandy

MODIFICATIONS *The teeth of sharks (above) show adaptations to cope with their various diets. Stages in the biting action of the great white shark (below): the mouth begins to open; the snout lifts as the upper jaw protrudes; the lower jaw slips forward; and closes again on the prey*

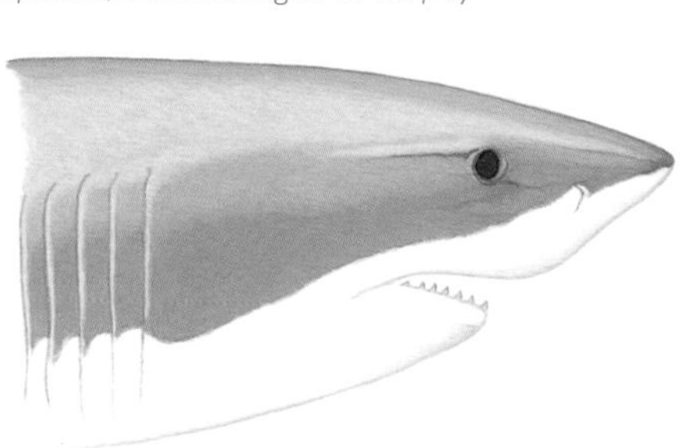

Stage 1

Stage 2

reef flats in search of stingrays, which they pin to the bottom with their head and devour. One of the most unusual predatory behaviors is that of reef interior hunters, such as reef whitetip, nurse, and epaulette sharks. The bodies of these species are so attenuated and flexible that they can swim into small holes in search of hidden crustaceans and fish prey, only to emerge from another hole on the other side of the reef.

Lethal Weapons

Sharks show many anatomical and behavioral adaptations for feeding, with the dentition of the jaw being particularly efficient. Species, such as the hornsharks and bonnethead sharks, that consume armored invertebrates, have small, sharp teeth at the front of the jaw for grasping their prey, and flat, molariform teeth at the back to crush the hard shell before swallowing. Larger requiem sharks have flat, triangular teeth with serrated edges to cut large fish and cephalopods into pieces before swallowing.

This tooth design reaches its climax with the large, triangular and serrated teeth of the lamnid great white shark, which can easily cut a 22 pound (10 kg) chunk of blubber from a whale body in a single bite.

Other species, such as the mako and sand tiger sharks, have long, thin, needle-like teeth that have become adapted for grasping large fish. The jaw and associated muscles form a highly efficient mechanism for the rapid capture, processing, and manipulation of many types of prey.

In the great white shark, the feeding action begins when the head and snout are lifted, and the lower jaw is simultaneously depressed. Once the jaw is fully open, muscle contractions force the forward rotation of the upper jaw, which detaches from the skull and comes completely out of the mouth. This action creates this predator's powerful and awesome bite.

"BITE AND SPIT" THEORY

Adult great white sharks are the major predator of elephant seals and sea lions, such as the group at right. These animals bask at the surface in many temperate coastal waters of the world. Surfers and skin divers are also sometimes attacked at the surface by great whites in these areas.

One similarity between encounters with both humans and marine pinnipeds is that the initial attack frequently involves a single, massive bite that inflicts a major, often fatal injury. Usually no flesh is removed until the subsequent bites.

This predatory behavior, unique to the great white shark, has led researchers to propose the "Bite and Spit" hypothesis. The prey is released after the first quick and powerful killing bite, aimed to incapacitate the victim. This behavior is thought to reduce the chance of injury to the shark during, for example, prolonged contact with a large, struggling elephant seal. Such a formidable opponent usually has dangerous teeth and nails and could weigh more than 1,000 pounds (500 kg).

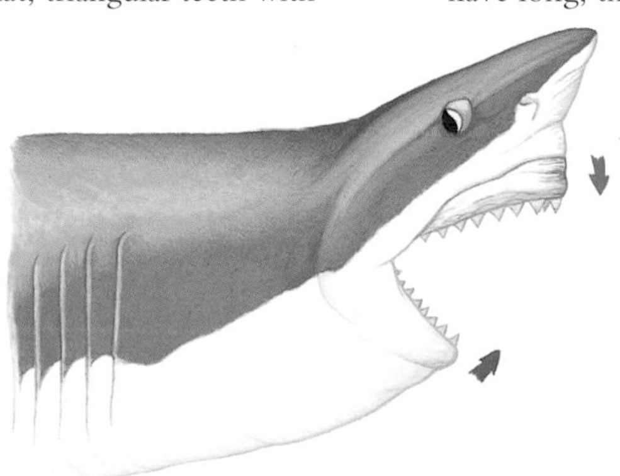

Stage 3

Stage 4

Daily Movements *and* Migrations

As advanced technologies tap into the ocean's secrets, we are gradually building up a picture of the way sharks use their environment.

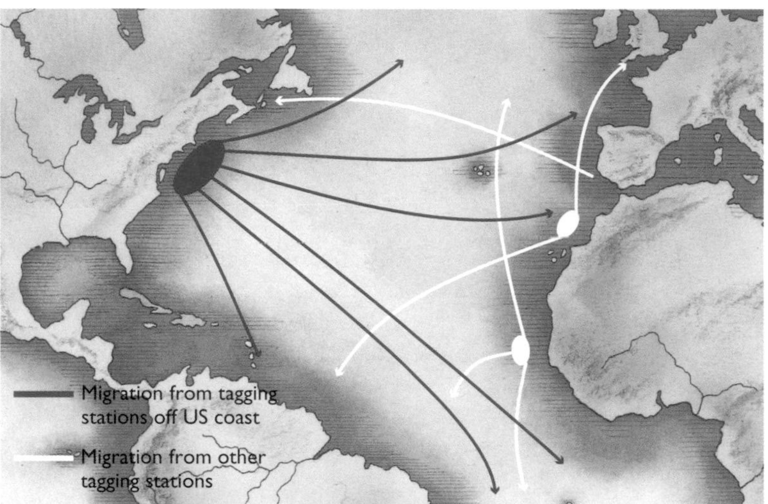

EPIC JOURNEYS *The map (left) shows the migratory patterns of the blue shark around the Atlantic Ocean, as revealed by an extensive tagging program. Individual animals may travel incredible distances each year.*

Spanning vast distances between continents, the world's oceans provide highways for the global migrations of many pelagic sharks. Other species never venture far from major landmasses, but travel long distances parallel to the shoreline or adjacent continental shelf.

Many such migrations are to follow movements of their prey while others are related to mating activities or pupping of the young. Much of our current understanding about shark movements comes as a result of tremendous human effort, and with the advent of new technologies, knowledge continues to expand.

Major Migrations

Because of seasonal changes in many local shark numbers, fishers and researchers realized long ago that sharks make large-scale migrations. Much of the relevant data about these movements comes from long-term tagging programs supported primarily by government agencies, researchers, and sport and commercial fishers.

The main tool is the dart tag—a numbered, labeled plastic streamer attached to a nylon or stainless-steel barb. Sharks are captured by hook and line, identified to species, sexed and, if possible, measured. The dart, attached to an applicator pole, is inserted under the skin usually near the first dorsal fin. The shark is then released unharmed to continue with its normal movements. If it is later recaptured, data on size, date of capture, and location are sent to the tagging agency.

The largest of these, the Cooperative Shark Tagging Program, is sponsored by the United States National Marine Fisheries Service and has been in operation since 1962. To date, more than 87,000 sharks of 46 species have been tagged by scientists and fishers off the eastern seaboard of North America. Of these, there have been nearly 4,000 returns covering 30 species.

Sharks are classified in three categories based on their migratory patterns. Local sharks are non-migratory species, such as the bull shark, nurse shark, and bonnethead shark. These sharks are found near the shore or above reefs, and seem to range within an area of only a few hundred miles.

Coastal pelagic sharks occur in deep waters above continental shelves. These include large species, such as the dusky, sandbar, tiger, and blacktip sharks, that are capable of migration distances in excess of 1,000 miles (1,600 km). The sandbar shark, for example, is known to migrate from the northeastern seaboard of North America to southern Mexico. Highly pelagic sharks, such as the mako and blue shark, make long, often transoceanic migrations across the deep basins of the Atlantic.

The longest linear movement by an individual was recorded for a blue shark tagged off the coast of the northeast United States and recaptured 300 miles (500 km) south of the Equator, a travel distance of 3,740 miles (6,000 km). Multiple recaptures of tagged blue sharks indicate regular transatlantic migrations over distances greater than 10,000 miles (16,000 km). Although shark tag and recapture data are relatively scarce in the Pacific, it is probable that blue sharks make similar long migrations between the coast of North America and Asia. While dart tagging is still valuable, it will be new technologies, such as satellite telemetry, that will eventually unravel the mystery of the global movements of sharks.

Daily Movements

New technology has emerged that is helping to record shark movements in their everyday environment, too. In recent years, many scientists have used ultrasonic telemetry transmitters, which are attached to the shark and tracked with a hydrophone from a boat or by a diver. These devices can be fitted with sensors to monitor depth, swimming speed, body or water temperature, or even stomach pH. Telemetry studies of the blue sharks off Santa Catalina Island, California, show that at certain times of year, individuals spend daylight hours not far offshore. After dark, they move in closer, presumably to feed.

Other studies show that tiger sharks associated with Pacific reefs move over a home range as large as 14 square miles (40 sq km) each day and make frequent vertical dives along the reef slopes at night, probably to feed. Other tropical reef species, such as the gray reef shark, may cover areas of about 11 square miles (30 sq km) each day. Within a given species, smaller sharks generally have smaller home ranges than do larger adults. For example, juvenile lemon sharks, which live in shallow reef flats near mangrove habitats, have a home range of less than ½ square mile (1 sq km), while adults use 20 square miles (50 sq km) or more.

Sharks also seem to pay visits to particular areas at regular times. For example, hornsharks found on temperate rocky reefs were observed to forage in the same area of the reef each day, rest in the same area of the rocky reef in the afternoon, and return to shelter in a single cave each night. Similarly, telemetered large gray reef sharks visit specific regions of the reef each day.

BUILDING THE PICTURE

A lemon shark swims past a monitor (top) that picks up a signal from an ultrasonic transmitter implanted in its body. A numbered tag from the University of Miami (above) carries instructions and a return address. A tiger shark (right) being tagged.

CHAPTER FIVE
RAYS

The secret pit of the ocean holds a universe of tangled infinities.

JOSEPH MACINNIS (b.1937), Canadian ocean explorer

IDENTIFYING *and* CLASSIFYING RAYS

Rays are among the most distinctive of the cartilaginous fishes but their classification is difficult and the subject of spirited ongoing scientific debate.

There are almost 600 living species of rays from some 18 families. Their body shapes have become highly modified and specialized. They are flattened in various ways and the pectoral fins and part of the body are joined to form a distinctive structure known as the "disc." This is typically wider than deep and may be wedge-shaped, oval, circular, or triangular. Members of major families are easy to recognize, but species can be confusingly similar in form.

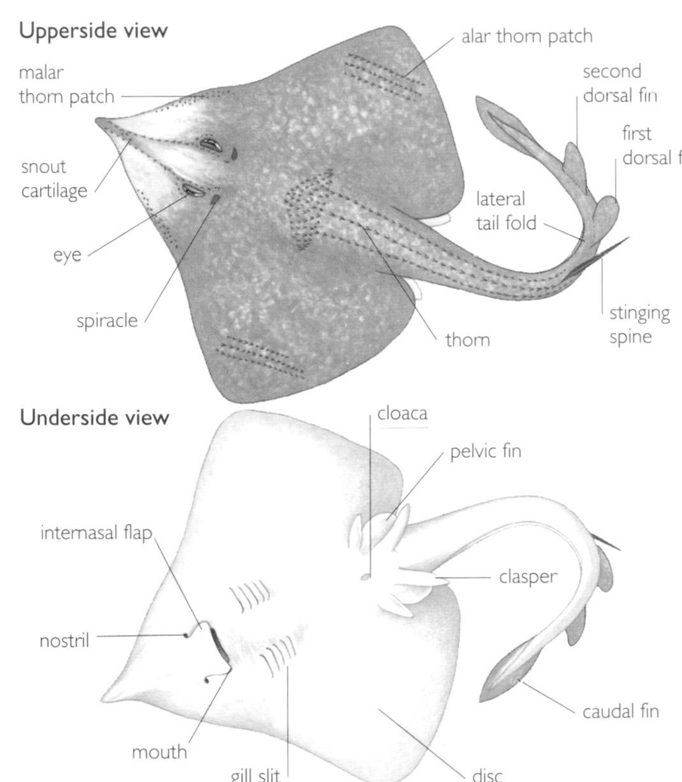

DISTINCTIVE FEATURES

Some shark groups, such as angelsharks and sawsharks, also have enlarged pectoral fins that resemble a small disc, but their gills are on the sides of the head. Rays, on the other hand, have five (or six) pairs of gill slits on the undersurface. In many ray groups, the head forms part of the disc and when the head is separate, the pectoral fins join the head in front of the gill slits. In bottom-dwellers, the eyes and spiracles are usually on top of the head. In a few blind electric rays, the eyes are covered with skin and difficult to see.

Some ray charactersistics are very useful for identification, for example, snouts that resemble saws, electric organs, enlarged pelvic fins that are joined to form discs, and lobe or horn-like projections on the snouts. The sexes can be distinguished at an early age. Male claspers are important in distinguishing species, because their shape and structure varies not only among families but also within them. They have been used extensively to

BODY LANGUAGE *Identifying the parts of ray (above). A bluespotted ribbontail ray (left) in Mabul, Malaysia.*

distinguish close relatives and also to assess evolutionary relationships between genera and species. The skin, thick in many rays, is either smooth with a coating of slimy mucus or may have a protective armor of strong bony tubercles or thorns. Size, shape, and location of these special types of denticle varies from species to species, which is important in identification.

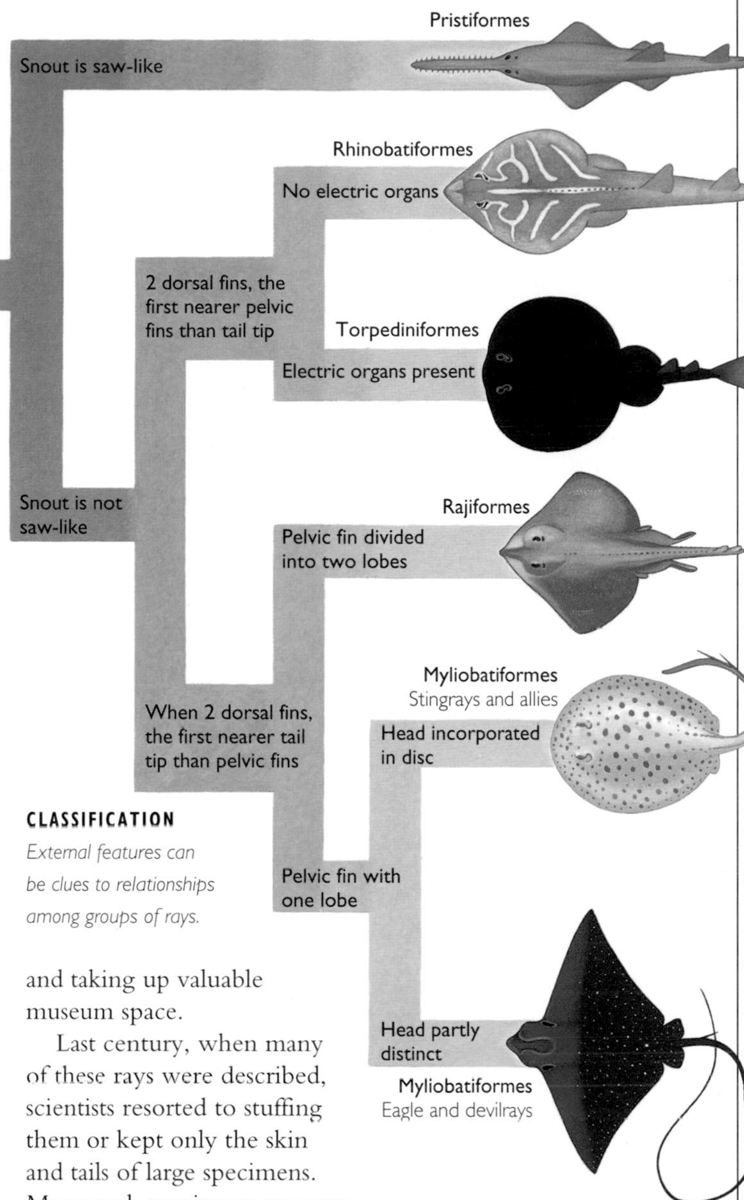

CLASSIFICATION
External features can be clues to relationships among groups of rays.

What Size Tells Us

With more than half of the species exceeding 20 inches (50 cm) in length, rays are among the largest fishes. The tail, which is often damaged, varies greatly in length from one specimen to another, so scientists prefer to express size in width. The gigantic manta ray may exceed 22 feet (6.7 m) in width and weigh several tons. The smallest, the short-nose electric ray, is less than 4 inches (10 cm) wide and weighs less than 1 pound (500 g). The average adult size varies greatly from family to family. While all numb-fishes are smaller than 3 feet (90 cm), the range for sawfish species is from 5–25 feet (1.4–7.6 m), and the highly diverse skates, with more than 280 species, vary from 8 inches to 8 feet (20 cm to 2.5 m).

Our knowledge of ray taxonomy is increasing only slowly. Unknown species lurk in the ocean depths, particularly in the Indo-Pacific where more than 50 new species have been discovered in the past decade. Inshore species are often mistakenly identified and need further study. Large adults can be bulky and heavy, making them difficult to collect, transport, and store, and taking up valuable museum space.

Last century, when many of these rays were described, scientists resorted to stuffing them or kept only the skin and tails of large specimens. Many such specimens are now lost or in poor condition.

Gathering Clues

Male and female rays can differ in shape and color, as can the young. To identify features that distinguish one species from another, taxonomists need to examine several specimens, including juveniles and mature males and females. For many species, this simply has not been possible.

When trying to identify a ray, it is important to note its external features. Is the disc large or small compared to the tail? Is the head separate from the disc? Is the tail broad and muscular, long and whip-like, or short and narrow? Does the tail have dorsal and caudal fins and where are they? All these important initial observations are needed to identify the ray's family group.

Beyond this point, the identification becomes more difficult and a knowledge of the species occurring within the area is usually needed. Each region has a unique ray fauna, with the species often having narrow distributional ranges. If you know where the ray was caught, the number of options can be reduced. Details of color, denticles, and placement of thorns are also vital clues.

THE EVOLUTION *and* RADIATION *of* RAYS

Given the difficulties in studying these interesting animals, it may be some time yet before the ray's evolutionary history is fully unraveled.

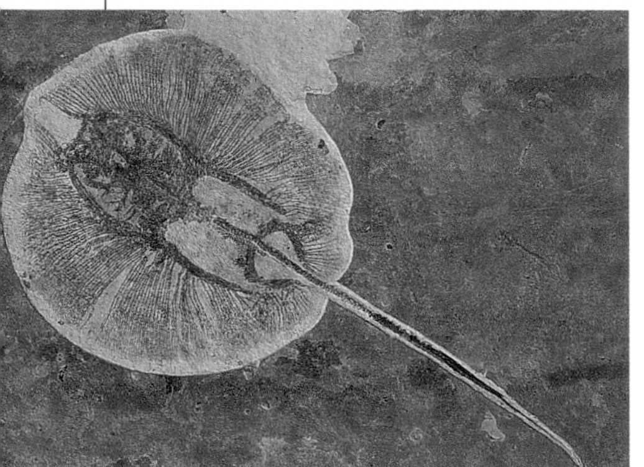

Rays evolved from sharks but there has been much debate about which groups are the oldest, and the sequence of their evolution. They belong to a major group of cartilaginous fishes called Squalea, which includes dogfishes, sixgill and sevengill sharks, angelsharks, and sawsharks. Ancestral rays may have resembled sawfishes and probably evolved during the age of the dinosaurs.

Guitarfishes and their relatives are thought to be among the oldest ray groups, and eagle rays, devilrays, and stingrays are the most recently evolved. Skates may be the immediate recent ancestors of either shovelnose rays or electric rays. Some ichthyologists believe that electric rays evolved before sawfishes. Yet another theory says that electric ray groups may have evolved from an ancestral guitarfish. The picture is unclear, so several classes of batoids have been proposed.

THE FOSSIL RECORD

The earliest known fossil rays date back to the Jurassic Period, more than 150 million years ago (mya). Most species are known from only a few teeth, denticles, and spines, but well-preserved whole bodies of ancient guitarfishes have been found. The appearance of these rays has changed little with time.

Sadly, the fossil record of many groups is incomplete. We know from examining the distributions of living rays and from Earth's geological history that several groups roamed those ancient seas for even longer than the fossil evidence suggests. While ray fossils of the Cretaceous (65–145 mya) are comparatively rare, they are common throughout Tertiary sediments (25–60 mya). Many such fossils are represented only by teeth, but whole fossil animals, including the stingray *Heliobatis*, trapped in coastal lakes when sea levels fell and the oceans receded, have been found in shales from the Green River, Wyoming, USA.

The oldest known fossil skates were found in sediments of a prehistoric sea dated to the late Cretaceous, some 70 mya. It has been suggested that these rays colonized the Pacific and Atlantic via an ancient marine pathway, the Tethyan Sea. But it is also probable that an old group of skates had an ancestor in the

ANCIENT AND MODERN *The white-spotted guitarfish (right) shares many characteristics with its fossilized ancestor* Heliobatis *(above) taken from Eocene deposits more than 35 million years old.*

seas around Gondwanaland, the ancient southern supercontinent. This group, which includes the rough skate, *Raja nasuta*, has species still living in the coastal seas of South America, New Zealand, and southern Australia. These three regions were connected to Antarctica in the Cretaceous Period, but later drifted apart. Since skates do not migrate across open oceans, they must have lived there before the break-up of Gondwanaland (about 80 mya). The oldest Antarctic fossils date from 50 mya.

Wide Distribution

Living rays, very successful fishes, are found in all oceans and seas on Earth. They are valuable in determining the evolutionary structure of the world's fish faunas because some of the groups contain species that are closely related but which have very restricted distributions. The eggs of many bony pelagic fishes drift in the open sea and are often transported to areas far from where they were laid. Young rays, on the other hand, are born alive or hatch from eggs laid on the bottom. Dispersal beyond their existing range depends almost entirely on the movements of the mother.

Unlike bony fishes, which produce eggs numbering millions in some species, rays have very few young at the end of quite a long gestation period. This limits how rapidly their populations can increase, so they rely instead on the survival of the few young they produce. If their numbers are affected by external influences, such as overfishing or loss of habitat, the survival of the species could be threatened.

Ray distributions also vary greatly from group to group. Sharkfin guitarfishes, devilrays, and sawfishes occur throughout the tropics but seldom visit cooler temperate waters. The ubiquitous skates live around the shelves and slopes of oceanic islands and all continents but have never been found near the coral islands of the Pacific. These are the dominant rays in cool waters but they are mostly confined to deeper waters in the tropics. Few of the families have restricted distributions, although the shorttailed electric rays (Hypnidae) are confined to Australian seas, and the river rays (Potamotrygonidae) are native to the South American rivers and lakes that drain into the Atlantic Ocean.

DISTANTLY RELATED GROUPS

The thornback skate (top), and the widely distributed sparsely spotted stingaree (above), probably have similar body forms because of the similarity of their lifestyles.

Rich Diversity

The shortnose electric rays (Narkidae) have an unusual distribution that includes the Indo-West Pacific (from Indonesia to Japan) and New Zealand, but not Australia. Within some families, genera may be quite restricted. Stingarees (Urolophidae) and whiprays (*Himantura*) have groups of species that occur in the Indo-West Pacific and off Central America but are quite distantly related to each other. Other groups have diversified greatly in some regions but less in others. Stingrays are much more diverse in the Indian Ocean than in the Atlantic.

The richest ray faunas are in the Indo-Pacific, from South Africa to Japan and Australia. About a third of all species occur off Australia and Indonesia. Atlantic faunas are smaller but still contain endemic species.

THE ANATOMY and BIOLOGY of RAYS

The secret lives of rays can be glimpsed by studying their anatomy and, in many cases, this is the best evidence we have.

We know details of the biology and ecology of only a small number of ray species. For example, while we are aware that most species live and feed on or near the bottom, we generally have a poor understanding of the more intimate aspects of their lives. Fortunately, a basic profile of a ray's life can be gleaned by examining its body features, such as shape, color, size, mouth structure, fin details, and internal anatomy. This field of study, known as ecomorphology, is becoming increasingly useful in predicting the lifestyles of many species of fish, including rays.

BODY SHAPE

Ray families vary greatly in shape, which makes them ideal subjects for ecomorphological studies. Their discs are well adapted for either a bottom-dwelling life or for swimming almost continuously above the bottom. The extent of flattening of the disc, its musculature, and its overall shape reflect the animal's preferred lifestyle. The tail, which is separate from the disc, is variably developed. The shorttailed electric rays (Hypnidae) have probably the shortest tails of all fishes. In contrast, the long, skinny whip-like tails of some stingrays, often several yards long, are among the longest found in fishes. In guitarfishes, the tail is comparatively broad, muscled, and powerful.

The dorsal and caudal fins vary greatly in shape, size and position among species. In some sawfishes and guitarfishes they are tall and shark-like, but in most other rays they are small. In the stingrays and eagle rays they are absent or rudimentary. One or more venomous stinging spines on the tail of many stingrays and stingarees are used to repel attacks by predatory sharks. Some eagle rays and butterfly rays also have stinging spines.

INTERNAL FEATURES

Ray skeletons, made almost entirely of cartilage, are highly modified, with the strong skull very flattened and a chain of small vertebrae that extends to the tip of the tail. The snout of guitarfishes and many skates is kept rigid by cartilage that extends from the front of the skull. This cartilage is absent in some species, such as the stingarees and stingrays, which need

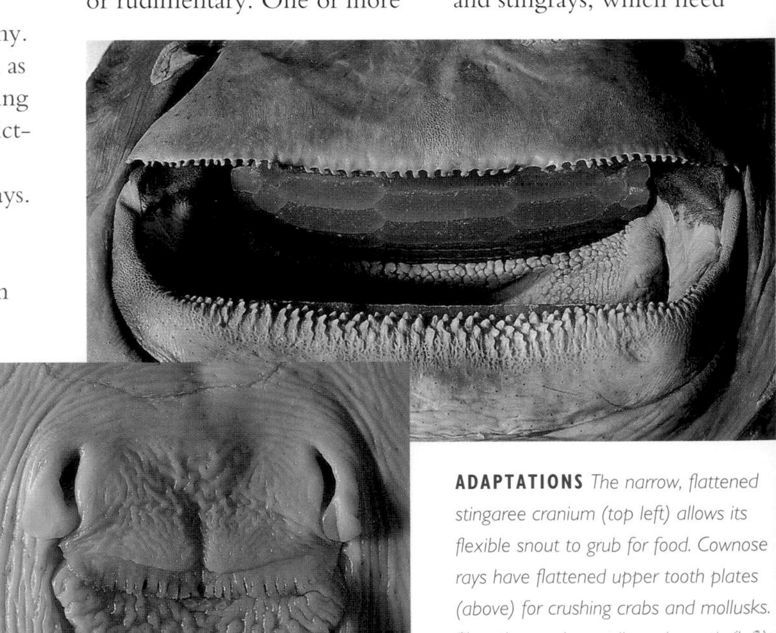

ADAPTATIONS *The narrow, flattened stingaree cranium (top left) allows its flexible snout to grub for food. Cownose rays have flattened upper tooth plates (above) for crushing crabs and mollusks. The stingaree's nostrils and mouth (left) house a well-developed sensory system for locating prey. A bat ray (right) consuming squid eggs.*

highly flexible snouts to grub for food. An animal's skeleton stops the body from flopping and provides attachment points for its muscles. The ray's disc is supported by numerous thin, pectoral-fin cartilages. These cartilages are flattened, densely packed and extend over most of the disc.

The brain of a ray is small and simple compared to that of a dolphin or a seal, but in ratio to body weight it is surprisingly large. In fact, this ratio is similar to that found in marsupials and birds. Of the cartilaginous fishes, rays are among the best endowed brainwise, with the manta ray having the largest brain of all.

All rays are carnivorous but most occupy a level below that of sharks in the food chain hierarchy. Where sharks are important predators on reefs and in open water, rays play a more significant role as predators on soft substrates. Large rays, including several torpedo rays, stingrays, and skates, are known to feed on fishes. However, small mobile invertebrates, such as sand worms, crustaceans, and mollusks, are more important dietary items. Algae and sedentary invertebrates, such as sea tulips, anemones, corals, and sponges, are rarely eaten.

TAIL STORIES

The stingray's whip-like tail (top) carries a venomous spine; the shovelnose ray's (above) is for swimming power.

Feeding Strategies

As the majority of rays are bottom dwellers, the mouth is located on the undersurface. Most rays feed by trapping prey against the substrate with their disc. Food is directed to the mouth by maneuvering the disc over the prey, or by manipulating the victim by means of the flexible disc flaps. Rays can be quite selective feeders and the various shapes of their mouth and teeth are an indication of their food preferences.

The bowmouth guitarfish, for example, has a contoured mouth with small, tightly packed, flattened teeth for crushing hard-shelled invertebrates. Eagle and cownose rays have a series of flattened tooth plates, rather like beaks, to crush crabs and mollusks. Torpedo rays have a very arched lower jaw studded with small spiny teeth. This can be thrust forward to suck up small fishes from the substrate. The cavernous mouth of the plankton-feeding manta ray is at the front of the snout. The teeth, which are not important in feeding, are minute and covered in skin in the lower jaw and totally absent in the upper jaw. Skates and most stingrays have compact rows of strong, pointed teeth in both jaws for simultaneously holding and crushing struggling prey.

The part of the sensory system used to find and gather food is well developed in rays. Sawfishes and most guitarfish have long, slit-like nostrils just forward of the mouth. The nostrils of other rays are partly covered with a broad, fleshy lobe, known as the internasal flap. This is covered in sensory pores and usually reaches the mouth. The pores form part of the ampullae of Lorenzini—an electroreceptor system for detecting electric fields produced by the nerves and muscles of other animals. Rays use them to detect predators, prey, and other members of the same species.

THE HABITAT *of the* RAY

These highly successful animals have adapted to all kinds of habitat and have found niches in oceans and seas all around the globe.

The majority of rays live exclusively in the sea, but some spend part of their lives in estuaries. A few have even invaded fresh water, living in rivers thousands of miles from the coast. Rays are important in marine communities, playing an integral part in the day-to-day life of the sea. Each has a discrete role—the common perception of a particular ray being just another ray is quite wrong.

For example, the lives of rays found in estuaries differ markedly from those living on outer continental shelves. Similarly, species living together in one area are biologically distinct from each other in some way. They may eat the same food, but they will have different seasonal distributions, reproductive methods, or prefer to live on different types of bottom. Most rays are highly efficient, and in some regions appear to have ousted bottom-dwelling bony fishes such as soles and flounders.

GLASS WALLS *This ray likes to rest on the smooth wall of its aquarium tank at Underwater World in Perth, Australia.*

BALANCING SALINITY

Rays living in estuaries must be able to overcome potentially severe ionic stresses from fluctuating salinity. In high-salinity environments, such as the sea, water diffuses out through permeable membranes of living cells in a process known as osmosis, and salts are gained. In fresh water, the reverse occurs, water diffuses into the animal, and salts are lost. Animals living in either environment need to balance their salt and water concentrations to survive. In brackish estuaries, this is made more difficult because the salinity of the water is changing continuously as river water mixes with the sea.

To achieve a balance, the ray adjusts its internal osmotic pressure to minimize the transfer of water through its membranes. In the sea, rays supplement chloride levels in the blood and tissue with nitrogen compounds, such as urea. Apart from some water taken up through the membranes of the gills and mouth, their bodies are almost impermeable, so rays can live in estuaries for short periods without the osmotic stresses experienced by bony fishes. Rays that live full-time in fresh water, such as the ocellate river ray below, have more difficulty. These rays need to reduce their osmotic concentration. To compensate, they have very well-developed kidneys and endlessly excrete large quantities of weak urine to remove excess water and minimize ionic losses.

DIFFERING LIFESTYLES

Rays occupy a variety of habitats in the sea. They are found inshore in very shallow water but extend offshore down into the abyss to depths exceeding 10,000 feet (3,000 m). Some rays are predominately pelagic, swimming tirelessly in midwater and rarely resting on the bottom. Others lie on or bury themselves in the substrate, only swimming off the bottom to browse for food, reproduce, or escape from predators. However, unlike some bottom-dwelling bony fishes, none of the rays live in burrows.

The habitat needs of rays are evident from their body

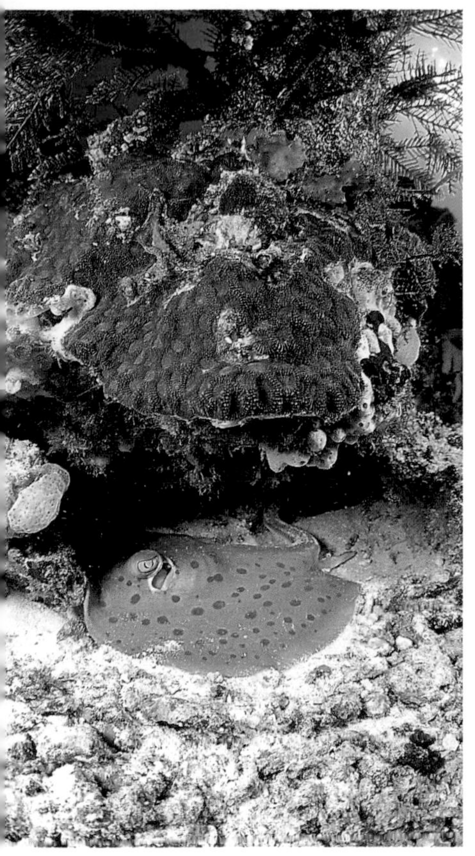

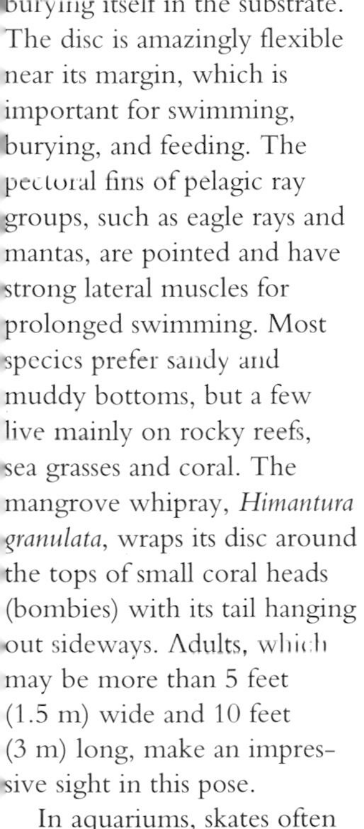

shapes and may be quite specific. A rounded, flattened body is ideally adapted to burying itself in the substrate. The disc is amazingly flexible near its margin, which is important for swimming, burying, and feeding. The pectoral fins of pelagic ray groups, such as eagle rays and mantas, are pointed and have strong lateral muscles for prolonged swimming. Most species prefer sandy and muddy bottoms, but a few live mainly on rocky reefs, sea grasses and coral. The mangrove whipray, *Himantura granulata*, wraps its disc around the tops of small coral heads (bombies) with its tail hanging out sideways. Adults, which may be more than 5 feet (1.5 m) wide and 10 feet (3 m) long, make an impressive sight in this pose.

In aquariums, skates often prefer to rest on the smooth, vertical glass walls, rather than on coarse rubble or rocky bottoms. Other rays living on reefs seek refuge on sandy patches among corals or under ledges.

Seasonal Changes

Some habitats are used seasonally or for only part of the day. Estuaries, tidal flats, and mangrove swamps are very important feeding areas for many tropical rays but few live there permanently. Instead, they move into these areas on the incoming tide and retreat as it recedes. Others move into some particular habitat for part of the year, perhaps to breed, and such seasonal migrations can be highly consistent from year to year.

Beyond the continental shelf break, demarcated by the 655 foot (200 m) isobath, lies the open ocean. Much of the deep-sea floor is muddy ooze. Some deep-water skates use their long, firm snouts, covered in sensory pores, to grub around in the soft upper layers. The equally long, but softer and more flexible snout of the sixgill stingrays (Hexatrygonidae) appears to be used like a finger to probe more deeply into the sediments for food.

Oceanic Mysteries

Devilrays live throughout tropical seas and migrate across the open oceans in water many miles deep. Their activities when far from shore are not well understood, but we believe they remain quite close to the surface.

One species of stingray is primarily oceanic and may venture into deep water. Unlike coastal rays, which typically have pale bellies, the pelagic stingray (*Pteryoplatytrygon violacea*) is black all over. Our knowledge of its distribution in the open seas is based on specimens hooked accidentally by longline fishers catching tuna.

HABITAT PREFERENCES *A blue-spotted ribbontail ray (top left) shelters under a ledge near Bunaken Island, Indonesia, while the stingray (below) is more at home swimming near the sandy sea floor surrounding the Bahamas.*

LIFE CYCLE *and* REPRODUCTION

Nature has equipped these creatures with marvelous ways to handle the hazards that arise during the dangerous time of conception and birth.

Rays use two types of reproductive strategy, egg laying (oviparity) or a form of livebearing (ovoviviparity) in which there is no placental attachment of the embryo to the mother. In all species, male rays, like sharks, fertilize females internally using their claspers, the modified inner edges of the pelvic fin. Claspers are present as a pair of minute lobes near the cloaca in young males at birth. They expand greatly in late adolescence and become firm with the development of internal cartilage when the male reaches sexual maturity. They are made up of many small cartilages, but their anatomy varies greatly among the ray families and even within certain genera.

The end of the clasper, known as the glans, carries many tiny structures, which may include hooks, spines, discs, plates, spongy tissue, and grooves. When the glans opens during copulation, these structures are responsible for maintaining contact within the female, as well as holding and transferring the semen. Lubricating fluid is produced in secretory glands at the base of each clasper. In some rays, this fluid may also block the female's oviduct, to prevent her from being fertilized again by another male.

COURTSHIP AND DEVELOPMENT

Copulation can appear violent and takes place in a variety of positions, either belly to belly, or back to belly with the claspers greatly twisted. The male often initially follows the female with his acutely sensitive snout close to her cloaca in search of chemical "green lights." Courtship usually includes some degree of nibbling or biting of the disc. The teeth of mature male skates are more slender and pointed than those of females, and probably help them to grasp the female during copulation.

Eagle rays use their flattened tooth plates to gouge the female's fins during courtship. Copulation can last just a few minutes or go on for hours, depending on the species. The act may take place on the bottom or in midwater. In each case, the teeth and body spines are important in helping the male maintain his position. In some skates, the male moves beneath the female and holds himself in place by the retractable alar thorns on top of the pectoral fins. Females may mate with several males in succession.

Skates are the only rays that do not give birth to live young. They lay leathery egg cases that are anchored or attached to the bottom. These are rectangular with long tendrils at each corner. Part of the egg case is usually sticky and shell bits and sand become attached,

PROPAGATION *A giant black stingray with its pup (top). Detail of a pair of male claspers (above) belonging to the eastern shovelnose stingaree. The ends are modified to hold the male in position while the sperm is delivered.*

weighting the egg case to the bottom. Embryos may take more than six months to develop so the cases have to be tough enough to avoid being eaten by predatory invertebrates and fishes. Some marine snails use their horny, rasping tongue to bore holes in the case and siphon out the contents.

In the ovoviviparous rays, the developing embryos either swallow nutrients secreted from the mother's uterus (as in torpedo rays), or absorb nutrients via string-like extensions of the uterus that reach the gut through the spiracles (typical of stingrays, eagle rays and butterfly rays). A newborn pup is sometimes more than 50 times heavier than the unfertilized egg.

Protective Measures

Sharp parts of young rays are likely to damage the mother at birth and in the uterus. Young sawfishes have a snout like the adult's, so the entire saw and its teeth are soft, flexible and covered with a membranous sheath at birth. The snout straightens and the teeth harden soon after. Similarly, the stinging spines of venomous rays are soft at birth. Some skates and stingrays that are very thorny as adults are born almost devoid of denticles. On the other hand, some mothers, for example, female electric rays, must avoid stunning and possibly killing their young. It has been found that torpedoes stop producing shocks in the presence of their pups and can be safely handled by humans. After the young are born, the rays revert to their usual habit of delivering shocks.

Rays have long gestation periods and produce relatively small litters, which makes them highly vulnerable to population collapses from over-fishing and habitat degradation. Many species also have a restricted range of distribution. These two factors make the group more fragile than most other marine animals, including bony fishes. Despite their obvious vulnerability, we have been slow to recognize their plight and their numbers continue to decline. Rays play an important role in the sea and the implications of their loss on the ecosystem are unknown.

THE MATING GAME

The breeding strategies of rays, which vary considerably among groups, are known for only a few of the more common species, such as the mating fiddler rays below. Round stingrays are segregated by sex outside the breeding season, with females occupying deeper parts of the continental shelf. Both sexes reunite inshore in late winter and spring to breed. In the morning, patrolling males locate receptive females, who make themselves obvious by resting on the substrate in harems, their bodies often in stacks. Groups of sexually inactive females, those we think may have already mated or are not reproductively active, remain buried in the shallows. During the afternoon, these females emerge to feed among sea grasses and the males become inactive. This daily cycle continues over a fortnight or so.

BIRTH PANGS *A sparsley spotted stingaree (left) in the process of giving birth, and a newborn stingaree pup (above) with umbilical cord still attached.*

SURVIVAL *and* DEFENSE

All animals face risks and rays have developed a powerful and surprising armory to defend themselves in the battle to survive.

The ray's ability to avoid and ward off predators is vital to its survival. Although they are relatively large fishes, they still have enemies and are a major food item for some species of shark. The ray's defensive armory includes electric organs, venomous spines, and hard bony thorns, also known as scutes. They can also make themselves difficult to detect by lying concealed in the silty or sandy substrate.

ON THE DEFENSIVE

The stinging spines (or stings) of rays, which are modified dorsal-fin spines, lie on top of the tail. The nearer the sting is to the tip, the more useful it becomes as a defensive weapon. It is a hard, flattened structure that tapers to a sharp point. The edges are serrated so that once driven into a victim, the sting either remains or tears the adjacent tissue when withdrawn.

Venom is produced and delivered in two narrow grooves running lengthways along the undersurface of the sting. The whole structure is covered by a thin skin which, when ruptured, releases its venom into the victim. Humans are frequent victims of ray stings but injuries are usually less severe than in shark attacks.

Longtailed rays, such as whiprays (*Himantura*), can use the tail to lash out when startled. The tail's effectiveness as a whip is lessened by the resistance of water, but this is partly compensated for by a covering of short sharp thorns that can severely lacerate unprotected skin. Despite this capability, these rays seem to use their tails on humans only in defense.

Sawfishes have been observed using the top of the snout as a bat to knock fishes away and laterally as a saw to lacerate. Large sawfishes can stun or kill fish as big as a grouper.

The shock-generating organs of the electric rays are among the most powerful found in fishes. Large torpedo rays can produce shocks of more than 200 volts. This is sufficient to knock humans off their feet or to stun an unsuspecting diver. Apart from defense against sharks, these organs are probably used to communicate, and to locate and stun prey. A kidney-shaped electric organ

TREATMENT OF RAY STINGS

The sting of a ray can be mildly painful to fatal, depending on the extent of the wound, its location, and the species of ray involved. The victim usually experiences immediate pain that increases in intensity over an hour or two. In most instances, the pain will abate within 6 to 12 hours. Victims of severe ray stings may experience breathing problems, nausea and vomiting, muscle cramping, and partial paralysis. Mechanical damage from the attack can also be fatal if the spine, pictured above, penetrates a vital organ.

Professional medical attention should be sought immediately. Meanwhile, any venom remaining on the surface of the wound should be washed away (fresh water is best, but salt water will do), and spine fragments removed. If the sting is on a limb, raise the limb higher than the victim's heart. The venom contains a large water-soluble protein that is destroyed by heat, so the wound should be washed in hot water (about 120 degrees Fahrenheit [50° C]) until the pain abates. Secondary infections can result if foreign bodies remain, so wounds are often X-rayed.

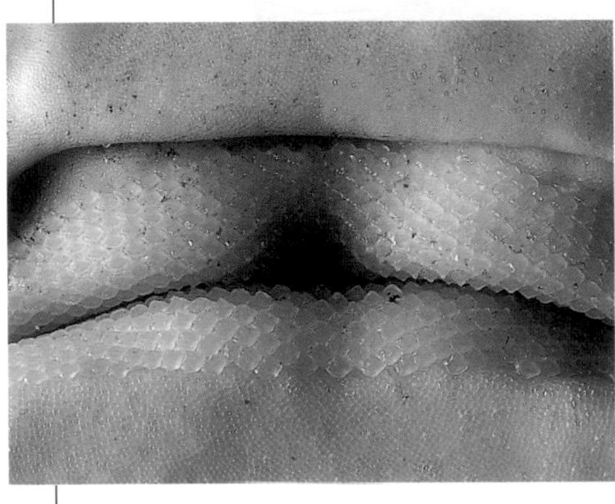

NON-SLIP GRIPPERS *The small teeth (above) of a shovelnose ray hold its prey firmly while it is crushed before swallowing.*

DEFENSIVE ARMORY *A porcupine ray (right) has a very rough upper surface consisting of plate-like denticles and sharp thorns (also present on the outer disc). The green sawfish (below) uses its saw both to cut and as a bat.*

is located lengthways near the middle of each side of the disc. Shocks can be delivered at will but quickly weaken in intensity. Some electric rays are known to rush at intruders to deliver a shock, but prey and predators alike are usually shocked accidentally when they wander over a concealed ray or strike it on the back.

Survival Tactics

Rays rarely use their teeth to retaliate. Eagle rays can bite if distressed, but are not likely to do so to deter predators, although surf fishers have had fingers crushed when removing hooks from a ray's mouth. Humans have also been bitten on the fingers when feeding stingrays. Recently, an oceanarium attendant who was wearing only scuba gear and swimsuit when hand-feeding a group of large whiprays, was severely lacerated by an over-exuberant ray.

The sensory capabilities of rays, such as sight, smell, vibration, touch, and electrical and magnetic impulses, are very well developed. The animal uses them in combination to survive. Signals to the brain supply the ray with a full picture of its surroundings. Rays are known to detect and use magnetic fields to locate prey, and they are also thought to use this sense to move along compass headings and detect ocean currents. Large rays migrating across open ocean, where senses such as sight and smell are of little use, probably use these capabilities to navigate.

Rays have their share of parasites. Particular species of rays become infected with adult tapeworms when they eat a smaller fish with a dormant cyst of the worm in its flesh. Digestive juices in the ray's stomach enable the cyst to hatch and the tapeworm grows to adulthood in the alimentary canal of its host. These worms, which may eventually grow to several yards in length, lay eggs that are passed into the sea with the ray's feces. These, in turn, may infect the ray's prey, thus continuing the life cycle.

Sometimes, small flattened crustaceans (copepods) and worms (monogeneans) are seen crawling on the skin within the ray's mucus, particularly on the head, near the cloaca, and on the tail. Unless present in large numbers, these parasites are rarely injurious to the ray.

Movement and Propulsion

The acrobatic gliding and rolling maneuvers of manta rays are well known to divers, but all rays ripple and glide with seemingly effortless grace.

Because they move in ways that vary greatly from group to group, the body shape and fins of rays are highly adapted to a pelagic existence or, more typically, to a life on the bottom.

Power and Grace

To understand the role of fins in movement, let us compare a ray with a glider. The pectoral and pelvic fins of the ray are equivalent to the wings, elevators, and ailerons of the glider, controlling horizontal stability and up-and-down movements. The tail fin and rudders (dorsal and caudal fins of the ray) are often more responsible for vertical stability, sideways movements, and steering.

Propulsion is mainly achieved either from the tail, by horizontal or lateral movement, or the pectoral fins, by vertical movement. Strongly built guitarfishes and sawfishes have powerful tails and relatively small pectoral fins compared with other rays. The tail muscles are arranged more as in sharks, and they move by laterally undulating the entire back half of the body. The pectoral fins are rather stiff and, rather than being flapped, are used to provide vertical control and stability. These rays also have well-developed dorsal and caudal fins, as do sharks, which enhance the swimming efficiency of the tail. The long lower lobe of the sharkfin guitarfishes provides lift.

Most rays have a well-developed disc, formed mostly from the pectoral fins. The tails vary from very short to several times longer than the discs. Except in some electric rays, the musculature is weak and plays a lesser role in propulsion. Skates and stingrays move by vertical undulations of the disc, either by flapping or sending ripple-like waves along the flexible disc edge. These ripples flow either from front to back to move the ray forward, or in reverse.

If only one side of the disc is moved independently, the

EFFORTLESS MOTION *Startled by something on the floor of the Coral Sea, a mangrove stingray (top) stirs up a great flurry of sand. A smoothtail mobula leaps out of the water (below).*

FLYING PROGRESS *Ripple-like waves along the edge of the disc enable the stingray (top) to move. A bat ray (right) changes direction by moving only one side of its disc.*

effect is like using oars on one side of a boat: the ray rotates. Movements of parts of the disc also enable the ray to dive, climb, turn, bank, or stop. Low-speed, finely controlled movements, not achievable by other bottom fishes, make rays incredibly maneuverable. This gives them a great advantage in seeking prey, enabling them to move around in the mud while still partly buried.

Some electric rays, such as numbfishes, use both disc and tail to move. On the bottom, delicate movements of the edge of its round disc allow the animal to forage around slowly. Above the bottom, it uses its well-developed tail and vertical fins to swim.

Distance Swimming

Mantas, cownose rays, and eagle rays are well adapted to a life that involves extended periods of swimming in open water. Most have long whip-like tails that serve no purpose in propulsion. Their powerful pectoral-fin muscles enable the stiff outer disc to flap like the wings of a bird. The center of the head and body are raised slightly on the downstroke and lowered on the upstroke. Unlike birds, they can flap one wing at a time to turn rapidly or beat a swift retreat by zigzagging away at great speed. This ability is used to foil predatory charges by sharks.

Unlike some bony fishes that drift passively in water currents or attach themselves to larger fish, rays are active continuously in open water. Some whiprays may seem passive at times when they ride on the backs of larger individuals, but apart from brief periods when copulating, they do not stay attached, as do lampreys and remoras.

Many rays are covered with a thick, slimy mucous coating to reduce drag. The mucus smooths out irregularities on the body surface and reduces surface tension. Apart from some stingrays and skates, rays seldom have large denticles and many are entirely smooth. The skin denticles make the body stiffer, so electric rays and stingarees with smooth skins generally have highly flexible discs capable of extremely delicate movements.

Rays lack the swim bladder of bony fishes and large oily liver that most sharks have to maintain neutral buoyancy, so unless they swim, they sink to the bottom. However, their enlarged pectoral fins give them one advantage over sharks. The flattened disc enables a ray to glide for long distances between active movements, which provides obvious benefits in conserving energy and may be useful in surprising prey. With their huge, lightweight discs, butterfly rays glide silently over the bottom searching for food and looking like stealth bombers.

Beating a Retreat

Rays are surprisingly good at retreating quickly from their resting position in the substrate if disturbed by a predator. They can turn quickly and accelerate rapidly at right angles to their original position. Others, including eagle rays and guitarfishes, prop on the tips of their pectoral fins in a racing start.

These animals differ in the way they retreat—eagle rays bear off by flapping one pectoral fin before accelerating, while guitarfishes twist the body and accelerate by using the tail. The powerful pectoral discs of eagle and manta rays enable them to move at great speed. Some species have been observed skipping along the surface, often leaping several yards clear of the water.

BEHAVIOR *and* CONSERVATION

With new technologies, studies of less accessible marine creatures, such as rays, are now possible, and we are slowly gaining an understanding of their place in the ecosystems of the sea.

The ecological role and behavioral complexity of rays have never been fully appreciated by humans. Because of their more fearsome reputation, sharks have generally stolen the limelight. Rays were once thought of as simple animals with uncomplex behaviors, but we now know them to be complicated animals with rather large brains and very well-developed sensory systems.

Knowledge of their behavior is still based largely on observations made by underwater divers and photographers, and studies of captive rays in oceanariums. Unfortunately, few of the species have been studied—they are generally less visible than terrestrial predators of a similar size and, among our marine fauna, they are considered less glamorous than seals and dolphins.

SOCIABILITY

Rays are basically sociable animals, often occurring in large groups of hundreds or even thousands of individuals. By sheer weight of numbers, schooling eagle rays may pose a nuisance to shellfish farms and they can decimate oyster beds. Farm managers place protective net fences around sites to keep them away, or sometimes try to entangle them in mesh nets. Rays resting in confined spaces, such as sand patches among reefs, will often rest on top of each other. Their skin is sensitive to touch and it has been observed that they seem to go into a trance if stroked.

Solitary rays are commonly seen among bony fishes at cleaning stations on coral reefs. They swim slowly above the bottom with gills and jaws open so that small wrasses can access the mouth cavities and spiracles to remove waste tissue and mucus. Parasites are also removed from the body.

They also share symbiotic relationships with other bony fishes, such as trevally, pilot fish, cobia, and remoras, which either swim together with the ray or attach themselves to its skin. These fish feed on food rejected by

SYMBIOSIS *Cleaner fish at work inside a manta ray's open mouth (top), and southern stingrays (right) hitching a ride by swimming on top of each other.*

CONSTANT COMPANY *The Pacific manta ray is usually accompanied by cleaner fish, in this case orange clarion angelfish, and often has remoras attached to its body.*

the ray or disturbed from the bottom by the beating of the ray's wings. Some rays live alone, presumably only socializing to mate. Like sharks, they sometimes occur in single-sex groups outside the breeding season.

Curiosity

Rays also differ greatly in their response to humans in their natural environment. Large stingrays are often inquisitive and will approach a diver cautiously. Sometimes they will threaten divers by quickly raising the tail over the back in a scorpion-like manner. The raising of the tail in a fixed upright pose by small stingarees is thought to be a territorial response.

Some whiprays swim in circles in front of an intruder with their long tails raised and trailing in an ominous display of defiance. Eagle rays and smaller stingrays tend to be shy and will depart rapidly if approached. Giant mantas are gentle and seem to be unafraid of humans in the sea.

Experiments on rays have shown that their strong instincts are supplemented by a reasonable learning capacity. Round stingrays (*Urobatis halleri*) have been conditioned to move to specific sites within a circular tank to obtain food. Correct strikes were rewarded with a herring meal, incorrect movements were given a solid prod. Using a reward system, bat rays have been taught to fetch little floats on their snouts.

Variety of Uses

Humans have used rays for many purposes through the ages. Japanese Samurai warriors used rough stingray skin covered in large denticles on the handles of their swords to provide grip. The tails have been used to make clubs and necklaces, the stings for spear tips, the skin for leather, and the flesh for food.

Large tonnages of rays are still being caught around the globe with little regard to their long-term sustainability as a resource. Catches are being monitored in only a few regions, so ray survival is becoming quite a serious conservation issue.

RAYS IN MYTH AND MEDICINE

The venomous barbs of rays, such as that of the southern stingray at right, earned notoriety long ago. Aristotle described rays as dangerous, and the Greeks noted that rays retained their venomous properties well after death. These powers were considered so great that plants and trees were expected to wither and die if a sting was scraped along their bark. It was believed that the flesh was also poisonous—native tribes in parts of the Indo-Pacific placed a taboo on eating it. Even today, artisanal fishermen of the region are reluctant to eat rays, and cut off the tails to avoid being stung. In Malaysian folklore, there are tales of a leviathan ray that lived beneath a gigantic sea mushroom.

The ray's sting is also thought to have magical properties. Malaysian witch doctors produced a magical potion, consisting of burnt and powdered spines mixed with fruit and needle-shaped crystals (calcium oxalate) derived from plants. Powdered and blended with the Christmas rose (hellebore), ray stings were used as an anesthetic in dentistry by the ancient Greeks. (Interestingly, alkaloids removed from hellebore are used today in the treatment of heart disease.) The Greeks also used the sting as a charm—when removed from a live ray and attached immediately to a pregnant woman's navel, it was thought to promote an easy labor.

In a world older and more complete than ours they move more finished and complete, gifted with extensions of senses we have lost or never attained, living by voices we shall never hear.
The Outermost House,
HENRY BESTON (1888–1968), American writer

CHAPTER SIX

SHARKS FIELD GUIDE

USING *the* SHARKS GUIDE

Knowing as much as possible about sharks and their appearance can only enhance your explorations of the watery world below the surface.

The accounts and illustrations in this field guide will help you to appreciate a wide range of sharks. Some are familiar sights over reefs and sand flats around the world. Others are much more infrequently seen. Using the guide, you may be able to confirm the rarity or perhaps novelty of a shark you see, photograph, or find as part of a catch. You might even discover a little-known shark, and your observations could help to advance scientific knowledge of these extraordinary creatures. To this end, some rarely seen species have been included in the guide in the hope of enlisting your assistance in the search for new information, to help unlock the secrets of the sea.

*The **main photograph** shows as much of the species as possible, given the constraints of photographing such wild creatures in circumstances and conditions that can be difficult.*

*The **common** and **scientific names** of each species. The species are grouped according to taxonomy.*

*The **text** provides information on the appearance of the shark, its common names, habitat, and where and what to look for when you want to find it. It also gives clues on how to differentiate between similar species, and supplies information, where known, about the shark's migratory habits and methods of reproduction.*

*The **secondary photographs** show details of particular features or amplify some aspect of the shark's habitat or behavior.*

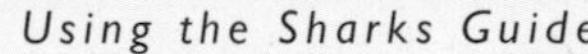

This ***illustrated banding*** at the top of the page is a visual pointer to indicate that the page is about a shark species.

This ***panel*** refers to the family of sharks that the species belongs to.

Quick-reference Field Notes panel

- *Distribution range of the shark*
- *Size*
- *Possible risks when encountering the shark*
- *Best time of day or year to observe the species*
- *Information on population numbers*

Color illustrations *supplement the text by showing some basic features of the shark.*

Frilled Shark

Chlamydoselachus anguineus

FIELD NOTES

- *Eastern Atlantic, western Indian Ocean, western and eastern Pacific*
- *Up to 6½' (2 m)*
- *Harmless*
- *Occasionally seen at the surface*
- *Not uncommon*

The frilled shark, or eel shark, has a long, slender body with an elongate tail fin, which gives it an almost eel-like appearance and one of its common names. A single small dorsal fin is located well back on its dark chocolate brown body, directly above the large anal fin. The pectoral fins are short and rounded. This shark has six pairs of large gill slits—most sharks have five—the first pair of which joins under the throat. The gills are surrounded by frilly margins of skin—hence the common name of frilled shark. Its snout is short, while the lower jaw is long, with the mouth almost at the tip of the snout rather than under the head.

The frilled shark's teeth have broad bases with three sharp cusps separated by two small intermediate cusps. Little is known about its diet, but with such teeth, it probably feeds on small deep-water fishes and squid.

Very little is known about the biology and ecology of this shark, the only living member of the frilled shark family. It is found on the bottom shelves and upper slopes around continents and large islands. Occasionally, it is seen near the surface in open waters, but it usually lives at a depth of 330–4,260' (100–1,300 m), so the only chance of observing it is from a deep-water submersible. It is sometimes collected as bycatch during bottom trawling.

Female frilled sharks bear 8 to 12 live young, about 16" (40 cm) long. Gestation is probably one to two years.

Thoughts on this shark's evolution are contentious. Some think it is a direct descendant of the primitive cladoselache sharks (see p. 70), but others say it is closer to modern forms.

snout with distinctive teeth and frilled gill margins

Broadnose Sevengill Shark

Notorynchus cepedianus

FIELD NOTES

- *Temperate regions of the South Atlantic, Pacific, and Indian Oceans*
- *To about 10' (3 m)*
- *Potentially dangerous*
- *Not usually seen by divers*
- *Not abundant*

The broadnose sevengill shark is immediately recognizable because of its seven pairs of gill slits—most shark species only have five pairs. Its other unusual feature is a single, small dorsal fin. It has a wide head with a short, blunt snout and small eyes. It is a large and powerful shark. Its silvery gray to brownish back and sides are speckled with numerous small dark and white spots, while the underside is pale. Juveniles have white margins on their rear fins.

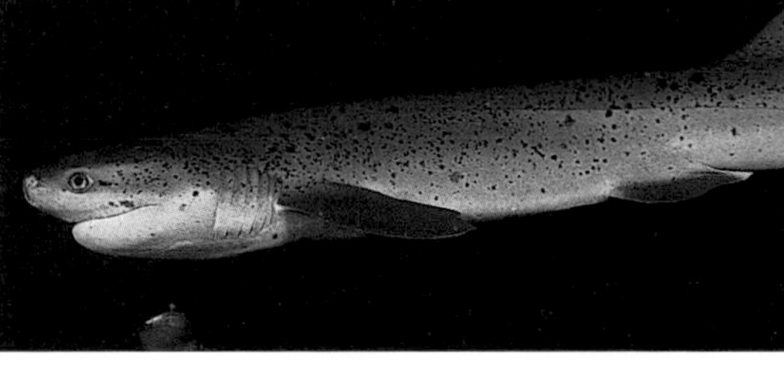

The seven gills and distinctive spots of a broadnose sevengill shark.

The teeth of the broadnose sevengill shark are very effective for cutting. The teeth of the upper jaw are jagged with cusps, except for a single middle tooth; the teeth of the bottom jaw are comb-shaped. The shark's diet includes other sharks, rays, bony fishes, seals, and carrion. It bites pieces of flesh from other sharks caught by gill nets and hooks.

The shark lives in temperate waters on continental shelves, at depths down to 450' (135 m). Although the species is widespread, it is not particularly abundant. It will often come close inshore in shallow bays and inlets, but does not rest on the seabed. This might explain why it is not commonly seen by divers. There are no records of it attacking people (except for divers in aquariums), but it will scavenge on human corpses. It is potentially dangerous. In captivity, it is aggressive when attacked, and it struggles vigorously to escape when captured.

Males mature at about 5' (1.5 m), and females at about 7' (2.2 m). They bear live young in shallow bays. Litter sizes vary, and can be as large as 82 pups. The pups are about 16–18" (40–45 cm) when born.

Bluntnose Sixgill Shark

Hexanchus griseus

The bluntnose sixgill shark has a massive body, with a long and powerful tail, which it uses to swim in a strong, constant motion. A single dorsal fin is located to the rear of the body, slightly in front of the anal fin below. The eyes are small, and set on the side of the wide, short-snouted head.

FIELD NOTES

- *Worldwide in northern and cold temperate to tropical seas*
- *5–16½' (1.5–5 m)*
- *Not dangerous unless provoked*
- *Most likely seen at night, year-round*
- *Common*

The shark has six pairs of gill slits. Only two other shark species have six: the frilled shark (see p. 136) and the bigeyed sixgill shark (*Hexanchus vitulus*). The latter belongs to the same family as the bluntnose sixgill shark, and can be distinguished from it by its more slender body and large eyes. It has five rows of saw-like teeth on each side of its lower jaw, whereas the bluntnose sixgill shark has six rows of similar teeth. Its upper jaw has smaller recurved teeth with a single cusp.

This large shark is a voracious predator of other large fishes, such as sharks, billfishes, dolphin, cod, and flounder, which it can quickly cut into bite-sized chunks with its teeth. It also takes smaller prey, such as herring, squid, crab, and shrimp.

The bluntnose sixgill shark is found both near the bottom and in the water column above continental and island shelves, at depths of 650–5,400' (200–1,800 m). It prefers dimly lit or dark waters, and is seen at night near the surface of the open ocean. Small sixgills move close inshore and forage near the bottom, but in coastal waters adults usually stay below 330' (100 m).

The broad, rounded snout of the bluntnose sixgill shark.

Females reach sexual maturity at about 14' (4.5 m). They produce up to 100 live young, about 28" (70 cm) long. Little is known about this shark's biology other than data from commercial fisheries—it is fished in many parts of the world for both its meat and its oil.

Prickly Shark

Echinorhinus cookei

The prickly shark is a spiny-skinned dogfish, one of two species of the bramble shark family. The bodies of both species are short and stout, the heads slightly flattened. There is a small spiracle behind each eye and in front of the first of five pairs of gill slits. Two spineless dorsal fins are located well back on the body above the pelvic fins. Anal fins are absent.

FIELD NOTES

- *Pacific, from the Americas to Hawaii, New Zealand, and Asia*
- *13' (4 m)*
- *Harmless*
- *Rarely seen, except when taken by commercial fisheries*
- *Fairly common*

The prickly shark is grayish brown with white around the mouth and underneath the snout, and black along its relatively large fin margins. Its denticles, usually about ⅕" (5 mm) wide at the base, are all over its body.

Little is known about the ecology and habits of this shark. It is primarily a deep-water species, dwelling in cold temperate to tropical seas on continental and island shelves and upper slopes at depths of from 36–1,390' (11–424 m). Individuals are seen occasionally in shallow waters. This slow-moving species is probably a suction-feeder of crabs and cephalopods near the bottom. It also takes fishes such as juvenile sixgill sharks, flatfishes, and herring. Females reach maturity at about 8–10' (2.5–3 m) long. They bear up to 24 live young, 16–18" (40–45 cm) long.

The related bramble shark (*Echinorhinus brucus*) gets its name from its much larger and very prominent spine-like denticles, about ⅗" (15 mm) in diameter at their base. They are scattered over the shark's body as well as on the underside of the snout in adults, and are sometimes fused into plates. The bramble shark is brown to dark gray above, with a lighter belly. It is most commonly encountered in the Mediterranean Sea and along the west coast of Europe and Africa.

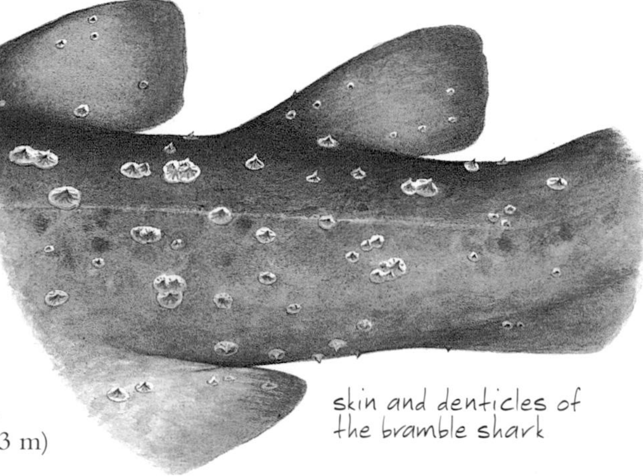

skin and denticles of the bramble shark

Common Sawshark

Pristiophorus cirratus

FIELD NOTES

- *Southern Australia, from southern New South Wales to mid-Western Australia*
- *Females to 5' (1.5 m); males to 4⅓' (1.3 m)*
- *Harmless unless provoked*
- *Year-round*
- *Common*

The common sawshark is also known as the longnose sawshark. Like all the sawshark family, it is immediately recognizable from its saw-like snout with a pair of barbels. Because of this snout, it can sometimes be confused with sawfishes (see p. 178). However, the sawshark's five pairs of gills are on the side of its head, while the sawfish's gills are underneath. Also, the sawfish does not have a pair of barbels.

The common sawshark is a slender shark with a slightly depressed and flattened body. It has an attractive patterning of darker bands and brownish spots and blotches on a pale yellowish brown background. This shark is found only in temperate waters in southern Australia. The southern, or shortnose, sawshark (*Pristiophorus nudipinnis*), also endemic to Australia, is found in a similar area. This brownish gray shark prefers to dwell on the inner continental shelf to depths of 230' (90 m); the common sawshark seems to prefer deeper water, on continental shelves and slopes to depths of about 1,015' (310 m).

Divers may find sawsharks lying on the sandy bottoms. They are timid and harmless, but will strike with their snout if handled. They feed by trailing their barbels along the bottom to locate the small bony fish that they eat. The teeth on the snout are probably then used for stirring up sediment to rouse the prey and strike it.

The common sawshark lives for more than 15 years. Like all sawsharks, it is ovoviviparous. Mature females appear to breed every 1 to 2 years, carrying from 3 to 22 young, with about 10 being the average. After about 12 months' gestation, the pups are born in shallow coastal areas. They are about 11–14½" (27–37 cm) long at birth.

snout of the southern sawshark

Pacific Angelshark

Squatina californica

Angelsharks are unusual, flattened sharks that are often mistaken for rays. They used to be called monkfish because the strange shape of their heads resembles the hood on a monk's cloak. The dozen species range along temperate coasts from shallow waters to more than 4,265' (1,320 m) deep. They are unique in having a blunt nose; the leading edge of their pectoral fins is free from the body; and the lower caudal fin lobe is longer than the upper.

FIELD NOTES

- *Eastern Pacific, from southeast Alaska, USA, to Baja California, Mexico, and from Ecuador to southern Chile*
- *To about 5' (1.5 m)*
- *Can bite if surprised or harassed*
- *Best seen at night*
- *Once common, now reduced due to heavy fishing pressure*

The Pacific angelshark is easily identified by its large eyes, a conspicuous spiracle, and a generally brown-gray coloration. During the day, it remains buried in sand on the bottom with only its eyes and head exposed, ready to burst upward out of the sand and ambush a fish or squid with its protruding, trap-like jaws and numerous spiky teeth. Occasionally, divers may encounter a Pacific angelshark swimming over sandy bottoms near kelp beds at depths of about 10' (3 m) and more. It can become aggressive if harassed—a diver or angler who foolishly grabs the tail of an angelshark soon discovers how quickly the shark can bite and how painful the bite can be.

Males and females are mature at about 3' (90 cm), and the female is ovoviviparous, producing eggs that are retained within her body. There are about 8 to 13 pups in each litter.

skin patterning

California Hornshark

Heterodontus francisci

Named for the spine in front of each dorsal fin, the California hornshark is one of nine living species of the family known as bullhead, horn, or Port Jackson sharks. The sharks of this family are unmistakable, with their blunt foreheads, pig-like snouts, and broad eye ridges. Their taxonomic name (from Greek for "mixed-tooth") refers to the small, pointed teeth at the front of the jaw and the blunt teeth at the rear. With these, they can grab soft-bodied fish and crustaceans, and crush sea urchins and the shellfish that they prefer.

California hornsharks have small dark spots on their bodies and fins. They live in cool, shallow waters, and lay curious, fist-sized, screw-shaped egg cases (always with a right-hand thread). The egg case is wedged into a rock crevice, and hatches after 6 to 10 months, depending on water temperature. During the day, divers find the sharks, as well as their egg cases, resting among large rocks in shallow-water kelp beds and at the base of boulders. At night, the sharks patrol for food out in the open.

California hornsharks are very popular in public aquariums. There, while sitting placidly on the bottom, they defy the commonly held belief that all sharks must swim in order to be able to breathe.

FIELD NOTES

- *Central California, USA, to the Gulf of California*
- *To 4' (1.2 m), but most adults less than 3' (90 cm)*
- *Generally sedentary; not dangerous*
- *Day and night, year-round*
- *Not uncommon; neither direct nor indirect sport or commercial fishing of species*

The egg case of a California hornshark.

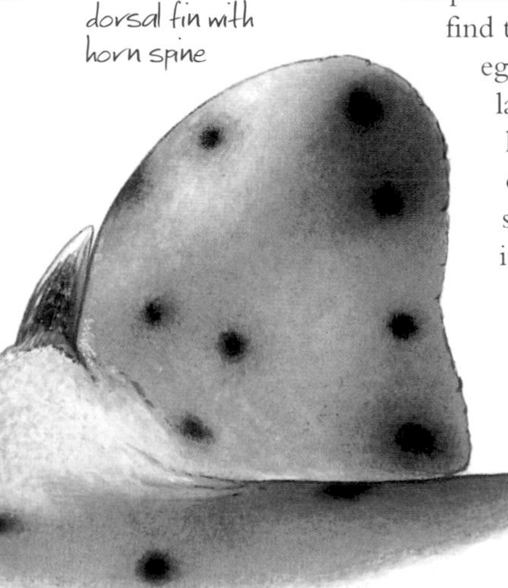

Port Jackson Shark

Heterodontus portusjacksoni

The Port Jackson shark, also called the oyster crusher or tabbigaw, is very similar to the related California hornshark (see opposite). It is brownish gray, with conspicuous, dark, narrow stripes in a harness-type pattern across the shoulders. Two other Australian bullheads, the crested hornshark (*Heterodontus galeatus*) and the zebra hornshark (*Heterodontus zebra*), have large crests above the eyes and a dark striped livery respectively. Port Jackson sharks are abundant and survive well in aquariums.

Although individuals may range over considerable distances, they favor certain reefs or caves, and usually return to this favored spot to rest during the day. Divers frequently encounter them in shallow water, in caves, and near rocks and at the base of seaweeds. Groups of adults move in and out of shallow water according to water temperature and breeding conditions.

FIELD NOTES

- *Southern Australia, from Queensland to mid-Western Australia, including Tasmania; rare in New Zealand*
- *To 5½' (1.7 m), but rarely larger than 4½' (1.4 m)*
- *Generally sedentary; harmless unless handled*
- *Mostly sighted at night, all year*
- *Not uncommon*

This species segregates by sex and maturity. In Australia, females and some males in the Sydney area move into shallow water in summer to mate. In August and September, females lay two eggs every 8 to 17 days among rocks in 16–100' (5–30 m) of water, often in a communal nursery. The female will wedge the pointed edge and flanges of the screw-shaped egg case into a rocky crevice using her mouth. The young hatch 9 to 12 months later and move into bays and estuaries. After a decade, they will have grown to 20–30" (50–75 cm) and have reached adolescence.

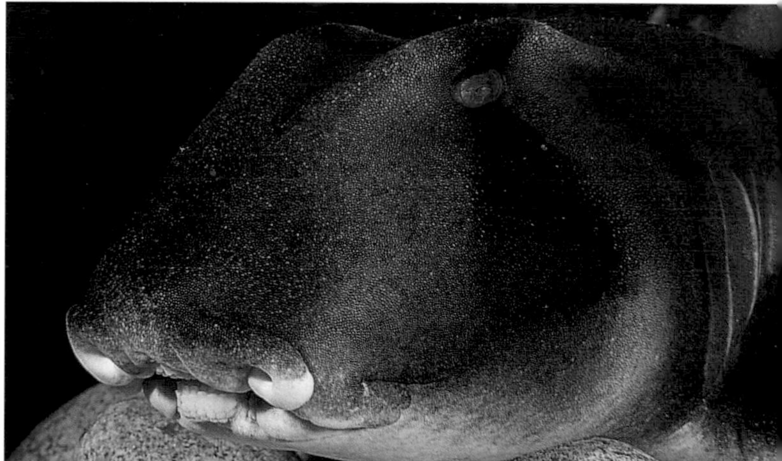

The distinctive pig-like snout and pointy front teeth of the Port Jackson shark.

Necklace Carpetshark

Parascyllium variolatum

FIELD NOTES

- Southern Australia
- Less than 3⅓' (1 m)
- Harmless
- At night, year-round
- Common

With its long, slender, and slightly flattened body, and its long but almost indistinct tail, the necklace carpetshark has a quite eel-like appearance. It is easily identifiable by its dark gray-brown body scattered with numerous white spots and the large black blotches on the edges of the fins. Most striking is the dark band, or collar, studded with small bright white spots that encircles the head like a necklace, hence its common name. It is also known as the varied carpetshark. Its spiracles are small, and its nostrils bear short barbels (probably for chemosensory purposes) and grooves that connect to the mouth.

Collared carpetsharks are closely related to nurse sharks and wobbegongs but are often mistaken for catsharks, which they resemble only superficially. Collared carpetsharks are distinguished by their mouth being located well in front of the eyes. The family has two genera: the *Cirrhoscyllium*, which have barbels on the throat, and the *Parascyllium*, which do not.

The necklace carpetshark is common on shallow rocky reefs along the southern temperate coast of Australia. It feeds and is active at night, and is often encountered by divers after dark. During the day it is difficult to spot because it rests either in caves or on the bottom, where it is perfectly camouflaged among the algae.

Little is known about this carpetshark's diet, but it probably feeds on invertebrates and small fishes. It is oviparous, laying egg cases with curled tendrils that anchor the cases to the substrate.

This necklace carpetshark, one of seven collared carpetsharks, is being attacked by a voracious 11-armed sea star.

Blind Shark

Brachaelurus waddi

FIELD NOTES

- Northern and eastern Australia
- Up to 4¼' (1.3 m)
- Harmless
- Secretive; most likely seen at night
- Common

Blind sharks get their name from their habit of closing their eyes when caught by fishers. The blind shark, along with the blue-gray carpetshark (*Brachaelurus colcloughi*), make up the blind shark family. They are closely related to bamboosharks, nurse sharks, and collared carpetsharks. Although often referred to as catsharks, they are related only distantly to them.

The blind shark has a stout, cylindrical, brown body, usually dotted with pale spots. Its two spineless dorsal fins are close together, with the first originating above the pelvic fins. It has very large spiracles positioned behind and to the side of the eyes. Its nostrils are well developed, with a pair of long, smooth nasal barbels, which are connected to the mouth by a groove that permits water that has passed over the olfactory organs to flow into the mouth. The blind shark can be distinguished from the blue-gray carpetshark by the presence of a small (symphyseal) groove in the middle of the chin, which the blue-gray carpetshark lacks.

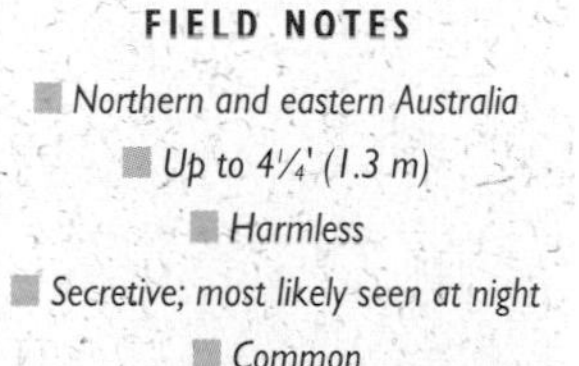

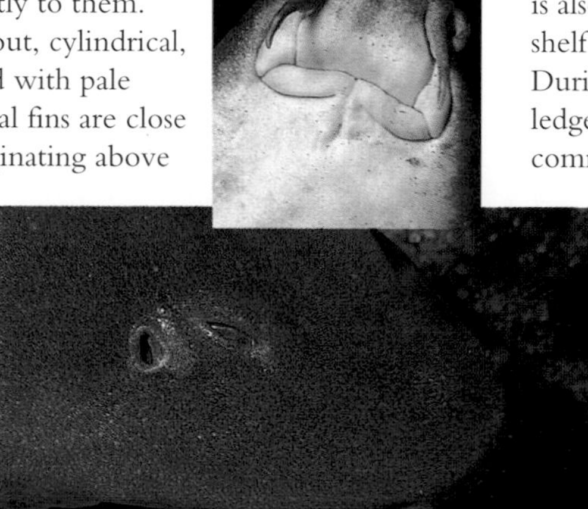

Snout and barbels from below (top) and from the side (above).

This shark inhabits shallow, warm temperate and tropical waters—it can occur in water just deep enough to cover it. It is also found on the continental shelf to about 490' (150 m). During the day, it shelters under ledges and in caves, and it is commonly observed by divers under ledges but is rarely seen out in the open. It emerges after dark to forage on the reef and the adjacent sandy areas for anemones, cuttlefish, and crustaceans.

Females reach sexual maturity when about 26" (65 cm) long, and give birth during summer to as many as eight young.

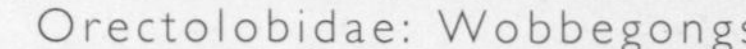

Tasselled Wobbegong

Eucrossorhinus dasypogon

Wobbegongs share many of the basic features of nurse sharks, blind sharks, bamboosharks, and collared carpetsharks. They have elongated bodies that are flattened, especially in the head region, and the two dorsal fins of similar size are set far back on the body. The broad, short pectoral fins are well adapted for a life on the reef bottom.

FIELD NOTES

- *Western Pacific*
- *10–13' (3–4 m)*
- *Dangerous when provoked, captured, or disturbed*
- *Year-round in many areas*
- *Common*

Tasselled wobbegongs are patterned with small, reticulated markings on a drab gray or brown background; the underside is white. These unusual sharks are distinguished by a very broad, flat head. The upper jaw is surrounded by many finely branched dermal lobes that appear as fleshy flaps hanging down over the mouth. The chin and sides of the lower jaw are also decorated with small, reticulated fleshy tassels. Within this mass of tassels are branched nasal barbels and grooves that channel the water leaving the nostrils to the mouth. The mouth is studded with sharp, narrow teeth, perfect for capturing the fish on which this shark preys.

A tasselled wobbegong's jaw, with branched, fleshy tassels.

Living in warm temperate to tropical seas, the tasselled wobbegong is a common member of tropical reefs of New Guinea, the north Australian coast, and Indonesia. During the day, it is commonly found in caves on the reef, where it feeds on sheltering fish. At night, it emerges to feed on small fishes and invertebrates. Females are believed to bear live young, about 8½" (22 cm) long.

Divers are most likely to encounter smaller individuals, about 3⅓' (1 m) long. Because of their markings, tasselled wobbegongs are difficult to see against the sea floor. There have been many reports of attacks on divers. Most are provoked by divers pulling the shark's tail or accidentally stepping on it. But in some cases, the attacks were apparently unprovoked.

Ornate Wobbegong

Orectolobus ornatus

FIELD NOTES

- Western Pacific
- 10' (3 m)
- Dangerous, particularly when provoked, captured, or stepped on
- Almost year-round
- Common

The ornate, or banded, wobbegong has large, black-bordered, saddle-shaped markings on the back. The body is flattened and wide from the head to the back of the trunk, where it quickly tapers to the tail. On each side of the head there are five or six dermal lobes. Each nostril bears a single barbel and there is a groove from the back of each nostril to the mouth. The teeth are long and slender, well adapted for grasping small fish prey.

This is one of four wobbegong species in the genus *Orectolobus*. While the relative position of these wobbegongs' fins is similar to that of the tasselled wobbegong (opposite), the fin lobes in *Orectolobus* are smaller in comparison to the body. *Orectolobus* also differs in having no dermal lobes or tassels on the chin or lower jaw. The back is smooth, which distinguishes sharks of this genus from the heavily tubercled cobbler wobbegong (*Sutorectus tentaculatus*), common on the southwest coast of Australia.

The ornate wobbegong is a large, common inshore inhabitant of temperate rocky and tropical reefs. During the day it rests in the open on rocky bottoms or table coral, or it sometimes hides under reef ledges. It becomes active at night, searching the reef for invertebrates and fishes to eat. Divers should be cautious because this species can easily camouflage itself against the sea floor, and it is considered dangerous—numerous provoked and unprovoked attacks have been documented. Females produce litters of up to 12 pups, each about 8" (20 cm) long.

Close-up of an ornate wobbegong's coloring.

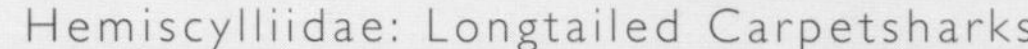

Epaulette Shark

Hemiscyllium ocellatum

FIELD NOTES

- Indo-West Pacific
- 3⅓' (1 m)
- Harmless
- Day or night, year-round
- Common

The 13 species of longtailed carpetsharks are subdivided into the epaulette sharks (*Hemiscyllium*) and bamboosharks (*Chiloscyllium*). These usually small fish have thin, slightly flattened, elongated bodies. The two relatively large, spineless dorsal fins are about the same size. The anal fin is far back on the underside, immediately in front of the caudal fin, from which it is separated by a notch. These short, stubby, paired fins are used by many species for "walking" across the bottom. Most juvenile longtailed carpetsharks have broad contrasting bands of color on the body. In adult epaulette sharks these bands become spotted, and a prominent black spot develops above the pectoral fins. The yellowish or brownish body of *Hemiscyllium ocellatum* is covered with dark brown spots, and the characteristic large black spot has a white ring around it. Its nostrils and mouth are almost at the tip of the snout, which is short and rounded like all the epaulette sharks.

The solid bands of color of the juvenile carpetsharks fade or disappear altogether in adult bamboosharks such as the brownbanded bambooshark (*Chiloscyllium punctatum*). It is a uniform brown as an adult. However, the adult slender bambooshark (*Chiloscyllium indicum*) is covered with small dark spots and bars, and has small side ridges. It has rounded dorsal fins and the pointed snout typical of the bamboosharks.

Longtailed carpetsharks are common inshore on coral and rocky reefs and in tide pools. Divers often encounter adults, but juveniles are rarely seen because they hide within the reef. These nocturnally active sharks feed on small benthic invertebrates and fishes. Many species lay eggs.

Adult brownbanded bamboosharks congregating on the bottom.

Nurse Shark

Ginglymostoma cirratum

No one is sure how the nurse shark got its name, perhaps from the sucking noise made by a feeding nurse shark, which sounds like a nursing baby. This fairly large bottom dweller is uniformly brown to gray-brown and has large, rounded fins. Noticeable barbels protrude from the nasal openings in front of the corners of its small mouth. A small spiracle behind and below each eye allows it to take in water over the gills when breathing.

Common over inshore coral reefs in tropical waters, it is probably the shark that snorkelers and divers in the Caribbean see most often. Although sluggish during the day, it is active at night, when it feeds on bottom-dwelling invertebrates, such as lobsters and other crustaceans, as well as snails, clams, octopus, squid, and any fish slow enough to be caught by its great gulping and inhaling style of feeding.

Because they are abundant and easy to capture, handle, and transport, nurse sharks are common residents of public aquariums. Behaviorists have used them to study learning in sharks, and have demonstrated that nurse sharks can be taught to react to novel situations.

These ovoviviparous sharks conduct an interesting courtship. Male and female swim in close synchrony, the male alongside or slightly behind and below the female. (Sometimes, a second male accompanies them to prevent the female from retreating.) When the male grabs the female's pectoral fin in his mouth, she rolls onto her back. He swims above her and inserts a clasper into her vent to deliver sperm.

FIELD NOTES

- *Eastern Pacific, from Mexico to Peru; western Atlantic, from Rhode Island, USA, to southern Brazil; tropical West Africa*
- *To 14' (4.25 m); rarely longer than 10' (3 m)*
- *Harmless unless provoked*
- *During the day, year-round*
- *Common, particularly in the Caribbean*

A nurse shark resting on a reef in the Bahamas.

Zebra Shark

Stegostoma fasciatum

The zebra shark is a lovely creature, found over tropical coral reefs. Its very long, broad tail and its coloring make it quite distinctive. The juvenile shark has zebra-like stripes (yellow on black), which give the shark its common name. It takes on a yellowish brown color with dark brown spotting as it reaches adulthood. Because of this adult coloration, it is also known as the leopard shark. (It cannot be confused with the other shark known as a leopard shark, a very different, cold-water species of the eastern Pacific, from the houndshark family (see p. 144).)

FIELD NOTES

- *Widespread in the tropical western Pacific and Indian Ocean*
- *To 11½' (3.5 m)*
- *Harmless*
- *More active at night, seen year-round*
- *Common*

The zebra shark has small barbels on its snout, a small mouth, and small eyes. Its teeth are pointed, with each tooth having two smaller, lateral, flanking points. Prominent ridges run along its flanks.

This is a sluggish species. Divers occasionally find one resting on the bottom during the day, propped up on its pectoral fins with its open mouth facing into the current in order to obtain oxygen more easily from the water. It poses no danger to humans. Its slender, flexible body allows it to wriggle into narrow crevices in the reef, searching for the shellfish, crustaceans, and small fishes upon which it prefers to feed.

The zebra shark is oviparous. It lays large, brown or purplish black egg cases, from 5–7" (13–18 cm) in length, that have fibers for attaching to the seabed.

Bunches of hair-like fibers secure the egg case of the zebra shark to the ocean floor.

Whale Shark

Rhincodon typus

The sole living member of its family, the whale shark is the world's largest living fish. Its massive, fusiform body reaches lengths in excess of 46' (14 m). It has alternating thin white vertical bars and columns of spots on a dark background, with long ridges along the upper side of the body and a prominent lateral keel. The narrow mouth extends across the full width of its flattened head. The eyes are small and far forward on the head. Each nostril has a small barbel and the gill slits are long and extend above the pectoral fins. Above the relatively small pelvic fins are the first of two dorsal fins. The powerful caudal fin is semicircular.

FIELD NOTES

- *Western Atlantic, eastern Atlantic, Indo-West, central, and eastern Pacific*
- *Up to 46' (14 m)*
- *Harmless*
- *Seasonally, day and night*
- *Common in some regions*

This shark swims slowly near the surface, consuming small crustacean plankton, small fishes, such as sardines and anchovies, and even larger fishes such as mackerel. It has well-developed internal spongy filters at the gill arches, which help to retain small prey within its huge mouth. This mechanism may impede the flow of water through the mouth during swimming, which limits the amount of plankton the shark can strain. So, as well as filter feeding, it can also pump water into its mouth to feed on concentrated patches of plankton.

The whale shark is found in all tropical and subtropical oceans, along coastal regions, and enters lagoons on tropical islands. It is mostly seen on the surface, where divers and snorkelers can swim with this gentle, curious creature (see pp. 234–5).

The whale shark is a livebearer. Pregnant females were recently found to contain hundreds of young, up to about 2' (60 cm) long.

A trevally disappears into the gaping mouth of the filter-feeding whale shark.

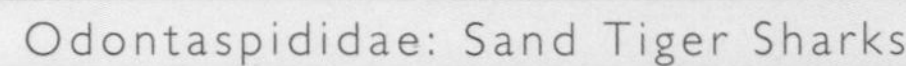

Sand Tiger Shark

Eugomphodus taurus

Depending on where you are in the world, the sand tiger shark may be known as the spotted raggedtooth or gray nurse shark. It is one of four species belonging to the sand tiger family, a group of large, fearsome-looking sharks that swim slowly with their mouths open, exposing long, narrow, needle-like teeth. Their bodies are stout, with two large dorsal fins. The elongated tails have a long upper lobe; there is a precaudal pit but no caudal keels.

FIELD NOTES

- *Western Atlantic, eastern Atlantic, western Indian Ocean, western Pacific*
- *10½' (3.2 m)*
- *Dangerous only when provoked*
- *Day and night; year-round in some regions, regional in others*
- *Common*

The sand tiger shark has a short, flattened snout. Its dorsal fins are about equal in size, with the first located closer to the pelvic fins than to the pectoral fins. It is bronzy above, gradually becoming paler below. Juveniles have reddish or brownish spots scattered on the tail and rear of the body, which tend to fade with age. There are three rows of large teeth on each side of the midline of the upper jaw.

This shark is found in shallow bays, sandy coastal waters, and rocky or tropical reefs from shallow waters down to about 655' (200 m). Divers often find large numbers in aggregations around rocky outcroppings in offshore waters. Essentially gentle sharks, they usually become aggressive only if provoked. Their diet consists of many species of large and small bony fishes, small sharks, rays, crustaceans, and squid.

The sand tiger shark is able to hover motionless in the water by swallowing surface air and holding it in its stomach, thus achieving near-neutral buoyancy. It is also known to make long coastal migrations for reproductive purposes. Reproduction is oviphagous. In each of the two uterine chambers, the first embryo to hatch, at about 6½" (17 cm), kills and devours the other developing siblings. The two embryos continue to feed on the other eggs inside the separate uterine chambers. After a gestation period of eight to nine months, the two live young are born, about 3⅓' (1 m) long.

A male sand tiger shark swimming, mouth characteristically open.

Goblin Shark

Mitsukurina owstoni

FIELD NOTES

- *Western and eastern Atlantic, western Indian Ocean, western Pacific*
- *11' (3.3 m)*
- *Harmless*
- *Not commonly seen*
- *Probably common*

Perhaps the most mysterious, and bizarre, of all sharks, the goblin shark is the only species of its family. Its light pink body is long but thin. The flesh has a soft, watery texture, which probably helps it to maintain neutral buoyancy, important in what is thought to be a slow-swimming species. The two dorsal fins are similar in size, while the anal fin is well developed. The tail consists almost entirely of a single long upper lobe.

This shark has an elongated snout flattened in the shape of a paddle. The nostrils are located immediately in front of the mouth. The teeth at the front of its narrow, pointed jaw are long and needle-like, ideal for grasping small fish. The teeth at the back of the mouth are small and form a crushing or grinding plate for processing captured prey The goblin shark probably feeds mostly on small fishes, crustaceans, and squid, and its paddle-like snout is thought to aid the electrosensory system in detecting and capturing a potential meal.

In addition, its jaw is highly specialized to project rapidly from the head. This makes the goblin shark a very efficient predator, capable of quickly grasping or sucking prey into its mouth in a single bite.

Very little is known about the biology and ecology of this shark. It occurs near the bottom on continental and island shelves and slopes, at depths of about 3,940' (1,200 m). Living in such deep waters, it is rarely seen or collected. However, it is occasionally found in shallow water near shore.

Until recently, no one had seen a living goblin shark. Early specimens had been preserved with the jaw in the extended position, which gave the shark a very weird appearance. However, we now know that when its jaws are closed, the very protrusible upper jaw fits tightly against the bottom of the skull.

upper and lower teeth

Megamouth Shark

Megachasma pelagios

FIELD NOTES

- *Throughout the world's oceans*
- *To 17' (5.2 m)*
- *Harmless*
- *Not likely to be seen by divers*
- *Known from 10 specimens*

The accidental capture of a large, black, blubbery shark off Hawaii in 1976 was the shark discovery of the century. The creature had become entangled in a deep-water net line. It had a large head, a huge distending mouth about 3⅓' (1 m) wide, and numerous small teeth. But other characteristics indicated a relationship with the ecologically disparate white sharks and makos. A new genus, species, and family of vertebrates was created, known as the megamouth shark. Its scientific name comes from the Greek to mean "giant yawner of the open sea."

Only nine more megamouth sharks have been found. The first six were all large males; more recently, a 12' (3.6 m) female, a 16½' (5 m) female, and a small, 6' (1.8 m) male have been observed.

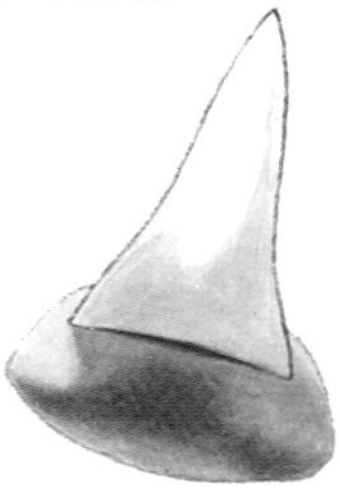

Not surprisingly, we know very little about the megamouth. It lives in the open ocean, often at great depths, which may explain the rarity of encounters. It appears to be a plankton feeder, like the whale shark (see p.127) and the basking shark (see p. 183). It swims slowly through the open ocean, filtering small shrimps and other prey from the water as it goes. It spends the day feeding in deep water and comes up to shallower water at night. The silvery lining of its mouth cavity is probably reflective, so that when shrimps and other luminous crustaceans enter the open, cavernous mouth, they may encourage others to enter.

upper and lower teeth

The great mouth filters huge amounts of water for tiny organisms.

Pelagic Thresher

Alopias pelagicus

FIELD NOTES

- Indo-Pacific
- Up to 11' (3.3 m); tail comprises half the total length
- Harmless and shy of divers
- Spring and summer
- Becoming less common in some areas because of heavy fishing

The pelagic thresher has a dark, countershaded body grading from gray above to white on the underbelly. It shares many of the features common to all the threshers (see p. 132), but the first dorsal fin of the pelagic thresher is closer to the pectoral fins. It has at least 30 rows of small teeth in each jaw; all the teeth bear a distinct cusplet in the tooth notch.

Widespread in tropical and subtropical Indo-Pacific seas, the pelagic thresher is commonly observed far from land, swimming at the surface. It also frequents the seaward edges of coral reefs and submarine seamounts. However, it is shy, and difficult for divers to approach. Occasionally, it makes excursions to depths as great as 490' (150 m). It feeds either near the surface or in deep waters on small fishes and squid, which it grasps and cuts with its small, sharp teeth.

The bigeye thresher (*Alopias superciliosus*) is known to reach 15' (4.6 m) in length. It is easily distinguished from the others by the deep grooves above its very large eyes, which are located almost on top of the head. It has large pelvic fins. Its pectoral fins are long, curved on the trailing margins and rounded at the tips. This species occurs in nearly all tropical and subtropical open oceans and coastal areas, from the surface to depths of about 1,640' (500 m). It is known to feed in the water column on pelagic mackerel, tuna, herring, and billfishes, as well as on bony fishes and squid near the bottom.

Female pelagic threshers reach reproductive maturity when about 8½' (2.6 m) in length. Embryos are cannibalistic in the uterus and only two live pups are born. These are almost 3⅓' (1 m) long. Bigeye threshers also bear cannibalistic pups, but litter sizes range from two to four, suggesting that some embryos coexist through gestation.

snout of the bigeye thresher

Common Thresher Shark

Alopias vulpinus

The common thresher is one of three thresher sharks. These large, pelagic sharks are immediately recognizable by their long tails. They have a short, conical snout, large eyes placed well forward on the head, and a husky, spindle-shaped body. The first dorsal fin is much larger than the second. The broad pectoral fins provide lift when swimming—these strong, active sharks have enough power to leap out of the water.

FIELD NOTES

- *Western and eastern Atlantic, Indo-West Pacific, central Pacific*
- *16½–20' (5–6 m)*
- *Not aggressive, but should be treated with caution*
- *During the day, almost year-round*
- *Becoming uncommon in many areas due to fishing pressure*

The jaws are relatively small, with remarkably efficient small, sharp teeth for capturing cephalopods and schooling fishes. They use the long tail to slap the water surface, frightening prey into tight groups to make capture easier.

Common threshers can be distinguished from their relatives by the position of the first dorsal fin, with its leading edge above the trailing edge of the pectoral fins. The pectoral fins are curved, with pointed tips. The body is dark blue-gray above, with a sharp, ragged break marking the edge of the white underside. There are prominent labial furrows at the sides of the jaws.

The common thresher shark is widespread in tropical and temperate waters. It is commonly seen swimming at the surface in coastal waters, but also occurs at depths of 1,150' (350 m) and more. It is best viewed from boats or by snorkelers in open water. While not aggressive toward humans, this is a large shark. Respect its power, and keep clear of its tail.

Females reach maturity at about 10' (3 m) long and produce four to six live young, about 5' (1.5 m) long. The thresher is targeted by fisheries for its fins and meat, and populations are diminishing in many coastal areas.

common thresher shark

Basking Shark

Cetorhinus maximus

The basking shark is the second largest fish in the world, after the other plankton filter feeder, the whale shark (see p. 127). Its huge size makes it easy to identify, as do its very broad gill slits that extend around the top and bottom of the head. The grayish brown body is streamlined and stout, with a strong crescent-shaped tail fin and lateral keels. The short snout is narrow and conical, with huge jaws that expand laterally when the shark feeds.

Basking sharks are frequent visitors to cold and warm temperate waters, where they take advantage of plankton blooms in coastal regions. They often enter large bays to feed. You will see them close to shore, swimming slowly near the surface with mouth wide open to form a very wide "net" for capturing the plankton. Water passes into the mouth and across the specialized gill rakers, which strain out the plankton before the water emerges through the gill slits. This feeding posture is in distinct contrast to the long but narrow mouth opening of a feeding whale shark.

Basking sharks are highly migratory, appearing seasonally in specific locations and supporting regional commercial fisheries—they are taken for their flesh and large liver.

Populations of basking sharks are often segregated by sex and size. Very little is known about their reproduction, but females reach maturity at about 13–16½' (4–5 m) long, and are thought to bear live young.

FIELD NOTES

- *Western and eastern Atlantic, western Indian Ocean, western and eastern Pacific*
- *33' (10 m)*
- *Possibly dangerous when attacked*
- *Seasonal, according to region; during the day*
- *Common in some regions, but depleted in others*

A feeding basking shark reveals its gill arches, which strain plankton from the water passing over them.

Great White Shark

Carcharodon carcharias

Also called the white shark, the white pointer, white death, and more, this is the largest flesh-eating shark. Star of film and literature, it strikes terror in many people, but little is known of its biology and behavior.

FIELD NOTES

- *Worldwide, along continental margins of all temperate seas and entering tropics*
- *Largest said to be 21¼' (6.6 m) and 7,300 lb (3,285 kg)*
- *Dangerous*
- *Africa: Dec–Feb; Australia: Jan–May; Mexico: Aug–Sept*
- *Nowhere abundant; protected in South Africa, Australia, Maldives, and California, USA*

The great white shark is a robust, torpedo-shaped, conical-snouted species with a normal assortment of dorsal, anal, and paired fins. Unlike most sharks, but like other mackerel sharks, the upper and lower lobes of its tail are almost equal in size. This indicates that it swims constantly (because it must swim to breathe) and sometimes rapidly.

The great white differs from its relatives in having nearly symmetrical triangular teeth with serrated edges. It is also huge. It prefers shallow, cool, coastal oceanic waters, but is occasionally seen as close to the equator as Hawaii, USA. During the day, adults search for the seals and sea lions that are an important part of their diet.

Great white sharks are responsible for the majority of unprovoked attacks on people in cool waters and they can kill humans. However, the number of attacks is usually fewer than 10 a year. By diving inside a steel cage, it is possible to see them in relative safety. Dives are organized off Baja California, Mexico, southern Australia, and South Africa.

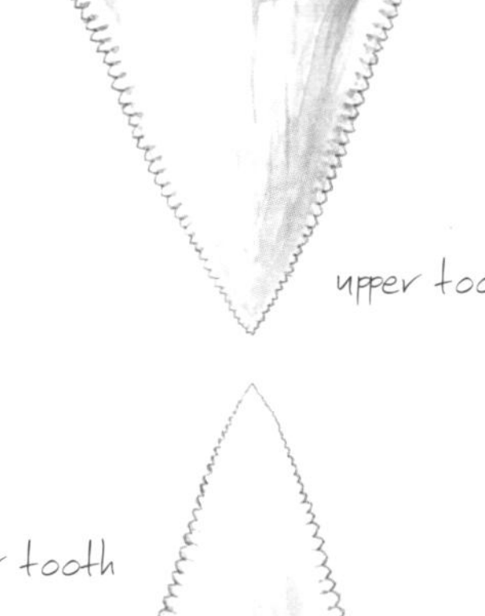

Females give birth to seven to nine live pups per litter, and are thought to produce only four to six litters in a lifetime. The young do not mature until about 10 to 12 years old, so the species is extremely vulnerable to overfishing.

Shortfin Mako Shark

Isurus oxyrinchus

The shortfin mako shark is also called the bonito or mako shark. It is the most spindle-shaped shark of the mackerel family, with a long, conical snout, short pectoral fins, and a crescent-shaped caudal fin. Its back is indigo blue, and the belly white. Its teeth are visible even when its mouth is closed—long, slender, smooth-edged daggers. The less common longfin mako (*Isurus paucus*) has longer pectoral fins and a blunter snout.

FIELD NOTES

- *Worldwide*
- *To 13' (3.95 m)*
- *Potentially dangerous*
- *During the day, year-round*
- *Not uncommon; however, reduced by developing fisheries*

The shortfin mako, the shark featured in Ernest Hemingway's novel *The Old Man and the Sea,* is well known as a sport fish, capable of spectacular leaps 20' (6 m) in the air when hooked and of achieving bursts of speed of more than 22 mph (35 km/h). It uses its speed to capture oceanic fish and squid. Large makos also catch billfish and cetaceans. One is known to have traveled 1,322 miles (2,128 km) in 37 days, an average of 36 miles (58 km) a day.

Shortfin makos live offshore in tropical and temperate waters, from the surface down to 490' (150 m). They are rarely encountered, but may be seen by open-water divers. They are dangerous and have attacked humans. However, attacks on fishing boats, when an angry mako leaps into a boat after being caught on the end of a fishing line, are more likely to occur.

Shortfin makos are viviparous, but lack a placental connection. Litters of 4 to 16 pups are common. Older embryos eat some of the eggs and smaller embryos while still in the uterus.

The very obvious teeth of the shortfin mako shark.

Salmon Shark

Lamna ditropis

FIELD NOTES

- *Subarctic waters of North Pacific, from Alaska to California, USA, and from the Bering Sea to Japan*
- *To 10' (3 m)*
- *Potentially dangerous*
- *Not seen by divers*
- *Abundant within center of range*

The salmon shark shares its generic name, *Lamna*, with the porbeagle (opposite). To the ancient Greeks, "Lamna" signified "a horrible monster of man-eating tendencies," and it was invoked to scare naughty children. The salmon shark and porbeagle are so similar that they were not recognized as two separate species until 1947. Generally speaking, if it lives in the North Pacific, it is a salmon shark; if in the Atlantic, it is a porbeagle.

The salmon shark shares the frightening appearance of all the mackerel sharks. However, it differs from the great white shark (see p. 134) in having smooth rather than serrated teeth, and from the mako sharks (see p. 135) in having a blue-gray rather than an indigo back. The feature that is found only in the salmon shark and the porbeagle is the secondary keel along the base of the tail.

Salmon sharks are heavy, torpedo-shaped predators. They have large, sharp, pointed teeth, and are well designed for chasing and capturing such fast-swimming oceanic prey as salmon and mackerel. Unlike most other mackerel sharks, they form schools of 20 to 30 individuals when feeding. They are not a threat to humans, mainly because they are not encountered by humans: salmon sharks inhabit the more frigid waters of the North Pacific, from the surface to depths of 500' (155 m), and they rarely come close to shore. They will consume the catch in fishing nets and sometimes become entangled in nets and lines.

Salmon sharks are viviparous, without a placental connection. As in related species, the embryos consume eggs and smaller embryos in the uterus. There are typically two to four young in each litter. They are born when they are about 26–28" (65–70 cm) in length.

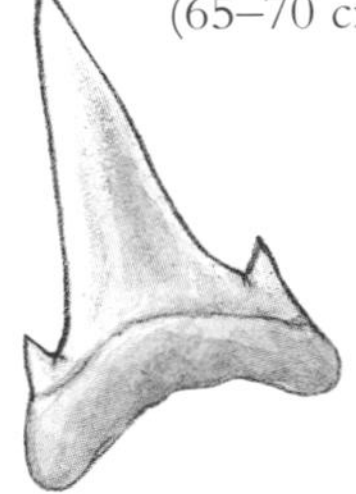

upper and lower teeth

Porbeagle

Lamna nasus

FIELD NOTES

- Cold waters of North Atlantic, South Atlantic, and South Pacific
- To 12' (3.7 m)
- Potentially dangerous
- Not seen by divers
- Common

The porbeagle and its North Pacific relative, the salmon shark (opposite), are the smallest of the five mackerel sharks. They are still an impressive sight at 350–500 lb (158–225 kg). The porbeagle's stout body is dark blue-gray to brown dorsally and white underneath. It has a patch of white on the trailing edge of the first dorsal fin. The porbeagle and salmon shark are the only sharks with a secondary keel at the base of their crescent-shaped tails. This efficiently cuts the water in its side-to-side swimming movement.

This fast-swimming shark inhabits the continental shelves in cold waters, down to depths of 1,210' (370 m). With its sharp, slender teeth, it feeds on mackerel and squid when it ventures into open waters, and also on cod, hake, flounder, and other bottom-dwelling fish. Like all mackerel sharks, but unlike most sharks that live on the bottom, the porbeagle must swim continuously in order to breathe.

It reproduces viviparously, without a placental connection. As with other mackerel sharks, the older embryos feed on some of the eggs and smaller embryos in the uterus.

The mackerel sharks are unique among sharks for their heat-exchanging circulatory system, which makes them, functionally, warm-blooded. They can capture the heat generated by their swimming muscles and, through a complicated arrangement of microscopic arteries and veins, use it to heat the blood. This blood is directed throughout their body, to the muscles, internal organs, and brain. As a result, their body temperature is higher than that of the surrounding water. This gives them increased muscle strength and allows more rapid nervous-system activity. The porbeagle has achieved the greatest body temperature elevation. Its body can be 20° F (11° C) warmer than the frigid North Atlantic Ocean that it inhabits.

tail with double keel

Coral Catshark

Atelomycterus marmoratus

The coral catshark is a rather small species with a striking body coloration of white spots on a dark background grading to a white underbelly. The dorsal fins, almost equal in size, have white spots on their tips. The tail fin is short.

Unique features include the short caudal fin, the long labial furrows at the corners of the mouth, and nasal flaps that extend to the front of the mouth. The eyes are set in front of large spiracles, which are used to move water into the gill chambers when the shark is at rest or feeding.

FIELD NOTES

- *Indo-West Pacific, from Pakistan to Papua New Guinea*
- *2' (60 cm)*
- *Harmless*
- *Seen mostly at night, almost year-round*
- *Common*

The Australian marbled catshark (*Atelomycterus macleayi*), which occurs in northern Australia, is similar in appearance to the coral catshark, but can be distinguished by the gray saddle-like markings along its back and small black spots over most of its body. With more than 100 species, the catshark family is the largest of the shark families. The name comes from the cat-like shape and color of the eyes.

Adult coral catsharks are commonly seen on shallow reefs in temperate and tropical waters. They live among coral branches and in the holes and tight crevices of the reef. With their very slender and flexible bodies, they can also be found swimming with sinuous movements near the bottom. They are more active during the night, when they feed on benthic invertebrates and small fishes.

Females reach sexual maturity when about 20" (50 cm) long. They lay purse-shaped egg cases, usually two at a time, with tendrils to anchor the cases to the bottom. The pups, about 4" (10 cm) long at birth, are rarely encountered. They probably spend their time sequestered within the reef, out of the way of predators.

A coral catshark swimming over a reef in the Philippines.

Swellshark

Cephaloscyllium ventriosum

The swellshark cannot be mistaken for any other shark. It has a broadly rounded snout and small dorsal fins on the rear half of the body, and is covered in large, spiky denticles. The patterning of dark brown blotches and saddle-like patterns on the yellow to brown background of its back, along with small dark spots on its belly and flanks, provides good camouflage for this sedentary shark. It has a wide, grinning maw laden with small, pointy teeth—very effective for capturing fish that carelessly swim by without noticing it.

Divers, too, frequently overlook swellsharks because of their camouflage. You will see them from 30' (10 m) to more than 200' (60 m) if you look carefully in caves and among shallow rocks and crevices around kelp forests. They are not dangerous unless handled and provoked. Swellsharks swallow water when distressed. They balloon themselves up in this way when positioned in a rock crevice or other narrow hiding place, until they are wedged tightly inside and are safe from potential predators.

FIELD NOTES

- *Temperate eastern Pacific, from central California, USA, to southern Mexico, and central Chile*
- *To 3⅓' (1 m)*
- *Harmless unless handled or provoked*
- *Active at night, secretive during the day*
- *Not uncommon*

The female swellshark lays large, greenish amber eggs among seaweeds. These purse-shaped eggs hatch after 7 to 10 months, depending on the temperature of the water. The young are about 6" (15 cm) long. The unhatched juveniles use their enlarged dermal denticles to pry themselves free of the egg case.

A small swellshark pup emerging from its purse-shaped egg case.

Striped Catshark

Poroderma africanum

FIELD NOTES

- *Eastern South Atlantic, western Indian Ocean off South Africa; possibly Madagascar and Mauritius*
- *3⅓' (1 m)*
- *Harmless*
- *Commonly seen at night*
- *Common*

The striped catshark is easily recognized by its pattern of solid horizontal stripes. Like the other two species that belong to the genus *Poroderma*, it has a stout, well-tapered body and a relatively short tail fin, and it lives off southern Africa. It also has barbels on the middle fold of the nasal flap, which extend back toward the front of the mouth. These barbels are short and usually end before the mouth. In contrast, the barbeled catshark (*Poroderma marleyi*) has relatively long nasal barbels; its body is covered with large, solid black spots. The leopard catshark (*Poroderma pantherinum*) also has longish barbels. It has a pattern of broken rings and small dark spots across its body.

The striped catshark inhabits temperate coastal waters, and is common on shallow inshore rocky reefs as well as in deeper waters to about 330' (100 m). This fish will hide in caves or rest in reef crevices during the day. At night, when it is most active, divers will see it moving about the bottom in search of food. Its diet is quite varied and includes small bottom-dwelling crustaceans, such as shrimp and crabs, small bony fishes, cephalopods, and mollusks.

Females reach sexual maturity when about 27" (70 cm) long. During the mating season, they lay two tendril-bearing egg cases every few days. The young emerge after five to six months and are about 6" (15 cm) long.

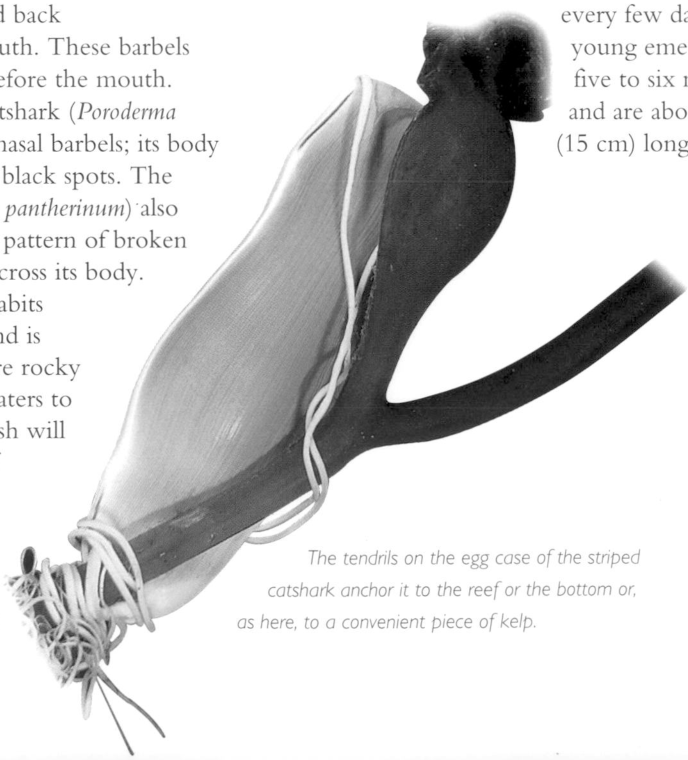

The tendrils on the egg case of the striped catshark anchor it to the reef or the bottom or, as here, to a convenient piece of kelp.

Smallspotted Catshark

Scyliorhinus canicula

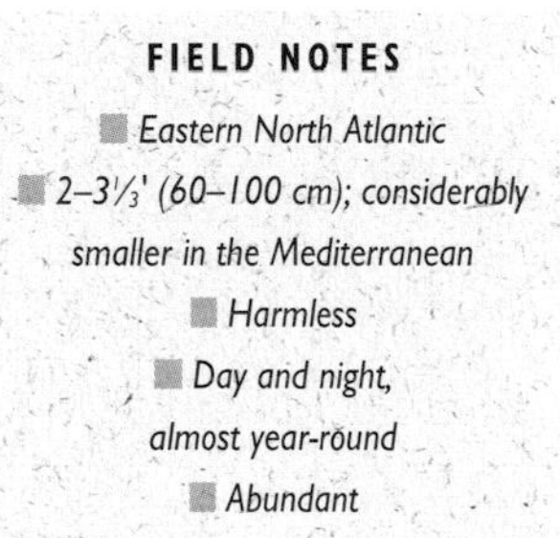

FIELD NOTES

■ *Eastern North Atlantic*

■ *2–3⅓' (60–100 cm); considerably smaller in the Mediterranean*

■ *Harmless*

■ *Day and night, almost year-round*

■ *Abundant*

The smallspotted catshark has a long, slender body and relatively short tail. Its head is slightly flattened and has large nasal flaps that project back to the edge of the mouth. There are neither labial furrows at the side of its mouth, nor barbels at its nostrils. The catshark's body is covered with small, usually dark, spots. Some sharks have an additional eight to nine dark, saddle-like shapes or blotches along their back. These markings are highly variable among individuals and in different locations.

This bottom-dwelling shark inhabits temperate waters. During the day, it can be found resting in open or sheltered areas on rocky reefs, sandy bays, and muddy bottoms. It also inhabits continental shelves in waters as deep as 330' (100 m). Like most catsharks, it is active at night, and divers may see it feeding on a wide variety of small fishes, mollusks, and crustaceans such as shrimp, crab, and lobster. Catsharks employ a quick biting action that sucks water into the mouth along with prey items.

Aggregations of females are found inshore during winter, where they are joined by males in spring. In late summer, the adult population migrates to deeper offshore waters to mate. The male bites the female during courtship, then coils around her to transfer sperm. Females move into shallow water to deposit their egg cases with tendrils for attaching among the rocky reefs or algal patches. After about nine months, the young emerge, measuring about 3½" (9 cm).

This species is commercially important in Europe for meat, fishmeal, and oil.

The slightly flattened head of the bottom-dwelling smallspotted catshark.

Soupfin Shark

Galeorhinus galeus

The soupfin shark is also known as the school shark or tope. It is a moderately slender shark, bronzy gray on the upper side and pale underneath. It has an unusually large subterminal lobe on the caudal fin. The small second dorsal fin is about the same size as the anal fin.

The soupfin shark is usually found on continental shelves and continental slopes in temperate waters. It feeds mainly on fish, squid, and octopus near the seabed or in the water column. Often preferring to congregate in schools, it lives to be more than 50 years old.

Although considered harmless, it is a very shy creature and encounters are unlikely. It will flee long before a diver arrives in its vicinity. Large numbers of newborn pups are sometimes caught inshore by anglers.

FIELD NOTES

- *Widespread: west coast of North America, east coast of South America, northeast Atlantic, South Africa, southern Australia, New Zealand*
- *Varies throughout the world, but up to 6½' (2 m)*
- *Not encountered by divers*
- *Abundant*

This species migrates long distances so pregnant females can give birth in cooler waters. Sharks tagged in England and Ireland have traveled to Iceland (1,530 miles [2,460 km]) and the Canary Islands (1,570 miles [2,525 km]). Sharks from the Californian region have been recaptured off British Columbia (1,000 miles [1,610 km]).

The soupfin shark is ovoviviparous. Litter sizes vary—a litter of 52 pups is the largest known. After a gestation of 12 months, the pups are born, 12–14" (30–35 cm) in length. Discrete, inshore nursery areas have been found in Australia, Argentina, and South Africa. Female sharks reach maturity at 8 to 10 years and breed only every second or third year. This low reproductive rate, combined with the soupfin's longevity, has made it vulnerable to overfishing for its meat, fins, and liver oil.

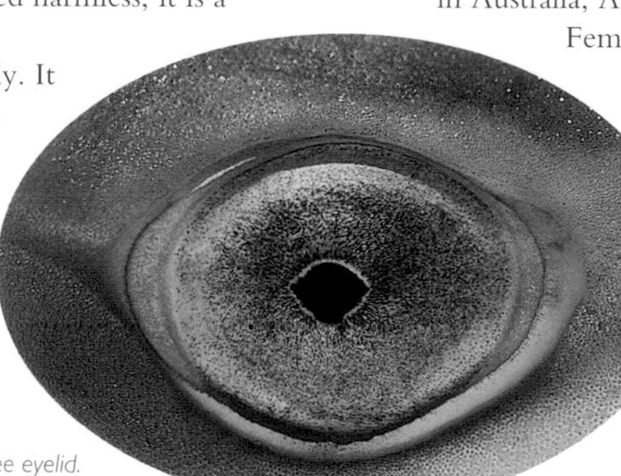

Close-up of the eye of the soupfin shark, showing the free eyelid.

Gummy Shark

Mustelus antarcticus

The gummy shark takes its name from its teeth. They are flat, and arranged in a pavement-like pattern, ideal for crushing rather than cutting its prey. This includes a wide variety of octopus, squid, crustaceans, and fish found on the sandy and rocky bottoms where it dwells.

FIELD NOTES

- Southern Australia
- Females to 5¾' (1.77 m); males to 4¾' (1.45 m)
- Harmless
- During the day, year-round
- Abundant

The gummy is a slender, bronzy gray shark with numerous white spots and sometimes black spots on its back and sides. A thin ridge runs along its back.

The dusky smoothhound (*Mustelus canis*) of the western Atlantic is another of the 20 or so species of the genus *Mustelus*. It is a slender shark, uniformly gray in color, and similar in biology and diet to the gummy shark.

Both species occur mainly in temperate waters on the continental shelf from the shore down. Some also dwell on the continental slope: the gummy shark to depths of 1,150' (350 m), the dusky smoothhound to 1,900' (580 m). They are abundant, and divers will often see them lying on the seabed in shallow coastal waters. Since they are harmless, they can be approached quite safely.

Tagging has shown that a small number of female gummy sharks make long migrations across the ocean off southern Australia—the longest known journey is about 1,140 miles (1,840 km). Most travel only relatively short distances.

The gummy shark is ovoviviparous. After a gestation of about 12 months, pups 12–14½" (30–36 cm) long are born in coastal areas. There are between 1 and 38 pups in a litter, with 15 being the average. They live for about 16 years. In the past there was concern about declining stocks, but these days they are fished sustainably—for their meat, which is popularly known as "flake."

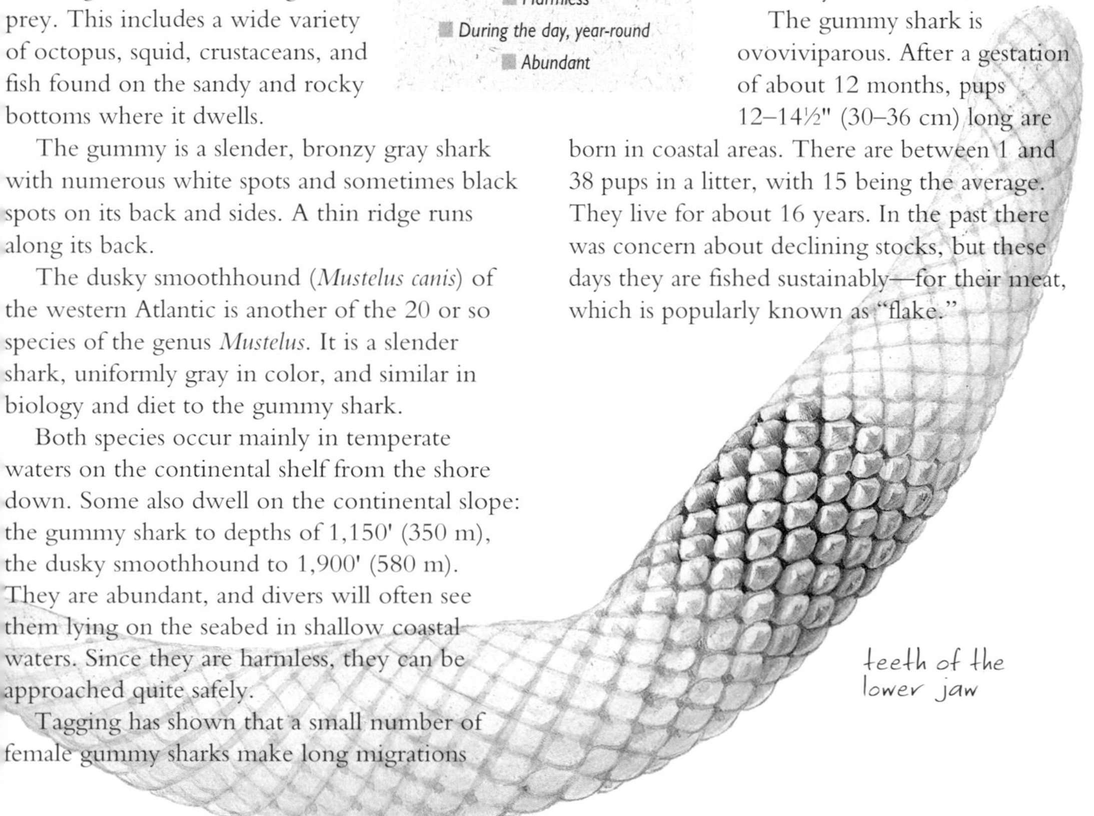

teeth of the lower jaw

Leopard Shark

Triakis semifasciata

Leopard sharks are regular and conspicuous inhabitants of most bays along the coast of northern California, USA.

They have attractive and elongated bodies, with a series of black spots and saddle-shaped markings on a generally gray background. This makes them popular occupants of public aquariums. They possess all the fins typical of a modern shark, but they do not need to swim in order to breathe. In fact, they are usually quite sluggish. They have small, pointed teeth, which they use to capture a wide variety of food, including fish, fish eggs, shrimp, crabs, and clams.

Each year, leopard sharks migrate from the inner bays to the outer coast of the temperate Pacific Northwest. Divers and kayakers will see them there, above the sandy or muddy bottoms of bays and along the outer coast. They are harmless, but because they are social and travel in schools, they are often caught in large numbers.

At maturity, males are smaller than females, but they ultimately grow to be slightly larger. Females produce up to 24 young every spring.

FIELD NOTES

- *Pacific coast from Oregon, USA, to Baja California, Mexico*
- *To 6' (1.8 m)*
- *Harmless*
- *Usually seen during the day, year-round*
- *Once extremely abundant, now becoming uncommon in places because of intensive sport and commercial fishing*

The striking markings (left) of the leopard shark; and its impressive array of small, pointed teeth (below).

Silvertip Shark

Carcharhinus albimarginatus

Silvertips are fairly large and slender sharks, dark gray in color. Their common name is derived from the distinctive white tips and margins on all their fins. The pectoral fins are narrow and pointed, and the first dorsal fin is narrowly rounded. Apart from these features, they look like many of the other gray requiem sharks that are commonly found out beyond the reef edge in warm tropical waters.

FIELD NOTES

- *Widespread in tropics from East Africa to Panama; not in the Atlantic*
- *10' (3 m)*
- *Aggressive, but not a significant risk*
- *During the day, year-round*
- *Common*

The teeth of silvertips are similar to those of other species that belong to the genus *Carcharhinus*. They are strongly serrated and narrowly pointed in the lower jaw, and sharp, serrated, and oblique in the upper jaw. They are ideal for catching and cutting the fish that they feed upon, such as reef wrasses and, in open water, tuna and flyingfish.

These sharks prefer offshore islands, coral reefs, and banks. However, they also enter lagoons, and it is here that you will encounter them often. Given their size and their aggressive behavior, you should always treat them with caution and respect. They have been known to harass divers, but reports of them actually attacking people are rare.

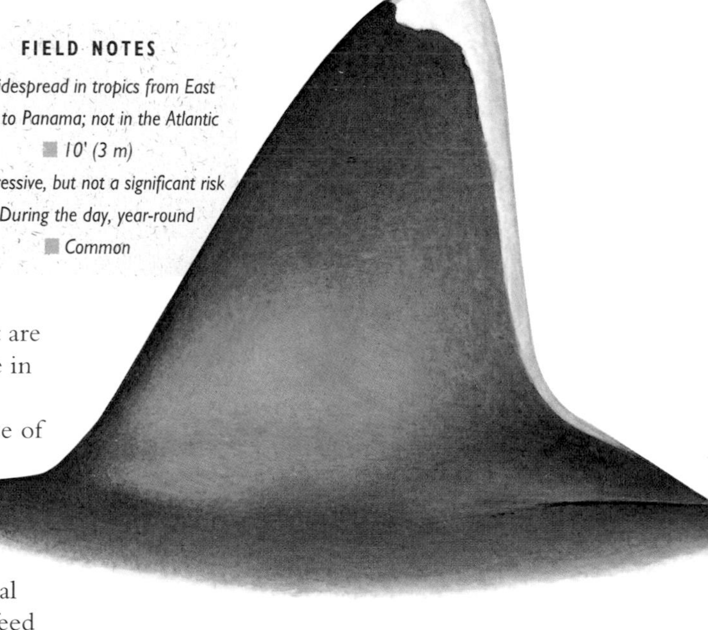

Silvertip sharks are viviparous; females usually have 5 or 6 pups to a litter, but there can be as many as 11. The young hatch after 12 months.

Experiments conducted using underwater sound have shown that silvertips are attracted to low-frequency sounds, probably because these frequencies mimic the sound made by an injured fish, potentially an easy meal.

Gray Reef Shark

Carcharhinus amblyrhynchos

The gray reef shark, or longnose blacktail shark, is similar in shape and general appearance to the silvertip shark (see p. 145), although usually smaller. It has a black edge on its tail. Some specimens have a narrow white edging on the first dorsal fin, but they lack the bold white-edged margins of the silvertip's tail and pectoral fins.

The teeth of the gray reef shark are triangular with fine serrations. It feeds on small reef fish. It is one of the most common sharks on Indo-Pacific coral reefs, and is seen in the reef passes. An inquisitive animal, it is attracted to the low-frequency underwater sounds and commotion caused by a speared fish—there are many stories of a gray reef shark taking a fish off the end of an unsuspecting spearfisher's spear.

If you startle one or get too close, it will perform a contorted threat posture. This includes wagging its head from side to side, sweeping its tail, depressing its pectoral fins, and arching its back. That should be ample warning to any diver—such behavior often precedes an attack. Sharks have severely bitten and injured divers, to threaten them, not to eat them.

FIELD NOTES

- *Central Pacific to Madagascar*
- *To 8' (2.5 m); rarely larger than 6' (1.8 m)*
- *Has attacked if threatened*
- *During the day, year-round*
- *Common*

The gray reef shark is viviparous. Female sharks give birth to up to six pups after a year's gestation. Pups are about 20–24" (50–60 cm) at birth and reach maturity after about seven years, when they are about 4¼' (1.3 m) long.

tail with black edge

The scars on the female gray reef shark at right are mementos of encounters with males during mating.

Bronze Whaler

Carcharhinus brachyurus

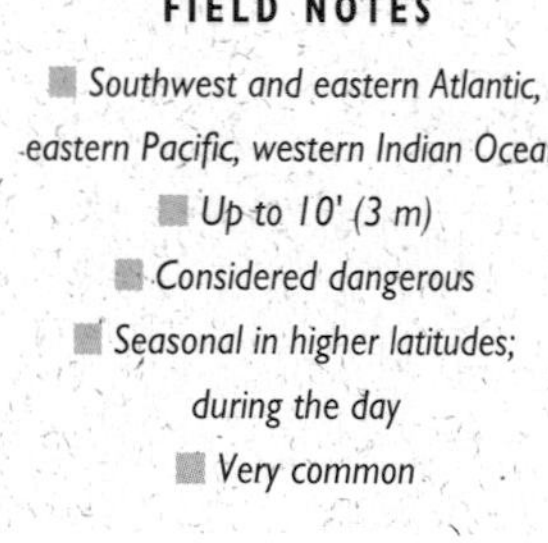

FIELD NOTES

■ Southwest and eastern Atlantic, eastern Pacific, western Indian Ocean

■ Up to 10' (3 m)

■ Considered dangerous

■ Seasonal in higher latitudes; during the day

■ Very common

The bronze whaler, also known as the copper shark, gets both common names from its brownish red, sometimes grayish red, coloring, which shades to white on the underside. It has a short band of pale pigmentation, like a white stripe, that extends down the side of the body almost to the pelvic fins. Apart from darkened tips on the pectoral fins of some individuals, there are no noticeable markings on the relatively slender body. The narrow snout is rounded at the tip. The upper lobe of its tail fin is broad and used for its powerful swimming motion. While the first dorsal fin is large, the second is far smaller.

The bronze whaler is found in most warm temperate and subtropical waters of the world, except along the eastern coastline of North America and the northern Indian Ocean. It is usually seen close inshore along rocky reefs and shallow bays, as well as in the deeper waters of continental shelves and around islands. This species is considered dangerous when excited by the smell of food, and while searching for food, is known to attack swimmers and bathers, probably attracted by their splashing.

Like many other requiem sharks, some populations of bronze whalers are known to make spring and summer migrations to waters in higher latitudes, probably to follow prey. Their diet consists of a wide variety of fishes, such as anchovies, sardines, mullet, hake, and jacks. They also feed on small elasmobranchs, such as spiny dogfish, sawfish, stingrays, and electric rays. Sea snakes and squid are also sometimes taken. Their teeth are pointed with many small serrations; those of the upper jaw have a rounded leading edge.

Little is known about the biology of the bronze whaler. Females are mature when about 8' (2.4 m) long. They produce between 13 and 20 young in each litter.

The claspers are visible on this male bronze whaler.

Silky Shark

Carcharhinus falciformis

FIELD NOTES

- Worldwide
- More than 10' (3 m)
- Potentially dangerous
- Year-round, usually during the day
- Common

This large, slender shark gets its name from the smooth, silky texture of its skin. Its body is nearly black to gray above, with no distinctive markings, and whitish underneath. There is a narrow interdorsal ridge on the back. The second dorsal fin is much smaller than the first, and has a trailing tip. The pectoral fins are long and narrow. The smoothly rounded snout is long and the upper teeth are tall, serrated, and nearly triangular in shape, while the lower teeth have a tall, narrow cusp that is only very weakly serrated.

The silky shark is widely distributed in nearly all tropical and warm temperate waters of the world. It is occasionally seen in waters close to shore, but is more common in oceanic waters, especially near large landmasses. A major pelagic species, it occurs at depths from 60' (18 m) to at least 1,640' (500 m). It is known to form schools segregated by sex—juveniles group in waters relatively close to shore, while adults gather farther out to sea.

It is not often encountered by divers, and while it is not responsible for many attacks, it should be treated with respect.

This shark is a fast swimmer and is capable of quick, darting movements. Its diet includes many small fishes, such as mackerel, tuna, mullet, and sea cats, and also invertebrates such as pelagic crabs and squid.

Females reach sexual maturity when nearly 7½' (2.3 m) in length, and give birth to 6 to 14 young per litter. The pups are about 29–31" (75–80 cm) long at birth. These sharks are commercially fished for their fins, meat, and liver.

A silky shark "flying" overhead in tropical Atlantic waters.

Galápagos Shark

Carcharhinus galapagensis

FIELD NOTES

- *Cosmopolitan in tropical seas, generally near oceanic islands*
- *To 12' (3.6 m)*
- *Potentially dangerous*
- *During the day, year-round*
- *Not uncommon in Hawaii, USA, and off Galapagos Islands, Ecuador*

The Galápagos shark is a large, grayish requiem shark without any distinctive markings. It looks similar to the gray reef shark (see p. 146) and the silvertip shark (see p. 145), except that it lacks their conspicuous white or black coloration on its fins. Its most distinctive feature is a ridge between its dorsal fins, but you would be wise not to get close enough to be able to make it out.

The Galápagos shark is generally not a threat to divers, and prefers to avoid them. However, although it has never attacked a diver, it can be aggressive and divers should always be cautious. Like the gray reef shark, it performs a seemingly awkward threat display before attacking a potential competitor or predator. It has attacked and eaten swimmers.

The shark was named in 1905 after specimens found in the waters of the Galápagos Islands. It has since been found around most tropical oceanic islands, ranging from inshore to well offshore. It prefers clear water, and can be seen beyond the deep reef edge, either near the surface or swimming in groups near the bottom. It feeds primarily on bottom-dwelling fish, squid, and octopus.

There are 6 to 16 young in a litter. They are born alive and remain in nursery areas, where the water is shallower than the area inhabited by the adults of the group. This is a not uncommon adaptation of a number of shark species to avoid cannibalism.

The long, rounded snouts and streamlined bodies of two Galápagos sharks.

Bull Shark

Carcharhinus leucas

This large, stout, and sluggish gray shark is widespread along continental coasts. It also enters rivers and lakes, and is therefore known by such names as the Lake Nicaragua shark and the Zambezi shark. It was also thought to be the rare Ganges shark, but this is now known to be a separate, distinct species.

The bull shark can tolerate highly salty sea water and fresh water—it has been recorded as far as 1,750 miles (2,800 km) up the Mississippi River and 2,500 miles (4,000 km) up the Amazon in Peru. It has ample opportunity to encounter, attack, and consume people. Because it has been confused with other similar-looking requiem sharks, it seems likely that it is responsible for even more attacks than those with which it is credited. This makes it more dangerous than the great white or tiger sharks.

In the Americas, it is usually found close to shore in estuaries and shallow marine habitats from just a few feet deep to 100' (30 m). The famous Matawan Creek incident of 1916, when sharks killed four people and injured one along the New Jersey shore over a 12-day period, was probably the work of bull sharks. It will eat almost anything it can capture, including other sharks, rays, fishes, turtles, birds, dolphins, mollusks, crustaceans, and things that fall overboard, such as cattle, dogs, rats, and people.

FIELD NOTES

- *All tropical and subtropical seas; also inland in fresh water*
- *To 11½' (3.5 m)*
- *Dangerous*
- *Not encountered by divers*
- *Common*

The bull shark has a unique appearance. It has a very blunt, rounded snout; small eyes; a pointed first dorsal fin; and dusky fin tips. It is viviparous, and selects estuaries as pupping grounds for litters of 1 to 13 pups, which are born after almost a year's gestation.

Because they live close to shore and in rivers and lakes, bull sharks are vulnerable to fisheries.

The bull shark's blunt, rounded snout is shorter than its mouth width.

Blacktip Shark

Carcharhinus limbatus

The blacktip shark takes its name from the black markings on the tips of the dorsal and pectoral fins and the lower lobe of the tail fin. The spinner shark (*Carcharhinus brevipinna*) has similar markings and a similar range, so the two species can be confused. The blacktip is a much stouter shark, however, and its well-developed first dorsal fin begins at about the middle of the pectoral fin. The spinner shark's first dorsal fin begins much farther back.

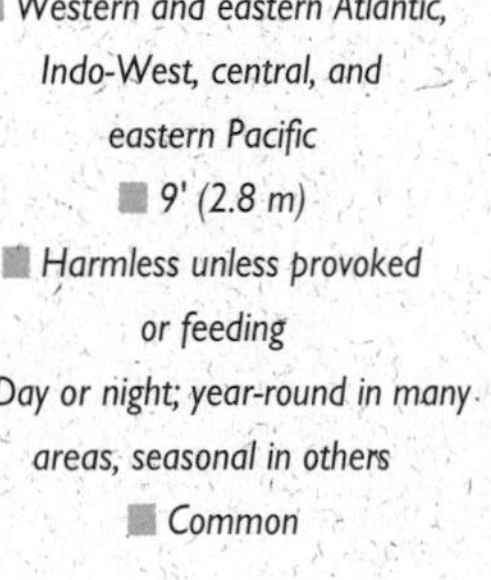

FIELD NOTES

- Western and eastern Atlantic, Indo-West, central, and eastern Pacific
- 9' (2.8 m)
- Harmless unless provoked or feeding
- Day or night; year-round in many areas, seasonal in others
- Common

The blacktip is a large gray or gray-brown shark, grading along the sides to a white underbelly and a white anal fin. A subtle white band usually runs along the side of the body. The snout is long and parabolic; the eyes are on the side of the head near the mouth's leading edge.

Blacktip sharks are found in all tropical and temperate waters of the world. They live at the surface above continental and island shelves, but will also frequent shallows along sand beaches, bays, and rocky coastlines in warmer months. They migrate along continental coasts in large schools, possibly for food or pupping.

Divers regularly see blacktips inshore. As long as there is no food stimulus present, they do not generally present a hazard. The blacktip's diet includes small schooling fishes such as sardines, anchovies, and menhaden, which the sharks feed on in the water column. On the seabed, they also eat bottom-dwelling fishes, crustaceans, and squid. They are often seen near shore jumping out of the water during feeding.

Two blacktip sharks in Bahaman waters.

Females reach maturity at about 5' (1.5 m) and produce 4 to 8 pups per litter, about 10" (25 cm) long, after a gestation of 10 to 11 months. South African blacktip populations appear to segregate, with mainly adult males and non-pregnant females grouped together.

Oceanic Whitetip Shark

Carcharhinus longimanus

The oceanic whitetip shark should not be confused with the sluggish, slender, and small-finned whitetip reef shark (see p. 162). The oceanic whitetip's enlarged first dorsal fin and long, paddle-shaped pectoral fins are unmistakable. These fins have conspicuous, mottled white tips; the fins of juveniles may also have black markings.

The oceanic whitetip is a large and stocky gray species, usually found far offshore, from the surface to depths of at least 500' (150 m). It prefers the open ocean, and can sometimes be seen from boats or encountered by divers in open water. Although it is generally slow moving, it is dangerous because it has powerful jaws, large teeth, and it will not hesitate to approach swimmers or small boats. It is probably responsible for many of the open-ocean attacks on people after air or sea disasters. It is most abundant in the tropics, but can also be found from coastal California, USA, to southern Australia, following the warm water masses.

FIELD NOTES

- *All tropical and subtropical waters*
- *To 13' (4 m)*
- *Potentially dangerous*
- *Day or night*
- *Once abundant, now reduced by overfishing*

Oceanic whitetips eat just about anything that they can catch in the open sea, including a variety of fishes and squid, whale carcasses, turtles, sea birds, and garbage disposed of at sea. They are aggressive and will dominate other shark species that are competing for food.

The litter size increases with the size of the mother—as many as 15 live pups are born after a gestation period of about a year.

mottled tail and fin tips

Blacktip Reef Shark

Carcharhinus melanopterus

FIELD NOTES

- *Indo-Australian Pacific to central Pacific*
- *To 6' (1.8 m)*
- *Potentially dangerous to waders; otherwise, not aggressive*
- *During the day, year-round*
- *Common*

Blacktip reef sharks are the most common sharks in the shallow lagoons and coral reefs of the tropical Pacific and Indian Oceans, along with whitetip reef sharks (see p. 162) and gray reef sharks (see p. 146). They are different from blacktip sharks (see p. 151), larger sharks with thin black tips on most fins that live mainly in the open ocean.

Blacktip reef sharks are easily recognized by the very distinct black marks on their fins, particularly the first dorsal and caudal fins. They also have a conspicuous white slash along their flanks. They are small to medium in size, with a short, blunt snout. Their teeth are narrow, sharp, and strongly serrated, designed for eating the reef fish that comprise their main food.

Divers and snorkelers commonly see these sharks patrolling in shallow waters from about 1' (30 cm) deep. Divers will find them in reef passes, while waders and snorkelers will see them in lagoons, their dorsal and caudal fins above the surface. On rare occasions, they have bitten waders on the legs and ankles, probably attracted by the splashing commotion made by the waders. They will attack speared fish, and are curious, but not aggressive, around divers.

Blacktip reef sharks are viviparous, with the yolk sac being attached by a placenta. Litters number from two to four. The pups are born after a gestation period of about 16 months. They are 13–20" (33–50 cm) long at birth.

In recent years, blacktip reef sharks have entered the eastern Mediterranean via the Suez Canal. Because they are a small, hardy species, a number of them have been captured in the central Pacific, off Christmas Island, and sent to public aquariums worldwide.

Black fin tips, particularly on the first dorsal and caudal fins, make this shark instantly recognizable.

Dusky Shark

Carcharhinus obscurus

The long, streamlined body of the dusky shark is brown-gray to gray above and white below. A faint pale stripe extends along the side of the body to the pelvic fins. In juveniles, the tip of the lower caudal fin and the undersides of the pectoral fins are notably dark or dusky, but this is indistinct in adults. The snout is relatively short and broad. The upper lobe of the caudal fin is well developed, indicating that this species is a strong swimmer. Its pectoral fins are long and curved on the trailing edge. Its second dorsal fin is much smaller than the first, and an interdorsal ridge is present.

FIELD NOTES

- *Western and eastern North Atlantic, western Indian Ocean, western and eastern Pacific*
- *To 13' (4 m); normally about 10' (3 m)*
- *Considered dangerous*
- *Day or night; seasonal in many regions*
- *Numbers dwindling in many areas*

Although divers occasionally see dusky sharks close inshore, this species occurs primarily above coastal shelves in offshore waters adjacent to the open ocean. It is widely distributed in warm temperate and tropical waters. While few attacks on humans are attributed to it, this is not a shark to seek out. Like many other large requiem sharks, it migrates into higher latitudes during warm months and more central latitudes during winter. The migratory pattern near South Africa appears to be complex and is at least partly related to pupping and nursery grounds.

The dusky shark has a varied diet that includes small schooling fishes such as sardines and anchovies, larger, fast-moving tuna and mackerel, and bottom-dwelling flatfishes and eels. It is also a significant predator of dogfishes, catsharks, smoothhound sharks, rays, and skates.

Females reach sexual maturity at about 9' (2.8 m). They mate in spring, and give birth after a 16-month gestation to litters of about 10 young that are up to 3' (95 cm) long.

Numbers of this species in the western Atlantic have fallen because of overfishing.

Dusky sharks patrolling off the coast of Australia.

Caribbean Reef Shark

Carcharhinus perezi

The Caribbean reef shark has a relatively stout body, gray or gray-brown above grading to white underneath. The first dorsal fin has a sharp point and a short, trailing tip. The pectoral fins are relatively long and narrow. It has an interdorsal ridge, and a blunt, rounded snout. The well-serrated upper teeth have broad bases and narrow cusps. The lower teeth also have broad bases and small serrations, but are narrow and straight. Such teeth are probably designed for a diet of bony reef fishes, small sharks and rays, and cephalopods.

FIELD NOTES

- *Western Atlantic and Caribbean, from Florida, USA, and Bermuda to southern Brazil, including parts of the Gulf of Mexico*
- *Up to 10' (3 m)*
- *Potentially dangerous*
- *Day and night, year-round*
- *Abundant*

Large numbers of these sharks occur on island reefs throughout the Caribbean Sea. It is a fast swimmer, but is known to rest in caves and under ledges during the day. It has been called the sleeping shark, although there is no evidence that it is actually asleep when resting.

Divers encounter Caribbean reef sharks in surface waters near shore, cruising over the bottom of coral reefs, or swimming along the reef drop-offs down to depths of 100' (30 m). In the Bahamas, it is possible to dive with them after they have been attracted to "shark feeds" (see pp. 214–15). While they are not particularly aggressive, they have been responsible for attacks on divers, especially in situations involving bait or spearfishing.

Very little is known about the Caribbean reef shark's biology. Females bear four to six pups per litter; these range from 2–2½' (60–75 cm) in length at birth. This shark is targeted by local fisheries for its meat, hide, liver oil, and for fishmeal.

A Caribbean reef shark, with another reef shark behind.

Sandbar Shark

Carcharhinus plumbeus

The most notable feature of this shark, also called the thickskin shark, is its strikingly tall first dorsal fin. It can be more than one-tenth of the length of this sizable shark, which usually reaches 6½' (2 m) and weighs 100 lb (45 kg), with some animals to 8' (2.4 m) and twice as heavy.

FIELD NOTES

- *Western and eastern Atlantic, western Indian Ocean, western, eastern, and central Pacific*
- *6½–8' (2–2.4 m)*
- *Not dangerous*
- *Day and night; seasonally abundant in many coastal areas*
- *Common, but declining in some regions because of overfishing*

The broad head is flattened. The streamlined body is gray or brown above, while the belly is white and the dorsal and tail fins both have dusky upper edges. In this strong-swimming species, the upper lobe of the tail fin is well developed. There is a ridge between the first and the far smaller second dorsal fins.

With broad, serrated upper teeth to cut up prey, the sandbar shark eats many fishes, including menhaden, eels, flatfish, other sharks, goatfish, skates, octopus, squid, and crustaceans.

Sandbar sharks live in tropical and temperate waters around the globe. Large schools range over continental and island shelves, with the schools often being segregated by sex. They can be found behind the surf zone on sandy beaches or at depths as great as 1,310' (400 m). Sometimes, divers see them near sandy beaches or rocky reefs, but they are not particularly aggressive. They prefer to swim near the bottom, often in large bays and estuaries, but do not move into fresh water.

Off the Atlantic coast of north America, females reach maturity at about 16 years of age. Mating occurs from spring through early summer, and females carry the developing young for 9 to 12 months. They retreat to shallow nursery grounds to give birth to 8 to 12 young, depending on the size of the mother. Pups are about 8½" (22 cm) long at birth.

The sandbar shark is heavily fished for its meat and fins.

Tiger Shark

Galeocerdo cuvier

FIELD NOTES

- Worldwide in tropical waters
- To 18' (5.6 m); possibly to 24' (7.4 m)
- Dangerous
- Very rarely seen
- Not common

This large, dangerous shark is to tropical waters what the great white shark (see p. 134) is to temperate waters. It is named for the dark stripes on its gray back, which are pronounced in juveniles (see above) but become pale or disappear in large adults. Its wide mouth, broad nose, barrel chest, and the slenderness at the base of its tail are distinctive. So, too, are its heavily serrated, cockscomb-shaped teeth. These, combined with its jaw strength, allow it to cut through the bodies of large sea turtles, as well as seals, sea lions, and cetaceans. It also has a liking for such spicy treats as venomous jellyfish, stingrays, and sea snakes. One of the few true shark scavengers, it has eaten cattle, pigs, donkeys, sheep, and humans that have fallen overboard.

Adult tiger sharks spend their days beyond the reef edge to depths of about 500' (150 m), except at certain times of the year, when they also come inshore during the day. They are active at night, and enter shallow reefs and lagoons after dusk to feed. In certain areas, they migrate between island groups to take advantage of colonies of young birds learning to fly over water.

Generally, tiger sharks are sluggish, but they can move quickly when feeding, and should be treated carefully on the rare occasions they are sighted. If you see one while diving, calmly leave the water, keeping it in sight at all times.

The tiger shark is the only ovoviviparous requiem shark. It has between 10 and 82 pups after a year-long gestation. The young are 20–30" (50–75 cm) at birth. They mature after about 4 to 6 years, and live for about 12 years.

upper and lower teeth

The shark's powerful body makes it capable of bursts of speed.

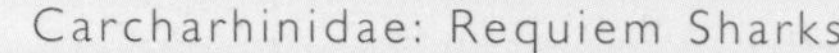

Lemon Shark

Negaprion brevirostris

This large, stout-bodied reef shark has a pale yellow-brown body with no obvious markings and a broad, flattened head. It is easily identified by its large dorsal fins, which are about equal in size. The anal fin, immediately below the second dorsal fin, is also large. The pectoral fins are long and curve back on the trailing edge. There is no lateral keel, and unlike many requiem sharks, it has no interdorsal ridge.

The only other species in the genus is the sicklefin lemon shark (*Negaprion acutidens*), found in the Indo-Pacific. The trailing edges of its pectoral fins are more curved than the lemon shark's.

The lemon shark is abundant in tropical reef systems, especially those with sea grass and associated mangrove habitats. It has adapted to be highly tolerant of shallow waters with low oxygen levels, such as warm-water mangrove swamps or bays, places where it is commonly observed. It has attacked humans, but is generally not considered aggressive, unless provoked.

Lemon sharks are active throughout the day and night. Among the Bimini Islands population, in the Bahamas, the level of activity seems to increase at dusk and dawn, possibly due to feeding. The diet consists of bony fishes, rays, crustaceans, guitarfishes, and mollusks. Some populations probably undertake lengthy seasonal migrations in search of food, because they are found in summer along sandy beaches and continental shelves in waters of high latitudes.

Females reach maturity when they are about 8' (2.4 m) long, and mate in spring and summer. About one year later, 4 to 17 live young, about 2' (60 cm) in length, are born.

FIELD NOTES

- *Western Atlantic, from New Jersey, USA, to southern Brazil; the Caribbean; possibly the west coast of Africa; eastern Pacific from southern Baja California, Mexico, to Ecuador*
- *11' (3.4 m)*
- *Harmless unless provoked*
- *Day and night; year-round in tropical regions*
- *Common*

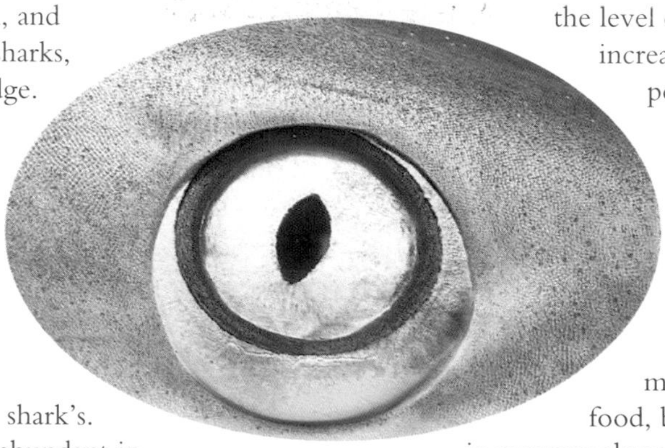

The eye (above) of the lemon shark is an effective hunting tool.

Blue Shark

Prionace glauca

FIELD NOTES

- Worldwide in open ocean
- To 12½' (3.8 m)
- Potentially dangerous
- During the day, year-round
- Previously very abundant, now reduced by heavy fishing

The blue shark, one of the most attractive sharks, is large and slender. Its upper body is indigo blue, the sides are bright blue, the belly markedly white. With its long, narrow, and pointed pectoral fins, long snout, and large eyes, it is unmistakable.

The blue shark is found in the open ocean throughout the tropics and into cooler seas. In the tropics, it often enters deeper, cooler water, while in temperate coastal waters it comes close to the edge of kelp beds, where divers may see it. It migrates regularly in the Atlantic, following the Gulf Stream to Europe, moving south along the African coast, then returning to the Caribbean.

Open-water divers may see these sharks, particularly if the sharks have been attracted by chum (berley). Dive operators offer tours using cages off southern California, USA (see p. 204–5), and elsewhere. Although attacks are unlikely, excited sharks have occasionally taken a nip at an unwary diver.

Blue sharks feed ravenously on large schools of squid, but are also very opportunistic and will decimate a floating whale or porpoise carcass. Fisheries consider them a menace because they attack nets and eat fish caught on lines. Once the most plentiful shark in the sea, they are now endangered through overfishing.

Although not yet observed, blue shark courtship is thought to be very lively. Males bite the females' shoulders; fortunately, their skin is three times as thick as that of the males. Females reach maturity when about five. They mate and store sperm for nearly a year, after which fertilization occurs. Litters of from 4 to 135 pups, depending on the size of the mother, are born alive the following year.

A blue shark (left) feeds on a school of northern anchovies off the California coast.

Milk Shark

Rhizoprionodon acutus

One of the most common small requiem species in the western Pacific and Indian oceans is the milk shark, a brownish red to gray shark with a white underbelly. Like the other sharks in this genus, it has a long, slender body, a parabola-like snout when viewed from above, and relatively large eyes near the tip of the mouth. The first dorsal fin is much larger than the second dorsal fin. The pectoral fins are short and stout, and the pelvic fins are small.

Long labial folds at the corners of the mouth distinguish the milk shark from all other requiem sharks in its range. The similar gray sharpnose shark (*Rhizoprionodon oligolinx*) inhabits coastal areas from the west coast of Africa, east to New Guinea and north to Japan. The Australian sharpnose shark (*Rhizoprionodon taylori*) ranges across the northern half of Australia. Both of these closely related species have very short labial furrows at the edge of the mouth.

Milk sharks are found in large numbers in coastal areas and continental shelves to depths of 655' (200 m). They spend most of their time in small groups or large schools foraging for food near the bottom, where they may be encountered by divers. Their diet consists of small fishes (herring, sardines, croaker, mojarra, and flatfish) and invertebrates (squid, octopus, snails, shrimp, and crabs). They are a major food source for large sharks. With barrier nets removing large predator sharks from beaches in South Africa, swimmers and divers are seeing more milk sharks off beaches there. They are no threat to humans, being quite harmless.

Females reach sexual maturity when about two years old and about 2½' (75 cm) long. They produce litters of one to eight live young, about 10" (25 cm) long at birth, after about a year's gestation. This shark is commercially important as a food source in many parts of its range.

FIELD NOTES

- *Eastern Atlantic, Indo-West Pacific*
- *Up to 6' (1.8 m); smaller individuals about 3⅓' (1 m)*
- *Harmless*
- *Day and night, year-round*
- *Common*

Caribbean Sharpnose Shark

Rhizoprionodon porosus

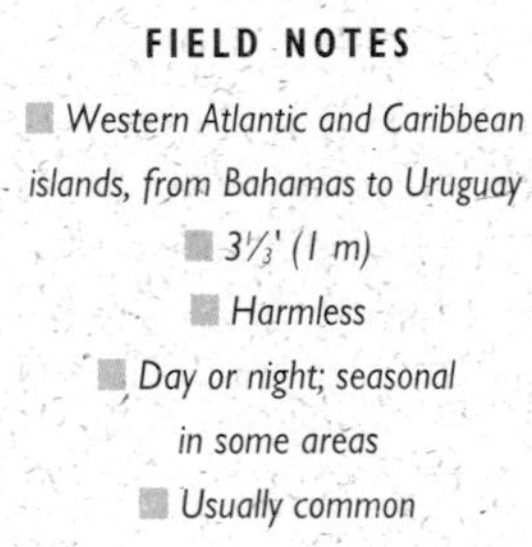

FIELD NOTES

- Western Atlantic and Caribbean islands, from Bahamas to Uruguay
- 3⅓' (1 m)
- Harmless
- Day or night; seasonal in some areas
- Usually common

The Caribbean sharpnose shark has a gray body that grades to white below. Like other *Rhizoprionodon* species, this small shark is slender, with a long, parabolic snout and relatively large eyes adjacent to the tip of the mouth. Its sides are sometimes scattered with white spots and the fins edged in white. The first dorsal fin is much larger than the second, and the pectoral and small pelvic fins are short.

Currently, there are thought to be six or seven species in the genus *Rhizoprionodon*. Although the taxonomic relationships among them are still under investigation, most species seem to have non-overlapping distributions in the tropical and subtropical latitudes of the world. The Caribbean sharpnose is similar to the Atlantic sharpnose shark (*Rhizoprionodon terraenovae*), which occurs in the Gulf of Mexico and also along the Atlantic coast of North America, but is distinguished from it by the number of vertebrae.

The Caribbean sharpnose is a common inhabitant of shallow inshore waters along continental and island shelves. It frequents sea-grass beds, coral reefs, and can tolerate the reduced salinity of estuaries. It is also collected at depths greater than 1,640' (500 m). Although common, this shy, harmless shark usually avoids contact with divers.

This species feeds on a variety of small fishes, and invertebrates such as snails and shrimp. It is a common prey for larger sharks. Gestation takes 10 to 11 months, with litters of 2 to 6 pups, about 1' (30 cm) in length, born in spring or early summer. This shark is taken for food and fishmeal by local and commercial fisheries.

A sharpnose shark swimming in tropical Bahaman waters.

Whitetip Reef Shark

Triaenodon obesus

The whitetip reef shark should not be confused with the larger and more graceful oceanic whitetip shark (see p. 152). It is a sluggish, fairly slender, gray requiem shark with conspicuous white tips on its dorsal and caudal fins.

It has medium-sized, pointed teeth with smooth edges, which are flanked by small cusps. Unlike most requiem sharks, it is not an effective fish hunter in open water. It feeds mostly on the bottom, taking advantage of its tooth structure and its short, broad snout to pursue prey into reef crevices, where they cannot escape. Like most reef sharks, it too falls prey to other, larger sharks and large reef groupers.

Whitetip reef sharks live close to shore, at depths of 26–130' (8–40 m). During the day, divers and snorkelers predictably find them resting in caves, particularly in Hawaii and the Galápagos Islands, or under rock and coral ledges. They are active at night and during slack tides. They can become accustomed to the sounds of boats and to spearfishers, and are aroused by the presence of divers, approaching them out of curiosity. Although this is not an aggressive species, foolhardy divers have lost a hand when feeding members squid and fish.

Whitetips are viviparous and bear litters of one to five pups. They are born after a short gestation period of at least five months and are 20–24" (50–60 cm) long at birth.

The flesh and liver of whitetips are consumed by humans. It is unique among sharks in having caused ciguateratoxin poisoning, a type of food poisoning with severe gastrointestinal and neurological symptoms.

FIELD NOTES

- *Red Sea, Indian Ocean, central Pacific, and tropical eastern Pacific*
- *Said to reach 7' (2.2 m), but rarely more than 5¼' (1.6 m)*
- *Potentially dangerous*
- *Year-round*
- *Common*

The whitetip reef shark uses its pointed, cusped teeth to grip and pull fish prey out of their hiding places in reef crevices.

Winghead Shark

Euspyhra blochii

The stout-bodied winghead shark is one of the smaller hammerhead sharks. The first dorsal fin is tall, and the second dorsal fin is set behind the anal fin. It is gray to brown above, grading to a white underside, with no conspicuous markings on the fins or body.

FIELD NOTES

- *Indo-West Pacific*
- *Up to 5' (1.5 m); commonly reaching 3⅓' (1 m)*
- *Harmless*
- *Day or night, usually year-round*
- *Common*

The winghead is easily identified by its broad wing-shaped head, the ultimate example of the cephalofoil, measuring about half the shark's total body length. The eyes are set far apart on the extremely broad head; this may have the effect of improving the shark's stereoscopic vision. The nares are located near the middle of the head, but the nasal grooves extend along almost its full width. These wide nasal grooves can sample a very large section of the water column, which may enhance the shark's ability to detect and locate odor sources. The electroreceptive ampullae of Lorenzini and mechanoreceptive lateral line on the wings have an extended distribution across the head. This may be useful for detecting and localizing prey, such as crabs, shrimp, cephalopods, and small fishes, buried in the sediment.

This poorly studied species is widespread along the coast of southern Asia in the Indian Ocean, and around islands of the western Pacific. It is also common in shallow tropical waters on continental and island shelves. It is exploited commercially in Southeast Asia, but because the winghead population has a high natural mercury content, it is not generally marketed elsewhere.

Females reach sexual maturity when about 3⅓' (1 m) in length. They mate in spring and give birth to 6 to 20 young, about 13–18" (32–45 cm) long, after almost a year's gestation.

wing-shaped cephalofoil

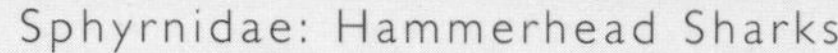

Scalloped Hammerhead

Sphyrna lewini

FIELD NOTES

- Western and eastern Atlantic, Indo-West, central, and eastern Pacific
- 10–13' (3–4 m)
- Not aggressive, but potentially dangerous
- Day or night; year-round or seasonal, depending on region
- The most abundant and widely distributed of the large hammerheads

The scalloped hammerhead, also known as the kidney-headed shark, belongs to a family of eight sharks with a unique specialization—the front of the skull expands laterally like a hammer to form a head structure called a cephalofoil. This serves many biological functions. Its wide, flattened shape adds lift during swimming, improving hydrodynamic efficiency. The increased surface area allows for the expansion of many sensory systems important for feeding. The eyes and nares are at the tips of the head; the electroreceptors and lateral line are over a wider area. Thus these fast, active sharks can capture large or elusive prey.

Scalloped hammerheads can be distinguished by the broad leading edge on the head, which is arched toward the back. There is a prominent indentation in the center with two smaller lobes on either side, giving a scalloped look. These sharks are found in most warm temperate and tropical waters. They occur in coastal areas above continental and island shelves, and in adjacent offshore waters to depths of nearly 1,000' (300 m). They enter shallow bays and estuaries, and aggregate around seamounts. Here, divers see them interacting, chasing, thrusting, shaking their heads, and biting each other. This behavior needs further study, but may be for social reasons, migration to feeding areas, or reproduction. They are often indifferent to divers, but do make close passes.

Their diet consists of bony fishes and cephalopods. Females bear 15 to 30 pups, 17–22" (43–55 cm) long at birth.

The unmistakable scalloped-looking head.

Great Hammerhead

Sphyrna mokarran

FIELD NOTES

- Western and eastern North Atlantic, Indo-West and eastern Pacific
- Up to 11½' (3.5 m); individuals more than 20' (6 m) long have been reported
- Few attacks recorded, but considered dangerous
- Day and night, year-round
- Common

The great hammerhead is easily identified by its thick, broad head, which has an almost flat leading edge, except for an indentation in the center. It is a large, stout shark, gray-brown above, grading to a paler color below. The first dorsal fin is extremely high and pointed, with a curved rear margin. The base of the anal fin is much longer than that of the second dorsal fin.

This species is distributed in nearly all warm temperate and tropical waters. It occurs in coastal areas above continental and island shelves, and in adjacent offshore waters to depths of about 260' (80 m). Divers are likely to see it in shallow waters close to shore, especially near coral reef drop-offs and adjacent sand habitats. It makes long migrations to cooler waters during the summer months.

The great hammerhead has a very keen olfactory sense, and is an impressive predator. Its diet consists of many mobile fishes associated with the water column, including sardines, herring, tarpon, and jacks, and benthic species such as grouper, sea cats, flatfish, and croaker. But this shark is best known for its preference for other elasmobranchs, such as stingrays, skates, and other sharks. In its voracious and unique predatory behavior toward stingrays, the great hammerhead uses the side of its head to pin a fleeing ray to the bottom. It then rotates its head to the side and cleanly bites off a large chunk of the ray's wing. It continues to circle and feed on the incapacitated prey until it has been totally consumed.

Females reach sexual maturity when about 10' (3 m) long. They usually produce 20 to 40 young per litter, and the pups are about 2¼' (70 cm) long at birth.

The very broad head allows for some unique feeding techniques.

Bonnethead Shark

Sphyrna tiburo

The bonnethead shark is a small hammerhead, and can be distinguished by its smooth, rounded, shovel-shaped head. Its body is plain gray-brown above, shading to a light color on the underside. The pectoral fins are short and straight along the rear margin. The anal fin is slightly concave but has no notch.

FIELD NOTES

- *Western Atlantic, eastern Pacific*
- *About 3⅓' (1 m); individuals 5' (1.5 m) long are known*
- *Harmless*
- *Day or night; year-round in many areas*
- *Common*

This shark frequents many different habitats within the temperate and tropical waters of its range. It is abundant in the surf zone, bays and estuaries, on coral and rocky reefs, and over sandy or muddy bottoms. It also inhabits waters of the continental shelf to depths of about 260' (80 m). Large schools migrate to warm latitudes in winter and to cooler latitudes during summer. Although harmless, it is timid and not easy to approach.

Bonnetheads have remarkable dentition, with small sharp teeth at the front of the jaw for grasping either its mate or a soft-bodied prey, and broad molar-like teeth at the back of the jaw for crushing hard-shelled invertebrates. It feeds primarily on invertebrates, crabs, shrimp, mantis shrimp, bivalves, snails, and cephalopods, as well as small bony fishes.

The behavior of this species has been well studied. Individual sharks exhibit specific types of behavior toward other individuals, including patrolling, head-shaking, jaw-snapping, hitting, and hunching. The function of such behavior is to establish and maintain dominance hierarchies and other agonistic relationships.

Individual populations are sometimes segregated by sex. Females reach sexual maturity when about 2½' (75 cm) long. They retreat to shallow bays and estuaries to give birth, delivering litters of 8 to 16 pups about 14" (35 cm) long.

The head of the bonnethead looks like a shovel.

Smooth Hammerhead

Sphyrna zygaena

FIELD NOTES

- Western and eastern North Atlantic, western Indian Ocean, western, central, and eastern Pacific
- 8–13' (2.5–4 m)
- Possibly dangerous
- Day or night; year-round in many areas
- Common

The smooth hammerhead has a cephalofoil that is long and narrow, its leading margin shaped in a smooth arch without a notch in the middle. Its body is olive to gray-brown above, becoming light on the underside. The tips of the pectoral fins are dusky on the bottom. The first dorsal fin is high, with a slightly curved rear margin. The pectoral fins are short and straight along the rear margin, while the anal fin has a prominent notch.

The smooth hammerhead is found in nearly all warm temperate and tropical waters. And while its distribution overlaps that of the scalloped hammerhead (see p. 164) and great hammerhead (see p. 165), the smooth hammerhead is mostly concentrated in temperate waters. It seems to prefer shallow inshore waters less than 65' (20 m) deep, and divers are especially likely to see it around rocky reefs. Divers need to take care, however, especially those who are spearfishing. It also occurs at the surface in the open ocean, and forms enormous schools to make long migrations to cooler latitudes during the summer, then returns to warmer waters for the winter months.

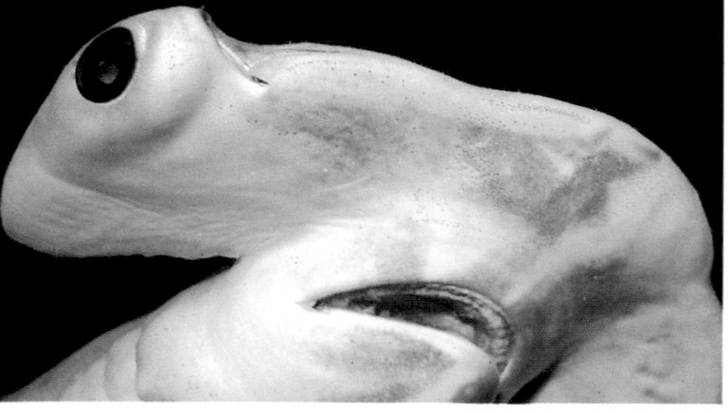

The smoothly arched leading edge of the cephalofoil, or head, of a juvenile.

The smooth hammerhead feeds on small schooling bony fishes such as herring and menhaden, as well as porgies and sea bass from the reef, and stingrays, skates, and other small sharks. Large crustaceans and cephalopods round out the diet.

Females reach sexual maturity when about 7½' (2.3 m) long, giving birth to large numbers of live young, between 29 and 37 per litter. The pups are about 22" (55 cm) long at birth.

SHARKS *of the* DEEP MIDWATERS

Below the euphotic zone, at depths of 650' (200 m), the sea is without the sun-driven photosynthesis that supports most life on Earth. Animals depend on dead and decaying plants and animals falling from above, or they venture to the surface to dine. Many small sharks from the dogfish family (Squalidae) ascend at dusk and return at dawn to the safety of the deep midwaters, relying on their large eyes and good vision in low light to detect prey. They also use their ventral bioluminescence to camouflage themselves from potential predators and prey.

BLACKBELLY LANTERNSHARK

Etmopterus lucifer

This small, stocky shark has spines in front of each dorsal fin. Its dorsal side and flanks are brownish, the underbody black, and there is no anal fin. It has blade-like teeth and feeds on squid, lanternfish, and crustaceans. A variety of features distinguish blackbelly lanternsharks from the other lanternsharks. These include the arrangement and number of their denticles, and subtle differences in fin size and coloration. It is closely related to *Etmopterus perryi*, the dwarf dogfish, which is a mere 8" (20 cm) long, and probably the smallest living shark.

The blackbelly lanternshark, widespread on outer continental shelves, lives on or near the bottom at depths of 590–2,700' (180–835 m). Its mode of reproduction is presumed to be ovoviviparous, like that of most sharks.

The 17 or more species of lanternsharks have numerous minute, bio-luminescent (light-producing) photophores

FIELD NOTES

- Southern oceans, also the China Sea and off the Philippines
- Males to 16" (40 cm); females to 13" (33 cm)
- Harmless
- Not encountered by divers
- Not uncommon

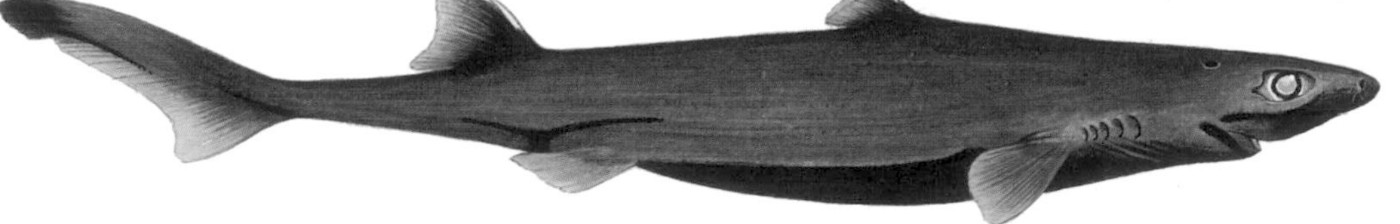

along the underside of their bodies. The light from the photophores is a means of camouflage because it "counter-illuminates" the shark. The shark produces just enough weak light on the underside of its body to equal the amount of down-welling light between it and the ocean's surface. Because of this optical illusion, it merges with the ocean and cannot be seen by potential predators, nor by unsuspecting prey.

Lanternsharks produce their own light by mixing a luciferin-like substrate with a luciferase-like enzyme. This differs from the method many fishes use, which relies on a symbiotic relationship with certain bacteria.

Pygmy Shark

Euprotomicrus bispinatus

Although it is a member of the dogfish family, the pygmy shark lacks the spines that normally precede the dorsal fins of other dogfishes. Its dorsal fins are quite small and on the rear half of the body. It has a bulbous head and an underslung jaw. It is generally black, with contrasting pale fins.

Pygmy sharks live in the open ocean, usually in temperate and tropical waters. They probably spend their days in deep water and migrate after sunset to the surface, covering as much as 4,900' (1,520 m) in either direction. This has been compared to a person walking 7 miles (11 km) every day. They migrate to follow their food supply, the deep-water crustaceans, squids, and bony fishes that make this same journey to feed on surface plankton at night, when there is less risk of being seen. Pygmy sharks have luminescent photophores on their underside. These help to camouflage the shark and perhaps help it to find a mate.

FIELD NOTES

- *Oceanic, north and south of the Equator*
- *Females to 10½" (27 cm); males to 8½" (22 cm)*
- *Harmless*
- *Not encountered by divers*
- *Not uncommon*

Pygmy sharks are ovoviviparous. They produce about eight young in a litter, and these are about 2½–4" (6–10 cm) long at birth.

Spiny Dogfish

Squalus acanthias

FIELD NOTES

- *Temperate and cold waters of the Pacific and Atlantic Oceans, Mediterranean, Black Sea*
- *Up to 4' (1.5 m)*
- *Harmless*
- *During spring and fall in temperate latitudes*
- *Common, but stocks are nearly depleted in many areas*

The spiny dogfish is also known as the piked dogfish or whitespotted spurdog. It is identified by a large spiracle behind each large eye, the presence of spines on the two dorsal fins, and the lack of an anal fin. It ranges from gray to brown in color, with small white spots above a light underside.

Spiny dogfish are cold-water sharks, preferring temperatures from 45–59° F (7–15° C). They are caught in waters down to about 2,600' (800 m) deep, but not exclusively in deep water. They form extremely large schools, routinely frequenting the shallow and coastal waters of higher latitudes in spring and fall, and migrating into deep waters during the cooler winter months.

The diet includes small fishes, such as cod, herring, menhaden, and haddock, as well as invertebrates such as krill, squid, scallops, and crustaceans. This species is extremely slow-growing and lives for up to 70 years. Females reach sexual maturity when 21 to 25 years old. They give birth to up to 20 live young, about 8–12" (20–30 cm) long, after a gestation of 18 to 24 months—the longest known for any of the elasmobranchs.

The spiny dogfish is of high commercial importance in many parts of the world. However, with its slow growth rate and low fecundity, it is very susceptible to overfishing, and has been overharvested in many regions.

SHARKS *of the* DEEP BOTTOMS

Some shark species live in the abyss, that portion of the ocean that is below the continental slope and covered by 13,000' (4 km) of sea water. This makes up two-thirds of the globe. For sharks such as some of the slow, lumbering sleeper sharks and gulper sharks, it is a cold place, usually 31° to 39° F (–0.6° to +4° C). It is almost completely dark, except for the light made by other animals. Pressure can be a thousand times that at the surface. Adaptation at such depths requires the ability to find and capture food, to avoid being eaten, and to find a mate—in the dark.

GREENLAND SHARK

Somniosus microcephalus

The Greenland shark is also called the sleeper or gurry shark. This gigantic dogfish is the only polar shark of the Atlantic. It lives in deep water to 1,800' (550 m) at temperatures of 36 to 45° F (2 to 7° C), only coming up to shallow water during the colder months. At such temperatures, it will not be encountered by divers, although it may be caught by fishers. It is a sluggish beast, and provides little resistance when captured. Nevertheless, it should always be handled carefully.

There are four or five species of sleeper shark. All have a short and rounded snout, a caudal fin with a well-developed lower lobe, and two small, spineless dorsal fins; they lack an anal fin. They vary in color, some being mottled, while others, such as the Greenland shark, range from pinkish to brown, black, or purplish gray.

The teeth of the Greenland shark's upper jaw are long and pointed, very different from

FIELD NOTES

- North Atlantic Ocean
- To 21' (6.5 m)
- Not encountered by divers
- Potentially harmful
- Not uncommon

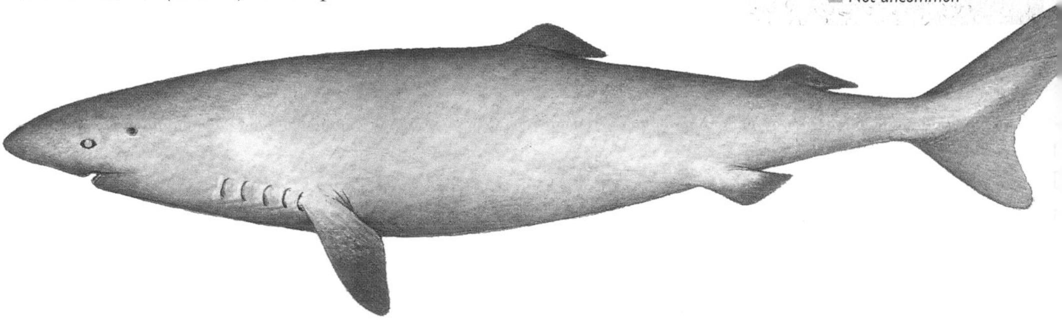

those of its lower jaw, which are strongly oblique, sharp, and close set. These teeth allow it to gouge large chunks of flesh from dead cetaceans, and probably to remove the heads of seals and sea lions rapidly before dining on the carcasses. It also eats fish such as salmon, and a variety of bottom-dwelling fishes.

That this sluggish shark can capture such wily and fast-moving prey may be because of small copepods that attach themselves to the corneas of the shark's eyes. Brightly luminescent, these copepods are thought to attract curious and hungry prey, which soon end up in the shark's cavernous maw.

Little is known about the Greenland shark's reproductive behavior. It was recently discovered to be ovoviviparous, bearing about 10 pups, 15" (38 cm) long, in each litter.

Spined Pygmy Shark

Squaliolus laticaudus

At 8" (20 cm) long, this deep-water dogfish rivals the dwarf dogfish (*Etmopterus perryi*) for the title of the world's smallest shark. At the moment, not enough specimens exist to make a final decision. The spined pygmy and its Australian relative, the smalleye pygmy shark (*Squaliolus aliae*), are unique in having a spine in front of the first dorsal fin but not the second. They are cigar-shaped, with a bulbous snout and a large spiracle behind the eye. Their upper jaw teeth are small and narrow; the lower teeth are larger and blade-like. Underneath, they have many luminous photophores, which serve to camouflage them from predators.

The spined pygmy dogfish lives in temperate and tropical waters, offshore near continental and island landmasses. Like other deep-water sharks, it makes a daily migration to feed. It ascends at dusk and feeds during the night on squid, shrimp, and midwater fishes, especially lanternfishes, then descends again at dawn. Unlike other species, it stops within 650' (200 m) of the surface, before heading down to ocean depths as great as 6,560' (2,000 m).

FIELD NOTES

- *All oceans*
- *Females to 10" (25 cm); males to 9" (23 cm)*
- *Not encountered by divers*
- *Harmless*
- *Uncommon*

Little is known about its reproductive biology, but it is likely to be ovoviviparous.

Prickly Dogfish

Oxynotus bruniensis

Among the most unusual looking sharks of the deep ocean bottom are the roughsharks (Oxynotidae). These small sharks have a stout body that is laterally compressed and bears a prominent ridge on the abdomen. Most notable are the high, spined dorsal fins with their forward extensions, which give the appearance of two sails. There is no anal fin. The head is slightly flattened, with large eyes, prominent spiracles, and small gill slits. The nostrils are placed relatively close together and the fleshy mouth is small and usually surrounded by labial furrows.

FIELD NOTES

- *Off southern Australia and New Zealand*
- *Up to 2⅓' (72 cm)*
- *Harmless*
- *Rarely seen*
- *Common*

One of four roughshark species, the prickly dogfish is distinguished by its forward-pointing first dorsal spine and its skin, which is covered with rough, prickly denticles. The body is gray or brown with whitish margins on the tips of the dorsal fins and trailing margins on the pectoral and pelvic fins.

The prickly dogfish occurs in temperate waters, dwelling at depths of about 165–1,640' (50–500 m). Very little is known of its biology. The diet consists of benthic invertebrates, such as segmented worms.

About seven young hatch from eggs that are retained inside the mother. The pups are born live when about 4" (10 cm) long.

Toothy Midwater Hunters

The deep waters of the open ocean are home to many small predatory sharks. These sharks have developed special features and behaviors that enable them to prey on the many organisms that live in their habitat, and thus survive in the dim to dark waters of the world's oceans.

Cookiecutter Shark

Isistius brasiliensis

Before its feeding behavior was discovered, this species was known as the "cigar shark." It is a small, brown shark with a short snout. Its cigar-like appearance is enhanced by its small dorsal fins being displaced to the rear of its body and by the lack of an anal fin. It also has a black collar around the back of its head.

The cookiecutter shark and its close relative, the largetooth cookiecutter shark (*Isistius plutodus*), have specialized suctorial jaws and lips, and razor-sharp, saw-like lower teeth. The shark forms a suction cap with its lips on the skin of its prey, then bites and swivels around to cut out an oval-shaped plug of tissue, just like a cookiecutter in pastry.

The cookiecutter shark's victims include large marlins, tunas, seals, whales, and dolphins, and it has even bitten the rubberized dome of a nuclear submarine. Scientists believe that it uses its bioluminescent light organs, which glow in the dark, to lure fast-swimming prey close, so that they can ambush them.

A tropical shark, it has been caught at the surface at

suction mouth and teeth

FIELD NOTES

- *Throughout the tropical oceans of the world*
- *To 20" (50 cm)*
- *Harmless*
- *Not seen by divers*
- *Probably not uncommon in deep oceanic waters*

night, but it normally inhabits depths as great as 11,500' (3,570 m). It is ovoviviparous, but nothing is known about the size of its litters.

Crocodile Shark

Pseudocarcharias kamoharai

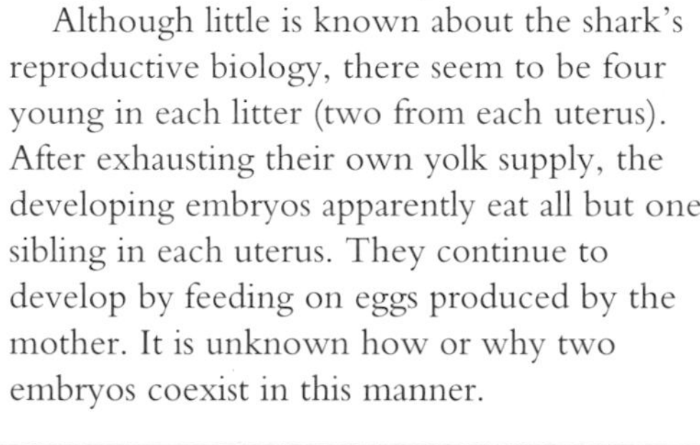

The crocodile shark, the only species of the family Pseudocarchariidae, is related to the sand tiger shark (see p. 128). Its muscular and highly streamlined body looks like a mini-torpedo. The first dorsal fin is about midway between the small pectoral and pelvic fins. The second dorsal fin is much smaller.

The body is dark brown above grading to lighter underneath, with dark blotches often scattered over the sides and bottom surfaces. The head is long, the snout conical, and the eyes large. The liver of this species contains squalene, a fine, low-density oil that increases the shark's buoyancy.

The crocodile shark is widespread throughout the open oceans of the world, from the surface to depths of about 1,970' (600 m). It is also sometimes seen offshore. It is probably a fast-swimming predator that chases small prey, either near the surface at night or down to 1,000' (300 m) in the mesopelagic zone during the day. The shark has powerful jaws and long, thin, needle-like teeth, which are similar in shape to those found in the larger mako sharks (see p. 135). This combination of jaws and teeth is designed for the crocodile shark to grasp its small midwater prey, including shrimp, lanternfishes, and squid.

FIELD NOTES

- *Tropical oceans throughout the world*
- *About 3 1/3' (1 m)*
- *Harmless*
- *Near the surface at night, probably year-round*
- *Common*

Although little is known about the shark's reproductive biology, there seem to be four young in each litter (two from each uterus). After exhausting their own yolk supply, the developing embryos apparently eat all but one sibling in each uterus. They continue to develop by feeding on eggs produced by the mother. It is unknown how or why two embryos coexist in this manner.

The characteristic wound inflicted by a cookiecutter shark shows clearly on the Pacific spotted dolphin at the top of this photo.

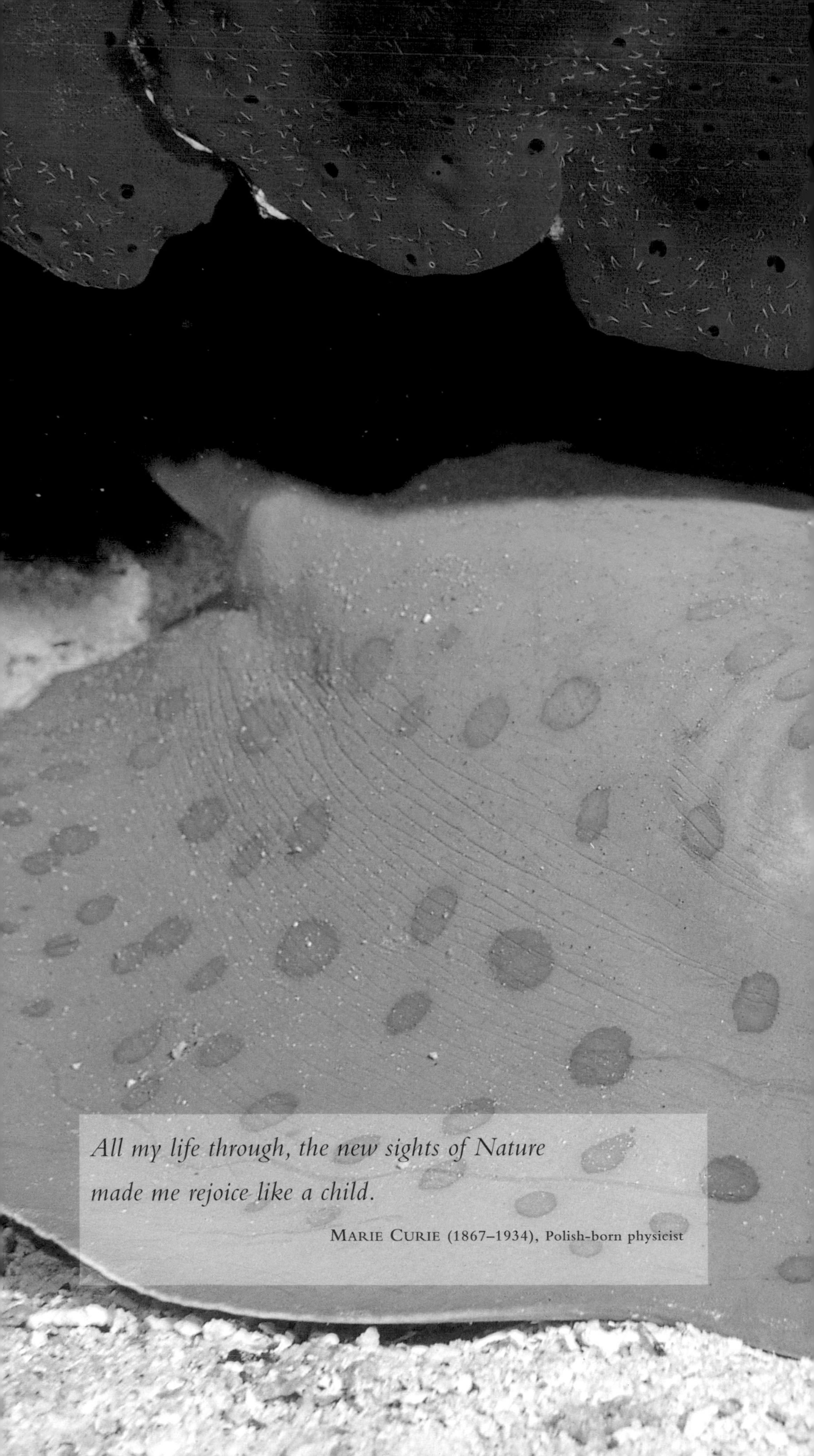

All my life through, the new sights of Nature made me rejoice like a child.

MARIE CURIE (1867–1934), Polish-born physicist

Chapter Seven
Rays Field Guide

USING *the* RAYS GUIDE

Get to know the rays in all their extraordinary shapes, sizes, shades, and perfectly adapted behaviors.

This field guide describes and illustrates just a few of the almost 500 species of ray that dwell in the world's oceans, estuaries, and rivers. At least one member of each family is featured here. Some rays are ubiquitous over tropical reefs, drop-offs, and sand flats, and can be curious about, even quite sociable with, snorkelers and divers. Many rays, however, never venture out of the cold, dark depths at the bottom of the ocean. Many more spend most of their days buried up to the eyes and spiracles in mud or sand. Given that they can be hard to find, the biology and behavior of most rays remain something of a mystery. But the next time you're wading in shallow water, watching where you're putting your feet, this guide will give you some insight into the rays you might encounter.

*The **main photograph** shows as much of the species as possible, given the constraints of photographing such wild creatures in circumstances and conditions that can be difficult.*

*The **common** and **scientific names** of each species. The species are grouped according to taxonomy.*

*The **text** provides information on the appearance of the ray, its common names, habitat, and where and what to look for when you want to find it. It also gives ideas on how to differentiate between similar species, and supplies information, where known, about the ray's migratory habits and methods of reproduction.*

__Color illustrations__ supplement the text by showing basic features of the ray, or a related ray species.

This **illustrated banding** at the top of the page is a visual pointer to indicate that the page is about a ray species.

This **panel** refers to the family of rays that the species belongs to.

Quick-reference Field Notes panel

- Distribution range of the ray
- Size
- Possible risks when encountering the ray
- Best time of day or year to observe the species
- Information on population numbers

Secondary photographs show details of particular features or amplify some aspect of the ray's habitat or behavior. In some instances, photographs showing other members of the ray's family are included.

Freshwater Sawfish

Pristis microdon

FIELD NOTES

- *Tropical Indo-Pacific; possibly Africa and the Americas*
- *Up to 21⅔' (6.6 m)*
- *Sometimes aggressive in captivity*
- *Rarely seen*
- *Endangered*

The sawfish family takes its name from its long, blade-like snout, edged with bony teeth, which resembles a crosscut saw. Sawfishes are easily confused with sawsharks (see p. 116) because they have a similar snout. However, the sawfish's gills are underneath its head rather than on the side, and it is much larger. Indeed, sawfishes are among the biggest fish in the sea.

Unlike most other rays, the sawfishes have a small disc and a shark-like tail. Most of them live inshore, in tropical seas. However, the freshwater sawfish usually inhabits tropical estuaries, rivers, and lakes. This slender, powerful sawfish is yellow to gray in color.

It is rare nowadays, so divers are unlikely to encounter it, and given that it is such a timid creature, it would probably flee at the first sign of a human. Anglers occasionally catch one on lines or in nets. It thrashes around wildly, and its saw teeth can cause serious injury. The saw is thought to be used offensively. The sawfish slashes it from side to side to stun the small fish upon which it feeds. Males also use their saws in battles during the breeding season.

The biology of the freshwater sawfish is not well known. Asian and Australian populations live almost exclusively in fresh water, but in Africa and the Americas, they also live in the sea. They are ovoviviparous. In Central America, they mate during summer in fresh water, where the pregnant females remain until they give birth five months later. Litters number up to 13, with pups being about 2½' (75 cm) at birth.

Sawfish populations have been seriously depleted this century through overfishing and degradation of their habitat. Many species are now rarely seen, and their plight is one of the major conservation issues of the sea.

snout from below

Bowmouth Guitarfish

Rhina ancylostoma

This unmistakable creature resembles something from prehistory. It has horny ridges with large thorns above and behind the eyes; a broad, flattened head; and gills on the underside of its small disc. All this is typical of a ray, but its powerful body with large, angular fins, and a tail with a pronounced lower lobe, are more shark-like—hence one common name, "shark ray." It is bluish gray to brownish, with large white spots. The shape of its mouth is also distinctive, undulating like a longbow.

FIELD NOTES

- *Tropical Indo-Pacific, from East Africa to Australia and Japan*
- *Up to 9½' (2.9 m)*
- *Not aggressive*
- *Year-round*
- *Uncommon*

The bowmouth guitarfish lives near the coast and around offshore reefs in tropical waters, down to about 295' (90 m). Scientists once thought it spent most of its time resting on the bottom, but its behavior in aquariums indicates that this ray swims actively for much of the day and night. Its tail is strong, and well adapted to prolonged swimming. It feeds mainly on crabs and large shellfishes by first restraining the prey against the sea bottom using its large head and pectoral fins. Then, with a series of short, sharp thrusts, it directs the prey into its mouth.

Divers sometimes find individual bowmouths resting near wrecks and coral bommies. They will not attack humans. They produce seven to nine live pups in each litter.

Trawl-net fishers occasionally take bowmouth guitarfish as bycatch. Along with the related white-spotted guitarfish (*Rhynchobatus djiddensis*), it is among the most sought-after elasmobranchs for shark fin soup. Consequently, there are concerns about overfishing.

The bowmouth guitarfish is likely to avoid humans, and certainly will not attack.

Atlantic Guitarfish

Rhinobatos lentiginosus

FIELD NOTES

- Northwestern Atlantic, from North Carolina, USA, to southern Mexico
- Reaches 2½' (75 cm)
- Harmless
- Year-round; most common off Florida, USA
- Reasonably common

Many of the 40 or so guitarfish species have a shovel-like head and a flattened, tapering tail. With a little imagination, their body shape resembles a guitar, hence their common name. The Atlantic guitarfish looks like some of the sharkfin guitarfishes in its general appearance. However, its dorsal fins are located closer to the tip of the tail (behind the pelvic fin tips), and the lower lobe of its caudal fin is much smaller than the upper lobe. It has a grayish to brownish upper surface with hundreds of small white spots. The adult Atlantic guitarfish differs from the related southern guitarfish (*Rhinobatos percellens*), which occurs from the Caribbean to Argentina, in having enlarged tubercles on the tip of its snout.

This is one of the smaller guitarfishes. It lives in warm temperate and tropical waters, mainly in the shallows from the intertidal zone to about 66' (20 m). Soft, sandy or muddy bottoms, or sea grasses, are its preferred habitats. It eats small, sand-dwelling mollusks and crustaceans, such as amphipods and small crabs. Some guitarfishes are fussy feeders, selectively ingesting only the nutritious parts of their prey. For example, they will crush clams in their mouth and spit out the shell and gritty bits.

The Atlantic guitarfish is most common off Florida. Swimmers and waders see it at low tide on urban beaches, swimming near the water's edge, its dorsal and caudal fins exposed and its snout probing the sand for food. In the Indo-Pacific region, juvenile plain grayish brown giant guitarfish (*Rhinobatos typus*) are also common inshore, as they search for food over sand flats and in mangrove swamps and estuaries.

Larger guitarfish species may have litters of up to 29, but the Atlantic guitarfish only has about 6 pups, each about 8" (20 cm) long. Males are sexually mature at 19" (48 cm) long. The females bear live young.

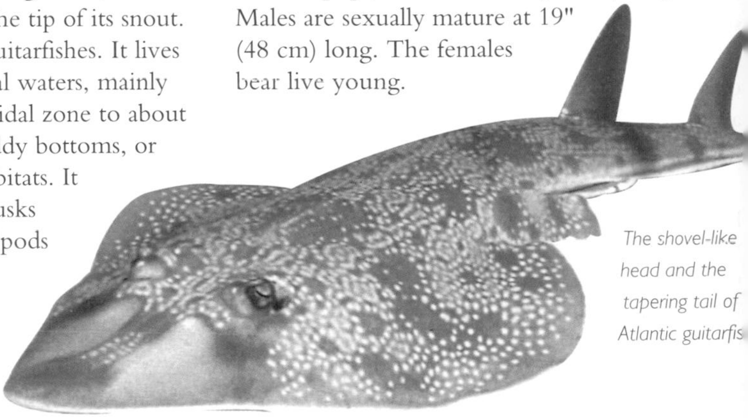

The shovel-like head and the tapering tail of Atlantic guitarfis

Thornback

Platyrhinoidis triseriata

FIELD NOTES

- *Eastern Pacific from California, USA, to Mexico*
- *Almost 3' (90 cm)*
- *Harmless; be wary of sharp thorns*
- *Year-round*
- *Once plentiful off southern California*

Thornback rays take their common name from the rows of large thorny spines along their back and sometimes their tail. They are similar to some round-snouted guitarfish found in other parts of the world. These distantly related groups probably evolved similar body forms to adapt to similar lifestyles in different parts of the world. The thornback's disc is short and broad, and the snout is evenly rounded rather than triangular. The fine segmented cartilages that form the skeleton of the outer disc reach almost as far as the snout tip. Two narrow cartilages link the snout tip to the skull.

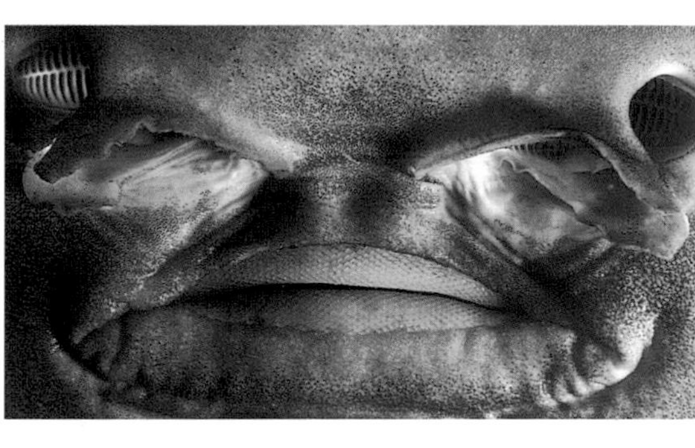

A close-up of mouth and nostrils on the underside of the thornback.

The brownish thornback has three rows of pale thorns. Its dorsal fins, near the tail tip, are of similar size, and the tail is much longer than the disc. It is similar to the Japanese thornback ray (*Platyrhina sinensis*), although this ray's thorns are confined to the central part of its disc and around the eyes; the thornback's run along the back and tail.

The thornback lives in temperate and subtropical waters, mainly inshore on sandy and muddy bottoms. Divers occasionally see one around kelp beds, where its brownish upper surface blends well with the dark substrate. It rests in small groups for much of the day, remaining partly buried, with only its thorns protruding. These are sharp, and are probably used defensively against its main predators, small sharks. Although it is harmless, this ray should be treated with caution.

Little is known about the thornback's general biology. It is not a powerful swimmer and so it seems unlikely that it undertakes any long migrations. It seems to be more active at night, feeding on sand worms, sea shells, and small crustaceans, such as crabs and shrimps. Mating occurs at the end of summer.

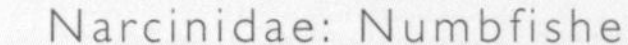

Lesser Electric Ray

Narcine brasiliensis

Possibly the best known of the numbfishes, the lesser electric ray is small and brownish with dusty blotches. It belongs to a family whose taxonomy and biology are not well understood. It has a flattened, oval-shaped disc, and large pelvic fins. Oversized dorsal and caudal fins cover most of the rear of its tapering tail. It eats mainly sand worms, although it also eats small fishes and crustaceans.

The kidney-shaped electric organs of this ray are located in the middle of the pectoral fins. They account for about a sixth of its body weight. Each organ consists of a honeycomb of 280 to 430 columns, containing several hundred electric plates, which deliver a shock of less than 37 volts. This is so weak that it is unlikely to be a means of defense or even of stunning prey. Nevertheless, some fishers claim to have been knocked off their feet after inadvertently stepping on a ray—probably more from surprise than from the intensity of the shock.

In winter, the lesser electric ray moves farther offshore in warm temperate and tropical waters.

FIELD NOTES

- *Central-western Atlantic from North Carolina, USA, to northern Argentina, including the Gulf of Mexico*
- *To 1½' (45 cm)*
- *Capable of delivering a weak electric shock; otherwise, harmless*
- *Summer*
- *Reasonably common*

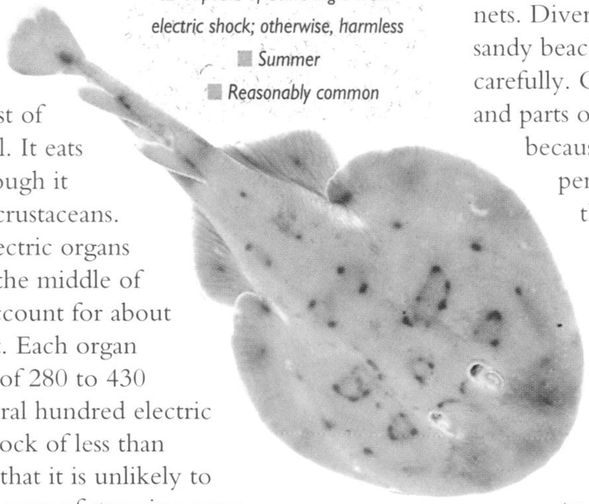

The lesser electric ray (below), showing the dusty blotches of its upper surface.

During summer, it usually inhabits very shallow waters near the shore, where it is often caught in beach and trammel nets. Divers may also see it off sandy beaches if they search carefully. Often, only the eyes and parts of the head are visible because it spends long periods concealed under the sand. Barefoot anglers and waders may accidentally step on a buried ray and receive a minor shock. But this is essentially a harmless creature, and you would have to annoy it before it would discharge its organs in response.

Female lesser electric rays venture into the surf zone in summer to bear 2 to 17 live young. Like many sharks and rays, the color pattern of the pups is more intense than in the adult. Pups average about 4¼" (11 cm) at birth.

Spotted Electric Ray

Narke japonica

FIELD NOTES

- Northwestern Pacific, from Japan to the South China Sea
- To about 16" (40 cm)
- Capable of delivering a weak electric shock; otherwise, harmless
- Year-round; hard to find
- Not uncommon

The spotted electric ray, also known as the Japanese numbfish, is one of the shortnose electric rays. This family of at least 12 species of small rays lives in the temperate and tropical Indo-Pacific, mainly on the outer continental shelf and upper slope, although the spotted electric ray does occur inshore. Like all the shortnose electric rays, its disc is almost oval in shape, with a short, thick tail—the general shape is like the numbfish's. It has only one dorsal fin.

The spotted electric ray is reddish brown, with black or white spots on the upper surface. Its snout is short, and like other members of the family, its eyes are small. It lives on sandy bottoms, often near rocky reefs, where it remains hidden for long periods of time. For this reason, although it is quite common, divers are unlikely to come across it. It can become aggressive when annoyed, and is capable of delivering a small electric shock (up to 80 volts), possibly for defensive reasons or to protect its territory. It feeds on small fish and crustaceans that live in the sand and sediment of its habitat. Its mouth is surrounded by a shallow groove, which allows the mouth to be projected forward to suck up the prey.

The female spotted electric ray gives birth to litters of up to five pups, which are born in early summer.

An unusual New Zealand relative, the blind electric ray (*Typhlonarke aysoni*), lives on the continental slope at depths of 655–2,950' (200–900 m). This little-known ray has minute eyes, concealed beneath a thin covering of skin, making them virtually useless for detecting prey. Instead, it uses electroreceptors. It also has a pelvic fin with a separate anterior lobe, which it can presumably use to prop itself up with when stalking prey.

blind electric ray

Shorttailed Electric Ray

Hypnos monopterygium

FIELD NOTES

- Only in Australian seas
- Probably 16" (40 cm), but reported up to 2' (60 cm)
- Not aggressive, but capable of delivering a powerful shock if touched
- Year-round; mostly seen at night
- Reasonably common

This ray is unique among the electric rays in having a very large, oval pectoral disc attached to a smaller disc formed from the pelvic fins. The ray takes on a most unusual shape if washed up dead on a beach, swelling in the hot sun to look like a flattened wooden coffin—its other common name is coffin ray. It has a very short tail, with two tiny dorsal fins near the equally small caudal fin. The soft skin lacks spines and denticles, and varies from a rather drab chocolate brown to pinkish or gray.

Shorttailed electric rays live near the coast in warm temperate and subtropical waters. They prefer sheltered habitats, such as muddy bays and estuaries, as well as the continental shelf to 720' (220 m). They are rarely seen because they conceal themselves so well. During the day they remain deeply buried, and they may also change color for camouflage.

This ray's electric organs, located centrally on each pectoral fin, are highly developed. They can deliver a strong shock to stun large prey and may also have a defensive role. Divers who accidentally place a hand on a ray's back will remember the experience for life. Adults feed at night, foraging for fish, worms, and crabs. The mouth of this ray is capable of taking surprisingly large prey, including flounders up to half the size of its body.

Little is known about the biology of this viviparous ray. Females grow larger than males, and bear pups 3–4½" (8–11 cm) long.

The underside of a male shorttailed electric ray (above). Only the eyes and spiracles of the ray (left) are visible above the sand.

Atlantic Torpedo

Torpedo nobiliana

The Atlantic torpedo is also known as the great or black torpedo ray. It is enormous, and at 200 lb (90 kg), it is certainly the largest of all the electricity-producing rays. It has powerful electric organs in the pectoral disc that can discharge up to 220 volts. The upper surface of its disc is positively charged and the lower surface is negatively charged. During discharge, sea water or an unsuspecting animal creates a path for the current to travel from one side of the "battery" to the other. Without this, the ray could even electrocute itself.

The Atlantic torpedo uses its electric organs in defense and for predation. They may also be used for sensory purposes to detect prey, or as a means of communication. Its back varies in color from dark blue to brown or black, and may be dotted with small white spots and black blotches.

FIELD NOTES

- *Eastern Atlantic, from United Kingdom to South Africa, including Mediterranean; northwestern Atlantic, from Nova Scotia, Canada, to Florida, USA*
- *Recorded up to 6' (1.82 m)*
- *If surprised or annoyed, produces a powerful electric shock capable of stunning a diver*
- *Year-round; rarely seen*
- *Not uncommon; more prevalent in temperate seas*

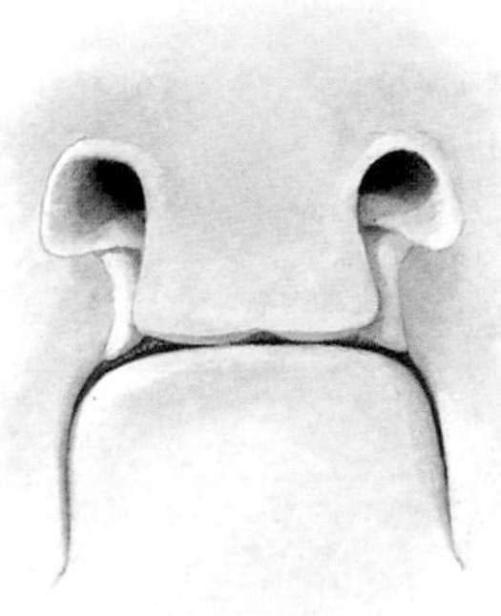

mouth and nostrils

All the torpedo rays have a large, flabby disc, broader than it is long, covered in smooth skin. The short tail has two dorsal fins, the first usually much larger than the second. The caudal fin has tall upper and lower lobes.

The Atlantic torpedo occurs inshore in temperate and tropical waters, to depths of about 1,475' (450 m). While it spends much of its time on the bottom, it is also known to migrate in open water. It is rarely encountered by divers.

Adults are efficient predators of bottom fishes such as small ground sharks, eels, flounders, and soles, whereas young torpedoes feed more on crustaceans. This ray prefers to stalk or ambush its prey under the substrate and eat it live (which makes it difficult to keep in aquariums).

For a ray, the Atlantic torpedo is highly fecund. Females are viviparous, delivering up to 60 pups after almost a year's gestation.

Rough Skate

Raja nasuta

FIELD NOTES

- Southeastern Pacific off New Zealand
- Reaches almost 3⅓' (1 m)
- Harmless
- Year-round; rarely seen by divers
- Common

The rough skate belongs to a group of skates whose common ancestor lived around the shores of the ancient Gondwana supercontinent more than 80 million years ago. This is indicated by the distribution of the modern-day group of skates, which are all found on the continental shelves off New Zealand, Australia, and South America.

The rough skate has a diamond-shaped disc with a very long, pointed snout. Its slender tail has three rows of thorns along its length, while its back is covered with minute prickles. It is usually grayish or brownish, with white spots and darker marbling. It occurs on soft bottoms to about 490' (150 m), usually beyond diving depths, although divers will occasionally see one.

Few details are known of the rough skate's biology. It lays horny, rectangular egg cases, which it attaches to the bottom by fine, thread-like tendrils. Eggs develop slowly and young hatch after several months. Recently hatched skates can be identified by a belly scar where the yolk sac was attached. Empty egg cases, called "mermaid's purses," are found washed up on beaches after storms.

Port Davey skate

A close relative of the rough skate is the recently discovered Port Davey skate (*Raja* sp.). Of the more than 280 skates in the world, it is the only one that lives in brackish water. It is confined to two estuarine bays in the remote southwest of Tasmania, off southern Australia. It has a long, stiff snout, more typical of deep-ocean skates. This is presumably used for grubbing around for food in the fine silty bottom on which it lives. Given its restricted distribution, the habitat needs of this skate left over from the prehistoric past are likely to be very specific. Its population is small, probably no more than a few thousand individuals. This makes it particularly vulnerable to habitat degradation and overfishing.

Round Stingray

Urobatis halleri

The round stingray, a member of the stingaree family, is plain brown with yellowish spots and reticulations. It has a circular disc, the upper surface of which is smooth, without tubercles. The related Cortez round stingray (*Urobatis maculatus*), from close by in Baja California and the Sea of Cortez, off Mexico, is similar in shape but has large black blotches over the disc. Stingarees can be mistaken for stingrays because of their similar body shape. However, stingarees have a shorter tail, which ends in a long, leaf-shaped caudal fin.

FIELD NOTES

- *Eastern Pacific, from northern California to Panama*
- *Reaches 22" (56 cm)*
- *Not aggressive; the stinging spine can cause minor injury*
- *Year-round*
- *Very common*

The round stingray lives mainly on muddy and sandy bottoms near the shore, to a depth of about 295' (90 m). In summer, it basks in warm shallow inlets, but remains in coastal waters during winter, only entering inlets to forage. It does not range far, rarely moving beyond an area of about a square mile. It seems sensitive to cold, and lives in water warmer than 50° F (10° C).

This ray feeds during the day on small bottom-dwelling crustaceans, bivalves, and sand worms. An efficient predator, it may use a combination of sight, smell, and vibration to detect prey. It uses its disc and mouth to "dig" for food in the substrate, and has also been seen nipping prey off sea-grass fronds. Divers may see a foraging ray in sheltered bays, or notice the outline of one buried in sediment.

Round stingrays mature early. The sexes segregate before the breeding season, and adult females live offshore until June, when they move in to coastal habitats to mate. Sexually aggressive males patrol the sandy strip between the deep sea-grass beds and the shore to select a suitable mate. He nibbles on her disc, then rolls beneath her and inserts a single clasper. Litters of one to six pups are born inshore in September, where they remain until maturity.

The underside of a juvenile round stingray.

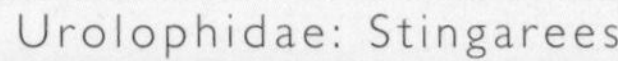

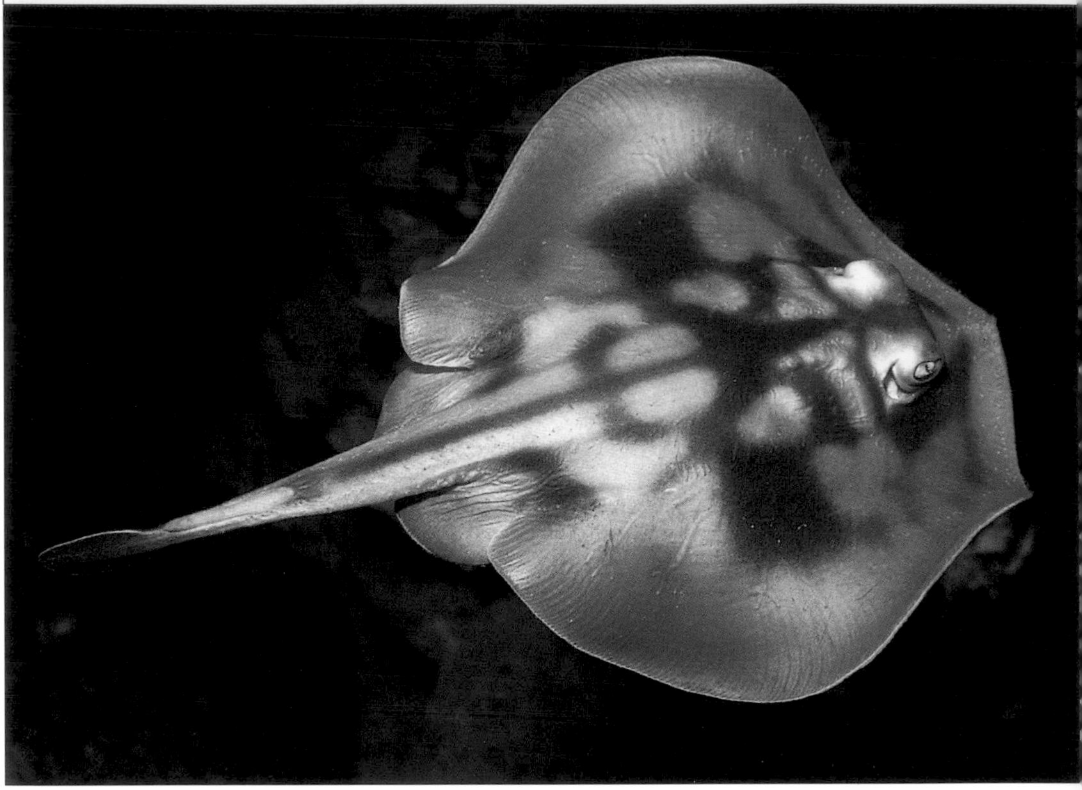

Banded Stingaree

Urolophus cruciatus

The banded stingaree is a highly distinctive ray, having smooth grayish to yellowish brown skin with a dark, banded pattern on its back, rather like a crucifix. Its tail is very short, fleshy, and highly flexible, usually with a single, large stinging spine on the upper half. If touched or provoked, the ray thrusts its tail toward its head, driving the spine and its venom into a victim. The pain varies from mild to excruciating, depending on the amount of venom and the location of the wound.

Adults are found concentrated in sheltered muddy bays and estuaries, although they are also common on sand patches near reefs and in caves. Divers and swimmers come across them all the time, frequently finding them with the more widely distributed, sparsely spotted stingaree (*Urolophus paucimaculatus*), a plain gray stingaree with a few white spots on its upper surface. The banded stingaree is quite inactive, and will often lie hidden under the substrate.

FIELD NOTES

- *Southwestern Pacific, off southern Australia*
- *Reaches 20" (50 cm)*
- *Not aggressive; however, the stinging spine can cause injury*
- *Year-round*
- *Very common*

This habit of concealment can cause problems for divers and swimmers, as it's very easy to kneel or place a hand on a ray's back accidentally and become the target of its thrusting tail. Net fishers have been stung when sorting through a catch, so gloves should be used for handling.

Stingarees are viviparous; litters of two to four are born after a gestation of about three months. Male banded stingarees mature at about 10" (25 cm). During spring, small groups of females can be found resting on the bottom with their tails raised over their bodies like scorpions. This behavior may be related to courtship; however, the lives of stingarees are not well understood.

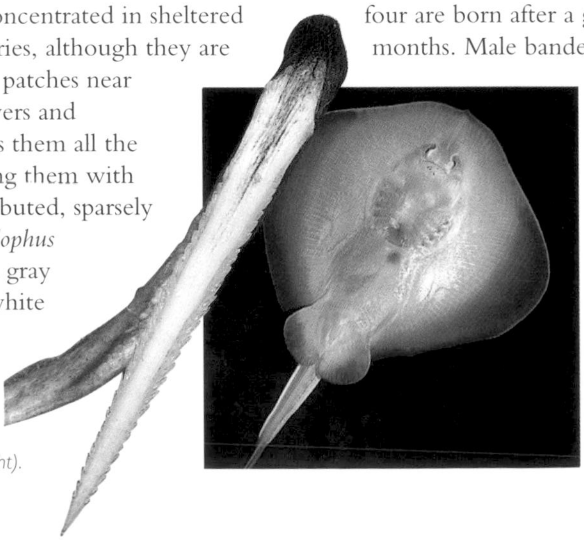

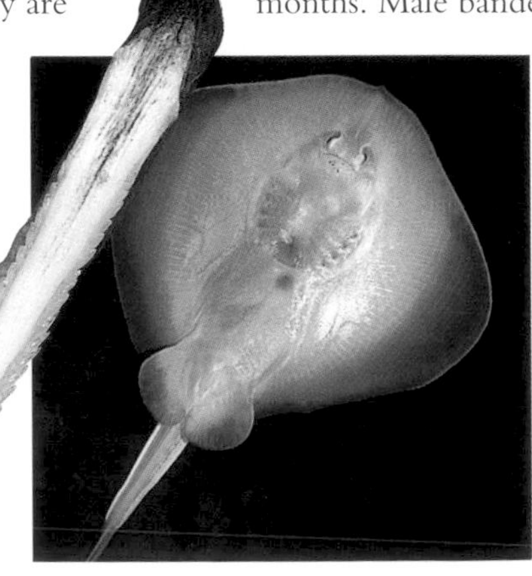

The venomous barb (right) of the banded stingaree, and the view from below of a spotted stingaree (far right).

Ocellate River Ray

Potamotrygon motoro

FIELD NOTES

- Rivers of Paraguay
- Up to 1' (30 cm) wide
- Not aggressive; however, the stinging spine can cause a potentially fatal wound
- Year-round
- Probably common

River rays are members of a small stingray family that lives in the large lakes and river systems of tropical South America. They are confined to freshwater habitats and may be found more than 1,000 miles (1,600 km) from the sea. Many species are similar in appearance but inhabit separate waterways. They resemble both stingarees and stingrays in shape. The disc is oval or circular, and the skin is mostly smooth and lacks large thorns. The tail is slender, without dorsal fins but usually with thorns down the middle, and it tapers away beyond a well-developed stinging spine.

The ocellate river ray has a distinctive pattern of dark rings that are biggest on the middle of its back. Smaller, more compact rows of rings are located around the edge. This river ray, from the rivers of Paraguay, lives partly buried in the mud and sand of back eddies and side channels. Once buried, it is very difficult to see, and is therefore easy to step on.

The stinging spine, which is located near the tail tip, can strike well forward, making it a formidable defensive weapon. And despite its small size, the spine can inflict a very nasty wound that produces agonizing pain—it is dreaded by the local fishermen, who catch this ray with nets. Deaths have been reported from stings on the abdomen and from secondary infections that result from unattended wounds.

Potamotrygon reticulata, *the reticulated freshwater ray (above), another South American river ray, in its natural habitat.*

Ocellate river rays breed between September and October, and the pups are born about five months later. The embryos gain nutrition while inside the mother from the egg yolk and the fluids secreted by her uterine tissues.

Rays that live in the sea need to store high concentrations of urea in the flesh and blood in order to osmoregulate (see p. 98) in their saline environment. However, freshwater river rays use far less urea to osmoregulate.

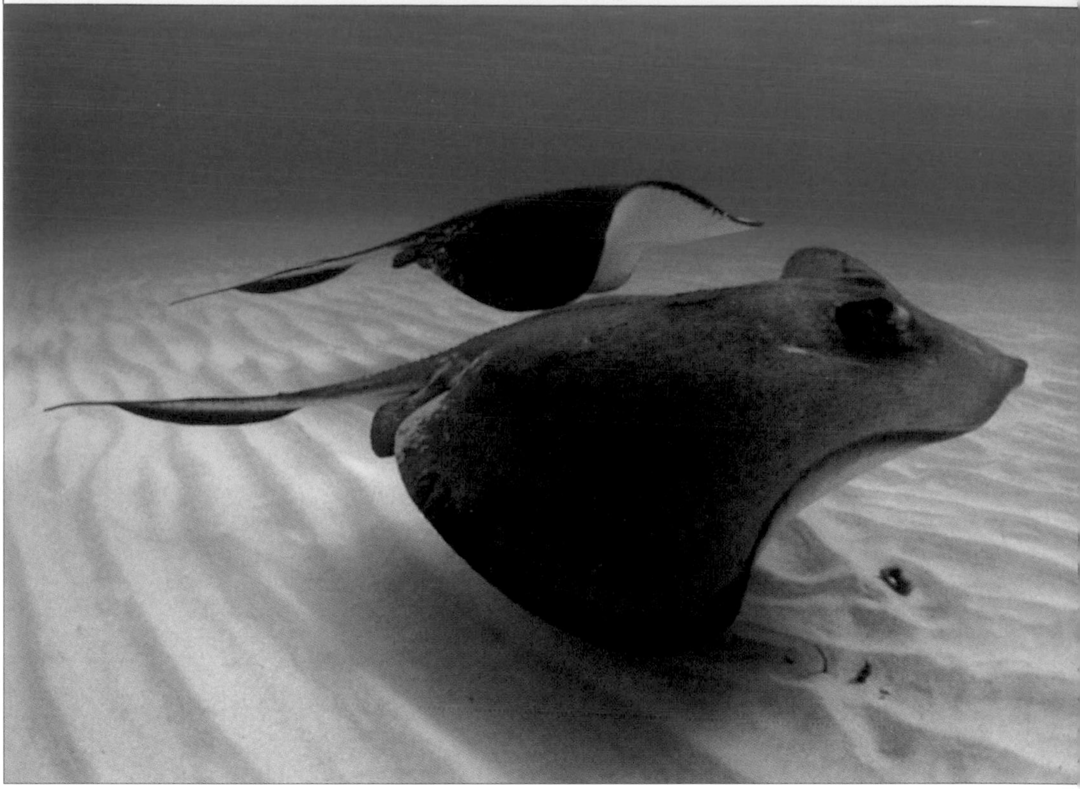

Southern Stingray

Dasyatis americana

The southern stingray has a large, flattened, somewhat angular disc, with a row of small tubercles running down its gray to brown back. The tail has a long skin fold along its undersurface and a low keel on top.

This stingray lives mainly in sandy habitats off beaches, in lagoons, and around sea-grass beds. It eats large invertebrates such as crabs, shrimps, and worms, and small bottom-dwelling fishes. It feeds mainly at night, remaining almost entirely concealed in the sand during the day. To dig into the substrate, it undulates the disc tips, dispersing the sand evenly.

Often, the first sign a diver sees is a pair of holes on the sandy bottom the ray's spiracles, easily mistaken for eyes. If approached with care, the ray usually stays still. The southern stingray is known for its social behavior with humans. At places in the Cayman Islands (see pp. 212–13), divers can hand-feed wild stingrays.

It is the long, dagger-like stinging spines on the tail that have given members of the stingray family their name and brought them unjustified infamy. Stingrays have been responsible for some human deaths, but in almost all recorded cases, the attacks resulted from the carelessness or stupidity of the victim. Always treat stingrays with respect, and under no circumstances attempt to ride one. As well as delivering venom, the big stinging spines of the largest stingrays are as sharp as a butcher's knife. Cuts from repeated thrusts can cause more damage than the venom, particularly if a vital organ is struck, but such defensive behavior is used only if the animal is threatened or harassed. Stingrays are typically gentle and inquisitive, easily domesticated, and very popular in aquariums.

FIELD NOTES

- *Central-western Atlantic, from New Jersey, USA, to Brazil*
- *At least 5' (1.5 m)*
- *Not normally aggressive; the stinging spine can cause serious injury*
- *Year-round*
- *Common in some areas*

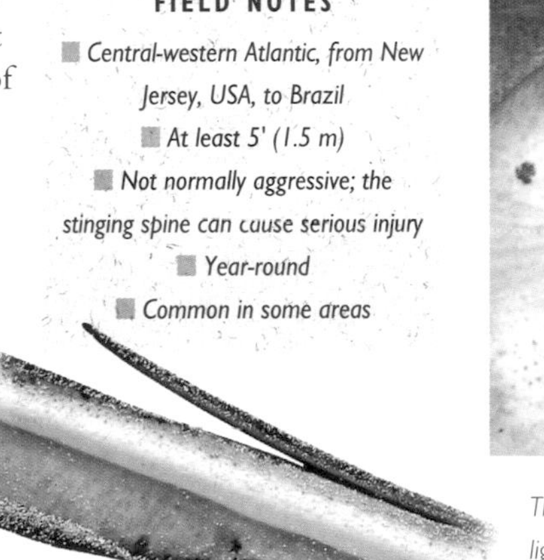

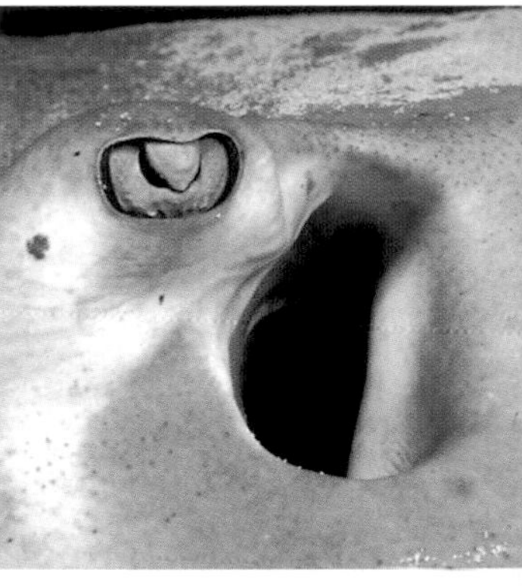

The eye, with pupil protected from daylight by the lappet shield, and spiracle (above), and the venomous spine (left).

Mangrove Whipray

Himantura granulata

This stingray belongs to a group known as the whiprays, which take their name from their very long, thin, flexible tails. Most of the whiprays, including the attractively patterned leopard whipray (*Himantura undulata*) and reticulate whipray (*Himantura uarnak*), live near tropical coasts throughout the Indo-Pacific. Some species, such as the huge and possibly rare freshwater whipray (*Himantura chaophraya*), have adapted to life in rivers and estuaries, and have been seen flapping around in the shallows of muddy rivers as far as several hundred miles from the open sea.

The mangrove whipray is oval in shape, with a thick disc about as wide as it is long. The rough upper surface is dark brown to grayish brown in the center of the disc, merging to brown to slate gray on the outer edges. This is usually scattered with fine white spots. The ray is white underneath, with dark spots along the edges. It has a distinctive white, whip-like tail without skin folds and with one or more stinging spines. When a ray has lost one of these stinging spines, it is usually possible to see a scar on the tail.

As well as occurring close inshore in tropical waters over sand flats and amongst coral, the mangrove whipray sometimes also dwells in mangrove habitats, as its name suggests. Divers occasionally encounter one in shallow waters. However, not a lot is known about the behavior and biology of this unusual stingray. Its diet includes small fishes and small crustaceans, such as crabs and shrimp. Females give birth to young that are about 11" (28 cm) wide and about 30½" (78 cm) in total length.

FIELD NOTES

- *Indo-West Pacific, from Micronesia, New Guinea, the Java Sea, to northern Australia*
- *At least 3' (90 cm) wide, possibly much larger*
- *Not aggressive; the stinging spines can cause injury*
- *Occasionally seen by divers*
- *Uncommon*

The leopard whipray is a large stingray with a distinctive, intricate pattern.

Bluespotted Ribbontail Ray

Taeniura lymma

The vivid ornamentation of the bluespotted ribbontail ray makes it immediately recognizable. It has bright blue spots on top of its flat, oval-shaped disc, and a distinctive blue stripe along each side of the tail. A broad flap of whitish or bluish skin extends along its undersurface to the tail tip.

The bluespotted ribbontail ray is found alone or in small groups, mostly in shallow water over reef flats. It has also been observed around coral rubble and shipwreck debris at depths of 65' (20 m). It moves over tidal flats, usually at high tide, to feed on sand worms, shrimps, hermit crabs, and small fishes. As the tide recedes, it retires to the protective covering of coral cervices. It rarely buries itself completely in the substrate, and divers and snorkelers will often detect this ray by its distinctive ribbon-like tail poking out from a crack or crevice beneath the coral.

FIELD NOTES

- *Tropical Indo-Pacific, from southern Africa and the Red Sea to the Solomon Islands*
- *Up to 2¼' (70 cm) long*
- *Timid; stinging spines can cause minor injury*
- *Year-round*
- *Very common*

This is the most abundant of the inshore reef-dwelling rays, and it is often encountered by divers and snorkelers in the Indo-Pacific region. The best viewing sites are over coral reef shallows and on sand patches beneath coral bommies.

Being rather timid, the ribbontail ray will usually swim away frantically if approached or disturbed by divers. The large eyes, which extend above the head on short stalks, give it excellent peripheral vision.

Unlike most other stingrays, its poisonous spines, often two in number, are located closer to the tip than the base of its tail. This enables these rays to strike at potential enemies well forward of their heads.

The bluespotted ribbontail ray produces about seven live young in every litter. Each pup is born with the distinctive blue markings of its parents, in miniature.

The tail of the bluespotted ribbontail ray is well armed, often with two venomous spines, set back near the tip.

Australian Butterfly Ray

Gymnura australis

The characteristic features of this unusual fish are best summed up by several of its common names—Australian butterfly ray, and also diamond ray and rattail ray. It has a very large and flat diamond-shaped disc with pectoral "wings" reminiscent of a butterfly. It is ornamented with a delicate greenish gray mosaic overlaid with a peppering of small black spots. The thin, stumpy tail, with its alternating black and white rings, has a small dorsal fin but no caudal fin. It also lacks a stinging spine, although related species may have a short one near the base of the tail.

FIELD NOTES

- *Off northern Australia and New Guinea*
- *Up to 2⅓' (73 cm) wide*
- *Harmless; lacks a stinging spine*
- *Rarely seen by divers*
- *Reasonably common in some areas*

Little is known about the butterfly rays, but their habits and diet are possibly similar to their relatives, the stingrays. They live mostly on the bottom in tropical waters, to depths of about 165' (50 m). They bury themselves deep into the sediments, their wafer-thin bodies needing only a shallow covering of sand for concealment. Not surprisingly, divers almost never see them. Their main food is a variety of crustaceans and small fishes, such as gobies and dragonets.

Males mature at about 14–16" (35–40 cm) and are much smaller than the largest females. Females bear live young, which are nourished while in the uterus partly from their yolk sac but mostly from fluid secreted by the uterine wall. An embryo lies in the uterus with its snout tucked in and its pectoral "wings" folded one over the other below its belly. Pairs wrap around each other head to head. The pups are born in this position and unfold soon after emerging from the mother.

The Australian butterfly ray is regularly caught as bycatch by prawn trawlers. Although they are harmless, they tend to flap around vigorously once on deck. One African species is said to grunt loudly by expelling trapped air from its mouth when brought on deck.

upper tooth

Spotted Eagle Ray

Aetobatus narinari

FIELD NOTES

- *Worldwide in tropical and temperate seas*
- *Reported to attain 11½' (3.5 m) in width but typically smaller, to 6' (1.8 m)*
- *Timid; the stinging spine can cause injury*
- *Year-round*
- *Common*

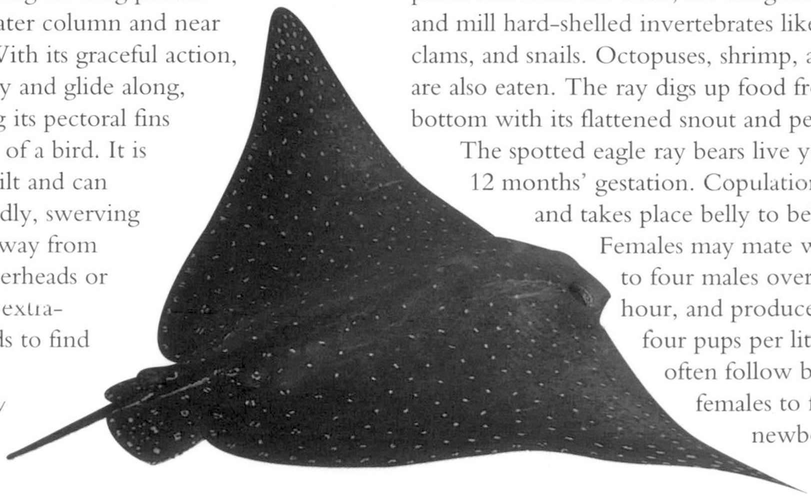

The spotted eagle ray is the most common and most widely distributed of the eagle rays. Its distinctive pattern of white spots or rings on its greenish to pinkish back makes it easily recognizable. Its flattened snout, like the beak of a duck, gives rise to its alternative common name, duckbill ray. A small stinging spine is located near the tail base.

The spotted eagle ray occurs near continents, islands, and atolls in tropical waters less than 200' (60 m) deep. It is extremely active, swimming for long periods both in the water column and near the bottom. With its graceful action, it appears to fly and glide along, slowly moving its pectoral fins like the wings of a bird. It is powerfully built and can accelerate rapidly, swerving and twisting away from hungry hammerheads or tiger sharks at extraordinary speeds to find safety in the shallows. Adults will frolic near the surface, at times leaping well clear of the water in a spectacular display. Their pectoral fins, when thus exposed, resemble a thrashing shark—causing more than one quick evacuation of a swimming beach. For a diver, the sight of a school of 100 or more of these rays cruising through clear blue water is an unforgettable experience. They may be wary if approached.

This ray's teeth, a series of flattened bony plates that form the beak, are designed to crush and mill hard-shelled invertebrates like oysters, clams, and snails. Octopuses, shrimp, and fishes are also eaten. The ray digs up food from the bottom with its flattened snout and pectoral fins.

The spotted eagle ray bears live young after 12 months' gestation. Copulation is brief and takes place belly to belly. Females may mate with up to four males over about an hour, and produce one to four pups per litter. Sharks often follow birthing females to feed on newborn pups.

A spotted eagle ray in full "flight."

Bat Ray

Myliobatis californicus

The bat ray has a broad, angular disc, from which the head protrudes in a rounded, lobe-like snout. It has a long whip-like tail (sometimes damaged by predators), with no caudal fin and up to five short stinging spines just behind the base. The spines, which are preceded by a small dorsal fin, are used to deter predators. Its heavily built body can be either smooth or have small spines along its midline or around the eyes.

This ray occurs alone or in groups, mainly inshore in temperate waters less than 165' (50 m) deep. It spends most time on the bottom, resting on kelp or in large hollows in the sand and mud when it isn't feeding. If disturbed, it will emerge from its hollow and prop itself up on the tips of its pectoral fins with its back arched in a "starting position." It may swim away with explosive acceleration if divers get too close.

The bat ray feeds on a variety of small animals, including shellfishes, crustaceans, and small bony fishes, which it grubs from the bottom. The diet changes with age. Clams are a favorite food of juveniles, while worms are eaten more often by adults. The teeth are fused to form grinding plates. Hard-shelled prey are partly ingested, heavily crushed by the jaws, and spat out. The nutritious flesh is then reingested selectively.

The mating behavior of the bat ray is fairly well known. The male swims in synchrony below the belly of a receptive female. Thorns around his eyes poke into the female's undersurface during mating, helping the couple to maintain position while the male twists a single clasper upward and into the cloaca. Up to 10 pups, each about 1' (30 cm) wide, are born a year later.

FIELD NOTES

- *Eastern Pacific, from the Sea of Cortez to Oregon, USA*
- *Up to about 6' (1.8 m)*
- *Harmless to divers; if handled carelessly, the stinging spine can cause a painful wound*
- *Year-round*
- *Common*

This school of bat rays, photographed gliding gracefully through Californian waters, is a remarkable sight.

Javanese Cownose Ray

Rhinoptera javanica

The Javanese cownose ray is dark grayish brown on the back. Its head is separate from the broad, diamond-shaped disc, and has a characteristic pugnose snout. This is concave at the front and overlays the rostral lobe, a lobe with such a marked indentation that it looks like two fleshy lobes rather than one.

FIELD NOTES

- *Indo-Pacific, from southern Africa to eastern Indonesia; possibly northern Australia*
- *At least 5' (1.5 m) wide*
- *One or more small stinging spines on the tail can cause a minor wound*
- *Year-round*
- *Not uncommon*

The Javanese cownose ray flaps its powerful pectoral fins in lazy, lateral undulations to swim almost continuously, rarely ever resting on the bottom. It swims mostly in groups—a related species, the Pacific cownose ray (*Rhinoptera steindachneri*), congregates in schools of more than 1,000. The Javanese cownose is most common along tropical coastlines and in shallow, muddy bays.

This large ray is thought to make daily migrations inshore to feed almost exclusively on bottom-dwelling crustaceans and bivalves. It exposes the buried shellfish by beating its "wings" near the bottom, then grabs it with its rostral lobes. It partly ingests the prey, crushes it between its strong tooth plates, spits it out, then retrieves and swallows the smaller fragments.

Divers sometimes see large schools working their way over shallow sand flats during the day, but this ray's timidity makes encounters rare.

Females copulate belly to belly with several males in succession. The young, one to six per litter, are nourished inside the mother, first by the egg yolk and then by uterine secretions.

A school of Pacific cownose rays near the Galapagos Islands.

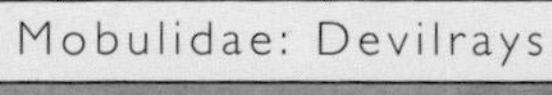

Manta Ray

Manta birostris

Mantas are the largest living rays and among the most majestic of fishes. Folklore may have inflated their width to more than 29½' (9 m), but the reality is still very impressive. A 16½' (5 m) manta found in the Bahamas weighed more than 3,000 lb (1,360 kg).

FIELD NOTES

- Worldwide in all tropical seas
- Reported to 29½' (9 m) wide, but probably to about 22' (6.7 m)
- Harmless unless provoked
- Year-round; numbers vary according to season and location
- Moderately common in most areas

The manta is related to the eagle and cownose rays, and has a similar diamond-shaped disc. But its tail is short and lacks a stinging spine, and its mouth is bordered by two long, lobe-like extensions of the pectoral fins—cephalic lobes. Mantas differ from smaller devilrays in having a relatively larger mouth, located at the snout tip rather than under the head. The color is not uniform, but is usually blackish above and pale below, with light and dark blotches.

Manta rays occur throughout the tropical seas of the world, and populations in each ocean may, in fact, be different species. They live inshore, close to the coast, as well as out in the open sea. They are mostly solitary or swim in small groups. Superbly adapted to pelagic life, they are both graceful and powerful movers, probably swimming almost continuously. They are seen along reef fringes near deep water and are also sighted from boats, as they bask or feed near the surface. Unless harassed, they are harmless.

A manta ray funnels microscopic plankton toward its mouth using the extended cephalic lobes, which remain folded spirally when not in use. Then, with a sophisticated filtering system, it sieves the plankton from the same water that it uses to breathe. Large rays also feed on pelagic crustaceans and small fishes and have been seen in feeding frenzies with sharks and other large predators.

Females produce one or two pups at a time, sometimes ejecting their young into the air when breaching.

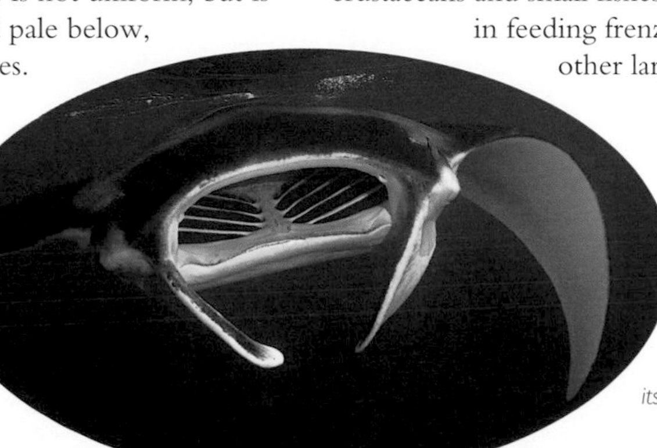

A feeding manta displays its huge gill arches.

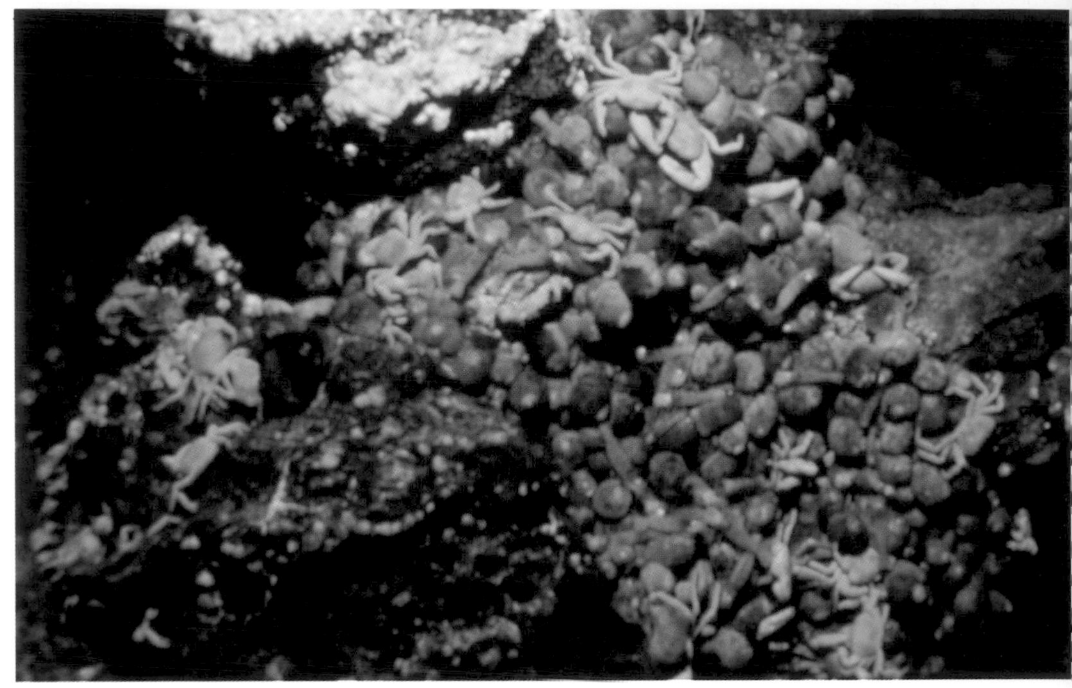

The Deep-water Rays

Almost half of the world's rays occur only in the cool, deep waters of the outer continental shelves and slopes. They are often caught accidentally during deep-sea fishing operations—this is really the only time they are encountered by people. Many of these species are new to science or are known from only a few specimens, so we understand very little about their biology and lifestyle.

Skates

Rajidae

Skates are the main group of deep-water rays. While a few true skates (Rajinae), also known as hard-nose skates, live in shallower waters close to shore (see p. 212), most of the 280 or so species live in deeper waters, on soft bottoms down to depths of 9,840' (3,000 m) or more. They are found throughout the world along continental margins, except around coral islands in the Pacific, the only place where they do not occur. Most have rather restricted ranges, and the skates of nearby regions are often quite distinct.

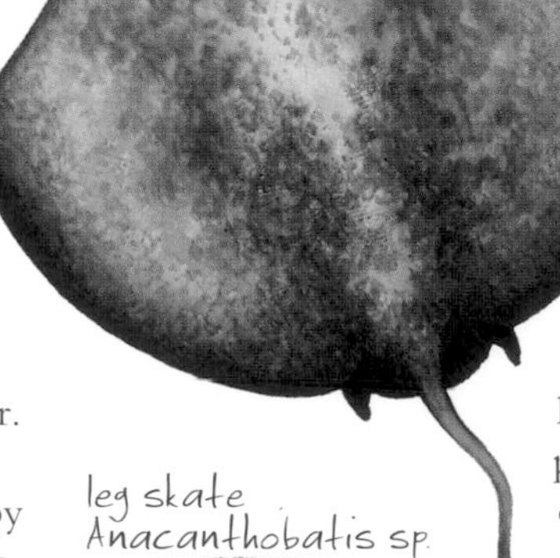

leg skate
Anacanthobatis sp.

The family is divided into two primary groups, the softnose skates (Arhynchobatinae) and the true skates (Rajinae). These groups are essentially similar in appearance. Their discs are very flattened and vary according to sex, ranging from round to almost diamond-shaped. They have a rather short, slender tail that usually has two small dorsal fins and a low caudal fin near its tip.

The main difference between the two groups is the flexibility of their snouts, which is based on the shape and strength of the supporting cartilage. As their name suggests, the softnose skates have a floppy snout, while most true skates have a firm and rigid snout supported by cartilage.

One of the most unusual groups of true skates is the leg skates (*Anacanthobatis*). They are small, evolutionally advanced rays with a very flattened, leaf-shaped disc and a thin tail without fins. Each pelvic fin is divided into two distinct lobes. The front lobes resemble thin legs and are presumably used for "walking" over the seabed. Mature males of some species have an extended,

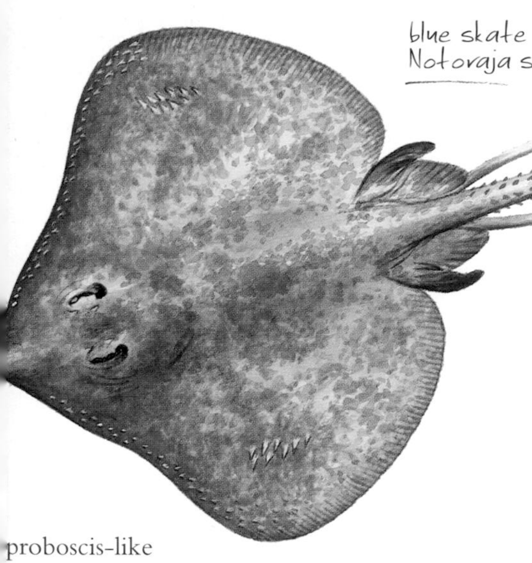

proboscis-like snout, which they use for probing around in the sediments for food. Most of the 18 or so known species of leg skate live on continental slopes. They are rarely caught, even by trawlers.

Skates vary greatly in size. The species of some genera, such as *Pavoraja*, are less than 16" (40 cm) long, with males maturing at about 11" (27 cm). Members of the more ubiquitous genus *Dipturus* may reach 6½' (2 m) long and weigh 200 lb (90 kg) or more.

The skin of skates is either smooth or covered in tiny denticles. Larger denticles, known as thorns, are sometimes present around the eyes and along the back and the upper surface of the tail. Mature males may have additional patches of very sharp thorns beside the eyes (malars) and also in the middle of each pectoral fin (alars), which they use to grasp females during mating. In many species, the alar thorns can be retracted into the disc, making them difficult to notice. However, they are well known to those who handle skates frequently, as is the sight of a careless angler with a skate dangling from a bloody hand.

Skates feed on bottom-dwelling animals, such as soft-shelled mollusks, sand worms, crustaceans, and small fishes. Some species are known to have rudimentary electric organs that may be used to locate prey.

Female skates are fertilized internally by the male's very well developed claspers, which have a series of hooks and spines for grasping the female during mating. The females lay horny egg cases and attach them to the ocean bottom with sticky threads and tendrils. The embryos may take from several months to more than one and a half years to develop and hatch. Young skates are virtually identical to the mother in shape, although their denticles and thorns develop and harden after birth.

Skates are caught for their meat. The wings, or pectoral flaps, fetch high prices and are eaten in some parts of the world. Given the limited distribution of some skates, they are susceptible to overfishing in certain regions.

Sixgill Stingrays

Hexatrygonidae

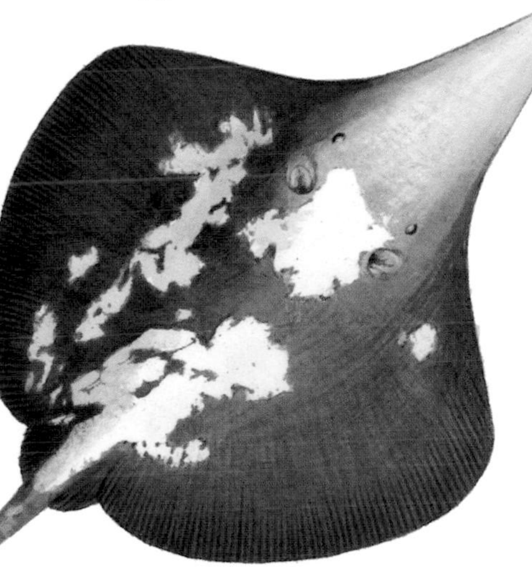

The sixgill stingray (*Hexatrygon bickelli*) belongs to the deep-water family of sixgill rays. They live on the midcontinental slopes of the Indo-Pacific, and are more closely related to stingrays than to skates.

The shape of the rear part of the disc and the tail, with one or two stinging spines and a caudal fin, is reminiscent of a stingaree. However, the body is flabby and the features of its head are distinctive and unique.

Unlike all other rays, which have five pairs of gill openings, this ray has six. It has very small eyes and a long, flattened, triangular snout filled with fluid. The snout, which is covered with sensory pores, is highly flexible and is used to detect food. A sixgill ray that had been trawled was observed moving the tip of its snout like a finger.

This ray is likely to bear live young, but like so many of the deep-sea rays, almost nothing is known of its biology.

The wonders of the sea are as marvelous as the glories of the heavens.

Matthew Fontaine Maury (1806–73), American scientist

Chapter Eight
Encounters *with* Sharks *and* Rays

USING ENCOUNTERS *with* SHARKS *and* RAYS

The challenge of observing sharks and rays can take you from the Red Sea to the Galapagos via the Great Barrier Reef.

The following pages feature 19 marine environments where you have the chance of coming face to face with a shark or ray in its own habitat. Some enthusiasts prefer particular types of encounters, or they become fascinated with certain aspects of the behavior of these mysterious creatures. Whatever your interest, careful planning is essential if you are to have the best chance of seeing sharks and rays in the wild. This guide will help you to choose the destination and diving experience that you seek.

*The **illustrated banding** is a visual pointe to indicate that the page is about a site.*

Vivid color plates give a graphic sense of the principal shark or ray that may be encountered at the site, or of unique features and particular types of flora and fauna that may be of special interest.

Ras Muhammad

Egypt

The parched landscape and rugged mountains of the Sinai Peninsula in Egypt seem lifeless. But beneath the sapphire waters of the Red Sea dwells a kaleidoscope of living color. Where the southern tip of the peninsula plunges into the sea at Ras Muhammad, incredible shallow reef flats near the shoreline give way to sheer coral walls disappearing into the depths below. Clouds of Anthias and glassfish shimmer among the undulating soft corals. And shafts of desert sunlight penetrate deep into the blue abyss to reveal patrolling gray reef sharks (see p. 146).

Shark Observatory, one of the best shark sites, is a stretch of the Ras Muhammad coral wall. Divers swimming here will see jacks, tuna, barracuda, and other pelagic marine life traversing the deep ocean. Only the wall is there to orientate you, with the seemingly bottomless sea dropping away beneath you. It is quite common to turn a corner and come face to face with several gray reef sharks searching for food or checking their territory for competitors. It is hard to decide who gets the bigger surprise, as the sharks veer out into the limitless blue and the divers kick toward the security of the wall.

Gray reef sharks are curious and territorial, and pay much attention to divers, circling constantly, coming and going, and sometimes even becoming slightly aggressive. But during December and January, you may have the rare privilege of witnessing groups of 5 to 10 gray reef sharks that completely ignore you because they are engrossed in mating behavior. Females circle in the water off the reef, within 30 feet (10 m) of you. A male will dash into the group, single out a female and pursue her, repeatedly biting her flanks. This action is thought to promote ovulation, and the female's thick skin has evolved to deal with it. While you are unlikely to see an actual coupling, these encounters provide opportunities for unique observations and rare photos or video footage.

Shark Reef and Jolanda Reef are two small submerged reefs just below the surface, a short swim from the tip of the peninsula. On their ocean side, these reefs again drop away in coral

Anthias, famous for their vivid color, dart about the coral reef (top); and the Red Sea and Sinai Desert (above).

220

*The **text** describes the habitat at the site, the species that can be seen here, and the behavior you might witness. It warns of possible hazards and advises on equipment that you will need to dive at the site. It also covers the other attractions of the region, the features likely to distract you from looking for sharks and rays.*

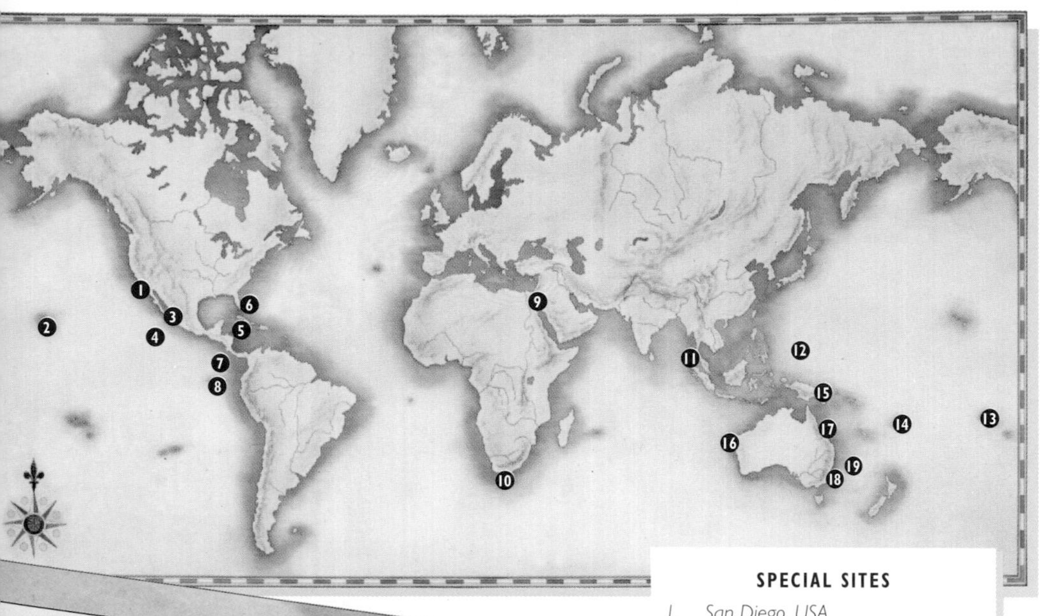

SPECIAL SITES

1. *San Diego, USA*
2. *Kona Coast, USA*
3. *Sea of Cortez, Mexico*
4. *Revillagigedo Islands, Mexico*
5. *Grand Cayman, Cayman Islands*
6. *The Bahamas*
7. *Cocos Island, Costa Rica*
8. *Galapagos Islands, Ecuador*
9. *Ras Muhammad, Egypt*
10. *Cape Town, South Africa*
11. *Similan and Surin Islands, Thailand*
12. *Yap and Palau, Micronesia*
13. *Rangiroa Atoll, French Polynesia*
14. *Mamanuca Islands, Fiji*
15. *Valerie's Reef, Papua New Guinea*
16. *Ningaloo Reef, Australia*
17. *Great Barrier Reef, Australia*
18. *New South Wales, Australia*
19. *Lord Howe Island, Australia*

Ras Muhammad

A reef shark patrols its territory (left); and a handsome yellowbar angelfish (below).

nother gray reef large ers and l also look whitetips oped and ds (see anta rays s one of ny manner of species could shallows at Jolanda Reef, wreckage from the sank in 1981, beautiful il rays (see p. 192) cruise

Marine Park is considered st dive sites. With its low reefs, coral walls, and t is a site for both divers to the reef is easy. Jeeps, live-aboards, and day boats operate from the nearby resort town of Sharm El Sheikh.

EQUIPMENT
Scuba and snorkeling equipment is available for hire or purchase, but the range is limited and expensive. If possible, bring your own. The Red Sea can be cool for a tropical destination, so 5 mm wetsuits are recommended for the cool season, and 3 mm wetsuits should be worn at other times.

SPECIAL FEATURES
Divers and snorkelers can see a spectacular variety of fish at Ras Muhammad, but two species are worth special attention. Giant Napoleon wrasse are particularly striking and endearing, and are likely to accompany divers in the hope of a handout—a practice discouraged these days. They look at you with big eyes that revolve like ball turrets as they seek out more generous divers. Yellowbar angelfish, unique to Africa and the Red Sea, have markings on their sides in the shape of Africa. KD 221

TRAVELER'S NOTES
Dive logistics Day boats, live-aboards, and shore-based diving from jeeps; pre-booking recommended
Accommodation Excellent range, from budget hotels to five-star resorts
Notes Very cosmopolitan dive travelers; be prepared for many different diving techniques and attitudes. Heed any political advisories for Egypt and neighboring countries

Traveler's Notes: *These provide brief details on when to visit, the weather, water temperature, and possible hazards that might be encountered. They also list the type of diving amenities that are available, live-aboards or day trips, and what level of accommodation to expect.*

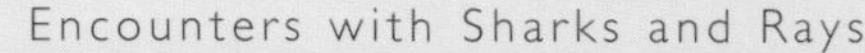

San Diego

United States of America

The California Bight lies between the southern Californian coast and Channel Islands, which dot the temperate Pacific waters off the American West Coast. The warm temperate marine communities of this region make it one of the world's richest oceanographic areas. Inshore is dominated by golden kelp forests. Offshore are the deeps of the blue-water channel. This is the place for diving with blue sharks (see p. 159).

A blue shark (above) eyes a diver in a protective chain-mail suit. Forests of giant kelp (left) thrive close to shore.

Dive boats transport groups of divers 12 to 15 miles (19 to 24 km) off the coast from San Diego. The Coronados Islands rise in peaks to the south; the long, rounded mountain of San Clemente Island breaks up the western horizon. All around is the vast Pacific, sometimes green, sometimes blue, some days glassy and sunlit, others choppy and covered in fog. April to September is the best time to dive to avoid the strong winds and big seas of winter.

The dive boat sets a sea anchor, then a roomy shark cage with a door at the rear is lowered over the side. This hangs about 10 to 15 feet (3 to 4.5 m) below the surface. A divemaster in a protective chain-mail suit (see p. 58) accompanies three divers to the cage. It feels strange to stand in a barred cage suspended in the open ocean, with the clear blue depths falling away, the invisible bottom more than a mile below. You wait, nervously, searching the vast, dimensionless space for a flash of brilliantly blue shark.

As soon as the divemaster, still outside the cage, begins to release bait and chum, they start to arrive—speeding, graceful blues—first 1, then 6, soon as many as 20. The sharks snap at the bait and bump the cage, wanting to test its taste and texture. In the midst of this rush of blue muscle, white teeth, and adrenalin, the practiced (and suit-protected) divemaster allows a small blue shark to bite his chain-mail-clad arm. Photographers, safe inside the cage only inches away, consume film faster

than the sharks do bait. You will soon become accustomed to the excitement, and revel in the spectacle. Elegant juveniles barely 2 feet (60 cm) long jet between adults up to 7 feet (2.1 m) and more, all feeding voraciously. A mako might race past in the distance, while strange, seemingly tailless mola molas (ocean sunfish) swim around at a leisurely pace.

The bait and chum are soon gone, and once the ocean current has dispersed any remaining food scraps, the blues begin to slip away, back into the vast ocean. Divers can now return to the boat, being especially careful as they go.

Equipment

Only scuba diving is possible in the shark cage. A full 5 mm wetsuit is recommended, but some divers prefer a dry suit as it can get cool waiting in the cage. Dive guides will help you get your weight right for the stationary cage.

Special Features

California gray whales migrate through the channel in winter on their way to their calving grounds in Mexico. Blue whales also visit the California Bight, and the second known specimen of the megamouth shark (see p. 130) was caught in the vicinity.

Harbor seals (right) visit the Channel Islands. Hilton's aeolid (below), a local marine snail.

You should explore the kelp forests close to shore. Beneath the canopy of massed fronds there are colorful fish, lobsters, eels, swellsharks (see p. 139), leopard sharks (see p. 144), California hornsharks (see p. 118), and even the occasional stingray. Watch especially for California's state marine fish, the bright golden (and pugnacious) garibaldi.

The Channel Islands, which can be visited by boat, are a refuge for seals, sea lions, whales, and sea birds. Back on the mainland, Sea World, in San Diego, offers one of the world's best introductions to living sharks. The Steven Birch Aquarium, of the famous Scripps Institution of Oceanography, has exhibits on local sea life and international marine research. LT

Traveler's Notes

When to visit *Best diving conditions Apr–Sept*

Weather *Temperate year-round; summer mornings can be foggy, clearing by midday; rain and rough conditions most likely Dec–Feb*

Water temperature *59–70° F (15–21° C)*

Dive logistics *Cage diving with scuba gear from day boats or live-aboards for trips of three days; pre-booking essential; shore diving and snorkeling around kelp beds and rocky points*

Accommodation *A wide selection is available in San Diego, ranging from budget motels to bed-and-breakfast guesthouses and five-star resorts*

Kona Coast

United States of America

The largest and most diverse of the Hawaiian islands is Hawaii, also called Big Island. Its western coast is known as the Kona Coast, and extends more than 85 miles (135 km). This area is a mecca for divers—calm, clear waters, massive corals, and abundant marine life. Among the many highlights are nightly manta ray "rush hours."

At night, the coastal luxury hotels in the Kona and Kohala districts shine floodlights over nearby rocky points into the shallows below. The powerful beams attract swarms of plankton, the smallest of sea creatures, and the food of choice for giant, filter-feeding manta rays (see p. 197). With the lights and the plankton come the mantas, ready to feed. Undoubtedly, they have been in the area for years, but "Manta Mania," the ad hoc festival of lights, people, and rays, is a recent phenomenon.

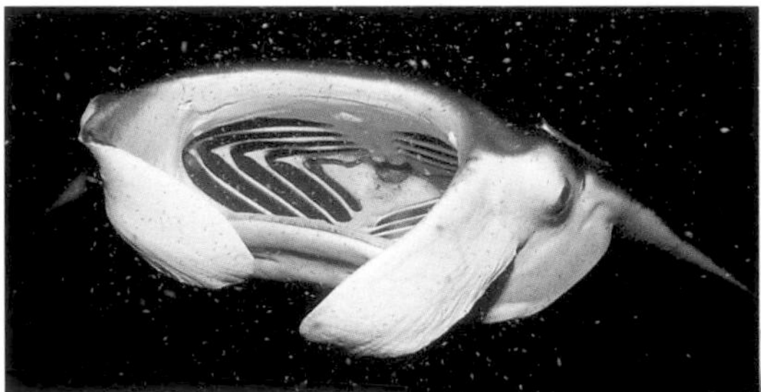

While there are no guarantees that the manta rays will show up, they usually do, especially on calm, moonless nights. Those who like to stay dry can watch them from a hotel balcony, or take one of the glass-bottom boats that depart from the harbor at Kailua-Kona. Alternatively, don snorkeling or diving gear and join these huge and graceful creatures in the water. Some snorkelers and divers are dropped off by dive operators' boats, while others simply swim out from shore. Night swims with rays can be enjoyed in many places along the coast. For a more private experience, ask a local diver.

A popular site is the area off Kona Surf Hotel at Keauhou Bay, about 6 miles (9.5 km) south of the town of Kailua-Kona. Here, the water is 15 to 20 feet (4.5 to 6 m) deep, usually with very

The open mouth of a feeding manta ray (left); and (below) the eastern coastline of Hawaii Volcanoes National Park.

A convoy of gray reef sharks (above); and a diver checks out a spotted pufferfish (left).

little surge. Floodlights make the water glow a luminous pale green. To a diver looking up from the bottom, the lights seem to blink occasionally. The blink is really huge mantas passing overhead, their 12 foot (3.6 m) wide bodies eclipsing the light.

The water is often so clear that you can see myriad tiny plankton swarming near the surface, and look into the open mouth of a feeding manta. And you can easily distinguish the gray and black spots on the ray's pure white underside as it passes close overhead in slow, balletic flight. It is a great temptation to touch or hold on to a passing manta, but such behavior is strongly discouraged.

Equipment

Snorkeling is the best way to see the manta rays. A Lycra suit or 3 mm wetsuit affords good protection and warmth. Dive operators are based around the Kona district and the town of Kailua-Kona; most offer rentals and sell a range of equipment.

Special Features

Hawaii is one of the best served and safest places to dive in the world. Dive boats cover the entire western coast, while excellent snorkeling areas also abound. Among bays, coves, lagoons, lava flows, and undersea lava tubes, an alert diver can find almost 600 species of fish—176 of them are found only in Hawaii.

Good encounters with a number of shark and ray species are possible. At particular sites along the western coast, you are likely to see whitetip and blacktip reef sharks, scalloped hammerheads, and eagle rays. You might also see whale sharks, tiger sharks, Galapagos sharks, gray reef sharks, even the occasional oceanic whitetip.

In winter and early spring, huge humpback whales fill these waters with song, vaulting into the air off Hawaii and the nearby island of Maui. Above ground, there is the spectacle of Hawaii Volcanoes National Park to be explored. LT

TRAVELER'S NOTES

When to visit *Fine year-round; best months for mantas May–Nov; humpback whale season Dec–May*
Weather *Warm days and cool nights; 70–85° F (21–29° C); gentle to brisk northeast trade winds; rainy Dec–Feb*
Water temperature *74–82° F (23–28° C)*
Hazards *Venomous animals include medusae and Portuguese man-of-war*
Dive logistics *Snorkeling from shore; day boats and live-aboards for week-long trips (pre-booking essential) offer access to sites along the Kona Coast*
Accommodation *A wide range, from beach camping and budget hotels to five-star resorts*
Notes *Bernice P. Bishop Museum, the archive of Hawaiian culture in Honolulu, has many artifacts relating to sharks*

Sea of Cortez

Mexico

The strikingly beautiful Sea of Cortez is formed by the long peninsula of Baja California to the west and the mainland of Mexico to the east. To people who live here or visit, the Gulf is clearly a special place, where stark, rocky desert meets this inland sea's sparkling waters.

Elephant Rock (above), off Isla Santa Catalina; and scalloped hammerheads approaching (left).

A complex system of currents divides the Gulf into a cooler northern half and a warmer southern half. Both offer fine diving, but fans of sharks and rays prefer the warmer waters around the major port of the Baja peninsula, La Paz, and adjacent islands. Divers usually fly to La Paz and join a live-aboard boat.

High on the desired site list is a seamount, El Bajo, just east of Isla Espiritu Santo. In this group of rocky pinnacles, 60 feet (18 m) below the surface, moray eels seem to occupy every crevice. Shoals of fish abound and Pacific manta rays (see p. 197), billfish, and an occasional finback whale or whale shark (see p. 127) may also swim by. But schools of hundreds of scalloped hammerhead sharks (see p. 164), with adults up to 12 feet (3.6 m) long, are the main attraction. The boat uses sonar to locate the underwater pinnacles and divers drop down to look up at the grand fleet of sharks, all headed in the same direction, schooling around the pinnacles. Despite continued study and many creative explanations, scientists are still not certain why the hammerheads do this.

Isla Las Animas to the north is one of the most exciting and colorful dive spots in the Sea of Cortez. Rock walls are dominated by sea fans and gorgonians and are dense with invertebrate life. Schooling jacks number in the hundreds and there are underwater caves for the adventurous, plus more opportunities for viewing the hammerheads and other pelagic species.

Isla Los Islotes, just north of Isla Espiritu Santo, hosts a sea lion rookery. The island's east end, with a drop-off into deep water with many detached boulders, is good for sighting big fish.

Although spearfishing is not permitted now, years of overfishing and careless practices have jeopardized the Gulf's ecological health. Baja's dive operators, Mexican and American alike, are dedicated to preserving its fragile beauty. The area is still rich in marine life, although numbers of large groupers and shellfish are declining.

Equipment

Dive shops in La Paz are well-equipped but it's best to travel with your own gear. Live-aboards provide weights and tanks. Night-diving is popular and worthwhile. Divers often bring good diving lights, batteries, and "cool light" sticks. On the boat deck, a 5 mm wetsuit can become unbearably warm, but it feels good in the water, especially during winter.

Special Features

Isolated small coral heads occur throughout the southern Gulf, but Cabo Pulmo, south of La Paz, can be said to have the only living coral reef on the Pacific coast of North America. Many reef fish will be recognized as relatives of central and South Pacific species. Farther offshore, fields of garden eels wave sinuously in the current, half their bodies burrowed into the sand while their big eyes search the water for plankton to snatch into mouths the diameter of a soda straw. Where rocks meet the sand at Cabo Pulmo and farther north toward La Paz, a sharp-eyed diver may see the rough-skinned Mexican hornshark, discovered near here in 1972.

In spring, the Sea of Cortez is a good place for sighting whales, including gray whales, finback whales, and the occasional 80 foot (24 m) blue whale. LT

TRAVELER'S NOTES

When to visit *Year-round; preferred diving season June–Dec*
Weather *Generally temperate to hot; 100° F (38° C) or more June–Sept; strong winds and tropical storms occur infrequently May–Oct*
Water temperature *70–80° F (21–27° C) June–Nov; 61–70° F (16–21° C) Dec–May*
Hazards *Variable weather conditions and occasional strong tidal currents*
Dive logistics *Day boats operate from La Paz and Cabo San Lucas; live-aboards offer 3–10 day excursions to Gulf Islands; pre-booking advised*
Accommodation *La Paz has a full range, from pensions, comfortable hotels, to high-rise luxury hotels*

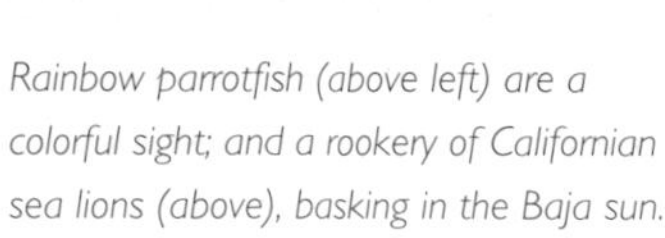

Rainbow parrotfish (above left) are a colorful sight; and a rookery of Californian sea lions (above), basking in the Baja sun.

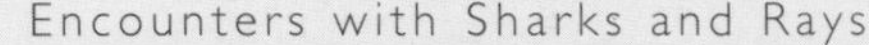

Revillagigedo Islands

Mexico

If a friend asks you to dive at "Revillagigedo," you could end up in the cold waters off Revillagigedo Island in Alaska. Or—and this is our recommendation—you could be diving in warm Mexican waters, far south of the tip of Baja California. Whichever island you visit, most people pronounce it "Ree-vee-yah-hee-hey-do."

The Mexican Revillagigedo archipelago is 300 miles (480 km) south-southwest of the tip of Baja and 370 miles (590 km) west-southwest of Cape Corrientes on the Mexican mainland. The islands, uninhabited except for a Mexican naval installation on Socorro Island, are made up of numerous pinnacles and oceanic rocks. The major islands, spread over a large distance, include San Benedicto, Roca Partida, Clarion, and the largest, Socorro, which rises to 3,707 feet (1,130 m) with 110 square miles (285 sq km) of emergent land. Like most Pacific oceanic islands, the Revillagigedos are volcanic—San Benedicto's last eruption took place in the 1950s.

The great attractions for divers are the large pelagic sharks and schooling tuna that share these remote waters with huge manta rays (see p. 197). As well as the scores of giant mantas, a typical visitor's species list includes large scalloped hammerheads (see p. 164), Galapagos sharks (see p. 149), tiger sharks (see p. 157), and schools of jacks, tuna, and wahoo.

Comfortable live-aboard dive vessels depart from Cabo San Lucas, on the tip of the Baja peninsula, and usually spend 7 to 10 days visiting Socorro and San Benedicto. Boiler Rock, a pinnacle at San Benedicto, is home to "the friendliest manta rays in the world," according to renowned underwater photographer and biologist Norbert Wu. Groups of five or six mantas are common, and they are not shy with divers. Part of the reason for their friendliness may be that they associate this area with fishes that provide a "cleaning

A school of scalloped hammerheads (top); a Pacific manta ray (left), with remoras and orange Clarion angelfish.

Roca Monument (left), Clarion Island; sightings of humpback whales (below) are often made in spring.

service." Young wrasses, damselfish, and other cleaner fish groom away dead tissue and parasites from the rays' gills, mouths, and body surfaces.

A close pass by a manta with a wingspan of up to 15 feet (4.5 m) may tempt a diver to grab on for a ride, but dive operators discourage this and so does the required permit from the Mexican government. Resist temptation and enjoy the glorious soaring dance of these huge rays as your bubbles caress their pale, muscled undersides.

Equipment

This is scuba diving for experienced divers only. A 5 mm wetsuit is recommended. Dive vessels provide weights and tanks and all the comforts of home, but bring reliable, well-tested, gear and a body that's in good physical condition. This is very rigorous diving in remote oceanic waters with strong currents.

Special Features

It's a long trip to the Revillagigedo Islands, but worth it, with the adventurous feel of an oceanic expedition. Watch for sea birds, dolphins, and whales—visitors in May might spot humpback whales.

Keep an eye out for other large pelagics, including schooling yellowfin tuna, and solitary toothy wahoos, 6 feet (1.8 m) blue-water predators that look like a cross between a tuna and a barracuda. Clarion Island gives its name to the rare and beautiful Clarion angelfish, a species unique to these Mexican waters. LT

Traveler's Notes

When to visit *Nov–May only, to avoid stormy Pacific waters and seasonal problems caused by offshore location*
Weather *Tropically warm; often windy*
Water temperature *70–80° F (21–27° C)*
Hazards *Strong currents, rough water, and the remoteness of the location*
Dive logistics *Large, comfortable live-aboards only; book well in advance; boats depart from San Diego, USA, or Cabo San Lucas, which is closer*
Accommodation *Cabo San Lucas offers a range of accommodation from lodges to luxury hotels*
Notes *This is a very rigorous outing, but it pays off in large numbers of approachable manta rays*

Grand Cayman

Cayman Islands

Three islands make up the Cayman group, islands of dense mangroves and lagoons, powdery beaches set in the Caribbean's aquamarine waters. The steep coral and limestone walls of the outer reefs offer grand diving, but the big attraction is inside the barrier reef of Grand Cayman, the opportunity to get close to southern stingrays (see p. 190).

The experience of wading, swimming, snorkeling, or diving with these huge rays is thrilling. They grow to 4 or 5 feet (1.2 or 1.5 m) wide, and have long, whip-like tails, complete with dagger-like stinging spines. They usually spend their days buried in the sand, but Cayman stingrays have overcome their characteristic shyness.

They were originally attracted by scraps from cleaned fish, because fishers and tourists used to clean their catch in the area. People began to feed them regularly, as they came to expect the visits. They are now quite gentle and tame, and seek out interactions with humans, who learn to enjoy the company of these fantastic creatures. Take a deep breath and stretch out on the sandy bottom to watch a ray fly gracefully overhead, its wings and gill slits moving slowly, its extraordinary mouth and nostrils like something from an unknown world. Or simply watch giggling children frolic with rays as wide across as the children are tall.

Southern stingrays (above) of the Caymans show off their tails. Vivid orange cup coral (left).

Cayman stingrays like to be fed, and have developed the manners of a starved dinner guest. If you don't have a squid or ballyhoo ready, the ray will move on after giving you a firm nudge.

There are two popular sites for "dancing" with rays. The most famous is the original Stingray City, on the west side of the Main Channel, close to Barker's Cay. This site is actually a wide, shallow, sandy channel spotted with coral heads. Visibility is usually excellent over the bright white sand. Tidal currents can cloud the water, but the rays come so close you can't miss them. Water depth varies from 6 to 8 feet (1.8 to 2.4 m). Take a boat to Stingray City, then simply drop off into the water and wade around in sneakers, with mask and snorkel.

Another good site, known as Sandbar, lies at the entrance to Rum Point Channel. The water is shallower here, never reaching more than chest high, and the sea floor is flat and sandy. The conditions are usually ideal.

The main challenge for the photographer is the popularity of the sites. You will have to vie for a prime position with many others. The best way of ensuring that you get clear views and good photos of the stingrays is to stay on the fringe and out of the crowd. The rays will check you out and leave if you offer nothing. By keeping your distance, you will get shots of these friendly rays, with and without people.

A Caribbean collage (above) of fish, corals, and sea fans. Dancing with the rays (left), an experience unique to the Caymans.

Equipment

You need only a pair of sneakers and a mask to see these southern stingrays. You can also snorkel or dive with them, and well-equipped dive shops rent and sell all kinds of snorkeling and scuba gear.

Special Features

Not to be missed is diving the Cayman Walls, a system of cliffs, slopes, canyons, and valleys encircling the islands. These are encrusted with massive elkhorn coral, bushy black coral, giant sponges, and delicate soft corals, and are home to vast numbers of fish. Look for small creatures, such as a button-sized flamingo tongue cowrie feeding on a purple sea fan. Eagle and manta rays cruise the outer reef walls in this protected marine park. LT

TRAVELER'S NOTES

When to visit *Year-round; May–Oct offer the best conditions*
Weather *Influenced by trade winds; cooler Nov–Apr, warmest June–Aug; watch weather patterns for tropical storms July–Sept*
Water temperature *Summer, 70–80° F (21–27° C); winter, a bit lower*
Hazards *Clear water and steep walls can tempt divers to dive too deep. Plan your dive and dive your plan. A recompression chamber is maintained at George Town Hospital, on Grand Cayman Island*
Dive logistics *Day boats to Stingray City; day boats and live-aboards serve the major Cayman dive spots and other islands; booking essential*
Accommodation *A full range, from rented houses and condominiums to luxury resorts; booking essential*
Notes *Holiday periods can be busy*

The Bahamas

The Bahamas consist of about 700 low-lying limestone cays, islands, and islets, only 20 of which are inhabited. Major islands include Grand Bahama, Bimini, Little Abaco, Abaco, Andros, New Providence (Nassau), Eleuthera, the Exumas, Long Island, and Great Inagua. The archipelago extends 600 miles (1,000 km) southeast from Grand Bahama, less than 60 miles (100 km) from the Florida coast of the United States, to Great Inagua Island, within 50 miles (80 km) of Cuba. With such an expanse, the Bahamas offer plenty of variety in dive locations. Every level of diving experience is catered to, and visibility is superb.

A lone sea star in crystalline Bahaman waters (top). Divers look on as Caribbean reef sharks circle in search of food (above).

Areas that specialize in shark dives are easy to spot from their names: Shark Alley, Shark Arena, Shark Junction, Shark Rodeo. These are open areas to watch free-swimming sharks. Cages are not used. Divers descend 40 to 60 feet (12 to 15 m) to a reef area well known to experienced dive operators. A divemaster joins the group and signals for the boat to lower a bait-filled metal or plastic box. The thawing bait inside soon attracts sharks. Most operators promise from 60 to 100 sharks feeding for an hour.

The old reliables are the graceful but stocky Caribbean reef sharks (see p. 155). These stream in by the dozen, circling the divemaster and bumping each other in their haste and excitement. Sometimes, the bulkier and bossier bull sharks (see p. 150) will move in (these have much larger first dorsal fins set farther forward than the Caribbean reef sharks). Very rarely, a tiger shark (see p. 157) may come by, but big as they are, tiger sharks tend to be shy around bull sharks.

Divemasters are well-trained and careful, but you are in the open with feeding sharks. Follow tips the guides give before the dive; maintain a discreet distance; stay calm and follow instructions.

In the excitement of the feeding, speeding sharks, it's easy to get confused and see only the

big picture, but it's a pity to miss the details, so here are some ways to slow down the action in your mind and to help you look more closely at this thrilling spectacle. Count the sharks. Can you tell the species apart? Are they all Caribbean reef sharks or are some bulls? How do the smaller sharks react to the larger sharks? Which are males and which females? (Remember to look at the pelvic fins. Adult males have long, paired claspers extending rearward; in immature males the claspers don't yet reach the margins of the pelvic fins.) Look at the gill slits. Are there any parasitic copepods or juvenile shark suckers there? Such careful and disciplined looking will enrich your shark-watching experience, especially in the Bahamas, where dozens of sharks create such a spectacle.

Divers are guaranteed close-up views of huge stingrays (above) and Caribbean reef sharks (left).

EQUIPMENT

Scuba diving is the only way to see the sharks. Equipment can be purchased or rented in larger centers, such as New Providence. Some gear is available in the more remote areas and on live-aboards, but it's best to bring your own. Weights are always provided. During the winter months, use at least a 3 mm wetsuit as the water cools considerably. Take your camera. Remember that nothing can be removed from the water.

SPECIAL FEATURES

Bahaman diving is big and superb, with steep walls, blue holes, large sharks. Take time to really look at the small things, too. Inside sponges lurk tiny golden gobies. Green sea grass shelters slender, delicate pipefish. Purple sea fans tolerate elegant flamingo tongue cowries that feed on the sea fans' soft tissue. Reef squid stare into your eyes, flash a colorful neon signal, then dart off. Don't miss these tiny miracles. LT

TRAVELER'S NOTES

When to visit *Year-round; summer is hot, but the sea refreshes*
Weather *Influenced by trade winds; cooler Nov–Apr, warmest June–Sept; watch forecasts for tropical storms*
Water temperature *From 70–75° F (21–24° C) in Feb to 82–88° F (28–31° C) in Sept*
Dive logistics *Day trips from Grand Bahamas and New Providence; live-aboards also; booking essential*
Accommodation *A wide range even on remote cays, from camping and comfortable dive lodges to luxury hotels; Walker Cay on Abaco Island has shore-side accommodation near Shark Rodeo*

Cocos Island

Costa Rica

Diving Isla del Coco (as the host country of Costa Rica calls it) is a high-seas adventure. A typical dive trip to Cocos begins with a flight to San José, in Costa Rica. An overnight stay in this capital city precedes the morning's three-hour bus trip to the coast, where the dive vessel departs. The 260 mile (420 km) crossing from Puntarenas to Cocos Island, over long, rolling Pacific swells (occasionally shortened to a steep chop), takes 32 to 36 hours. The lush green island, once a favored pirate haunt, is washed by 300 inches (7,620 mm) of rain annually and consequently streams with rivers and waterfalls.

Cocos is famous for what have come to be affectionately called "LLPs" or "Large Legendary Pelagics" ("pelagic" is the oceanographic term for "open sea"). The LLPs of note are silky sharks (see p. 148), scalloped hammerhead sharks (see p. 164), Galapagos sharks (see p. 149), huge manta rays (see p. 197), the occasional whale shark (see p. 127), and schools of tuna and jacks.

Once the vessel arrives, it becomes the mother ship for groups of divers using roving skiffs to reach the diving sites. To justify the long trip to Cocos, most operators stay for a full seven days of diving, with three dives a day. The ship anchors and the skiffs stay mobile to pick up divers surfacing in the strong currents. Deep diving, fast currents, and plenty of sharks are all thrilling aspects of Cocos diving.

One popular dive spot is a small rock spire on the north side of the island, called Manuelita. This can be a very strenuous and exciting outing. Typically, divers chance the bottom at 140 feet (45 m) to get upward views of schooling scalloped hammerheads shyly aggregating in the murky depths. Currents can be unpredictable, and sometimes flow from different directions at various depths. During your descent to deeper waters, several 12 to 15 foot (3.6 to 4.5 m) manta rays may make lazy barrel rolls close by.

At Punta Ulloa, about 100 whitetip reef sharks are a frequent sight, sharing the area with

Circling sailfish, just some of the large creatures seen at this site.

A magnificent manta ray (above) with two remora companions; and countless squirrelfish (left) swimming on a Cocos Island reef.

dozens of large marbled ribbontail rays, 4 to 6 feet (1.2 to 1.8 m) across. Whitetips come in all sizes, alone, in pairs, and in groups. Most divers lose count after the first 50. Dirty Rock and Viking Rock usually offer lots of whitetip reef sharks (see p. 162) and numerous scalloped hammerheads too, congregating in water about 120 feet (35 m) deep. The mix often includes a few large Galapagos sharks.

Scalloped hammerheads are abundant on the deep reefs and spires off Cocos. Scuba divers describe them as generally shy, elusive, and difficult to approach within close range. To get good close-up photographs, divers make use of rebreathers (which produce fewer bubbles and make less noise than other types of breathing apparatus). Hammerheads like to stay in deeper, colder, murkier depths, and you can count on seeing them below 120 feet (35 m), although solitary individuals may wander into shallower depths. Most of the LLPs can be seen while diving no deeper than 100 feet (30 m).

Equipment

This is an active dive trip for experienced divers able to handle strong currents and deep diving. At least a 5 mm wetsuit is essential. Bring reliable gear, a good dive computer, and a body in good physical condition. Nitrox and rebreathers are available on some dive boats that serve Cocos, as are weights and tanks.

Special Features

An attentive diver can find all kinds of interesting fish and invertebrates, but the big fish are the main attraction. If you tire of open-water sharks, drop to a ledge and get close to a whitetip reef shark. There are hundreds in the area. LT

TRAVELER'S NOTES

When to visit *Mar–Sept*
Weather *Cocos Island can be wet; offshore weather can be windy, with rough seas; trust the skipper to make a safe crossing and find the lee*
Water temperature *Varies with currents; surface can be 80–82° F (27–28° C), with thermoclines dropping to 65–70° F (18–21° C)*
Hazards *Strong currents and deep diving in a remote area*

Dive logistics *Live-aboards for 11-day trips, offering 7 full days of diving; advance bookings with dive charter operators are necessary*
Accommodation *Large, comfortable live-aboard vessels are necessary because of the long ocean passage to Cocos Island; they accommodate between 12 and 22 divers*
Notes *This is a trip for avid and experienced divers only*

Galápagos

Ecuador

Politically part of Ecuador, the Galápagos Islands are a remote evolutionary showcase. This archipelago of volcanic islands only five million years old sits astride the Equator and is washed by three major ocean currents. Many of the species of sharks, rays, and reef fishes that live in Hawaii are also here, but only in the Galápagos can you see marine iguanas and penguins basking on a black lava coastline.

Most visitors to this natural treasury fly first to the Ecuadorean capital of Quito, and then west 600 miles (1,000 km) off the coast of South America to the small Galápagos islet of Baltra. Live-aboard charter vessels pick up visitors and, accompanied by a government-licensed naturalist guide, the adventure begins.

Sharks and rays are seen almost anywhere among the many islands, but the favored spots for shark diving are two remote rock islands, Isla Darwin and Isla Wolf, 100 miles (160 km) north of the main group. Here the water is usually warm and clear, and the underwater fauna is large and abundant. Schools of scalloped hammerheads (see p. 164) number in the hundreds; green sea turtles paddle by in their dozens; eagle rays coast above the bottom; and mantas (see p. 197) barrel-roll in midwater, then break the surface. Whitetip reef sharks (see p. 162) rest on the bottom beneath overhangs before venturing forth for a meal of reef fish. A large whale shark (see p. 127) may pass through on its way south. The species list is long and thrilling, and includes sea lions, barracudas, fur seals, and false killer whales. Pacific cownose rays, rare in open waters, gather in large numbers in enclosed mangrove bays. Hot spots include Tortuga Negra on Santa Cruz Island and Elizabeth Bay on Isabella Island. Locals call them *raya dorada*, or golden ray, for their rich color.

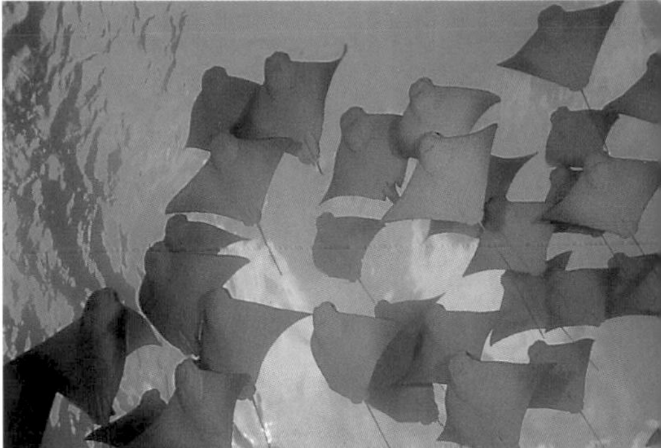

Crowds of cownose rays (above) gather in sheltered mangrove bays; a marine iguana (below), seen only in the Galápagos Islands.

Pinnacle Rock (above), Bartolomé Island; a green sea turtle (right).

The first Galápagos shark (see p. 149), collected here in 1904, was named in honor of the islands, but they are now known to occur throughout the world's tropical waters. Graceful and strong, they are seen swimming either alone or in small groups, and should be treated with caution. The Galápagos hornshark, unique to the Galápagos and adjacent South American coastline, lives on the bottom or in rocky crevices. Its large black spots contrast with its cream body.

Divers must pay attention to currents and surging swells. Huge boulders on the bottom look stationary but have only recently been moved by the ocean's power. One diver has described the surging swells as leaving divers "feeling like guppies in a washing machine." The shallower rocky reefs are home to fascinating invertebrates and fishes.

Equipment

You are strongly advised to bring your own dive gear. Booking through a dive-travel operator will ensure that your live-aboard vessel is equipped for scuba diving (many boats here serve only shore excursions, with limited snorkeling). The mix of currents creates a range of surface water temperatures, and there are marked thermoclines. A 5 mm wetsuit with hood is recommended year-round. Galápagos is not recommended for inexperienced divers because of its remoteness and strong currents.

Special Features

Visiting the Galápagos to see only sharks would be worse than visiting Africa to see only lions. There are thousands of reasons to come here; most of them involve animals and plants, both land and marine. Nowhere else can you see coral reef fishes, penguins, sea lions, marine iguanas, and flightless cormorants all on the same day. At the Charles Darwin Research Station at Puerto Ayora, Santa Cruz Island, conservationists are trying to save the endangered giant tortoise.

Prepare for your visit by reading some good books on Galápagos natural history, including young Charles Darwin's accounts of his adventures. LT

TRAVELER'S NOTES

When to visit *Year-round, but best in late Feb–May*
Weather *Equatorial; warm to hot; cooler season from May–Dec; hotter season Jan–May*
Water temperature *Variable with location and depth; from 65–80° F (18–27° C)*
Hazards *Blue-water diving with strong currents; this is not for novices*
Dive logistics *Live-aboards only; book packages through dive operators*
Accommodation: *Live-aboards only, booking essential; hotels and guest-houses at Puerto Ayora, Santa Cruz Island, but little or no diving support*
Notes *Be aware of the political climate in Ecuador; check government advisories*

Ras Muhammad

Egypt

The parched landscape and rugged mountains of the Sinai Peninsula in Egypt seem lifeless. But beneath the sapphire waters of the Red Sea dwells a kaleidoscope of living color. Where the southern tip of the peninsula plunges into the sea at Ras Muhammad, incredible shallow reef flats near the shoreline give way to sheer coral walls disappearing into the depths below. Clouds of Anthias and glassfish shimmer among the undulating soft corals. And shafts of desert sunlight penetrate deep into the blue abyss to reveal patrolling gray reef sharks (see p. 146).

Anthias, famous for their vivid color, dart about the coral reef (top); and the Red Sea and Sinai Desert (above).

Shark Observatory, one of the best shark sites, is a stretch of the Ras Muhammad coral wall. Divers swimming here will see jacks, tuna, barracuda, and other pelagic marine life traversing the deep ocean. Only the wall is there to orientate you, with the seemingly bottomless sea dropping away beneath you. It is quite common to turn a corner and come face to face with several gray reef sharks searching for food or checking their territory for competitors. It is hard to decide who gets the bigger surprise, as the sharks veer out into the limitless blue and the divers kick toward the security of the wall.

Gray reef sharks are curious and territorial, and pay much attention to divers, circling constantly, coming and going, and sometimes even becoming slightly aggressive. But during December and January, you may have the rare privilege of witnessing groups of 5 to 10 gray reef sharks that completely ignore you because they are engrossed in mating behavior. Females circle in the water off the reef, within 30 feet (10 m) of you. A male will dash into the group, single out a female and pursue her, repeatedly biting her flanks. This action is thought to promote ovulation, and the female's thick skin has evolved to deal with it. While you are unlikely to see an actual coupling, these encounters provide opportunities for unique observations and rare photos or video footage.

Shark Reef and Jolanda Reef are two small submerged reefs just below the surface, a short swim from the tip of the peninsula. On their ocean side, these reefs again drop away in coral

walls, and are another favorite area for gray reef sharks and other large pelagic fish. Divers and snorkelers should also look out for oceanic whitetips (see p. 152), scalloped and great hammerheads (see pp. 164–5), and manta rays (see p. 197). This is one of those sites where any manner of species could turn up. And in the shallows at Jolanda Reef, amid the remaining wreckage from the MV *Jolanda*, which sank in 1981, beautiful bluespotted ribbontail rays (see p. 192) cruise among the corals.

Ras Muhammad Marine Park is considered one of the world's best dive sites. With its crystalline waters, shallow reefs, coral walls, and wealth of marine life, it is a site for both divers and snorkelers. Access to the reef is easy. Jeeps, live-aboards, and day boats operate from the nearby resort town of Sharm El Sheikh.

A reef shark patrols its territory (left), and a handsome yellowbar angelfish (below).

Equipment

Scuba and snorkeling equipment is available for hire or purchase, but the range is limited and expensive. If possible, bring your own. The Red Sea can be cool for a tropical destination, so 5 mm wetsuits are recommended for the cool season, and 3 mm wetsuits should be worn at other times.

Special Features

Divers and snorkelers can see a spectacular variety of fish at Ras Muhammad, but two species are worth special attention. Giant Napoleon wrasse are particularly striking and endearing, and are likely to accompany divers in the hope of a handout—a practice discouraged these days. They look at you with big eyes that revolve like ball turrets as they seek out more generous divers. Yellowbar angelfish, unique to Africa and the Red Sea, have markings on their sides in the shape of Africa. KD

TRAVELER'S NOTES

When to visit *Best diving conditions during warm months, June–Oct; more variable visibility and risk of rough seas during cool season, Nov–Feb; sharks and manta rays more in evidence during the mating season, Dec–Feb*

Weather *Arid desert climate, hot days, cooler at night; very little rain; cool winds during Nov–Feb make days cool and nights quite cold*

Water temperature *70–82° F (21–28° C)*

Dive logistics *Day boats, live-aboards, and shore-based diving from jeeps; pre-booking recommended*

Accommodation *Excellent range, from budget hotels to five-star resorts*

Notes *Very cosmopolitan dive travelers; be prepared for many different diving techniques and attitudes. Heed any political advisories for Egypt and neighboring countries*

Cape Town

South Africa

To dive with great white sharks is the ultimate thrill for shark watchers. Dyer Island, a two-hour drive east of Cape Town in South Africa, offers the possibility of viewing and cage diving with great whites. This very special area is actually comprised of two islands. The main island, Dyer, is home to a huge marine bird population; the second, Geyser Island, hosts almost 13,000 Cape fur seals. Separating the two islands is a shallow channel, roughly 160 yards (150 m) wide and 550 yards (600 m) long, nicknamed Shark Alley. Great white sharks patrol this protected channel to hunt fur seals, and this area is without doubt one of the great white shark meccas of the world.

Jackass penguins (above), Dyer Island; Cape fur seals (left) at Geyser Island.

Divers are transported the 5 miles (8 km) to the site from nearby Gansbaai by a well-equipped deep-sea cabin cruiser, or in speedboats from Kleinbaai harbor. Once in the channel, most operators deploy a specially designed three-person cage that floats at the surface. Although divers need no fins and don't venture more than 7 feet (2 m) beneath the surface, all are required to have a minimum scuba-diving qualification. Divers can make two to four dives a day, taking turns in the cage. Non-divers can view the activity from the deck or flying bridge of the boat, as the sharks often break the surface in search of bait. One tour operator uses a shark-viewing capsule, which forms part of the boat and offers a 180 degree view of sharks through thick safety glass.

Although sharks are abundant here (on one occasion, researchers working in the area tagged 18 great whites in 7 hours), chumming assures a good turnout. Sometimes the sharks leap boisterously out of the water, but the typical approach is more subdued. First, there is a slight bulge on the glassy surface caused by the shark's bow wave, then two vortices form behind a large dorsal fin as it breaks the surface and a 15 foot (4.5 m) shark heads straight for the bait.

The Twelve Apostles (above), Cape Town. Note the very pointed nose of the great white shark (left), from around Dyer Island.

On deck, watchers are at first mesmerized by the sight, then excited, then eager to jump into the cage and look the creature in the eye. Once in the cool water, the excitement can be elevated by the murky background, out of which the great creatures suddenly emerge. Or, depending on conditions, visibility may permit you to spy a large shark from some distance away.

The high likelihood (claimed to be at least 80 percent) of seeing great white sharks makes Dyer Island and adjacent areas appealing for shark watchers. However, this is also an important research site for the study of the biology and behavior of great whites. Be sure to select a dive operator who cooperates with the ongoing scientific and conservation activities here.

Equipment

Some dive operators supply all diving equipment but it is always best to provide your own mask, regulator, and wetsuit—fins are not needed in the cage. A dry suit is best for these waters, but a 6 mm wetsuit will give minimum protection.

Special Features

Rocky Dyer Island and the surrounding islands host thousands of Cape fur seals, Cape gannets, jackass penguins, whales, and dolphins. Specially organized dives into the enchanting and balletic world of the Cape fur seal are offered at Seal Island, about 18 miles (30 km) from Cape Town on the Atlantic side of the Cape of Good Hope. Or try whale watching at De Kelders, near Gansbaai, where southern right whales come within 100 feet (30 m) of the rocks. These giant mammals visit this coast to mate and calve from mid June to late December; you can see up to 30 as they come to rub their bodies on the kelp.

The Cape of Good Hope also has more than 50 marked wrecks for divers to explore. LT

TRAVELER'S NOTES

When to visit *High season Feb–Sept, almost 100% likelihood of sightings; low season Oct–Jan, about 80% likelihood*
Weather *Usually pleasant, temperate; sometimes stormy and windy, or still and foggy*
Water temperature *58–65° F (14–18° C)*
Dive logistics *Day boats; day trips from Cape Town; overnight trips or 10-day excursions based at Gansbaai; book through dive operators*
Accommodation *A range of accommodation in Cape Town; guesthouses at Gansbaai, some self-catering*
Notes *During winter (June–Aug), high shark activity, but weather only permits trips to the island one or two days a week*

Similan and Surin Islands

Thailand

The Similan and Surin Islands are located in the tropical waters of the Andaman Sea, about 70 miles (110 km) northwest of Phuket, Thailand. Huge granite boulders rise out of the aquamarine water like ancient sentinels. On land, there are quiet bays of talcum-powder sand and groves of palm trees. Underwater, the boulders descend 115 feet (35 m) to the sandy sea floor, with every boulder covered in spectacular soft corals, gorgonians, and sponges. These undersea gardens are home to the zebra, or leopard, shark (see p. 126), one of the most endearing and beautiful of sharks.

Divers descend into the warm, calm waters of the Andaman Sea to discover that visibility is excellent, varying from 40 to 100 feet (12 to 30 m). The gentle currents bring nutrient-rich waters to the area, which help create the spectacular diversity of corals and marine life.

Sooner or later, you will come across a zebra shark resting comfortably on the sand floor among the brilliant reefs. They are gentle and harmless, and will let you come quite close, occasionally even within a few feet. Scuba divers are more likely than snorkelers to see zebra sharks. It is very pleasant to lie on the sand alongside a shark your own size and feel completely safe. This beautiful creature usually stays quite still and you can see remoras moving about on its skin. Eventually, the shark swims off gracefully through the coral canyons, its long tail moving with an undulating, sensuous, almost hypnotic motion.

A diver takes a very close look (right) at a zebra shark, also known as a leopard shark. Above, a striking clown triggerfish.

An underwater seascape of soft corals and lionfish (above), and a bay (below), in the Similan Islands.

The islands are visited by live-aboard dive boats operating out of Phuket. (Day boats also offer tours to reefs and islands just off Phuket, where zebra sharks and plentiful marine life can be viewed.) Today, the nine islands in the Similan group are mostly uninhabited and are designated the Similan Islands National Park, protecting the flora, fauna, and marine life of the area.

Equipment

Scuba and snorkeling equipment can be hired from local dive centers and resorts in Phuket. Lycra suits will suffice, but divers often find a 2–3 mm wetsuit is better, as sometimes cool water thermoclines occur in this region.

Special Features

The Similan Islands offer a rare example of differing underwater environments. On the west-facing side, the brilliant colors and unexpected shapes of soft corals and sea fans cover the giant granite boulders. This is in startling contrast to the pastel hues of the hard corals usually populating coral reefs, and which you can find growing prolifically on the eastern side of the islands. Thus, in the same group of islands, you are able to observe the best of both coral worlds.

As well as the tropical fish you'd expect to see—including butterflyfish, angelfish, and orange Anthias—the reefs of the Andaman Sea contain some unique marine life. The Andaman Sea Crown of Thorns sea star, in iridescent red and purple, can be found eating contentedly and blending in perfectly among the soft corals. These sea stars are a necessary part of the reef's delicate ecosystem. The world's most spectacular triggerfish, the clown triggerfish, is also resident, and can be approached.

Between February and May, the lucky visitor may also encounter a whale shark swimming near Richelieu Rock, in the Surin Islands. KD

TRAVELER'S NOTES

When to visit *Best during the dry season, Nov–Apr; sunny, calm seas*
Weather *Tropical climate, 77–89° F (25–31° C)*
Water temperature *79–82° F (26–28° C)*
Hazards *Very wet during the monsoon season in Sept*
Dive logistics *Snorkeling or scuba diving from live-aboard boats for trips of 2–12 days; pre-booking recommended*
Accommodation *A wide range of resorts, hotels, and guesthouses is available in Phuket*

Yap and Palau

Micronesia

The island groups of Yap and Palau in the western-central Pacific, along with the outlying Truk (also known as Chuuk) group 1,000 miles (1,600 km) to the east, offer many dive possibilities. Sharks and rays, the abundant tropical marine life, an extraordinary geography, rich local cultural customs, and arguably the best wreck diving in the world, make Micronesia a favored spot for divers.

Sharks patrol the glorious reef (above). The Seventy Islands National Park (left), Palau.

Yap

Almost unheard of a decade ago, Yap is today renowned for opportunities to get close to manta rays (see p. 197). A combination of tidal barrier-reef channels and favorable weather patterns allows diving with them year-round. Mantas regularly move into two channels for feeding and cleaning. From June through October, locals recommend Goofnuw Channel on the eastern side, where mantas are dispersed over five distinct spots. Milli Channel, on the western side, offers Manta Ridge, where visibility can exceed 100 feet (30 m). Divers cling to the rocks along a ledge about 30 feet (10 m) down while overhead, mantas cruise through the channel.

At both locales, mantas congregate during tidal changes as plankton is funneled out of the lagoon and mangrove areas. Huge volumes of food-rich water are flushed through to the hovering mantas. Some soar directly over your head, close enough to touch, but any such interference with their movements is prohibited.

Palau

To many divers, Palau is the top tropical dive spot in the world, while to biologists it is a treasury of both land and sea biodiversity. There are more than 100 different dive sites in the vast coral lagoon and adjacent islands, offering diving unlike anywhere else in the world. Thousands of marine species inhabit the region, including manta rays, barracuda, large and small sharks, and an impressive invertebrate fauna ranging from giant clams to the chambered nautilus.

Palau is unusual in having atolls, high volcanic islands, and its famous uplifted limestone rock

islands all in one area. The edge of the barrier reef is nearby, with magnificent wall diving at such legendary sites as Blue Corner, a pass between lagoon and open sea where sharks abound. Divers share swift-flowing tidal waters with gray reef sharks (see p. 146), blue marlin, manta rays, dogtooth tuna, and Napoleon wrasse. Nearby Big Dropoff and New Dropoff are other favorite spots to drift along in the current, about 30 feet (10 m) down, with the coral-studded bottom passing below and gray reef sharks cruising by in search of a meal.

Equipment

Main centers on all island groups have dive shops, but it is best to bring your own gear. This is warm-water diving but Lycra suits and 3 mm wetsuits protect divers from abrasions and stinging plankton, and on cooler night dives. Scuba diving is the only way to see life in the passes, but the clear waters and glorious reef development also make for superb snorkeling.

Longnose hawkfish on a sea fan (left). Some Palau lakes harbor Mastigias jellyfish (below).

Special Features

One Micronesian dive experience not to be missed is the wreck diving at Truk. This cluster of 12 tiny volcanic islands and many lesser islets, in a large lagoon girdled by a coral reef, was heavily bombed during the Second World War. The great lagoon is now a graveyard for the wrecks of more than 100 planes and ships, which provide a dramatic background for diving amid the richness of Micronesian marine life.

Inland "lakes" on Palau host large populations of unique jellyfish. Extensive outer reefs offer a phenomenal diversity of invertebrate life, including black corals, giant sea fans, sponges, and stony corals, and some dive operators will even grant your wish to swim with a live chambered nautilus. LT

TRAVELER'S NOTES

When to visit *Year-round; manta mating season at Yap, Nov–Mar*
Weather *Good year-round; trade winds May–Nov*
Water temperature *82–86° F (28–30° C)*
Hazards *Be extra alert when wreck diving; poisonous spiny trees on Palau*
Dive logistics *Day boats and live-aboards from all islands; a live-aboard amphibious airplane based at Palau visits outer islands, including Yap. Pre-booking before departure essential*
Accommodation *Palau has luxury hotels; Yap and Truk have comfortable hotels and lodge accommodation*
Notes *Yap offers best combination of indigenous culture and dive sites. Nitrox and rebreathers, and training in their use, are available on Yap and Truk*

Rangiroa Atoll

French Polynesia

To the northeast and east of Tahiti is a set of low-lying atolls and islands once known as Tuamotu, the Dangerous Archipelago. The largest of the 80 islands is Rangiroa, some 40 miles (65 km) long and 20 miles (32 km) across. In fact, Rangiroa is the second largest atoll in the Pacific Ocean and its lagoon could accommodate the entire island of Tahiti.

The lagoon at Rangiroa Atoll (above) stretches away endlessly. Red brick soldierfish (left) shelter in a pass.

Because of its size, Rangiroa offers far more than the usual excitement of a coral atoll. Steep reef faces drop off to almost 1 mile (1,600 m) deep and swift tidal currents rush through the narrow openings in the reef between lagoon and open sea. At full tidal flood, currents can exceed 5 knots, far too fast to swim against. Although tidal extremes are slight (up to 2 feet [60 cm]), the volume of the lagoon and the narrowness of the passes assure fast-flooding currents when the tide turns. It is these passes that offer Rangiroa's most exciting diving, and that includes sharks.

The order for the day is "go with the flow." Dive boats drop divers off inside the lagoon so they can swim down 20 to 30 feet (6 to 9 m) and be swept along in the current (to be picked up later out in the open sea by the boat). This is the closest you can get to underwater flying. Imagine soaring from lagoon to open sea while sharing "air space" with a range of sharks, manta rays (see p. 197), and Napoleon fish. Soaring over rich reef growth, you can look down on delicate reef fishes struggling to hold position in the lee of coral heads. You may pass a cave with at least 20 nurse sharks (see p. 125)—perhaps you can return to investigate later.

Outside the reef, where the food-rich and sun-warmed lagoon water meets the water of the open sea, whole food chains are concentrated. Eggs, spawn, larvae, and juveniles born on the reefs of the lagoon meet the predators—sharks, mantas, barracudas, jacks, dogtooth tuna, and mahi-mahi. There is nowhere better to see predation in action than around a flushing pass.

Gray reef sharks (left) wait outside a reef pass for a meal to be served up to them by the tide. A Titan triggerfish (below).

The principal diving spots in Rangiroa include Avatoru Pass, one of the two larger passes at 165 feet (50 m) wide. It is noted for Napoleon fish and manta rays, as well as gray reef sharks (see p. 146), leopard rays, and an impressive fish fauna, especially snappers and jacks.

Tiputa Pass is shorter and not as deep as Avatoru, but it ends with a steep drop-off. Dolphins are often seen in the pass and divers have also reported sailfish and marlin. Drift diving with the current here brings shouts of joy from divers. Photographers are recommended to stay at the end of the group to photograph their buddies in the middle of the action. Gray reef sharks, whitetip reef sharks (see p. 162), and hammerheads guarantee excitement.

Le Failles is a two-hour chartered boat trip across the lagoon. This spectacular dive site on the outer side of the atoll offers rich coral growth and interesting canyons and caves. Shelter in a canyon and see gray reef sharks and perhaps the odd silvertip passing against deep blue space.

Equipment

Scuba equipment is available for hire, but if possible, bring your own. Lycra bodysuits or 3 mm wetsuits afford protection from scrapes and keep you warm during long exposures.

Special Features

Every fragment of the land on atolls such as Rangiroa was formed by once-living reef plants and animals. Long ago, volcanic Rangiroa was a high island of black lava, like Hawaii or the Galapagos Islands are now. Slowly, the black rock has sunk into the sea and the living reef has continued to grow. Now, the low-lying atoll is just the tip of a thick limestone cap on a basaltic platform far below. LT

Traveler's Notes

When to visit *Year-round, but best Nov–Apr*
Weather *Excellent, although trade winds can blow strongly across low-lying atoll; sun protection is always necessary*
Water temperature *Up to 80° F (27° C)*
Dive logistics *Day boats essential to dive the passes; pre-book through local Polynesian dive shops; also live-aboards*
Accommodation *Packages from Tahiti by air include live-aboards or, more frequently, lodge-like shore accommodation; booking essential*
Notes *Pass diving is a challenge for beginning divers, and local guides expect some experience. Plan your trip carefully to permit ample diving between the infrequently scheduled flights*

Mamanuca Islands

Fiji

Fiji consists of more than 300 islands scattered over 42,000 square miles (108,800 sq km) of tropical ocean. The only drawback to visiting the region is selecting a single place to stay. Some visitors choose a live-aboard vessel for 7 to 14 days and visit a number of dive sites. Others settle in a shore-based resort and concentrate on the rich variety at hand.

The gray reef shark (above) can be seen in gangs at some sites on the reefs in Fijian waters. A dazzling male blue ribbon eel (far right).

Closest to the visitor's arrival point at Nadi International Airport is the Mamanuca Group (pronounced Mama-nutha). Within this group, Mana Island is a popular choice. The calm, clear waters surrounding the island are protected by a barrier reef, making it an ideal place to learn how to dive or to refine your skills.

One of the best areas for viewing sharks and rays in the Mamanucas is the Supermarket. With coral walls extending about 100 feet (30 m), it is the home of gray reef sharks (see p. 146) and their calmer relatives, nurse sharks (see p. 125) and whitetip reef sharks (see p. 162). Divers drop to the sandy bottom near the reef wall and watch their Fijian dive guide confer with the sharks. Like a generous host at a social gathering, the guide offers chunks of fish on the end of a pole spear. Sharks are cultural resources in Fiji, and some dive guides belong to Fijian shark clans—their job is to protect sharks from entanglement in fishing gear.

Nearby Gotham City is known for its batfish. This rich reef also has abundant triggerfish, barracuda, surgeonfish, and all manner of schooling basslets and damsels. The underwater ecosystem here is typical of the Mamanucas.

The whole Fiji region is full of sharks, and not only the ubiquitous whitetip. Live-aboard vessels have secret spots to share with visiting divers at locations where local Fijian owners have granted permission for diving adventures. These locales offer large gangs of gray reef sharks, both individual and schooling hammerheads and, near reef drop-offs, large silvertip sharks (see p. 145).

Beds of soft coral (above)—the whole area offers wonderful diving; one of Fiji's many islands (left).

Equipment

All resorts offer weights and tanks, and many also provide regulators and buoyancy vests. Some resorts rent camera or video gear, but most do not. Lightweight wetsuits, vests, or Lycra dive skins are highly recommended. During warm months, a 3 mm wetsuit is a good idea. For cooler times, a 5 mm wetsuit is better. Scuba diving is necessary to see the sharks, but the reefs can be explored with snorkel gear.

Special Features

Located far from major population centers, Fiji's reef system has, for the most part, not been over-exploited, overfished, or damaged. A traditional land-tenure system rigorously protects tribal lands and waters from misuse. This system means, too, that divers and dive operators must have the permission of the owner to dive in a specific area, including sites that may seem remote and unused.

The reefs that this system protects and allows divers to enjoy are glorious. Imagine soaring along the top of a vertical wall, blue water below you, passing under black coral trees and colonies of soft corals taller than you are. Or consider returning to the same spot at night to watch the hundreds of glowing firefly-like lights, which are the headlamps of flashlight fish, emerging from their daytime hiding spots to seek a nocturnal meal of plankton.

Shallower reef areas are home to hundreds of species of coral and reef fish, including bright blue ribbon eels. The males have elongate yellow nasal tubes that give them a scary, threatening appearance, but they are lovely creatures, and harmless as well. LT

TRAVELER'S NOTES

When to visit *Year-round; best weather in dry season (May–Oct)*
Weather *Daytime temperatures 68–86° F (20–30° C); mild, dry May–Oct; wetter, warmer Nov–Apr (wet season); highest rainfall and humidity in Jan–Feb; east-southwest trade wind*
Water temperature *Temperature 80–83° F (27–28° C) from Nov–Apr; 78–80° F (25–26° C) May–Oct*
Hazards *Stonefish and medusae*
Dive logistics *Snorkeling and scuba diving from the shore, live-aboards or day boats; booking essential*
Accommodation *There is a full range of accommodation, from thatched fales to comfortable lodges and resorts; some resorts cater exclusively to the needs of divers*
Notes *Fiji is friendly and hospitable and has a rich culture*

Valerie's Reef

Papua New Guinea

The tropical waters and string of islands forming the Bismarck Archipelago lie to the north of the spectacular mountainous mainland of Papua New Guinea. Among the islands of the New Hanover group in the archipelago, hundreds of coral reefs rise to within 30 feet (10 m) of the surface. One of these, Valerie's Reef, is home to a large group of silvertip sharks (see p. 145).

Valerie's Reef had no name until the recent discovery of the silvertips. It was named in honor of Valerie Taylor (see p. 59), renowned shark authority and underwater photographer. Silvertip sharks are the most impressive and largest of the reef shark family, and Valerie's Reef has become the most famous site in the world for guaranteed silvertip shark encounters.

Divers (above) admire a gorgonian coral. The lacy scorpionfish (left) can inflict a painful wound with its spines.

Between 9 and 12 large, female silvertips, ranging in size from 6½–10 feet (2–3 m), live around the reef area. They congregate on the reef as soon as a dive boat appears—they were once fed regularly from visiting dive boats and still associate the sound of the motor with food. It can be a little daunting at first to look into the water and see several sharks waiting for you. But these large, powerful creatures are well behaved. They are waiting to accompany you on what is, initially, a heart-stopping swim to the reef. Once there, you feel less vulnerable, and are able to watch the sharks patrolling their habitat. They cruise slowly and gracefully through the clear, warm water, circling over the beautiful coral gardens and making occasional inquisitive approaches. The silvertips seem to have a social order, and the smaller sharks respect the larger ones.

These sharks are calm and confident, and do not harass divers. However, silvertip sharks can be dangerous if overstimulated or provoked. Swim beneath the surface to avoid splashing. Always wear dark gloves and keep your hands

close to your body to avoid them being mistaken for fish scraps. Dive in buddy teams and give yourself time to get used to the sharks' behavior. Always make your own way back to the live-aboard at the end of a dive rather than signal for a pick-up by the tender. These are small boats with outboards, and the sound of the motor starting excites the sharks, which then dash toward the boat.

The best access to the reef is by live-aboards operating out of Kavieng, on New Ireland, but it is also within range of day boats. The silvertips are accustomed to divers, and photographers will have opportunities for close-ups, wide angles, and even to capture multiple sharks in one shot.

Equipment

Scuba diving is recommended rather than snorkeling. The sharks perceive scuba divers as just another predator. But with so many sharks competing for food at one reef, a snorkeler might attract the wrong kind of attention. You will need normal scuba equipment. The water is very warm so a 2–3 mm wetsuit will be quite adequate for all dives.

A female silvertip shark (above) patrols the reef; and (left) a local fishing canoe.

Special Features

Papua New Guinea is regarded as one of the top 10 dive locations in the world, and it's easy to get distracted from shark and ray encounters. The diversity of corals and fish and the variety of ship and plane wrecks from the Second World War are astounding. The region is also famous for some very rare and bizarre marine species. These include the lacy scorpionfish, an ornately patterned scorpionfish, and the flamboyant cuttlefish, a small, beautiful creature that lays its eggs inside sunken coconuts. *Octopus horridus* is often seen in these waters—no one has yet discovered if it is poisonous or not.

Papua New Guinea also has some of the world's most diverse, unique, and unspoilt indigenous cultures. The people of the Gazelle Peninsula near Kavieng are famous for their fire dancing, so consider a stopover on the way. KD

Traveler's Notes

When to visit *All year round*
Weather *Very warm, tropical; no distinct wet season*
Water temperature *79–82° F (26–28° C)*
Hazards *Malaria*
Dive logistics *Scuba diving from day boats or live-aboards; the snorkeling is excellent, but is not recommended where there are sharks*
Accommodation *Hotels in Kavieng; excellent live-aboards, booking essential*
Notes *Heed security advisories, particularly in the capital, Port Moresby*

Ningaloo Reef

Australia

In the remote far north of Western Australia, 161 miles (260 km) of coral fringing reef are washed by the tropical waters of the Indian Ocean. The reef is protected as Ningaloo Reef Marine Park. Whale sharks (see p. 127), the gentle giants of the oceans, congregate here in large numbers each year from late March to early May.

The higher temperatures of the Indian Ocean in summer and the full moons in March and April trigger a mass explosion of synchronized spawning of the corals of Ningaloo Reef. The coral spawning coincides with the congregation and mass spawning of millions of other marine life forms. This extraordinary phenomenon provides a bountiful food supply, which is what attracts the large numbers of whale sharks to Ningaloo Reef.

The possibility of diving with these huge, slow-moving sharks brings thousands of divers and snorkelers from around the world. Nothing prepares you for the enormous size of one of these creatures, and the feeling of awe as it materializes out of the blue haze, its massive head filling the view, its tiny eye watching. Divers can swim alongside the shark as it moves majestically through the ocean, occasionally opening its cavernous mouth to feed, always accompanied by an entourage of juvenile jacks, pilotfish, cobia, and a mass of remoras. Caution is necessary as the wide sweep of the shark's powerful tail can easily stun or disable a diver.

A whale shark (above) dwarfs a snorkeler. The vast Ningaloo Reef Marine Park (left).

There are numerous dive tours operating out of Exmouth, the gateway to Ningaloo Reef. A spotter aircraft works with the dive boats to help locate the sharks. Fast and maneuverable, the dive boats repeatedly drop divers off ahead of the shark, picking them up when the shark has moved on, then overtaking the shark to drop them off in front again. Whale sharks may swim slowly, but trying to keep up with them is still tiring. Snorkeling is easier than diving. The sharks spend a great deal of time on the surface, and a snorkeler can swim faster and operate from the dive boat more comfortably than a scuba diver.

Strict rules have been introduced to protect the whale sharks from stress during the season.

There is a total ban on divers touching or riding the sharks, and there are limits on the number of divers in the water with a shark at any one time and on the amount of time they can spend with it. Strobes (flash units) are not allowed. Tour operators must have a permit and boats have a restricted approach zone of 100 feet (30 m).

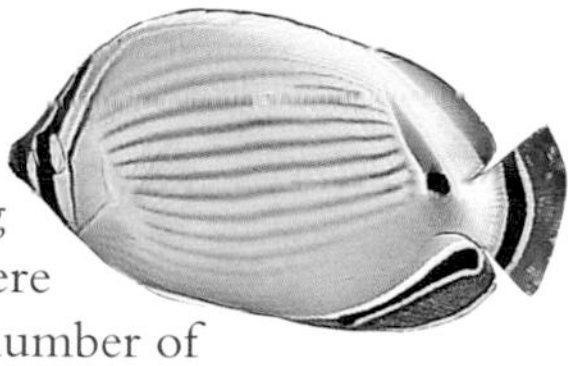

Oval butterflyfish (above left) thrive on the reef; and corals caught in the act of spawning (above right), an annual event.

Equipment

Snorkeling is an ideal way to see whale sharks. Consider using a high-tech snorkel and high-performance fins, because you will do a lot of swimming in seas that vary from flat to choppy if the wind picks up. A full-length Lycra suit is also a good idea; it will protect you from marine stingers (nothing deadly) and sunburn.

Special Features

Ningaloo Reef does not have world-class coral but it does boast a wealth of marine life. A dive at the Navy Wharf at Exmouth is also very rewarding—the rich artificial reef has an incredible diversity of fish species, including resident tasselled wobbegong sharks (see p. 122).

Cape Range National Park

Ningaloo Reef Marine Park is parallel to the rugged landscape of North-West Cape and the Cape Range National Park. It was formed when ancient beds of rock were pushed up from the ocean floor between 1.6 and 5 million years ago. The rocks contain fossils of the huge teeth of the prehistoric shark *Carcharodon megalodon*. This awesome predator, estimated to measure more than 40 feet (12 m), is believed to be an extinct relative of the great white shark. It could once be found throughout the oceans of the world. Local rangers and guides conduct tours to these extraordinary fossil sites. KD

TRAVELER'S NOTES

When to visit *Late Mar to early May*
Weather *Warm, tropical, very sunny; afternoon sea breezes*
Water temperature *73–79° F (23–26° C)*
Hazards *Occasional cyclones*
Dive logistics *Snorkeling or scuba diving from day boats; some live-aboard boats, but not essential for good access*
Accommodation *Hotels, caravans, and camp sites in Exmouth*
Notes *Avoid operators without spotter planes. Book your dive tours and accommodation before departure. Plan a minimum of five day's diving to guarantee many encounters*

Great Barrier Reef

Australia

The Great Barrier Reef, off Australia's northeast coast, is the only living thing that can be seen from space. Much of the 1,430 miles (2,300 km) of reef is protected as the Great Barrier Reef Marine Park. It is the pristine home to an extraordinary diversity of coral, invertebrates, and fish—including sharks and rays.

The problem for the enthusiast who wants to see sharks and rays is the enormous choice of sites here. Many dive boats also visit the oceanic reefs of the Coral Sea, 115 miles (185 km) offshore. Some sites virtually guarantee encounters.

Lady Elliot Island is a small coral cay at the southern end of the Great Barrier Reef. It has one of the few resorts actually out on the reef. A dive at Lady Elliot is wonderfully simple. Divers or snorkelers wade into the water to explore the fringing coral reef surrounding the island. The reef descends into 65 feet (20 m) of water, where you will find zebra sharks—also known as leopard sharks (see p. 126)—usually resting on the sand near large coral heads. Manta rays (see p. 197) can arrive at any time, flying overhead like huge spaceships. The hardest decision for the diver is whether to look up for mantas, down for zebra sharks, or to be distracted by fish, turtles, and coral gardens.

The giant clam (left), with its blue-green mantle, needs strong sunlight to grow. Yellow soft corals (above) put on a show for divers.

Another extraordinary site—for scuba divers only—is Scuba Zoo at Flinders Reef, out in the Coral Sea. A giant shark cage has been permanently stationed here at a depth of 65 feet (20 m). As soon as the dive boat moors, up to 40 reef sharks appear, cruising the deep reef slope beyond the cage. Divers can feel very vulnerable as they swim down through open water to the cage, but the sharks keep their distance, moving about on the bottom like gray shadows. They are mostly gray reef sharks (see p. 146), with some whitetip reef sharks (see p. 162) and silvertip sharks (see p. 145).

Once everyone is inside the cage, a divemaster hauls down a container of fish. When the

Looking down over Lady Musgrave Island (above), in the Bunker Group. Gray reef sharks (left).

lid of the container is pulled off and the food is released, dozens of sharks descend on the bait, tearing it apart in a feeding frenzy. They are so close to the cage, you can hear their teeth crunching on bone. Within minutes, the baits are entirely consumed and it is all over. The sharks continue to dash about, excited by the odor of blood and the tiny pieces of fish meat floating in the current. Divers remain in the cage until the current has dispersed all food remnants and the sharks have resumed their normal, relaxed behavior. Only then is it safe to leave the cage and move among the sharks, taking photos in less restricted circumstances.

If your air supply is low because of all the excitement, you can head back to the boat. The sharks will patrol the area and make close passes to inspect divers before dispersing into the deep blue void again.

Equipment

A one-piece, 2–3 mm wetsuit will suffice in the warmer waters of northern Queensland. A 5 mm suit is recommended for southern Queensland. Bring your own equipment if you are planning a live-aboard excursion, as equipment is generally not available for hire on board.

Special Features

The incredible diversity of marine life and the grandeur of the reef are impossible to ignore. Some unique creatures include sea snakes, stonefish, giant clams, and spider shells. During the Australian spring, turtles come ashore to lay eggs, and the mass, synchronized coral-spawning of the Great Barrier Reef occurs for several nights after the October and November full moons. At the Cod Hole off Lizard Island, up to 20 giant potato cod regularly interact with divers. KD

TRAVELER'S NOTES

When to visit *Good conditions almost year-round; occasional strong winds; cyclone season late Dec–Apr*

Weather *Warm to very hot, tropical conditions; consistently dry, except during the cyclone, or wet, season*

Water temperature *72° F (22° C) in southern Queensland to 82° F (28° C) in northern Queensland; cooler June–Aug*

Hazards *Venomous animals include the lionfish, stonefish, sea snakes, box jellyfish (or sea wasp), cone shell, and blue-ring octopus. None is aggressive and accidents are rare, but learn to identify these species and their behavior*

Dive logistics *Day boats (be prepared for long trips to get out to the reef); live-aboards, trips of 4–8 nights, mostly from Cairns and Townsville, pre-booking recommended*

Accommodation *From camping to five-star resorts ashore or on coastal islands; also on several islands out on the reef; pre-booking recommended*

Notes *Shark feeding not permitted inside the Marine Park*

New South Wales

Australia

The coast of New South Wales, on the eastern seaboard of Australia, is dotted with towns and cities, lined by sandstone cliffs and beaches, and edged by the temperate waters of the Tasman Sea. Here, there are underwater worlds to explore with a diverse range of sharks and rays.

Jervis Bay (above), on the east coast of Australia. The restless sand tiger shark (left), which feeds only at night.

Seal Rocks

Just over 185 miles (300 km) north of Sydney, Seal Rocks is renowned for its large schools of resident sand tiger sharks (see p. 128), also known as gray nurse or spotted raggedtooth sharks. They congregate in packs of 5 to 20, and occasionally even 40, around the spectacular underwater rock formations, in the large reef gutters and sea caves.

Sand tiger sharks have a fearsome appearance, with their long, hooked teeth perpetually protruding from their mouths. However, these are gentle, fish-eating animals that will not attack. They generally have no fear of small groups of divers, and scuba divers can swim safely among them, observing their characteristic circling pattern and photographing them at very close range. Sometimes, they make a sudden, determined approach and the diver has to get out of the way fast. It is quite a thrill to lie on the sea floor and watch that mouth and those teeth pass only a few feet above your head. A careful search in the gutters on the sea floor will often reveal sand tiger shark teeth, shed during mating or feeding.

Day trips from Forster are offered year-round by several dive operators. Although larger congregations occur between November and July, there are always sand tiger sharks to be seen.

Jervis Bay

Jervis Bay, a sheltered bay about 115 miles (180 km) south of Sydney, features a rugged sandstone coastline, pure white beaches, and protected coves. Each year during August and September, thousands of Port Jackson sharks (see p. 119) converge on this area to mate and lay their bizarre, spiral-shaped egg cases. Divers

Swimming in the midst of a mating group of Port Jackson sharks (above); and the extraordinary spiral egg case (left) of the Port Jackson shark.

exploring the bay from boats will come across large groups of exhausted females lying about in gutters, caves, and hollows on the reef. Single males patrol the reef, probably looking for receptive females.

During November and December, most of the adult sharks disperse. But a careful search of the bay's sand flats will reveal newly hatched Port Jackson sharks, each a perfect replica of its parents, except for its fins, which seem too large for its tiny body.

These sand flats are covered with many species of algae, sponges, invertebrates, and sea pens—an ideal habitat for angelsharks, eastern fiddler rays, and shorttailed electric rays (see p. 184). Electric rays can give an unwary diver a severe shock if they are touched or harassed.

Jervis Bay also has huge sea caves and giant boulder reefs covered in vividly colored sponge gardens. Spotted and ornate wobbegongs—most unusual sharks with beautifully decorated skin (see p. 123)—lie perfectly camouflaged among the sponges, waiting for passing prey. Divers have occasionally been bitten simply because they disturbed a wobbegong they had not seen.

Equipment

Use snorkeling equipment in the shallow coves and foreshores of Jervis Bay to see mating Port Jacksons and also skates, but scuba diving is recommended at all other sites. In summer, wear a one-piece 5 mm wetsuit; in winter, use a two-piece 5 mm wetsuit.

Special Features

Around Jervis Bay lives the biggest member of the cuttlefish family, the giant Australian cuttlefish. More than 3⅓ feet (1 m) long, its colors change with its emotions. It will try to bluff by raising its large tentacles if you seem to be a competitor for its territory, but as long as you only observe, encounters are usually spectacular stand-offs. Also look out for the weedy sea dragon, with its delicate coloring. KD

TRAVELER'S NOTES

When to visit *Year-round*
Weather *Warm Oct–Mar, cool Apr–Sept; no distinct rainy season; unpredictable*
Water temperature *57–70° F (14–21° C)*
Hazards *Rough seas during periods of strong offshore winds*
Dive logistics *Forster: day boats only; Jervis Bay: live-aboards or day boats, both offering equally good access*
Accommodation *Good-quality hotels, guesthouses, camping, and caravan sites at all locations*
Notes *An excellent region for self-driving, camping, and exploring a diverse range of dive locations and sighting the plentiful marine species*

Lord Howe Island

Australia

The flamboyant Spanish dancer (left), a nudibranch, or sea slug. The view of Lord Howe Island (below) from Mount Eliza.

Tiny Lord Howe Island stands alone in the Tasman Sea, about 745 miles (1,200 km) north-east of Sydney, Australia. It is an extinct volcano, its peaks rising sheer from sapphire-blue subtropical waters that support coral reefs. These corals have formed a beautiful shallow lagoon, home to giant black stingrays and Galapagos sharks (see p. 149), as well as many indigenous species of fish.

At Comet's Hole, groups of giant black stingrays rest, camouflaged in the sand. When they move, it is an extraordinary sight. They rise languidly off the sea floor, creating a cloud with the sand that was covering them. It streams off their bodies and trails in their wake. Divers and snorkelers can move among the resting rays or follow those that are swimming. Sometimes, you will see a ray pause close to the bottom and use a flapping motion to disturb the sand and uncover prey, which it blankets with its wide body so the prey cannot escape. It then maneuvers itself until its mouth has located the prey.

If you get too close to a ray, it will raise its thick tail high above its back like a lance and make aggressive stabbing movements into the water column. There is no doubt as to the outcome should you venture any closer.

Young Galapagos sharks enter the lagoon with the rising tide and leave before it falls. The best place to see them is at Erscott's Hole. Because this area is also full of beautiful fish and coral, divers may be concentrating on something else when the sharks first appear. They are fast, frisky, and a little wary, and usually circle on the edge of visibility before dashing in to take a close look at you. A small, sleek shark speeding toward you is bound to get the adrenalin going, but they are simply curious.

A Galapagos shark (above) circles inside the coral lagoon. The rare Lord Howe Island woodhen (left); and a giant black stingray (far left).

Occasionally, divemasters add a little bait to the water to encourage the sharks to come closer, and up to a dozen usually appear. They will continually come up to investigate divers—several sharks approaching at once can be very exciting. If one gets too insistent, a light tap on the nose will result in its rapid departure, leaving you in awe of its speed and streamlined design.

The lagoon is an excellent site for snorkelers and scuba-diving beginners. Even non-divers can view this pristine world from the glass-bottom boats that make daily excursions into the lagoon. Scuba divers can use a fast day boat for single dives in the lagoon or for offshore dives on the reefs surrounding the island.

Equipment

Basic snorkeling equipment will suffice and is available for hire, as is scuba equipment. Scuba divers should use a ⅛ inch (3 mm) or 3⁄16 inch (5 mm) wetsuit. Be sure to bring a compact waterproof dive light for night dives.

Special Features

Lord Howe Island is a World Heritage Area. Its isolation and its position at the crossroads of the Tasman and Coral Seas have encouraged the development of many unique and endemic species of animal, bird, and marine life. It is an important bird sanctuary, providing a haven for many nesting seabirds, as well as the Lord Howe Island woodhen, one of the world's rarest birds. This flightless creature was almost extinct, but a rescue breeding program has seen its numbers increase gradually.

Divers and snorkelers should also seek out some of the unique fish species, including the doubleheaded wrasse, the wide-band anemonefish, and the Spanish dancer, a red and white nudibranch that resembles the ruffles on a flamenco dancer's dress. KD

TRAVELER'S NOTES

When to visit *Nov–May*
Weather *Cool, tropical summer, Oct–May; occasional unpredictable strong winds and regular rainfall; no distinct wet season*
Water temperature *68–75° F (20–24° C)*
Hazards *The banded scalyfin, a very aggressive small fish, has a bite that can draw blood; swim away from its territory*
Dive logistics *Glass-bottom boats and day boats for snorkeling or scuba diving; pre-book during peak season, Dec–Jan*
Accommodation *Small resorts and guesthouses, fully catered or self-catering; pre-book Dec–Jan*
Notes *Only 400 tourists are allowed on the island at one time. Pack a waterproof coat for rainy spells and a warm jacket for cool evenings*

WHALES, DOLPHINS, *and* PORPOISES

The sea never changes and its works,
for all the talk of men, are wrapped in mystery.

Typhoon,
JOSEPH CONRAD (1857–1924), Polish-born English essayist

We need another and a wiser and perhaps a more mystical concept of animals.

The Outermost House,
HENRY BESTON (1888–1968), American writer

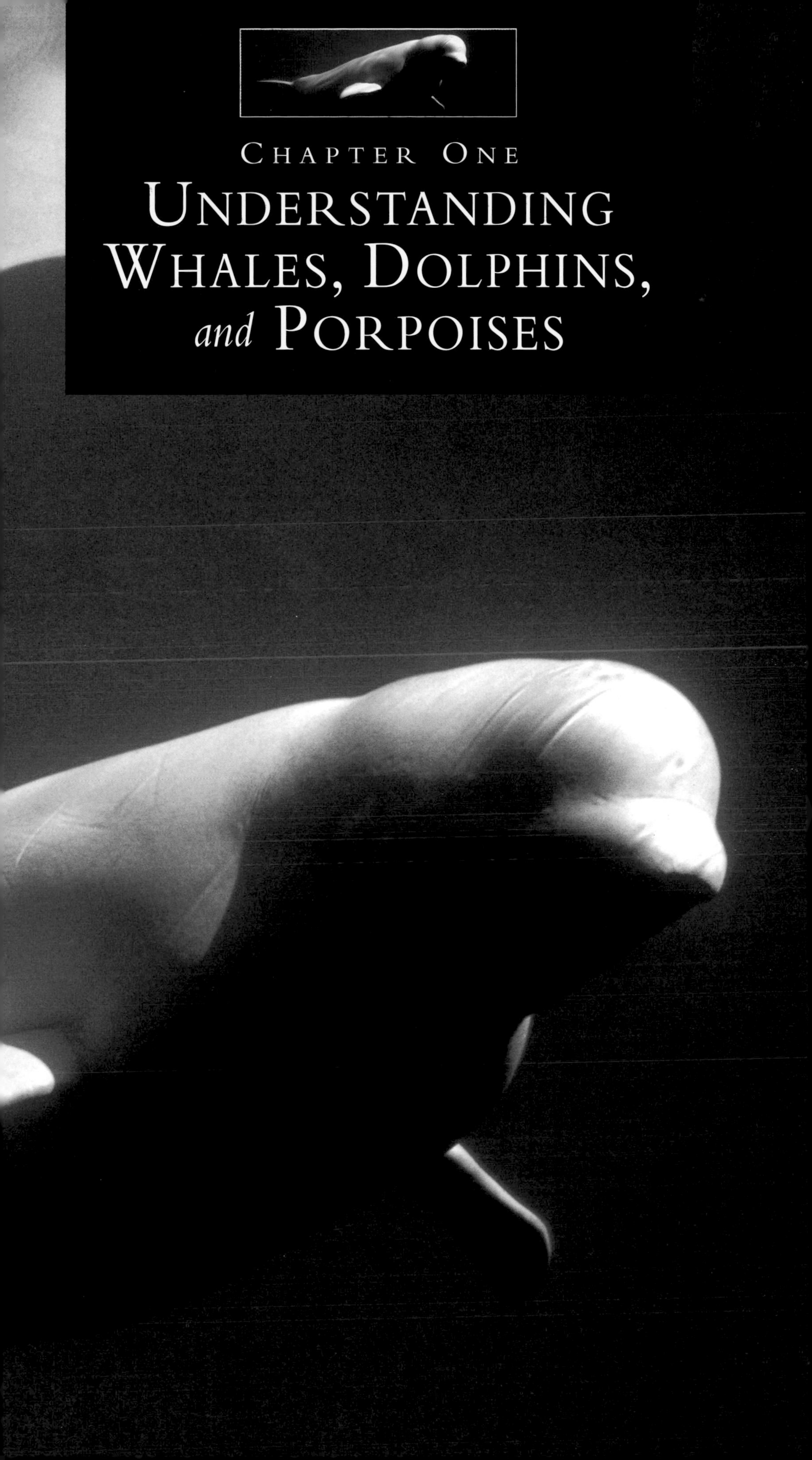

Chapter One
Understanding Whales, Dolphins, *and* Porpoises

The World *of* Whales, Dolphins, *and* Porpoises

Whales, dolphins, and porpoises belong to a single group of marine mammals known as the cetaceans.

A total of 81 different species are currently recognized by whale experts although, as research progresses, new ones are still being discovered. A strange skull, for example, was found in the Juan Fernández Islands, off the coast of Chile, in June 1986. After nearly a decade of painstaking examination and scientific discussion, a team of whale experts finally concluded that this discovery was new to science. It was named Bahamonde's beaked whale in 1996, making it the most recent cetacean species to be formally recognized. Although believed to be a living species, no live representatives of this whale have yet been seen.

Meanwhile, a number of other cetacean species have been split in recent years. In 1995, for example, the common dolphin was officially separated into two distinct species, now known as the long-beaked common dolphin and the short-beaked common dolphin.

Infinite Variety

Inevitably, whales, dolphins, and porpoises share many features in common. Yet they also come in an impressive variety of shapes, sizes, and colors; live in many different marine and freshwater habitats; and have developed a bewildering variety of adaptations for survival in their underwater world.

Some live in shallow water close to shore, or in major rivers and estuaries, while others live so far out to sea that they probably never set eyes on land from the day they are born until the day they die. Some are fairly common and widespread, while others are on the verge of extinction.

They range in size from several small dolphins and porpoises, as little as 4 feet (1.2 m) in length, to the enormous blue whale, which can grow to more than 98 feet (30 m) in length, almost as long as a Boeing 737. Some species are brightly colored, with a motley collection of spots and stripes, several have striking black-and-white markings, while others are a relatively drab brown or gray. Some are long and slender, others short and robust. Some have tall, scythe-shaped dorsal fins; other species have much smaller, triangular fins; and several have no fins at all. There are even variations among individuals of the same species: between males and females, youngsters and adults, and among populations in different parts of the world.

Special Appeal

There is something special and particularly appealing about cetaceans. This is difficult to put into words, and impossible to prove, yet it is a feeling shared by a great many people.

PHYSICAL VARIATION *The short-beaked common dolphin (top). Atlantic spotted dolphins (right). At the far right, is the curved fin (top) of a short-finned pilot whale, and the small dorsal fin (bottom) of a humpback whale.*

CHAMPIONS *Sperm whales, such as the one shown above, have made the longest and deepest dives ever recorded.*

Some claim it is because of their apparent intelligence; others are in awe that air-breathing mammals, like us, are able to thrive in such an alien underwater world. Some people are inspired by their ability to explore places out of our reach, experience things we will never experience, and see things we will never see. Others see them as we would like to see ourselves—free, graceful, compassionate, peaceful, and full of energy.

Undoubtedly, the amazing sense of mystery surrounding these enigmatic creatures is itself a major part of their appeal. We now know that many of our early assumptions about them were wrong or, at least, were not entirely accurate. Yet the more we learn about these incredible creatures, the more intriguing their story becomes.

RECORD BREAKERS

Perfectly adapted to life underwater, whales, dolphins, and porpoises are the record breakers of the animal kingdom. Here are a few examples:

- The blue whale is the largest animal on Earth. The heaviest ever recorded was a female weighing 209 tons (190 tonnes), caught in the Southern Ocean in 1947. The longest was another female, also landed in the Southern Ocean, in 1909, measuring 110 feet 2 inches (33.5 m) from the tip of her snout to the end of her tail.
- The low-frequency pulses made by blue whales and fin whales, when communicating with members of their own species across enormous stretches of ocean, have been measured at up to 188 decibels—the loudest sounds emitted by any living source.
- The longest and most complex songs in the animal kingdom are sung by male humpback whales. Each song can last for half an hour or more and consists of several main components.
- The humpback whale also undertakes the longest documented migration of any individual mammal (a record previously believed to be held by the gray whale). One humpback, for example, was observed at its feeding grounds near the Antarctic Peninsula and, less than five months later, was seen again at its breeding grounds off the coast of Colombia. The shortest swimming distance between these two locations is 5,176 miles (8,334 km).
- The sperm whale is believed to dive deeper than any other mammal. The deepest known dive was 6,560 feet (2,000 m), recorded in 1991. It was made by a male sperm whale diving off the coast of Dominica, in the Caribbean. Indirect evidence suggests that sperm whales may be able to dive to depths of at least 10,000 feet (3,000 m). The record for the longest dive by any mammal is also held by the sperm whale; on 11 November 1983, biologists working in the southwest Caribbean listened to five sperm whales clicking underwater during a dive lasting an astonishing 2 hours 18 minutes.

THE OCEAN REALM

With seas and oceans covering more than two-thirds of its surface, planet Earth might more appropriately be called planet Water.

CHANGING HABITATS *Giant kelp forests (above right) off Catalina Island, California, with a brilliant golden orange fish, a garibaldi, swimming among the tall kelp growth. A humpback in the cold waters of the Antarctic (above left).*

Seas and oceans are often treated as a single entity, like tropical rain forests, deserts, or mountains. But they contain many distinct habitats as different from one another as grassland is from woodland. These include rocky or sandy coastlines, estuaries, mud flats, mangrove swamps, coral reefs, salt marshes, kelp forests, open ocean, and ocean depths.

In the scientific world, the marine environment is usually subdivided into four major ecological zones. First is the intertidal or littoral zone, which is underwater at high tide and exposed to the air at low tide. Sandy beaches, salt marshes, mud flats, and mangrove swamps are all intertidal habitats; they are rarely used by cetaceans themselves, but are critically important as the breeding grounds of fish and other prey species.

Next is the continental shelf or sublittoral zone, the shallow area of sea closest to a continent. The continental shelf typically extends seaward to a distance of about 45 miles (70 km), but tends to be wider off low-lying regions and narrower off mountainous regions. It dips gently from the shoreline to an average depth of about 650 feet (200 m) and is a rich source of food for cetaceans and other predators, especially in temperate zones.

The continental slope, or bathyal zone, comes next. This dips much more steeply from the edge of the continental shelf to the ocean bottom. It typically ends at a depth of about 3,500 feet (1,100 m) or more.

The ocean bottom itself, or abyssal plain as it is often known, is the fourth zone. It is extremely flat—more so than almost anywhere else on Earth—and occupies more than 40 percent of the oceanic area. Its depth is highly variable from region to region, but averages about 13,000 feet (4,000 m). Few animals live in its inhospitable, cold, dark waters. In some parts of the world, the abyssal plain is punctuated by ocean trenches and troughs that reach phenomenal depths. The deepest point is the Marianas Trench in the western Pacific, which drops to at least 35,800 feet (11,000 m).

DEPTH CHANGES

Even within these major ecological zones, there are different habitats at different depths. For example, the deeper you move down the water column, the darker it gets: the different colors of sunlight disappear, one by one, as depth increases (red is absorbed first, followed by orange, then yellow, green, and, ultimately, blue). As well as affecting visibility, this also influences the distribution of animal life in the water column. Where there is light, there are minute plants to sustain minute animals, which, in turn, are preyed on by larger animals.

Meanwhile, deeper water also means greater pressure: for every 33 feet (10 m) you descend, pressure increases by about 1 atmosphere. This means that a sperm whale diving to a depth of, say, 6,500 feet (2,000 m) has to be able to withstand pressures of as much as 200 atmospheres.

THE WARM, SHALLOW WATERS *of the Atlantic, in the Bahamas, are perfect for Atlantic spotted dolphins (above).*

Water temperature is also affected by depth and has a major impact on many biological, chemical, and physical processes in the sea. Oceans tend to have different layers of temperature, though the precise structure varies seasonally and from region to region; the temperature change from one layer to another frequently acts as a substantial barrier to different marine creatures. There is also great variation in the surface temperature of the sea in various parts of the world. It is highest at the equator, where it can sometimes reach 105 degrees Fahrenheit (40° C) in shallow tropical lagoons, and lowest in the high polar regions, where it can fall as low as 28 degrees Fahrenheit (–1.9° C).

Cetacean Habitats

Unfortunately, we know very little about the specific habitat requirements of most whales, dolphins, and porpoises. It is clear that each species, or population, tends to choose waters of a particular depth and temperature range but, within these requirements, many other factors have to be taken into consideration.

Their distribution is often affected by the pattern of major ocean currents. The Earth's rotation causes surface currents to flow clockwise in the Northern Hemisphere, which results in warm tropical waters moving farther north along the east coasts of continental land masses. So the distribution of warm-water species frequently extends farther north than might otherwise be expected. In the Southern Hemisphere, surface currents move anticlockwise, so cold polar waters move farther north along the west coasts of continental land masses. As a result, cold-water species frequently range surprisingly close to the equator.

Distribution is also affected by a process known as upwelling. Areas of upwelling are caused by a combination of seabed geography, winds, and currents, which bring cold, nutrient-rich water from the ocean depths up to the surface. Food is particularly abundant in these areas, which, inevitably, tend to attract large numbers of cetaceans and other top predators.

AWAY FROM THE OCEAN

The marine environment is not the only one inhabited by cetaceans. Four river dolphins, for example, live in some of the largest, muddiest rivers in Asia and South America. The Amazon River dolphin, in particular, can be found more than 2,000 miles (3,200 km) inland in some areas.

Several other cetaceans regularly inhabit fresh water. Some travel freely between river and sea but often there are separate riverine populations that seem to spend all their lives in fresh water; for example, finless porpoises (below) in the Yangtze River, China; tucuxis in the Amazon and Orinoco rivers, South America; and Irrawaddy dolphins in several major river systems of the Indo-Pacific.

Is It a Whale? a Dolphin? or a Porpoise?

The common names used for animals can be confusing at the best of times, but whales, dolphins, and porpoises are in a league of their own.

The words "whale," "dolphin," and "porpoise" are misleading. They have no real scientific basis and are the cause of much confusion. In theory, whales are the largest of the cetaceans, dolphins are of medium size, and porpoises are the smallest. But this does not always work: some whales are smaller than the largest dolphins, and some dolphins are smaller than the largest porpoises.

The situation is even more complex in North America, where small cetaceans of all kinds are commonly referred to as porpoises.

There are six "whales," in particular, that should really be called "dolphins." Despite their names, the killer whale, short-finned pilot whale, long-finned pilot whale, false killer whale, melon-headed whale, and pygmy killer whale are all members of the dolphin family, Delphinidae. It could be argued that the killer whale would more appropriately be called the killer dolphin (although most experts prefer to call it the orca, since it does not really deserve to be called "killer" at all). To add to the confusion, these six species are often grouped together as the "blackfish," which is particularly strange since not all are black and, of course, none is a fish. Ironically, there is even a "dolphinfish" that is really a white-fleshed saltwater fish.

Other species have equally confusing names, but for different reasons. The two right whale dolphins were named after northern and southern right whales (since all four species have finless backs). Curiously, not all white-beaked dolphins have white beaks. The Irrawaddy dolphin lives in the Brahmaputra, Ganges, Mekong, and Makakam rivers, and in the coastal waters of southeast Asia, as well as in the Irrawaddy River. And Indo-Pacific hump-backed dolphins living east and south of Sumatra, in Indonesia, do not have humps.

VARIATION *The orca (left), or killer whale, seen here displaying its teeth, is not a whale, but a member of the dolphin family. The huge southern right whale (above) is able to filter small food items with its prominent comb-like baleen plates.*

At the same time, many cetaceans are known by umpteen common names in at least as many languages. Thus the long-snouted spinner dolphin, spinner dolphin, long-beaked dolphin, rollover, and longsnout are all the same species. Likewise, the fin whale is also known as the herring whale, the finback, finner, common rorqual, and razorback. Even on the few occasions when everyone agrees on a name, there can be disagreement over the spelling, as in bottlenose, bottlenosed, and bottle-nose dolphin.

Classifying Cetaceans

The solution is to think of modern cetaceans in terms of two distinct groups, instead of three: the toothed whales, or odontocetes, which possess teeth; and the baleen whales,

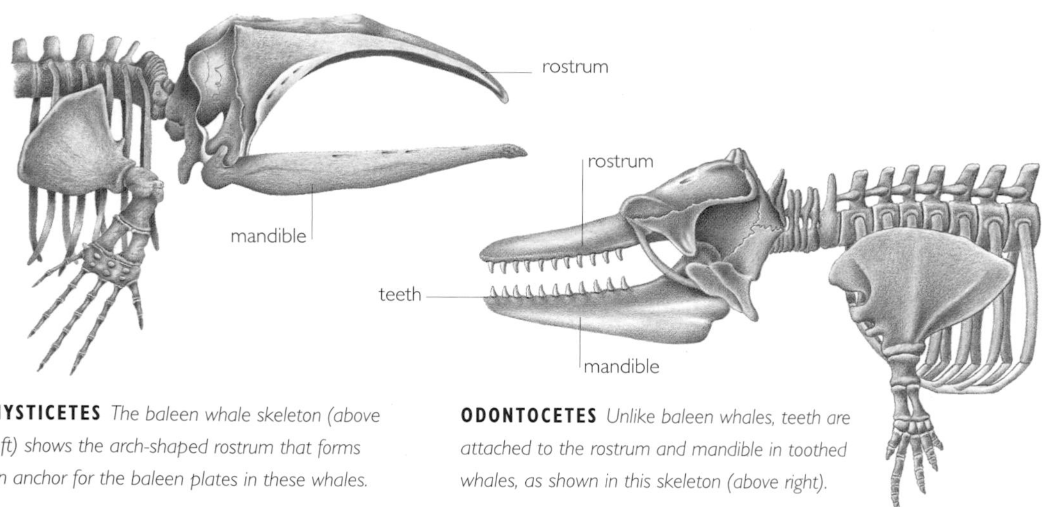

MYSTICETES *The baleen whale skeleton (above left) shows the arch-shaped rostrum that forms an anchor for the baleen plates in these whales.*

ODONTOCETES *Unlike baleen whales, teeth are attached to the rostrum and mandible in toothed whales, as shown in this skeleton (above right).*

or mysticetes, which do not. These groups have a strong scientific basis, and avoid all the confusion normally associated with "whales," "dolphins," and "porpoises."

The vast majority of cetaceans are odontocetes. There are 70 species in all, including all the oceanic dolphins, river dolphins, porpoises, beaked whales, and sperm whales, as well as the narwhal and beluga. The number, size, and shape of their teeth varies enormously. The long-snouted spinner dolphin, for example, has the most teeth, with the exact number varying from 172 to 252. At the other extreme, a number of species have only two teeth and, in many females, even these do not erupt (so they appear to have no teeth at all).

In the main, odontocetes feed on fish and squid, although some also take a variety of crustaceans, and a few take marine mammals.

The mysticetes comprise the remaining 11 species and make up for their lack of numbers by including many of the large and most popular whales, such as the blue, gray, humpback, and bowhead. Instead of teeth, they have hundreds of furry, comb-like baleen plates, often referred to as whalebone, which hang from their upper jaw. These are tightly packed inside the whales' mouth, and have stiff hairs that form a sieve-like structure to filter food out of the sea water. Mysticetes feed mainly on small schooling fish or crustaceans, such as krill and copepods.

There are other, more subtle, differences between odontocetes and mysticetes. Toothed whales, for example, are recognizable by their single blowholes, while baleen whales have two blowholes side by side.

WHALES, DOLPHINS, AND PORPOISES

FAMILY		No. of SPECIES
Baleen whales (Mysticetes)		
Balaenidae	right whales and bowhead whale	3
Neobalaenidae	pygmy right whale	1
Eschrichtiidae	gray whale	1
Balaenopteridae	rorqual whales	6
		Total 11
Toothed whales (Odontocetes)		
Kogiidae	pygmy and dwarf sperm whales	2
Physeteridae	sperm whale	1
Monodontidae	narwhal and beluga	2
Ziphiidae	beaked whales	21
Delphinidae	oceanic dolphins	33
Iniidae	boto (Amazon River dolphin)	1
Pontoporiidae	Yangtze River dolphin and franciscana	2
Platanistidae	Indus and Ganges River dolphins	2
Phocoenidae	porpoises	6
		Total 70

BOTO, OR AMAZON RIVER DOLPHINS, *(above), found only in the Amazon and Orinoco River basins, are toothed whales.*

NAMING WHALES, DOLPHINS, *and* PORPOISES

Naming whales, and working out which ones are closely related, is a challenging but very important branch of whale research.

Mention *Balaenoptera musculus* to most people and the chances are they will have no idea what you are talking about. But the eyes of a group of whale biologists will light up immediately. The reason is simple—*Balaenoptera musculus* is the scientific name for a blue whale.

Admittedly, "blue whale" is the more appealing of the two names. It is certainly the easier one to remember, so it is not surprising that most people use it in preference to *Balaenoptera musculus*. What causes endless problems is that species often have common names in many languages. The blue whale, for example, has several alternative names in English, as well as lots of foreign ones: *shiro nagasu kujira* in Japanese, *blåhval* in Norwegian, *ballena azul* in Spanish, *baleine bleue* in French, and so on. Its scientific name, on the other hand, is used by whale biologists throughout the world, whatever language they speak. Since no species has more than one scientific name, and no two species have exactly the same scientific name, there is no room for confusion. So by using this system, biologists in different parts of the world can always be sure they are talking about exactly the same kind of whale.

The scientific name is Latinized and is written in italics or underlined. It normally consists of two different words: the first begins with a capital letter and identifies the genus, while the second begins with a lower-case letter and identifies the species. There might also be a third word to identify the subspecies (if there is one).

THE PRINCIPLES OF TAXONOMY

Another reason for assigning a unique scientific name to each species is to place it within a structure of relationships in the animal kingdom. Biologists classify all living things by arranging them in groups, according to their similarities and differences. This very specialized science is known as taxonomy.

It is rather like working out an enormously complex family tree. The basic unit is the species, which is defined as a population of animals whose members do not freely interbreed with members of other populations. A genus is simply a group of closely related species. In the same way, a group of closely related genera (plural of "genus") forms a family; then closely related families are grouped into orders, closely related orders into classes, and so on.

This is the theory of classification, and it works

BRINGING ORDER *Swedish naturalist Carolus Linnaeus (left) evolved the system of classification still used today. A southern right whale (above left).*

CLASSIFYING THE MINKE WHALE AND HUMPBACK WHALE

Minke and humpback whales are classified in the following way:

	Minke	Humpback
Kingdom	Animalia (animals)	Animalia (animals)
Phylum	Chordata (chordates)	Chordata (chordates)
Subphylum	Vertebrata (vertebrates)	Vertebrata (vertebrates)
Class	Mammalia (mammals)	Mammalia (mammals)
Order	Cetacea (cetaceans)	Cetacea (cetaceans)
Suborder	Mysticeti (baleen whales)	Mysticeti (baleen whales)
Family	Balaenopteridae (rorquals)	Balaenopteridae (rorquals)
Genus	*Balaeonoptera*	*Megaptera*
Species	*acutorostrata*	*novaeangliae*

THE SCIENTIFIC NAME Balaenoptera musculus *immediately identifies the blue whale (above) as a filter feeder.*

very well—most of the time. In practice, though, scientific names and groupings sometimes have to be changed as new information comes to light, or when biologists disagree over the details of a particular grouping. It is also necessary, in some cases, to add extra groupings (subspecies, subfamilies, and suborders) to deal with more complex relationships within the system.

Classifying Cetaceans

Taxonomy's real challenge is in establishing which animals are most closely related. All of the whales, dolphins, and porpoises are related to some extent, but clever detective work is needed to determine the different levels of these particular relationships.

Early taxonomists classified cetaceans almost entirely on their external appearance, but this was never a satisfactory system. At its crudest, it was tantamount to assuming that all men with gray beards and bald heads must be related. It sometimes resulted in unrelated species being linked, and closely related species being kept apart.

These days, classification of cetaceans is highly sophisticated. Taxonomists gather information from many disciplines, including physiology, behavioral biology, ecology, paleontology, and even biochemistry.

DNA Classification

Recent work in the field of biochemical research, especially on the analysis of DNA (deoxyribonucleic acid), has had a particularly dramatic impact on the classification of the animal kingdom. In essence, it enables scientists to measure the level of relationships among species in an extraordinarily precise way.

DNA is the basic genetic material found in all animals. It is a kind of instruction manual for the design and assembly of the body's proteins. Every cell in an animal's body contains an exact replica of this manual and almost all the "pages" go to making it what it is—a human, a dog, a humpback whale, a long-snouted spinner dolphin, and so on. The small number of "pages" that are left help to distinguish one individual from another—just as one person's fingerprints are different from everyone else's, no two animals have exactly the same DNA.

Making sense of all the similarities and differences in DNA is a highly complex process, but it has already resolved a number of long-standing uncertainties in the classification of whales, dolphins, and porpoises and other wildlife.

FEATURES *The humpback whale (left) breaches more frequently than other baleen whales. The minke whale (below) takes its species name,* acutorostrata, *from its slim, pointed head.*

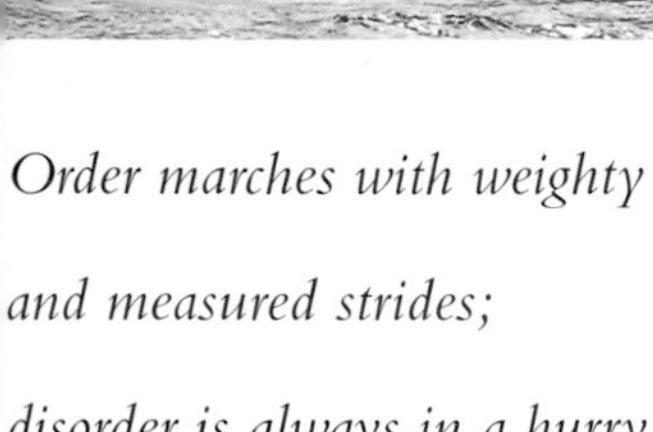

Order marches with weighty

and measured strides;

disorder is always in a hurry.

Maxims,
NAPOLEON BONAPARTE
(1769–1821), Emperor of France

How Little We Know

The lives of most whales, dolphins, and porpoises are still shrouded in mystery.

Despite a flow of new information, we know surprisingly little about the majority of cetacean species and our knowledge of the others is frustratingly patchy. We have learned enough to start asking the right questions, yet the deeper we delve, the more we realize there is still to learn.

The problem is that these are among the most difficult animals in the world to study. They often live in remote areas far out to sea, spending most of their lives underwater, and showing little when they rise to the surface to breathe. No wonder, as one researcher commented at a recent conference, that our knowledge of many species has only progressed from almost nothing to just a little.

STRANDING *of long-finned pilot whales provides an opportunity for a post-mortem (right). A baby dolphin is examined in the laboratory (below).*

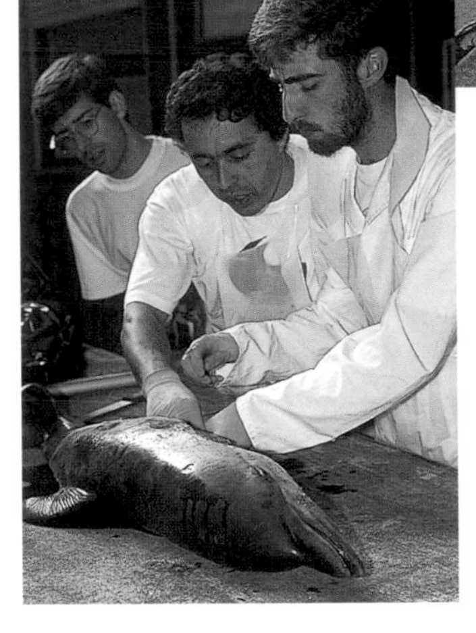

Dead Animals

In the early days of cetacean research, the little information we had came mainly from dead animals washed ashore or killed by whalers and fishers. Even today, professional post-mortems can teach us a great deal about poorly known species, such as beaked whales. A single cetacean carcass can provide an amazing amount of data that, when combined with other data, becomes invaluable.

The precise details of a post-mortem depend largely on the aims and objectives of the study, and the information required. Typically, it consists of three distinct stages, often carried out by different people with a diverse range of skills. The first stage takes place on site (if the animal cannot be easily transported) or in a laboratory, and involves a general overview: everything from taking external body measurements and noting its general physical condition to identifying its sex and checking its reproductive status.

The second stage, normally in a laboratory, involves a much more detailed analysis: estimating the age of the animal, checking key body tissues for pollutants, identifying its stomach contents, examining genetic material, and much more. The final stage can often be the most time-consuming, and usually takes place in an office in front of a computer screen. This is the analysis of all the results. What do they mean? How do they compare with findings of similar studies? Are they statistically significant? What further research needs to be done? These and other questions have to be answered before, finally, the work can be written up and published in a scientific journal.

Captive Animals

In the mid-1800s, another source of information became available. Since then, biologists have been able to study captive animals—usually dolphins and other small species that can be confined in a concrete tank—with varying results.

On moral grounds, many people would argue against keeping cetaceans in captivity for research purposes (or for any other reason). But there are also concerns about the research itself. Inevitably, an animal in captivity will behave abnormally—at least part of the time—and this can give a thoroughly distorted picture of its behavior under natural conditions. Even if it is in a large enclosure, it will be unable to carry out all the normal activities of its wild relatives. At the very least, conclusions drawn from research on captive animals have to be treated with caution. Many studies can be carried out satisfactorily only under natural conditions.

But there are advantages in studying cetaceans under controlled conditions. They can be observed at close range for 24 hours a day. Knowing their age, sex, reproductive status, and level of dominance is another major benefit enabling researchers to study their biology and behavior in the most minute detail. It is also useful to be able to undertake specific scientific experiments, under tightly controlled conditions, on everything from sleep requirements to the physiology of diving.

Going Out to Sea

A great deal of information can be obtained only by studying the animals, wild and

> *Knowledge is the true organ of sight, not the eyes.*
>
> *Panchatantra,*
> ANON (c. fifth century),
> (trans. by FRANKLIN EDGERTON)

free, in their natural environment. Few people took up this enormous challenge until the late 1960s and early 1970s, and it is only in the past decade or so that research into wild cetaceans really developed into the sophisticated and popular branch of natural science we know today.

Early pioneers focused mainly on counting whales, dolphins, and porpoises at sea. Observers were posted at lookouts on land, in boats, or in light aircraft, and used relatively simple methods to calculate population and group sizes. These days, there is still no perfect way to count cetaceans, but the techniques are being refined all the time and modern surveys take into account everything from the number of animals likely to have been missed along a cruise track to varying sea and weather conditions. At the same time, research has gone well beyond mere population estimates to social and behavioral studies, combined with careful note-keeping, resulting in many exciting discoveries in recent years.

Patience

Despite the difficulties, it is an exciting time to be involved in wild whale, dolphin, and porpoise research. We are just beginning to understand the intricacies of their natural behavior, diving capabilities, social organization, feeding techniques, and many other aspects of their daily lives. In fact, in recent years, growth in our knowledge has been nothing short of remarkable.

The main requirement for any study of them is patience. It can take many years to collate all the tiny snippets of information necessary to assemble a single coherent picture. It is something like putting together an enormously complicated jigsaw puzzle, one piece at a time, in which every individual piece raises new questions. The main difference, of course, is that the complex cetacean puzzle will never be completely finished.

GATHERING DATA *A captive bottlenose dolphin (above) is studied by biologists. Feces collected in the Sea of Cortez (right) will be examined later in a laboratory to reveal what blue whales are eating.*

Accuse not Nature; she hath done her part;

Do thou but thine.

Paradise Lost,
JOHN MILTON (1608–74), English poet

CHAPTER TWO

SAVE *the* WHALES

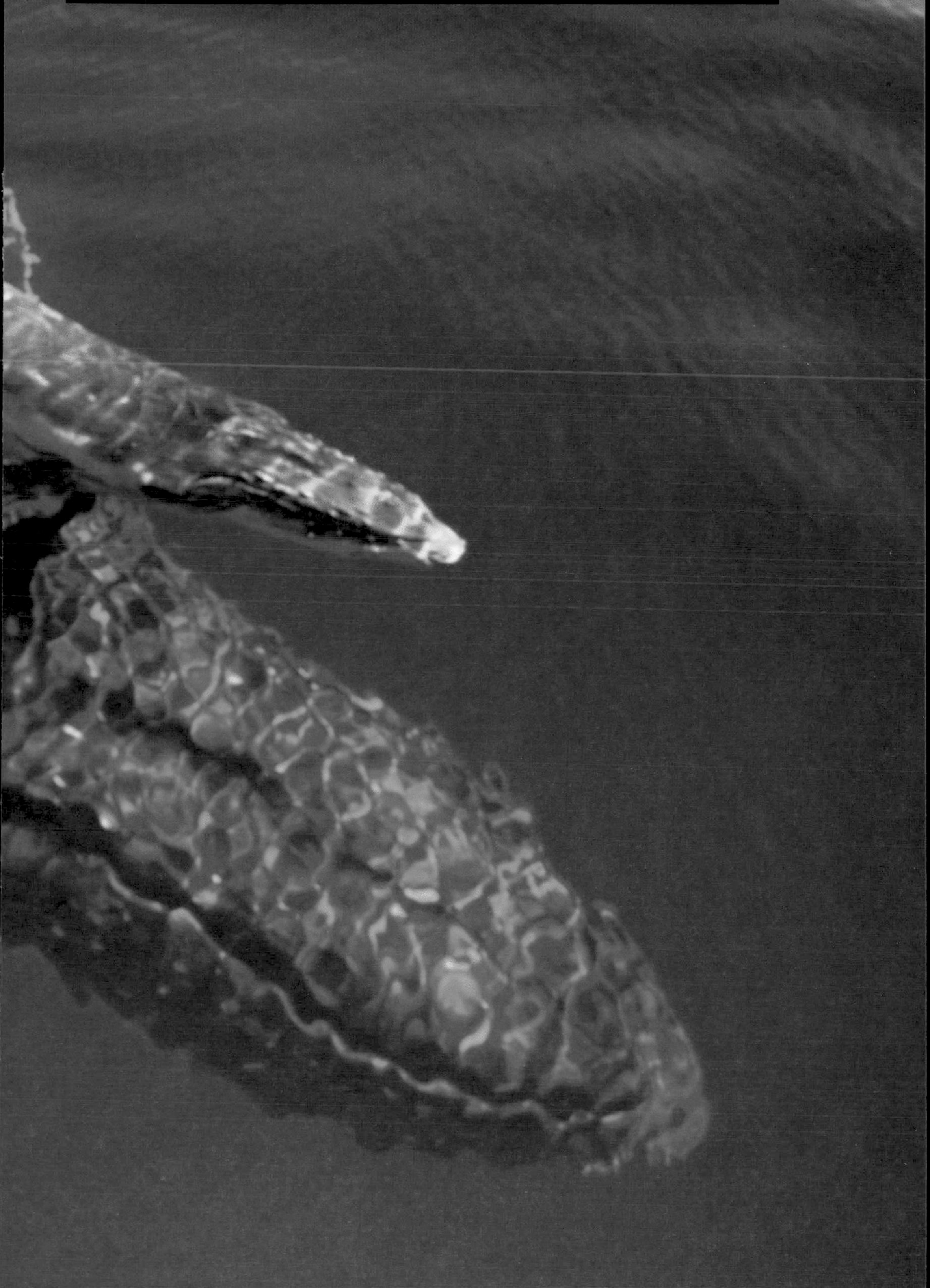

THE HEYDAY *of* WHALING

Since its early beginnings nearly 1,000 years ago, commercial whaling has had a long and checkered history.

MORE RECENT TIMES *Several whales are being weighed (above) at a railway station in Durban, South Africa in 1939.*

Its origins are unrecorded, but the first large-scale commercial whaling was probably by Basques from the coasts of France and Spain. By 1200, they were hunting right whales in the Bay of Biscay, and had found a market for nearly every part of the whale carcass—even the excrement was used as a red fabric dye.

By the beginning of the seventeenth century, Britain, Holland, and other nations had realized whaling's potential and were busy competing for control of the richest grounds. The American whaling industry began soon after, in the 1640s, when early colonists first ventured from the green shores of New England to hunt right whales.

In many ways, the next 200 years were like the gold rushes that later swept across western North America. Like prospectors searching for big strikes, whalers moved relentlessly from one hunting ground to another, killing all the animals in one place, then moving on to the next. Whaling rapidly developed into a major industry and, on the way, exposed new worlds to the mixed blessing of Western civilization.

THE AMERICAN WHALER

Everyone involved in a whaling expedition was taking a risk. Ship owners gambled many thousands of dollars to outfit their vessels. While some ships came back with their holds full again and again—making their owners exceedingly rich—others left on their maiden voyages and vanished without trace—causing the owners to lose their investment completely.

Officers and crew, on the other hand, gambled not with money, but with their lives. Many never made it home from their long and hazardous journeys. If they didn't become the victims of violent storms, rogue whales, reefs, accidents, disease, or fighting, they often jumped ship.

An American whaling vessel typically left port with a crew of about 30–35 men. These included the captain, 4 harpooners, 4 mates, a cooper (for making and repairing barrels), a steward, a blacksmith, a cook, a cabin boy, and

WHALING SCENE *A nineteenth-century whaler flying the American flag.*

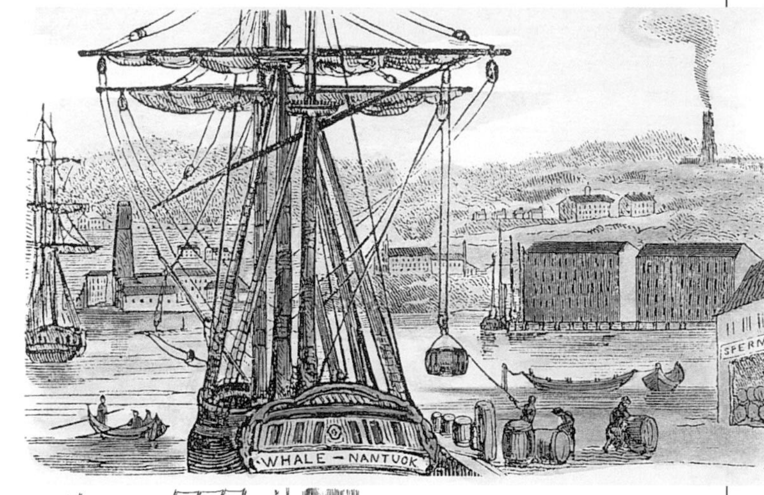

ARTISTS' IMPRESSIONS *An 1852 engraving (right) of a whaling ship at a New England port. An undated print (below) shows a seaman being flogged.*

15–20 ordinary seamen. While the captain and his mates lived in fairly comfortable accommodation toward the stern of the vessel, the ordinary seamen lived together in cramped, dark, filthy conditions near the bow.

Food was a constant source of complaint. Hardly anyone ate whale meat because the taste was considered too strong, but the alternatives were little better. Occasionally, they would be able to trade for fresh meat, fruit, and vegetables, but the basic diet was salted pork or beef, with thick, hard crackers, and coffee or tea. Floating the crackers in a hot drink, until the maggots crawled out and could be skimmed off, was a common practice.

It was also hard for wives and girlfriends left behind. Many whaling voyages lasted for four or five years, and there were no guarantees the men would ever return. Communications were almost non-existent, despite a system of makeshift "post offices" in some parts of the world. In the Pacific, for example, ships heading out to the whaling grounds would leave letters on the Galápagos Islands in a wooden box covered by an enormous tortoise shell, ready to be picked up by other ships heading home. But it was a rather hit-and-miss affair—one woman wrote more than a hundred letters to her husband during his voyage, yet he received only six.

As word filtered out from the ports of New England, home to the American whaling armada, the romance of whaling was soon outweighed by real-life stories of danger, cramped and filthy conditions, tyrannical officers, boredom, and the reality of long absences from home. A popular saying at the time was "One voyage on a whale ship is one too many." One log keeper on the Yankee whale ship *Brewster* commented: "My opinion is that any man who has a log hut on land with a corn cake at the fire and would consent to leave them to come … on a whale voyage is a proper subject for a lunatic asylum."

With so much bad publicity, combined with the rapid expansion of whaling after 1815, New England seaports were soon finding it hard to recruit competent crews. It was even harder by the mid-1800s, when the industry had to compete with the lure of free land and gold in the West. Unscrupulous "shipping agents" were often hired to assemble ordinary seamen—by whatever means necessary. They rounded up naive young men from up and down the eastern seaboard, and across the Midwest, tempting them with false promises of money and adventure. Worse still, it was not an uncommon event for men to wake up after a night on the town with a massive hangover in a rock-hard bunk on their way to whaling grounds hundreds or thousands of miles from home.

In an age before petroleum or plastics, there were huge amounts of money to be made from whaling—but they rarely filtered down to the crew. Everyone received a percentage of the net value of the cargo: the ship's owner received about 66 percent; the captain up to 10 percent; the mates, harpooners, and coopers up to 1 percent each; the ordinary seamen about 0.6 percent; and the cabin boys no more than 0.4 percent. Even then, a variety of "expenses" were deducted from these meager wages and, ultimately, the lowly crew earned considerably less than unskilled workers on shore.

Modern Commercial Whaling

A series of technological advances in whaling vessels, killing equipment, and hunting methods spelled disaster for the world's whales.

Modern commercial whaling really began in the mid-nineteenth century, when the Norwegian whaler Svend Foyn developed an explosive harpoon that could be fired from a bow-mounted cannon. Foyn's invention was the first in a remarkable series of developments that revolutionized the whaling industry over a period of about 60 years, and greatly increased the number of whales being killed.

Other major advances included faster and more maneuverable catcher boats; longer and stronger harpoon lines; better winches to relieve some of the strain as the whales struggled for their lives; machinery for inflating the carcasses with air, to make them float; and enormous factory ships that could process the whales far out to sea. New and improved techniques for processing whale products were also developed and, meanwhile, navigational aids improved, weather forecasting became more accurate, and new technology helped to make whaling much safer.

ABUNDANCE *The aquatint (above) of a painting published in 1825 shows a South Sea whale fishery in the early days.*

SVEND FOYN 1809–94

Norwegian Svend Foyn (left) has been dubbed the inventor of modern whaling. Indirectly, he is probably responsible for the deaths of more whales than anyone else in the business.

Born in 1809, he grew up in a small harbor town called Tønsberg, near the capital, Oslo. From an early age, he was determined to be a seaman, even though his father had died at sea when he was just four years old. He embarked on a career in the coastal freight business, but left that in 1846, and turned his attentions to sealing. Hunting seals around Jan Mayen, a tiny Arctic island between Iceland and Spitzbergen, quickly made him rich. But when the profits began to decline in the early 1860s, he began to look for new challenges.

He had noticed large numbers of whales, mainly fin and blue, on his trips to and from the sealing grounds. Realizing that they had somehow escaped the attentions of whalers, he decided to have a go at hunting them himself. A deeply religious man, he later wrote that "God had let the whale inhabit [these waters] for the benefit and blessing of mankind and, consequently, I considered it my vocation to promote these fisheries."

During the years that followed, Foyn transformed the whaling industry by building the first steam-driven catcher ship and developing an explosive harpoon that could be fired from a fixed cannon.

He was active to the end of his life and died, as an 85-year-old, while sponsoring a whaling expedition to Antarctica.

KEY TECHNOLOGICAL DEVELOPMENTS IN MODERN WHALING

Until just over a century ago, the technique of whaling had barely changed for more than 700 years. Whalers chased their quarry in open rowing boats, and normally killed them with hand-held harpoons, just as the Basques had done when they hunted right whales in the Bay of Biscay during the eleventh century. But in the 1850s, the era of modern commercial whaling began with a vengeance—and the whalers have not looked back since.

1852 The first successful explosive harpoon (above) was invented by an armorer from Connecticut, United States. Known as the bomb-lance, it consisted of an explosive missile armed with a time-delay fuse that killed or mortally wounded the whales—normally at a safe distance from the whalers.

1857 The first auxiliary steam engines were installed in British whaling ships and, in the years that followed, many other whalers installed similar engines in their vessels.

1859 The first purpose-built steam whaling ships were successfully launched. The extra power gave them increased speed and safety, although once on the whaling grounds, the whalers continued to hunt from traditional rowing boats.

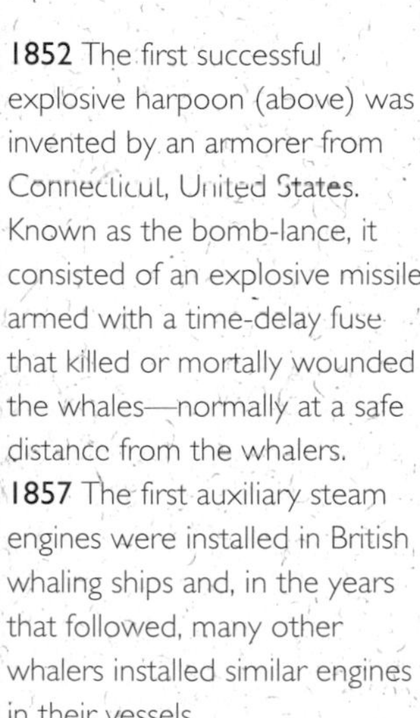

1863 Norwegian sea captain Svend Foyn built a new, 82 foot (25 m) steam-driven schooner called the *Spes et Fides* (meaning "Hope and Faith"). The first of the modern whale catchers, this combined the functions of the open rowing boat and the ship in a single vessel. It was relatively easy to maneuver and yet fast enough to chase the whales by itself. (A similar vessel, from the 1890s, is seen above.) No species of whale, no matter how fast a swimmer, was now safe.

1865 A whaling captain from New Bedford, in the United States, invented the darting gun, a kind of explosive harpoon with the accuracy of a conventional harpoon.

1868 After several seasons of experimentation, Svend Foyn developed an explosive harpoon that could be fired from a cannon mounted on a swivel in the bow of a whaling vessel (shown below, manned by skipper Duncan Greys). The cannon was solidly made to absorb the recoil and so well balanced that it could be aimed with great accuracy. Screwed to the tip of the harpoon was a grenade, consisting of a detonator and a sack of black gunpowder in a steel container equipped with barbs. The barbs were designed to open on impact, ensuring that the harpoon was firmly embedded in the animal's flesh, and the grenade exploded inside its body two or three seconds later. This awful weapon precipitated an enormous increase in whaling worldwide and is still in use today, albeit in modified form.

1925 The growth of the whaling industry was limited by a need to return constantly to shore-based stations to process the whales. The final dramatic development, floating factory ships (such as this one below, whaling in South Georgia), solved this problem. The new ships were designed to accompany fleets of catcher boats far out to sea and, with stern slipways to winch the whales on board, gave a new level of efficiency to the hunt. It was in 1925 that the first factory ship arrived on the Antarctic whaling grounds.

The Aftermath *of* Whaling

In the space of a few hundred years, untold millions of great whales were killed around the world.

The final death toll is shocking: about a million sperm whales, at least half a million fin whales, more than 350,000 blue whales, nearly a quarter of a million humpbacks, and literally hundreds of thousands of others. Two million whales were killed in the Southern Ocean alone. Some years were particularly bad: in the 1930–31 season, 28,325 blue whales were killed; more than 30 years later, in 1963–64, no fewer than 29,255 sperm whales met their death—we still had not learned the lessons of the past. Today, we are left with merely the tattered remnants: in most cases, no more than 5–10 percent of the original great whale populations remain.

By the time the animals were given official protection it was almost too late and, indeed, some species may never recover. The rarest whale in the world, the northern right whale, came so close to extinction that, even after more than 60 years of official protection, its population is represented by only about 300 survivors. Meanwhile, the bowhead whale has all but disappeared from vast areas of its former range.

But there is some good news, as well. Against all the odds, several species appear to be bouncing back. The gray whale (top) is the ultimate success story. The North Atlantic stock was probably wiped out by early whalers, and only a remnant population survives in the western North Pacific. But in the eastern North Pacific, it has made such a dramatic recovery that it is now believed to be at least as abundant as in the days before whaling. Meanwhile, there has been a dramatic increase in blue whale numbers off the coast of California, where about 2,000 animals gather for the summer and autumn (the largest animals on Earth have shown little sign of recovery elsewhere). Humpbacks and southern right whales are also making a comeback in many places.

No Whales: No Whaling

Different whales have been in vogue at different times during the history of commercial whaling. Their popularity depended on the market value of their products, the whaling techniques available at the time, and the availability of the species (which, naturally, declined as whaling intensified).

Right whales were the first targets for commercial whalers and have been hunted for hundreds of years, since the eleventh century. Named for being the "right" whales to hunt, they were easy to approach, swam slowly, lived close to shore, had a tendency to float when dead, and provided large quantities of valuable oil, meat, and baleen. As their numbers declined, and whalers ventured farther

FAST SWIMMER *The blue whale (left) was too difficult to catch until the introduction of explosive harpoons and steam-powered vessels.*

Whom man kills, him

God restoreth to life.

'Fantine," *Les Misérables,*
VICTOR HUGO
1802–85), French novelist

ut to sea, sperm whales and ther species became the new ocus of attention. The swift nd powerful blue whale was afe from whaling until the ate 1800s, when explosive arpoons and steam-driven essels became widely avail- ble, but it soon became the ost sought-after species. hen, as blue whale stocks ere depleted, whalers shifted heir attentions to fin whales. ne by one, the great hales were hunted lmost to the point of xtinction. The minke hale became sought fter only when its arger relatives could o longer support the haling industry; it is ow the only whale eing hunted commer- ially and within the onfines of international law.

YING INDUSTRY

s the number of whales eclined, the whaling industry tself was threatened with xtinction. But it was not ntil the twentieth century hat whalers realized that their wn survival depended on an bundance of available whales. ventually, they joined forces nd adopted the 1931 Con- ention for the Regulation of Whaling, which began, albeit ather inadequately, to regulate he industry. The Interna- ional Whaling Commission IWC) was created in 1946, nd has been responsible for egulating whaling ever since.

WORLDWIDE PROTECTION

The first whale to be given worldwide protection from commercial whaling was the bowhead, in the early 1930s. Most other species have been afforded regional or worldwide protection in the years since. This culminated, in 1986, with a moratorium on commercial whaling which, finally, granted worldwide protection for all the great whales.

Unfortunately, the killing often continued long after official protection was declared (and, in some cases, continues still today) but the following dates still have considerable significance:

1931 Bowhead whale (became US law in 1935)
1935 Northern right whale
Southern right whale
1946 Gray whale (pictured right)
1966 Humpback whale
Blue whale
1979 Sei whale (except in the Denmark Strait west of Iceland)
1984 Sperm whale
1986 IWC moratorium takes effect

PROTECTED *The humpback (left) and southern right whale (below) populations are recovering since the introduction of whaling bans.*

WHALING IS CRUEL

Despite all the advances made in the whaling industry, it is still virtually impossible to kill a whale humanely. It is extremely difficult to hit the vital organs of a moving animal—from a moving vessel—regardless of the accuracy of the harpoon gun.

Most whales are killed within a few minutes—which is bad enough—but some struggle in agony for much longer. In 1993, for example, a minke whale took 55 minutes to die a slow, lingering death at the hands of Norwegian whalers. It is hard to imagine the pain and suffering it experienced after an explosive harpoon had blown a huge, gaping hole in the side of its body. Japanese whalers use electric lances to kill harpooned whales, in a vain attempt to speed up the process. But the electric charge is insufficient to induce death and probably causes even more suffering. Discussions at the 1997 IWC meeting suggest that electric lancing may be phased out.

As one ex-whaler commented: "If whales could scream, whaling would have stopped many years ago."

The International Whaling Commission

Since 1946, government representatives from around the world have met every year, under the auspices of the IWC, to discuss whaling.

Originally, the IWC was established to make possible the orderly development of the whaling industry. It actively encouraged the development of whaling and, as a result, more than two million whales were killed during the organization's first 30 years—despite the advice of scientists on the Scientific Committee.

More recently, the IWC has been working toward better protection of cetaceans But some of its 39 member countries are still strongly pro-whaling. Consequently, IWC debates are frequently passionate and heated, and often involve behind-the-scenes politicking, bribery, and frequent threats.

Whale Peace Treaty

In 1982, there was a major breakthrough when IWC members voted for an indefinite moratorium on commercial whaling. But this world peace treaty for the whales left too many loopholes to work effectively. Since then, an incredible 57,391 whales have been killed, including minke, fin, sei, Bryde's, humpback, gray, sperm, and bowhead whales. Even since 1985–86, when the whaling ban actually came into effect, Japan, Norway, Iceland, Russia, Korea, and indigenous whalers in several other countries, have killed some 21,760 whales between them.

In 1994, members of the IWC approved the Southern Ocean Whale Sanctuary, covering an area of some 20 million square miles (50 million sq km) around Antarctica. The sanctuary was designed to protect a critically important feeding ground for seven species of great whale. But even this is not sacrosanct, since Japan continues to hunt minke whales within the "protected" area.

Two countries, Norway and Japan, continue to hunt whales in blatant defiance of world opinion and the intentions of the IWC. Far from bringing their whaling activities to an end, they are steadily expanding them.

Norway officially objected to the moratorium and so, under IWC rules, is legally entitled to continue hunting whales. In the first 11 years after the ban, its industrial whaling fleet killed 2,011 minke whales. Meanwhile, its annual quota, set by the Norwegian government itself, is steadily increasing; and its whaling fleet of several dozen vessels spreads farther out across the northeast Atlantic.

Initially, Japan took the same course of action, but then withdrew its objection and renamed its whaling "scientific research." This takes advantage of another

COMMERCIAL AND SCIENTIFIC WHALE CATCHES UNDER THE IWC

Country	Region	Species	1994	1995	1996
Norway	Northeast Atlantic	Minke whale	279	217	388
Japan	North Pacific	Minke whale	21	100	77
Japan	Antarctica	Minke whale	330	440	440
Total:			630	757	905

DEAF EARS *The IWC meets (top) in Brighton, Britain, but Norwegian whalers continue to operate in spite of bans. A minke whale (left) is winched aboard.*

'HE GERLACHE STRAIT *(above) is* *›art of the vast Southern Ocean Whale* *anctuary in Antarctica.*

najor loophole: the IWC allows any number of whales o be taken "for purposes of cientific research." A limited mount of research is undertaken, yet no new knowledge s being gained, and the whale carcasses are processed commercially. In the same 11-year period since the noratorium, Japan has killed ›,083 minke, 634 Bryde's, ınd 400 sperm whales.

HISTORY OF ABUSE

Many whaling nations have a checkered history of undernining, ignoring, and abusing he international regulations established to protect whales. For example, in the early 1990s, it was discovered that Russia had been falsifying its whaling data for more than 30 years. As well as killing protected species, it had grossly exceeded its IWC quotas for other species. In April 1996, 6½ tons (6 tonnes) of Norwegian whale meat was confiscated by Japanese customs officials. Disguised n a mackerel shipment, it was the first instalment of a 66-ton (60-tonne) shipment of whale meat due to be smuggled into the country.

The United States and other IWC members have tried to make illegal whaling and smuggling more difficult, but such illegalities show that, where profit can be made, science, conservation, and international law are of small concern to the whaling industry.

THE FUTURE

Recent years have witnessed some dramatic developments at the IWC. At the 1996 meeting, several countries announced their opposition to whaling under any circumstances. This was a controversial position to take—there were fears that it may prompt whaling nations to leave the IWC altogether—yet it reflected a moral view shared by millions of people worldwide.

Then, at the 1997 meeting, Ireland proposed limited commercial whaling in coastal waters, on the understanding that the meat could not be traded internationally and that all other whale hunts should stop. Unfortunately, the proposal was taken seriously and is to be discussed at the next meeting. Only time will tell how the IWC will evolve. But one thing is certain: the whales are not saved yet.

PIRATE WHALING

Untold numbers of whales have been killed every year by so-called pirate whalers, who circumvent international regulations by registering their vessels under the flags of non-IWC members. During the 1970s and early 1980s, the temptation of profits lured companies based in at least 11 countries into the business of pirate whaling. But many of their vessels had rather obscure origins. One active pirate whaling ship, for example, was called the *Sierra* (inset picture) and hunted whales throughout the Atlantic Ocean until it was eventually impounded in South Africa and sunk by saboteurs in 1980. Jointly owned by a Norwegian businessman and a large Japanese fishing company, it was registered in Liechtenstein, flew a Somali flag, and had a South African crew. The Norwegian captain carried Japanese meat inspectors on board. It labeled its illegal catch "Product of Spain" and sold it through the Ivory Coast to Japan.

Even today, pirate whaling still exists. Evidence of one such operation in the mid-Atlantic came to light as recently as the summer of 1997, when sailors on trans-Atlantic yachts approaching the Azores from the west, reported dead and dying whales afloat on the surface or tied to buoys. At least one factory vessel and its catcher boat are believed to have been involved, and evidence suggests that at least some of their victims were endangered sperm whales.

Captive Cetaceans

Is there any justification for taking cetaceans from the wild and keeping them in captivity—or is it done purely for financial gain?

Whales, dolphins, and porpoises are the undisputed stars of aquariums, marine parks, and zoos around the world. Every year, millions of people flock to see them "kissing" their trainers, fetching balls, jumping through hoops, performing somersaults, and making synchronized leaps in special choreographed shows.

Since the first bottlenose dolphins were taken into captivity more than a century ago, at least 25 species have suffered a similar fate. Today, Pacific white-sided dolphins, false killer whales, belugas, orcas, Irrawaddy dolphins, and many others are being held in a collection of netted pools, concrete tanks, and even hotel swimming pools. Although a few of these are bred in captivity, the vast majority are still being taken from the wild. During 1997, for example, a pod of orcas was driven ashore by fishers in Japan; half the struggling animals

were taken for sale to marine parks and aquariums.

It is not surprising that, for years, animal-welfare and conservation groups have been campaigning for a total ban on the capture of wild cetaceans. They would also like to see captive animals being released, where possible.

Cruelty

The people who keep whales, dolphins, and porpoises argue that captivity is a simple trade-off. The animals lose their freedom and natural companions in return for escaping the two biggest problems of life in the wild: going hungry and being eaten. But animal-welfare groups argue that cetaceans are completely unsuited to life in captivity, so keeping them in small tanks and pools is both immoral and cruel.

In the early days, a great many animals died during the first few hours or days after capture, and the remainder rarely survived more than a few months. Even today, when we understand more about their requirements, the transition from life in the wild to confinement can be most traumatic. Unknown number die in the process of transition

Their final destinations include a bewildering range of establishments, from badly run zoos where they are poorly treated, to professional marine parks that provide the best care money can buy. The best establishments have coastal enclosures that are filled naturally with sea water and flushed with every new tide; they are often several acres in size and fairly deep. The animals are kept in carefully structured family groups, fed on varied and healthy diets, and have regular checkups by experienced veterinarians.

Unfortunately, such facilities are in the minority. Most consist of bare and

Fetters of gold are still fetters and even silken cords pinch.

English proverb

"AMBASSADORS?" *The argument is that facilities such as Vancouver Public Aquarium, British Columbia (above), and Sea World, Orlando, Florida (left and below left), provide the only opportunity most people will ever have to experience live cetaceans.*

featureless concrete tanks, with filthy water, and sometimes no natural sunlight. The animals are kept alone, or with unfamiliar company, and have to adapt to an unhealthy diet of dead fish. Sometimes, the captives simply cannot cope. They swim in circles, stop vocalizing, become aggressive or depressed, and may even harm themselves.

EDUCATION

One of the main arguments for keeping cetaceans in captivity is education. The protagonists claim that captive animals act as "ambassadors" for their wild relatives. But animal-welfare groups argue that few captive facilities make use of the great potential for educating and informing the public. If there is any educational element, it merely pays lip service to the concept of an "informative commentary."

Choreographed shows are particularly contentious. Trainers argue that they are educational, and that they keep the animals physically and mentally fit. But animal-welfare groups claim that they are just cheap entertainment for profit—and do little more than perpetuate the domineering and manipulative attitude we have toward nature. Moreover, the animals are often forced to perform—in some cases, they are even starved until they get it right.

At the end of the day, it is not essential to see whales and dolphins in real life to understand and appreciate them. After all, it is possible to learn about the Moon without actually standing on it. So while a live animal is more likely to trigger the emotions than words, photographs, or films, these could all be used as strong "second bests." Meanwhile, there are some exciting possibilities for the future, including computer technology that could simulate virtual-reality encounters with whales and dolphins where they really belong—in the oceans, wild and free.

CAN CAPTIVITY HELP TO PROTECT ENDANGERED SPECIES?

Despite many claims to the contrary, most marine parks and aquariums do nothing to protect endangered whales, dolphins, and porpoises. Simply keeping endangered species in captivity has no practical benefit and is not conservation. In fact, the opposite is usually true, because taking the animals from the wild can be a significant drain on local populations.

One particular species, however, is so rare that its only hope of survival may lie in semi-captivity. The Yangtze River dolphin, or baiji, is the world's rarest cetacean. Fewer than 100 are believed to survive in the wild. It faces so many threats—overfishing, dangerous fishing hooks, riverbank development, dam construction, pollution, and heavy boat traffic—that it is already doomed in its natural home in the Yangtze River, China.

So far, there has been little success in capturing a handful of the elusive survivors to establish a small breeding colony in the relative safety of a semi-natural reserve. But unless this last-ditch effort is successful, there are genuine fears that the baiji could disappear altogether within a decade. Even if this program is successful, whether or not the baiji (seen left) can ever be returned to the wild remains another matter.

THE IMPACT *of* FISHERIES *on* CETACEANS

The number of whales, dolphins, and porpoises drowned in fishing nets is staggeringly high—possibly amounting to millions of animals every year.

In the high-tech scramble to meet a growing worldwide demand for seafood, it is not only fish stocks that suffer—cetaceans and other wildlife are victims, too. Blame rests squarely on the introduction of increasingly destructive fishing methods and the sheer scale of many modern fisheries.

We are still a long way from identifying the precise impact of most fisheries on cetaceans, let alone enforcing practical solutions. But there is little doubt that urgent action is needed if we are to avoid disastrous population declines. In some cases, a simple modification to either the nets or the fishery management systems can have a positive effect. But far more drastic action, such as seasonal closures of some fisheries, may be the only effective long-term solution.

OVER-EXPLOITATION OF FISH STOCKS

Overfishing is one of the major conservation crises of the 1980s and 1990s and the sheer scale of many modern fisheries could be a major threat to whales, dolphins, and porpoises.

Put simply, fish are being taken faster than they can reproduce (see the harvest of dog salmon, below, in China). According to the Food and Agriculture Organization of the United Nations (FAO), 70 percent of commercially important marine fish stocks are fully fished, over-exploited, depleted, or slowly recovering. Yet the global fishing fleet—subsidized by many governments—continues to expand.

The impact of such intensive fishing on cetacean populations is largely unknown, but as the level of human competition for dwindling fish stocks intensifies, common sense suggests that there will be less available for cetaceans and other wildlife to eat. It certainly does not bode well for the future.

DRIFT NETTING

First used on a colossal scale in the mid-1960s, this is probably the most indiscriminate method of fishing ever devised. A single drift net can be up to 30 miles (48 km) in length. Normally released at dusk, it is allowed to drift with the ocean currents and winds before being retrieved the following day, or several days later. It is virtually undetectable as it hangs in the water, and catches literally everything in its path. There are thousands of miles of these "walls of death" floating around the world's seas and oceans at any one time—more than enough to circle the Earth at the equator.

In recent years, the world has slowly begun to wake up to the dangers of drift netting, and a UN resolution on nets longer than 1.6 miles (2.5 km) was finally agreed in December 1992. But even a net of this size poses a considerable threat to marine life and, of course, in defiance of the resolution, many fisheries continue to use much longer nets.

INDISCRIMINATE *An endangered vaquita is accidentally caught in a net, along with the target species. Cetaceans drown when they can't surface for air.*

COASTAL GILL NETS

These are used in shallow, coastal waters. Made of the same nylon monofilament line as drift nets, and equally difficult for cetaceans to detect underwater, they either float at the surface or are anchored near the seabed. Cheap and durable, they are popular in many parts of the world. The

FISHERIES *are keen to avoid trapping large cetaceans, such as the humpback caught in a fishing net (right), because they damage the nets. A recently trialled acoustical "pinger" that can be attached to the invisible nets holds great promise.*

gill-net problem stretches from New Zealand to Sri Lanka and from Canada to Britain, bringing death to a great many small cetaceans every year. It is even possible that dolphins and porpoises are attracted to the nets by all the trapped fish—and then become entangled themselves.

Tuna Fishing

The tuna-fishing industry has received a great deal of adverse publicity, and deservedly so, since it has killed more dolphins in the past 35 years than any other human activity. It is directly responsible for the deaths of some 6 to 12 million spotted and spinner dolphins, and several other species. Indeed, during the worst period, the 1960s and early 1970s, the industry was killing as many as half a million dolphins a year.

The problems began in 1959, when a new kind of net, the purse-seine net, was introduced to catch yellowfin tuna in the eastern tropical Pacific (a stretch of ocean extending from southern California to Chile and covering an area roughly the size of Canada).

It arrived at a time when yellowfin tuna fishers began to use the presence of dolphins to find their quarry (tuna and dolphins often swim together, but only the dolphins have to surface for air). "Fishing over porpoise," as the practice became known, increased tuna-fishing profits substantially but also sentenced millions of dolphins to slow, lingering deaths in the great canopies of loose netting.

PURSE-SEINE NETTING *With this method, tuna and dolphins are encircled in a net. The bottom is then drawn up tight to form a bag with the animals trapped inside. Divers sometimes help the dolphins out over the edge of the net.*

After years of public outrage, the tuna-dolphin slaughter continues—but on a much smaller scale. The tuna-fishing industry is now governed by a variety of rules and regulations, ranging from special escape hatches in the nets (which allow trapped dolphins to be released) to the presence of official observers on tuna-fishing boats. The introduction of "dolphin safe" or "dolphin friendly" tuna, in 1990, was another step in the right direction, but there is still no independent enforcement scheme to check the truth of such claims. Already, less reputable tuna companies have been caught cheating.

In 1992, some governments signed the Agreement for the Conservation of Dolphins, known as the La Jolla Agreement. This sets dolphin mortality limits for each vessel participating in the fishery and has been an enormous success: the death toll has since fallen to about 4,000 dolphins per year. This is still too high and, worse still, there is mounting evidence to suggest that dolphins are being set on by tuna-fishing fleets in other parts of the world—so the problem could now be repeating itself.

CARING *for* WHALES, DOLPHINS, *and* PORPOISES

Although whales, dolphins, and porpoises continue to be killed by myriad human activities around the world, there is still hope for the future.

It is only natural that, from time to time, everyone involved in whale conservation feels a sense of despair and helplessness. But progress is being made, albeit slowly, and the attitudes of governments and other key decision makers are gradually changing. In the past decade, there have been many success stories, from the establishment of the Southern Ocean Whale Sanctuary, surrounding Antarctica, to the passing of a new law to ban dolphin hunting in Peru. But there is still a huge amount to be done and there will always be setbacks.

WHAT'S THE ANSWER?

There are no easy solutions to most of the problems facing whales, dolphins, and porpoises. The issues are complex and there are often many vested interests involved. Solutions do exist, but they are often complex themselves and it may be many long years before they are put into effect.

The work undertaken by organizations such as the British-based Whale and Dolphin Conservation Society, the largest charity of its kind dedicated to the conservation, welfare, and appreciation of cetaceans, is necessarily wide ranging. It includes anything from the development of good working relationships with key politicians to working toward a feeling of mutual respect and cooperation with local fishers.

It involves encouraging and assisting schoolchildren to take an interest in conservation, and focusing world attention on key issues, such as commercial whaling and destructive fishing methods. It entails producing action plans for saving endangered species, or populations, and developing realistic economic alternatives to hunting and killing. It involves undercover operations to gather important information on a wide range of illegal activities, improving the enforcement of existing laws and regulations, and much more. Above all, constant vigilance is essential because, even when important progress has been made, it can always be weakened or revoked.

HOW CAN YOU HELP?

Concerned individuals really can make a difference. Without public support, there would be no money for conservation groups to carry out their vital work; and, without public pressure, there would be no incentive for key decision makers to take essential action. At the end of the day, there would be very few conservation success stories.

If you would like to help whales, dolphins, and porpoises, here are some ideas:

- Join a like-minded conservation group.
- Write letters of protest to key decision makers, organize petitions, and actively support conservation campaigns in other ways.
- Raise money through such activities as walks, bike rides, parachute jumps, and other sponsored events.
- If you have a special skill that might be of benefit to cetaceans (perhaps you are a journalist, a filmmaker, a printer, or a computer expert, for example), offer to donate some time and expertise.

EDUCATION *Whale lectures increase awareness and help secure the future of cetaceans.*

PROTESTS

Activists in Vienna form a bloody whale tail (above) to protest against Norwegian whaling. When Greenpeace monitored drift-net fishing in the North Atlantic, a French patrol tug (left) attacked Rainbow Warrior.

THE RAREST WHALES, DOLPHINS, AND PORPOISES IN THE WORLD

Species and Distribution	Population	Notes
Yangtze River dolphin or baiji		
Yangtze River, China (middle and lower reaches)	Fewer than 100 (possibly fewer than 50)	Now very little chance of rescuing this species. It is likely to become the first cetacean to become extinct in historical times
Vaquita or Gulf of California porpoise		
Extreme northern end of the Gulf of California (Sea of Cortez), Mexico	Fewer than 200	Has the most restricted distribution of any marine cetacean; most commonly seen around the Colorado River delta
Northern right whale		
Western North Atlantic (occasional records from eastern North Atlantic and eastern North Pacific)	Fewer than 320	Officially protected for more than 60 years, it has never recovered from being hunted almost to extinction by commercial whalers
Indus River dolphin or bhulan		
Indus River, Pakistan (mainly along 100 mile [160 km] stretch between Sukkur and Guddu barrages, or dams)	Fewer than 500	Since the 1930s, barrages have split the dwindling population into isolated pockets
Hector's dolphin *(inset picture)*		
Coastal waters of New Zealand (most common around the South Island)	Fewer than 4,000	The world's rarest marine dolphin, threatened mainly by incidental catches in coastal gill nets
Ganges River dolphin or susu		
Ganges, Meghna, Brahmaputra, and Karnaphuli river systems of India, Bangladesh, Bhutan, and Nepal	Fewer than 4,000	The population is split into two by the Farakka Barrage

Special note: population estimates are unavailable for many cetaceans, so it is possible that some poorly known species are even rarer than the ones on this list; at the same time, some species survive in slightly higher numbers, but are at least as endangered.

- If you own a company, or are employed by a company that you think may be interested in working with a conservation group for the benefit of cetaceans, investigate the possibilities for joint promotions and corporate sponsorship.
- Try to bring whales, dolphins, and porpoises into your life in as many ways as you can: if you are a teacher, tell your class about them; if you are a parent, tell your children; and if you are at work, tell your colleagues and anyone else who will listen. After all, the best way to gain support for cetaceans is through word of mouth.

Chapter Three
Origins *and* Adaptations

They live in the midst of the sea, like fish;
yet they breathe like land species.

Histoire naturelle des cétacés,
Bernard Germain Lacépède (1756–1825), French naturalist and author

EVOLUTION *and* RADIATION

In the 50 million years of their history, whales and dolphins have shown many adaptations.

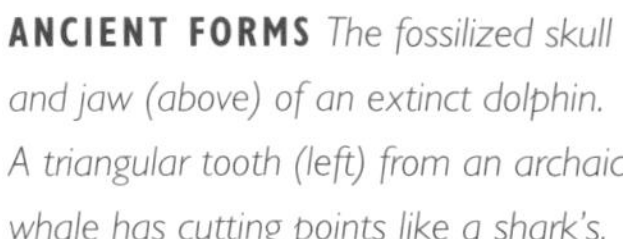

ANCIENT FORMS *The fossilized skull and jaw (above) of an extinct dolphin. A triangular tooth (left) from an archaic whale has cutting points like a shark's.*

Mammals are the dominant large land animals of the modern world. But, for about two-thirds of their evolutionary history, while dinosaurs dominated the Earth, they were small and probably rather insignificant. The earliest mammals, from about 210 million years ago, were shrew-sized species now known mainly from fossils of tiny teeth. There is little fossil evidence of large mammals until about 65 million years ago. Perhaps dinosaurs were so successful that there was no place in the world's ecology for larger mammals with the lifestyles familiar today.

After the mass extinction of dinosaurs 65 million years ago, mammals diversified widely and rapidly. They became the dominant land animals, with an average size perhaps that of a cat. Size, however, can vary from tiny (shrew) to enormous (larger than an elephant) for some extinct land mammals. Mammals diversified in feeding habits, including many specializations on the basic pattern of herbivore or carnivore. New environments were invaded worldwide, from seashore to mountains. Some mammals moved underground, and others to the treetops or to the air. Several groups took to water.

ORIGINS OF WHALES

The ancestors of whales and dolphins are known from 50-million-year-old fossils found in India and Pakistan. These fossils represent small, perhaps dolphin-sized, amphibious mammals that lived in a shallow subtropical seaway—the Tethys Sea, between the Indian subcontinent and Asia. Later, continental drift pushed India into Asia, closed the Tethys Sea, and upthrust the Himalayas. Ancient marine rocks containing whale bones are now exposed on land.

Among the archaic whales, called archaeocetes, is *Pakicetus*, found in sediments deposited in river or shallow marine settings. Skull bones, teeth, and a lower jaw point to a small cetacean, perhaps less than 6½ feet (2 m) long, which had a limited ability to hear underwater. Other early archaeocetes retain a pelvis and hind limbs, but probably swam by up-and-down movements of a strong tail, as do living cetaceans. Overall, these animals mark an early transitional amphibious stage in the shift from land to sea.

The land-dwelling relatives of early cetaceans were even-toed hoofed mammals, the cud-chewing artiodactyls. Supporting evidence for this comes from studies on living species, particularly on DNA, chromosomes, blood composition, and soft-tissue anatomy. So, sheep and cattle are among the closest living relatives of whales and dolphins.

ANCESTORS *The forebears of cetaceans lived on land and may have been dog-sized animals that looked like* Mesonyx *(right).*

TRACES OF THE PAST
The fossil whale (left) found in Antarctica is thought to be 35 million years old, while the skull and jaws of an archaic baleen whale (below) is about 25–30 million years old.

To identify the exact ancestors, we must turn to the fossil record. One extinct group, the mesonychids, appears to include the ancestors of archaic whales. These comprise a range of mostly medium-sized (perhaps dog-sized) animals that lived in ancient Asia, Europe, and North America. They showed diverse feeding habits. Perhaps cetaceans evolved when one line of mesonychids took to feeding on fish in rivers or estuaries, rather like otters.

Radiation

During their early history, about 50 to 35 million years ago, archaeocetes diversified and spread from the tropics to temperate waters. Skull form became more complex, to aid underwater feeding and hearing, and the hind limbs were reduced to small vestiges.

About 35 to 30 million years ago, the ancestors of baleen whales and of toothed whales and dolphins evolved rapidly. These were the first mysticetes and odontocetes. Mysticetes showed a new feeding style, that of filtering their prey from the water. This behavior allowed whales to crop the extensive food resources of the polar oceans. Early fossil mysticetes filter fed using sieve-like teeth. Baleen evolved by about 30 million years ago, and has been a key feature of mysticetes since.

Fossil odontocetes from about 30 million years ago probably echolocated, using high-frequency sound to navigate and detect prey. This behavior has been a feature of odontocetes since then.

Once the basic "modern" behaviors of filter feeding and echolocation appeared, cetaceans diversified dramatically from about 25 million years ago toward modern days. They ranged from poles to tropics, from near shore to open ocean, from surface to great depths, and even invaded fresh waters. But, there was an ongoing ecological "jostling for position" in the world's waters, so that some groups of cetaceans diversified as others declined to extinction. About 12 to 15 million years ago, for example, the first true dolphins, porpoises, and white whales appeared. After that, some groups that were more primitive declined and gradually disappeared. These changes may also relate to changing food resources and marine circulation.

The last main turnover among cetaceans was about four million years ago, about the time our ancestors first walked upright in Africa. As climate gradually deteriorated before the ice ages, the last groups of archaic mysticetes and odontocetes disappeared, leaving a fairly modern cetacean fauna.

Body Shape

Major changes in body shape probably occurred 50 to 35 million years ago during the time four-legged amphibious proto-whales evolved into fully oceanic forms. Hind legs became smaller and were eventually lost, and tail flukes developed. Though there is no sure fossil evidence, we can guess that, at this time, external ears and body hair disappeared and perhaps the dorsal fin evolved. The forelimb changed into a flipper with an inflexible elbow. Later, early odontocetes probably developed the bulbous forehead and single blowhole seen in living species. Odontocetes also evolved a wide range of upper-jaw forms, from short and wide to long and narrow. Among baleen whales, throat grooves probably appeared in rorqual lineages within the past 10 million years.

MAMMALS or FISH?

Cetaceans are fast-moving, fully aquatic carnivores. They have a streamlined and maneuverable body propelled by a tail rather than by limbs.

Cetaceans show many fish-like features that are adaptations to life in water. These are over-printed on basic, underlying mammalian structures.

MAMMAL VARIATIONS

Cetaceans have a body form that lacks the projecting parts seen in most mammals. The skin is normally smooth, with hair present only as facial bristles in young cetaceans and a few adult baleen whales. The expressive "face" typical of land mammals is largely obscured by blubber. Most mammals have forward-facing nostrils, but the equivalent blowhole in living cetaceans is on top of the head. Farther toward the back, dimples on the sides of the head mark the position of the ears, but there are no external ear pinnae (flaps or lobes). Most of the cetaceans have a short and rather inflexible neck, and head movement is limited.

Behind the head, forelimbs are fin-like, without visible elbows and fingers. Generally, there are only small bony limb remnants, hidden far inside the body, with no hint of legs. The genitals don't protrude, other than for sexually active males, and there is no scrotum. Adaptation to aquatic life is a trade-off; some mammalian features cannot be lost fully but must be retained in modified form.

Perhaps the most obvious fish-like features are the dorsal fin and tail flukes. The dorsal fin may be used for stability, as well as heat regulation or even, in some species, as a sexual characteristic. But in some cetaceans, the dorsal fin is small, and in a few it is absent. It is not clear how this sort of variation affects swimming ability. Horizontal flukes are present at the tip of the tail. These flukes are supported only in the midline by the hindmost tail vertebrae, and otherwise are constructed of tough non-bony tissues.

FULLY ADAPTED *The fin-like forelimbs (above) of an orca have become pectoral fins, with no elbows or fingers.*

CETACEANS AS MAMMALS

Most mammals are active land-dwellers with a high metabolism, and a constant warm body temperature. Body structures match these basic adaptations. Breathing air is fundamental; the nose is well developed, and lung breathing is helped by a diaphragm and thoracic ribs. A four-chambered heart pumps blood to the lungs and body. The genitals and anus are separate. Mammals carry the fetus in the uterus, suckle the young, and show complex patterns of reproductive and parental care. Cetaceans show all these features. More subtle mammalian features are also important. For example, the ear contains three tiny bones, the lower jaw is composed of a single bone, and the vertebrae in the backbone are separated into different regions from front to back.

Cetaceans inherited their basic swimming movements from distant land-dwelling ancestors. Fast-moving land mammals flex the body up and down, in contrast to the side-to-side movements of many reptiles and amphibians. Such movement is linked with rapid fore-and-aft motion of the limbs, seen well in a galloping or bounding nammal. Cetaceans also flex he spine vertically, although hey don't use fore- and hind imbs for movement. Rather, oowerful muscles above and oelow the vertebrae give rise o tendons that run back, via a narrow peduncle, to power he tail flukes. Overall, propulsive muscles, tendons, and vertebrae act to beat the flukes up and down, providing hrust. Most cetaceans can also bend the body sideways.

Different cetacean species have different sizes and distributions of swimming muscles, and different shapes of flukes. Also, there is a wide range of swimming speed and maneuverability among species. Dall's porpoise, for example, s a remarkably fast oceanic odontocete, while some of he river dolphins, such as the boto, are slow yet very maneuverable. Broad correlations between body structure and swimming performance are not well understood.

OTHER MARINE MAMMALS

Demands of aquatic life have been solved in different ways by the other two marine mammal groups: the pinnipeds (walrus, sea lions, and seals) and the sirenians (manatees and dugong).

All pinnipeds are powerful swimmers, and are superbly adapted to life in the sea, yet they have not made a total break from land. All their feeding is done at sea but they have to come ashore (or, in some cases, onto ice) to molt, rest, and breed. It is this need to return to land that accounts for the more typically mammalian features found in pinnipeds, but lost in cetaceans or sirenians. In particular, pinnipeds are unusual in having four webbed limbs, armed with claws at the ends of all the digits, and (in most cases) a dense coat of fur. The fur seals and sea lions can even use all their limbs to walk around on land (in true seals, the hind limbs are greatly modified for swimming, and cannot support the body).

Unlike cetaceans, seals have a social system which is clearly adapted for the land: smell, body posture, size (sexual dimorphism), and development of hair (such as the "mane" in some male fur seals and sea lions) all play a behavioral role.

Sirenians are fully aquatic. They also lack external hind limbs and have tail flukes. But sirenians are quite different from cetaceans in body form and habits. These slow-moving shallow-water herbivores feed on sea grass, and live only in warm waters.

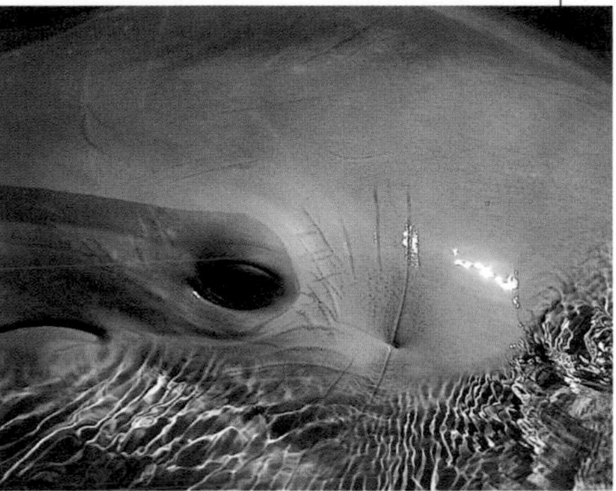

VESTIGES *Hairs on the upper jaw of a gray whale calf (right) are its only remaining body hair. The dimple on the bottle-nose dolphin's head (below right) is a vestigial ear opening.*

MAMMALIAN *features of a harbor seal (below) include fur and facial whiskers.*

What is more enthralling to the human mind than this splendid, boundless, colored mutability!—life in the making?

Adventures in Contentment,
DAVID GRAYSON, (1870–1946),
American journalist

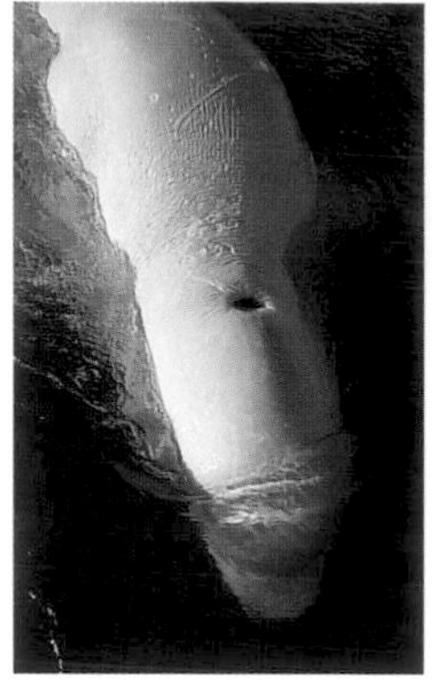

Living Underwater

Whales and dolphins show dramatic adaptations for life underwater. Changes in almost every body system make them quite unlike other mammals.

Land-dwelling mammals have load-bearing limbs to support and move the body. Because cetaceans live in water, a buoyant medium, limbs are not needed for support or propulsion.

Thermal and vascular adaptations of cetaceans are quite distinctive. Like other mammals, cetaceans maintain a constant warm internal temperature. Blubber insulates against the chilling effects of water and heat-conserving countercurrent exchange systems reduce heat loss in blood that circulates near the surface. Because of their body size and proportions, cetaceans have a problem getting rid of excess heat generated by exercise. Many species use countercurrent exchange systems in the flippers, dorsal fin, and flukes to radiate or conserve excess heat.

Land mammals need water to maintain the correct salt balance in the body. So, how do cetaceans deal with water and salt? Ingestion of salt during feeding, and from swallowed water, seems unavoidable, but we don't understand salt-balance mechanisms well. Probably, the complex cetacean kidney helps in the excretion of excess salt.

Sleeping Without Drowning

Sleep for humans means reduced muscle activity and reduced consciousness. Blood pressure and breathing rate drop, and the eyes close. Cetaceans apparently don't sleep quite the same way. In aquariums, animals rest quietly near the surface, or at the surface with the blowhole exposed. The breathing rate is lower than usual, and the eyes may close. But, breathing still seems to be voluntary, pointing to a wakeful level of consciousness. Anecdotal evidence points to some species, particularly the sperm whale, as sleeping soundly for long times at the surface, so much so that they can be a hazard to shipping. Some species rest during the day, but are more active at night.

Evolution of the Blowhole

We can breathe through either nose or mouth, but cetaceans breathe only through the blowhole (nostril). Cetaceans have effective structures to close the blowhole underwater. In mysticetes, the two blowholes are blocked by large nasal plugs. During breathing, the plugs are retracted by fast-acting muscles that originate on the upper jaw in front of the blowholes. (In humans, the same muscles lie between the lips and nose.) The action is remarkably fast, occurring in the brief interval that the whale breaks the water.

Odontocetes have a more complex blowhole, because the nasal passages are modified for sound generation (see p. 288). Two nasal plugs are still present, but they are buried far inside the head where they close off the more internal parts of the nasal passages. The single, external blowhole is a neomorph (or new

SLEEP *A beluga with blowhole open (top). A southern right whale (left) rests quietly at the surface of the water.*

THE BENDS AND NITROGEN NARCOSIS

Deep diving is hazardous for air breathers. Narcosis, a narcotic condition of stupor or insensibility, is caused by breathing air under pressure. And the bends (decompression sickness) is caused by surfacing too quickly from the depths, so that dissolved nitrogen suddenly bubbles out of the blood causing pain in joints and tissues. Yet although some cetaceans, such as the sperm whale (above left) and ziphiids, dive deep and long, with rather fast descent and ascent, they don't appear to be affected. Mechanisms that prevent the problems may include: diving with rather small volumes of air, thorax and lung collapse at depth (air squeezes from lungs into the windpipe, thus reducing nitrogen absorption), rapid transmission of nitrogen from blood to lungs at the end of a dive, and reduced circulation of blood to the muscles.

structure), which is an evolutionary change unique to odontocetes. The odontocete airway, unlike that in humans, is quite independent from the mouth and throat. Part of the larynx fits into the nasal passages at the back of the palate, so that food processing and breathing are separate.

Maintaining Buoyancy

In most mammals, the body's center of buoyancy lies forward of the center of gravity, so that the animal floats with the head raised. Marine mammals, however, have a lifestyle that requires the body to be submerged except when breathing. Head and body orientation can be changed by ballasting (weight redistribution) or by hydrodynamics (swimming movements). Ballasting can involve lightening some bones, as seen in the porous and fat-filled vertebrae of some mysticetes. Alternatively, additional dense bone can be deposited, for example, in the ribs.

Ballasting is understood poorly for living cetaceans, but has been studied in some fossil species and also in sirenians (manatees and dugong). It seems to be linked with slow swimming speeds. For faster marine mammals, swimming movements maintain appropriate head and body posture. It has been argued that the spermaceti in the forehead of the sperm whale is used to help maintain buoyancy, but it seems more likely that the forehead has a function in sound transmission.

Swimming Modes in Cetaceans and Fish

Fast-moving fish and cetaceans are superficially similar: in both, the body is streamlined to reduce drag, fins are used to maneuver and stabilize, and a crescent-shaped tail beats to provide thrust.

In detail, there are many differences between cetaceans and fish. Fish show many more swimming techniques. Varied body undulations (including eel-like wriggling) may be involved. Cetaceans do not use rhythmic movements of the limbs as their main method of propulsion, whereas many fish and swimming land mammals (such as humans) do. Instead, cetaceans move the tail up and down, rather like body movements of a running land mammal (see p. 63).

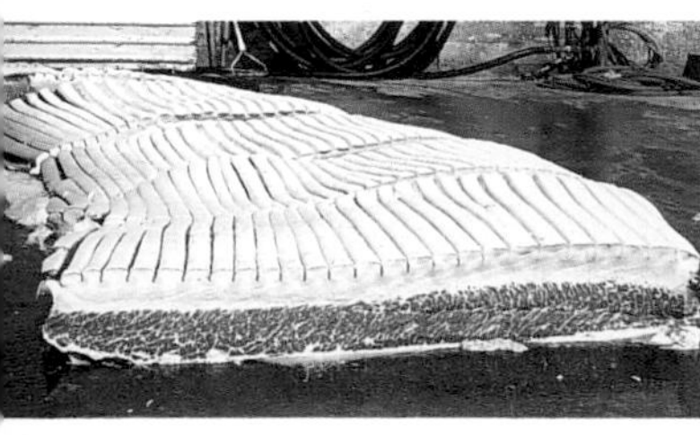

INSULATION *A layer of blubber and muscle such as this one from a fin whale (left) insulates cetaceans against the cold.*

FEEDING—BALEEN WHALES

Filter feeding is linked to many aspects of baleen whale structure and behavior, such as the huge head and mouth, large body, migration, and polar feeding.

STRAINER *Some frayed baleen hairs from the inner surface are visible in this outer view of the baleen plates of a gray whale. These form a sieve-like mat that traps food inside the mouth.*

Baleen whales are unusual mammals. Although enormous, they feed on tiny prey, filtering food from huge volumes of water in a remarkable harvesting operation.

BALEEN PLATES

Mysticetes (baleen whales) filter feed using baleen plates that hang from the roof of the mouth. Each baleen plate is thin, wide, and long, shaped like a narrow-based triangle, and formed of tough, flexible, organic material similar to hair or fingernail. Each plate grows down from the gum. A plate is formed internally of tiny, elongate tubules that are exposed as hairs where the plate is worn along its inner edge. Different species have varying numbers, sizes, and colors of baleen plates (light, dark, or mixed).

Although it originates from the gum, baleen is not related to teeth. Teeth do occur in embryonic mysticetes, but they are resorbed before birth, leaving mysticetes with no teeth in either the upper or lower jaw. Fossils show that baleen whales arose from toothed ancestors. The geologically oldest mysticetes had well-developed teeth, perhaps associated with baleen; but by approximately 30 million years ago, no trace of teeth remained in many of the mysticete groups.

GULPING

Baleen whales show two main feeding strategies, "gulping" (or "swallowing") and

HUMPBACK FEEDING

Humpback whales show remarkably diverse feeding patterns. Feeding may involve lunges through prey shoals by a single whale, or synchronized group feeding, in which several humpbacks strike prey shoals together. They may even "herd" scattered prey into clusters that can then be caught more easily. A whale may swim on its side for better maneuverability, or circle around, disturbing the water and causing frightened prey to cluster. The whale then lunges through the shoal of food. In bubblenet feeding (left), humpbacks produce columns of bubbles that also cause prey to cluster tightly. A single, large, bubble net, produced by a continuous spiral of exhaled air, is believed to work just like a conventional fishing net. One or many whales may circle underwater, and then swim through the center of the net to catch their clustered prey.

"skimming." Gulping is common among rorquals. These whales have many external grooves, or pleats, below the mouth and throat. A gulping whale lunges at shoals of prey with its lower jaw dropped and the mouth wide open, and engulfs a huge volume of water and prey. Throat, or ventral, grooves allow the mouth cavity to increase greatly, forming an expanded pouch below the throat and thorax. With the mouth closed, water is forced out across matted baleen hairs and between baleen plates, so that food is trapped. The food is then swallowed.

GIANT MOUTHFULS

As the humpback whale (above) lunges to engulf a shoal of fish, throat pleats expand and then contract to force water through the baleen filter hanging from the upper jaw. The arched upper jaw and baleen of this southern right whale (left) are clearly visible as it skims for food.

Other features are linked with gulping. The lower jaws are bowed out, to increase mouth volume. Jaw-closing muscles have unusual orientations on the skull, to help close the widely opened jaw. Upper jaw bones are only loosely attached to one another, perhaps to reduce stress across the skull. Some specialized behaviors, such as bubble-net feeding (see box), are also associated with gulp feeding.

Skimming

Right whales feed differently, moving slowly at or near the surface, and forcing a stream of water across their very long baleen plates to skim off food. Feeding is more or less continuous, in contrast to the short, dramatic bursts of gulpers. Unlike balaenopterids, the narrow upper jaw is remarkably arched to hold the long baleen, giving the skull a most unusual appearance. There are no throat grooves.

Some balaenopterids use both skimming and gulping techniques, although most are gulpers. The gray whale is mainly a bottom feeder. It stirs up mud or silt, then filters small bottom-dwelling invertebrates from the slurry. It may also suck up prey.

Individually and overall, mysticetes eat a wide range of food. In the Southern Ocean, the main prey is the small, shrimp-like crustaceans called krill (euphausiids). Krill occur mostly at shallow depths, where they feed on small algae. It is not clear how baleen whales find krill swarms, but smell is possibly used. Copepods (another group of small, free-swimming crustaceans) are also an important source of food.

Northern mysticetes take a broader range of food, including krill, copepods, and amphipods (the group that includes sand hoppers). Schooling fish, such as herring and capelin, and mollusks, including squid and pteropods, also are taken.

Antarctic minke whales with body weights around 6.5 tons (6 tonnes) eat an average of 80–260 pounds (40–120 kg) of krill per day during a 120-day feeding season. Consumption for the larger sei whales, which mature at about 20 tons (18 tonnes), is less certain. Estimates are as high as 1,600 pounds (720 kg) of food per day, but they are known to eat at least 220–440 pounds (100–200 kg) daily. During a 130-day feeding season, bowhead whales, which may exceed 55 tons (50 tonnes), generally consume an estimated 1,100–3,300 pounds (500–1,500 kg) of food daily.

FEEDING—TOOTHED WHALES *and* DOLPHINS

Toothed whales and dolphins characteristically use echolocation as a feeding tool.

TOOTH VARIATIONS *A few examples of the teeth of odontocetes: (from left) the Ganges River dolphin, the harbor porpoise, the spiral tusk of a male narwhal, the sperm whale, and the strap-toothed whale.*

Toothed whales and dolphins (odontocetes) hunt and eat relatively large, single prey. This is a more generalized and more adaptable feeding method than the filter feeding of baleen whales. Feeding adaptability explains the greater diversity of odontocete species and range of habitats. The proportions of jaws and skull in different odontocetes hint at their feeding habits. Generally, long, narrow jaws allow a fast-closing forceps-like action, but not such a strong grip. Conversely, short and usually broad jaws provide power rather than fast action.

Ancient fossil odontocetes had triangular teeth with multiple cutting points. Over time, these teeth evolved into the simplified conical teeth of most odontocetes seen today. Occasionally, delicate "tusks" projected from the tip of the jaws. Some fossils suggest rather different feeding habits from those of living species. For example, an extinct bizarre dolphin from Peru may have been a suction feeder like the modern walrus.

Most odontocetes now have uniformly simple conical teeth that vary little from front to back. These homodont teeth probably function just to grasp food, in contrast with the more varied teeth used for complex food processing in most mammals. Yet there are interesting anomalies within this general pattern. The teeth of the rough-toothed dolphin, for example, have a wrinkled surface. It is not clear how such rough surfaces function. In the harbor porpoise, the teeth are spade-shaped and compressed from side to side; presumably, they shear food rather than merely holding it. Orca teeth are large, robust, and rooted in strong, short jaws adapted to bite chunks of meat out of large prey.

Odontocetes commonly have more teeth than usual for mammals. Sometimes, there are scores of teeth in each side of the jaw, as in the common dolphin and the franciscana. Squid-eating species, on the other hand, often have greatly reduced numbers of teeth.

VARIETY OF FOODS

Varied jaws and teeth among odontocetes suggest that different species have evolved

FAST GRABBER *The Amazon boto's long, powerful jaws (left) hold numerous rough-surfaced teeth. At the back of the jaw, these are quite wide and low.*

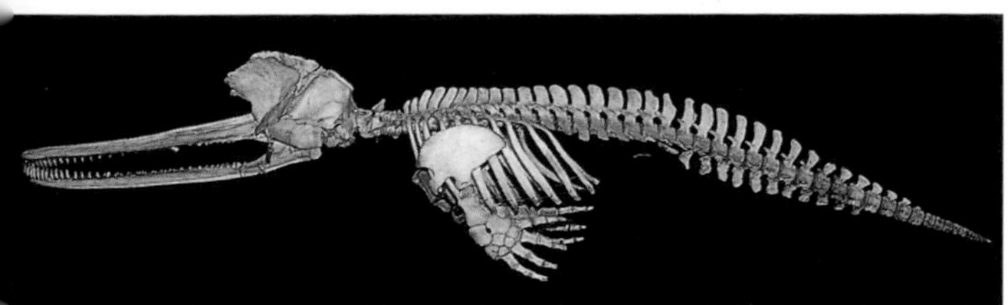

FORCEPS ACTION *Narrow jaws in the Ganges River dolphin (left) carry interlocking, needle-like teeth.*

to specialize on different sorts of food, thus reducing competition. Strangely, many odontocetes are quite flexible in their choice of food. For example, spinner dolphins in the open ocean feed on mid-level fish, squid, and shrimp, but in shallow seas they may eat bottom-dwelling and reef organisms. Striped dolphins take mainly squid in some parts of their range, but mid-water fish in other regions.

A few odontocetes clearly are specialists with no close competitors. One, the Ganges River dolphin, has very narrow, long jaws with interlocking needle-like teeth. These jaws allow fast grabbing of mobile prey. The Ganges River dolphin usually swims on its side, perhaps for better maneuverability.

Male beaked whales (family Ziphiidae) commonly have one pair of highly distinctive protruding lower teeth, but females lack large, functional teeth. In males, teeth originate at the jaw tip (Cuvier's beaked whale), or well back along the jaw (Sowerby's whale). Male ziphiids often carry elongate subparallel scars on the body, apparently from fighting.

In the strap-toothed whale, a broad tooth from each side of the lower jaw curves up and over the upper jaw, greatly limiting the extent to which the mouth can open.

Given other sophisticated behavior in cetaceans, it is no surprise that cooperative hunting occurs in odontocetes. Groups of tucuxi (found in South American rivers and coastlines) may encircle fish schools in a coordinated attack. Small groups of orcas have been known to harass and attack individual mysticetes, working cooperatively to remove the soft tissues around the mouth. And in estuaries along the eastern shore of North America, bottlenose dolphins engage in a form of cooperative hunting (see p. 305).

SPERM WHALES FEEDING

The sperm whale is the largest odontocete and, with its strange teeth and huge face and forehead, is one of the more peculiar. Peg-like erupted teeth in the narrow lower jaw fit into sockets in the broad upper jaw. Upper teeth are vestigial and buried in gum tissue, but fossils indicate that in ancestral sperm whales, the upper teeth were functional.

Sperm whales routinely dive (right) to feed in very deep water, where they can take giant squid. These rapid-growing squid may have mantles more than 6½ feet (2 m) in length, and tentacles more than 32 feet (10 m) long. Sperm whales are believed to use echolocation to find their prey and probably use suction feeding to take the squid. (Whales with deformed jaws have still been able to eat, which indicates that teeth don't play a critical role.) There is no conclusive evidence of fierce deep-sea fights between squid and whales. Indeed, whales have such a size advantage that the contest is very one-sided. Less dramatically, medium-sized squid and, for near-shore sperm whales, a range of fish are also important as food.

SENSING *the* UNDERWATER ENVIRONMENT

Water is a dense medium to which the sensory systems of cetaceans have adapted remarkably well.

Cetacean sensory systems are well adapted to detect water-borne signals, which have unexpected characteristics. For example, sound travels at about 1,120 feet (340 m) per second in air, but in water it is about 4.5 times faster. Yet, cetaceans can detect and interpret this sound. Dissolved scent moves fast in air, but slowly in water, and a mammalian nose is not structured for sniffing water.

Light is important in surface waters, but even here, eyes must work with blue rather than a full range of color. Water provides buoyancy, which partly counters gravity, and allows much more three-dimensional movement. This, in turn, must be monitored in ways land mammals rarely have to do.

IMPORTANCE TO WHALES

Sound (see pp. 286 and 288), sight, and touch seem to be as important to cetaceans as to other mammals. These senses function in navigation, communication, feeding, and breeding, and work with all the other senses to monitor the environment continually. But other senses are understood in only a general way, because of the lack of detailed study. We know or guess that relevant detectors are present and are used, but we don't understand exactly how they work. These other senses include taste, smell, and the detection of gravity, acceleration, pressure, temperature, and magnetic fields.

SIGHT

The cetacean eye operates in a setting where temperature and pressure can change rapidly, where light levels range from near-sunlight to complete dark, and where swimming brings a buffeting stream of particles and small organisms. Thick mucus helps to protect the eye, while muscles can partly close the lid, or can retract, or perhaps even push out the eye. Internally, the rather thick eye lens lacks the ciliary muscles that, in other mammals, adjust lens shape and focus.

Because the eye is also focused for the dense medium of water, cetaceans out of water are quite short-sighted. Yet, captive animals clearly can see in the air, and may perform complex movements that require rapid visual and body coordination. Such behavior indicates better binocular vision than expected for animals with eyes on the side of the head. Wild animals sometimes "spyhop," looking about with the eyes generally directed ventrally (downward relative to body axis).

Underwater, vision seems to be important in shallow, sunlit waters. Variable color patterns in some species hint at a role for visual recognition of individuals. The eye of the Ganges River dolphin, which lives in muddy waters is very reduced, with no lens. It must rely on echolocation and touch for navigation and communication.

I SPY *Although probably short-sighted in air, the humpback whale (left) must be gathering information visually when it spyhops. A close-up of the eye of a gray whale calf (top).*

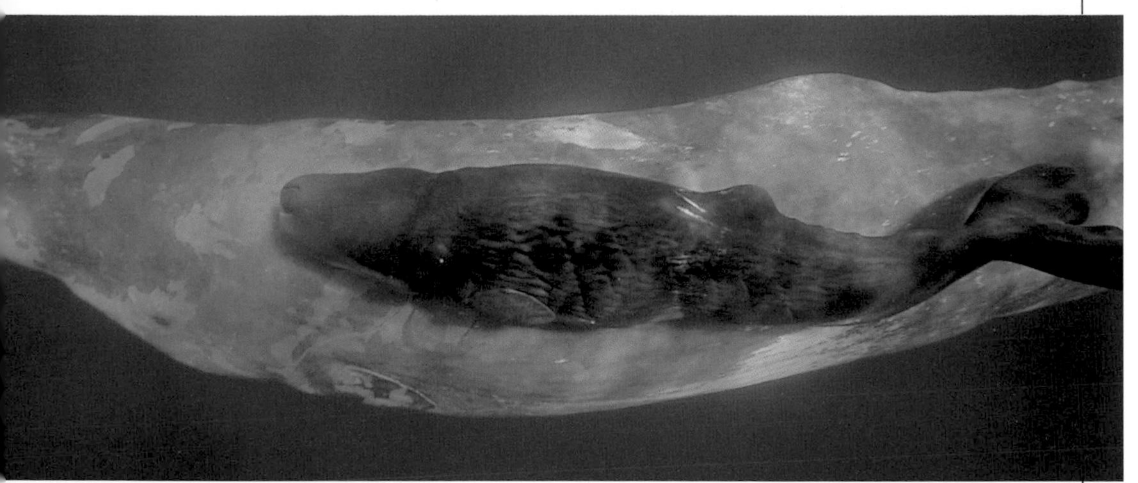

TOUCH *A sperm whale mother and calf (above) caress constantly. The tongue of the bottlenose dolphin (left) has taste buds and captive animals show preferences for particular foods.*

Touch

Whales and dolphins are very sensitive to touch. It is clearly important socially, because rubbing and sexual contact—with the same or opposite sex, and sometimes a different species—is common. Touch receptors, which may be densely packed in the skin, perhaps also function as pressure sensors in diving.

Cetaceans lack the prominent sensory whiskers of many other mammals, but scattered sensory hairs occur in many species. Young odontocetes often have a few coarse hairs along the upper lip, and adult mysticetes usually have well-developed lip hairs.

Taste and Smell

Anatomical study of the tongue shows that taste buds are present. Captive dolphins can identify a modest range of experimental tastes. Also, captives may have quite particular food preferences, again hinting at a key role for taste. It is suspected that taste is important in recognizing the different body secretions used in social signaling, such as sexual receptivity or danger. A small sensory organ, Jacobson's organ, occurs at the front of the mouth in a few species. Perhaps this further broadens tasting abilities.

The sense of smell is a little contentious. Within the nose, mysticetes still have a small olfactory cavity, with scroll-like bones for nasal sensory tissues, and olfactory nerves, but the size points to a very reduced sense of smell compared with land mammals. Recent studies show that plankton produce a distinctive gas, dimethyl sulphide, which might allow mysticetes to track their prey by smell. The olfactory nerve has not been identified conclusively in odontocetes, and there is no separate olfactory cavity. Smell was presumably lost as the nasal passages evolved into the complex sound generators used in echolocation.

Seeing, hearing, feeling, are miracles, and each part and tag of me is a miracle.

"Song of Myself," *Leaves of Grass,* Walt Whitman (1819–92), American poet

Other Senses

The presence of pressure-compensating mechanisms in cetaceans points to the existence of appropriate sensors. During diving, for example, the middle ear cavity must be pressurized with air if hearing is still to function. Yet, details of these sensors are uncertain.

As in all mammals, the three tiny semicircular canals in the inner ear of cetaceans monitor acceleration and gravity. In cetaceans, the canals are smaller than might be expected, hinting at a reduced role in detecting rotation and acceleration.

The mineral magnetite (iron oxide) is a key biomagnetic material that occurs in many organisms, including some cetaceans. Biomagnetism allows animals to orient relative to the Earth's magnetic field. For cetaceans, biomagnetism may play a role in migrations and perhaps mass strandings. But, at the anatomical level, it's not clear how cetacean magnetite functions.

VOICES *from the* DEEP

All whales and dolphins deliberately make a wide range of sounds and use them in communication.

Cetaceans make good use of the properties of sound underwater. Sound can be better than sight for long-distance communication both under and above water. It travels nearly five times faster in water than in air, and low frequencies may travel very long distances. Odontocetes also use the high frequency sounds they produce to echolocate (see p. 288).

VOCALIZATIONS

As a group, cetaceans produce sounds that range from very low to very high frequencies. Some individual species also have a wide frequency range, and most species produce several different styles of sound. Baleen whale sounds include rather low-frequency moans, belch-like sounds, bellows, snorts, bubble sounds, knocks, grunts, and yelps. Dolphins produce higher frequency whistles, squeaks, and clicks, singly, or in bursts, or in a continuous stream. Dolphins can also make "jaw-clap" sounds in conflict situations. Other noises, like splashes and slaps made by the body, may also be used to communicate.

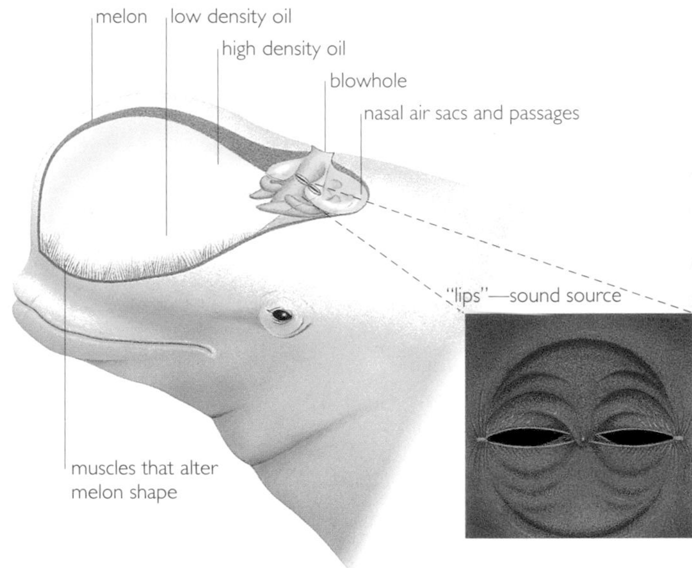

SOUND PRODUCTION *We are still learning how sounds are produced by belugas, but the high-frequency sounds used in echolocation are probably focused in the melon.*

HOW SOUNDS ARE MADE AND HEARD

Mammals usually make sounds using the larynx, a complex structure in the airway to the lungs. Elastic vocal cords in the larynx vibrate as air passes across them. Despite years of study, though, it is still not clear how, or even if, cetaceans use the larynx to produce sound. A laryngeal source has been suggested for baleen whales, in the absence of other convincing sound generators, but there are no vocal cords in mysticetes. Perhaps other parts of the larynx help to produce sound. Mysticetes also lack the complex soft tissues near the blowhole

DEFENSE MODE *These Atlantic spotted dolphins are squawking to issue a threat.*

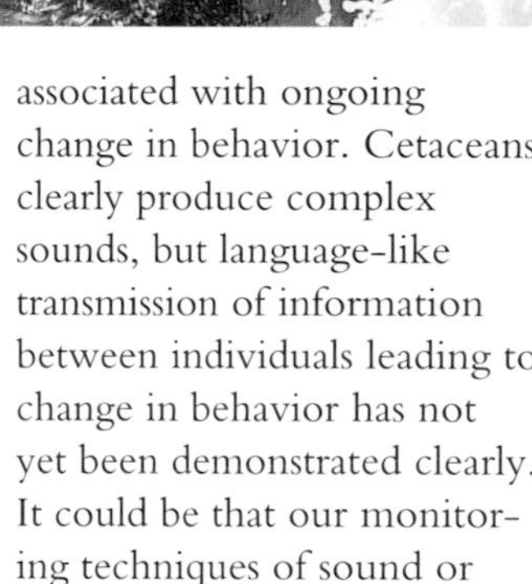

SOUNDS AND DIALECTS IN ORCAS

The orca (inset) produces complex "discrete calls"—distinctive sounds that may act as acoustic "identity badges" for individual pods. These calls, mostly pulsed, repetitive sounds that are stereotyped enough for humans to recognize basic patterns, are common during travel and foraging. This suggests that they are signals that help to coordinate activity. Each pod has a distinct and rather stable dialect, but calls vary slightly among individuals, perhaps because of the way each learns the calls when young. Orcas also produce more variable calls, used when the animals are close together resting or socializing.

which, in odontocetes, produce the high-frequency sounds used in echolocation. Vocal folds occur in odontocetes, but it is not clear if these produce the whistles reported for many species.

Sound is received in the ear by an amplification chain of three tiny ear bones that transmit sound to detectors in the inner ear. But how does sound get to the start of the amplification chain? The ear canal, which in humans and other mammals is open, is closed by a wax plug in mysticetes, and is vestigial in odontocetes. In odontocetes, sound travels from the side of the head to a thin "acoustic window" or "pan bone" in the lower jaw. From there, a fat body directs sound to large ear bones and then to the amplification chain.

How mysticetes hear is not clear, for although extinct species had a "pan bone" of sorts, living species lack this feature. In both odontocetes and mysticetes, the left and right ears are isolated from one another by complex air-filled sinuses inside the head. These sinuses probably help cetaceans to better detect the direction of the sound source.

LONG-DISTANCE CONTACT

Low-frequency sound travels long distances underwater. Baleen whale sounds have been detected from hundreds of miles away, and distances of thousands are possible. In the ocean, differences in salinity and temperature create extensive bodies of deep water which, because of their unusual density properties, may act as long-distance sound channels, transmitting low-frequency sounds even across entire oceans.

LANGUAGE STUDIES

Whatever we might want to believe about the acoustic behavior of whales and dolphins, years of study have not identified language in the human sense. In human language, variation in the order or context of familiar words produces widely varying meanings, and our words are associated with ongoing change in behavior. Cetaceans clearly produce complex sounds, but language-like transmission of information between individuals leading to change in behavior has not yet been demonstrated clearly. It could be that our monitoring techniques of sound or behavior are too crude.

HUMPBACK WHALE SONGS

Male humpback whales (inset) sing under the water, producing a complex series of low grunts, squeals, chirps, whistles, and wails. A song is made up of anything from two to nine separate themes, which are sung in a specific order, and can last from a few minutes to as long as half an hour.

Songs are produced mainly in tropical (winter) breeding grounds, but singing may also occur in the cold-water feeding grounds in summer and autumn. In any one ocean basin, whale populations sing the same distinctive song. Over time, each song changes progressively, but all the whales manage to keep up with the changes. The function of songs is not clear. Some researchers suggest they may form part of sexual behavior, others suggest that they may help to maintain social order.

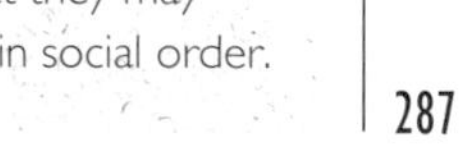

Echolocation

Toothed whales and dolphins are skilled echolocators, using sound to navigate and to hunt prey.

An echolocating dolphin sends out an intense beam of sound, usually at high frequency. This bounces off an object and returns as an echo, helping the animal to determine its distance, position, and size.

Echolocating odontocetes produce close-spaced clicks of broad-spectrum sound. Clicks, usually at high to very high frequencies, vary in structure, with each species having distinct frequencies and patterns.

Echolocation is known for certain in only a dozen or so species studied in captivity. But all the wild odontocetes studied also produce similar sounds to captive animals. This points to echolocation as a key behavior pattern in all odontocetes—sperm whales, pygmy sperm whales, beaked whales, the Ganges and Indus river dolphins as well as other river dolphins, true dolphins, porpoises, narwhals, and belugas. Strangely, though, echolocation is not used all of the time by all species. Orcas, for example, echolocate to hunt fish, but don't always use it when hunting other cetaceans or seals. (Visual hunting is better to find prey which, because of their own good hearing ability, could detect an approaching predator.) Also, it seems that there is a learned component to echolocation—it does not just come naturally to all animals.

NO HIDING PLACE *A bottlenose dolphin (above) using echolocation to find tiny fish hiding in sand. Echolocation works by bouncing a beam of sound off objects (right) and evaluating the echoes.*

How Does It Work?

Odontocetes produce the sounds used in echolocation in the complex soft tissues of the nasal passages, inside the forehead between the skull and the blowhole. A large, fatty, internal structure, the melon (see diagram p. 286), apparently helps to transmit sound forward and out into the water as a narrow beam. In the sperm whale, the skull itself probably acts as an acoustic reflector to further refine the sound beam.

Theoretically, when sound is transmitted through different media, such as bone, tissue, and water, a loss of efficiency would be expected. It is not clear how odontocetes avoid "transmission loss" for outgoing and returning sound.

Echolocation requires complex identification of different sorts of sound. The target distance is determined from the length of time it takes for an echo to return, but this means that outgoing sound must be distinguished from faint echoes. Also, the sensitive ear must be isolated from the intense noise of the sound-producing region. Isolation is provided by complex air-filled sinuses inside the head. These probably also separate the left and right ears from each other, allowing directional (left–right) hearing.

Returning sound is picked up at the side of the head and is transmitted to the ear via a succession of structures: the "pan-bone" in the jaw, a fat body, a large ear bone (which functions instead of an eardrum), and an amplification chain of three tiny bones (see p. 285). Within the ear, the cochlea, a spiraled organ, detects sound and passes acoustic signals to the brain. Just how the brain processes and interprets the signals is uncertain.

Why Is It So Important?

Echolocation works in the absence of light, and is effective in turbid waters both

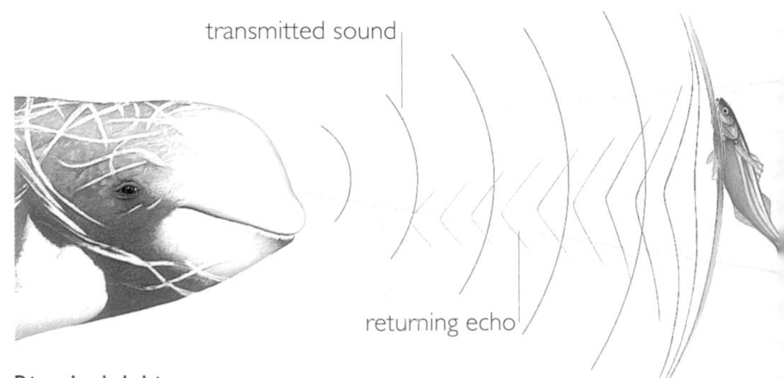

Risso's dolphin

near the shore and in rivers (where there is much suspended sediment), and also in dark, deep waters below about 150 feet (45 m). So, echolocation opens almost all waters of the world to the odontocetes. Judging from the form of fossil skulls and ear bones, odontocetes were able to echolocate from their earliest beginnings, about 30 million years ago. This complex behavior may help explain why odontocetes have diversified more in structure and lifestyle than any other group of marine mammals.

Echolocation, Sonar, and Radar

Odontocetes use sound exactly as humans use sonar, except that we've used sonar for about 50 years while they have been echolocating for millions. Sonar uses emitted sound and its returning echo to detect the presence, distance, and position of objects. Like odontocetes, bats also use this mechanism. Many other mammals (such as rodents, insectivores, and carnivores) hear high frequencies, but there is little clear evidence that they echolocate. Radar, invented by humans, involves essentially the same principles of emitted energy and returning echo, but uses radio waves rather than sound.

How Efficient Is Echolocation?

It was observations on captive odontocetes that led to the recognition of echolocation. In the 1950s, it was shown that blindfolded dolphins could swim easily among obstacles without collisions, and that dolphins could navigate well in the dark. Experiments have shown that some species can echolocate well enough to detect targets about 1⁄16–1⁄8 inch (1.5–3 mm) in diameter, from distances up to 10 feet (3 m). Some dolphins reportedly can discriminate between ball bearings 2 inches (5 cm) in diameter and those of 2.5 inches (6.5 cm). Generally, it seems that odontocete sonar is a short- to intermediate-distance sense, which operates best up to about 30 feet (10 m).

FINE FOCUS *An Atlantic spotted dolphin has no trouble catching a tiny needlefish.*

APPROPRIATE MEANS *While the two orcas (above) may track prey, especially fish, by echolocation, they will spyhop to decide on a strategy for the capture of these emperor penguins.*

Do Baleen Whales Use Sonar?

High-frequency sounds have been recorded occasionally from baleen whales, such as minke and blue whales. These sounds are a minor component of the wide range of noise produced by mysticetes, and they lack the structured form produced by echolocating odontocetes. Mysticetes also lack the complex nasal passages which, in odontocetes, generate echolocation sounds. It seems, therefore, that mysticetes do not use sonar in any major way.

Whale Migration

The annual seasonal movement of whales between feeding and breeding areas is known as their migratory cycle.

The seasons drive the migrations of all creatures, including a number of whales. Seasonal effects are greatest in high latitudes, where long summer days and melting of sea ice bring about massive blooms of microscopic plant plankton, or phytoplankton. These are eaten by krill, copepods, and other zooplankton, which in turn feed birds, seals, squid, fish, and whales. When polar seas freeze over in winter, biological production slows and many species migrate to warmer climes, to waters comparatively devoid of marine life.

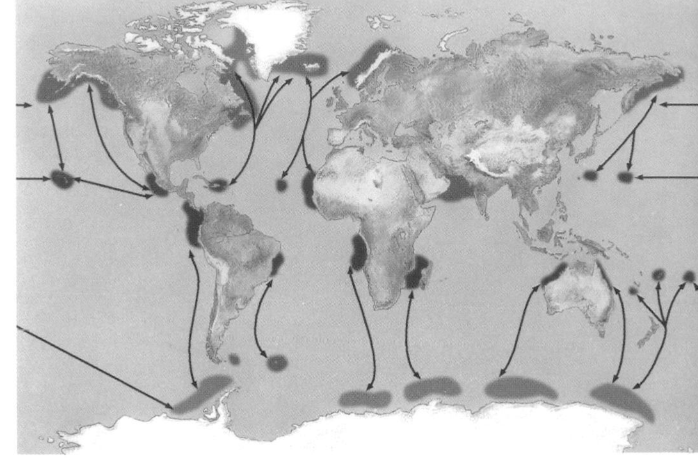

NO BOUNDARIES *This map shows the migratory patterns of the different populations of humpback whales. The fin whale (above left), is a fast and powerful migratory traveler.*

Baleen Whales

Baleen whales are the greatest cetacean rovers, spending almost as much time traveling as they do on their breeding and feeding grounds. Except for Bryde's whales, which remain in warm waters year-round, all baleen whales make essentially north–south migrations between cold-water feeding areas for summer, and temperate to tropical breeding areas for winter.

Pacific gray whales show a typical pattern. In early winter, perhaps in response to various hormonal changes initiated by shortening days, they move south to breed in the warm, shallow lagoons along the Mexican coast. From February, they migrate north to feed along the coast of Alaska and in the Beaufort Sea. Mothers with newborn calves remain in the breeding areas longer than the others, to allow their calves to gain strength for the long swim ahead.

Humpback whales show a similar pattern. In the North Atlantic, they breed around the West Indies, migrating up the western side of the Atlantic Ocean in spring, to disperse in summer feeding areas between the Gulf of Maine and Iceland. A smaller population migrates between Norway and west Africa and the Cape Verde islands. North Pacific humpbacks breed along the coast of Mexico, around the Hawaiian Islands and southern islands of Japan, feeding along the coasts of the northern Pacific Rim.

The seasons are reversed in the Southern Hemisphere, so humpbacks breed between June and October along the tropical coasts of the southern continents, and around Pacific islands such as New Caledonia and Tonga. These populations summer in the krill-rich Southern Ocean surrounding Antarctica. The greatest confirmed migration by any individual mammal is that of the humpbacks that summer on the Antarctic Peninsula, south of Cape Horn, and breed off the coasts of Colombia and Costa Rica. In the Arabian Sea, one unusual population of humpbacks does not migrate, because its warm breeding waters support abundant marine life for food.

Most southern right whales remain in the mid-Southern Ocean, but some feed at the edge of the Antarctic pack ice. Their coastal breeding grounds lie mainly along the southern coasts of Africa, South America, and Australia. The breeding destinations of blue, fin, sei, and minke

STEADY PACE *Although humpbacks (right) can move at 5 miles (8 km) per hour, they rest and socialize often, and average about 1 mile (1.6 km) per hour overall on their epic journeys. A migrating gray whale yearling calf (below) plays in a kelp forest off the Californian coast.*

whales are almost entirely unknown, but probably lie in warm, deep, tropical waters.

Toothed Whales

Most toothed whales do not have the well-delineated migrations typical of baleen whales. Many are nomadic rather than migratory. Orcas were long thought to migrate away from Antarctic waters, but at least some of them breed and winter in the ice. One species whose migration is understood is the sperm whale, which has a unique pattern. While female sperm whales and immature males remain in temperate to tropical waters during summer, mature males migrate to polar waters to feed on vast quantities of squid, rejoining the nursery schools in winter to breed.

Why Migrate?

In terms of energy, migration is a huge commitment. Baleen whales are believed to fast throughout much of their migration, living on their blubber and fat for up to eight months of the year. In the case of a female that calves on migration, total weight loss may be as high as 50 percent. In a fully grown blue whale cow, this may represent a loss of some 89 tons (81 tonnes). Migrating whales probably have a "tight energy budget."

The conventional view is that birth and early development in warm water is important for calves, and that insufficient food remains in the feeding areas during winter. But bowheads, orcas, belugas, and narwhal raise their young in very cold water, and plankton supports huge numbers of Antarctic seals, penguins, fish—and many whales—during the winter.

It is possible that before continental drift, migratory endpoints were much closer, and that whales have simply continued to visit these points as they drifted farther apart. Perhaps baleen whales breed away from Antarctic waters to avoid predation on their calves by orcas, which do not migrate. Some animals not involved in breeding forgo migration, saving a huge expenditure of energy. Many minke whales winter in the Antarctic sea ice, and about half of the Southern Hemisphere adult female humpbacks in any year do not reach the breeding grounds. Instead, they may remain in feeding waters year-round, putting on condition for the next year's cycle.

Large rorquals, such as blue and fin whales, are the most powerful travelers, with one fin whale recorded as averaging 10½ miles (17 km) per hour over 2,300 miles (3,700 km).

UNIQUE PATTERN *Of the sperm whales (below), only the adult male migrates long distances.*

...As they fell down sideways they splashed the water high up, and the sound reverberated like a distant broadside.

Journal of a Voyage Round the World,
CHARLES DARWIN (1809–82), English naturalist

Chapter Four
Social Life *and* Behavior

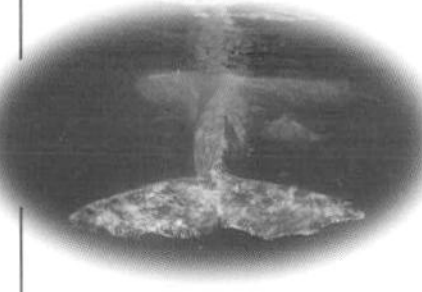

Living Together

The social organization of cetaceans is often a consequence of the ecology of their prey, and the degree of cooperation required to catch it.

One of the most fascinating things about watching cetaceans is observing their social lives. There are three overriding priorities: feeding, reproduction, and avoiding predation. Mothers and calves form the basic unit of society common to all cetacean species, but beyond this, differences start to emerge.

Feeding may be the single most important factor in determining the nature of cetacean societies. The single greatest division is between baleen whales and toothed whales. One group has baleen plates, used to swallow large numbers of small schooling prey; the other has teeth, to grasp single, larger prey.

Toothed Whales

Toothed whales occupy a vast diversity of aquatic habitats, from the deep polar oceans to equatorial rivers and estuaries. Their group size varies from almost solitary, to great aggregations of thousands of animals. Although toothed whale groups are usually more stable and larger than those of baleen whales, species such as river dolphins are found in very small groups, or even singly. They live in a stable environment in which their prey is more or less evenly dispersed, and they have to contend with fewer predators.

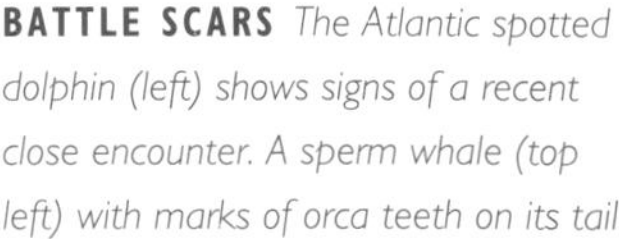

BATTLE SCARS *The Atlantic spotted dolphin (left) shows signs of a recent close encounter. A sperm whale (top left) with marks of orca teeth on its tail.*

Dolphins that live along coastlines face more predators, and their food is more clumped, so they tend to be found in larger groups. The largest cetacean groups are those of oceanic dolphins, which travel widely in search of scattered patches of prey. They move in small, closely related, permanent groups, which may amalgamate with similar groups to form temporary herds of thousands.

The close relationships within toothed whale societies give them their stability. Most species are female-centered: that is, adult females form the stable nucleus of the group. Males leave at puberty to join other groups, thus avoiding inbreeding. There are rare exceptions to this, such as orcas and pilot whales, in which all members remain with one group for life, and mating occurs between two such groups. This leads to a very high degree of social cohesiveness and cooperation, well demonstrated in coordinated hunting by orcas.

Another well-known and often tragic illustration of the cohesiveness of toothed whale groups is the phenomenon of mass strandings (see p. 310). Science cannot yet comment on the personal relationships among individual whales, but dry genetic theory predicts that it is worth the risk to help related companions if your shared genes then have a better chance of surviving.

Social life, however, is not

GROUP OF TWO *This pair of humpbacks (left) may be foraging or merely enjoying each other's company.*

INDEPENDENT *Some toothed whales, such as the Amazon river dolphin (left), are often found alone or in small groups.*

all sweetness and light. Hierarchies of dominance exist, in which subordinate animals are forcefully reminded of their place. These are most clearly seen in captive dolphins that cannot avoid each other. In the wild, dominance may be used to settle access to food, or to mates.

Body language and underwater sounds express social status, but conflict often becomes physical. Tooth rake marks are very common in many toothed species, and indicate the frequency of aggressive interactions in everyday life. In some beaked whales, males have a single pair of teeth used for display or fighting, and many animals are covered with linear scars.

Baleen Whales

Much of what we know about baleen whales comes from the two most easily observed species, humpbacks and southern right whales. Social organization in feeding areas derives from the nature of their food source—usually scattered patches of small fish or crustaceans, better utilized by small groups. In such diverse humpback feeding areas as the Gulf of Maine and the Antarctic, the most common group size is two. Where their gender has been determined, they are either females, or a male and a female. It has been found in recent years that these pairs may be together over several years, suggesting that these animals form good foraging "teams." It may also be, of course, that like dogs, horses, and humans, they simply prefer the company of certain whales over others. Mature males do not associate in feeding areas, perhaps unable to put aside the intense rivalry of the breeding season.

Little is known of the social lives of other rorquals. Large aggregations are sometimes seen where there is abundant food. In Antarctic waters, one group of nearly 50 fin whales and another of 25 blue whales were sighted. There was also a report of nearly 1,000 minke whales feeding on a huge swarm of krill. Yet almost nothing is known of social interactions within these species. Blue whales have been reduced to such low numbers, particularly in the Southern Hemisphere, that contact and socializing may be quite difficult for them.

In breeding areas, once again, most of what we know comes from humpback and southern right whales (see pp. 308 and 343). On breeding grounds, humpback social groupings are usually small and unstable. Groups of up to eight humpback males compete aggressively to escort females prior to mating, but there do not seem to be long-term associations among males as there are with right whales. After weaning, juveniles tend to be solitary, becoming more social with age.

It's them as take advantage that get advantage i' this world.

Adam Bede,
George Eliot
(1819–80), English novelist

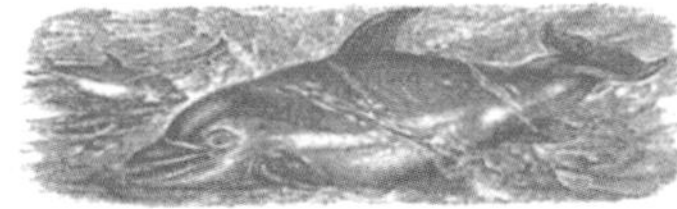

MATING *to* BIRTH

There is nothing more important in the lives of cetaceans than the perpetuation of their own genes, and hence their species.

Animals have an inbuilt compulsion to reproduce. Each of the 81 cetacean species has evolved a unique combination of timing, behavioral strategies, and physiological adaptations to ensure that it survives.

Compared to many other mammals, cetaceans have low reproductive rates. This is because they grow slowly and do not mature sexually for at least five or six years (much longer than some other species), and almost invariably give birth to only a single calf, which takes a year or more to reach independence.

This low reproductive rate is offset by the fact that they are generally long-lived, with females capable of bearing many calves during their life.

INTIMATE MOMENT *Atlantic spotted dolphins mating (with male underneath).*

BREEDING CYCLE

Scientific study of the ovaries and testes of dead whales and dolphins over many years has resulted in an understanding of the animals' breeding condition at various seasons. From these, it appears that reproduction is a cyclical activity. In many species, the breeding cycle is intimately linked to the seasons and, in the case of migratory species, to migration.

This is particularly so in baleen whales, which have a surge in hormonal activity in both sexes as they approach the breeding areas, possibly stimulated by changes in day length or water temperature. The exception is the tropical Bryde's whale, which breeds throughout the year.

Some oceanic dolphin species have two breeding peaks—in spring and in fall. Other species, such as coastal bottlenose dolphins, may breed throughout the year, as their environment changes little with the seasons.

This linked breeding and migratory cycle means that the breeding season is short and intense. The gestation, or

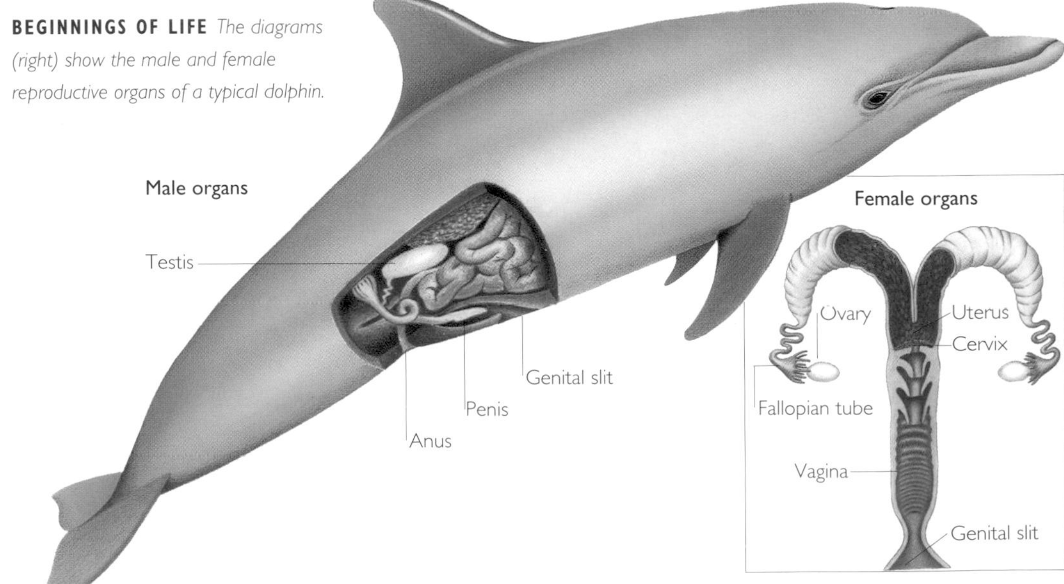

BEGINNINGS OF LIFE *The diagrams (right) show the male and female reproductive organs of a typical dolphin.*

CHOOSE YOUR WEAPON *Male narwhals may use their spiral tusks to gain supremacy over sexual rivals.*

Birth, and copulation, and death. / That's all the facts when you come to brass tacks.

Sweeney Agonistes,
T. S. ELIOT (1888–1965),
American-born English poet

pregnancy period, in many species is usually around 12 months, so mating occurs on the calving grounds. The female will return a year later to deliver her calf.

Huge energy demands on breeding females, including fasting during migration, mean that only very rarely do they breed in consecutive years (although a humpback cow has been seen with new calves in three consecutive years). More often, there is a breeding cycle of two or three years in baleen whales. In many toothed whales, the cycle is even longer, because gestation may be longer (up to 18 months in sperm whales) and calves stay with their mothers for longer.

MATING

Once males and females arrive at the breeding areas, complex mating systems come into play. No species of cetacean is monogamous: they are either promiscuous (males and females have multiple partners, as is common among right and gray whales and many dolphins), or polygynous (males mate with multiple females, as seen among sperm whales, orcas, and narwhals).

The songs of polygynous male humpbacks advertise a smorgasbord of choice for females. Intense competition among males often follows, as they attempt to displace each other to become a female's "principal escort" as a prelude to the gentler acts of courtship and mating.

Males of other species use a variety of strategies, from the mating alliances of bottlenose dolphins (see p. 304) to narwhals, which may use their spectacular tusks in jousts for supremacy, often with fatal results. In right whales, sperm competition (see p. 308) is a more peaceful solution. Males, not necessarily related, may actually help one another to mate, then let their sperm fight it out on the way to the ovum (although they are not above raking each other with barnacle-covered callosities). Larger penises are seen in animals that employ sperm competition, as extra length may give a competitive edge.

CONTEST *As two Atlantic spotted dolphins are mating, a rival male blows bubbles in a bid to cut in.*

Females are not mere passive recipients of all this male activity. Females have their own priorities, which are to mate with a suitable male, and to raise their offspring successfully. While mature males are usually ready to mate, females may be in a non-breeding phase of their cycle, or may exercise their right to choose a mate.

It is difficult for a male cetacean to force a female to mate against her will. Females may signal their sexual status in various ways, perhaps by means of hormonal secretions in the urine, or by subtle behavioral cues that are obvious to prospective mates.

PREGNANCY

In migratory species, such as humpback and gray whales, newly pregnant females are the first to leave the breeding areas and return to summer feeding grounds. A pregnant female must rapidly put on enough fat to sustain her and her growing fetus through the coming year. This is a difficult task, bearing in mind that most baleen whales fast during migration. Near-term cows are among the first to return to the calving area, as early calving allows more time for the calf to grow before it, too, must migrate.

BIRTH to DEATH

Although their lives are perilous from birth, many cetaceans have a life expectancy comparable to that of humans.

Except in captivity, the birth of cetaceans has rarely been witnessed. It is a dangerous time, both for the mother, who may be distracted by her labors, and for the calf, which relies on its mother (and possibly "aunts," or helpers). While captive dolphins have been seen to bear their young tail-first underwater, a gray whale calf in Baja California emerged head-first, above the surface. For cetaceans, single births are the norm, with the calf being typically a third the length of the mother.

Once the calf has emerged, the mother guides it to the surface for its momentous first breath. This is the start of a close bond which in some species will persist for life. In others it is severed in a year.

Once mating has taken place, the father's role is finished, although adult males may defend closely related calves or those that have a high chance of being their offspring. In species such as sperm and pilot whales, defense of the young is a communal responsibility.

EARLY LIFE

For the first few weeks of life, a calf rarely strays from its mother's side, and the two are in frequent physical contact. Small, weak, and defenseless, calves cannot dive deep or swim far, and require constant feeding in order to grow to a size where they can begin to fend for themselves. As they grow, they become bolder and venture farther from the safety of their mother or their group. Feeding bouts become longer, but fewer. Growing calves, like other young animals, can be insistent about being fed, and southern right whale cows, at least, have been seen to refuse to feed their calves, provoking what can only be called tantrums.

Cetacean milk is very rich, consisting of about 40 percent fat. The lactation period varies considerably. Humpbacks feed their calves for nearly 11 months, while minke, sei, and fin whales lactate for between 4 and 6 months. Blue whales lactate for seven months, during which the calf will grow at a rate of about 180 pounds (85 kg) per day to nearly 25 tons (23 tonnes).

All baleen whales gradually wean their young after the first year of life. Southern right whales appear with their calves at the breeding area exactly 12 months after giving birth. They simply leave their calves and depart. At this point, the calves become

NURTURE *A humpback (top left) and her calf. A sperm whale calf (left) will nurse for several years, in some cases up to 15 years. Part of the umbilical cord can be seen still attached to the belly of the newborn sperm whale (below).*

Life is a gamble at terrible odds—if it was a bet, you wouldn't take it.

Rosencrantz and Guildenstern are Dead,
TOM STOPPARD
(1937–), English playwright

CLOSE BOND *The sei whale (left) will provide rich milk for her calf for between four and six months.*

juveniles, and appear to have little further contact with their mother. This may be the basis of the apparently loose social ties in baleen whale society. In contrast, most toothed whales feed their calves for 2 years or more, with some old sperm whale cows still nursing calves that are 10 to 15 years old.

After a young cetacean has left its mother, it must make its way in a dangerous world. Mortality is highest during the first years of life, as disease, predators, parasites, pollution, injuries, deaths in fishing gear, vessel strike, and hunting take their toll. There are some unexpected causes of death and injury, such as a dolphin being suffocated by an octopus covering its blowhole, and whales have been found with billfish spears embedded deeply inside them. Mortality rates are difficult to calculate, but it is believed that a majority of whales reach adulthood.

Growing Up

As cetaceans grow, their play behaviors eventually become the serious activities of life. Playful contests between young males become the mating battles of adults, and animals such as orcas actively teach their young the foraging and hunting techniques that are essential for survival.

Alliances that are important for mating and feeding success are made. When cetaceans near sexual maturity, their lives change. Baleen whales generally mature early, at around five to seven years old, with sexual maturity being related to body size. In depleted populations (such as Antarctic sei whales) individuals have increased access to food, so growth is faster, and sexual maturity is achieved earlier. In toothed whales, young males that have lived within their mother's group reach puberty and most leave to join groups of other young males. In sperm whales, full sexual maturity is correlated with size, with the larger males not maturing until the age of 20 or more, and smaller females at 10 years.

HOW LONG DO CETACEANS LIVE?

A general rule in nature is that smaller animals live shorter lives. Harbor porpoises, one of the smallest cetacean species, live only 15 years or less, while it seems that some large whales may survive for 100 years. Bottlenose dolphins live for about 50 years in the wild. Until now, age could be determined only by examining a cross-section of a toothed whale's tooth, or a cross-section of the waxy earplug that forms inside a baleen whale's ear. Both of these are built up in layers, each of which corresponds to a yearly cycle. Layers also form in the very thin band of cement just beneath the outer enamel of the tooth, allowing for the most accurate calculations. Now, with the photographic identification of natural markings, it is possible to study the lives of individual whales from birth to death, without harming them.

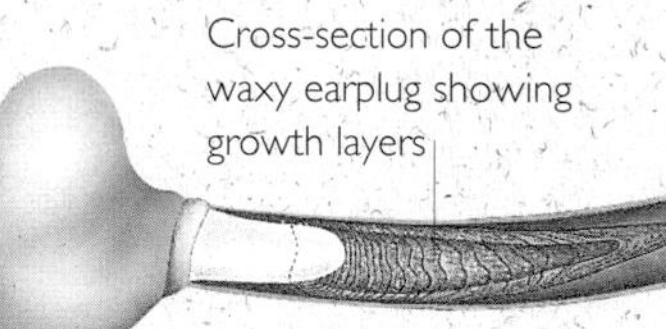

Cetacean Intelligence

Many cetaceans have relatively large and complex brains, but does this make them "intelligent?"

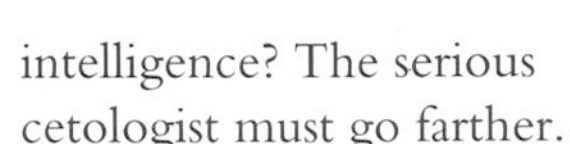

Even in humans, "intelligence" is a loaded term. It can mean many things—the ability to know, to analyze using reason and judgment, to think fast, and to understand. But what does variation in human intelligence mean? And how can we identify intelligence in other species?

Intelligence Quotient

Human intelligence is related to context. How we measure someone's intelligence is highly dependent on setting. Assessments of human intelligence—IQ tests—are standardized to allow easy comparison of results, so it is ironic that standardization brings loss of context.

Beyond behavioral testing, structural features of the nervous system have been used to gauge intelligence between species. Many studies of mammals have looked at the cerebral hemispheres—the largest parts of the brain. In those lobes, a well-developed outer layer (cortex) seems to indicate higher intelligence. Another measurement, the encephalization quotient, an index of brain size to body size, also seems to be linked with intelligence. Species with a bigger brain than expected for their body size appear to be more intelligent.

There are many anecdotes about cetacean intelligence which involve, for example, belief in interspecies communication between human and dolphin, and even extrasensory perception (ESP). Can we get beyond this level of anecdote in our understanding of cetacean intelligence? The serious cetologist must go farther.

In general, cetacean brains are larger than expected for their body size (relative to other mammals) so that the encephalization quotient is high. Their large brain size points to a need for information processing which is related to complex hearing, communication, and movement. This relative brain size, though, is not always high: small river dolphins and the large sperm whale have smaller than expected brains.

Behavioral tests have been used extensively for cetaceans, but because cetaceans are non-manipulative, and don't modify their environment in the way that most mammals do, it is not clear what these tests may mean.

Ability to Learn

Studies on a few captive species of odontocetes show that they can quickly learn complex physical routines. Captives learn to respond to

LEARNED BEHAVIOR *The orca (top) is playing with a young sea lion. Often, a pup is stunned or killed in this way. The learning ability of the dolphin (left) is studied at a dolphin research center.*

CARE-GIVING BEHAVIOR *An adult short-finned pilot whale (right), together with some other members of the pod, closely guard a dead calf.*

different human gestures or sounds, modifying their behavior in response to subtle changes in the instruction given. There is some evidence that learned information is transmitted from one animal to another. But human-like language, with its implications for intelligence, has not been identified clearly. For wild animals, there is strong evidence that odontocetes all have the ability to echolocate, but there is also a strong learned component in successful echolocation.

Problem Solving

The activity of cetaceans in the wild shows that many species use very sophisticated problem-solving behaviors. Cooperative bubblenet feeding in humpback whales (see p. 280), and beach capture of seals by orcas, are examples of complex monitoring and physical co-ordination. Wild cetaceans show care-giving (epimeletic) behavior that may involve supporting a calf or sick animal. Some species show clear group defensive behavior. So, cetaceans produce complex responses to rapidly changing environments. If these behaviors are learned, they indicate high intelligence, but if they are genetic (instinctive), they are not such persuasive evidence.

How Whales Compare with Other Animals

Encephalization quotients are high for most cetaceans. And, fossils show that cetacean brains became large quite early on in evolutionary history, long before the increase in human brain size. But brain size alone has to be interpreted carefully, because other animals with absolutely and relatively small brains can show extremely complex behaviors. Pigeons, for example, have small brains, yet complex flight patterns. Among mammals, bats have tiny brains, yet they use highly sophisticated echolocation to detect prey and determine complex flight paths. Perhaps a key feature of many cetaceans is that, compared to many mammals, they have a complex and human-like folding of the cortex in the cerebral hemispheres. Parts of the brain that process sound are also well developed.

HOW HUMAN-LIKE IS CETACEAN INTELLIGENCE?

What can we make of similarly large and complex brains? In humans, brain complexity and intelligence are apparently linked with sophisticated language and with manipulation of the environment. Cetaceans don't modify their environment in the human sense or, indeed, as other mammals do, and a human-like language has not been demonstrated. Brain complexity perhaps relates to sound processing. It is not clear why brains should be similarly complex in odontocetes and mysticetes, which produce and use different sorts of sound. We have far to go before we can really understand if cetaceans are intelligent and what their intelligence might mean.

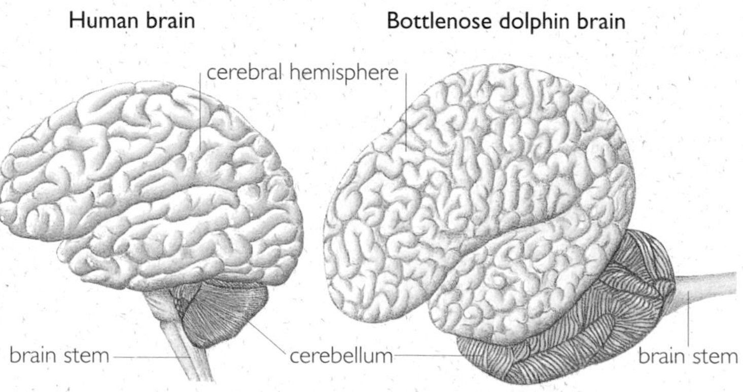

Interpreting Behavior

One of the most mystifying things about cetaceans is trying to work out just what they are doing while you are watching them.

Behaviors vary from the dramatically obvious, to the almost invisibly subtle. While it takes much study to gain a comprehensive knowledge of the behavior of a species (and we are far from achieving this for any species), it is possible to learn something of the types of cetacean behaviors and so make some sense of our observations.

MYSTERIOUS URGE *Pec-waving (top) is a common activity of humpbacks. A breaching humpback (above) may repeat its leap many times.*

Leaping and Porpoising

Probably the most popular image of cetaceans is that of a leaping, porpoising, or breaching animal. These are all behaviors in which the whole body, or most of it, breaks clear of the water. Smaller animals, such as dolphins, generally leap and this may signal a general state of excitement, or perhaps something more specific. Off Argentina, dusky dolphins leap to show that they have found aggregations of fish and that more dolphins are needed to herd them so all the group may have a feed. Many species leap, but none so spectacularly as the spinner dolphin. Their spinning leaps are thought to coordinate and synchronize behavior within groups.

Although superficially similar to leaping, porpoising is not a social behavior but an energetically efficient method of travel. Small cetaceans clear the water when surfacing to breathe, as air offers less resistance to movement than water. Nevertheless, a high degree of synchronization is often seen among porpoising animals, and it is an eye-catching sight when large schools are on the move.

Breaching

One of the grandest sights in nature is a breaching whale. This is the term given to the leaping of cetaceans. The animal seems to burst from the water in slow motion. Humpbacks are probably the most prodigious breachers, and individuals have been seen to breach more than 100 times consecutively. A number of explanations have been proposed, ranging from simple *joie de vivre*, through the dislodging of parasites (such as barnacles and remoras), to getting a better look at boats, or warning away intruders. All of these may be true, but breaching is certainly a visible and audible form of communication, although what is being communicated is difficult to know. In one case, a humpback calf that had been separated from its mother breached for at least two hours. Breaching may follow disturbance by boats, or by other whales. Sometimes it seems contagious, and mothers and calves, or other pairs of cetaceans, often breach in unison.

Headrises and Spyhopping

Other behaviors where the head breaks the surface include headrises, in which the animal's head lunges briefly out of the water while moving forward, and spyhopping, a similar behavior, but usually while the whale remains stationary. Whales often spyhop to scan their surroundings, as visibility in air is usually much greater than underwater. Whales may spyhop to inspect boats, and orcas in Antarctica spyhop to examine seals and penguins resting on ice floes.

CHAMPIONS *Spinner dolphins (above) spin their bodies rapidly around their long axis while they are in the air.*

Fins and Flukes

A different set of behaviors involves waving or slapping the pectoral fins or the tail flukes. "Pec-slapping" is commonly seen in humpback whales, which lie on their sides, slapping their long pectorals against the water surface, to produce a resounding crack that can be heard at a considerable distance. Pec-slapping can also be used more gently between courting animals close to one another. Right whales and many other species use their pectoral fins for reassurance, or to caress one another during courtship.

Tail flukes have functions other than propulsion. They are defensive weapons, and right whales, for example, have only to point their flukes at another animal to send a clear warning to stay away. Many species slap their flukes on the water, or "lobtail," as it is called. As with breaching and pec-slapping, this sends a visible and audible signal, with a variety of meanings. It may be a leisurely, almost lazy, activity used by socializing whales, or it may be a forceful threat. In extreme examples, open-boat whalers often had their boats smashed by lobtailing whales. Southern right whales also use their flukes in another way—called "sailing." They hold their flukes vertically out of the water for extended periods. Whether they are actually sailing, cooling themselves in the breeze, or simply enjoying the sensation of the wind, is not known.

Bow Riding

Another familiar behavior is bow riding, when dolphins, in particular, ride, almost without effort, in the pressure wave created ahead of the bow of a vessel or the head of a whale. Larger whales, such as orcas, also bow ride. When observing bow-riding dolphins, you will often notice other behaviors signifying aggression or sexual activity. These include biting, butting, exerting dominant status to drive another animal out of the bow wave, and overt sexual activity, including copulation.

WHAT'S GOING ON? *Humpbacks often indulge in boisterous pec-slapping (left). The spyhopper (below) in this pod of socializing melon-headed whales, may simply be wanting a better view.*

Bottlenose Dolphins

The best known cetacean species is the bottlenose dolphin. Because it lives along coastlines in many parts of the world, it is the most often seen and best studied cetacean species in the wild.

Studies, some of them extending over more than 20 years, of coastal bottlenose dolphin societies have enabled a detailed understanding of their behavior and social organization. The lives of their offshore relatives, which live in the open sea, are much less well known.

Social Units

A long-term study at Sarasota Bay, Florida, by Dr. Randall Wells and colleagues, identified four types of social units: a mother-calf pair, groups of subadults of either sex, adult females with their calves, and adult males. The way these groups interact is largely determined by the breeding biology of the species. In this "fission-fusion" society, individuals constantly leave and rejoin groups.

Male Bonding

Bottlenose dolphins are slow breeders; females calve only every four to five years, so females in mating condition are rare in a population at any given time. As a result, males have developed strategies to make the most of mating opportunities when they occur.

Males leave their mother's group at puberty and join groups of subadults. As they age, they form smaller and smaller groups, until fully mature males form alliances of just two or three animals. At Shark Bay, in Western Australia, these alliances have been seen to cooperate in subduing and herding mature females, presumably as a prelude to mating. This treatment of females is often rough, with frequent pushing, buffeting, biting, and vocal threats, and females are often unwilling participants. Males sometimes cooperate to herd females; at other times they compete, and even fight for females. There appear to be social hierarchies, often dominated by the largest males, and much time is spent reaffirming bonds. The pecking order can be seen when they are feeding on discarded fish from trawlers—some stay aside to let others get the best discards.

CLOSE CONTACT *The bottlenose dolphins (above and top) socialize and play in a variety of ways. Mother and calf (left) will maintain a long association.*

COOPERATIVE EFFORT *Bottlenose dolphins driving fish up onto a river bank.*

Female Networks

While male alliances appear to be among the most lasting bonds in bottlenose society, some female associations also last for many years. Suckling of calves can continue for four years or more, and some female calves may accompany their mothers for life. Other calves join subadult groups with a preponderance of males, in which social behavior is explored and developed.

Many adult females form loose, changing networks. In broad biological terms, males devote their energies to impregnating as many females as possible, while females devote their energies to the raising of offspring. There is no breeding advantage to females in forming permanent close relationships, but they can call on their associates when assistance is required for feeding, defense, or in some cases, repelling amorous males. In some cases, "aunts" will assist a female in giving birth.

Dolphins frequently stroke and caress each other, and sexual behavior, including copulation, is used casually, apparently indiscriminately, to reaffirm bonds. Aggressive contact is also common, with the scars from tooth raking seen on a majority of animals. Eavesdropping with hydrophones reveals that angry squawks, clicks, and pops accompany aggressive behavior.

Bottlenose dolphins also show a decidedly unsocial phenomenon—the occasional solitary animal that is never seen in company with other dolphins, and which lives a life apart from the security offered by a group. Occasionally these loners associate with humans instead, perhaps to satisfy a need for company. We do not know if they have left voluntarily or have been driven out.

Cooperation

Cooperative behavior is regularly seen in feeding bottlenose dolphins. Indeed, they have a remarkable ability to adapt to a wide variety of feeding situations, and have devised clever ways to catch prey. In South Carolina, they are known to cooperate to drive fish up onto a muddy river bank, then beach themselves briefly to grasp the flapping fish.

While animals that spend their lives together are likely to exhibit a high degree of coordination, cooperative feeding does not necessarily imply altruism—by agreeing to cooperate, all benefit as individuals. When searching areas with less prey, bottlenose dolphins often forage singly or in small groups.

Some populations or communities of bottlenose dolphins reside in bays or estuaries where there is a constant food supply. They sometimes forage outside in open water, but generally remain in a restricted area—their "home range." Within a "community home range," individuals may have preferred foraging areas. Along coastlines, small populations may live in overlapping home ranges, which they patrol in search of food, traveling in groups for defense. One such community comprises about 100 Sarasota Bay dolphins. Mating probably occurs among such adjacent groups.

TACTILE CONTACT *Social relationships are constantly reinforced with touching, from gentle caresses to more violent pushing.*

Sperm Whales

An animal of extraordinary appearance, the sperm whale has equally extraordinary habits.

Herman Melville, in his classic story *Moby Dick*, declared the sperm whale king of whales, and expressed the fascination seafarers, and whalers in particular, felt for this archetypal whale. The largest of the toothed whales, the sperm whale is the deepest of all divers, possibly descending as far as 10,000 feet (3,000 m) in its search for squid. It is found in all seas from the equator to the edge of the polar ice.

MUTUAL GOOD *Sperm whales in the North Atlantic (right and below) appear to have different levels of association, perhaps moving in and out of groups in response to the amount of food present.*

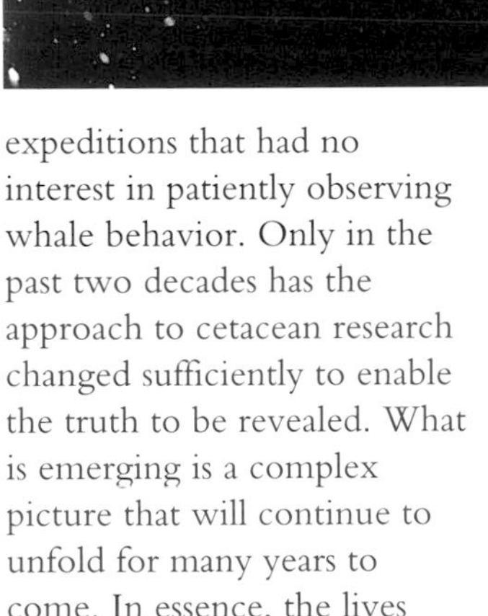

Early Perceptions

The perception of the social organization of sperm whales was for many years based on aspects of human society. Mature males are much bigger than females, and it appeared that sperm whale society was dominated by powerful males who maintained harems of females and their young. These harem masters ruled by defeating challengers in combat, leaving the females only for the annual summer migration of males to feed in polar or subpolar waters.

These perceptions fitted the observable facts at the time, when sperm whales were mainly encountered by whaling expeditions that had no interest in patiently observing whale behavior. Only in the past two decades has the approach to cetacean research changed sufficiently to enable the truth to be revealed. What is emerging is a complex picture that will continue to unfold for many years to come. In essence, the lives of mature males and females are quite different.

Nursery Schools

At the center of sperm whale society is the so-called "nursery school," comprised of adult females and immature animals of both sexes, including suckling calves. These schools are found near oceanic islands, seamounts, and continental shelves in equatorial to temperate regions, rarely straying north or south of 45 degrees latitude. Off the Galápagos Islands, a research team led by Hal Whitehead found three levels of association within nursery schools. Small groups, called "units," average 13 animals and remain together for years and possibly for life. These units often join into "groups," which average 23 animals and remain

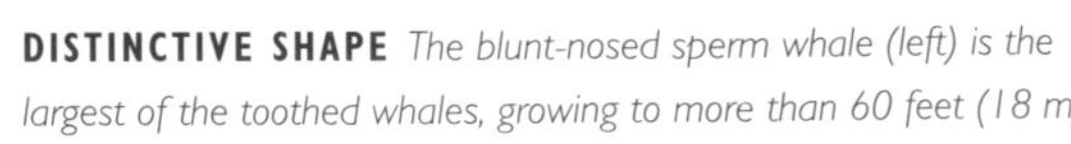

DISTINCTIVE SHAPE *The blunt-nosed sperm whale (left) is the largest of the toothed whales, growing to more than 60 feet (18 m).*

EAVESDROPPING ON SPERM WHALES

In 1983, Dr. Hal Whitehead and several companions sailed into the Indian Ocean in the tiny 33 foot (10 m) sloop *Tulip*, to begin a program of sperm whale research in the Indian Ocean Whale Sanctuary—particularly in the area off the east coast of Sri Lanka. This was the first time that such research had been attempted. Tracking groups of whales day and night by their underwater clicks, they used the small, self-sufficient vessel to locate and stay with the whales for periods of days and weeks. They identified and got to know individuals and gained unique insights into their social organization, behavior, and ecology.

Geographical remoteness and increasing civil strife made it impracticable to continue the research in Sri Lankan waters, so in 1985 Hal (pictured below), his wife Lindy, and their colleagues continued their research around the Galápagos Islands in the equatorial east Pacific. There they continue to record and unravel the complex social relationships and communication of these mysterious whales, and to throw new light on their feeding and diving behavior, and ecology. With Hal Whitehead's entry into the field, the study of sperm whales entered a new phase.

together for about a week. Several groups may then join into "aggregations," which form for only hours, and average 43 whales. It is likely that the more abundant the food, the larger the groupings.

There is a high degree of social cooperation within these nursery schools. It is obvious that a nursing mother who must dive deep for up to half an hour or more to feed, needs help to protect her calf, which must remain near the surface. Within permanent units, the care of calves is a shared responsibility. Females born into such a unit will probably remain with it for life, developing strong ties to its other members. Young males, on the other hand, apparently leave, or are made to leave, on reaching puberty between 7 to 10 years of age.

Bachelor Schools

Young males then join other socially immature males in "bachelor schools," which live separate lives from the nursery schools, although they may occur in the same area. As the males mature, they continue to associate with males of a similar age, and form smaller bachelor schools. Finally, when they become physically mature at around 27 years of age, other males become competitors rather than allies, and from that point, males are more often solitary. Indeed, fully grown bulls have come to be regarded as almost always solitary. They make very distinctive underwater vocalizations that may serve to keep them apart. However, the presence of broken teeth and jaws, and extensive scarring on their heads indicates that fighting does occur among mature males.

It seems that males compete for access to the reproductive females in a nursery school, and only one male at a time will mate with the females in a school. He will usually stay with such a school for only a matter of hours, before moving on to find another school. Yet in whaling days, mature males often defended nursery schools that they were attending: the sinking of the whaler *Essex* in 1820 seems to have been an example of this.

Southern Right Whales

Southern right whales have revealed a social system of surprisingly subtle complexity.

In 1970, the study of southern right whale society was initiated by Roger Payne and his then wife Katherine at Península Valdés, Argentina, where it had been noticed that these whales gathered every year. This was exciting news, because right whales, both southern and northern, had been comprehensively slaughtered by whalers during the nineteenth century, and even after their protection in 1935, their recovery had been hampered by illegal poaching.

For the same reason that they were once the easiest whales to kill, southern right whales are the easiest species of cetacean to study—during their breeding season, they congregate very close to shore, often in shallow bays. As a result, they can be easily observed from headlands and cliffs in areas such as the Gulf of San José at Península Valdés without being disturbed. This is a mating and calving area, and Roger and Katherine soon became aware that a rich tapestry of social life was unfolding before them.

FASCINATING STUDY *A female southern right whale (above) and calves at the Head of Bight, South Australia. Roger Payne and Katherine Payne (below) watching a southern right whale in the Gulf of San José, Argentina.*

Mating

Like many other species, right whale females mate with a succession of males. Males move from female to female, seeking those that are sexually receptive. Unlike humpbacks and some other whales, there is little violent competition between males for reproductive access to females; indeed, right whales are generally most peaceable. Instead of physical competition, right whales engage in "sperm competition." Males have the largest testes in the animal kingdom, each pair weighing about one ton and producing copious quantities of sperm.

It is thought that actual competition occurs among sperm (see p. 297), with males waiting patiently for each other to finish, provided the female is willing. There seem to be alliances among males to help each other by restricting a female's movements so that they can mate more easily. If a female, larger than the male, doesn't want to mate, it is difficult to force her to do so. She may move into very shallow water to dissuade her suitors, turn on her back, or simply swim away from them.

Social Customs

It was long thought that right whales were basically solitary, and did not form lasting relationships. But females seem to form preferred groups with other females, at least within seasons. Whale researcher Stephen Burnell has studied southern rights at a major calving site at Head of Bight,

South Australia, since 1991. Mothers tend to keep newborn calves apart from other whales, but as they grow and begin to explore their environment, they are allowed to interact with other whales, usually mothers and calves.

Not all mothers and calves are acceptable: some are threatened if they approach, others ignored, while favored ones may approach. It is not uncommon to see a female with two calves swimming beside her, while the mother of one of the calves patiently waits, submerged, nearby. Occasionally, a calf will leave with the wrong mother, and then its own mother must turn and rush back to it. Meanwhile, small groups of subadults may prowl like teenagers in a shopping mall, looking for action.

Physical Communication

Right whales are extremely tactile animals, and subtle in their behavior. While whales such as humpbacks are very vocal and probably mediate much of their behavior by the use of underwater sound, right whales spend a good deal of their time in physical contact

EASY VIEWING *A group of three subadult whales (above) visit a female and calves at Head of Bight, South Australia. Close-up (right) of a southern right whale breaching.*

with others, although socializing adults also vocalize. A right whale will signal its displeasure at being approached by another whose company it does not want, not by some extravagant display, but simply by orienting its body so that its flukes, its main weapon, point at the interloper. This message is picked up at a considerable distance, and usually provokes a change in course away from the unwelcoming individual. Courting adults make surprisingly sensuous use of the pectoral fins, stroking and caressing one another.

Mothers and very young calves are in almost constant touch, and as the calves grow and explore farther away, they frequently return for reassurance. This is partly related to their feeding: young calves feed frequently, but in short bursts, while older calves feed less often, but for longer. The gentleness of a cow with a boisterous calf has to be seen to be believed. Since the calf depends on the cow's milk supply, and this is not infinite, discipline is sometimes needed.

Yet, despite the closeness between mother and calf during the first few months of life, the following season when they return to the breeding area, the mother promptly abandons her well-grown offspring, and returns to the Southern Ocean feeding grounds, leaving the yearling to make its own way in society. As yet, there is no evidence of a special relationship between mothers and calves in later years. Newly weaned yearlings soon learn to associate with others, perhaps including calves they met during their first season.

The Mystery *of* Strandings

Of all the varied aspects of cetaceans' lives, none has such a grip on the public imagination as strandings.

HIGH AND DRY *Beached false killer whales at Seal Rocks, on the east coast of Australia in 1992.*

Usually well covered by the media, the sight of a large group of whales or dolphins dying on a beach, or being pounded by surf, provokes feelings of pity, incomprehension, and impotence. How do such superbly adapted marine animals come to be out of their element and helpless?

Types of Strandings

Animals may be alive or dead when stranded; they may be alone or in groups, sometimes very large. The great majority of whales, dolphins, and porpoises die out at sea, and are either consumed by sharks while still afloat, or their bodies may sink and be eaten by the small animals of the sea floor. The bodies of stranded dead animals have probably drifted ashore with winds or currents while still inflated with the gases of decomposition. These are usually single animals, unless there is a fatal epidemic afoot within a local population. Sometimes dead strandings give vital clues to the cause of death, which may include net entanglement, ship strike, or toxic pollution.

Why Do They Strand?

Humans have long been perplexed by live strandings. Prehistoric humans would certainly have used stranded cetaceans for food and other useful products, and are likely to have had their own explanations of why these animals had come ashore. The Greek philosopher and natural historian Aristotle, among the first to write of the phenomenon, had the sense to admit that whales strand "for no apparent reason."

More recently, speculation has abounded, and for many years cetacean "suicide" was a popular theory. Strandings have even been linked to extraterrestrial life and cosmic events. Another theory proposes that the animals are trying to return to their evolutionary roots on land.

More sensible explanations have come from serious studies, which have revealed that the species that strand most often, and in greatest numbers, are those that form cohesive social groups and are commonly found in deep water away from coastlines. These include pilot whales, false killer whales, and sperm whales. Their unfamiliarity with the coastline may be a factor. Species that spend much time along coastlines, such as humpback and southern right whales, rarely strand.

Deep-water animals may follow prey inshore; indeed, sperm whales, considered to be the deepest diving whale, have recently been found feeding in very shallow water off New York. Other correlations suggest that whales have navigational "malfunctions." Serious infections of parasitic worms are sometimes found in the ear canals or the brain, which may affect the whales' coordination, orientation, balance, and hearing. Weakness

RARE EVENTS *A single juvenile humpback (left) in Western Australia, and more than 400 long-finned pilot whales (below) stranded in Catherine Bay, New Zealand.*

or confusion caused by injury or disease may drive animals into the shallows, where life can be prolonged a little without drowning.

Coastal topography seems to play a crucial part. Many strandings occur where there are gently sloping beaches. In such places, perhaps the echolocation signals of toothed whales are deflected away by the sloping bottom, indicating open water ahead.

In New Zealand, headlands of a certain configuration are thought to shepherd whales into dangerous waters, particularly when adjacent to a shelving bottom. Sandbars shift with time, perhaps confusing even animals that are familiar with an area. Weather may also play an important part in many strandings: onshore winds and heavy seas could hamper cetaceans retreating from a dangerous situation in shallow water, especially on a falling tide.

Another possibility is that cetaceans may navigate using anomalies in the Earth's magnetic field. Migratory birds and marine turtles, for example, have this ability, and magnetite, a mineral involved in geomagnetic navigation in other animals, has been found in the brains of some cetaceans. Such a capability could help to explain the whale's marvelous ability to navigate over great tracts of apparently featureless ocean.

Yet such a sense could also lead cetaceans astray. In Britain, a correlation has been noted between strandings and locations where magnetic lines of force cross the coast at right angles, although another study in New Zealand has shown no such correlation.

The worst stranding on record was a herd of more than 400 long-finned pilot whales in New Zealand in 1985, but there have been many others involving scores or hundreds of animals. The key may be in the strong social bonds among members of many toothed whale societies. If an individual is sick, injured, or dying of old age, the lifetime habit of assisting group members in trouble is not broken because of proximity to shore.

This may seem noble or foolish, but such social structures are the key to survival for these species. This was not understood for many years, and the notion that they were bent on suicide was reinforced because rescued animals often restranded immediately. In reality, they were showing an extreme reluctance to leave their fellows, possibly even their mothers or calves.

IN THE SHALLOWS *The slope of the beach at Seal Rocks, Australia, may have disoriented these false killer whales.*

There's nothing like a jaw-to-jaw encounter with a friendly shark or whale to get the juices running.

SYLVIA A. EARLE (b. 1936), American marine biologist and conservationist

CHAPTER FIVE

IN *the* FIELD

GETTING *into the* FIELD

Once you have decided to take your interest in whales to the practical stage of going out to look for them in the wild, how do you go about it?

The world of cetaceans is vast and varied, and options for viewing them depend on what you can afford in time and money and, to a certain extent, on where you live. A resident of Monterey, California, or of Sydney, Australia, will find it easier to go whale watching than someone living inland.

The first step is to find out where and when whales, dolphins, and porpoises can be found. The activities of many species are influenced by the seasons, and there is a wealth of information concerning the time and place different species can be found. Watching Whales, Dolphins, and Porpoises (page 390) features 28 locations where you are most likely to encounter cetaceans. Like migrant birds, the movements of whales cross national boundaries, so it is possible to see the same population of, for example, gray whales feeding in the Gulf of Alaska in July, and then breeding along the Pacific coast of Baja California, Mexico, in February. In many areas, cetaceans are present year-round. Some areas are famous for sightings of one species; others host many.

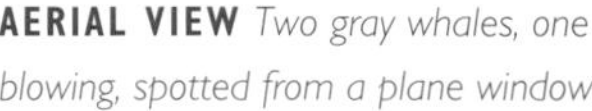

AERIAL VIEW *Two gray whales, one blowing, spotted from a plane window.*

BACKGROUND DATA

Take the time to do some research, according to your interests. Perhaps there is a coastal area that you have long wished to visit, and you may be able to combine your visit with whale or dolphin watching. On the other hand, if you are interested in a particular species, you could plan your holiday around their movements.

While there are many whale-watching sites of world importance and reputation, successful encounters with cetaceans are possible at many lesser known areas. Local knowledge can be obtained from natural history museums or the National Marine Fisheries Service in the United States (or the equivalent government wildlife authorities elsewhere). You could also consult the commercial whale-watching industry or local residents of particular areas. Check out the information available on the Internet. Extend your knowledge by joining a volunteer group that organizes whale-watching activities, including counts and surveys of scientific value. This way, your love of whale-watching provides valuable help.

TYPES OF ENCOUNTER

What sort of whale-watching experience do you want? Would you like to experience the brief, close encounters offered by commercial whale-watching vessels? Would you prefer the more leisurely, less intrusive approach of observing coastal migrations from the shore? Or are you likely to take your own vessel into waters frequented by cetaceans? Going whale watching by yourself gives you flexibility of timing and movement. On the other

INTERACTION *Atlantic spotted dolphins enjoy playing with a snorkeler who is using an underwater scooter.*

Blue seas ... are the domain of the largest brain ever created, / With a fifty-million-year-old smile.

Whale Nation,
HEATHCOTE WILLIAMS
(1941–), English poet

hand, placing yourself in the hands of others may give you access to whales you otherwise cannot have, as well as to the knowledge and expertise provided by professionals.

Remember that watching whales and dolphins usually requires patience. If you are short of time, by all means join a scheduled cruise, and take your chances—you may or may not see the animals. The more time you spend watching for cetaceans, the more varied and interesting behavior you will see.

The range of whale-watching experiences is very broad. You can wade with bottlenose dolphins at Monkey Mia in Western Australia, observe humpbacks from inflatable boats on the Antarctic Peninsula, or river dolphins from a wooden boat on the Amazon. You can watch the passing of migrating gray whales from Californian headlands, or feeding fin whales in the Gulf of St. Lawrence in Canada. You can watch humpback whales glide over the warm shallows of Silver Bank in the Dominican Republic, or sperm whales diving off the South Island of New Zealand.

A rise in some baleen whale populations since whaling ceased, coupled with the increase of global tourism and commercial whale watching, means that many more people are now encountering cetaceans than even a decade ago. Backed by unprecedented levels of public interest, this has increased awareness of and concern for dolphins and whales, and has had considerable economic benefits for many coastal communities. Numbers of recreational boaters have also grown sharply, and they often encounter whales. Never before has there been such scope for the cetacean enthusiast.

COLD COMFORT *Watching humpbacks near Melchor Island, Antarctic Peninsula.*

NEW FRIENDS *A tourist feeding the dolphins at Monkey Mia, Shark Bay, Western Australia.*

PREPARING *for a* FIELD TRIP

Like any outdoor activity, whale, dolphin, and porpoise watching requires careful preparation, for comfort, safety, and enjoyment.

Once you have decided where and when you wish to look for whales, there are several things to consider. Will you be on the water, or on land? Are you going to be exposed to the elements for long periods of time? Will you be in a remote area?

If you are going to sea and you don't know if you are prone to seasickness, you should assume that you are. Consult your physician or pharmacist for an approved remedy, such as acupressure patches or oral medication.

PROTECTION

Remember that when you board a commercial whale-watching vessel, you should be shown what safety equipment is on board, and where it is stowed.

Whale watching in all its forms involves some exposure to the elements: wind, sun, rain, heat, cold … even sleet and snow. It is essential that you are prepared for any conditions you might meet. Not only will being caught unprepared (so that you become sunburnt, wet, or cold) spoil your experience, it may even be dangerous.

So think about where you're going and what climatic conditions you can expect—not only the average, but the extremes. You may be surprised. Tropical regions, for example, do not always exhibit the "balmy breezes" of the tourist brochures. Often the trade winds blow at almost gale force, sometimes for weeks at a spell. Desert regions, such as Baja California in Mexico, can be witheringly hot and windy, while mild temperate regions, such as southern Australia, can experience sudden cold changes, even in summer. It is best to be over-equipped with warm and dry clothing if possible—one of your companions may need extra protection one day.

Windproof wet-weather gear and a good sunscreen are probably the most important items, particularly if you are on the water. When dressing for cold conditions, use the "layer principle"—several relatively light layers of clothing, which trap insulating air between them. In this way, when temperatures change, a layer or two can be donned or shed. Hypothermia and sunstroke are killers, and with current levels of ozone depletion, ultraviolet radiation is a serious health risk. Deep tans no longer make sense, but sunscreens do. Good sunglasses, either polarized or UV-proof, will protect your eyes from the intense glare on water, and also make it easier to see whales in bright conditions. Remember that about 35 percent of body heat is lost from the head, so take a warm hat or cap, whatever the conditions.

BE PREPARED *You never know what the weather might do so always have warm, waterproof clothing and protection against the sun and glare off the water.*

PERSONAL COMFORT

The inner person also needs looking after during long sessions searching for cetaceans. Snack food is always welcome, and cold or hot drinks may be essential in extremes of climate. Each adult will need about 2 pints (1 L) of fluid per day, considerably more in hot, dry conditions. A vacuum flask is a good investment for both hot and cold drinks or soups.

You may wish to prepare for periods of boredom, when

ESSENTIAL REFERENCE
A reliable field guide (below) can be used to check distinguishing features, such as the flukes of this humpback (left) sighted at Stellwagen Bank, New England.

whales are not to be seen. You can read (a good time to read up about cetaceans), sketch or paint, watch birds, or simply watch and listen to the sea in its changing moods.

Whale-watching Gear

The basic equipment needed for watching cetaceans is quite simple: something to see them with, and information to help identify what you see.

Most important of all are binoculars, the eyes of any observer of wildlife, and they should always be close at hand. A good pair of binoculars will convert that distant splash into a living animal. They will enable you to identify whales at a distance, and to follow details of their behavior and the subtle features of their appearance that would be invisible to the naked eye. If you can afford to buy a good pair of binoculars, they are well worth the extra expense. Buying cheap ones may be false economy, as their poorer optics give a lower quality image, and tire the eyes more.

You should select a pair of binoculars between 7x and 10x magnification—the number of times closer an object appears through the binoculars than with the naked eye. Anything less than 7x is not powerful enough, and any more than 10x is probably too heavy, and hard to hold steady. You will notice when looking at binoculars that two numerals are given, for example, 7x50, or 8x40. This second numeral (50 or 40) refers to the diameter of the front lens in millimeters (1 inch = 25 mm). The greater this number, the more light the lens lets in and the more effective it is in low-light conditions. But this also results in heavier binoculars. You have to find a balance of weight, viewing clarity, and power that suits you. More expensive binoculars, of the roof-prism type, tend to be more compact and lighter for a given magnification, while porro-prism ones are bulkier and heavier. Waterproof binoculars are more costly.

Spotting telescopes are useful, especially for land-based watching and on cruise ships, but are too powerful (generally between 15x and 60x) to keep steady on small boats. From land, to watch a distant whale, they are ideal, but they can't replace binoculars, and are usually used after a sighting has been made with binoculars or the naked eye.

You should also have at hand a good field guide to cetaceans, such as this book, or perhaps one that specializes in the area where you are. Watching whales becomes much more interesting when you know which species you are observing. You can then put your own observations into a framework of what is known about the species, such as its migrations and behavior.

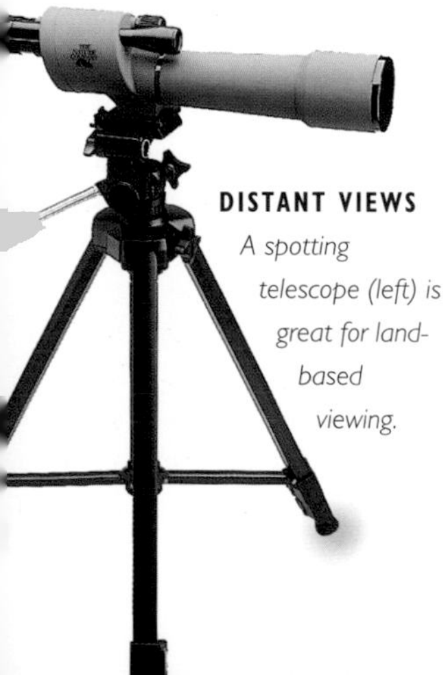

DISTANT VIEWS
A spotting telescope (left) is great for land-based viewing.

Whale Watching *from the* Shore

There's a world of whale watching to be had from land, which in its own way offers as much as vessel-based experiences.

OFFSHORE *Whale watchers line the cliff top (left) to see gray whales off the west coast of North America each year.*

In the minds of many people, the archetypal image of whale watching is that of close encounters from the deck of a whale-watching vessel. But when you consider the vast extent of the Earth's coastlines, and how often many species can be found close to land, the potential for shore-based watching becomes obvious. With a little knowledge of where to go and what to expect, visits to coastal regions may take on the added excitement and satisfaction of watching cetaceans as they move and live along the coast.

Shore-based watching is free, you can do it independently any time you like, you can take your time, and combine it with your travels. You can do it in weather too rough for whale-watching vessels (although whales are difficult to spot in rough conditions), and you can enjoy the often beautiful and wild coastal scenery. Most important, you will not affect the behavior of the animals, because you are not intruding upon their environment.

The main disadvantage of shore-based watching is that you must depend on the animals coming within viewing range. It is frustrating, for example, to see the splashes of a school of dolphins or the blows of a very large whale, off near the horizon, without any hope of being able to identify them. You must also be prepared to be patient and often to see nothing.

Where to Go

Many scientific studies take advantage of the ease with which cetaceans can be observed from land. Migratory gray whales tend to swim within 5 or 6 miles (about 10 km) of land, occasionally coming within a stone's throw while passing the Pacific coast of the United States. They can even be seen in the surf. The cliffs of Point Reyes, California, provide spectacular views of migrating whales, as do many of the headlands of northern California. In a few key areas of Washington State and British Columbia, orcas and other species may be observed from shore. Much farther north, bowhead whales stream around Point Barrow, Alaska, on their migration into the Beaufort Sea. The east coast of the United States offers less scope for shore-based whale watching. In the Southern Hemisphere, humpbacks are seen daily during their migration past Cape Byron, Australia's easternmost point, also well known for its surfing bottlenose dolphins. Off the arid Nullarbor coast of South Australia, southern

right whales congregate at the base of limestone cliffs for months during the breeding season, making this arguably the best whale-watching site in the world. They mate and rear their calves virtually at the watcher's feet, oblivious to the attention they are receiving. The Gulf of San José in Patagonia, Argentina, offers similar chances to observe right whales from shore, as does the Cape Whale Route of South Africa.

Cetaceans often enter fiords and bays to feed or rest. Bottlenose dolphins are the most commonly sighted coastal cetacean worldv because of their habit o coming close inshore. are often seen in harbo creeks, and estuaries. Some may become habituated to human contact, as has occurrec at Monkey Mia, in Western Australia, where interaction between humans and dolphins has reached such levels that it has been necessary to regulate the contact. Similar situations have developed elsewhere, and in some places, humans even swim with dolphins.

Planning Encounters

There are two ways to plan your expedition. Either choose an area you wish to visit, or select a species of particular interest. Obviously your choices are somewhat limited, as not all species closely approach land on a regular basis. Many species, such as sperm whales, are found in deep water and are usually observed from boats. Your options will also be dictated by the seasons, and by the seasonal movements of the cetaceans themselves.

Obviously, coastlines with high cliffs or headlands will offer the best prospects for viewing cetaceans. When you are viewing from a cliff top, the horizon is many times farther away than when you are viewing from sea level, and many a pleasant hour can be spent tracking the distant blows of whales as they move along a coast. Binoculars or a spotting scope are a must, and you will develop the knack of finding a comfortable position where you can remain for hours. Wind and sun can take their toll, so find a sheltered spot if possible, and be prepared with hat and sunscreen. You may be able to camp at a suitable lookout: nothing is more enjoyable than the first sighting of the morning as you sip your coffee or tea.

With migrating species, such as gray and humpback whales, face the direction from which the whales are likely to come, and be patient. Occasionally scan around, looking for anything out of the ordinary—a fleeting dark shape, a splash, or the puff of a whale blow. Blows may be visible for 5 miles (8 km) or more through binoculars.

During migrations, there may be a constant stream of whales all day, with several pods visible at once. Try to follow individual pods, remembering that whales may submerge for 10 minutes or more. When waiting for whales to resurface, look ahead of where they dived—they usually maintain the same speed, whether at the surface or submerged.

MIGRATIONS *The movement patterns of many species are well known. Southern rights (left), swim close to shore. A mother and calf (above).*

JOINING THE FUN *Windsurfers find a novel way (left) to see humpback whales close to the shoreline in Bonavista Bay, Newfoundland, Canada.*

WHALE WATCHING *from* BOATS

Vessel-based whale watching takes you into the whale's domain, and offers experiences of an immediacy that cannot usually be gained from land.

The phrase "vessel-based whale watching" includes a wide range of experiences—from paddling a kayak among whales, to spending an afternoon on a commercial whale-watching boat, to viewing them from a ferry, or the bridge of a luxury cruise liner during an ocean voyage. These experiences fall into two categories—take yourself, or let someone else take you there.

ON YOUR OWN BOAT

Almost any boat can be used for whale, dolphin, or porpoise watching. The suitability of certain types of craft depends on the location, weather, water conditions, the operator's experience, and an awareness of how to behave around marine mammals (see p. 322). In sheltered waterways, small, fragile craft, such as sea kayaks or rowing boats are sometimes used to approach cetaceans. Only fully proficient users of such craft should share the water with whales. Although usually considerate toward small boats, when whales are engaged in vigorous activities, such as feeding or social interactions, they may easily bump or swamp a small craft that has drifted too close, and this is no time to learn self-righting techniques.

Some vessels have less impact than others. Vessels under sail obviously create little underwater noise. Low-revving engines have less effect than, say, the high-pitched whine of an outboard motor at speed, which can disrupt cetacean communication and behavior at a considerable distance. Speed itself is a problem: if you are in an area frequented by marine mammals, proceed slowly and keep a sharp lookout. Also consider having a propeller guard fitted, as whales, dolphins, and manatees are increasingly the victims of propeller strike.

Many people encounter whales while using small power craft, such as the runabouts used by recreational anglers. Operating any craft on open waterways is a serious undertaking, and you should not only be proficient in boat handling, but you should also be provided with suitable safety and communication equipment, and know how to use it. Warm and waterproof clothing, together with sufficient food and drink, are essential.

Once you have sighted whales or dolphins, it's time to abide by the whale-watching regulations (see p. 322). However, there is nothing to stop whales and dolphins being drawn to you. One of the most enjoyable of all whale-watching experiences is to have a vibrant group of dolphins bow riding—jostling for prime position in the pressure wave at the bow; clicking, whistling, and making eye contact with humans peering down from only a yard or so above. If you are moving at high speed

BRAVING THE COLD *(right) in Zodiacs to watch humpback whales in the pack ice of the Antarctic Peninsula. A dusky dolphin (above) riding the bow wave of a small boat, Kaikoura, South Island, New Zealand.*

CLOSE ENOUGH *Kayaker meets orcas (above) in British Columbia, Canada.*

when dolphins approach, slow down. They prefer slower speeds, and will stay with you longer if you do so.

Whales and dolphins seem to enjoy the silent movement of yachts, and dolphins will often bow ride for extended periods with a yacht under sail. Whales are drawn to yachts, perhaps because they are of a comparable size, and are vaguely whale-shaped. If whales are encountered while sailing, you may wish to heave to nearby, and wait to see if they will approach you, as they often will.

Commercial Operators

Commercial whale watching is a booming industry in many parts of the world, and has been an economic lifeline for many coastal towns, including ex-whaling communities. Most people experience their first close contact with whales and dolphins through such commercial operations, which can provide some truly memorable experiences.

Most commercial operators are responsible, and have a genuine concern for the well-being of the whales. They interpret natural history and behavior for their clients, and most people come away from such experiences with a heightened understanding of and concern for the magnificent animals they have been privileged to see. But because whale watching has become such a competitive industry, ethics are sometimes sacrificed to gain an edge. To provide spectacular displays, such as breaching, for their customers, some operators harass whales. You can exercise responsibility by choosing operators with a good reputation, or by pointing out infractions, should they occur, to the operator.

HYDROPHONES

The calls of cetaceans are an important part of their social interactions. Many people have heard the famous songs of humpback whales, but all cetaceans "vocalize" at various times. The world of underwater sound that can be accessed by hydrophones, underwater microphones, can be a revelation. Apart from the moans, cries, and clicks of cetaceans, there are the beautiful calls of seals, the snapping clicks of shrimp, and the astonishing variety of sounds made by fish. You may also hear how pervasive are the sounds of boats.

The technology for listening in on whales and dolphins is simple and relatively inexpensive. Hydrophones (inset picture) are lowered 20–30 feet (6–9 m) into the water from a stationary boat. These are connected to a pre-amplifier, which magnifies the signal before it passes to a cassette recorder. Complete off-the-shelf units or hydrophone and pre-amp components are readily available from mail-order suppliers of electronic and scientific equipment.

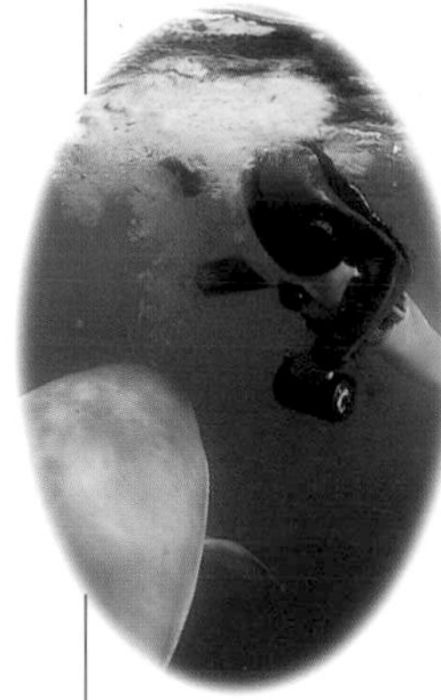

Whale-watching Guidelines

Some countries now have whale-protection legislation in place—with whale-watching guidelines being an important component.

These guidelines may have the force of law, and are designed to reduce the potential disturbance of cetaceans by vessels and aircraft. One reason such guidelines are necessary is the physical welfare of those aboard the vessels (see p. 320), who may be at risk in situations where whales feel harassed. The main reason, however, is the welfare of the whales, because they are vulnerable to disturbance and harassment, even when it is unintended.

Underwater sound is a very important form of disturbance to cetaceans that is frequently overlooked because it is invisible. Sound travels much faster and farther through water than in air. A cetacean's sense of hearing is acute and it uses sound for communication, navigation, and finding food. Many vessels produce engine or propeller noises that are so loud that they can be detected from miles away, so at close range they could disturb many species. Just as important, some frequencies are more of a problem than others, depending on the hearting and vocal ranges of the species concerned.

It is thought that whales can detect sounds made by an icebreaker 18 miles (about 30 km) distant. Even the sounds of aircraft can penetrate water: a low-flying jet fighter passing overhead was detected by hydrophone at a depth of 60 feet (18 m). With these facts in mind, the potential for disturbing whales by a group of noisy whale-watching vessels or low-flying aircraft becomes more obvious.

DISTRESS SIGNALS *The beluga whale (above left) and the humpback (above) are both blowing underwater, a possible sign of disturbance.*

Physical Intrusion

There is also the issue of physical disturbance. The presence of boats (combined with greatly increased noise levels as the vessel approaches) within or near a group of whales, or even a single whale, can disrupt their normal activities. Whales and dolphins live their lives according to strict time and energy budgets and, often, can ill afford to be distracted from vital behaviors, such as breeding, feeding, or nursing calves, to avoid craft that may be disturbing them.

Boats can physically threaten whales by violating "polite" distances, or they can separate whales from others in the pod, which is particularly serious in the case of mothers and calves. Low-flying aircraft, particularly helicopters, may appear threatening to cetaceans.

Cetaceans respond to the attentions of humans in different ways. If they are approached carefully and considerately, they may simply carry on as they were, minding their own business. They may decide to break from what they were doing and come to investigate the vessel, which is just what the whale watcher wants. If the attention is unwelcome, they may show it in various ways.

The ability to read these changes in behavior is the key to success, and anyone who

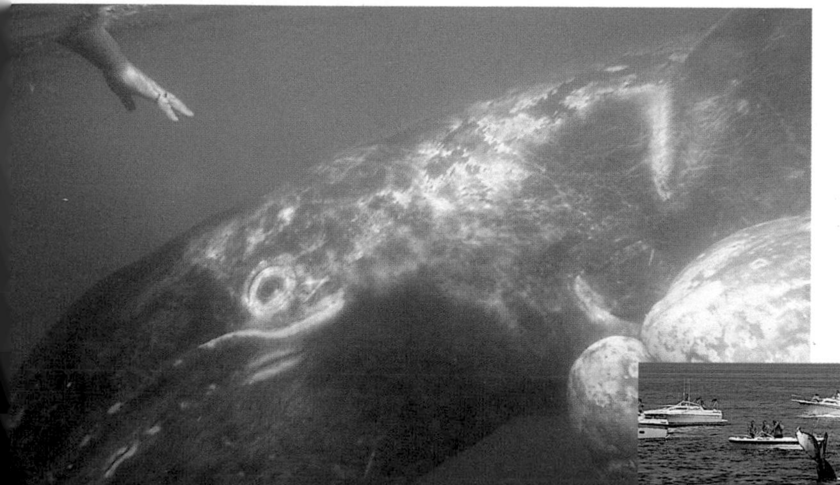

HARASSED *A tourist reaches down to pet a gray whale (left) in Baja, Mexico. The humpback (below) may be lobtailing because it feels vulnerable—a result of overcrowding by whale watchers in New England*

intends to watch whales regularly should acquire the skill. At the first sign of disturbance, such as an unusual or abrupt change in behavior (see below), you should back off immediately.

SIGNS OF HARASSMENT "Harassment" is persisting in following or approaching whales when they are exhibiting escape or disturbance behaviors. If you are not sure if you are disturbing the animals, give them the benefit of the doubt. Escape or disturbance behaviors include: rapid changes in speed or direction; increased breathing rate; prolonged diving or changing course underwater; blowing underwater, or loud "growling" blows at the shielding of calves by their mothers; tail slapping, tail slashing or breaching, or making threatening "rushes" past the boat. These may all (but not always) indicate that the whales are upset by your presence. One problem is that some of these behaviors are spectacular, and some unscrupulous individuals are known to harass whales deliberately to get a spectacular response. This very exploitative view of cetaceans ignores their needs.

As a member of the whale-watching public, you should regard it as your responsibility to become aware of the relevant standards and behaviors. Try to base your own personal guidelines on the most stringent available.

You may feel moved to request that others, including commercial operators, abide by them. But remember that guidelines are not based on biological realities, they are a compromise that gives the whale-watching public what it wants: a reasonably close view of whales. While the legal minimum approach distance is usually 110 yards (100 m), cetaceans will usually be well aware of you before you reach that point, and may be moving to avoid you. Chasing a whale to bring it to the legal minimum distance may constitute serious harassment. The responsible whale watcher knows when to leave the animals alone.

HOW TO APPROACH A WHALE

Never pursue a whale that seems disturbed by your actions and never separate whales in a pod. If seriously alarmed, whales may change direction, or remain submerged for longer than usual, or even leave the area. Avoid making loud noises. When approaching in a boat, either (A) position your craft 330 yards (300 m) ahead and to one side of the animal and wait quietly for it to pass, or (B) approach slowly from the side, never closer than 110 yards (100 m). Swimmers should leave 33 yards (30 m) clear. (Illustration not to scale.)

Chapter Six
Identifying Whales, Dolphins, *and* Porpoises

Greatest of all is the Whale, of the Beasts which live in the waters,
Monster indeed he appears, swimming on top of the waves,
Looking at him one thinks, that there in the sea is a mountain,
Or that an island has formed, here in the midst of the sea.

Abbot Theobaldus (c. 1022)

Identification Techniques

Identifying cetaceans at sea can be frustratingly difficult, and even the world's experts are unable to identify every animal they encounter.

Developing the skills necessary to tell the species apart can be satisfying, but the animals do not make it easy. They spend most of their lives hidden from view underwater, and even when they come to the surface to breathe, they often disappear before it is possible to get a good look. When they do reveal more of themselves, or stay on the surface for longer, many of them look remarkably similar and are almost impossible to tell apart. There is even a great deal of variation within each species, and no two individuals look exactly alike: they vary in color and size, behave differently, and their dorsal fins are not uniform.

The simple fact that whales and dolphins live in the sea adds yet more complications. Imagine trying to get an accurate impression of an animal on the move, while struggling to keep your balance on a rolling, slippery deck. Adverse conditions, such as a whitecaps, high winds, heavy swell, driving rain, or even glare from the sun, add to the challenge.

Despite all these potential difficulties though, there are ways of identifying whales, dolphins, and porpoises. In fact, it is quite possible for anyone to recognize the relatively common and distinctive species and, eventually, many of the more unusual ones as well. All it requires is a little background knowledge and some practice.

The best approach is to use a relatively simple process of elimination. Run through a mental checklist of key features every time a new animal is encountered at sea. The more features you are able to take into account, the better chance you have of making a positive identification. Ultimately, this process becomes almost automatic, and you learn to recognize a particular species by its unique combination of features or, in bird-watching jargon, its own "jizz," a slang term for "general impression of size and shape."

CHARACTERISTICS *of the pygmy right whale (below, top), typical of baleen whales, could never be confused with those of toothed whales, such as the Atlantic white-sided dolphin (below, bottom).*

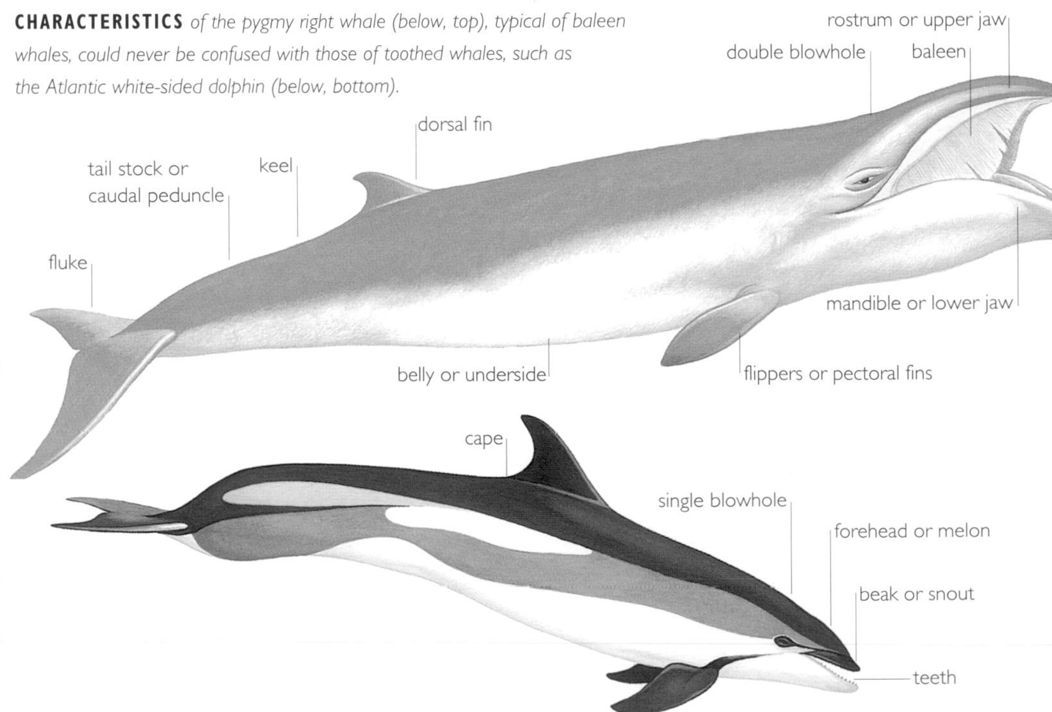

NOTEWORTHY *The tall dorsal fins of three males (right) identifies this as a pod of orcas. The distinctive heart-shaped or V-shaped blow (far left) is characteristic of the gray whale. The prominence of the beak of this common dolphin (below) is one of its distinguishing features.*

IDENTIFICATION CHECKLIST

Becoming familiar with the most obvious features of your subject will help greatly.

Geographical location There are not many places in the world with records of more than a few dozen species of whales, dolphins, and porpoises. So taking the location into account immediately limits the number of possibilities.

Habitat Just as woodpeckers inhabit woodlands rather than shores, and giant pandas prefer mountains to wetlands, most whales, dolphins, and porpoises are adapted to specific marine or freshwater habitats.

Unusual features The tall dorsal fin of the male orca, the long tusk of the male narwhal, the extraordinary curved teeth of the male strap-toothed whale, and highly distinctive features of some other species can often be useful for a quick identification.

Size Estimating size accurately at sea is notoriously difficult, unless a direct comparison can be made with the length of the boat or something else in the water. But simply deciding whether the animal is small, medium, or large can help to eliminate a range of possibilities.

Color and markings Distinctive markings and bright colors can be useful identification features. However, since colors at sea vary according to water clarity and light conditions, they can also be quite confusing if they are at all subtle.

Dorsal fin The size, shape, and position of the dorsal fin varies greatly among species and a few species have no fin at all. While rarely enough alone, such details can be useful in combination with other features for making a positive identification.

Flippers It is rarely possible to see the flippers, or pectoral fins, clearly—but their length, color, shape, and their position on the animal's body, vary greatly from one species to another.

Body shape The animal's overall shape can sometimes be useful, although many whales, dolphins, and porpoises rarely show enough of themselves to give a satisfactory impression.

Beak In oceanic dolphins, and some other toothed whales, the presence or absence of a prominent beak is a particularly useful identification feature.

Flukes Some large whales lift the flukes high into the air before a dive, others do not. This distinction alone can help with identification, but it is also worth checking the shape of the flukes, which vary considerably from species to species.

Blow or spout The blow is immensely useful for identifying larger whales. It varies in height, shape, and visibility among species and, especially on calm days, can be all that is needed for a positive identification.

Dive sequence The way in which a whale, dolphin, or porpoise breaks the surface to breathe, and then dives again, is known as its dive sequence. In some species, this is very distinctive, although differences in others can be quite subtle.

Behavior Most whales, dolphins, and porpoises have been known to breach, pec-slap, lobtail, and perform other well-known behaviors at one time or another. But they all have slightly different techniques, and some are more active at the surface than others.

Group size The number of animals seen together is a useful indicator; some species are highly gregarious while others tend to live alone or in small groups.

BODY SHAPE *and* SIZE

Whales, dolphins, and porpoises have broadly similar body shapes, but they vary greatly in size and, on closer inspection, reveal many subtle differences.

IDENTIFYING FEATURES *A clear view of the flipper of a short-finned pilot whale (above). A bottlenose whale (left) has a bulbous forehead and dolphin-like beak.*

On land, it is possible to estimate the size of animals with considerable accuracy, using trees, telegraph poles, bushes, rocks, buildings, and a host of other recognizable objects to provide the essential element of scale. But it is notoriously difficult to estimate the size of a whale or dolphin, a bird, a boat, or anything else in a vast expanse of "empty" sea. If 10 people were asked to estimate the size of a whale or dolphin, chances are there would be 10 completely different answers.

If the animal comes close enough to the boat, it may be possible to make a direct comparison: a whale roughly two-thirds the length of a 100 foot (30 m) vessel, for example, is clearly about 65 feet (20 m) long. But most of the time, it is necessary to estimate the size without the benefit of such a comparison.

Despite the difficulties involved, this is not a major problem for identification purposes. The trick is simply to decide whether the animal is small (up to 10 feet [3 m]), medium (10–33 feet [3–10 m]) or large (more than 33 feet [10 m]). Don't try to be accurate to the nearest few inches, or even feet, because this scale will instantly narrow down the number of possibilities: 42 species are "small," 28 species are "medium," and only 11 species are "large."

BODY SHAPE

Unfortunately, many whales, dolphins, and porpoises rarely show enough of themselves to reveal their overall body shape. But when they leap into the air, or are visible underwater, this can be an immensely useful aid to identification. The huge, rotund body of a right whale, for example, is quite different to the long and relatively slender body of a fin whale. Many of the differences between species are far more subtle to the untrained eye, but with a little practice, they can easily be recognized.

NEW ZEALAND'S *Hector's dolphins (left) have unusually rounded dorsal fins.*

DORSAL FINS

The character of the dorsal fin is rarely enough on its own for a positive identification, especially as it varies greatly from one individual to the next, but it can be useful in combination with other features. The key variables to look for are its size, shape, and position on the animal's body.

The blue whale's dorsal fin is distinctive for being small and stubby, and for its location three-quarters of the way along the animal's back. In

Leviathan …

Upon earth there is not

his like …

The Bible,
BOOK OF JOB 41:33

contrast, the sei whale has a tall, sickle-shaped fin, located much farther forward. The male orca has an unmistakably tall dorsal fin, reaching an incredible height of up to 6 feet (1.8 m), while the dorsal fin of many hump-backed dolphins sits on an elongated hump in the center of their back. Hector's dolphins have distinctive rounded fins that are likened to Mickey Mouse ears.

Only eight species have no dorsal fin at all: the finless porpoise, the southern right whale dolphin, northern right whale dolphin, narwhal, beluga, northern and southern right whales, and the bowhead whale. A number of others, including most of the river dolphins, the Irrawaddy dolphin, sperm whale, and gray whale, have only tiny dorsal fins or small humps.

FLIPPERS (PECTORAL FINS)

It is rarely possible to get a clear view of the flippers, or pectoral fins, when watching whales, dolphins, and porpoises at sea. Humpbacks sometimes wave their enormous flippers in the air, which is handy for identification purposes, but they are the exception rather than the rule. In most species, the flippers remain well hidden—except during a breach or a close encounter when the water visibility is particularly good.

However, the length, color, and shape of the flippers, as well as the position on the animal's body, vary greatly from one species to another and can be useful in conjunction with other identification features. They can be short or long, narrow or broad, drab or strikingly colored, and come in a range of combinations in between.

Interestingly, the length of the flippers is one of the few ways of distinguishing a short-finned pilot whale from a long-finned pilot whale at sea.

BEAK OR NO BEAK

The presence or absence of a long, well-defined beak is a valuable identification feature in many toothed whales. In some species, the beak is distinctive and clearly demarcated from the forehead, while in others it is barely noticeable or even absent. Pilot whales, for example, have bulbous foreheads with indistinct beaks, while bottlenose whales have similar foreheads with dolphin-like beaks.

The 27 species of oceanic dolphin are difficult to tell apart at sea, but simply checking for the presence or absence of a beak immediately cuts the possibilities by half.

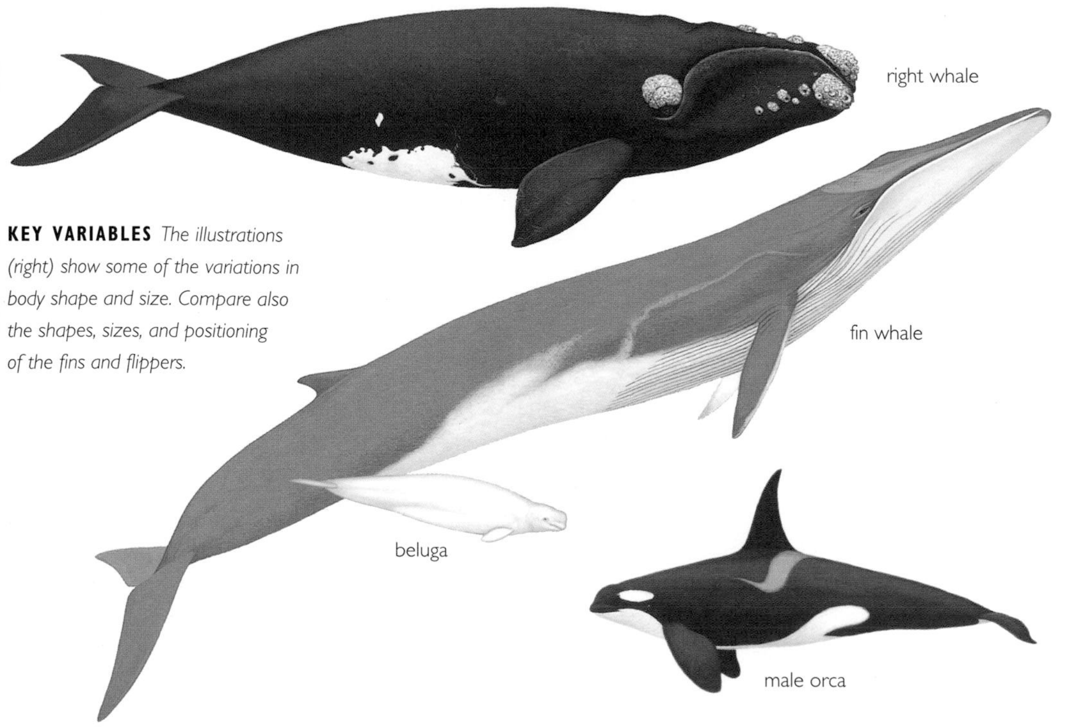

KEY VARIABLES *The illustrations (right) show some of the variations in body shape and size. Compare also the shapes, sizes, and positioning of the fins and flippers.*

Dive Sequence

The way in which some whales, dolphins, and porpoises break the surface of the water to breathe, and then dive again, can be sufficiently distinctive to make a positive identification.

The dive sequence is particularly useful when identifying large whales, although there are many factors to take into account. For example, the way a whale breaks the surface can vary according to its age, if it is feeding or engrossed in breeding activities, the speed at which it is traveling, the depth from which it has surfaced, and whether it is feeling stressed or relaxed.

The sequence also varies if the whale is simply catching its breath or about to embark on a deeper dive. A gray whale, for example, may break the surface to breathe half a dozen times before diving, but may raise its flukes only on the final occasion. Normally, it is this final dive sequence that is the most revealing for identification purposes.

Among the large whales, seven species regularly lift their flukes high before diving: gray, blue, bowhead, northern and southern right, humpback, and sperm. Raising the flukes is a useful identification feature in itself although, unfortunately, none of these whales fluke every time; on some dives they prefer to keep their flukes below the surface. The shape and design of the flukes can also be useful for identification, since they vary considerably from species to species. Sperm whales, for example, have broad, triangular flukes, while gray whales have flukes which have noticeably convex trailing edges.

Bryde's, minke, sei, and fin whales almost never lift their flukes on a dive. Inevitably, though, there are exceptions: several fin whales in the Sea of Cortez, Mexico, for example, lift their flukes on a regular basis.

Minke Whale

The minke whale has a very distinctive dive sequence. First to appear is normally its sharply pointed snout, which breaks the surface at a slight angle. As the rest of the head comes into view, it drops to a much shallower angle, the whale begins to blow and

DIVE SEQUENCES

The dive sequence is often a useful tool for identification purposes.

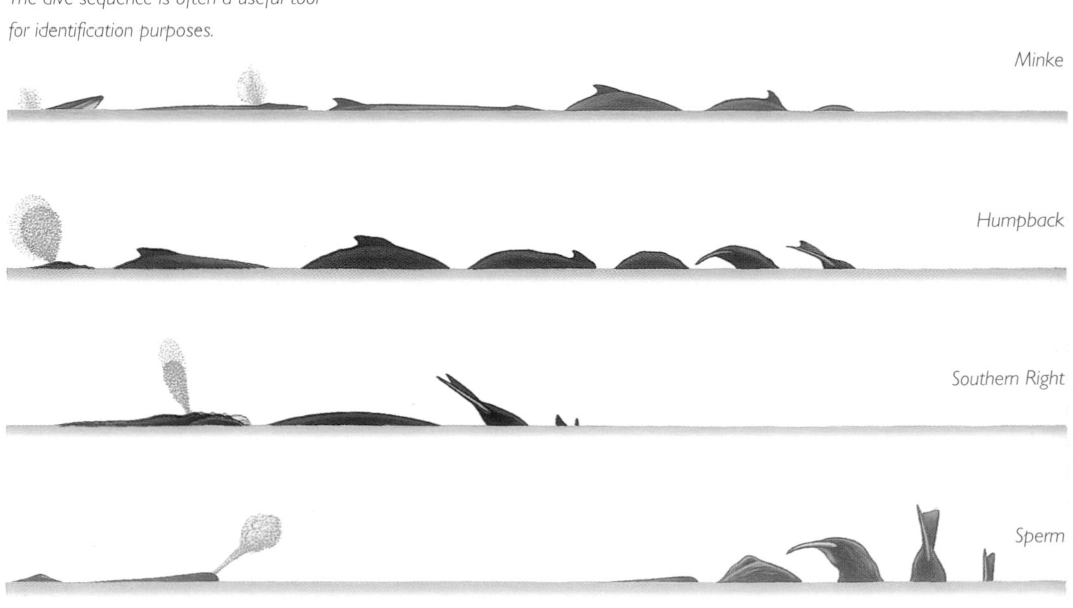

EXCEPTION TO THE RULE *This fin whale in the Sea of Cortez, Mexico, is lifting its flukes as it dives.*

then the blowholes appear. The blowholes and dorsal fin are often visible at the same time, distinguishing the minke from all other members of its family except the sei whale and smaller youngsters of other species. Toward the end of the dive sequence, the back and tail stock begin to arch strongly, in preparation for a long dive, but the flukes do not appear above the surface.

Humpback Whale

When a humpback whale surfaces to breathe, its splash guard and blowholes appear above the surface first. Then its low, stubby dorsal fin comes into view, and its distinctive sloping back forms a shallow triangle against the surface of the sea. As the humpback arches its body, forming a much higher triangle, the hump on its back is especially evident. Toward the end of the dive sequence, while the dorsal fin drops below the surface, the tail stock is strongly arched and the whale rolls forward. As it steepens its angle of descent, its flukes begin to appear above the surface and the distinctive black-and-white markings on the underside are clearly visible from behind.

Southern Right Whale

The head of a southern right whale is usually held high out of the water as it surfaces to breathe, showing its distinctive callosities. After the whale has produced its characteristic V-shaped blow, its head disappears below the surface and only the smooth, broad, finless back is visible. Free of barnacles and callosities, the back is also very distinctive. The whale normally raises its flukes when diving, but sometimes may "false-fluke" and not lift them out of the water.

Sperm Whale

The sperm whale frequently remains motionless when catching its breath, although it may swim leisurely. As it lifts its head for a final breath, only two-thirds of its body length is normally visible. The sperm whale then straightens and stretches its body, gently arches its back and briefly disappears. It accelerates and reappears a little farther on. Arching its back until it is high out of the water, making the rounded hump and "knuckles" along the upper side clearly visible, it then throws its flukes and the rear third of its body high into the air and drops vertically, with barely a ripple.

Small Cetaceans

Some small cetaceans also have distinctive dive sequences. The harbor porpoise often rises to breathe in a slow, forward-rolling motion, for example, making it appear as if its dorsal fin is mounted on a revolving wheel; both the Indus and Ganges river dolphins may surface at such a steep angle that their entire head and beak can be seen above the surface; and the dwarf sperm whale simply drops out of sight, rather than rolling forward at the surface like most other small whales.

While it can be immensely useful, the dive sequence is not a foolproof means of identification. The trick, as always, is to use it in combination with other features.

DISTINCTIVE DIVES
Before diving, gray whales (left) always lift their flukes, while dwarf sperm whales (below) just drop down below the surface.

Blow Shape *and* Size

Experienced whale watchers can often tell one species from another just by the height, shape, and visibility of their blows, or spouts.

"Thar she blows!" was once a familiar cry from the mastheads of whaling vessels. For a long time, whalers believed that the animals squirted water from their heads. Pliny the Elder went so far as to suggest that a sperm whale could fill a boat with water from its spout to capsize it. People were often warned to keep out of the spray, which was claimed to be so unbelievably smelly it could cause disorders of the brain. According to another popular myth, if touched by the spray, human skin would peel away as if burned by a flame. Even Herman Melville commented that "if the jet is fairly spouted into your eyes, it will blind you."

What Is the Blow?

Despite the myths, it is not water being spouted from a whale's head but air. As the animal surfaces to breathe, its blowhole opens and there is an explosive exhalation followed immediately by an inhalation. The blowhole closes tight once again, and the whale dives. The process takes no more than a few seconds, even in the largest of whales.

BLOWHOLES *Toothed whales, such as the bottlenose dolphin (left), have a single blowhole; baleen whales, such as the humpback (below), have two.*

No one really knows what makes the blow so visible. It is normally whiter and easier to see in cold weather, which suggests that it probably includes water vapor that condenses in cold air. It also contains a small amount of sea water, originally trapped in the area around the blowhole, which is then blown into a fine spray. A third ingredient may be oil droplets and mucus from the whale's air sinuses, windpipe, and lungs—producing a kind of giant sneeze.

Identifying the Blow

Small whales, dolphins, and porpoises tend to have small, brief blows that are rarely visible and normally do not have a recognizable shape. In contrast, most large whales have very distinctive blows and, in calm weather, these can be recognized even from a considerable distance.

There are a number of variables, however, that must be taken into account. In wet or windy conditions, the shape of the blow can easily be distorted. Even in good weather, V-shaped blows may look like single columns if viewed from the side. Also, the power, height, and shape of a blow varies according to the size of the whale, what it is doing, how long it has been underwater, and so on. The first exhalation after a deep dive may be a thunderous blast heard nearly a mile away, while subsequent blows are less powerful and may even differ slightly in shape.

MARVELS *A nineteenth-century engraving (left) of a whale blow from a German picture book; and the side-on view of the blow (far top left) of the gray whale.*

Distinctive whale blows (head-on view)

BRYDE'S WHALE
The thin, hazy blow produced by Bryde's whale is variable in height, although, typically, it rises to about 10–13 feet (3–4 m); it is rarely distinctive from a distance, especially if the whale begins to exhale before breaking the surface.

SEI WHALE
Sometimes described as shaped like an inverted cone, or a pear, the sei whale's blow appears as a single, narrow cloud; it resembles the blows of fin and blue whales, but reaches a height of only about 10 feet (3 m). It is also not as dense.

SPERM WHALE
The sperm whale's unique, angled blow is extremely distinctive, especially on windless days, and projects to a height of 6½ feet (2 m) or more. Since the blowhole is on the extreme left-hand side of the forehead, the blow is projected forward and to its left.

BOWHEAD WHALE
With two widely separated blowholes, the bowhead whale produces a rather bushy, V-shaped blow; the two diverging clouds of spray rise directly upward to a height of about 23 feet (7 m).

FIN WHALE
The fin whale's strong, straight blow appears as a tall, narrow column of spray; it is usually 13–20 feet (4–6 m) high, and can be seen from a considerable distance.

RIGHT WHALES
The right whale produces a distinctive V-shaped blow, having widely separated blowholes like the bowhead. The plumes rise to a maximum height of about 16½ feet (5 m).

BLUE WHALE
Blowing as soon as its head begins to break the surface, the blue whale produces a spectacular column of spray rising to 29½ feet (9 m) or more. The tallest and strongest blow of all whales, it is noticeably slender and upright.

GRAY WHALE
The gray whale's bushy blow is normally described as V-shaped, but sometimes the two plumes meet in the middle and produce a distinctive heart shape; they normally rise to a height of 10–15 feet (3–4.5 m).

HUMPBACK WHALE
Rising to a height of about 8–10 feet (2.5–3 m), the single bushy blow of the humpback whale is surprisingly visible and distinctive; it is usually wide relative to its height, and can occasionally be clearly V-shaped from a distance.

COLOR *and* MARKINGS

It is sometimes possible to identify cetaceans by their background colors, body patterns, and markings such as stripes or eye patches.

Some whales, dolphins, and porpoises have such unique colors that they are virtually unmistakable. The ghost-like, uniformly light color of the beluga is a particularly good example: superbly camouflaged for life in the Arctic, this whale can be surprisingly difficult to pick out among whitecaps or floating ice, but its white, grayish white, or yellowish white body makes it extremely easy to identify.

Other species can be recognized by a distinctive marking or unique combination of markings. There is nothing quite like Heaviside's dolphin, for example. The front half of its body is uniformly gray and the rear half predominantly blue-black. It has dark flippers, dark patches around its eyes and blowhole, white "armpits," and a white underside; there is even an unusual white finger-shaped lobe on either side of its tail stock. Not surprisingly, the combination of these features alone is usually enough for a positive identification.

The patterns formed by distinctive markings are sometimes as significant as the colors themselves. There are two recognized species of common dolphin, for example, and many color variations, but they all share one feature: an elaborate crisscross or hourglass pattern on either side of the body.

EFFECTIVE CAMOUFLAGE *While difficult to spot among ice floes, belugas (above) are easy to identify because of their distinctive uniformly light color.*

There is a single point where the dark color under the dorsal fin, the tan or yellowish side patch, the pale gray tail stock, and the white or creamy underside all meet in the middle—and it makes a splendidly reliable identification feature. The only other species with an hourglass pattern on its sides is the appropriately named hourglass dolphin, but its hourglass is rather crude in comparison, and is in black and white.

Some markings, of course, are a little more tricky to use for identification purposes, either because they are especially subtle or because they are not always visible. Minke whales, for example, are broadly similar in color to several of their larger relatives, but many (particularly in the Northern Hemisphere) have distinctive white bands on their flippers. The size and shape of the bands vary, and they are often hidden from view, but in a good sighting, they can be enough to make a positive identification.

SIGHTING CONDITIONS

Unfortunately, colors at sea vary according to the water clarity and light conditions.

IDENTIFICATION *The minke whale (left) has a distinctive white band on the flipper, especially in the Northern Hemisphere. The extent of black and white coloring (below) varies among Dall's porpoises.*

Even in fine weather, these can change dramatically from hour to hour, day to day, and season to season. The same whale may appear quite different, depending on whether it is observed at dawn, in the bright midday sun, or after sunset. Alternatively, if the sun is low on the horizon, it may cast dark shadows over the whale, giving an impression of stripes or other markings. Similarly, if the whale is backlit, it will appear much darker than if the sun is shining from the front. Cloudy conditions, or rain, may alter its appearance yet again.

One of the best examples of this variability is the background color of the blue whale. It is a pale blue-gray color but, at the surface, it often takes on the color of the sea and sky. It can probably reflect more colors than any other whale: as the sun drops below the horizon, and darkness falls, a blue whale may turn from blue to yellow and orange, then red, lavender, dark gray and, ultimately, to black.

Individual Variations

Another potential pitfall is that members of the same species do not always look exactly alike (see p. 354). Although they do not, as many birds do, change their markings in the breeding season, their markings may alter as they grow older. Males and females sometimes have different colors and patterns on their bodies, and their appearance may also vary on an individual basis. To identify beaked whales by color alone, for example, is risky, because there is so much variation from one animal to another (and besides, little is known about the coloration of live beaked whales).

As always, caution is essential, even with species that appear to have distinctive background colors, body patterns, and markings. Dall's porpoises, for example, are very striking: they are predominantly jet black, with a prominent white patch on their belly and sides. But this white patch varies enormously in size—resulting in a wide range of individuals from all black to all white, and with an endless number of variations in between. So just because an animal does not look exactly like an illustration in a field guide, do not assume that it is another species altogether. Just to be sure, check other diagnostic features as well.

DISTINCTIVE CRISSCROSS *All common dolphins can be identified by the elaborate hourglass pattern on their sides.*

Unique Features

Some whales, dolphins, and porpoises are instantly recognizable by unique features such as scarring, unusual teeth, or strange growths.

It is always wise to check more than one feature before making a positive identification. But a number of species are so distinctive that, with a reasonable sighting, they cannot easily be confused with anything else. Following are some of the most striking examples.

STRIKING FEATURES *The scars of a Risso's dolphin (left) and the crease in its forehead are unique. The huge, squarish head of a sperm whale (below).*

Strap-toothed Whale

Female strap-toothed whales are almost impossible to identify at sea, but the males are among the few beaked whales that are really distinctive. They have two extraordinary teeth (see p. 359), which grow from the middle of the lower jaw, curl upward and backward, and then extend to wrap around the top of the upper jaw.

In older animals, these teeth can grow to a length of 12 inches (30 cm) or more, and may actually meet in the middle. When this happens, they form a muzzle, preventing the whales from opening their jaws more than a couple of inches.

Despite this apparent handicap, males can still catch squid, their main prey, by using their mouths like vacuum cleaners. Indeed, the teeth may even help—by acting as "guardrails" to keep the food on a direct path to their throats.

Risso's Dolphin

Any good-sized dolphin that looks distinctly battered is likely to be a Risso's dolphin (see p. 379). The extensive body scarring on adults is caused by the teeth of other Risso's dolphins and, to a lesser extent, by confrontations with squid. Young animals are relatively unmarked and the scarring becomes more pronounced with age.

Risso's dolphin also has a deep vertical crease down the center of its forehead, which is visible at close range and is another feature unique to this species.

WEAPON *The distinctive, twisted left tooth of the narwhal (left) is commonly broken off as a result of fighting.*

Sperm Whale

Even though it rarely shows much of itself at the surface, the sperm whale (see p. 352) is easy to identify at sea. It is the only large whale with an enormous, squarish head (typically measuring about a third the length of the body). This is particularly huge and distinctive in adult males.

It has three other unique features: it is the only large whale with a single blowhole, an angled blow, and an unmistakable prune-like skin.

Narwhal

The male narwhal has two teeth (see p. 386). The one on the right normally remains invisible, but the one on the left grows to a remarkable length. It pierces the animal's upper lip, develops into a long tusk and eventually looks rather like a gnarled and

DISTINCTIVE APPENDAGES *A good view of the humpback's unmistakably long flippers (above) as it breaches.*

twisted walking stick. (When viewed from the root, it always spirals in a counter-clockwise direction.) It is probably used in establishing sexual dominance, rather like the antlers in male deer.

At least a third of all narwhal tusks are broken, but unbroken tusks reach an average length of about 6½ feet (2 m) and, in extreme cases, may exceed 10 feet (3 m). Approximately 1 male in 500 has two tusks and 1 female in 30 grows a single tusk.

Northern and Southern Right Whales

The two right whales (see pp. 343 and 344) are instantly recognizable by the areas of roughened skin on their enormous heads. These are called callosities, and occur on the rostrum, the chin, the "cheeks," and the lower lips, as well as above the eyes and near the blowholes. Their function is unclear, although they may be used in some way in aggressive interactions.

Realistically, the only way to tell a northern right whale from its southern relative is by the geographical location; fortunately, for identification purposes, there is no overlap in their range.

Humpback Whale

The humpback whale's exceptionally long flippers, or pectoral fins, are unmistakable. They typically measure about 15 feet (4.6 m) in large animals, but grow up to one-third of the length of the whale—making a potential maximum of more than 18 feet (5.5 m). No other whale has flippers anywhere near as long (see p. 351).

Humpbacks also have unique black-and-white markings on the underside of their tails, which are clearly visible when they raise their flukes before a deep dive.

From space, the planet is blue, / From space, the planet is the territory, / Not of humans, but of the whale.

Whale Nation,
HEATHCOTE WILLIAMS
(1941–), English poet

Bryde's whale

Bryde's whales and sei whales are strikingly similar in both size and appearance. At a distance, they can be extremely difficult to tell apart and, for many years, were frequently confused. However, Bryde's whales are unique in having three longitudinal ridges on their head (other baleen whales in the same family have just one) and are therefore unmistakable at close range (see p. 347).

The prominence of the two outer ridges is, unfortunately, variable and, in some individuals, one or both may be difficult to detect at sea. So it is always wise to look for other identifying features as well—just to be certain.

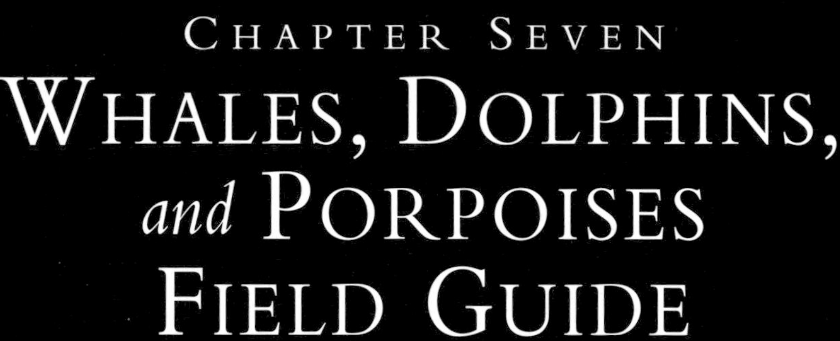

Chapter Seven
Whales, Dolphins, *and* Porpoises Field Guide

Of all animals, none holds sway over so vast a dominion; their watery realm extends from the surface to the bottommost depths of the sea.

Histoire naturelle des cétacés,
Bernard Germain Lacépède (1756–1825), French naturalist and author

USING *the* GUIDE *to* CETACEAN SPECIES

Getting to know whales, dolphins, and porpoises in all their extraordinary shapes, sizes, colors, and perfectly adapted behaviors is a pursuit that can easily become a rewarding obsession.

The field guide describes and illustrates some of the many species of whale, dolphin, and porpoise that dwell in the world's oceans, estuaries, and rivers. It describes important features and behaviors that might help you to identify an animal you have sighted or photographed, and gives the range in which you might expect to find each species. The more information you have, the better you will be able to appreciate the cetaceans you encounter.

*The **main photograph** shows as much of the species as possible, given the constraints of photographing such wild creatures in circumstances and conditions that can be difficult.*

*The **common** and **scientific names** of each species. The species are grouped according to taxonomy.*

*The **text** provides information on the appearance of the whale, dolphin, or porpoise; its common names; habitat; and where and what to look for when you want to find it. The text gives ideas on how to differentiate between similar species, and supplies information about the cetacean's migratory and feeding habits, and breeding grounds. Also discussed are the history of its encounters with humans, such as whalers, and the extent to which these encounters and environmental damage have depleted the cetacean populations.*

***Secondary photographs** highlight a distinctive behavior you may observe, or details of particular features that help identify the species. In some cases, part of the cetacean's habitat is shown.*

This **illustrated banding** at the top of the spread indicates that it is about a cetacean species.

This **panel** refers to the cetacean family to which the species belongs.

Quick-reference Field Notes panel

- *Size from sexual maturity to maximum length of male and female; average size of calf at birth*
- *Main food*
- *Habitat*
- *Range of the cetacean*
- *Status: IUCN category and other notes*

***Color illustrations** supplement the text by showing basic features of the particular whale, dolphin, or porpoise.*

Gray Whale

Eschrichtius robustus

FIELD NOTES

- *Male: 36½–48' (11.1–14.6 m); female: 38½–49' (11.7–14.9 m); at birth: 15' (4.6 m)*
- *Various benthic amphipods, polychaetes, isopods, tube-worms*
- *Inshore to open ocean*
- *Coastal North Pacific*
- *Not listed on IUCN Status list; was intensively whaled, Californian stock is apparently healthy, but Korean stock remains low*

Whalers called gray whales "devilfish," mainly because of the ferocity of the mothers when separated from their calves. Whale watchers are still advised to avoid coming between mothers and calves. Young gray whales, however, can be "friendly," coming to the side of boats and even lifting them partly out of the water.

Mature gray whales carry lice and barnacles, as well as numerous scars and marks. Young gray whales are darker than the adults, and have no barnacles or lice. Adults have robust bodies, bulkier than rorqual whales, but much slimmer than right whales. The dorsal fin, only a small hump, is followed by 6 to 12 knuckles extending down the back to the flukes. Gray whales are often active at the surface, spyhopping, breaching, and at times lobtailing and surfing in shallow water.

The gray whale is a messy eater and is the only whale that is known to feed often in the sand and mud, sucking up benthic amphipods, as well as considerable water, sand, and stones. For some reason, most gray whales feed by rolling onto their right side, but a few are "left-handed" feeders.

Each year, gray whales in the eastern North Pacific make the 12,400 mile (20,000 km) round trip between Mexico and Alaska. The cruising speed on migration is about 1 to 3 miles (1.6 to 4.8 km) per hour. A few, mainly younger whales, make a shorter journey from Mexico, stopping off in the area from northern California to British Columbia.

With its blotchy complexion, often dirty face, and chunky profile, the gray whale might seem an unlikely Californian hero. Yet everyone respects a survivor. Eastern Pacific gray whales, nearly extinct in the late nineteenth century, are now thought to number more than 20,000.

Gray whales, a characteristic mottled gray and easily identified, are frequently spotted close to shore while migrating.

Northern Right Whale

Eubalaena glacialis

Right whales were so called because the early Basque whalers considered them the "right" whales to hunt—full of oil and easy to catch. The northern right whale is the most endangered whale in the ocean. Its numbers have been reduced to about 300 in the North Atlantic, and possibly a handful in the North Pacific.

FIELD NOTES

- *Male: 49–54' (14.9–16.4 m); female: 51–60' (15.5–18.3 m); at birth: 16'+ (4.9 m+)*
- *Copepods and other zooplankton*
- *Inshore and offshore*
- *Temperate and subpolar waters of the Northern Hemisphere*
- *Endangered*

A large, bulky animal, the northern right whale is mostly black with distinctive patches called "callosities" on its head. These patches are covered in whale lice—cyamid crustaceans—which make them appear whitish yellow, orange, or pink. The largest patches, above the eyes and around the tip of the rostrum, are arranged in unique patterns that are used to identify and keep track of individuals.

Northern right whales are unlikely to be confused with other animals since they are the only large whales within their temperate range without a dorsal fin and with callosities on the head. But even the clear sight of a flipper or a fluke is enough for most whale-watch skippers or naturalists to identify them. The flippers are broad and the spatulate shape is unique; the flukes are wide, with a smooth, concave trailing edge and pointed tips, and a deep median notch.

Northern right whales sometimes breach or roll around in the water. When females are ready to mate, they call for males then turn on their backs to play "hard to get" as males charge in from various directions. The males jostle to stay next to the female, waiting for her to roll over to breathe. Then they try to mate. Such behavior can continue for hours.

Once victimized by whalers, the right whale is today a victim of its feeding habits. In some prime right whale areas, shipping traffic needs to slow down to avoid slow-moving right whales as they sift copepods from the water.

The distinctive callosities are clearly visible on these right whales nuzzling each other.

Southern Right Whale

Eubalaena australis

Southern right whales have healthier numbers than their northern relatives, but they are still considered "vulnerable" because of intensive whaling. Protected since 1935, along with the northern right whale, the southern right whale (see also p. 308) has been recovering slowly, but probably numbers no more than 3,000 to 5,000.

FIELD NOTES

- *Male: <50' (<15 m); female: <54' (<16.4 m); at birth: 15'+ (4.6 m+)*
- *Copepods, euphausiids and other zooplankton*
- *Inshore and offshore, mainly coastal*
- *Temperate and subpolar waters of the Southern Hemisphere*
- *Vulnerable, was intensively whaled*

The southern right whale (as well as the northern right whale) has unique callosities on its head, diagnostic of the species as well as individuals. In 1970, Roger Payne and colleagues in Argentina began studies on the southern right whale, among the first photo-identification studies of whales in the world.

Southern right whales and northern right whales (see p. 344) look almost identical, but are considered to be different species. There are small cranial variations between the two species, and they are reproductively isolated. When the southern right is on its calving and nursing grounds, the northern right is half a hemisphere away feeding. Some researchers have noted that southern right whales have more callosities on top of their lower "lip" and fewer on the head than the northern species.

Southern right whales engage in behavior known as sailing—raising their flukes into the wind and using them as sails. This behavior appears to be a form of play—although it is never seen among northern right whales—and is a popular activity in the strong, steady winds off Argentina.

In the austral winter months, southern right whales mate and calve in the inshore waters of Chile, Argentina, Brazil, South Africa, southern Australia, and some Southern Hemisphere islands. Most of them migrate to remote southern waters nearer Antarctica to feed during the austral summer. Less is known about their habits and where they go during the main feeding season.

A southern right whale on its breeding grounds, off Argentina.

Bowhead Whale

Balaena mysticetus

FIELD NOTES

- *Male: 39½–59' (12–18 m); female: 46–65½' (14–20 m); at birth: 11½'+ (3.5 m+)*
- *Euphausiids, copepods, swimming mollusks, and sea jellies*
- *Near pack ice and along leads*
- *Cold arctic and subarctic waters*
- *Vulnerable, was intensively whaled, still hunted off Alaska, Canada, and Russia*

The bowhead spends its life following the advance and retreat of Arctic ice. For the long winter, it lives in total darkness in cold waters. In the short summer, the 24-hour sunshine brings an explosion of life and a world bathed in light.

Bowheads are very rotund, with huge heads containing the longest baleen of any whale. Each side of the jaw contains 250–350 plates which grow up to 10–13 feet (3–4 m), and rarely, reaching 17 feet (5.2 m).

Within their home range, size and bulk alone make bowheads distinctive. The arctic toothed whales, the narwhal and beluga, are both much smaller. Compared to gray, right, or any of the rorqual whales, bowheads have smooth skin and are black all over, except for white to gray areas on the tail stock and around a "necklace" of black spots on the chin.

The few whale watchers who get a chance to meet this whale generally see only two slightly raised humps on the water. The first is the head, followed by the deep indentation behind the blowhole and then the broad, rounded, black back with no dorsal fin.

Bowheads travel in groups of three or fewer, but form larger groups on the feeding grounds. Despite their size and slow-moving nature, they do breach and often raise their tail flukes before diving. They make frequent low sounds, especially while migrating, and may passively echolocate by listening to the echoes of their own sounds off the ice.

Bowhead whales were the second main species—after the right whale—to be targeted by the commercial whaling industry. Driven to commercial extinction, today only a few are taken each year off Alaska, Canada, and Russia by Inuit and other native people.

baleen plates of the bowhead whale

Minke Whale

Balaenoptera acutorostrata

The minke whale was formerly called the little piked whale or little finner in some parts of the world. The smallest and most abundant of the rorqual whales, it is found in all oceans, almost to the edge of the ice. Minkes are the only baleen whales still being regularly hunted by commercial whalers. Estimates of the population are therefore controversial, but they range from 500,000 to 1,000,000 individuals worldwide.

A slim whale with a sharply pointed head, the minke surfaces, blows, and rolls through the water, its dorsal fin appearing briefly before it dives. The minke's smaller size (slightly larger than an orca), compared to other baleen whales, provides the first indication of the species. A good way to identify a minke is to look for the white band on the flippers. This is clearly visible at medium to close range as a white patch just below the surface beside the animal. In some parts of the world, however, the flippers are all black.

When seen up close, the back of the minke whale is swathed in variable areas of dark and light pigmentation. These marks have been used to photo-identify and keep track of individuals.

On their feeding grounds minkes are often seen in pairs, although the numbers can reach up to 100 in a feeding area where food is plentiful. Minkes tend to feed steadily with little concern for boats or people, but sometimes, in certain places, they can exhibit curiosity around boats, even swimming beside a boat for 30 minutes or more.

FIELD NOTES

- *Male: 22–32' (6.7–9.8 m); female: 24–35' (7.3–10.7 m); at birth: 8'+ (2.4 m+)*
- *Schooling fish and various invertebrates*
- *Inshore to offshore*
- *Cold polar to tropical world waters*
- *Insufficiently known, currently being hunted*

A minke at the edge of the ice in Antarctica.

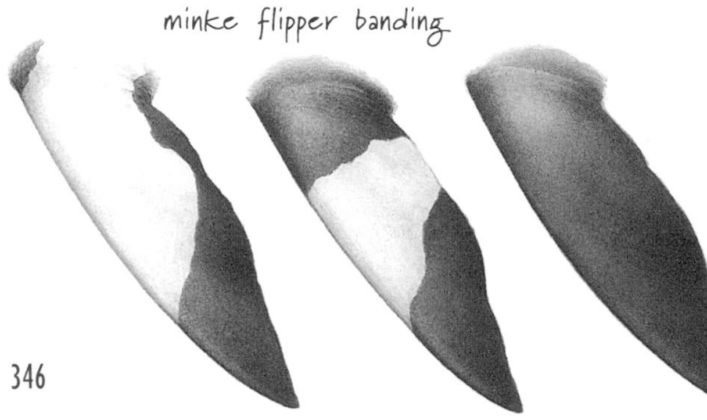

Bryde's Whale

Balaenoptera edeni

Bryde's whales are unique among baleen whales because they spend the entire year in the tropical and subtropical zones, in waters more than 68° Fahrenheit (20° C). They make only short migrations—or none at all—and never visit cold waters. Sometimes called the tropical whale, the Bryde's (pronounced broo-dess) whale is named after Mr. J. Bryde, who helped build the first whaling factory in Durban, South Africa, in 1909.

FIELD NOTES

- *Male: 39–47' (12–14 m); female: 41–51' (12.5–15.5 m); at birth: 11' (3.4 m)*
- *Fish and some invertebrates*
- *Inshore to offshore*
- *Tropical and subtropical world waters*
- *Insufficiently known, has been whaled to some extent*

Smaller than the sei whale, Bryde's whale is slender with short flippers, a prominent, curved-back dorsal fin, and the classic rorqual head—narrow with a pointed snout and numerous throat grooves that enable the mouth to expand when feeding. It is dark above and light on the throat and belly, and the skin is sometimes spotted with circular scars. The most distinguishing characteristic is the set of three parallel ridges on the top of the head extending from the tip of the beak to the blowhole. Sei and other baleen whales have only one ridge down the center.

Typical feeding behavior can be observed at two key sites. In the Gulf of California, Mexico (above), the resident whales feed alone, or may be found in groups of up to five or more, although they are usually widely separated on the feeding grounds. In Tosa Bay, Kochi Prefecture, Japan, the 15 or more resident Bryde's whales feed alone or in mother-calf pairs. Commonly seen here when the animal breaches is the pinkish tinge to the throat and belly. Bryde's whales in both areas will approach whale-watch boats.

There may be separate inshore and offshore populations in various parts of the world. As photo-identification studies are fairly recent, much has yet to be learned.

Bryde's whale head

sei whale head

Sei Whale

Balaenoptera borealis

FIELD NOTES

- *Male: 42–60½' (12.8–18.5 m); female: 44–69' (13.4–21 m); at birth: 15' (4.6 m)*
- *Euphausiids, copepods, amphipods, small fish, squid*
- *Offshore*
- *Tropical to subpolar world waters*
- *Vulnerable, was intensively whaled*

The sei is the middle whale in size in the series of Balaenopterid rorquals (from smallest to largest: minke, Bryde's, sei, fin, blue). It looks like a typical rorqual, with the characteristic narrow snout; the erect, curved-back dorsal fin; and the slender flippers.

At a distance, sei whales are easily confused with the rorquals closest to it in size: Bryde's whales and fin whales. However, Bryde's whales have three ridges on the top of the head, while the sei whale has a single ridge from the tip of the rostrum to the blowhole (see p. 347). The sei whale is smaller than the fin, and unlike the fin, has symmetrical coloring on either side of its head. You can easily tell a sei from a fin by observing both sides of the whale's head just as it surfaces.

Feeding behavior is varied. Like right whales, sei whales skim for copepods, swimming steadily through the water to catch their food, rather than lunging and gulping like other rorquals. For this reason, their ventral pleats are short and the baleen fringes fine. However, in the Southern Hemisphere, krill is the main food, but they will turn to copepods and amphipods. Sometimes great numbers of sei whales follow prey into prime fishing areas. They usually travel in groups of two to five individuals, although on good feeding grounds, many more, often well spaced, are observed.

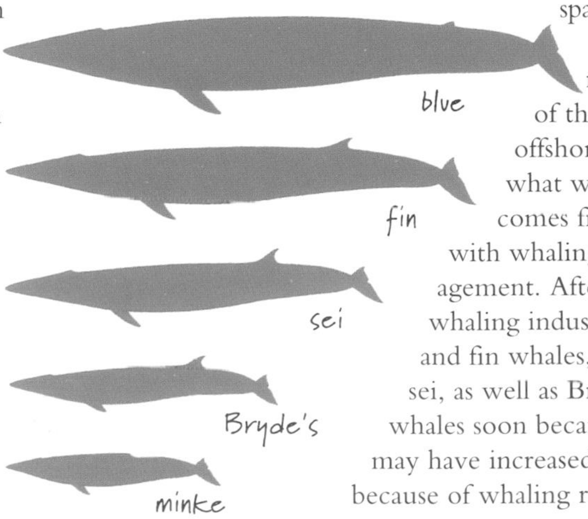

Sei whales are rarely seen because of their preference for offshore waters. Most of what we know about them comes from studies associated with whaling or whaling management. After the commercial whaling industry ran out of blue and fin whales, whalers turned to sei, as well as Bryde's whales. Sei whales soon became scarce, but they may have increased in recent years because of whaling restrictions.

Fin Whale

Balaenoptera physalus

The second-largest living animal after the blue whale (see p. 350), the fin whale's record length is about 88½ feet (27 m). Because of its size and cosmopolitan presence, it was extensively whaled from the late 1800s in the North Atlantic, then in the North Pacific and the Southern Ocean. By the 1930s, when blue whale numbers began to decline, fin whale catches had increased in the Southern Ocean. In the 1970s, seriously declining stocks were protected from whaling, although some commercial whaling continued in the North Atlantic until 1985. Native whaling still occurs off Greenland.

FIELD NOTES

- *Male: 58–82' (17.7–25 m); female: 60–88½' (18.3–27 m); at birth: 19½'+ (5.9 m+)*
- *Schooling fish, euphasiids and other invertebrates, copepods, squid*
- *Inshore to mostly offshore*
- *Warm temperate to polar world waters (usually migratory)*
- *Vulnerable, was intensively whaled*

Individual fin whales are identified by the V-shaped chevron behind the head, the back pigmentation, and dorsal fin marks.

At sea, the fin whale is most likely to be confused with blue and sei whales. All others are much smaller. However, the fin whale has a dramatic asymmetry which whale watchers can easily observe: white on the lower right side of the head; black on the lower left. Sometimes, if the whale is feeding, you can also see the mostly white baleen on the right side; the baleen on the left side is dark gray.

Fin whales are one of the more commonly seen whales in the Northern Hemisphere—they can be seen close to shore off Iceland, eastern Canada, New England, Baja California, and in the Mediterranean. They can also be encountered, although less often and perhaps a little farther offshore, in the Southern Hemisphere, including in the Antarctic.

Fin whales rarely breach or spyhop when being observed and normally just keep feeding. They are often observed alone or in pairs, but on feeding grounds up to 10 or 20 can be found together, with 100 or more at times loosely grouped. In the St. Lawrence, they often travel in pods of 5 to 10, swimming and feeding together in a tight group.

A photo-identification catalog has been set up for the North Atlantic and many researchers are contributing their photos and sightings in an effort to learn more about these animals.

Blue Whale

Balaenoptera musculus

FIELD NOTES

- *Male: 65½–101½' (20–31 m); female: 69–110' (21–33.6 m); at birth: 19½'+ (5.9 m+)*
- *Euphausiids with some squid, amphipods, copepods, red crabs*
- *Offshore*
- *Tropical to polar world waters (migratory)*
- *Endangered, was intensively whaled*

Almost every aspect of the blue whale's appearance and natural history provides another footnote for the record books. This is the largest living animal, but the largest known blue is subject to debate. The "best" record appears to be at least 110 feet (33.6 m) long and a weight of 209 tons (190 tonnes). It was a female—the largest baleen whales are females.

A newborn blue whale measures at least 19½ feet (5.9 m). Biologists have made estimates about its first year of life: a baby blue whale drinks 50 gallons (190 L) of milk a day, adding about 8 pounds (3.6 kg) of weight per hour, or 200 pounds (90 kg) a day. At about eight months of age, when the calf is weaned, it can measure close to 50 feet (15 m) long and weigh about 50,000 pounds (22,700 kg).

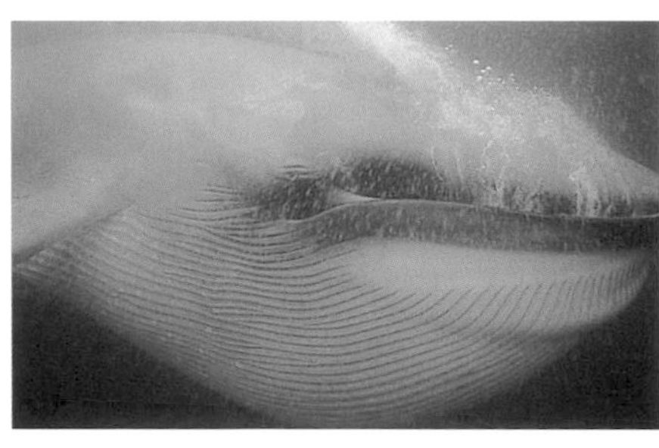

A blue whale gulps a big mouthful of food and water.

Blue whales are so much larger than other whales that distinguishing them is usually easy. Compared to the next largest, the fin whale, the blue whale's spout is thicker and taller. If you cannot see the fin whale's white markings on the right-hand side of the head, look for the shape of the head. Seen from above, a blue has a wide, almost U-shaped rostrum, whereas the fin whale has a more V-shaped head with a pointed snout. In a certain light, it is possible to see the characteristic mottling of the blue whale's back and sides. The mottling picks up reflected blues of the sea and sky, which is the origin of its common name. Individual whales can be identified by the blotchy pigmentation.

At sea, blue whales usually feed alone or in pairs, often widely spaced, probably because they need to work large areas.

Fast-moving for their size, blue whales are thought to be able to exceed 19 miles (30 km) per hour. In the late nineteenth century, they were pursued relentlessly; by the 1950s, blue whales were endangered. Only an estimated 6,000 to 14,000 remain in the world's oceans.

Humpback Whale

Megaptera novaeangliae

The most popular whale on whale-watch trips, the humpback seems happy to perform: it lifts its head out of the water, waves its long, massive flippers, splashes its tail, rolls over in the water, and more than anything else, leaps out of the water. It tends to move close to boats, as if attracted by watchers, and shows little shyness toward humans. There are more spectacular pictures of humpbacks than of any other whale.

FIELD NOTES

- *Male: 36–57½' (11–17.5 m); female: 36–62½' (11–19 m); at birth: 15'+ (4.6 m+)*
- *Various schooling fish, invertebrates*
- *Mainly inshore, but also offshore*
- *Tropical to polar world waters*
- *Vulnerable, was intensively whaled, numbers probably increasing*

The humpback whale is classed as one of the rorquals, but some aspects of its anatomy differ. Compared to the slim, sleek, classic rorquals (see p. 347), the humpback is bulkier, and its skin is knobby and covered in barnacles. The dorsal fin is reduced to a fleshy hump, or hook, that sits on a sort of platform on the back. The tail is not smooth but ragged on the trailing edge. More than anything else, the flippers seem greatly out of proportion. At up to 16 feet (5 m) long, they are the longest appendages of any animal.

Although said to be slow-moving, humpbacks are capable of impressive bursts of speed during mating and fighting. Their feeding behavior is more versatile than other baleen whales and includes bubblenetting (see p. 281).

Humpbacks are seen singly, in pairs, or in groups of up to 15 animals. Mothers and calves stay close for the first year, but on the mating grounds they are often joined by male "escorts."

Humpbacks usually lift their flukes before a deep dive. The flukes have a distinct pattern on the underside, which varies from almost white with black markings, to almost black with only a few white markings. Several thousand humpback individuals have been photo-identified by their fluke markings and have become part of a huge catalog on whales in the North Atlantic, North Pacific, and in the Southern Hemisphere.

A humpback surfaces—its mouth full of fish from bubblenetting.

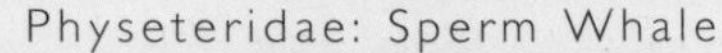

Sperm Whale

Physeter macrocephalus

In many ways, the sperm whale can claim the title "lord of the sea." It ranges throughout most of the world's oceans, except the high Arctic. It has the largest brain of any animal, and is the largest toothed whale—the male can be as long as 65½ feet (20 m). It seems fitting that Herman Melville chose the sperm whale for his novel *Moby Dick*.

FIELD NOTES

- *Male: 36–65½' (11–20 m); female: 27–56' (8.2–17 m); at birth: 13' (4 m)*
- *Deep-water squid, including giant squid and larger fish*
- *Offshore*
- *Tropical to subpolar world waters*
- *Insufficiently known, but still exist in some numbers*

The sperm whale has a number of physical features that make it almost instantly identifiable. At a distance, first seen is often the spout, which is directed forward and a little to the left (the blowhole is on the left side of the forward portion of the head). At closer range, you can see the low hump that barely passes for a dorsal fin, followed by a series of bumps leading to the tail.

The skin can be splotchy, with scratches on the head, and the middle to rear parts of the body prune-like. When a sperm whale breaches, the huge head, up to a third of the body length, is visible. Careful observation reveals white areas around the mouth.

Sperm whales spend most of their lives in either nursery or bachelor schools (see p. 306–7). A nursery school includes females of all ages plus immature males. Mature bulls visit during the breeding season. A bachelor school includes males that are sexually mature, or nearly so. Differences between male and female sperm whales are pronounced. Mature males can be one and a half times the length of mature females. Most females have calluses on the dorsal hump, which males rarely do.

Sperm whales make long, deep dives, possibly up to 10,000 feet (3,000 m) that can last up to two hours. Before diving, they lift their flukes. Although never witnessed, their battles with giant squid are the stuff of legend. Scars on the bodies of sperm whales, and giant squid beaks found in the stomachs of dead sperm whales, provide compelling evidence.

Sperm whales usually congregate in nursery or bachelor schools of up to 50 animals.

Dwarf Sperm Whale

Kogia simus

Whale-watch tours from the Gulf of California in Mexico, Dominica in the Caribbean, and the Tañon Strait in the Philippines, have encountered this little-known, dolphin-sized whale repeatedly. In the Caribbean it is often difficult to tell it apart from its close relative, the pygmy sperm whale. These two whales were declared separate species as recently as 1966.

FIELD NOTES

- *Male: 7–9' (2.2–2.7 m); female: 7–9' (2.2–2.7 m); at birth: 3½' (1.1 m)*
- *Deep-water squid and octopus, fish, invertebrates*
- *Offshore*
- *Tropical to temperate world waters*
- *Insufficiently known*

Underwater, and when found stranded on beaches, the heads of both look shark-like. The dwarf sperm whale is a little smaller than the pygmy sperm whale, but the dorsal fin is larger and more erect—somewhat like a bottlenose dolphin's dorsal fin. Either a glimpse of the head, or a few minutes' observation at sea, will confirm that this isn't a dolphin; the challenge is to distinguish a dwarf sperm from a pygmy sperm whale.

When resting, the dwarf sperm may float lower in the water than the pygmy sperm whale. It is slow-moving and drops directly below the surface instead of continuing to swim forward as it dives. It often travels alone or with a companion, although groups of up to 10 are sometimes seen.

Pygmy Sperm Whale

Kogia breviceps

The shark-like head, false gill markings, and under-slung lower jaw make the pygmy sperm whale look like a fish at first glance. At sea, it rises slowly to breathe, then drops. The dorsal fin is small compared to its overall body size and smaller than a bottlenose dolphin's or a dwarf sperm whale's—two cetaceans with which it could be confused. It is difficult to make a positive identification except during rest periods when it floats at the surface, its head and back exposed and only its tail hanging limply in the water. There are usually up to six animals in a group.

FIELD NOTES

- *Male: 9–11' (2.7–3.4 m); female: 8½–9½' (2.6–2.9 m); at birth: 4' (1.2 m)*
- *Deep-water squid and octopus, fish, invertebrates*
- *Offshore*
- *Tropical to temperate world waters*
- *Insufficiently known*

A warm-water, offshore species, these whales frequently strand on beaches, especially in South Africa, New Zealand, southeastern Australia, and on the east coast of North America. Most of what we know about them comes from strandings. Rarely seen in the wild, whale-watch tours off Dominica have encountered them recently. They seem to be shy animals, seldom approaching boats. When frightened, they may release brown fecal material that clouds the water and may work as a decoy, like squid ink.

Pygmy sperm whale

Cuvier's Beaked Whale

Ziphius cavirostris

FIELD NOTES

- *Male: 17½–22½' (5.3–6.9 m); female: 17–21½' (5.1–6.6 m); at birth: 7'+ (2.2 m+)*
- *Deep offshore cephalopods, some fish and crustaceans*
- *Offshore*
- *Tropical to cold temperate world waters, including Mediterranean Sea*
- *Insufficiently known*

One of the most abundant and widespread beaked whales in the world, Cuvier's is one of the three most watched beaked species (along with Baird's beaked whale and the northern bottlenose whale).

The first details of this species were published in 1823 when the French anatomist Georges Cuvier created a new genus and described what he thought to be an extinct whale. In the 1870s, it was realized that Cuvier's fossil represented a living species, and numerous disparate beaked whale findings from all over the world were re-identified as Cuvier's beaked whales.

The forehead slopes gently to a slight beak. Because the head, often visible as the animal swims, has a shape reminiscent of a goose's beak, Cuvier's beaked whales are sometimes called goose-beaked whales. Often depicted as brown or black, their color varies from individual to individual. Older males, for example, have extensive white areas from the beak to the top center of the body. The whales are heavily scarred—particularly the older males—from the teeth of other males. The two teeth erupt only in males and can be seen protruding from the tip of the lower jaw. Barnacles sometimes grow on the teeth.

The dorsal fin, often the first feature seen at sea, is curved back like that of a dolphin or minke whale, and is positioned far back on the body. Cuvier's beaked whales travel alone (usually older males) or in groups of up to 25, although more commonly 10 or fewer. They arch their back steeply and sometimes raise their tail when diving deep. They may stay down 20 to 40 minutes while hunting for deep-sea fish and squid.

It is difficult to predict sightings, but Cuvier's beaked whales are sometimes seen on whale-watch trips in the Mediterranean, Hawaii, the Canary Islands, and off South America en route to Antarctica.

lower jaw and teeth of Cuvier's beaked whale

Northern Bottlenose Whale

Hyperoodon ampullatus

The northern bottlenose whale, particularly an older male, has a large bulbous forehead and a prominent tube-like beak. The female is smaller with a less pronounced forehead and beak. Both sexes regularly approach ships, and this behavior has made them more likely to be hunted, studied, and, more recently, whale-watched than the other beaked whales.

FIELD NOTES

- *Male: 24–32' (7.3–9.8 m); female: 19–28½' (5.8–8.7 m); at birth: 11½' (3.5 m)*
- *Squid, some fish and invertebrates*
- *Deep waters offshore*
- *Cold temperate waters of the North Atlantic*
- *Insufficiently known, heavily whaled but healthy population in the Gully*

Resident in the cooler waters of the North Atlantic, northern bottlenose whales can be reliably found in the Gully (see p. 411). The whales make dives of 3,280 feet (1,000 m) or more, using their superb sonar system to pursue deep-water squid in the black depths.

Many researchers have watched them playing and socializing; leaping out of the water, and touching one another. Long-term relationships have been observed among whales of the same sex, but not among mixed sexes. Using photo-identification, the researchers have shown that about 230 northern bottlenose whales use the Gully, and that they do not make seasonal migrations. They are among the few whales known to spend the entire year in cold waters.

Northern bottlenose whales have been hunted more than any other beaked whale. In the late nineteenth century, Scottish whalers used to call the old northern bottlenose whale bulls "flatheads." Tens of thousands have been killed since then. Scientists disagree about the extent to which the species has been depleted, and its current status. Increased awareness of northern bottlenose whales through responsible whale watching in the Gully and other parts of their range, may help secure the future for this "friendly" and attractive species.

The bulbous foreheads of northern bottlenose whales protrude above the surface.

Baird's Beaked Whale

Berardius bairdii

Baird's beaked whales inhabit the deep offshore waters of the northern North Pacific. The species was discovered in 1882 when researcher Leonhard Stejneger picked up a four-toothed skull on Bering Island. The following year, he published his discovery, honoring his colleague, Spencer Baird, with the species name. Baird had also worked in Alaska and had just been appointed Secretary of the Smithsonian Institution.

Yet long before this large, up-to-42 foot (12.8 m) beaked whale was classified, the Japanese were catching it with hand harpoons as part of coastal whaling. Today, the Japanese still capture 40 to 60 annually, mainly in the waters off the Boso Peninsula, near Tokyo, and off Hokkaido Island in the north.

Baird's is probably the largest of the beaked whales, with a long beak like a bottlenose dolphin. Unlike most other beaked whales, the males and females both have teeth that erupt: one large pair at the tip of the protruding lower jaw and a smaller pair just behind them. In older animals, the teeth can be worn down to the gums. The bulging forehead is broader and more bulbous in males than females, although females on average are larger. Baird's beaked whales stay in tight social groups ranging from 3 to 30 or more individuals.

Like other beaked whales, Baird's beaked whales dive deeply. Dive times can reach up to 67 minutes, but 25 to 35 minutes is more common. The scarring on their back indicates that there is probably a great deal of play or aggression within the groups.

The chance to see this species in the wild affords a rare opportunity to meet a beaked whale in action. Even for a seasoned whale watcher, who may have met orcas, gray, humpback, right, and sperm whales, a beaked whale encounter would be something special.

FIELD NOTES

- *Male: 30–39' (9.1–12 m); female: 32–42' (9.8–12.8 m); at birth: 15' (4.6 m)*
- *Deep-sea cephalopods, crustaceans, and fish*
- *Offshore*
- *Warm to cold temperate waters of the North Pacific*
- *Insufficiently known, still hunted off Japan*

lower jaw and teeth

Blainville's Beaked Whale

Mesoplodon densirostris

FIELD NOTES

- Male: <19½' (<5.9 m); female: <15½' (<4.7 m); at birth: 6½'+ (2 m+)
- Squid and other cephalopods
- Offshore
- Temperate to tropical deep ocean waters
- Insufficiently known

In 1972, a young male Blainville's beaked whale came ashore on a New Jersey beach. It was alive, and James G. Mead from the Smithsonian Institution drove to the scene and tried to save it. The whale lived for three days, and died without revealing much. Mead has since worked hard to learn more about the mysterious beaked whales.

Blainville's beaked whale was one of the early beaked whales to be identified. In 1817, Henri de Blainville managed to describe it from a small piece of the jaw, which was the heaviest bone structure he had ever seen, denser even than elephant ivory. This also gave rise to its other common name: the dense-beaked whale.

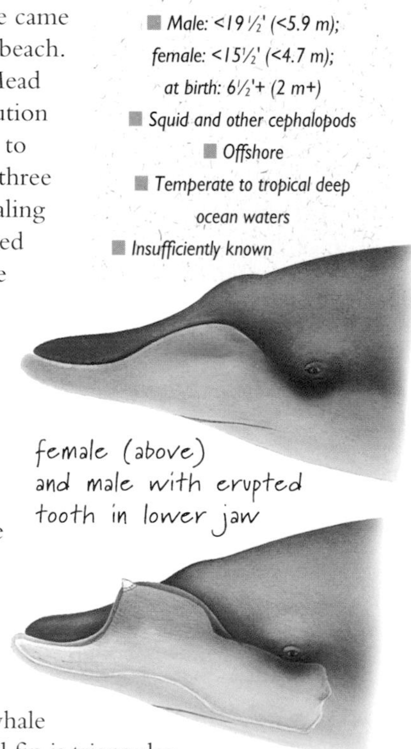

female (above) and male with erupted tooth in lower jaw

The Blainville's beaked whale forehead is flat and the dorsal fin is triangular or curved back. One of the beaked whales with a high-arched jawline, the male has two large teeth on the crest of the arch that grow forward and protrude from both sides of the closed mouth. The female has a beak lighter in color, a less prominently arched lower jaw and, as with most other beaked whales, no erupted teeth.

Traveling in groups of up to 6 (occasionally up to 12), Blainville's beaked whales are often heavily scarred, particularly the males. Circular scars probably come from cookie-cutter sharks and various parasites, while the long, white lines may come from fights with other males. Their deep dives for food can last for up to 45 minutes.

This whale turns out to be one of the more widely distributed beaked whales, commonly stranding on oceanic islands on both sides of the equator. It has been seen on whale-watch trips off Oahu in Hawaii, where researchers were able to photograph the male's head as it surfaced headfirst at a sharp angle, the sun gleaming on the barnacles that covered the two large teeth.

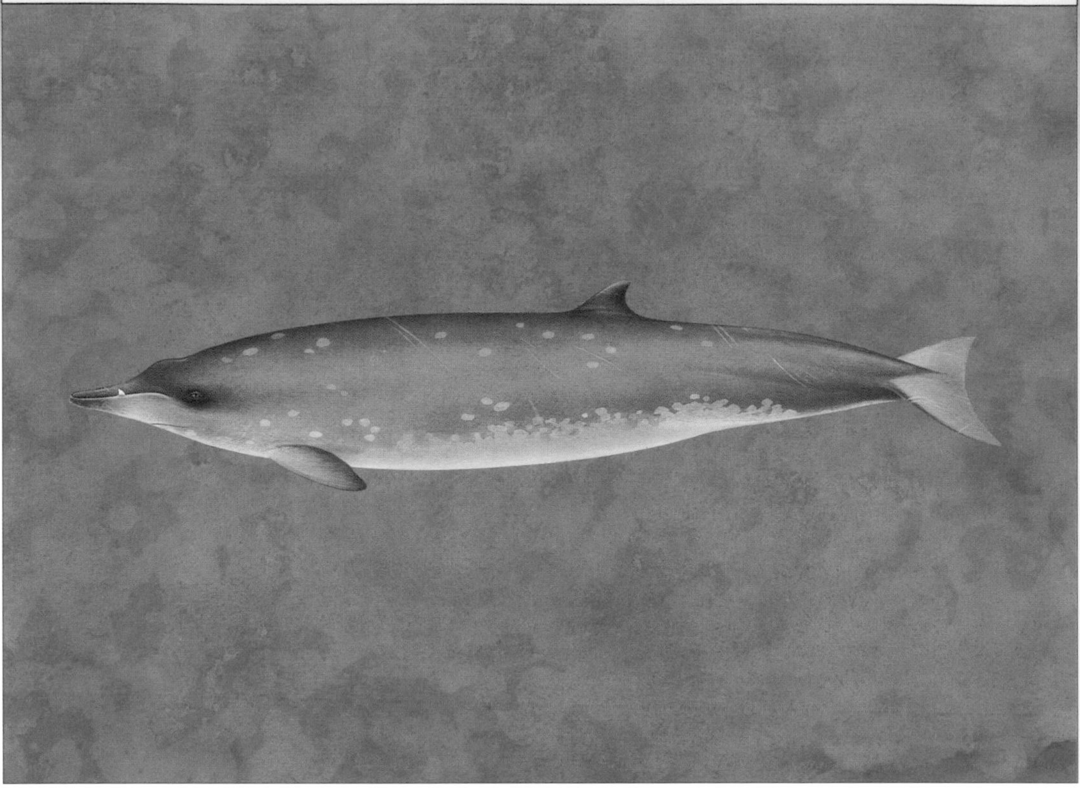

Sowerby's Beaked Whale

Mesoplodon bidens

FIELD NOTES

- *Male: 18' (5.5 m); female: 16½' (5 m); at birth: 8' (2.4 m)*
- *Squid and small fish*
- *Offshore*
- *Cold temperate North Atlantic, including North Sea*
- *Insufficiently known*

More than one naturalist has called Sowerby's the "North Sea beaked whale." Although its range extends across the North Atlantic, this whale is most likely to be found in the northern North Sea. It was first discovered off north-eastern Scotland in 1800. A male had stranded in the Moray Firth and the skull was collected. A couple of years later, James Sowerby, an English watercolor artist, painted a picture of the skull and how he imagined the animal looked. When the pictures were published, he used the Latin name *bidens*, meaning "two teeth," to name the species. Because this was the first beaked whale ever described, the teeth seemed unusual but, in fact, although the position often varies, the males of many species of beaked whale have two protruding teeth in the lower jaw.

The two teeth in the Sowerby's male are located about halfway along the fairly straight mouthline of the lower jaw and are visible even when the mouth is closed. If you could approach close enough at sea, this would be the best way to distinguish them from other beaked whales. Compared to other whales found in the North Atlantic, Sowerby's has a smaller head, longer dolphin-like beak, smaller dorsal fin, and flukes with no median notch. It is smaller than the minke whale.

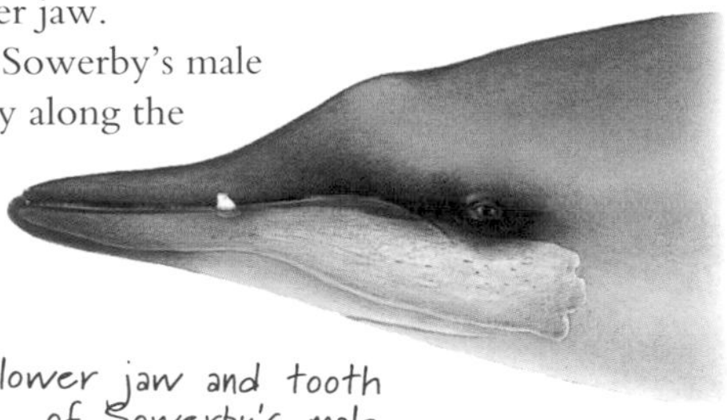

lower jaw and tooth of Sowerby's male

Although Sowerby's was the first beaked whale to be named, it remains one of the more elusive. It has rarely been seen alive at sea. Although a few have stranded on beaches, basic natural history data, such as the contents of the stomach, have not been recorded.

In the early 1970s, a calf and its dying mother were found on a beach in Belgium. A Dutch aquarium tried to rehabilitate the calf, which was 9 feet (2.7 m) long and weighed 408 pounds (185 kg). This provided a chance to see how the animal swam, tucking its flippers into its side and doing all the propulsion and steering with its tail (dolphins use their flippers to steer). Its lack of fine steering ability led to the animal's death as it hit the walls of the small pool.

Strap-toothed Whale

Mesoplodon layardii

FIELD NOTES

- Male: 19' (5.8 m); female: 20' (6 m); at birth: 7' (2.2 m)
- Squid
- Offshore
- Cold temperate circumpolar waters in the Southern Hemisphere
- Insufficiently known

The strap-toothed whale presents one of the puzzles of the whale world. The two teeth in the lower jaw of the male grow up and over the upper jaw, sometimes wrapping right around it. In this position, the jaw can open only a little way, so how does the male strap-toothed whale catch food, much less swallow it? Perhaps it sucks up its food (squid) from the tight corners of deep offshore canyons. The teeth are not needed for chewing—the female survives with no erupted teeth. Some researchers claim that "wrap-around" teeth may function as guard rails to funnel food into the mouth. Most likely the teeth are a sexual characteristic, and help determine the fittest males for mating. The variety of tooth formations originally led to the naming of at least four new species, but in time, scientists recognized that they were all the same species.

At up to 20 feet (6 m) long, the strap-toothed whale is one of the largest beaked whales. At home in the cold temperate Southern Hemisphere, it has turned up on the beaches of Chile and Argentina including Tierra del Fuego, southern Africa, New Zealand, and Australia.

The Southern Hemisphere has produced three new species of beaked whales since the early 1990s. The pygmy beaked whale, *Mesoplodon peruvianus*, up to 12 feet (3.7 m) long, was found in fish markets and on beaches in Peru. The smallest of the beaked whales, it was officially named in 1991. Bahamonde's beaked whale, described in 1995, turned up in the Juan Fernández Islands, 800 miles (500 km) off the coast of Chile. A species called simply "unidentified beaked whale A" has been seen at least 30 times in the eastern tropical Pacific, but it has never been found stranded. A fresh male specimen will be needed to confer full species status and to give it a name.

Beaked whale authority James Mead, of the Smithsonian Institution, has said there may be more beaked whale species still to be discovered. Keep a lookout on deep-sea boat trips: you may be the one to encounter a whale no one has ever seen before.

wrap-around teeth of male

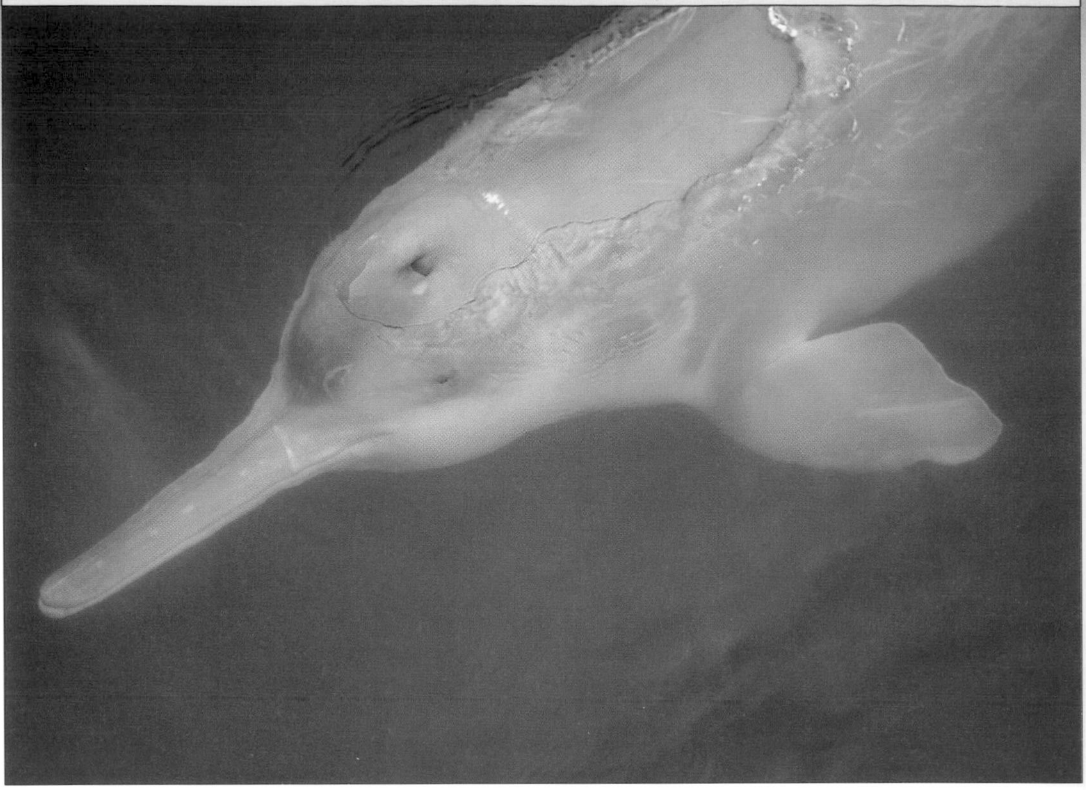

Baiji

Lipotes vexillifer

Only 80 years after it was first described in scientific literature, the Yangtze River dolphin, or baiji, is on the brink of extinction. Despite more than a decade of international conservation efforts, the baiji remains the most endangered of cetaceans.

FIELD NOTES

- *Male: 6½–7½' (2–2.3 m); female: 6½–8' (2–2.4 m); at birth: 3' (0.9 m)*
- *Small freshwater fish*
- *Yangtze River in China*
- *Endangered, may soon be extinct*

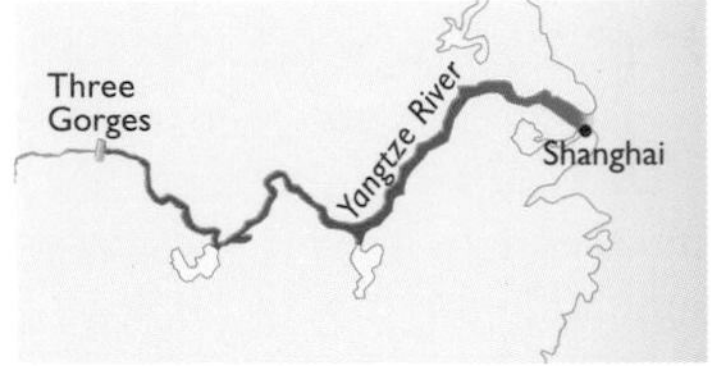

Baiji are found only in the dark blue area of the Yangtze River, as shown above.

It has a stocky body about the size of an adult human. Like other river dolphins, it has tiny eyes and a long, narrow beak. Its coloring appears white or gray at a distance, but close up looks dark bluish gray on the back fading to grayish white on the belly. The triangular dorsal fin is set low, and the flippers are broad and somewhat rounded.

It is most active from early evening to early morning. People who have been lucky enough to find baiji see them alone or in groups of up to six where tributaries join rivers, especially around shallow sandbanks. The species is quiet, reserved, and difficult to approach. In calm conditions, the blow may be heard as a high-pitched sneeze, although this quick spouting sound is difficult to distinguish from that of the finless porpoise, the only other cetacean species in its range. Cetacean sightings in the Yangtze River often turn out to be finless porpoises, because these are more numerous, more visible, and easier to approach.

The baiji was declared a National Treasure of China and has been protected since 1975. Parts of the river have been declared a natural reserve, but this initiative has had little real success in protecting the baiji because of continual boat traffic, fishing, and industrial development along what is one of the world's busiest waterways. The baiji's genus name *Lipotes* comes from the Greek meaning to be "left behind." This refers to its limited range and may yet prove to be its epitaph.

A baiji stamp (right) issued by the Chinese government to win support for conservation.

Boto

Inia geoffrensis

The boto, the largest and most commonly seen river dolphin, is the only one of the five river dolphin species to support regular commercial tours. It is noted for its pink coloring and is variously called the pink porpoise, pink dolphin, or the Amazon River dolphin. The color, however, varies according to sighting conditions, the animal's age, and individual variation. Some botos are bluish gray, while others appear almost white; younger animals are gray.

The only other dolphin to share its habitat in the Amazon and Orinoco regions, is the tucuxi which looks like a small bottlenose dolphin. The boto is larger, with a long beak, broad flippers, a bulbous melon, and a hump instead of a dorsal fin. Its physique is almost ungainly. The large cheeks are so chubby that they may even hamper the dolphin's vision when it is hunting, and this may be the reason that it often swims upside down.

FIELD NOTES

- *Male: 6½–9' (2–2.7 m); female: 5–7½' (1.5–2.3 m); at birth: 2½' (0.7 m)*
- *At least 50 species of fish*
- *Tropical river*
- *Amazon and Orinoco river basins*
- *Vulnerable*

Botos are said to be more active in the early morning and late afternoon, and if so, they follow the pattern of many tropical rain-forest creatures. They are usually seen alone or in pairs, although groups of 10 or 15 may be observed in the dry season when the river levels are low, or if there is plenty of food.

The boto has the widest distribution and largest population of all the river dolphins. It is less affected by human population pressures than the three river dolphins of Asia, but the destruction of the tropical rain forest is causing boto numbers to decline. Conservation lessons learned from the more endangered Asian river dolphins are being applied to the boto, but only time will tell if it has a long-term future.

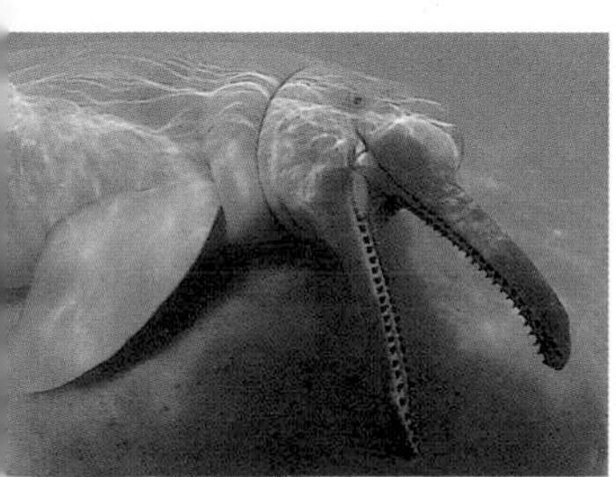

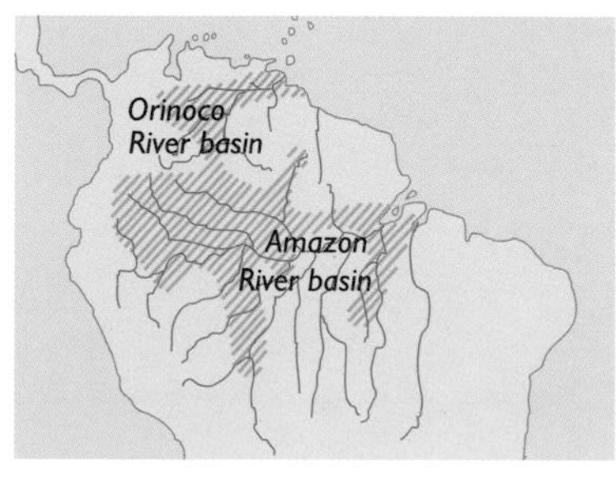

The mouth (left) is fitted with 46 to 70 teeth. Botos' range (above) covers a wide area.

Tucuxi

Sotalia fluviatilis

Tucuxi, the "other dolphin" of the Amazon and Orinoco, is smaller and more plainly colored than the pinkish boto, or Amazon River dolphin (see p. 361). Pronounced too-koo-she, the tucuxi is a "river dolphin" by habit but not a member of the group of five river dolphin species that have evolved to live only in rivers. Although some tucuxi dolphins spend their entire lives in the river, many more live along the coastal area of the western Atlantic from southern Brazil and north, to Panama. These two separate populations vary only slightly, although the coastal form grows larger than the riverine form. One of the smallest dolphins, the chunky tucuxi resembles the bottlenose dolphin in overall body shape. Along the coast, it may be confused with the bottlenose, but the tucuxi is much smaller, with a smaller triangular dorsal fin.

FIELD NOTES

- *Male: <7' (<2.2 m); female: 4 ½–7' (1.4–2.2 m); at birth: 2'+ (0.6 m+)*
- *Variety of fish, mainly schooling; cephalopods*
- *Inshore shallow coast and rivers*
- *Tropical waters of the western Atlantic Ocean, including the Amazon and Orinoco rivers*
- *Insufficiently known, killed accidentally in nets*

Tucuxi travel in groups of 2 to 7, although larger groups may consist of as many as 20 in fresh water and 50 along the coast. They engage in typical dolphin behavior, leaping, spyhopping, flipper slapping, and lobtailing, but do not bow ride. Along the coast of Brazil, the sight of a tucuxi leaping high out of the water then crashing back on its side is a familiar one. It then rejoins its family and swims on.

For years, in Brazil, the tucuxi has been killed in purse-seine and gill nets, as well as shrimp traps. Recently, Brazilian researchers have begun to study the coastal form in southeastern Brazil, photo-identifying individuals and following them from year to year. The most popular dolphin-watch tours in South America are to see the tucuxi living around Santa Catarina Island, in Brazil. Every week, thousands of people go dolphin watching there on sail and motorboats.

Watching the larger coastal tucuxi, off Rio de Janeiro.

Indo-Pacific Hump-backed Dolphin

Sousa chinensis

In 1765, Swedish explorer Per Osbeck was amazed to find "snow white dolphins at play in the China Sea." In recent years, the "pink dolphins" of Hong Kong have become a great attraction, but just as tours became popular in the mid-1990s, Hong Kong's new airport threatens to destroy the hump-backed dolphins' locally favored habitat.

FIELD NOTES

- *Male: <10 ½' (<3.2 m); female: <8' (<2.4 m); at birth: 3 ½' (1.1 m)*
- *Fish, crustaceans, and mollusks*
- *Inshore coastal, estuaries and mangroves*
- *Warm temperate to tropical waters of the Indian Ocean and western Pacific*
- *Insufficiently known*

The Indo-Pacific hump-backed dolphin can often be identified purely by its surfacing behavior (see Atlantic hump-backed dolphin below). It lives in the shallow coastal waters of southern and eastern Africa, including the Red Sea, extending east along the coast to China, the Indonesian archipelago and northern Australia. Its taxonomy is still being argued, and there may be two species, or at least two distinct populations. Those west of Sumatra have a fatty hump or platform below the dorsal fin, while those east and south of Sumatra have no platform but a taller dorsal fin. The color seems to vary locally, as well as among age groups and individuals. The back is mainly dark gray, but can be almost white or even pink. On the underside, they are light gray.

Indo-Pacific hump-backed dolphins often swim with other dolphins, mainly bottlenose, but also spinner dolphins and finless porpoises. They rarely bow ride or approach boats.

Atlantic Hump-backed Dolphin

Sousa teuszii

For as long as local people can remember, the mullet fishers of Mauritania have waited for Atlantic hump-backed dolphins to help them drive fish into their nets. Resident only in shallow coastal waters of West Africa, these dolphins are often found in the estuaries and mouths of rivers and around mangrove swamps.

FIELD NOTES

- *Male: 6 ½–8' (2–2.4 m); female: <7 ½' (<2.3 m); at birth: 3' (0.9 m)*
- *Mullet and other schooling fish*
- *Inshore coastal, estuaries and mangroves*
- *Subtropical to tropical waters of the eastern Atlantic (west African coast)*
- *Insufficiently known*

Juveniles, darker in color and without a hump, breach frequently and adults chase each other around at high speed, perhaps displaying courtship behavior. Atlantic hump-backed dolphins sometimes associate with bottlenose dolphins in the herding of fish. They are closely related to the Indo-Pacific hump-backed dolphins, but their ranges do not overlap and they usually have fewer teeth.

Atlantic hump-backed dolphin

Both hump-backed dolphin species present an odd sight as they swim in groups of up to 7 and rarely more than 25 individuals. Each animal first lifts its long, slender beak out of the water. There is a clear glimpse of its big torso as it arches its back, displaying the small dorsal fin that sits on a raised platform. The animal then appears to pause—unlike the surfacing behavior in other dolphins—and either dips below or flips its tail and dives.

Rough-toothed Dolphin

Steno bredanensis

From a distance, as it surfaces and moves rapidly along, the rough-toothed dolphin looks like a bottlenose dolphin, or even a spotted or spinner dolphin. It sometimes travels among these other species. However, at close range, a rough-toothed dolphin is more easily identified than others.

FIELD NOTES

- *Male: 7–8½' (2.2–2.6 m); female: 7½–8' (2.3–2.4 m); at birth: 3' (0.9 m)*
- *Offshore cephalopods and fish*
- *Mainly offshore*
- *Warm temperate to tropical world waters*
- *Insufficiently known*

The name rough-toothed dolphin comes from the fine, vertical ridges on the teeth, but these are impossible to see in the wild. An ungainly, often scarred, primitive-looking cetacean, the rough-toothed dolphin may be the "ugly duckling" of dolphins. The head is sometimes described as having a reptilian appearance. The large flippers look too big for the animal and are set far back on both sides. Its body often has scratches and scars, and bite marks from cookiecutter sharks. Only the curved-back dorsal fin looks like that of an "ordinary" dolphin.

The rough-toothed dolphin is rarely seen and studied because of its preference for deep waters beyond the continental shelf. In recent years, however, they have been encountered more often around Hawaii, the Bahamas, and off Ogasawara, Japan. The rough-toothed dolphin is gregarious, traveling in groups of 10 to 20, and sometimes up to 50 or more at a time. They may bow ride but rarely do a full breach. Instead, when traveling fast, they skim the water with just the head visible—a behavior called porpoising. They often stay at the surface only briefly, perhaps because they are busy feeding at depths on small schooling fish and squid.

Rough-toothed dolphins are sometimes captured by accident and killed in tuna purse-seine and other nets. They have been killed in small numbers around Japan, Sri Lanka, and the Caribbean, but little is known about this species and more work needs to be done.

Rough-toothed dolphins porpoising near the Azores Islands.

Bottlenose Dolphin

Tursiops truncatus

The bottlenose dolphin is the archetypal dolphin, found around the world, from cooler temperate to tropical waters. It lives both inshore and offshore, and is the active dolphin that leaps, bow rides, bodysurfs, splashes its tail, and approaches boats and swimmers more than any other dolphin. The lone, sociable dolphins that have mixed with humans for years, such as Fungie in Ireland and the dolphins of *Flipper* fame, are also mainly of this species.

FIELD NOTES

- *Male: 8–12½' (2.4–3.8 m); female: 7½–12' (2.3–3.7 m); at birth: 2½'+ (0.7 m+)*
- *Fish, cephalopods, invertebrates*
- *Inshore to offshore*
- *Temperate to tropical world waters*
- *Insufficiently known, overall numbers substantial but some populations threatened*

Bottlenose dolphins are mostly gray with a lighter or white underside, a short but definite beak, and a prominent curved-back dorsal fin. The flippers are pointed. The body is robust, but there is great variation in adult size, from 7½ to 12½ feet (2.3 to 3.8 m). Size and other features vary according to whether the dolphins live inshore or offshore and in what part of the world. Through photo-identification studies, researchers have learned that coastal bottlenose dolphins reside in or return to the same areas year after year. Females with calves stay together, using the most productive areas of the community home range; males form long-term bonds with each other and range farther afield as they get older. Sometimes the males venture into the range of nearby bottlenose dolphin communities, traveling from one female group to another.

Bottlenose dolphins have long associated closely with humans.

The food habits and hunting behavior of bottlenose dolphins vary greatly. They adapt their behavior to local circumstances and conditions, and only orcas eat a greater variety of food. Clever, cooperative feeding habits occur in South Carolina and Baja California, where dolphins chase fish onto the shore, then roll up on the beaches, completely out of the water, to grab the fish on the beach. Bottlenose dolphins are sometimes involved with humans, to their mutual advantage, in corralling and catching fish (see p. 423).

Atlantic White-sided Dolphin

Lagenorhynchus acutus

The Atlantic white-sided dolphin was first described scientifically in 1828. Long before this, these dolphins were well known to early fishers and whalers in the North Atlantic. The names for these species of lively dolphins all referred to their habit of jumping clear out of the water as they moved. Norwegians called them "springhval," Germans "springer," and to eastern Canadians, they became "jumpers."

FIELD NOTES

- *Male: 7–9' (2.2–2.7 m); female: 6–9' (1.9–2.7 m); at birth: 3½' (1.1 m)*
- *Various fish and squid*
- *Inshore to mainly offshore*
- *Cold temperate waters of the North Atlantic Ocean*
- *Insufficiently known*

Identifying this dolphin is easy; you just look for the bright yellow patch on the rear flanks. This flashes briefly as the dolphin moves through the water. You may also glimpse the subtle white band on each side below the dorsal fin, which gave this dolphin its common name.

Traveling in groups of up to 100, Atlantic white-sided dolphins are a favorite of whale watchers on tours off Scotland, Ireland, Iceland, Massachusetts, and Newfoundland. The dolphins often accompany whales; they may be feeding on similar prey at times, but for the dolphins, it seems to be more of an opportunity to be sociable. Herds of up to 1,000 dolphins have been seen on occasion in offshore areas.

White-beaked Dolphin

Lagenorhynchus albirostris

The white-beaked dolphin shares most of its North Atlantic range with the Atlantic white-sided dolphin. But it ventures farther north into subarctic waters, making it the most northerly occurring of all dolphins. It is the most robust of all the "lag" dolphins (those belonging to the genus *Lagenorhynchus*) with the thickest blubber layer.

FIELD NOTES

- *Male: 8–10' (2.4–3 m); female: 8–10' (2.4–3 m); at birth: 4' (1.2 m)*
- *Offshore schooling fish, cephalopods, crustaceans*
- *Inshore to mainly offshore*
- *Cold temperate to subarctic waters of the North Atlantic Ocean*
- *Insufficiently known*

In spite of the common name "albirostris," meaning "white beak," the beak, when it can be seen in the wild, is often not white, but gray or even black in parts of its range. The best way to distinguish this species from the Atlantic white-sided dolphin is by checking the rear flanks. White-beaked dolphins have a grayish patch; a bright yellowish patch indicates an Atlantic white-sided dolphin.

These dolphins are welcomed on whale-watch tours off Iceland, Norway, Newfoundland and other areas of eastern Canada, Greenland, the Faeroes, and Ireland. They often churn the water, creating, like Dall's porpoise, a "rooster tail" effect.

White-beaked dolphins are powerful swimmers.

Pacific White-sided Dolphin

Lagenorhynchus obliquidens

This exclusively North Pacific dolphin acquired the species name "obliquidens," meaning "slanting tooth," because of its slightly curved teeth. This feature was noted by the fish taxonomist Theodore Nicholas Gill of the Smithsonian Institution, who gave the species its name after examining three skulls that had been collected near San Francisco.

FIELD NOTES

- *Male: 5½–8' (1.7–2.4 m); female: 5½–8' (1.7–2.4 m); at birth: 3½' (1.1 m)*
- *Offshore fish and squid*
- *Mainly offshore but sometimes inshore*
- *Cool temperate waters of the North Pacific Ocean*
- *Insufficiently known, killed accidentally in net fishing*

Within their range, Pacific white-sided dolphins are most likely to be confused with common dolphins, as both travel in large groups and have light side patches. However, the Pacific white-sided has a short, thick snout unlike the beak of the common dolphin. It also has a thin, gray stripe along both sides, extending from the head, curving down below the dorsal fin, and ending in a large, white, rear flank patch. Pacific white-sided dolphins often have two-color dorsal fins, dark on the front half and gray or white on the back.

"Lag" dolphins are all acrobatic and sociable. The Pacific white-sided may be the most acrobatic and sociable of them all. They often swim in groups of up to 100, although offshore assemblies of 1,000 to 2,000 are common. Their sociable natures also extend to other cetaceans, particularly northern right whale dolphins. They often ride the waves—from the bow and wake of boats and from the surf. Intensely curious, they will sometimes inspect boats.

Pacific white-sided dolphins often steal the show on offshore whale-watch trips. They can be seen from British Columbia (Vancouver Island), southeast Alaska, California (particularly southern California and Monterey), Mexico, and Hokkaido, Japan. These dolphins live mainly offshore, but will come closer at certain times of the year, particularly in deep-water areas. A photo-identification study along northeastern Vancouver Island, where they sometimes come into inshore waters, has cataloged hundreds of these dolphins.

Acrobatic Pacific white-sided dolphins.

Dusky Dolphin

Lagenorhynchus obscurus

The dusky dolphin was one of two *Lagenorhynchus* dolphins, or "lags," described by John Edward Gray in 1828—the other was the Atlantic white-sided dolphin. Gray saw only a drawing of a dusky dolphin based on a skull and stuffed skin from the Cape of Good Hope, South Africa. He called the species "obscurus" for its dusky coloring.

FIELD NOTES

- *Male: 7' (2.2 m); female: 6' (1.9 m); at birth: 2' (0.6 m)*
- *Squid, and fish such as anchovy, bottomfish*
- *Inshore to continental shelf waters*
- *Temperate waters of South Africa, New Zealand, southern Australia, and southern South America*
- *Insufficiently known*

Resident in the coastal and shelf waters of South Africa, New Zealand, southern Australia and southern South America, duskies in different areas have slightly different patterns on their back, but all have proved to be the same species.

At sea, the best way to identify a dusky is to look for the light face and short blunt rostrum with the hint of a beak. The dorsal fin is curved back, pointed, and often has two colors, a variable pattern of dark in the forward area and light in the rear. Look for the two-prong blazes of white, pointing forward on each rear flank.

The duskies are one of the most acrobatic of dolphin species, their slim, light bodies executing extraordinary leaps and somersaults. Once one dolphin starts leaping, others often follow. They seem to enjoy contact with boats and people, and are popular on whale- and dolphin-watching trips from Patagonia, Argentina and Kaikoura, New Zealand.

One of the first-ever dolphin photo-identification studies was carried out on the herds of duskies off Patagonia. Researchers found that the same dolphins stay there throughout the year. In summer, they come together to socialize and rest, but separate into smaller groups to feed.

The highflying, acrobatic breach of a dusky dolphin thrills dolphin watchers off the coast of Kaikoura, New Zealand.

Fraser's Dolphin

Lagenodelphis hosei

This tropical, deep-water dolphin, first described in 1956 and identified in the wild in the 1970s, can now be seen with some regularity on whale-watch trips. In some areas they avoid boats, but in South Africa they ride the bow waves, and have become a welcome feature of whale-watch tours in the Caribbean and the Philippines.

In 1955, cetologist Francis Charles Fraser found a mislabeled skeleton in the British Museum collected 60 years earlier in Sarawak. He placed the specimen somewhere between *Delphinus*, the common dolphins, and *Lagenorhynchus*, the "lag" dolphins, so he invented an intermediate genus: *Lagenodelphis*.

FIELD NOTES

- *Male: 7½–8½' (2.3–2.6 m); female: 7–8½' (2.2–2.6 m); at birth: 3½' (1.1 m)*
- *Various fish, squid, shrimp*
- *Mainly offshore or deeper waters*
- *Subtropical to tropical world waters*
- *Insufficiently known*

At sea, Fraser's dolphins have a striking color pattern with a dark band stretching from the face to the rear underside and bordered above by a gray or whitish line. The dark band can be very wide and dark in males and its intensity may increase with age. Otherwise, the back is dark brownish gray and the belly is pink or white.

Fraser's dolphins often travel in groups of 100 to 500, and occasionally the group can be as large as 1,000. They sometimes associate or feed with other species of tropical toothed whales and dolphins.

Hourglass Dolphin

Lagenorhynchus cruciger

Hourglass dolphins live in deep waters offshore in the Southern Ocean between Antarctica and the major continents. In the early 1820s, a French expedition off Antarctica watched these dolphins frolic around their ship and named them "cruciger," or cross-bearing. The common name, hourglass dolphin, is derived from the dramatic white, double patches along the flank, which seem to crisscross along the animal's sides. These prominent markings make it fairly easy to identify this robust dolphin.

FIELD NOTES

- *Male: 5' (1.5 m); female: 6' (1.9 m); at birth: <3½' (<1.1 m)*
- *Small deep-water fish and squid*
- *Offshore*
- *Cold temperate Southern Hemisphere to Antarctic waters*
- *Insufficiently known*

Not shy, the hourglass dolphin is seen riding the bow or stern waves of fast ships, and swimming parallel to slower vessels. It usually travels alone or in groups of up to 7, but occasionally up to 40 are seen in a group. They may travel with other dolphins and whales. Although these dolphins are encountered more often, their remote habitat and range prevent regular study; there remains much to learn.

The hourglass dolphin of the Southern Ocean is easily identified.

Commerson's Dolphin

Cephalorhynchus commersonii

In 1767, as Louis Bougainville's round-the-world expedition approached Tierra del Fuego, Philibert Commerson, a French physician and botanist aboard, noted his delight at seeing striking black-and-white dolphins moving at great speed around the ship. It was not until 1922, however, that these dolphins acquired full recognition and their current scientific name.

FIELD NOTES

- *Male: 4½–5' (1.4–1.5 m); female: 4½–5' (1.4–1.5 m); at birth: 2½' (0.7 m)*
- *Inshore fish, crustaceans, and squid*
- *Mainly inshore*
- *Cold temperate waters of southeastern South America, Falkland Islands, and Kerguelen Islands*
- *Insufficiently known*

Identifying a Commerson's dolphin in the inshore waters of Argentina and Chile, where it is often encountered, is easy. It usually has a distinctive rounded dorsal fin, and dramatic black-and-white markings rather like an orca. A wide, white band between the blowhole and the dorsal fin completely encircles the dolphin. On either side of this white band are the black head and flippers, and the black dorsal fin and rear portion. Around the Kerguelen Islands in the southern Indian Ocean, the dolphin's black-and-white patterns are dark and light gray.

The shape of the black patch on the underside of a Commerson's dolphin indicates the sex. On a male, it is shaped like a raindrop; on a female it is shaped like a horseshoe.

Commerson's dolphins eagerly ride waves at sea or as they break on shore. They show no fear of boats, often riding the bow and stern waves, but their sometimes erratic swimming behavior makes it difficult to keep track of them. Maneuvering through fast, swirling rapids, they are agile swimmers. Typically, they travel alone or in groups of 2 to 15. Occasionally 100 or more are seen.

Popular with dolphin watchers, Commerson's dolphins can be seen from shore as well as from boats within their limited, remote range. Their movements and behavior are being studied in southern Patagonia, using photo-identification methods.

Easily identified by their striking markings, Commerson's dolphins rest near the Falkland Islands.

Hector's Dolphin

Cephalorhynchus hectori

New Zealand's own dolphin, the Hector's dolphin, is one of the smallest cetaceans, at only about 4½ feet (1.4 m) long. It has a complex color pattern of gray, black, and white. Moving in groups of two to eight animals in the waters around New Zealand, they surface frequently to breathe, showing little of their stout bodies. Hector's dolphins differ considerably from bottlenose and other dolphins. Although it is easy to miss them because of their low profile and small size, the best way to identify them is by their characteristic rounded dorsal fin.

FIELD NOTES

- *Male: 4–4½' (1.2–1.4 m); female: 4½–5' (1.4–1.5 m); at birth: 2'+ (0.6 m+)*
- *Fish and squid*
- *Inshore, including estuaries*
- *Coastal New Zealand waters*
- *Indeterminate, killed accidentally in gill nets*

Mother and calf sighted off Banks Peninsula.

Hector's dolphins inhabit muddy river mouths and shallow bays, often swimming among rocks close to the shoreline. They rarely venture more than 5 miles (8 km) from land. They breach, lobtail, spyhop, and engage in most of the dolphin play behavior familiar to watchers.

The best place to observe Hector's dolphins is around the Banks Peninsula, in New Zealand's South Island, where regular tours are offered. They can also be viewed from various other ports on the South and North islands, including the popular whale-watch port of Kaikoura. They can even be seen from shore, often near rocks or entering estuaries and rivers, sometimes swimming a little way upstream.

Hector's dolphins can be attracted to boats, particularly slow-moving boats, although they seldom bow ride. Dolphin watchers sometimes find that these dolphins will swim alongside the boat for a time, often swimming in its wake.

In the past, Hector's dolphins were caught for bait, and currently they are trapped accidentally in trawls and especially gill nets. Some parts of their habitat near the Banks Peninsula have been protected, but to save this declining species, more near-shore areas around New Zealand will have to be declared no-go zones for coastal gill nets.

Southern Right Whale Dolphin

Lissodelphis peronii

François Peron, a naturalist aboard *Géographe*, a French expedition to Australia in 1800, was amazed to see these finless dolphins near Tasmania: the first finless dolphins a scientist had ever noted. The common name of this dolphin, and its northern relative, is "right whale" dolphin. (The right whale is many times larger, but also lacks a dorsal fin.)

Compared to the northern right whale dolphin, the southern species has larger white areas on its body. On its low-angle leaps, the white beak and forehead present an odd profile. These so-called "mealy-mouthed porpoises" have largely white flippers with either a dark leading or trailing edge, and patches of white on the leading edge of the upper sides of the flukes. The underside is entirely white.

Mainly resident in the cool, deep, temperate waters of the Southern Ocean, these dolphins extend into subantarctic waters. They may be seen on tours near the Falkland Islands, en route to the Antarctic, and off New Zealand, Argentina, Chile, and South Africa.

FIELD NOTES

- *Male: >7' (>2.2 m); female: <7½' (<2.3 m); at birth: 2½'+ (0.7 m+)*
- *Squid and a variety of fish (lanternfish)*
- *Offshore*
- *Cool temperate to subantarctic waters of the Southern Hemisphere*
- *Insufficiently known*

Northern Right Whale Dolphin

Lissodelphis borealis

This lithe animal with its smooth back, devoid of a dorsal fin, presents a graceful dance as it skims the waves in low-angle leaps. Traveling at speed in groups of up to 200, often with Pacific white-sided dolphins, they look like so many balls bouncing across the water.

Discovered in the mid-nineteenth century, nearly 50 years after its close southern relative (above), the northern species is dark, except sometimes on the tip of its lower jaw, on its chest and the underside of the flukes. Because it has no dorsal fin, it is unlikely to be confused with any of the other cetaceans within its range.

Confined to the cool, deep, temperate waters of the North Pacific, northern right whale dolphins were considered rare until cetacean biologists Stephen Leatherwood and William A. Walker studied them in the mid-1970s. They made numerous sightings, finding as many as 3,000 in one group. Today, these dolphins are more often seen traveling in groups of 5 to 200 on late summer and autumn whale-watch tours to the Monterey submarine canyon. They sometimes bow ride.

FIELD NOTES

- *Male: 7–10' (2.2–3 m); female: 6½–7½' (2–2.3 m); at birth: 2½'+ (0.7 m+)*
- *Variety of fish and squid*
- *Offshore*
- *Temperate waters of the North Pacific*
- *Insufficiently known, commonly caught in net fishing*

A northern right whale dolphin bounces across the surface.

Short-beaked Common Dolphin

Delphinus delphis

One of the most common of all dolphins, this fairly large dolphin is easily distinguished by the hourglass pattern on its side. This makes a dark "V" shape below the dorsal fin, almost like a reflection of the fin. At one time or another, more than 20 species have been proposed and discarded for variations of this geographically widespread species. The case for at least one other species has recently been generally accepted (see below). The description of behavior that follows applies to both forms; specific anatomical differences are dealt with in the entry below.

FIELD NOTES

- *Male: 5½–7' (1.7–2.2 m); female: 5–6½' (1.5–2 m); at birth: 2½'+ (0.7 m+)*
- *Small fish and cephalopods*
- *Mainly offshore*
- *Temperate and tropical waters, including inland seas (Black Sea)*
- *Insufficiently known, but taken in many fisheries worldwide*

Common dolphins travel in groups of 10 to 500 in most areas, with up to 2,000 or more in the eastern tropical Pacific. These herds are so acrobatic and boisterous that the noise of their approach can often be picked up from miles away. Their high-pitched sounds can sometimes be heard as they bow ride.

Although common dolphins are killed in significant numbers in tuna and other fisheries, numbers are thought to be considerable.

Long-beaked Common Dolphin

Delphinus capensis

For decades, it has been known that various stocks of common dolphins look different. In 1994, a new species of dolphin was created by the splitting of common dolphins into short-beaked and long-beaked species. The short-beaked common dolphin kept the original scientific name and the new species took a new name, "capensis." Based on anatomy as well as genetics, the differences between the two species are consistent in at least several parts of the world. However, even within the two species, there is still variation.

FIELD NOTES

- *Male: 6½–8½' (2–2.6 m); female: 6–7½' (1.9–2.3 m); at birth: 2½'+ (0.7 m+)*
- *Various small fish and cephalopods*
- *Coastal*
- *Temperate and tropical world waters*
- *Insufficiently known*

short-beaked (above) and long-beaked

The long-beaked common dolphin has a muted color pattern, with less contrast between the dark and the white (or yellow) parts of its body. Subtle differences include a slightly longer, less chunky body; a less rounded head; and a thicker, dark line between the beak and the flipper. But the most noticeable is that the long-beaked form has a longer beak than the short-beaked form.

Little is known about this dolphin's behavior at sea, apart from what is generally known about common dolphins. However, because of its strong coastal presence, it makes up a sizable proportion of the sightings of common dolphins.

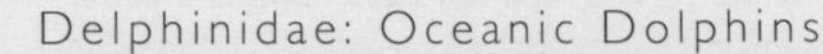

Spinner Dolphin

Stenella longirostris

The spinner dolphin—also known as the rollover, longsnout, long-snouted spinner dolphin, or long-beaked dolphin—is famous for its fantastic spinning leaps, in which a dolphin breaches high out of the water then rolls on its longitudinal axis making up to seven complete turns. Few, if any, dolphins leap as high or as often, and no others, except the clymene dolphin, are known to spin. Spinner dolphins are frequently observed around Hawaii, Mexico, and Japan.

If you can't see them spinning, the best way to distinguish these dolphins from other dolphins within their range is by looking at the long, thin beak, the dark gray stripe from eye to flipper, and the usually well-defined three-toned coloring of the body, ranging from dark on the top, to gray to light on the belly. Also, the dorsal fin, particularly in some populations, stands erect.

The motion of the longitudinal spin can be seen in the twist of the body.

FIELD NOTES

- *Male: 5½–8' (1.7–2.4 m); female: 5½–7' (1.7–2.2 m); at birth: 2½'+ (0.7 m+)*
- *Various fish and squid*
- *Offshore*
- *Subtropical and tropical world waters*
- *Insufficiently known, many killed in fishing nets*

There are several forms of spinner dolphins. In the eastern tropical Pacific alone, where they have been intensively studied due to their association with yellowfin tuna, there are three forms, each with slight differences. There are apparently other forms in other parts of their wide range.

At sea, spinner dolphins often approach boats to bow ride and may stay for as long as half an hour—longer than most other dolphins. They travel in groups of 5 to 200, although often up to 1,000 or even more swim in mixed schools with pantropical spotted and other dolphins.

Because of its acrobatic talents, the spinner was one of the first dolphins to be captured for aquariums in the North Pacific, but they have a poor survival record. The main threat to spinners has come from tuna fisheries which have caused the deaths of many hundreds of thousands of spinner dolphins. Although the kills are much fewer today, their numbers have apparently not returned to original population sizes.

Clymene Dolphin

Stenella clymene

FIELD NOTES

- Male: 6–6½' (1.9–2 m); female: 6–6½' (1.9–2 m); at birth: 2½' (0.7 m)
- Small fish and squid
- Mainly offshore
- Subtropical and tropical waters of the Atlantic Ocean including Gulf of Mexico
- Insufficiently known

Originally described in 1846, the clymene, also known as the short-snouted spinner dolphin, was not considered a valid species until recently. Its external color pattern looked more like the spinner dolphin (see opposite page) with which it had long been confused. In 1975, however, William Perrin and his colleagues found that the skulls of some spinner dolphins from the coast of Texas resembled the original clymene dolphin from the British Museum. In 1981, the clymene dolphin received full species status.

The distribution of the clymene and the spinner overlap in the North Atlantic, although the spinner is found farther south, even into the tropical South Atlantic. Distinguishing spinner and clymene dolphins can be difficult at sea. The clymene is a little more robust than the spinner dolphin. It is also said to have a less pronounced triangular dorsal fin, but this alone isn't sufficient for identification due to the dorsal fin variation among spinner dolphins. Up close, the clymene dolphin has a shorter beak, a dark line which sometimes looks like a mustache on top of the beak, and a darker cape which dips close to the white areas on either side of the dorsal fin.

Normally, the clymene dolphin's leaps are not as high, and its spins not as numerous as the spinner dolphin, but it is the only other dolphin besides the spinner to make longitudinal spins, rather than somersaults. They sometimes bow ride and occasionally approach boats. In feeding areas they associate with other small dolphins such as common and spinner. School size is much less than for the spinner dolphin—usually fewer than 50 animals.

Little yet is known about this dolphin—its distribution, habits, and status. Some are killed for meat by local fishers in the eastern Caribbean.

A dark line on top of the beak helps identify a clymene.

Pantropical Spotted Dolphin

Stenella attenuata

Often called "spotters," or simply spotted dolphins, the pantropical spotted dolphin is a delightful sighting on any marine nature tour. They travel with ships, charging to the bow or stern to ride the waves. They make long, low leaps clear of the water as they swim along, and their breaches are high and frequent, if a little less acrobatic than the spinner dolphin.

There are two recognized species, the pantropical and the Atlantic (see opposite page), but there may be additional species named as more is learned about the taxonomy of these dolphins. In the eastern Pacific alone, there are at least two main forms within the pantropical species, one coastal, the other offshore. The coastal species is larger and more robust, with a thicker beak and more spots.

FIELD NOTES

- *Male: 6½–8½' (2–2.6 m); female: 6–8' (1.9–2.4 m); at birth: 2½'+ (0.7 m+)*
- *Small fish and cephalopods*
- *Coastal to offshore*
- *Mainly tropical, some subtropical and warm temperate world waters*
- *Insufficiently known, caught in tuna purse-seine nets, more abundant south of the equator*

Even though its spots provide the best clue to identification, this is not always straightforward. At a distance and in some lights, the spots don't always show up, and pantropical populations in the Gulf of Mexico and around Hawaii have few, if any, spots. Bottlenose dolphins and both species of hump-backed dolphins also have some spotting at times, although usually not on the back. Finally, pantropical spotted dolphins are unspotted at birth. As juveniles, they acquire dark spots on their bellies, followed by light spots on the back.

Tuna purse-seine fishing, particularly in the eastern tropical Pacific, has seriously depleted numbers of these dolphins. Pantropical schools are located by plane and ship, and nets are set around them to catch yellowfin and skipjack tuna. Hundreds of thousands of dolphins per year were killed in the 1960s and 1970s until conservation measures began to take effect in the late 1980s. Although not endangered, these dolphins still suffer high losses.

Except for a cookie-cutter shark scar, no spots are obvious on these "spotters" sighted near Hawaii.

Atlantic Spotted Dolphin

Stenella frontalis

FIELD NOTES

- *Male: 6½–7½' (2–2.3 m); female: 6½–7½' (2–2.3 m); at birth: 3'+ (0.9 m+)*
- *Various fish and cephalopods*
- *Inshore to offshore*
- *Tropical, subtropical, and warm temperate waters, of the Atlantic Ocean*
- *Insufficiently known, caught in Atlantic tuna purse-seine nets*

The two Atlantic spotted dolphin juveniles (above) have yet to develop their spots.

Since the early 1980s, several generations of Atlantic spotted dolphins have been visiting and swimming with dolphin watchers in the clear, shallow waters of the northern Bahamas. The dolphins' movements have been recorded in synchronization with their sounds, allowing for the development of a behavioral ethogram, or catalog of behavioral patterns. Researchers have found generally small schools of 1 to 15 individuals. Larger numbers sometimes join up temporarily. The schools have a fluid structure, with dolphins often joining and splitting into subgroups, as do the well-studied bottlenose dolphins, yet there are also long-term bonds. Like the pantropical spotted dolphin and most other closely related oceanic dolphins, the Atlantic spotted dolphin bow rides, breaches, and plays at every opportunity.

The Atlantic spotted dolphin is found only in the tropical to warm temperate Atlantic. In this area, their range overlaps with the pantropical spotted dolphin and confusion is possible at sea. The main differences between the two, noticeable at close range, are that the Atlantic spotted dolphin is generally more robust, more spotted, and often darker (which helps the spots show up better). The spots develop as the animal matures. As with pantropical spotted dolphins, there are two forms, coastal and offshore, with considerable variation within each group. With an Atlantic spotted dolphin that is not very spotted, typically an offshore form, its robust body is close in overall appearance to that of a bottlenose dolphin.

Beloved of dolphin watchers on the northern fringes of the Caribbean, Atlantic spotted dolphins are still hunted for food in the eastern Caribbean by local fishers. However, cetacean-watch tours from St. Vincent, Grenada, and Dominica are giving visitors and locals the pleasure of watching these animals at sea.

Striped Dolphin

Stenella coeruleoalba

FIELD NOTES

- *Male: 6–8½' (1.9–2.6 m); female: 6–7' (1.9–2.1 m); at birth: 3½' (1.1 m)*
- *Various fish, cephalopods, and sometimes crustaceans*
- *Offshore*
- *Warm temperate, subtropical, and tropical world waters*
- *Insufficiently known, accidentally killed in fish nets and hunted in Japan*

The first to appreciate the delicate beauty of dolphins were the ancient Greeks, who painted them in frescoes. Several thousand years later, we can see that their inspiration was undoubtedly the striped dolphin.

These beautiful animals look almost hand-painted. With an upward brush stroke toward the dorsal fin, the light gray flank divides the dark back and the white or pink belly. But the best identifying feature is a thin, dark stripe with a feathery, dark streak below it, extending from the black beak, around the eye patch to the underside of the rear flank. There are also one or two dark bands between the eye and flipper.

At sea, striped dolphins are easy to identify at medium to close distance. Their acrobatic, often aerial behavior ensures that the characteristic stripe will be seen. Like other *Stenella* dolphins, they manage tailspins and somersaults, as well as breaching to great heights, up to 23 feet (7 m), or three times their length. They bow ride in the Atlantic, but there are fewer reports of this behavior in the Pacific or Indian Oceans. Apparently, they are more easily alarmed than other dolphins, and will turn tail and streak away—in the Pacific they are called "streakers." Herds number 100 to 500, but can be up to 3,000. In some areas, such as the Mediterranean, however, group size is fewer than 100.

Like several other dolphins, they sometimes travel above yellowfin tuna, which has led to them being killed, although in fewer numbers than spotted, spinner, and common dolphins. A much more serious threat is Japanese drive fishing, which kills thousands. There are also killings near Sri Lanka, as well as accidental catches during Mediterranean netting operations.

The dark stripe is easily seen on these striped dolphins, as they race along with flying leaps.

Risso's Dolphin

Grampus griseus

The Risso's dolphin is a robust, blunt-headed oceanic dolphin. Larger than any other cetacean that carries the name "dolphin," it is sometimes informally grouped with the "blackfish" because of its size and blunt head.

This dolphin is easy to identify. It is heavily scarred, ghost-like, and looks like no other species, although from a distance the tall, curved-back dorsal fin might be confused with an orca or bottlenose dolphin.

FIELD NOTES

- *Male: 8½'–12½' (2.6–3.8 m); female: 8½'–12' (2.6–3.7 m); at birth: 4½' (1.4 m)*
- *Squid and other cephalopods, fish, and crustaceans*
- *Offshore*
- *Tropical, subtropical and temperate world waters*
- *Insufficiently known*

As seen here, the torso of the blunt-headed Risso's dolphin is larger than that of the bottlenose dolphin.

Also called the gray dolphin, or the gray grampus (a literal translation of its scientific name), the Risso's dolphin is gray on the back and sides, and white on the belly. On the head and just in front of the dorsal fin, the coloring is light gray, sometimes white. All appendages (the dorsal fin, flippers, and flukes) tend to be darker than the rest of the body. The body becomes lighter as the animals age, and older animals can be almost white. Younger animals have few, if any, scars, while mature animals carry a wide range of scratches, blotches, and spots.

Why do these dolphins have so many scars? The Risso's dolphin has between 4 and 14 teeth near the tip of the lower jaw. There are rarely teeth in the upper jaw. Some of the scars come from the teeth of other Risso's dolphins, possibly playing or fighting with each other. However, it is thought that some of the scarring may come from squid bites. Limited stomach studies reveal the dolphin's preference for squid.

Photo-identification studies have been started recently off central California and in the Azores. Risso's dolphins are found in groups of 3 to 50, but sometimes up to 4,000. Compared to other cetaceans, they have been little studied, and not much is known about their status. Many Risso's dolphins have been killed accidentally in gill nets around Sri Lanka.

Irrawaddy Dolphin

Orcaella brevirostris

This blunt-nosed, little dolphin with the stubby, almost non-existent dorsal fin makes few waves. Traveling through the inshore waters of southeast Asia, Indonesia, and northern Australia, its low profile is more often missed than recognized. Named after the Irrawaddy River of Myanmar (formerly Burma), it is also sometimes known as the Mahakam River dolphin, after a river in eastern Borneo (Kalimantan) where it lives hundreds of miles upstream.

FIELD NOTES

- *Male: 7–9' (2.2–2.7 m); female: 7–7½' (2.2–2.3 m); at birth: 2½'+ (0.7 m+)*
- *Fish, cephalopods, and crustaceans*
- *Inshore and rivers*
- *Subtropical and tropical waters of the Indian and western Pacific Oceans*
- *Insufficiently known*

The Irrawaddy dolphin has many attributes which put it in the family of oceanic dolphins, but some researchers consider it close to the beluga family—it looks a little like a beluga. In the wild, this dolphin can be confused with the finless porpoise which is, however, much smaller and has no dorsal fin. From a distance, they may even sometimes be confused with dugongs.

Irrawaddy dolphins travel in small groups, usually fewer than 6 but sometimes up to 15 individuals. They occasionally make low-angle leaps, lobtail, breach, and spyhop, and they have been known to spit water. However, above-surface behavior is uncommon, and there are no reports of bow riding.

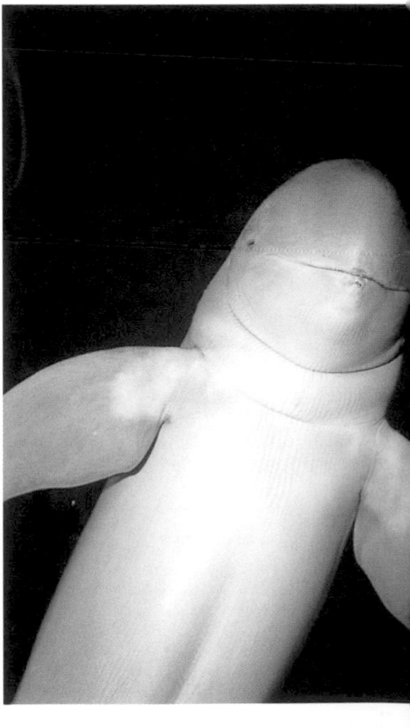

With its blunt, rounded head, indistinct beak, flexible neck, and straight mouth-line, the Irrawaddy dolphin looks a little like a small beluga.

The Irrawaddy's chosen habitat is in tropical rivers, estuaries, and inshore coasts, which means that it comes into frequent conflict with people and industry. It is killed accidentally in shark gill nets in Australia as well as in fish traps and other nets within its range. But more serious threats to the Irrawaddy dolphin arise from the destruction and degradation of its habitat by riverbank development and the construction of dams.

Melon-headed Whale

Peponocephala electra

FIELD NOTES

- *Male: 7–9' (2.2–2.7 m); female: 7½–9' (2.3–2.7 m); at birth: 2'+ (0.6 m+)*
- *Various small fish and squid*
- *Offshore*
- *Tropical and some subtropical world waters*
- *Insufficiently known, killed accidentally through gill nets and other fishing methods*

The melon-headed whale was originally thought to be a "lag" dolphin, similar to the Pacific white-sided dolphin. In 1965, a herd of 500 swam into Suruga Bay, Japan, 250 of which were caught and killed. After studying them, scientists decided this species deserved its own genus.

Melon-headed and pygmy killer whales (see below) are difficult to distinguish at sea. The melon-headed whale, however, has a slender, torpedo-shaped body with shorter, narrower flippers with pointed tips. But the most distinctive difference is the head. The melon-headed whale has a slim, pointed head, while the pygmy killer whale has a rounded head.

Melon-headed whales generally travel in large, tightly packed herds of 100 to 500, with occasional herds of 1,500 to 2,000. They may bow ride and spyhop, but usually steer clear of boats. They have a reputation for being fierce; when two groups were captured for marine aquariums in the Philippines and Hawaii, they attacked their handlers. The best places to find melon-headed whales are off Cebu Island in the Philippines, the east coast of Australia, Hawaii, and in the eastern Caribbean, especially around Dominica.

Pygmy Killer Whale

Feresa attenuata

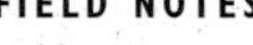

FIELD NOTES

- *Male: 6½–9½' (2–2.9 m); female: 7–8' (2.2–2.4 m); at birth: 1½'+ (0.5 m+)*
- *Various smaller fish and squid*
- *Mainly offshore*
- *Tropical and subtropical world waters*
- *Insufficiently known*

Pygmy killer whale, off Florida's Atlantic coast.

The pygmy killer whale is as little known as the melon-headed whale with which it shares almost the same habitat and range. It also has a similar appearance. It has been reported to herd and attack dolphins in the South Atlantic and the tropical Pacific. Like melon-headed whales, pygmy killer whales have been captured several times for marine aquariums and have proved aggressive.

Compared to the melon-headed whale, the pygmy killer whale has a more rounded head and flipper tips, and a darker cape. Skull comparisons of stranded specimens also show fewer teeth. In general, they travel in much smaller groups—fewer than 50 is typical. They are commonly encountered near Dominica, around St. Vincent, Hawaii, and parts of southern Japan. They occasionally bow ride and breach, but aerial behavior is otherwise rare. Most of the time, they tend to avoid boats. A glimpse of these whales is an unusual and welcome sight.

False Killer Whale

Pseudorca crassidens

FIELD NOTES

- Male: 12–19½' (3.7–5.9 m); female: 11½–16½' (3.5–5 m); at birth: 5½' (1.7 m)
- Various fish, cephalopods, rarely dolphins
- Mainly offshore
- Tropical, subtropical, and sometimes temperate world waters
- Insufficiently known

The false killer whale, sometimes also called "pseudorca," is a warm-water resident of the world's oceans. Like orcas and pilot whales, it has a complex social nature. Smaller than pilot whales and orcas, the false killer is much larger than any other "dolphin." All three are among those sometimes called "blackfish."

The false killer whale has a long, slender head and slim body. The dorsal fin looks like a young orca's—prominent and curved back and not wide at the base like a pilot whale's. Compared to two other blackfish, the pygmy killer whale and melon-headed whale with which it is most often confused, the false killer whale is much longer and larger. The head is all black (no white lips, as found in some other blackfish). The flippers are unique, if you can manage to glimpse them as the animal swims along or bow rides: there is a prominent hump that looks like a bend or elbow halfway along the leading edge of each flipper.

False killers are fast, acrobatic swimmers—acting more like playful, inquisitive dolphins than pilot whales or orcas. They often breach, sometimes landing on their sides or backs with a great splash. They travel in pods of 10 to 50, although several hundred are sometimes seen in a superpod, or grouping of more than one pod. Both sexes and all ages travel together. False killer whales are often involved in mass strandings; the largest recorded was of more than 800 animals.

False killers are hunted off China, Japan, and the Caribbean, and they are also sometimes killed accidentally in fish nets, including tuna purse-seines and pelagic gill nets. They have a reputation for stealing fish off lines and from nets. They have also been reported to attack dolphins escaping from tuna nets and there is one case of them attacking and killing a humpback whale calf near Hawaii. Their usual diet, however, is fish and cephalopods.

The slim body of a false killer whale is seen when it breaches.

Orca

Orcinus orca

The largest of all dolphins, the orca is found in all seas, from the equator to the polar ice. It is among one of the most widely distributed animals on Earth. Until quite recently it had the reputation of a fierce killer. Its other name, "killer whale," comes from eighteenth-century whalers who saw orcas feeding on other whales and dolphins. As top predator in the sea, the orca's diet extends to several hundred known species—a more diverse and extensive diet than that of any other whale or dolphin. There is no known case of a wild orca ever killing a human.

FIELD NOTES

- *Male: 17–29½' (5.1–9 m); female: 15–25½' (4.6–7.7 m); at birth: 6'+ (1.9 m+)*
- *Numerous fish, squid, and marine mammal species, including blue whales; even gulls, penguins, turtles*
- *Inshore and offshore*
- *Equatorial waters to polar ice*
- *Insufficiently known, hunted and captured in recent years off Japan, Iceland, Antarctica, and other areas*

Its white eye patch, gray saddle patch, and black back make the orca easy to identify at sea. The underside is entirely white and the flippers are all black. The tall dorsal fin of the male, unique among cetaceans, can be recognized even at a great distance. In a mature male, it can be up to 6 feet (1.9 m) high; at half the male's height, even the female dorsal fin is tall. The flippers are broad and rounded and more than 6 feet (1.9 m) long in mature males.

A mother orca, on the right, travels with her two offspring, a juvenile and a full-grown male.

A 25-year study off British Columbia and Washington State, has found that orcas stay in long-term social groups, or pods, for life, an average of 29 years for males and 50 years for females. Residents live in close family pods of 7 to 50 and subsist on fish; transient pods of 1 to 7 feed on marine mammals. The two groups do not mix.

Orcas can be reliably seen on tours around Vancouver Island, off Antarctica, Norway, and Iceland, and occasionally in many other areas. They are very curious and will approach close to boats to inspect them. Traveling in close-knit groups, they make a great display of activity, spouting loudly, spyhopping, breaching, and lobtailing. Youngsters will sometimes ride the bow or wake. Orcas have been hunted in the past few decades, some of them taken alive as part of the world aquarium trade.

Short-finned Pilot Whale

Globicephala macrorhynchus

Short-finned pilot whales range through offshore, warm temperate and tropical seas, making deep dives mainly to feed on squid. Pilot whales are so intensely social that they are almost never seen alone.

FIELD NOTES

- *Male: 20–22' (6–6.7 m); female: 17–18' (5.1–5.5 m); at birth: 4½'+ (1.4 m+)*
- *Squid*
- *Offshore*
- *Warm temperate and tropical world waters*
- *Insufficiently known, exploited to some extent, but not extensively*

Identifying short-finned pilot whales is fairly easy. They sometimes travel with dolphins, such as bottlenose dolphins, but they are much larger and their black bodies are darker—most dolphins tend to be gray. The short-finned pilot whale's dorsal fin is broad based and set far forward on the back. Its head is rounded and bulbous. The only animal likely to be confused with this whale is its close relative, the long-finned pilot whale (see opposite page).

Short-finned pilot whales resident in the warm waters off Tenerife in the Canary Islands have been studied, with 445 individuals photo-identified as part of long-term behavioral research. Here, scientists have found that the whales prefer water depths of about 3,300 feet (1,000 m). Typical group size is 10 to 30, but some pods are as large as 60. Like orcas, pilot whales live a long time, with females known to survive up to 65 years.

Short-finned pilot whales rarely breach, but sometimes spyhop. They can be seen on whale-watch trips in the Bahamas; in the eastern Caribbean; in the Azores; in Kochi Prefecture, off Japan; in the Tañon Strait, the Philippines; and around Hawaii.

Although not hunted to the same extent as long-finned pilot whales, several hundred short-finned pilot whales are killed every year off Japan, as well as a few in the eastern Caribbean by local fishers. In Japanese waters, there are two forms of the species.

Both pilot whale species have some variation and separation of populations. In future, this may lead to scientists isolating another species.

Short-finned pilot whales with a yearling calf, Azores Islands.

Long-finned Pilot Whale

Globicephala melas

Both species of pilot whale are sometimes called "potheads," a name that was given, as many whale names were, by the hunters who first encountered them. The name is based on the resemblance of the pilot whale's head to a black iron cauldron, or pot. The long-finned pilot whale is still hunted persistently in the North Atlantic Ocean.

FIELD NOTES

- *Male: 13–25' (4–7.6 m); female: 10–18½' (3–5.6 m); at birth: 6' (1.9 m)*
- *Squid*
- *Offshore*
- *Cold temperate to subpolar North Atlantic and Southern Ocean*
- *Insufficiently known, extinct in North Pacific, still hunted in North Atlantic*

long flipper

short flipper

Like the short-finned pilot whale, the long-finned is a family animal, traveling in groups of 10 to 50, and sometimes up to 100 or more. There are reports of thousands seen together in great superpods. Any sighting of a group of black, medium-sized whales with rounded heads and very wide, thick, curved-back dorsal fins, is bound to be of pilot whales. Young long-finned pilot whales will sometimes breach, but this is rarely observed in an adult.

In a few temperate waters of the world, the distribution of short-finned and long-finned pilot whales overlaps, making it difficult to tell the two apart. Externally they look alike, except that the long-finned has longer flippers (pectoral fins) and a few more teeth. It is difficult, however, to see flippers, much less teeth, at sea. At times, positive identification may be impossible. It's no wonder that mariners usually write "pilot whales" in their logbooks, refusing to try to distinguish between the two. But in most areas, distribution is quite enough to determine the species.

Long-finned pilot whales inhabit cold temperate to subpolar waters in both the Northern and Southern Hemisphere, except in the North Pacific. The species lived in the North Pacific off Japan until at least the tenth century, but has since completely disappeared.

The long-finned pilot whale often strands on beaches and is possibly subject to more mass strandings than any other cetacean. Frequent strandings occur on Cape Cod, in southern Australia, New Zealand, and southern South America. Because of their social ties, when one pilot whale strands, the others remain with it.

Narwhal

Monodon monoceros

The tusk of the narwhal may well be the source of the unicorn myths. The tusk is actually a tooth. Narwhals have two teeth, both in the upper jaw. In females, they rarely erupt. In males, the left tooth erupts, penetrating the upper beak and spiraling out up to 10 feet (3 m). The tusk is primarily for display and is used to compete for females (the largest tusked male may get the female). The scratches on the head of many males may result from comparing tusks, and perhaps a little sparring. The sound of two tusks hitting is like the "clack" from musical sticks. The tusk is mostly hollow and an estimated one in three tusks is broken.

FIELD NOTES

- *Male: 13–20½' (4–6.2 m), not including tusk; female: 11–16½' (3.4–5 m); at birth: 5'+ (1.5 m+)*
- *Wide variety of fish including herring, cod, halibut, salmon; cephalopods, crustaceans*
- *Mainly offshore*
- *Arctic Ocean and adjacent bays and straits (except western Canada to eastern Russia)*
- *Insufficiently known, some taken by native hunters*

the erupted left tooth of a male

The narwhal, with the beluga, is a member of the family of "white whales" (Monodontidae) which are considered whales by some and dolphins by others. They have many characteristics of larger dolphins, but also qualify as a separate family of toothed whales.

Tusked narwhals are unmistakable. Only the females and calves, which normally live in separate groups from the males, may be confused with belugas. Narwhals and belugas have a similar head with a bulbous forehead and the hint of a beak. Narwhals sometimes turn whiter with age, but most are considerably darker and splotchy compared to the uniformly light color of the beluga. Narwhals have only a slight hump instead of a dorsal fin, whereas belugas have a dorsal ridge that shows up as a series of dark bumps. Finally, narwhals have distinctive flukes with convex trailing edges that make the flukes appear to be put on backward.

Narwhals have been hunted for centuries by European and Inuit peoples, and today they are still hunted in northern Canada and Greenland.

A narwhal's splotchy skin distinguishes it from a beluga.

Beluga

Delphinapterus leucas

The beluga, sometimes called the white whale, is one of the most vocal of all cetaceans. The sounds can often be heard clearly above water or through the hull of a boat.

With their all-white, sometimes yellowish, body, belugas are distinctive. The calves are dark to brownish gray at birth and whiten as they age, reaching pure white between the ages of 5 and 12.

As an arctic animal, the beluga is robust and blubbery. The body is wrinkled and flexible to an extent found in few other cetaceans. The head with its rounded forehead is small compared to the body. The forehead changes shape and the lips can appear rounded as they vocalize. Belugas have a visible neck and can move their head from side to side, giving them the ability to look behind.

At sea, belugas can be difficult to find. With a small dorsal ridge and no fin, belugas have a low profile, and they rarely leap. However, they swim slowly, surface often, and their white bodies contrast with a dark sea. They spyhop often and show curiosity toward boats. In rivers, such as the Churchill in Manitoba, or the St. Lawrence-Saguenay, finding them is much easier.

FIELD NOTES

- *Male: 12–18' (3.7–5.5 m); female: 10–13½' (3–4.1 m); at birth: 5'+ (1.5 m+)*
- *Large variety of fish, various crustaceans and other bottom-living invertebrates*
- *Inshore including estuaries and rivers in summer, sometimes offshore*
- *Arctic and subarctic waters (including St. Lawrence River)*
- *Insufficiently known, population reduced by hunting*

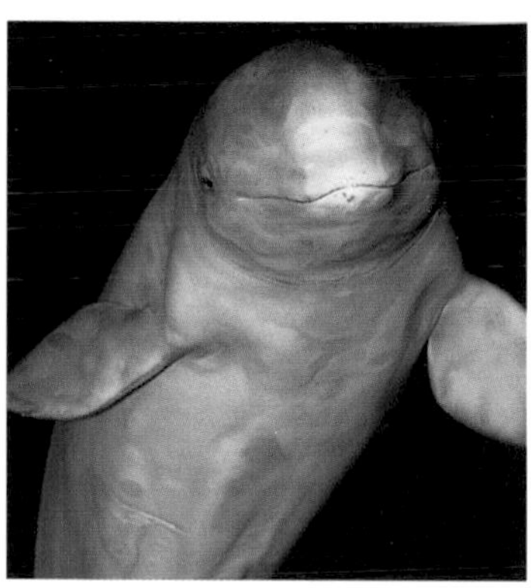

An inquisitive beluga shows its flexible neck and blubbery body.

Belugas travel in groups of 5 to 20, although more than a thousand may congregate around the estuaries and in rivers to feed in the summer. They have been known to swim hundreds of miles up rivers in Russia, Canada, and northern Europe. They have little fear of shallow waters, and if stranded are often able to wait and refloat on the next tide.

Belugas have been hunted by Russian, European, and native people for many centuries. A large number of belugas are still taken for food, and numbers are down in some areas. Greater concerns, however, come from the effects of oil and gas activities and chemical pollution.

Dall's Porpoise

Phocoenoides dalli

The hyperactive Dall's porpoise acts more like an excited dolphin than a shy, retiring porpoise. Resident in the cold temperate North Pacific, Dall's porpoises will race around whale-watching boats, even riding the bow. Traveling just beneath the surface at estimated speeds of up to 35 miles (56 km) per hour, they push up a distinctive spray that looks like a "rooster tail." They don't leap out of the water, but the excitement they create on a whale-watch tour can last for hours.

FIELD NOTES

- *Male: 6–8' (1.9–2.4 m); female: 6–7' (1.9–2.2 m); at birth: 2½' (0.7 m)*
- *Hake, herring, mackerel, capelin and other small fish; squid*
- *Inshore and offshore*
- *Warm temperate to subarctic waters of the North Pacific Ocean*
- *Not well known, many killed in western Pacific hunts and in fishing nets*

Most Dall's porpoises are black with a white belly and lower flanks, and with fringes of white on the tail and dorsal fin. There are several forms of the species and the various color patterns on the dorsal fin and body may represent subspecies or races. Dall's porpoises are two to three times the bulk of other porpoise species. They were first noted by American zoologist William H. Dall as large, "porpoise-like" animals. His sightings were made off the coast of Alaska in the 1870s.

Harbor Porpoise

Phocoena phocoena

The harbor porpoise is the most commonly seen and studied member of its family, even though it is generally wary of boats and little of its body shows when it surfaces. Once glimpsed, it can be recognized by its low dorsal fin and absence of a beak. The upper body is gray to black, including the small flippers and flukes. The white on the belly and flank turns to gray as it extends high up the sides.

The blow of the harbor porpoise is rarely seen but can be heard. Whale watchers unimpressed at first with the idea of seeing porpoises, come to enjoy the familiar "pop" of its spouting.

FIELD NOTES

- *Male: 6' (1.9 m); female: 6' (1.9 m); at birth: 2½' (0.7 m)*
- *Variety of inshore and offshore fish, herring, mackerel, and anchovy*
- *Inshore to offshore*
- *Coastal waters of temperate to subarctic North Atlantic and North Pacific*
- *Still exist in large numbers*

Found mainly in cool, coastal waters throughout the Northern Hemisphere, the porpoise travels in groups of two to five, surfacing about eight times a minute with a slow, forward-rolling motion. When feeding, it might surface to breathe about four times every 10 to 20 seconds before diving for 2 to 6 minutes.

It is the shortest lived cetacean, rarely surviving past the age of 12 years. Even this short life is threatened by humans. It gets caught in fishing nets, is still hunted in a few areas, and has suffered habitat loss near urban areas and shipping lanes.

Harbor porpoises tend to travel in small groups.

Finless Porpoise

Neophocaena phocaenoides

This light-colored Asian porpoise is distinguished by its lack of a dorsal fin. Instead, it has a low ridge studded with small, wart-like tubercles along its back. It is one of the smallest cetaceans, and with its bulbous forehead, it looks a little like a tiny beluga.

Finless porpoises often travel in groups of up to 10 individuals, and are found feeding in rivers, estuaries, and mangroves where fresh and salt water mingle. They also travel upriver and out to sea, but most are found no more than 3 miles (5 km) from shore. Like the closely related Dall's and harbor porpoises, the finless porpoise is an active animal, and can often be seen darting from side to side as part of its routine. Usually only 1 or 2 are seen at a time, but groups of up to 50 have been reported in feeding areas.

They sometimes spyhop, and at such times the eyes may be visible—about half of all finless porpoises have bright pink eyes.

Living near large population centers in Asia, finless porpoises have suffered considerable habitat destruction from shipping traffic, dams, and pollution. It must be expected that the tremendous human population growth in Asia will continue to have an impact on this species for decades to come.

FIELD NOTES

- *Male: 5–6' (1.5–1.9 m); female: 4½–5½' (1.4–1.7 m); at birth: 2' (0.6 m)*
- *Small fish; prawns; squid; cuttlefish*
- *Coastal waters, estuaries, and rivers*
- *Tropical and warm temperate waters from Japan to the Persian Gulf*
- *Not well known, some populations reduced by habitat destruction*

Vaquita

Phocoena sinus

Vaquitas are found only in shallow lagoons in and around the Colorado River delta in the northern Gulf of California, Mexico. They are locally called Gulf of California porpoise, or cochito. Studies of the animal often involve long periods of searching with few sightings. Like some other porpoise species, vaquitas may well avoid boats.

One of the smallest cetacean species, the inconspicuous vaquita grows to only 5 feet (1.5 m). Its distinctive triangular fin is large compared to the rest of the body, and at first sight might seem shark-like. Most "encounters" have been with dead animals accidentally caught in gill nets.

Despite bans, illegal gill netting has persisted for many years. In June 1993, the Mexican government established the Upper Gulf of California Biosphere Reserve to protect the vaquita and its habitat. It remains to be seen whether there are enough left to save the species.

FIELD NOTES

- *Male: 4½' (1.4 m); female: 5' (1.5 m); at birth: 2½' (0.7 m)*
- *Grunts, gulf croakers, and other fish; squid*
- *Inshore*
- *Warm temperate waters in the northern Gulf of California*
- *Endangered, may be too few left for the species to recover*

A vaquita retrieved from a gill net.

The greatest resource of the ocean is not material but the boundless spring of inspiration and well-being we gain from her.

JACQUES COUSTEAU (1910–97), French diver and photographer

CHAPTER EIGHT
WATCHING WHALES, DOLPHINS, *and* PORPOISES

USING *the* GUIDE *to* WATCHING CETACEANS

Opportunities to watch and learn about cetaceans are offered in key areas of the world, from the Arctic to Antarctica.

The following pages feature 28 special areas, divided into 7 regions, all of which are exciting and reliable places to watch whales, dolphins, and porpoises. The species you are likely to encounter, and the behavior you may observe, are complemented with information, as well as tips, on how best to watch these magnificent creatures. This guide will give you an insight into what to expect in each area, alert you to the unexpected, and help you select a whale-watch trip according to your interests.

The ***illustrated banding*** *indicates that the spread is about a special area.*

Vivid photos *give a fresh perspective on whales, dolphins, or porpoises that may be encountered in each area, or of unique features that may be of special interest to the visiting whale watcher.*

The ***text*** *describes the ambience of an area, or sometimes of a particular spot, and how to get there. It lists some of the species likely to be found, and why the animals are there, and explains some of the behavior you may observe. It also points out unusual cetaceans or other attractions you may want to include in your trip.*

Watching Whales, Dolphins, and Porpoises

Hawaii

West Coast of North America

Every Christmastime, humpback whales return to sing, fight, mate, and raise their calves in the tropical blue waters off Hawaii. Humpbacks make their winter homes near these islands, which are checkered with tropical forest, pineapple and coffee farms, and topped with volcanoes. From hotels on the west side of Maui, it is possible to watch the humpbacks as they arrive; they make occasional approaches opposite Lahaina's Front Street, so be prepared.

Migrating from Alaska, the female humpbacks often arrive first, some heavy with calf, others having just given birth. The males arrive later in search of a partner. In the late 1970s, biologists in Maui first witnessed humpback whales fighting. The fighting seems to follow extended bouts of singing among the males who apparently compete to escort and mate with females. Many of the females start these fights or get involved in them by emitting streams of warning bubbles toward ambitious males. Blood can sometimes be seen on the tail or back of a whale or in the water, but the injuries are usually only superficial.

A humpback nearly clear of the water as it breaches (above) close to shore. A spinner dolphin (left) executes a breathtakingly high, spinning leap.

The shallow, warm sea between the islands of Maui, Molokai, and all around Lanai is the prime area in Hawaii for humpbacks and the core area of the Hawaiian Islands National Marine Sanctuary, which was set up mainly to protect these whales. The best access is through boat tours from Lahaina or Kihei on Maui's west side. Maui is a short plane flight from the international airport at Honolulu on the nearby island of Oahu.

The humpback tours usually include sightings of bottlenose dolphins, which often accompany

404

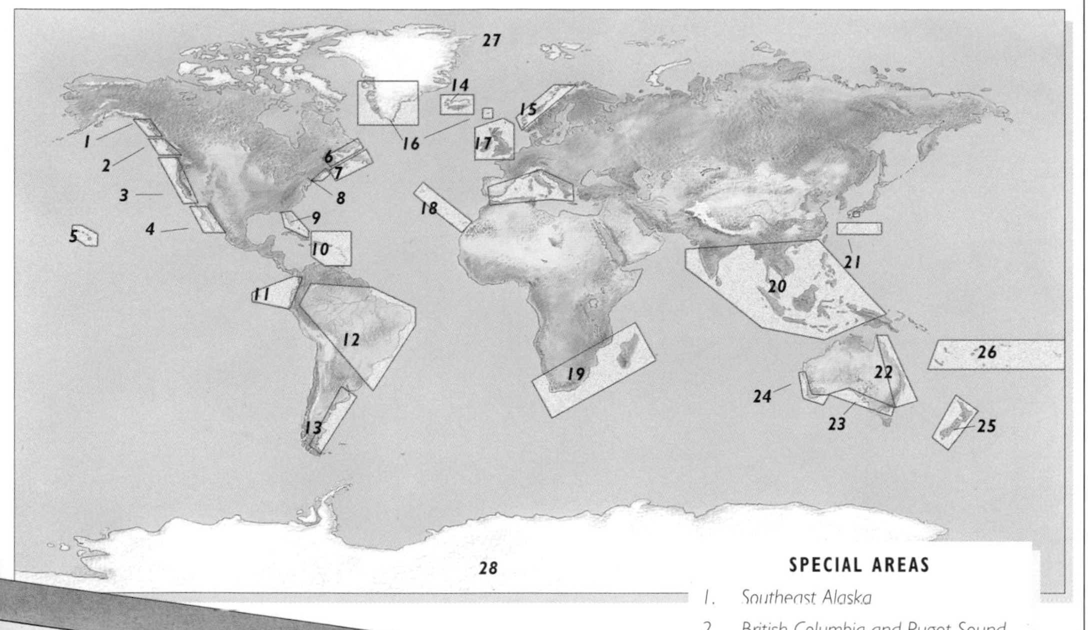

SPECIAL AREAS

1. Southeast Alaska
2. British Columbia and Puget Sound
3. California, Oregon, and Washington
4. Baja California
5. Hawaii
6. St. Lawrence River and the Gulf
7. The Maritimes and Newfoundland
8. New England
9. Florida and the Bahamas
10. The Caribbean
11. Ecuador and Colombia
12. Brazil and the Amazon River
13. Argentina
14. Iceland
15. Norway
16. Greenland and the Faeroe Islands
17. Britain and Ireland
18. Canaries and Azores
19. South Africa and Madagascar
20. South Asia
21. Japan: Ogasawara and Okinawa
22. East Coast Australia
23. Southern Australia
24. Western Australia
25. New Zealand
26. Tonga and Other Pacific Islands
27. The Arctic
28. Antarctica

Hawaii

ɔacks. As in other
lolphins will ride a
wave, but here they
ke of a whale as well.
the humpbacks
ated with the
npanionship, and
ve seen humpbacks
ls at the dolphins,
urage them and
ay. Beneath the
beside your boat,
e dolphins—
wear polarizing
the glare—or
mming, the bubbles from their
g a trail through the water.
her main Hawaiian islands offer
watching and a chance to see a
pical cetaceans. Although
focus on the humpbacks,
u will see include bottlenose
s, false killer
, and even
les. From the
spinner
r high leaps
in through
hroughout
er
re wide-
tours,
auai.

Close behind the powerful tail of a short-finned pilot whale (above). The rugged, volcanic coastline of Kauai (left).

SPECIAL FEATURES
From the main street of Lahaina, signs of whale-watching culture date from the 1970s. In front of the Pioneer Hotel, once home to whaling captains waiting for South Seas postings, about 20 whale-watch boats are berthed, each with its signboard displayed. You can see glass-bottom boats, Chinese junks that look like pirate ships, motor cruisers, Zodiac inflatables, schooners, and trimarans. This is a rare opportunity to go window-shopping for the best whale-watch tour. Key features to look for are an on-board naturalist or nature guide, and a boat equipped with hydrophones, through which you can hear haunting humpback songs.

TRAVELER'S NOTES

When to visit Late Dec–Apr for humpback whales, largest concentrations in Feb and Mar; year-round: spinner, bottlenose, and pantropical spotted dolphins, false killer whales, short-finned pilot whales, and many others
Weather Warm to hot; sometimes strong Kona winds bring rain and high seas
Types of tours Half- and full-day tours, some extended multi-day expeditions; inflatables, sailboats, and large whale-watch boats
Tours available Maui: Lahaina, Kihei, Maalaea; Hawaii (big island): Keauhou, Kailua-Kona, Kohala Coast, Honokohau; Oahu: Honolulu, Kaneohe. Kauai: Hanalei
Information Hawaii Visitors Bureau, 2270 Kalakaua Avenue, Suite 801, Honolulu, HI 96813. Ph. 1 808 924 0266

405

Traveler's Notes: *These provide brief details on the best time to see cetaceans, the weather, and possible sea conditions. They also list what types of tours are available, points of departure, and contact details for bookings or further information.*

WEST COAST of NORTH AMERICA

Home of the earliest whale-watch tours, the West Coast offers excellent opportunities to sight a wide diversity of cetaceans.

A juvenile gray whale near the Channel Islands, off California.

The world's first commercial whale watching occurred in southern California in early 1955, when Chuck Chamberlin, a fisherman from San Diego, put out a handmade sign that said "See the Whales—$1." The whales were gray whales that migrated along the west coast of North America every winter. The trips proved a steady seller and, four years later, Raymond M. Gilmore, a marine scientist, began the first trips to be led by a naturalist. By the late 1960s, Gilmore and others were leading trips to Baja California to encounter the gray whales mating and raising their calves in Scammon's Lagoon.

At the same time, more and more people began to gather at coastal California lookouts, especially during weekends in the winter, to look for spouting gray whales. The whale-watching craze spread north and south along the coast, following the gray whales' migration path.

In the early 1970s, as whaling finally came to a halt around North America and the whales started returning to coastal waters, more than 20 fishing and other communities became involved in the whale-watching business. From California, north to Washington State, and south to Baja California, whale watching became a way for those who fished or worked in the travel industry to earn some money through winter.

Whale watching grew steadily on the West Coast and soon spread to Hawaii. At first, humpback tours were conducted from Lahaina on Maui, but today, tours leave from all the main islands and encounter a variety of tropical dolphins as well as the humpbacks.

Alaska joined the ranks, with humpback whales again the main attraction. In British Columbia, the orcas became the first toothed whales to be commercially watched, and trips to see them soon rivaled the popularity of tours to spot some of the large baleen whales.

In the late 1970s, seabird and other tours to the waters off San Francisco and Monterey, California, began turning up some amazing finds from August to October: blue and humpback whales, and a wide assortment of other species. As the whale-watching business flourished, these important areas for whales, birds, and fish soon became candidates to be declared marine-protected

A humpback close to the shore of Lahaina, Maui, Hawaii.

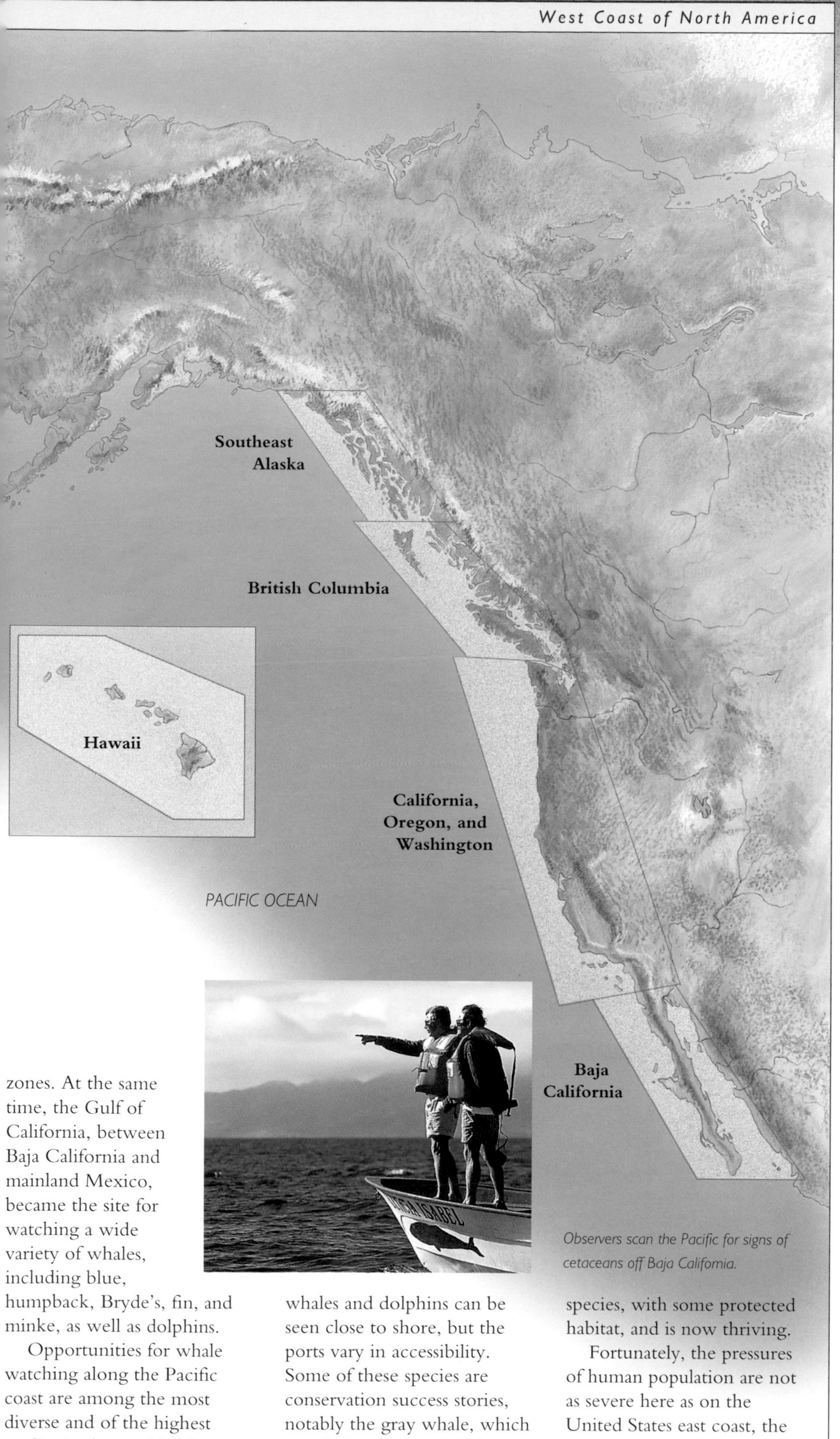

Observers scan the Pacific for signs of cetaceans off Baja California.

zones. At the same time, the Gulf of California, between Baja California and mainland Mexico, became the site for watching a wide variety of whales, including blue, humpback, Bryde's, fin, and minke, as well as dolphins.

Opportunities for whale watching along the Pacific coast are among the most diverse and of the highest quality in the world. Most whales and dolphins can be seen close to shore, but the ports vary in accessibility. Some of these species are conservation success stories, notably the gray whale, which was declared a protected species, with some protected habitat, and is now thriving.

Fortunately, the pressures of human population are not as severe here as on the United States east coast, the St. Lawrence, and in Europe.

Southeast Alaska

West Coast of North America

The grandeur of the humpback whale fits the majesty of southeast Alaska, where there is the feeling of being in the presence of nature without bounds. The visitor can sense what the world must have been like before humans arrived on the scene: deep fiords filled with salmon, small schooling fish, and plankton; walls of mountains with tall, dense stands of conifers; glaciers moving at their own slow pace; lush, untouched islands; open sea; and fins and flukes wherever you look.

Whale watchers are treated to the sight of a humpback breaching, its flippers outstretched as if taking flight (above). A minke whale (below).

Southeast Alaska is where "bubblenet feeding" (see p. 280) by humpbacks was first seen and studied. The humpbacks come to Alaska each year from Mexico and Hawaii, and use this technique to round up small schooling fish.

Besides humpbacks, various other whales and dolphins are seen. Orcas patrol the straits and island passages in pods of 10 or more whales. They are here to feed on salmon, although other orcas, the so-called "transients," come to feed on porpoises, seals, and other marine mammals, which sometimes includes whales. Judging from the orca teeth marks on many humpback whale tails, they try, but are not often successful. Minke whales, feeding on plankton and small schooling fish, can also be found all along the southeast Alaskan coast, as well as Dall's and harbor porpoises, Pacific white-sided dolphins and, less frequently, fin whales.

Whale-watching vessels in southeast Alaska range from giant cruise ships to tiny one-person kayaks. Some tours use medium-size motor boats in and around Glacier Bay and Gustavus, the main port for whale-watch boats in southeast Alaska. These tours are day trips, but the cruise ships and kayaks make multi-day tours.

Alaska is the world's number three cruise ship destination; only the Caribbean and Europe

Humpbacks, after a cooperative "bubblenet feed" (above). Watchers on a cruise ship (left) in Glacier Bay.

attract greater numbers. Summer cruise ships run from California, Seattle, and Vancouver through the Inside Passage to various ports in southeast Alaska. Twenty years ago, cruise ships did not stop for whales. If whales were seen, it was in passing and a matter of luck. Cruise ships then began to advertise their tours using pictures of orca pods and humpback whales as they cavorted against the backdrop of tall conifers, mountains, and glaciers. Customers now demand that ships stop for whales and to be guaranteed sightings.

Today, many cruise ships take a few hours or even a half-day excursion to spend time with the whales, usually in Icy Strait, near Gustavus, and Glacier Bay. Cruise ships are too large and unmaneuverable to approach close to wildlife, but for many people, this is their only chance to see whales. Some cruise ships launch inflatable boats for close-up observation, but the best whale watching normally occurs from medium-size tour boats, such as dedicated whale-watch boats, sailboats, and converted fishing boats.

Special Features

Wildlife is a big part of all tours to southeast Alaska. Besides the high-profile humpback whales and orcas, you can see harbor seals and Steller sea lions on remote rocky islets. Southeast Alaska has the highest density of black bears in the world. To see brown bears and eagles feeding on spawning salmon in the rivers, the Pack Creek Cooperative Management Area/Stan Price State Wildlife Sanctuary has camping and guided trips in July and August. Access is gained from the west side of Seymour Canal and Admiralty Island, 28 miles (45 km) by air or boat south of Juneau. Another popular site, farther south, is Anan Creek Bear Observatory, on the mainland near Wrangell Island.

TRAVELER'S NOTES

When to visit *June–early Sept humpbacks, minke whales, orcas, Pacific white-sided dolphins, Dall's and harbor porpoises. Bubblenetting humpbacks best in June–early July*
Weather *June–Sept cool to cold on water and subject to extreme changes, including fog and rain; Aug prime month for weather, seas, and whales*
Types of tours *Multi-day cruises on small and large cruise ships and kayak expeditions; day trips on fishing, sail, inflatable, and whale-watch boats*
Tours available *Gustavus, Pt. Adolphus, Glacier Bay, Ketchikan, Juneau, Petersburg, Elfin Cove, Wrangell Island, and Sitka; also long-range cruise ships from Seattle, Vancouver, Prince Rupert, and San Francisco*
Information *Alaska State Division of Tourism, E-28, Juneau, AK 99801 Ph. 1 907 465 2010*

British Columbia and Puget Sound

West Coast of North America

Along the British Columbia and Washington coast, the towering dorsal fins of orcas cut through the mist. They have become emblems of the Northwest—visible in everything from Kwakiutl and Haida native totem poles to road signs and tourist brochures. At sea, the tall angularity of the fins matches the tall, snowcapped peaks behind. But more often, it is the sound of orcas spouting, like shotgun fire on a still morning, which alerts you to their approach.

Pacific white-sided dolphins delight watchers with acrobatics off the British Columbia coast.

You may see orcas almost anywhere through the Inside Passage or outer coast—from land, ferry, cruise ship, or whale-watch tour boat. The best chance, however, is in two prime spots—western Johnstone Strait-Blackfish Sound (the better spot) and southern Vancouver Island.

Many of the boat tours for western Johnstone Strait-Blackfish Sound depart from Telegraph Cove, a town on northern Vancouver Island. Telegraph Cove, where the main street is a boardwalk that winds along the water, is a half-day drive north from Victoria, or you can fly in to Port Hardy from Vancouver and drive to "the cove." Tours will escort you on half-day or full-day trips to meet the orcas.

A typical whale watch usually starts with bald eagles, harbor seals, and sometimes sea lions. Orcas and other cetacean species, including Dall's porpoises, harbor porpoises, minke whales, and Pacific white-sided dolphins, are often seen. More than 10 pods of orcas regularly patrol Johnstone Strait. Although they come mainly to feed on salmon, a day in the life of an orca pod includes periods of rest, play, and socializing. At such times, they often interact with whale-watch boats, playing up for the cameras. A little farther out to sea, off the north and southwest coast of Vancouver Island, humpback whales are sometimes found, but these areas are less accessible to marine tourism. Some tours will end the day with a salmon barbecue back at the port.

The other good spot for orcas is off southern Vancouver Island. Resident to the waters of this

A photographer's paradise: an orca (above) breaches with the tree-clad coast of San Juan Island as a spectacular backdrop; and (right) a pod of orcas in formation with a bull in the foreground.

area and northern Washington State, are 3 pods, comprising about 100 whales. The best boat access is from either Victoria, or Friday Harbor on San Juan Island in Washington. You can reach San Juan Island by car ferry from Anacortes, Washington. In Friday Harbor, don't miss the Whale Museum on First Street. This is dedicated to orcas and other marine mammals in the area and has both research and educational programs. On the west side of San Juan Island there are good land-based lookouts for orcas.

Gray whales migrate along the length of the British Columbia coast. The best place to see them is by boat from Ucluelet and Tofino, or from the shore in Pacific Rim National Park, near Tofino, during the northerly migration in March and April. Some young gray whales stop here for the summer to feed (for most grays, the full northern migration terminates off western Alaska). They spend their days diving in muddy shallows, eating small shellfish and other organisms, and churning the water to brown.

Special Features

Harbor seals and California and Steller sea lions can be seen on rocky islets along the coast. The most accessible locales are Race Rocks at the southern tip of Vancouver Island and Sea Lion Rocks off Long Beach in the Pacific Rim National Park. In many other spots along the coast of Vancouver Island, bald eagles prey on salmon and other fish. The eagles take advantage of the best sea views from tall, mature trees. When the tide changes in Johnstone Strait, dozens of eagles divebomb for fish, with the occasional mid-air fight between sparring eagles. Talons locked, they fight over the food until they hit the water.

TRAVELER'S NOTES

When to visit *Mar–Apr gray whales (west Vancouver Island); May–Sept orcas, Pacific white-sided dolphins, Dall's porpoises (nth Vancouver Island), harbor porpoises (sth Vancouver Island), gray whales (west Vancouver Island)*
Weather *Mar–June, often rainy and cold on water; July–Aug, cool on water but usually dry, fog especially mornings on west coast Vancouver Island*
Types of tours *Half- and full-day tours, multi-day expeditions; inflatables, sailboats, and large whale-watch boats; some whale watching from ferries*
Tours available *British Columbia: Alert Bay, Telegraph Cove, Port McNeill, Sointula, Tofino, Ucluelet, Victoria, Nanaimo; Puget Sound area: Anacortes, Bellingham, Friday Harbor, Seattle*
Information *Tourism British Columbia, Parliament Buildings, Victoria, BC V8W 2Z2, Ph. 1 800 663 6000; Department of Trade & Economic Development, 101 General Administration Bldg., AX-13, Olympia, WA 98504, Ph. 1 800 544 1800*

California, Oregon, and Washington

West Coast of North America

A school of blunt-nosed Risso's dolphins (above) seen off the coast of California, west of Monterey.

As regular as the seasons, gray whales come and go on their annual migrations up and down the west coast of North America. With a glassed-in observatory and outdoor overlook, Cabrillo National Monument draws tens of thousands of whale watchers each year who often cheer when gray whales spout. There are numerous lookouts all along the west coast of the continent. Many quiet headlands with good sea views are known only to local people, and whale watching here can be a more contemplative experience. A leisurely driving tour along Highway 1 would allow you to follow the migration of gray whales as they move south or north over a seven-month period.

From late October to December, they arrive off the coast of Washington State from Alaska. Fresh from a summer of feeding in the far north, they are headed for mating and calving grounds in the Baja California lagoons. Off the Oregon coast, the southern migration peaks in the last week of December and the first week of January. Continuing south along the Californian coast, the greatest numbers are seen in the latter half of January. By February, the first gray whales are already starting to appear off southern California on their way back north. The first wave arrives off Oregon in late February and continues through early March. The last stragglers, many of them females with calves, pass along the coast of northern California to Washington in May.

Watching gray whales from land has been a popular activity for decades. For a closer, if colder and wetter look at the action, boat trips depart from some 35 ports along this stretch of coast. Slopping around in the sea alongside these mighty mammals, you can only marvel at their endurance—swimming 12,400 miles (20,000 km) a year back and forth from Alaska to Mexico.

Whale-watching trips encounter various species depending on how far offshore they go and how knowledgeable the operator is. From

A gray whale (above) swims through kelp off the California coast. Keen whale watchers (left) in southern California waters.

northern Washington, for example, boat tours trying to catch the last of the gray whales may meet orcas, harbor porpoises, and Pacific white-sided dolphins. Off California, pilot whales, orcas, bottlenose dolphins, and even northern right whale dolphins are sometimes seen.

Special Features

In the late 1970s, dedicated seabird cruises, taken during August to October to the offshore canyons and banks west of San Francisco and Monterey, began to encounter dolphins and a variety of whales, such as blues and humpbacks. In all, there have been sightings of 26 cetacean species, almost a third of all species, including sporadic sightings of a number of rare beaked whales. Besides blue, humpback, and summering gray whales, the most commonly seen are minke and fin whales; Pacific white-sided, Risso's, and northern right whale dolphins; and Dall's and harbor porpoises. The whales are here to feed, while many of the smaller cetaceans remain in the area year-round. Other marine mammals are often sighted. This extraordinarily rich marine area extends from the Monterey Submarine Canyon opposite Moss Landing in Monterey Bay to Cordell Bank, some 60 miles (100 km) northwest of San Francisco. It has been protected in three continuous marine sanctuaries—Cordell Bank, Gulf of the Farallones, and Monterey Bay National Marine Sanctuary, the largest, extending along 300 miles (485 km) of coast, to some 50 miles (80 km) out to sea.

TRAVELER'S NOTES

When to visit *Dec–May migrating gray whales; June–Sept summering gray whales, north California to Washington; Aug–Oct blue, humpback, and other whales and dolphins off the coast of central California*
Weather *June–Sept cool to cold on water, even when hot on land; Oct–May, California to Washington, cold, rainy*
Types of tours *Half- and full-day tours, multi-day expeditions; inflatables, fishing, sail, and large whale-watch boats*
Tours available *California: Avila Beach, Balboa, Dana Point, El Granada, Fort Bragg, Hollister, La Mesa, Long Beach, Monterey, Morro Bay, Oceanside, Oxnard, Point Arena, Redondo Beach, San Diego, San Pedro, Santa Barbara, Santa Cruz, Ventura; Oregon: Charleston, Depoe Bay, Garibaldi, Newport; Washington (west coast only): La Push, Neah Bay, Westport*
Information *Department of Trade & Economic Development, 1121 L Street, Suite 103, Sacramento, CA 95814, Ph. 1 916 324 5853; Economic Development Department, 595 Cottage Street, NE, Salem, OR 97310, Ph. 1 503 986 0123; Department of Trade & Economic Development, 101 General Administration Bldg., AX-13, Olympia, WA 98504, Ph. 1 360 753 5600*

Baja California

West Coast of North America

Baja California, or "lower California," which extends south from the California border with Mexico, is one of the most important areas in the world for whales. In terms of whale watching, there are two dramatically different regions. The first is the open Pacific coast with its sheltered lagoons. Here, friendly gray whales may nudge your boat or ease it up and out of the water, a breathless and rather nerve-racking experience. Don't forget your wide-angle lenses. The other is the Gulf of California, between Baja and the mainland coast of Mexico. This is one of the most species-diverse cetacean and marine areas in the world. Motoring out from the desert coasts of Baja, you feel as if anything could happen.

The blue whale (above), largest living organism on Earth, feeds in the Sea of Cortez in winter.

Baja California first became known as the winter home of the gray whale—a magical place beside the desert where the whales gather to socialize, mate, and raise their calves. The gray whale, which spends part of its year in the lagoons, was once reduced to near extinction. In the mid-nineteenth century, whalers led by Captain Charles M. Scammon discovered the entrance to the Pacific coastal lagoon that would bear his name. The whalers killed almost every gray whale. When Scammon's Lagoon was designated the world's first whale sanctuary in January 1972, gray whales were considered highly endangered. Besides Scammon's Lagoon, the whales are found along the coast in Magdalena Bay and San Ignacio Lagoon. Today, after many years of protection, the gray whales are thought to have recovered fully.

Whale-watching trips to the lagoons can be arranged as part of a 7- to 10-day trip out of San Diego on a self-contained boat. Other visitors drive to Guerrero Negro, near Scammon's Lagoon, and Adolfo López Mateos, at Magdalena Bay, and hire small Mexican boats called "pangas." Land-based whale watchers can stay at several permanent campsites at Magdalena Bay

A gray whale calf breaching (above) in a Baja lagoon. Magdalena Bay (right), an area where gray whales congregate in winter to socialize and breed.

and San Ignacio Lagoon. The idea of sleeping out in the land of the "desert whale" provides a wonderful sense of community, despite the sandy sleeping bags and basic living conditions.

At the south end of the Baja California peninsula, from San José del Cabo and east coast ports, such as Loreto and Bahia de los Angeles, another world opens up—the Gulf of California, also known as the Sea of Cortez. Here you can see fin, humpback, sperm, short-finned pilot, and minke whales, as well as various dolphins including common, bottlenose, and Pacific white-sided. Moreover, it is one of the best places in the world to find blue and Bryde's whales—two species not often seen by whale watchers. Day trips into the Gulf of California are popular, but most people take one- to two-week boat excursions out of La Paz with a small group of participants. They live aboard the boat and are guided by naturalists who know the area.

Special Features

In 1993, Mexico's newest reserve, the Upper Gulf of California and Colorado River Delta Biosphere Reserve, was established to protect the vaquita, the small, endangered porpoise that lives only in this part of the world. You may not spot a vaquita but, by way of consolation, humpbacks are sometimes encountered, and fin whales are often seen. Tours leave from the popular tourist town, Puerto Peñasco, in the state of Sonora, just south of the Arizona border. Even though ecotourism is relatively new in this area, it may well become very popular with the excellent birding prospects, the desert and its wildlife, the nearby volcanoes, and diverse cetacean life.

TRAVELER'S NOTES

When to visit *Jan–Apr, gray whales live in the lagoons of Baja California, blue, Bryde's, humpback, fin, and minke whales move into the Gulf of California; year-round, Pacific white-sided, common and various tropical dolphins, bottlenose dolphins (in gray whale lagoons and in the Gulf of California)*

Weather *Dry, clear, warm winters; wind, especially on the Pacific side, can make it cool at sea*

Types of tours *Multi-day expeditions, some day trips; inflatables, pangas, sailboats, and medium-size cruise ships*

Tours available *La Paz, Ensenada, Tijuana, Rosarito, San Diego*

Information *Gobierno del Estado de Baja California Sur, Coordinación Estatal de Turismo, Km. 5.5 Carret. al Norte, Edif. Fedepaz, Apdo. Post. 419, La Paz, Baja California Sur, Mexico, Ph. 52 112 31702*

Hawaii

West Coast of North America

Every Christmastime, humpback whales return to sing, fight, mate, and raise their calves in the tropical blue waters off Hawaii. Humpbacks make their winter homes near these islands, which are checkered with tropical forest, pineapple and coffee farms, and topped with volcanoes. From hotels on the west side of Maui, it is possible to watch the humpbacks as they arrive; they make occasional approaches opposite Lahaina's Front Street, so be prepared.

Migrating from Alaska, the female humpbacks often arrive first, some heavy with calf, others having just given birth. The males arrive later in search of a partner. In the late 1970s, biologists in Maui first witnessed humpback whales fighting. The fighting seems to follow extended bouts of singing among the males who apparently compete to escort and mate with females. Many of the females start these fights or get involved in them by emitting streams of warning bubbles toward ambitious males. Blood can sometimes be seen on the tail or back of a whale or in the water, but the injuries are usually only superficial.

A humpback nearly clear of the water as it breaches (above) close to shore. A spinner dolphin (left) executes a breathtakingly high, spinning leap.

The shallow, warm sea between the islands of Maui, Molokai, and all around Lanai is the prime area in Hawaii for humpbacks and the core area of the Hawaiian Islands National Marine Sanctuary, which was set up mainly to protect these whales. The best access is through boat tours from Lahaina or Kihei on Maui's west side. Maui is a short plane flight from the international airport at Honolulu on the nearby island of Oahu.

The humpback tours usually include sightings of bottlenose dolphins, which often accompany

the humpbacks. As in other areas, the dolphins will ride a boat's bow wave, but here they ride the wake of a whale as well. Sometimes, the humpbacks become irritated with the constant companionship, and researchers have seen humpbacks wave their tails at the dolphins, trying to discourage them and drive them away. Beneath the water's surface beside your boat, you can glimpse dolphins—especially if you wear polarizing sunglasses to cut the glare—or even whales swimming, the bubbles from their blowholes leaving a trail through the water.

Most of the other main Hawaiian islands offer whale or dolphin watching and a chance to see a wide variety of tropical cetaceans. Although whale-watch tours focus on the humpbacks, other cetaceans you will see include bottlenose and spinner dolphins, false killer whales, pilot whales, and even the rare beaked whales. From the big island of Hawaii, spinner dolphins—famous for high leaps during which they spin through the air—can be seen throughout much of the year. Other cetacean tours, and more wide-ranging marine nature tours, leave from Oahu and Kauai.

Close behind the powerful tail of a short-finned pilot whale (above). The rugged, volcanic coastline of Kauai (left).

Special Features

From the main street of Lahaina, signs of whale-watching culture date from the 1970s. In front of the Pioneer Hotel, once home to whaling captains waiting for South Seas postings, about 20 whale-watch boats are berthed, each with its signboard displayed. You can see glass-bottom boats, Chinese junks that look like pirate ships, motor cruisers, Zodiac inflatables, schooners, and trimarans. This is a rare opportunity to go window-shopping for the best whale-watch tour. Key features to look for are an on-board naturalist or nature guide, and a boat equipped with hydrophones, through which you can hear haunting humpback songs.

TRAVELER'S NOTES

When to visit *Late Dec–Apr for humpback whales, largest concentrations in Feb and Mar; year-round: spinner, bottlenose, and pantropical spotted dolphins, false killer whales, short-finned pilot whales, and many others*
Weather *Warm to hot; sometimes strong Kona winds bring rain and high seas*
Types of tours *Half- and full-day tours, some extended multi-day expeditions; inflatables, sailboats, and large whale-watch boats*
Tours available *Maui: Lahaina, Kihei, Maalaea; Hawaii (big island): Keauhou, Kailua-Kona, Kohala Coast, Honokoha; Oahu: Honolulu, Kaneohe. Kauai: Hanalei*
Information *Hawaii Visitors Bureau, 2270 Kalakaua Avenue, Suite 801, Honolulu, HI 96813, Ph. 1 808 924 0266*

EAST COAST of NORTH AMERICA

The East Coast of North America offers some of the world's most popular ports for whale watching.

The first commercial whale watching on the east coast of North America occurred in Canada. A summer trip by members of the Zoological Society of Montreal in 1971 took them down the St. Lawrence River to see belugas and large baleen whales. It was so successful that more trips were organized. In 1975, the Dolphin Fleet of Provincetown, Massachusetts, entered the whale-watch business, based largely on humpback whales, and the idea spread up the coast of Maine to the Canadian Maritime provinces and Newfoundland. By the late 1980s, the success of whale watching on the North American east coast eclipsed the West Coast in numbers, and this area leads the world with more than 1.5 million whale watchers every year.

A pristine beach in Nova Scotia, the Maritimes.

Most of the activity in northeast North America is centered around the feeding grounds of large baleen whales from May to November. It was partly the search by scientists for the mating and calving grounds of some of these whales that led to whale watching in the Caribbean from January to April. In the early 1980s, trips to see Atlantic spotted dolphins had started in the Bahamas, off Florida—the first commercial tours anywhere to offer a chance to swim with wild dolphins. In 1986, the Silver Bank Humpback Whale Sanctuary, north of the Dominican Republic, was established.

Throughout the region, science and education have gone hand in hand with commercial whale-watching development—more so than anywhere else in the world. Photo-identification studies have produced excellent records and catalogs, and databases of sightings have been set up for each baleen whale species in the North Atlantic. If researchers in the Caribbean encounter a certain humpback mother and her newborn calf, researchers in New England might photograph them a few months later when the whales come north to feed, documenting

Watching one of the 3,000 humpbacks that winter in the Silver Bank Humpback Whale Sanctuary.

Swimming with wild Atlantic spotted dolphins in the Bahamas.

the growing calf until it is time to move south again. Over several years, behavioral portraits of individual animals have emerged, as well as precise records of movements, associations, entanglements in nets, and other life events.

East Coast whale watching has benefited from having easy access from large cities. The popularity of the whales has helped with conservation measures, such as the designation of a marine-protected area at Stellwagen Bank, off Massachusetts. However, these large populations centers have had an impact on cetaceans from shipping traffic, marine pollution, and other human factors. Great care will be needed to manage whale watching and protect the habitat to ensure that cetaceans and humans have a shared future to enjoy.

St. Lawrence River and the Gulf

East Coast of North America

In many places, large whales come close to shore, yet there are few areas where a variety of large whales can be seen far upstream in a river. When the ice thaws in the St. Lawrence River, warm-water upwellings from the open sea are carried upstream in submarine trenches. These drive nutrient-rich water to the surface, which results in an explosion of marine life throughout the food pyramid. Whales arrive as soon as the river can be navigated, swimming upstream to take advantage of this wealth of food.

A fin whale (left), part of a photo-identification program.

In the province of Quebec, Canada, at the Saguenay-St. Lawrence Marine Park, 230 miles (370 km) upstream from the mouth of the river, belugas and fin and minke whales can be seen. Farther downstream are humpbacks and even blue whales. On the north shore of the river lies Tadoussac, formerly a sleepy summer tourist town and now the bustling main whale-watch center in eastern Canada. Thousands of people pass through here every week in summer, and it is now one of the three largest whale-watch areas in the world, along with New England and the Canary Islands. Most of the operators in Tadoussac are French Canadian, and some of the shipboard narratives are given in English and French.

From Tadoussac, as well as neighboring towns along the hilly north side of the river, it is possible to take day tours to see mainly fin and minke whales. For the best chance of seeing blue whales, choose a boat from Les Escoumins, 22 miles (35 km) from Tadoussac, or farther downstream. All along the north shore of the river, and in several spots along the south shore, are whale-watch lookouts and additional ports from which other tour companies depart. At the river mouth on the north shore, the Pointe-des-Monts lighthouse provides a superb lookout for blue and other whales.

The dedicated whale watcher, however, will follow the road even farther to the northern Gulf of St. Lawrence, reaching the Mingan Islands near Anticosti Island. The village of Mingan is the home of the Mingan Island Cetacean Study, which has a superb museum and visitor center,

Rugged whale watching (above) in the Gulf of St. Lawrence. A beluga (left) surfaces in the St. Lawrence River.

and a whale-watch and scientific program. Visitors are invited to watch and sometimes assist in blue whale research. This group pioneered photo-identification of blue whales.

The program also focuses on fin, minke, and humpback whales, as well as Atlantic white-sided and white-beaked dolphins, and harbor porpoises. Day tours and week or 10-day excursions are offered. Whale watching is more rugged here, bouncing around in rubber inflatables while dressed in Mustang survival suits (provided by the research team), but it affords a rare chance to see how cetacean research is carried out.

Special Features

Where the St. Lawrence and Saguenay rivers meet is the southernmost area in the world to see belugas. They can be sighted from the lookout at Pointe Noire or during tours that depart from Tadoussac. The boats don't target the belugas since they are endangered. They are likely to be seen only at some distance. The image of their ghostly white bodies, however, leaves a lasting impression, and if the boat carries a hydrophone, there's a chance of hearing their constant sounds.

Now reduced to about 500 individuals from a population of several thousand, the St. Lawrence belugas have had to endure contaminants and pesticides from the heavy industrial use of the river system, including extensive shipping traffic and effluent outflows upstream from large United States and Canadian cities on the Great Lakes.

Every year, belugas are found stranded and are examined by a dedicated research team. But, there are still some new calves appearing every year and the youngsters, bluish gray beside their white mothers, sometimes poke their heads out of the water or come close to a whale-watch boat to investigate.

TRAVELER'S NOTES

When to visit *St. Lawrence at Saguenay River: June–Nov fin, minke whales, belugas, harbor porpoises; Les Escoumins to Pointe-des-Monts, river and north shore of gulf, especially Mingan Islands: June–Nov fin, minke, humpback whales, occasional orcas, Atlantic white-sided dolphins, harbor porpoises and blue whales in Aug–Nov*

Weather *July–Sept cool to cold on the water, fog common, some heavy summer rains, snow by mid-Oct or Nov*

Types of tours *Half- and full-day tours, some extended multi-day expeditions; inflatables, sailboats, and large whale-watch boats; good land-based whale watching*

Tours available *St. Lawrence River, Quebec: Tadoussac, Baie-Ste-Catherine, Grandes-Bergeronnes, Les Escoumins, Godbout, Baie-Comeau, Baie-Trinité, Pointe-des-Monts; Gulf of St. Lawrence, Quebec: Longue-Pointe-de-Mingan, Havre-Saint-Pierre; Gaspé Peninsula: Rivière-du-Renard, Gaspé*

Information *Tourisme Quebec, CP 979, Montreal, Quebec H3C 2W3, Ph 1 514 873 2015*

The Maritimes and Newfoundland

East Coast of North America

The Maritimes are the Canadian seaboard provinces of Nova Scotia, New Brunswick, and Prince Edward Island. The Bay of Fundy, between Nova Scotia and New Brunswick, is well known for having the highest tides in the world. This makes for tide rips and tricky currents, especially around the various islands, and contributes to the famous "Fundy fog." These conditions may have discouraged whalers and made the bay a refuge for wildlife.

Watchers observe a humpback (left) in Newfoundland waters. A pod of rare northern bottlenose whales (below) swimming in the Gully.

In August 1980, on a routine marine mammal aerial census of the bay, 19 northern right whales were counted on one day. This led to intensive research and it is now known that there are still about 300 northern right whales in the North Atlantic. Some stay in the Bay of Fundy from August to November and, even though there are so few, sightings are reliable. During this period, the bay becomes a feeding and nursery area for mothers and calves that appreciate the sheltered waters. Access is by tours from southwest Nova Scotia and eastern New Brunswick, especially from North Head on Grand Manan Island. Other adult whales go to open waters in Browns Bank and Roseway Basin south of Nova Scotia. Only occasional multi-day tours visit this far offshore area.

Humpback, fin, and minke whales are also common in the Bay of Fundy, with sei and sperm whales farther offshore. The western side of the bay is famous for high concentrations of harbor porpoises, which can be seen from land, from ferries to Grand Manan Island, and from whale-watch boats. The porpoises hunt in groups and move rapidly through the water. Unlike dolphins, they tend to avoid boats and do not ride bow waves.

Newfoundland has sheer cliffs from which the whale watcher can view fantastic seabird colonies and abundant whales coming in close to shore. Locals have given unusual names to the common cetaceans. The ever-present harbor porpoises are called "puffing pigs," and dolphins are referred to as "squid hounds." Humpback whales are common

A humpback falls back into the water after breaching (top) in the Newfoundland fog. The small town of Yarmouth (above), in Nova Scotia, is almost encircled by water.

and fin, minke, and long-finned pilot whales are also seen. The Atlantic white-sided and white-beaked dolphins are seen year-round, and less often (mainly in summer) sei, blue, killer, and sperm whales are sighted.

Visit Cape St. Mary's, on the Avalon Peninsula about 125 miles (200 km) from St. John's, for the chance to see humpback, minke, and pilot whales, as well as Atlantic white-sided dolphins. Other good land-based lookouts on the Avalon Peninsula are Cape Race, Holyrood Arm, and Bay de Verde. Besides land-based viewing, there are numerous boat tours all around Newfoundland that venture out to meet the whales.

Special Features

About 100 miles (160 km) out to sea in the North Atlantic off eastern Nova Scotia, lies the Gully, a deep canyon beloved by northern bottlenose whales (see p. 355). This is the only known place this rare beaked whale can reliably be seen. Proposed as a protected area, the Gully contains large concentrations of plankton, fish and squid. These attract not only bottlenose whales but others, such as blue and sperm whales and, from the warmer waters farther south, several species of dolphin including common, bottlenose, and even striped dolphins.

Of these, northern bottlenose whales are the prize residents and the most commonly seen. There are an estimated 230 bottlenose whales using the Gully—mothers, calves, juveniles, and larger males with their characteristic square heads. Researchers have found their natural behavior a little difficult to study because they are so curious about boats. For the whale watcher who has seen the more common whale species, this provides a new and unforgettable experience.

TRAVELER'S NOTES

When to visit *June–Oct fin, humpback, minke whales, various dolphins and harbor porpoises; Aug–early Nov northern right whales, Bay of Fundy and off Nova Scotia*
Weather *June–Aug cool to cold; fog especially in Bay of Fundy; Sept–Oct colder but often clearer*
Types of tours *Half- and full-day tours, extended multi-day expeditions; inflatables, sailboats, whale-watch boats; some whale watching from ferries*
Tours available *New Brunswick: Grand Manan, Leonardville, Fredericton; Nova Scotia: Halifax, Tiverton, Westport (Brier Island), Cheticamp, Capstick; Newfoundland: St. John's, Bay Bulls, Trinity, Twillingate*
Information *Tourism New Brunswick, Box 6000, Fredericton, NB E3B 5H1, Ph. 1 800 561 0123; Tourism Newfoundland, Box 8700, St. John's, NF A1B 4J6, Ph. 1 709 729 2803; Tourism Nova Scotia, Box 519, Halifax, NS B3J 2R7, Ph. 1 902 490 5946.*

New England

East Coast of North America

Lifted high out of the water, the 16 foot (5 m) black-and-white flippers of the humpback whale, the longest appendages of any animal, can be easily seen above the often white-capped seas of the New England coast. It was here that the humpback whale acquired its name, *Megaptera novaeangliae*, which translates as "great winged New Englander." When whale watching started here in the mid-1970s, humpbacks would occasionally approach boats. Over several years, certain ones got used to the boats and began to interact with whale watchers, leaping repeatedly out of the water and waving flippers and flukes.

The fin whale, seen above surfacing, can grow to 80 feet (25 m); Atlantic white-sided dolphins (below right) at Stellwagen Bank.

Besides humpbacks, more than six species of whale and dolphin—minke, fin, right, and pilot whales, as well as Atlantic white-sided dolphins and harbor porpoises—come to these waters and use the area as a summer feeding ground. The focal point is Stellwagen Bank, a 19 mile (31 km) long submerged sandbank that runs north–south between the tip of Cape Cod and Boston's north shore, at Cape Ann. This massive mound is invisible to whale watchers, but just 65–100 feet (20–30 m) below the sea surface lies a rich ecosystem. Extending across Massachusetts Bay, Stellwagen Bank influences ocean currents and upwellings, both of which help to create high levels of nutrients that support plant plankton and zooplankton, the basis for these important fishing grounds. In 1993, after successful lobbying by whale watchers, an 842 square mile (2,180 sq km) area around the bank was designated a National Marine Sanctuary, an important step in conservation.

The rarest visitors to Stellwagen Bank, indeed the rarest of all whales, are the northern right whales. In April, they sometimes enter Cape Cod Bay and swim so close to shore that they can be photographed against the old clapboard beach houses and traditional homes of Provincetown lining the shore. After April, right whales are seen sporadically in the area and along the Maine coast through October. They are most reliably seen in the Bay of Fundy (see p. 410).

The wide expanse of Cape Cod Bay (above). The distinctive flippers of a humpback whale, Stellwagen Bank (left).

The right whales charge through the water, mouths open, in search of copepods, as do basking sharks in the area, while humpbacks and other whales operate by encircling sand lance, herring and other small fish, and krill. Seeing which whales are present gives biologists an idea of which fish or plankton will be found in high concentrations at the time.

Southern New England is one of the most popular whale-watching areas in the world. With some 30 companies offering tours from 17 communities, whale watching here offers excellent value for money. Most trips carry naturalists and, because of competition, the cost is less than elsewhere. Many trips feature scientists who do their work on board, photographing whales they know by name. More than almost anywhere else, a whale-watch trip to Stellwagen Bank often turns into a grand social occasion in which the naturalist guides and scientists introduce whales by name as they are spotted. They tell stories and exchange gossip about their favorites—who's traveling with whom and which mothers have new calves are the talk of the day.

Special Features

The Stellwagen Bank National Marine Sanctuary offers much more than whales. Boat trips to the sanctuary and along the coast encounter some 40 species of resident marine birds, including loons, shearwaters, storm petrels, gannets, phalaropes, fulmars, puffins, and murres. Migratory birds also stop here. Harbor and gray seals spend part or all of their year in the region, along with various sea turtles, including leatherback, green, loggerhead, and Kemp's ridley sea turtles.

TRAVELER'S NOTES

When to visit *Apr–May humpback, right, minke, fin, and small cetaceans; June–Oct all whales are common, except right whales, which are seen only occasionally; Aug–Oct northern right whales off northeast Maine from Lubec*
Weather *Warm to hot especially from Massachusetts ports May–Aug, it can be cool out on the sea; rain is most likely in Apr–early May*
Types of tours *Half- and full-day boat trips; some extended multi-day trips; large whale-watch boats*
Tours available *Massachusetts: Provincetown, Nantucket, Barnstable, Plymouth, Boston, Gloucester, Newburyport; New Hampshire: Rye, Hampton Beach, Portsmouth; Maine: Bar Harbor, Kennebunkport, Lubec, Northeast Harbor, Ogunquit, Portland, Boothbay Harbor*
Information *Massachusetts Office of Travel and Tourism, 100 Cambridge St., 13th Floor, Boston, MA 02202, Ph. 1 617 727 3201*

Florida and the Bahamas

East Coast of North America

The Commonwealth of the Bahamas includes more than 700 low-lying islands and 2,000 cays, only 24 of them inhabited. They form a chain extending some 500 miles (800 km) southeast from Florida.

In the mid-1970s, in the waters north of Grand Bahama Island, film-makers discovered that herds of Atlantic spotted dolphins regularly approached boats and photographers in the water. The dolphins appeared so reliably that researchers became interested, and several dive and tour companies began taking people on multi-day tours to meet the dolphins, watch, and sometimes swim with them. Some of the best and most popular tours, organized by an American scientist, helped pay for research into the dolphins' behavior.

Atlantic spotted dolphins (above) are easily seen in the clear, shallow waters.

The shallow water is relatively calm and extraordinarily clear, the bottom white and sandy, so dolphins can be easily observed in what must be among the best conditions in the world for watching wild dolphins underwater. This has afforded a chance to learn about the dolphins' elaborate behavioral repertoire.

Three dolphin generations on, small groups of Atlantic spotted dolphins still come to boats and swim with snorkelers. The boats typically anchor for several days about 30 miles (48 km) from land on the shallow sandbank, part of Little Bahama Bank, in only 20 feet (6 m) of water. There are an estimated 80–100 dolphins in the population around this sandbank, but only up to 10 are usually seen together. Sometimes bottlenose dolphins travel with the Atlantic spotted dolphins, or they may be seen separately.

The trips are accessible on 3- to 11-day tours from Florida or through West End and Port Lucaya on Grand Bahama Island. They depart aboard dive boats, sailboats, and motor cruisers from May to September, although there are some trips in winter and at other times of the

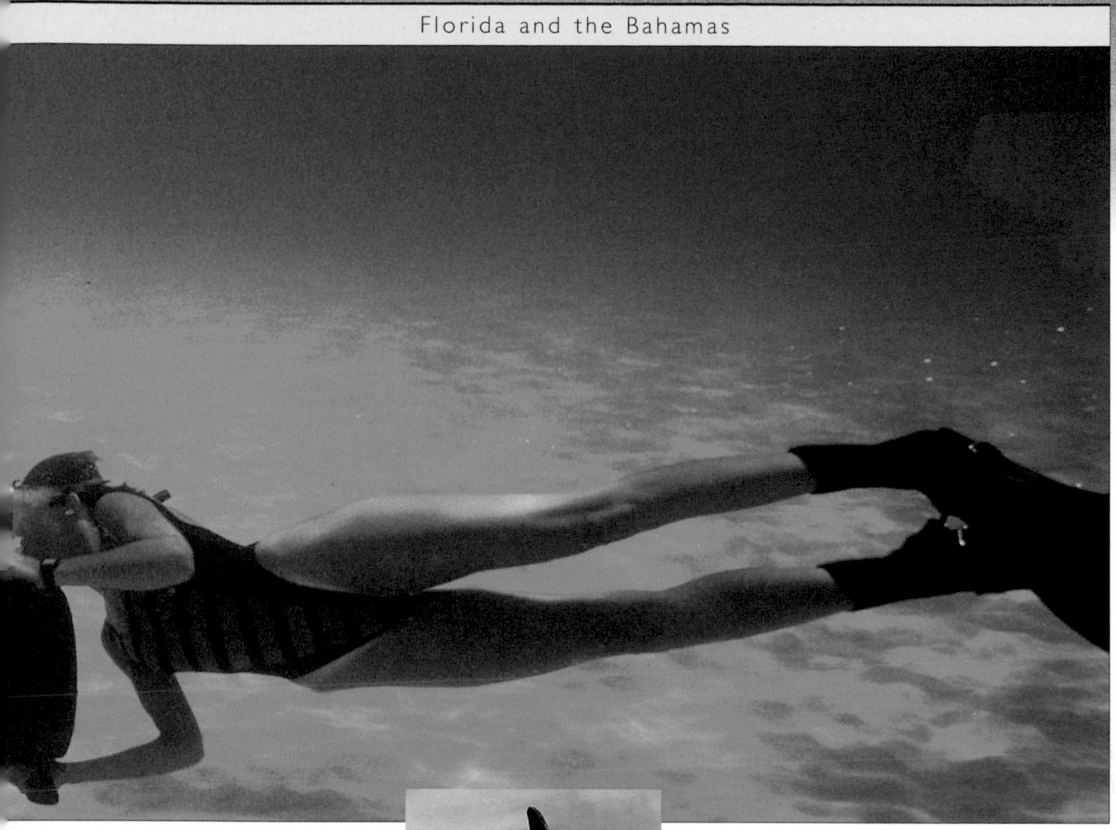

Spotted dolphins are invited to play (above) with a snorkeler using an underwater scooter. A bottlenose dolphin (right).

year. The dolphins live year-round in these waters, but there is less wind and the seas are generally calmer from May to September. Many of these multi-day trips, often on the way to or from Florida, spend a day cruising in the deeper open waters of the Gulf Stream. There, other cetaceans are sometimes seen, including rough-toothed and other tropical dolphins and short-finned pilot and sperm whales.

In Florida, bottlenose dolphins can be seen from Atlantic and Gulf Coast beaches and sometimes in the intracoastal waterway, along with manatees, diving pelicans, and other wildlife typical of Florida. Particularly good sites for shore-based dolphin watching are in the Florida Keys, the Gulf panhandle, and around Sarasota on the Gulf Coast. For offshore viewing, one long-standing tour operator offers day trips from Key West, about 200–250 days a year, depending on the weather. Inquire locally for information about other operators.

Special Features

For the past few years, a number of special one-week marine mammal survey expeditions have been offered through Earthwatch. These trips started out mainly as whale surveys but now focus on the flora, fauna, and culture of the northern Bahamas. Some 16 species of whale and dolphin have been recorded. Besides the Atlantic spotted and bottlenose dolphins, the surveys have recorded sperm, humpback, false killer, and short-finned pilot whales, as well as several species of rare tropical beaked whales. The surveys cover the marine habitat around hundreds of islands, from mangroves and shallow sandbanks to deep trenches, so they may yet find more surprises. The trips depart from Great Abaco Island. For information, contact Earthwatch (see below).

TRAVELER'S NOTES

When to visit *For Atlantic spotted and bottlenose dolphins year-round; May–Sept best for Bahamas, although some tours at other times of year. Check hurricane reports June–Oct*
Weather *Warm to hot, generally calm during May–Sept*
Types of tours *Mainly 3–11 day expeditions to Bahamas (book in advance); some day tours in Florida waters; inflatables, sailboats, motor cruisers, and dive boats*
Tours available *Florida: Key West; Florida to Bahamas: Jupiter, Dania, Fort Lauderdale, Indialantic, Miami Beach; Bahamas: West End, Port Lucaya, Freeport (Grand Bahama Island)*
Information *The Bahamas Tourist Office, 255 Alhambra Circle, Suite 425, Coral Gables, FL 33134, Ph. 1 305 442 4867; Florida Division of Tourism, 126 Van Buren Street, Tallahassee, FL 32399, Ph. 1 904 487 1462; Earthwatch, 680 Mt. Auburn Street, Box 403, Watertown, MA 02272, Ph. 1 617 926 8200*

The Caribbean

East Coast of North America

The sperm whales lie motionless on the surface, their wrinkled backs exposed. They spout one by one, each explosion followed by a hollow, dull whine as they suck in fresh air. When the whales dive, watchers can see the rest of their bodies in the clear Caribbean waters. The seas of the Caribbean make for idyllic whale and dolphin watching. Most visitors come for the beaches, or for sailing or cruising holidays, but it is also a good place to see a wide variety of cetaceans.

Bottlenose dolphins love to ride a boat's stern wave (left). The humpback whale (below right) is tail-breaching in Silver Bank Humpback Whale Sanctuary.

In 1988, the island paradise of Dominica became the first place in the eastern Caribbean to offer whale watching. Trips depart near Roseau and rely on a resident group of 8 to 12 sperm whales found in the deep waters just off the west coast. Besides these, there are pilot whales, false killer whales, and spinner and spotted dolphins. Pygmy sperm whales, rarely seen anywhere else in the world, are often found in the warm waters around Dominica. Bottlenose, Risso's, and Fraser's dolphins are also encountered, as well as orcas, dwarf sperm whales, and melon-headed whales. Dive-boat operators on Martinique and Guadeloupe, the main islands near Dominica, now offer tours to see sperm and other whales.

In the eastern Caribbean, there is excellent spinner and spotted dolphin watching off St. Vincent and the Grenadines. Based out of Arnos Vale, on the big island of St. Vincent, the tours are almost year-round, although mid-December to mid-February can become windy. Farther south, Grenada has several dolphin-watch operators who take visitors to see spinner, spotted, and bottlenose dolphins, with a chance to see short-finned pilot and sperm whales. The Kido Project in Carriacou offers youth environmental projects that include dolphin watching on a catamaran—a chance for young people to become inspired and motivated by encounters with cetaceans.

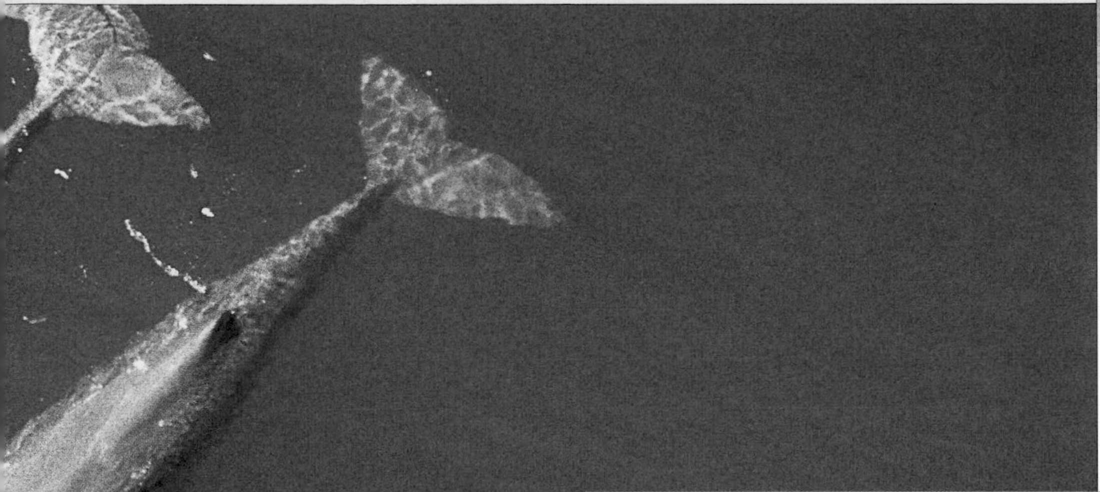

The squared head shape of the three sperm whales (above) surfacing together is unmistakable. Clear sea and lush vegetation (right) make the Caribbean a popular destination.

Some 3,000 humpbacks gather in the relaxed, warm-water setting of the Caribbean, and there's a good chance of seeing tail-lashing females and singing males. The key area is the Silver Bank Humpback Whale Sanctuary, north of Dominican Republic. The whales also gather on Navidad Bank in Samaná Bay, on the west side of Puerto Rico, and north of the British and American Virgin Islands. Whale watchers who have met individual humpbacks on the feeding grounds off New England and eastern Canada may encounter the same animals in the Caribbean. North Atlantic humpbacks use the Caribbean for singing, mating, and calving, much as the North Pacific humpbacks use Hawaii, Mexico, and southern Japan. In winter, the tropical seas around these areas resound with singing humpback whales.

Special Features

Since the early 1990s, Paul Knapp Jr. has invited several hundred people each winter (Dec 30–Apr 15) to listen to male humpback whales singing in the waters north of Tortola. Visitors concentrate on sounds delivered by high-quality hydrophones and speakers. Even when the whales are some distance away, well out of sighting range, the sounds coming into the boat can be quite loud. No need to travel long distances, or wait for calm seas. Just slip into a comfortable boat, drop a hydrophone over the side, lie back and listen. Such a "whale-listening" tour gives a new dimension to the experience of whale watching.

TRAVELER'S NOTES

When to visit *Jan–Apr humpback whales; year-round sperm whales and various dolphins; inquire locally as tour operating seasons vary (for example, St. Vincent, dolphins, Apr–Sept)*
Weather *Warm to hot, seas sometimes rough; tours often confine activities to the lee side of islands. Storms sometimes Aug–Oct; rainy season varies, but seasonal daily rain may last for only part of a day*
Types of tours *Half- and full-day tours, some extended multi-day expeditions in Dominican Republic; inflatables, sailboats, and large whale-watch boats*
Tours available *Dominican Republic: Samaná, Puerto Plata, Santo Domingo; Puerto Rico: Rincon; US Virgin Islands: Long Bay, St. Thomas; British Virgin Islands: Road Town, Tortola; Guadeloupe: Le Moule; Dominica; Roseau; Martinique: Carbet; St. Vincent: Arnos Vale; Grenada: St. George's, Carriacou (Grenadines)*
Information *Caribbean Tourism Organization, 80 Broad Street, 32nd Floor, New York, NY 10004, Ph. 1 212 682 0435*

South America

South America has everything from river dolphins deep in the jungle to the great southern right whales off Patagonia.

Galápago Islands

Commercial whale-watching tours in South America started in Argentina in 1983. As early as 1970, Roger Payne began his photo-identification work on southern right whales at Península Valdés, Patagonia. Many whale and dolphin researchers from around the world made treks to this area through the 1970s and early 1980s, and their fascinating stories of Patagonia and the whales and dolphins living in the sheltered bays of the peninsula spread worldwide.

Even before whale study and research began in Patagonia, cetacean watching was a part of jungle excursions to the Amazon as well as boat tours around the Galápagos Islands. But the success of whale watching in Argentina has led to the expansion of dolphin watching along the coast of Brazil and in the Amazon basin, and the initiation of new whale-watch tours along the coasts of both Ecuador and Colombia.

All the other countries in South America, except land-locked Paraguay, have at least some cetacean-watching activity, and even where there are no commercial tours, there are still viewing opportunities from land. Wherever you go, along the coast and up rivers, keep your eyes open.

Many of the large whales are visitors to South America. They spend part of their year feeding in the Antarctic waters and then swim north to warmer climates, heading either east or west of Tierra del Fuego to reach the South Pacific or South Atlantic. In most cases, the migration stops south of the equator, but certain humpbacks cross the equator and move as far north as Colombia and Costa Rica—the longest migration by an individual whale as yet documented.

A southern right whale starts to breach off Patagonia, Argentina.

South American waters provide mating, calving, and nursery grounds for the large whales, while the smaller whales and dolphins live here year-round and find both their food and mates in the same waters. Southern South

In the waters off the Galápagos Islands live dolphins and other marine life.

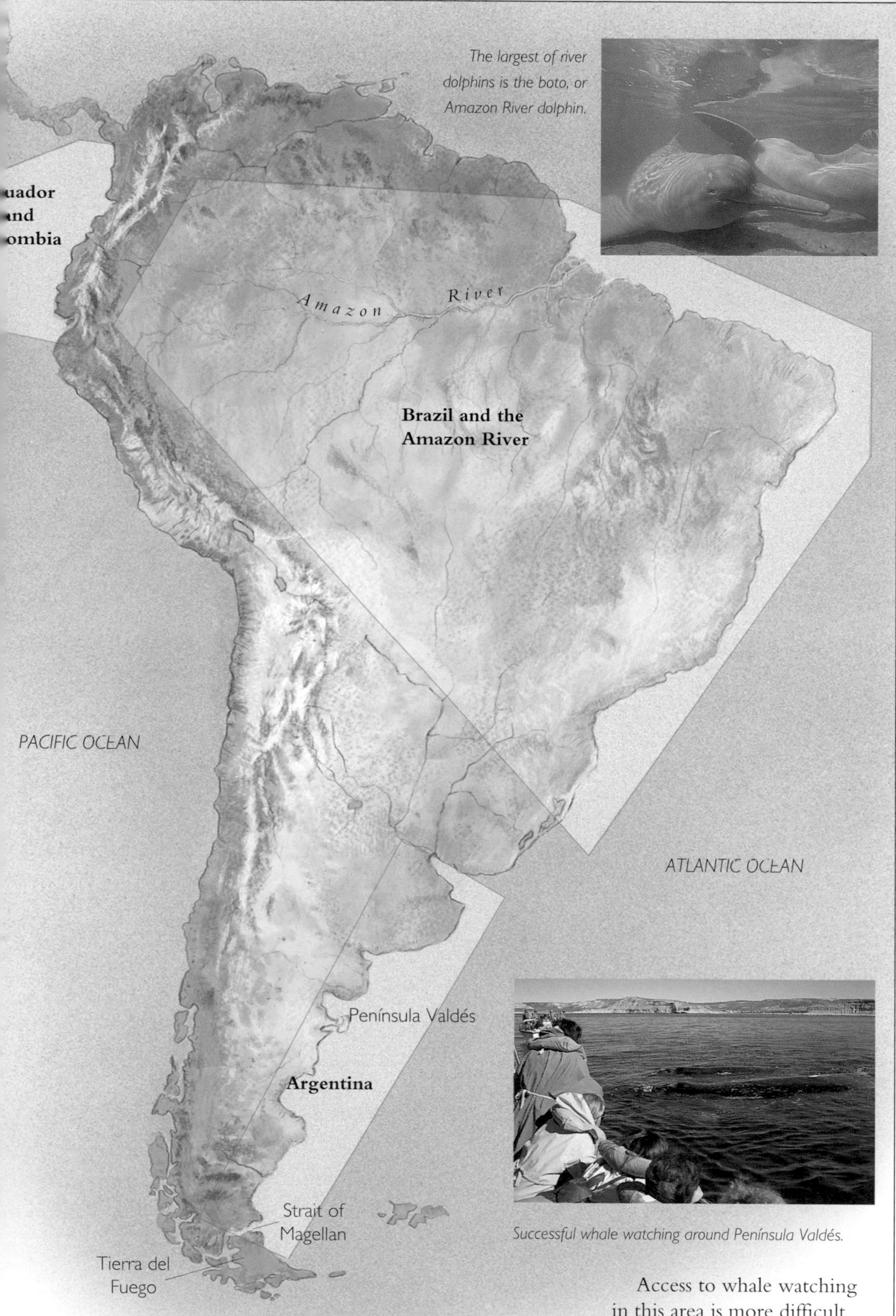

The largest of river dolphins is the boto, or Amazon River dolphin.

Successful whale watching around Península Valdés.

America has a great diversity of unusual species: at least six dolphins and porpoises are found mainly or only in these waters, especially off Chile and Argentina. As well, some of the rarer beaked whales are seen in the offshore waters or stranded on the beaches of southern South America, including two new species of beaked whale described as recently as the early 1990s.

Access to whale watching in this area is more difficult than in North America and some other parts of the world. But the thrill of seeing river dolphins, the big southern rights, or rare dolphins in and around the Strait of Magellan make this a unique and interesting region to visit.

Ecuador and Colombia

South America

Whale watching in the northwest corner of South America is hot and steamy, and offers the chance to meet some rare tropical species as well as migrating whales. Ecuador and Colombia are relatively new to whale-watch tours. Ecuador has long been famous for its offshore Galápagos Islands, and Colombia has a long coast on the Caribbean, but the best whale watching in Ecuador and Colombia occurs along the Pacific coast. The main attraction is Southern Hemisphere humpback whales, which cross the equator on their extraordinarily long migration. They migrate from the Antarctic, where they feed in the austral summer, to Colombia and Ecuador, where they breed—a round trip of 10,351 miles (16,668 km).

Humpback whales charging through the water off Gorgona Island.

In Colombia, humpback research is centered around the island of Gorgona, which is located 35 miles (56 km) offshore from the mainland. During the whale-watch season from August to October, the best place to depart for on-the-spot tours is from the mainland at Juanchaco. Some of the whale-watching boat owners lease cabins on the beach at Juanchaco and also offer package tours that depart from Cali and Buenaventura. Besides the humpback whales, it is possible to see various dolphins, including bottlenose, as well as orcas and false killer whales.

In Ecuador, whale watching of seasonal humpback whales is offered from June to mid-September along the mainland coast out of Machalilla National Park and the fishing ports of Puerto López and Salango. Many whale-watch trips head from the park to the island of La Plata, which is an excellent area for humpback whales. For land-based whale watching, the Hotel Punta

Gorgona Island (above), where researchers study humpbacks. The primeval Galápagos landscape (left).

Carnero, at Punta Carnero, can offer superb views, from a viewing platform or some of its seaside hotel rooms, of humpback whales spouting, lifting their white flippers, and breaching.

The best time in Ecuador for other cetaceans is December to May, with sun and calm seas on most days. Bottlenose and pantropical spotted dolphins patrol the inshore waters. Farther out to sea, look for sporadic visits by Bryde's and false killer whales; orcas; striped, common, and Risso's dolphins.

There is reliable bottlenose dolphin watching in the estuary of the River Guayas in the Gulf of Guayaquil. Some 400 to 500 dolphins live in the river year-round, but the best months to feel soft breezes and have a dozen dolphins splashing beside your boat are June through November.

SPECIAL FEATURES

The Galápagos Islands, located 600 miles (975 km) offshore in the equatorial Pacific, were one of the first international ecotourism destinations. The Galápagos Marine Reserve dates from 1959 and the islands were opened to organized tourism in 1970. Today, all the waters around the Galápagos are a whale and dolphin sanctuary.

Visitors can sometimes see bottlenose, common, and spinner dolphins near the islands. Farther offshore are sperm whales and Bryde's whales, but it is usually necessary to take overnight tours to see them. Various international operators take people on nature tours that include dolphins and the odd whale as part of the natural history experience, but few trips feature cetaceans.

Even cetacean-oriented tours include visits to see the extraordinary range of island habitats from lava deserts to tropical forests, to encounter the amazing endemic species that include marine iguanas and giant tortoises, and to visit the Charles Darwin Biological Research Station.

TRAVELER'S NOTES

When to visit *Year-round: bottlenose, pantropical spotted, and other dolphins Ecuador and Galápagos; offshore Ecuador: spinner dolphins, orcas, sperm, and Bryde's whales; June–Sept humpback whales Ecuador, and Aug–Oct Colombia*
Weather *Coastal Ecuador and Colombia hot, humid year-round, sometimes rainy during humpback whale season; the Galápagos are drier, best months for sea conditions Mar–Aug, although year-round possible*
Types of tours *Half- and full-day tours, extended multi-day expeditions; inflatables, sailboats, small motorboats, and small cruise ships*
Tours available *Ecuador: Guayaquil, Quito, Machalilla National Park, Puerto López, Salango; Colombia: Cali, Buenaventura, Bahía, Juanchaco, Ladrilleros, Bahía Solano, El Valle, Chocó*
Information *Fundación Ecuatoriana para el Estudio de Mamíferos Marinos (FEMM), Velez 911 y 6 de Marzo, Ed. Forum, 5to. piso, Of. 5-16, PO Box 09 01 11905, Guayaquil, Ecuador, Ph./Fax: 593 4 524 608; Estación Científica Charles Darwin, Isla Santa Cruz, Galápagos, Ecuador*

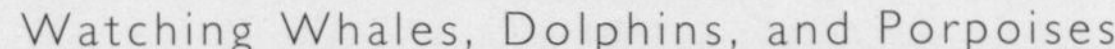

Brazil and the Amazon River

South America

Watching pink dolphins with long beaks splash and chase fish through the brown, muddy water of the Amazon is a strange sight, even on a jungle safari. Many local and native Indian people thought botos, or Amazon River dolphins, brought bad luck and tried to avoid them, and this reputation has effectively protected the dolphins. Although botos are not dangerous, they are highly curious and playful. People in boats report that the dolphins grab the paddles in their mouths and even rub their backs on the undersides of boats.

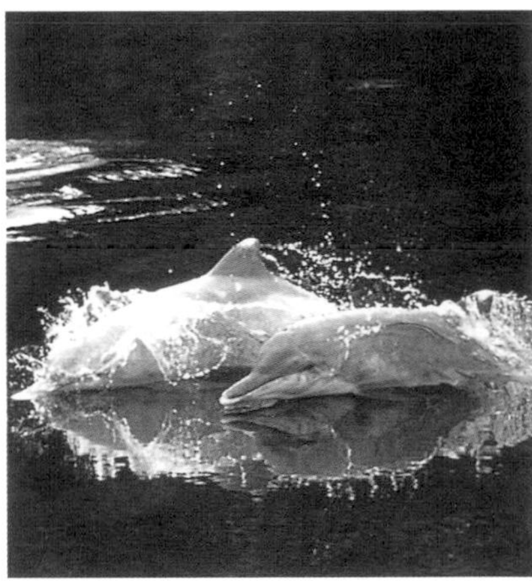

The tucuxi (above) is found along the Brazilian coast and in the Amazon River region.

Botos are found only in the tropical rain forest of South America. This covers much of the vast Amazon and Orinoco river basins that drain more than half of South America, including parts of Brazil, Bolivia, Peru, Ecuador, Colombia, Venezuela, and Guyana. You are able to see botos in all of these countries. The best ports to depart from include Leticia and Puerto Nariño in southern Colombia; the Pacaya-Samiria Reserve in eastern Peru; and Manaus and various other ports on the Brazilian Amazon with its many large tributaries.

Many cetacean watchers have heard of the boto, but few realize that there is also another dolphin that is seen on river-dolphin and rain-forest excursions. It's called tucuxi. Classed as an oceanic dolphin, its range includes the Amazon and Orinoco rivers. The difference between the two dolphins is evident when you see them together. The tucuxi looks sleek and streamlined, while the pinkish boto is an awkward-looking, angular animal, with huge, broad flippers, a beak full of tiny teeth, and pinholes for eyes.

The tucuxi is most commonly found living along the Atlantic coast of Brazil, and is the most popular cetacean for whale and dolphin watchers in Brazil. It can be seen on sailboat tours from the north-central coast of Santa Catarina Island. Other cetacean tours in Brazil focus on spotting southern right whales from the cliffs in a breeding and calving area near the south end of Santa Catarina Island; humpback whales in the

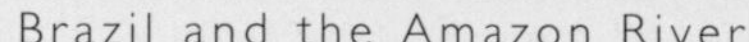

Boto (above) spotted in the waters of the Amazon River. A river safari through the jungle (left) uses the Amazon and its tributaries as a highway.

National Marine Park of Abrolhos, some 25 miles (40 km) offshore from southern Bahia; and spinner dolphins at Fernando de Noronha archipelago in Pernambuco. Bottlenose dolphins can also be seen in many places, including year-round from the southern coast of Santa Catarina.

Special Features

In Santa Catarina, some distance south of the main southern right whale area on Santa Catarina Island, you may witness rare and extraordinary cooperation between humans and dolphins. Some 200 bottlenose dolphins reside inshore around the mouth of a large lagoon near the coastal city of Laguna. The dolphins come close to shore year-round, except during July and August, for mullet fishing. The mullet fishery, which uses traditional hand nets, supports more than 100 families. For long periods, some 25–30 dolphins in various groups help the fishers by driving the fish closer to shore and into the nets. The dolphins benefit by being able to take some fish as well.

In 1993, Laguna declared the lagoon an ecological sanctuary for dolphins. In the future, Laguna may offer tours for the southern right whales, which come close to shore near Imbituba between June and September, but the right whales as well as the dolphins are best and most easily observed from land.

TRAVELER'S NOTES

When to visit *Year-round: river dolphins in Amazon-Orinoco but best during low-water seasons as dolphins are more confined, and you avoid rainy season; tucuxi dolphins at Santa Catarina Island, spinner dolphins at Fernando de Noronha archipelago, both in Brazil. June–Sept/Oct: southern right whales southern Santa Catarina Island. June–Dec humpbacks in National Marine Park of Abrolhos in Brazil*

Weather *Amazon-Orinoco hot, humid conditions; in southern Brazil, whale season is cold, windy, even from lookouts, often rough on the water*

Types of tours *Half- and full-day tours, some extended multi-day expeditions; inflatables, sailboats, motorboats, canoes, and river ferries; some watching from land*

Tours available *Brazil: Florianópolis, Caravelas, Manaus; Colombian Amazon: Bogotá, Leticia, and Puerto Nariño; Peru: Iquitos*

Information *Oceanic Society Expeditions, Fort Mason Center, Building E, San Francisco, CA 94123, Ph. 1 415 441 1106; International Wildlife Coalition/Brasil, C.P. 5087, 88040-970, Florianópolis, SC, Brazil, Ph./Fax 55 48 234 1580*

Argentina

South America

Fabled Patagonia, celebrated by explorers, biologists, and modern writers, is the remote southern region of Argentina. Called by one writer "the uttermost part of the Earth," Patagonia comprises the provinces of Chubut, Río Negro, Santa Cruz, and the territory of Tierra del Fuego.

Patagonia is a semiarid tableland full of sheep farms, mineral deposits, and vast open areas. Much of the coastline is stark, windswept cliffs, but halfway down the long Patagonian coast, a large peninsula, called Península Valdés, juts out. This provides two large gulfs and, within them, some sheltered bays that are favored by the rare southern right whale.

In the 1970s, Patagonia became famous in the cetacean world when scientist Roger Payne (see p. 308) moved his family to a cliff-side house to study right whales. He and later researchers developed the individual photo-identification method for these whales, and he recorded their sounds and most intimate behavior.

Arriving every July, southern right whales use the waters around Península Valdés to mate, calve, raise their young, and sometimes play. As Payne and his family witnessed, the afternoon show begins as the winds reach 20 miles (32 km) per hour off the Patagonian coast. One by one, the southern right whales raise their broad tails

Tail high, a southern right whale (above) "sails" across the bay in the sheltered waters around Península Valdés, Patagonia.

high out of the water and "sail" across the bay; then they dive and return to repeat the maneuver. To see one of these huge tails sailing past from a small boat, is an awesome sight.

Day tours to watch southern right whales leave from the towns of Puerto Madryn, Trelew, and Puerto Pirámide; for seven-day or longer package tours, book ahead through international tour operators. All tours go through, or leave from, Buenos Aires. Package tours can include visits to elephant seal, sea lion and seal rookeries,

An orca (above) teaches her calves how to catch sea lions, then return to the water. A whale-watch boat (left) at Puerto Pirámide.

Magellanic penguin colonies (at nearby Punta Tombo), as well as land-based excursions into Patagonia itself.

Península Valdés is the place to witness acrobatic dusky dolphins and the drama of orcas attacking sea lions. Orcas feast on them during the pupping season from mid-February to mid-April. At Punta Norte, on the other side of Península Valdés, there is a special viewing area where you can see the orcas patrolling the shallows and charging right out of the water onto the beach to pick off young sea lions.

Special Features

Many experienced cetacean watchers long to spend time in southern Patagonia. Several cetacean species are found only around the tip of southern South America (including the waters of either or both Argentina and Chile). The best studied of these is Commerson's dolphin, a small black-and-white dolphin, which can be seen on dolphin-watch tours out of Puerto Deseado in the far south of Argentina. These dolphins appear in the same season as the southern right whales, but spring weather is poor in these far southern waters and the best viewing season is December to March. This overlaps with part of the period when orcas grab the young sea lions off the beach at Península Valdés. Whale watchers who miss the right whale season at Patagonia can see Commerson's dolphins and orcas instead. It is also possible to see indigenous Peale's dolphins, but to spot some of the other rare small cetaceans found only off southern South America, you need to join a long-range cruise which includes the Strait of Magellan.

TRAVELER'S NOTES

When to visit *Mid-July–Nov southern right whales at Península Valdés, Patagonia, best Sept–Oct; orcas year-round but catch sea lions on beaches mid-Feb to mid-Apr; Dec–Mar Commerson's dolphins and Peale's dolphins near Puerto Deseado*
Weather *Mid-July–Nov cold during right whale season, cool at sea even on best days for dolphin watching in Dec–Mar*
Types of tours *Mainly extended multi-day expeditions, some day tours locally; inflatables, fishing boats, sport-fishing boats, sailboats, kayaks*
Tours available *Buenos Aires; Chubut province: Puerto Pirámide, Puerto Madryn, Rawson, Trelew; Santa Cruz province: Puerto San Julian, Puerto Deseado*
Information *Oficina Informática Turística (Tourism Information Office), Avenida Santa Fe 883, 1059 Buenos Aires, Argentina, Ph. 54 1 312 2232 or 312 5550*

EUROPE *and* AFRICA

Greenland

The spiritual home of dolphin watching since the days of Aristotle, Europe and Africa are excellent for land-based, scientific, and educational whale watching.

Commercial cetacean watching in Europe and Africa started in 1980, when a Gibraltar fisherman began offering boat tours to see three species of Mediterranean dolphin. By the mid-1980s, trips were being offered in France, Britain, Ireland, and Portugal to see dolphins. At the same time, interest in land-based watching of southern right whales was growing on the South African coast, but it wasn't until the end of the 1980s that whale and dolphin watching really took off there. In addition, substantial industries started up in Norway, Italy, and the Canary Islands followed closely by the Azores.

Whale watching for sperm whales and various baleen whales out of Andenes, in northern Norway, is in many ways a model for successful ecotourism. Experienced naturalists, or nature guides, and scientists work on board whale-watch boats, and a museum and whale center are located in the town. Watching whales here has become a learning experience as well as simply good fun.

In Italy, guided fin whale tours out of Porto Sole and San Remo, near Genoa, have become popular. In the Azores, there is an amazing diversity of cetaceans and both land- and boat-based whale watching.

The Canary Islands, off southern Morocco, have had the fastest growth in whale watching of anywhere in the world. Between 1991 and 1996, the number of people watching whales increased from fewer than 1,000 to an estimated 500,000 visitors a year taking trips on at least 46 registered boats, owned by some 31 companies. This makes the Canary Islands one of the three largest whale-watch destinations in the world, along with southern New England and the St. Lawrence River. There are outstanding opportunities for observing local short-finned pilot whales and various dolphins. However, few operators carry naturalists on board, so make enquiries about who the responsible operators are.

Cornish coast (above); a dolphin off the coast of Cornwall (above right).

Aside from the Canary Islands, Europe and Africa have been responsible for some of the finest whale-watch tours. In South Africa and Ireland, in particular, thoughtful and well-developed walking tours have given participants a chance to see whales during guided tours along the cliffs.

From Italy, Greece, Croatia, and France, along with some other countries, participants may sign up for 3–10 days to accompany scientists on high-quality tours

A dolphin (left) swims and leaps alongside watchers aboard an inflatable tour boat on the Mediterranean.

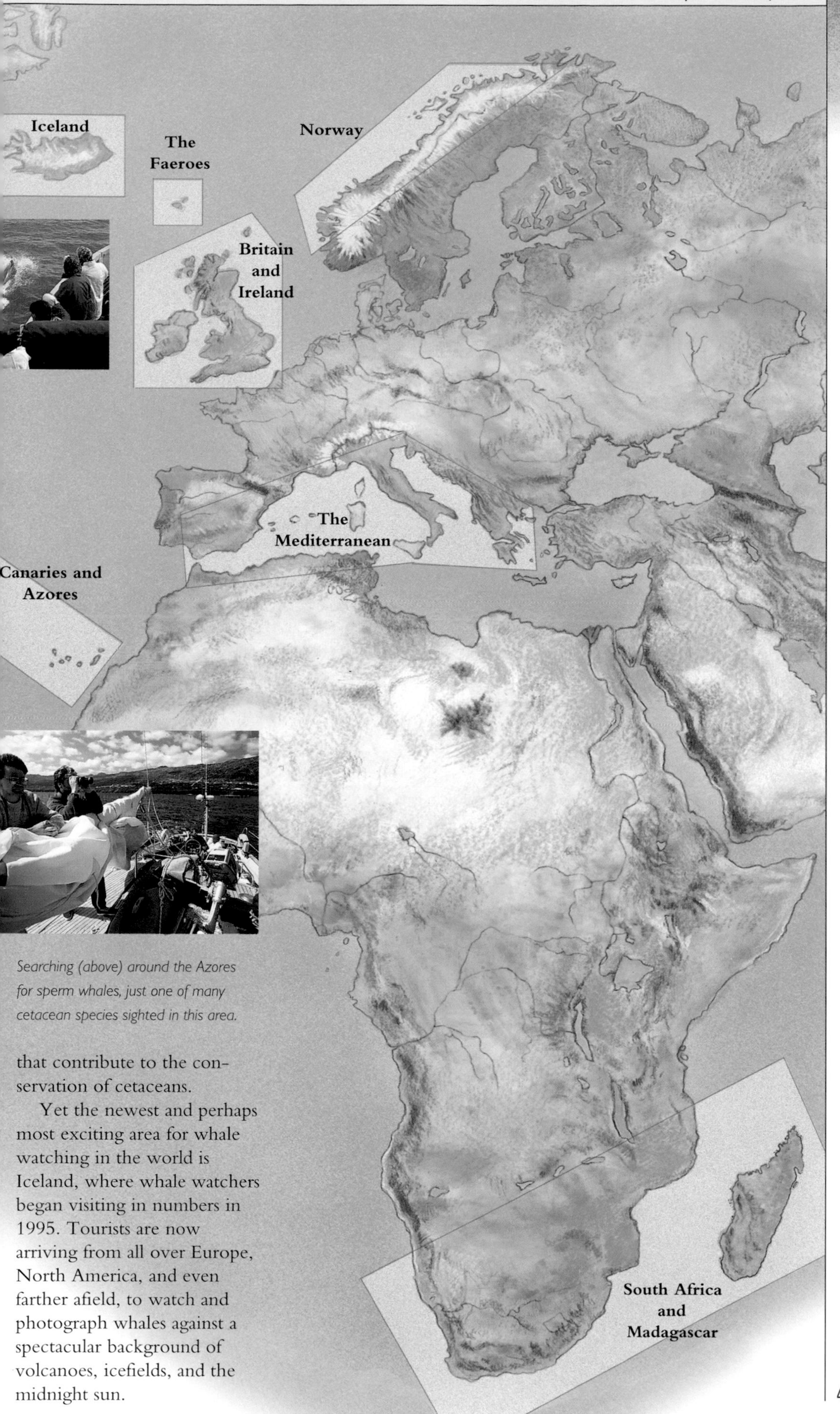

Searching (above) around the Azores for sperm whales, just one of many cetacean species sighted in this area.

that contribute to the conservation of cetaceans.

Yet the newest and perhaps most exciting area for whale watching in the world is Iceland, where whale watchers began visiting in numbers in 1995. Tourists are now arriving from all over Europe, North America, and even farther afield, to watch and photograph whales against a spectacular background of volcanoes, icefields, and the midnight sun.

Iceland

Europe and Africa

At an hour past midnight, in the full sun of early summer, minke whales are spouting and terns diving—all scooping and swallowing tiny fish. Lulled by flat, calm seas in the shadow of snow-capped peaks off north-eastern Iceland, a boatload of whale watchers sights a pod of playful whales, their spouts and broad backs gleaming in the sun.

A minke whale (above) is bathed in the warm glow of the midnight sun as it surfaces near Húsavík, northern Iceland.

Lying just below the Arctic Circle in the far North Atlantic Ocean, Iceland is roughly midway between North America and Europe. Icelandair, Iceland's national airline, offers one- to three-night stops in Iceland for Europeans or North Americans crossing the Atlantic, at no extra charge. To date, no other scheduled airlines stop in Iceland.

More than ever, people today are headed toward Iceland for whale-watching and nature excursions. Whale-watching sites have opened up in various villages and towns around the country. Besides minke whales, fin, killer, sperm, sei, humpback, and blue whales can be seen, along with Atlantic white-sided dolphins, white-beaked dolphins, and apparently shy harbor porpoises.

Although midnight whale watching in late June can be enjoyed from various parts of the country, Húsavík, a fishing village in northeastern Iceland, has become the center for whale watching. Friendly minke whales provide the main interest during the whale-watch season. Humpback whales are sometimes encountered, and, several times every year, blue whales (normally feeding farther offshore) come into the bay and feed for a few days or a week. Whales are sometimes seen from the town and, by boat, often within an hour of leaving the dock.

At Höfn, in southeast Iceland, where whale watching started in 1991, whale watchers board a 150 ton (135 tonne) lobster fishing boat to see humpback and minke whales, as well as harbor porpoises and sometimes orcas. On the west coast, 10–12 miles (16–19 km) offshore from Stykkishólmur, blue and sperm whales can be

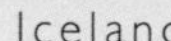

Iceland offers visitors a wealth of wildlife, such as the humpback whale (above) breaching, and a close-up view of a minke whale for whale watchers near I lúsavík (right).

spotted on full-day trips that include visits to thriving seabird colonies and also to the famous Snaefellsjökull glacier, location for the movie *Journey to the Center of the Earth.*

Other whale-watch ports around the country include Grindavík, Keflavík, Arnarstapi, Ólafsvík, and Dalvík. Some of the operators, such as at Húsavík, use sturdy wooden Icelandic fishing boats customized for whale watching, while others use newer fishing boats.

Access for all tours is through the international airport at Keflavík, with a transfer to the national airport in nearby Reykjavík for ports in northern Iceland, including Húsavík. Whale watching is possible on day tours, while some visitors come as part of a guided package tour. Such trips can be designed around whale-watching activities or might include other nature and cultural tours.

Special Features

In northeastern Iceland, near Húsavík, there is superb bird watching in the Lake Myvatn area. Species include some rare ducks. There is regular volcanic activity nearby, which can be seen in hot, sputtering mudholes and a lunar-like landscape. It was here that American astronauts trained for their moon walks.

From Höfn, on the southeastern coast, there are excursions by skidoo or snowmobile across Vatnajökull, Europe's largest icecap. In the southwest, from Grindavík, close to Reykjavík, tours visit Eldey Island, the last stand of the great auk—a flightless marine bird that lived on the island before being driven to extinction. Eldey Island is now the site of a huge gannet colony.

TRAVELER'S NOTES

When to visit *May–Sept several cetacean species (humpback whales more in early summer, orcas in late summer); best period June–Aug*
Weather *Cold on the water; rain and rough seas intermittent; snow is possible early and late in whale-watch season*
Types of tours *Half- and full-day tours, some extended multi-day expeditions; fishing boats and large tour boats*
Tours available *Húsavík, Höfn, Dalvík, Hauganes, Stykkishólmur, Keflavík, Grindavík, Arnarstapi, Ólafsvík*
Information *Icelandic Information Center, Bankastraeti 2, 101 Reykjavík, Iceland, Ph. 354 562 3045*

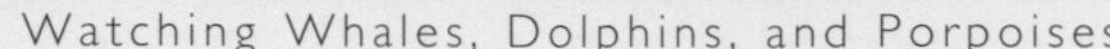

Norway

Europe and Africa

In the rugged seas off northern Norway, sperm whales break the water, their long backs sliding up and down the waves like logs adrift. These sperm whales, all males, come here to feed on squid. Sperm whales are the largest of the toothed whales, and have the biggest brains of any animal. Almost certainly a part of that brain power is employed in their complex sensory systems, which enable them to hunt and catch squid in the blackness of submarine canyons.

Guillemots and kittiwakes nesting on an island (left) in the Norwegian Arctic.

The colorful fishing port of Andenes, which has its own airport (accessible through Oslo), is the most northerly place in the world from which to see sperm whales; it is also one of the best. Here, the continental shelf is closer to shore than anywhere else in Norway, little more than two hours away by boat. The four- to five-hour tours are offered twice a day from the end of May to mid-September.

During the summer months, Andenes—located on Andøy Island, which is connected to the mainland by bridges—is awash with visitors from some 40 countries, most coming for whale-watching trips that may be the most culturally diverse in the world. The brochures are printed in three or four languages, and multilingual naturalists travel on each trip. The naturalists are keen Scandinavian scientists who do some of their photo-identification and other work on the boats. In this way, whale watching in Norway has significantly contributed to the development of cetacean field work in northern Europe.

Besides sperm whales, other cetaceans sometimes encountered include minke, fin, and pilot whales, white-beaked dolphins, orcas, and harbor porpoises. In June and July, daylight lasting almost 24 hours allows time to appreciate every aspect of nature—and to find the whales. Some 95 percent of trips successfully spot whales, and the main tour operator guarantees that if whales are not seen, a free trip will be provided.

South of Andenes along the Norwegian coast, in an area called Tysfjord, the military-like formations of orcas herding herring close to

An orca (above) in Norwegian waters. On day tours (left) from Tysfjord, northern Norway, sightings of orcas are guaranteed.

shore every autumn lend a touch of drama to the dark, moody Norwegian fiords. The prime viewing period is short (10 October to 20 November), with daylight extending to only four to six hours a day at that time. Sometimes the orcas can be seen from land but almost always within an hour or two of departure from the dock. The popularity of these tours caused traffic jams on local roads and in the fiords in recent years, but operators and researchers are trying to improve the situation. Access is through Narvik Airport, about an hour and a half away.

Special Features

In the Andenes area, on or near Andøy Island, visitors are offered a wide range of activities. One of Norway's better bird cliffs, on Bleiksoy Island, is just off the western side of Andøy. Two-hour tours visit the colony, where 70,000–80,000 pairs of puffins, 6,000 pairs of kittiwakes, and numerous cormorants, storm petrels, common guillemots, and fulmars breed.

Two of several local museums of special interest to nature lovers are Hisnakul—a new museum that covers local bird life, fisheries, the moors, geology, and the northern lights—and the Andenes Whale Center, a museum of whales, whale research, and north Norwegian whaling. At the Whale Center, there are slide shows and daily public lectures on whale behavior, research, and ecology. In addition, visitors can obtain a memento of their whale-watch trip, in the form of a diploma and badge, by joining the Royal International Whale Safari Club. Membership funds are used to support the research and information activities of the Whale Center, which is affiliated with the whale-watch operation in Andenes.

TRAVELER'S NOTES

When to visit *Late May–Sept in the Andenes area for sperm and other whales and dolphins; Oct–mid-Nov around Tysfjord for orcas*
Weather *Cold on the water late May–Sept in Andenes and Oct–Nov in Tysfjord; Tysfjord has very short days (few hours daylight by mid-Nov)*
Types of tours *Half- and full-day tours, some extended multi-day expeditions; inflatables, sailboats, and large boats*
Tours available *Andenes, Nyksund, Myre, Stø, Storjord*
Information *Andøy Reiseliv, Tourist Information, P.O Box 58, N-8480 Andenes, Norway, Ph. 47 76 11 56 00*

Greenland and the Faeroe Islands

Europe and Africa

Greenland, the second largest island in the world after Australia, is made up mostly of an icecap up to 14,000 feet (4,300 m) thick. Greenland's 55,900 residents are mainly Inuit people who arrived from North America around 2,500 BC, along with Norse settlers, who followed after Eric the Red's landing in AD 985. A self-governing territory of Denmark, Greenland today remains more remote and expensive for local travel and amenities than adjacent northern Canada to the west, or Iceland to the east, but its whale watching has a character all of its own. Tiny, often colorful villages built on icy fiords offer superb baleen and toothed whale watching. The island's deeply indented coast provides shelter for mariners inside icy bays with craggy shores. Greenland has a productive marine environment that attracts plankton and other invertebrates, fish, seals, dolphins, and whales.

The most popular summer site to see whales is out of Paamiut (Frederikshåb) on the relatively warm southwest coast. Humpback whales come here to feed and, with any luck, you can get a photograph of them lifting their giant flukes with a drifting iceberg or glacier as the backdrop. Greenland humpbacks are arguably the most energetic or adventurous humpbacks in the North Atlantic. These whales come from the Caribbean, passing through feeding grounds in the Gulf of Maine, the St. Lawrence River, and off Newfoundland to feed around Greenland's waters. Their choice of location for summer feeding is probably determined by the areas they were first taken to as calves.

Tourists in small inflatable boats check out a tide-water glacier (above) around Prince Christian Sound, in southern Greenland.

Besides humpbacks, tours out of Paamiut often encounter fin and minke whales feeding in large numbers in areas with massive plankton blooms. After a good feeding bout, whales can frequently be seen leaping and cavorting, and some may even come over to your boat to investigate, rolling on their sides at the surface or spyhopping to catch a glimpse of the whale watchers.

North along the west coast of Greenland, from the Disko Bay area, there are boat charters,

A humpback breaching (above). A flotilla of fishing boats (left) moored in Klaksvik, Faeroe Islands.

as well as kayaks for rent, to see whales close up, especially at Aasiaat and Ilulissat (Jakobshavn). Imagine kayaking with fin whales and puffing porpoises moving alongside you at water level. In September and October, belugas and fin whales may be sighted. Although the days are short, for whale watching, you might find narwhals farther offshore.

The Faeroes comprise 18 islands connected by bridges and small ferries. From these Danish self-governing islands, located between Iceland and Scotland, dolphins and sometimes whales can be seen on boat tours and from shore. Classic Faeroese Viking boats offer bird-watching and nature tours. Although the gregarious pilot whales are hunted here, the marine nature opportunities are still outstanding. Many visitors ask to watch whales and dolphins, to visit steep seabird cliffs, and to see local seals.

Special Features

Just 28 miles (45 km) east of Ilulissat (Jakobshavn) is the most active glacier in the Northern Hemisphere, producing an estimated 20 million tons (18 million tonnes) of ice every day. Greenland Tourism offers a range of nature, glacier, cultural, and historical tours by helicopter, boat, kayak, and dogsled. Don't miss the seabird cliffs in spring and early summer on Mykines and other Faeroe islands. Access is through Tórshavn.

Fin whales (above) spotted off the coast of Greenland, where they feast on plankton.

TRAVELER'S NOTES

When to visit *June–Aug Greenland; Sept–Oct whales common but weather can be poor; May–Oct Faeroes*
Weather *Cold on the sea, rain and snow a possibility*
Types of tours *Half- and full-day tours, some extended multi-day expeditions; kayaks, fishing boats, large touring boats*
Tours available *Greenland: Paamiut (Frederikshåb), Aasiaat, and Ilulissat (Jakobshavn) in Disko Bay, Ammassalik; the Faeroe Islands: Tórshavn, Sandur*
Information *Greenland Tourism a/s, Postbox 1552, DK-3900 Nuuk, Greenland, Ph. 299 22888; North Atlantic Marine Activity Ltd., PO Box 1371, FR-110 Tórshavn, Faeroe Islands, Ph. 298 12499; Joan Petur Clementsen, FR-210 Sandur, Faeroe Islands, Ph. 298 86119*

Britain and Ireland

Europe and Africa

Britain and Ireland serve as the summer feeding areas for some whales, and provide year-round habitat for various groups of resident dolphins. Cruising through island passages dotted with castles and crofts, boat tours meet playful minke whales and bottlenose dolphins—the two most commonly sighted species. With their tag-along friendliness, they are welcome companions. It is also possible to see white-beaked, common, Atlantic white-sided, and Risso's dolphins; harbor porpoises; long-finned pilot whales; and orcas in the waters surrounding Britain and Ireland.

Scotland is becoming one of the headquarters for small-cetacean watching in Europe. Educational study tours directed toward minke whales have become popular offshore from the Isle of Mull. Risso's dolphins, and sometimes harbor porpoises and orcas, can also be seen. Off northern Scotland, an eight-hour ferry crossing from South Ronaldsay, in the Orkney Islands, to the Shetland Islands, provides one of the better runs for regular cetacean sightings in the British Isles.

The Moray Firth of Scotland offers the most northerly resident population of bottlenose dolphins in the world, and can be accessed by rail and air through the city of Inverness. Here, the bottlenose dolphins can be seen from land, feeding and playing. The best time for viewing is two to three hours before high tide from North Kessock, near the site of a small marine research base that monitors the dolphins and local seals.

In England, bottlenose dolphins are found off Cornwall and appear to move regularly between there and Cardigan Bay, Wales. However, the dolphins are more reliably seen out of Wales, with almost year-round day tours offered from New Quay, in Dyfed. Sightings are also sometimes made of common and Risso's dolphins, pilot, and even minke whales on extended day trips.

In the green country of coastal southern Ireland, the cetacean walking tour with bed

Fungie, the famous Dingle dolphin, leaping for tourists watching from a boat off the Dingle Peninsula, County Kerry, Ireland.

The rugged coastline of the Orkney Islands, off northern Scotland (above). Risso's dolphins (right) are seen off Britain and Ireland, mainly in deep water.

and breakfast, and pub stops, is an Irish innovation. Some of the best tours are those to Mizen Head and Clear Island, in County Cork. From two vantage points, Blannarragaun and the Bill of Clear, 12 cetacean species have been spotted, including harbor porpoises; Risso's, bottlenose, common, Atlantic white-sided, and white-beaked dolphins; and minke and long-finned pilot whales. A good source for information on current sightings is the Cape Clear Observatory. There is a ferry service to the island and a variety of accommodations available. Boat tours are also in operation to Mizen Head and Clear Island, along with other offshore areas.

In western Ireland, in the Shannon River estuary, some 60 resident bottlenose dolphins can be seen on year-round boat tours from Carrigaholt.

Special Features

Communities in both Britain and Ireland have long had relationships with solitary friendly bottlenose dolphins. Dolphins named Freddy, Donald, Percy, and Simo were some of those who befriended people and took up residence in British coastal waters for two to three years. The latest dolphin is Fungie, who moved into Dingle Harbour, County Kerry, Ireland, in the mid-1980s, and began approaching and following boats. Leaping and spyhopping, he has entertained more than a million visitors since then, at the rate of up to 150,000 people a year. There is no way to predict how much longer he will stay—by 1996, he had remained longer than most others. Fungie has already done his bit to get many people interested in cetaceans. In future there will no doubt be other solitary dolphins seeking human company.

TRAVELER'S NOTES

When to visit *Year-round dolphins but best seen May–Oct; Apr–Oct minke whales in western and northern Scotland; June–Aug prime whale- and dolphin-watching season*

Weather *Cool to cold on the water; rain possible, even in summer, especially in western parts of Britain and in Ireland*

Types of tours *Half- and full-day tours, extended multi-day expeditions, inflatables, sailboats, and large whale-watch boats; some whale watching from ferries; land-based whale watching*

Tours available *Britain: (England) Cornwall; (Wales) New Quay, Milford Haven; (Scotland) Dervaig (on the Isle of Mull), Mallaig, Oban, Gairloch, Cromarty, Inverness; Republic of Ireland: Carrigaholt, Dingle, Schull, Castlehaven, Kilbrittain, Clifden*

Information *British Tourist Authority, Thames Tower, Blacks Road, Hammersmith, London W6 9EL, England, Ph. 44 181 846 9000; Irish Tourist Board, Baggot Street Bridge, Dublin 2, Ireland, Ph. 353 1 602 4000*

Canaries and Azores

Europe and Africa

The Canary Islands, just 60 miles (100 km) off the northwest coast of Africa, due west of southern Morocco, include seven main and several uninhabited islands. Tenerife, the base for most of the whale watching, has a pale red volcanic landscape, with the highest point at 12,198 feet (3,781 m). Tourism development has taken over parts of the island, but it is still possible to see the traditional cave-like houses carved into the mountains.

Many whale-watch boats depart from Los Cristianos and Colón, near Playa de las Americas, on the southern end of Tenerife, accessible through two international airports. Tenerife is one of the few places in the world to offer year-round whale watching and, since the mid-1990s, along with southern New England and Quebec, it has become one of the three most popular whale-watch areas in the world. Choose your trip carefully though, not just based on price, but by looking for boats that offer naturalist guides and those that contribute to local research and conservation.

The warm, deep waters around Tenerife support a resident population of at least 500 short-finned pilot whales. These whales, between the size of a bottlenose dolphin and an orca, and sharing behavioral habits of both, live in tight family groups. Their characteristic bulbous heads, hook-like flippers, and long bodies can be seen in the clear waters as they swim just beneath the surface before diving deep to hunt squid. Bottlenose dolphins are often encountered, along with the pilot whales, within an hour of leaving port.

Common dolphins off Pico, Azores (above) and the pale red cliffs (below, far right) along the southern coast of Tenerife, the Canaries.

Whale and, especially, dolphin watching has recently spread to Gomera, Lanzarote, and Gran Canaria. Some of the other islands offer chances to see inshore bottlenose dolphins (Gomera), or to sail in search of sperm whales and various beaked whales (Gomera, Lanzarote).

In the Azores Islands, in the North Atlantic west of Portugal, whales have long been a topic of conversation. Once a whaling center, they now offer whale watching from May to October, especially from the islands of Pico and Faial.

Whale watching in the Azores is small scale compared to the Canary Islands, but the diversity of whales is greater. Sperm whales are a reliable sight, along with bottlenose, common, Risso's, spotted, and striped dolphins, plus short-finned pilot whales and various beaked whales. Few places in the world are as good for sighting rare beaked whales. A wide range of other species can also be seen.

Relics of the old whaling days, vigias, or watch towers, such as the one seen above on Faial, are now used for research. Part of a large resident population of short-finned pilot whales (left) off Tenerife, in the Canaries.

Special Features

In the Azores, traditional small boat-based whaling with hand harpoons was carried on until 1985, with three additional whales taken in 1987. Now the "vigias," or lookout towers where the whalers kept watch for the whales, have been restored by whale-watch companies. Many of them, especially on Pico and Faial where whale-watch tours are offered, are open to visitors. You may meet researchers who do some of their tracking of the whales from vigias.

One of the best is Vigia da Queimada, which allows sightings for up to 18 miles (30 km) on a clear day, within a radius of 200 degrees from east to west. At this distance, sperm whales and many other deep-water cetaceans can be seen. In Lajes, on the island of Pico, you can take a marked three-hour walk designed for whale watchers. This includes the Vigia da Queimada, the whaling museum, the old whalers' boathouse, and the whaling factory.

TRAVELER'S NOTES

When to visit *Year-round Canaries: short-finned pilot whales, bottlenose, common, and many other tropical dolphins, along with small, toothed whales. May–Oct Azores: sperm, other whales, but whales may also be seen before and after this period*
Weather *Canaries: subtropical year-round with cool, refreshing winds; sometimes hot, sandy desert winds from Africa make whale sighting difficult, but there are usually 300 good whale-watching days per year; May–Oct Azores: seas windy, cool to cold*
Types of tours *Half- and full-day tours, some extended multi-day expeditions; sailboats and large whale-watch boats*
Tours available *Canary Islands: Los Cristianos and Puerto Colón, near Playa de las Americas, on Tenerife, Gomera, Lanzarote, Gran Canaria; Azores: Horta on Faial; Lajes on Pico*
Information *Servicio de Turismo, Plaza de España S/N, Bajos del Palacio Insular, 38003 Santa Cruz de Tenerife, Tenerife, Canary Islands, Spain, Ph. 34 22 239 592; Azores Tourism Office, Casa Do Elogio Colonia Alema 9900, Horta-Açores (Azores), Portugal, Ph. 351 922 3801*

South Africa and Madagascar

Europe and Africa

The Republic of South Africa has developed land-based whale watching to a fine art. Where the warm waters of the South Atlantic sweep around to meet the Indian Ocean, the main season for southern right whales is July to November. The whales come in close to shore then, to mate and raise their calves. Best access is through Cape Town, where you can rent a car and drive along the "Cape Whale Route." Along this ocean-front road, which extends from Cape Town east along the coast, there are dozens of lookouts along the rocky coastline that provide superb right whale watching. The whales come so close to shore that they are seen even from hotel rooms and local restaurants.

Shore-based whale watching in Hermanus, South Africa, is a learning experience (above).

Hermanus, some 60 miles (95 km) east of Cape Town, is the center of activity, attracting tens of thousands of visitors from around the world. It has a festival atmosphere through the whale season; a "whale crier" strolling through the town blows a bass kelp horn to alert locals and visitors to sightings of right whales. He wears a small billboard showing locations of the sightings. Anyone interested is given a map and directions. The sounds on the horn also employ a sort of whale Morse code to indicate current sighting locations that change from day to day, sometimes from hour to hour. Special naturalist-led walking tours are offered by various tour companies in the town. A naturalist takes you to the best sites along the rocky cliffs and talks about the whales as you watch and wait.

At present there are no boat-based whale-watch tours to see right whales in South Africa, but it isn't necessary as they come so close to shore. Bottlenose and Indo-Pacific hump-backed dolphins can also be seen from shore in many

Bottlenose dolphins (above) are seen year-round in Madagascar and South Africa. Magellanic penguins (right) in Cape Province.

places along the coast, such as Plettenberg Bay. In the west of the country, out of Lambert's Bay, there are boat tours to see Heaviside's dolphin, found only in southwestern Africa. There are also a few boat tours on which humpback and Bryde's whales are seen.

Across Mozambique Channel, northeast of South Africa, in the Indian Ocean, is the island of Madagascar. The world's fourth largest island, at 229,000 square miles (593,000 sq km), it is almost the size of California and Oregon put together. Although more and more of its tropical forest has been cut down in recent years, this large subtropical island offers many natural wonders, and sightings of various dolphin species.

On Madagascar's east coast, around the island of Nosy Boraha (also known as Sainte-Marie), humpback whales return every year from July to September to mate and raise their young. In Andampanangoy, boat tours can be booked through local hotels and outdoor sports shops. In addition to humpback whales, sperm whales can be spotted farther offshore, while inshore to offshore, bottlenose, spinner, and Indo-Pacific hump-backed dolphins are commonly found throughout the year.

Special Features

With many parks close at hand in South Africa and Madagascar, visitors will want to experience rain forest, savannah, and the vast coast. Rare primates, such as lemurs, and other endemic flora and fauna are attractions on Madagascar. The Masoala Peninsula, adjacent to the prime humpback whale area, has pristine lowland rain forest where red-ruffed lemurs live.

A South African wildlife area close to the whale-watching sites is the Cape of Good Hope Nature Reserve. There are also a number of easily accessible colonies of Magellanic penguins well worth visiting in the Cape Province region.

TRAVELER'S NOTES

When to visit *July–Nov southern right whales in South Africa; July–Sept humpback whales, and a chance to see mating behavior and calves in Madagascar; year-round bottlenose, Heaviside's, and Indo-Pacific hump-backed dolphins*

Weather *July–Nov in South Africa weather mixed with rain and strong winds alternating with warm-to-hot temperatures; July–Sept, humpback season in Madagascar, warm weather even at sea*

Types of tours *Mainly land-based lookouts and tours; boat tours for dolphin watching in South Africa; small-boat and fishing-boat tours in Madagascar*

Tours available *South Africa: Hermanus, Plettenberg Bay (various), Lambert's Bay; Madagascar: Andampanangoy*

Information *South African Tourism Board (SATOUR), Private Bag X164, Pretoria 0001, Republic of South Africa, Ph. 27 123 470600*

ASIA

As Japan leads the way, whale watching, and especially dolphin watching, is catching on in fishing villages and beach resorts all over Asia.

Whale watching is proving its worth as a source of income in Asia, a vast region with important fishing economies where many people depend on the sea for their livelihood.

In April 1988, the first Japanese whale-watching expedition departed from Tokyo for the Ogasawara Islands. This trip, reported worldwide, was so notable because Japan remains both a whaling nation and a consumer of whale meat. Since 1988, Japanese whale watching has flourished. Some 25 communities around the country now offer whale- and dolphin-watching tours. With a whale-watching season of only three months a year, the Ogasawara whale-watch industry provides half of the year's tourist income to the islands. That is twice the revenue from agriculture and almost half that of the most important industry—fishing.

In some communities, the local government or fishing collective sponsors whale watching. In other areas, local fishers, dive operators, and even some professional people have organized the whale-watch tours. Many Japanese travelers have experienced whale watching in Hawaii, Canada, or Baja California, so it was perhaps inevitable that they would take ideas back to their own country. The surprise is how popular it has become. More than 60,000 people a year—most of them

Searching for whales near Krakatau volcano (above), in Indonesia. A pod of dwarf sperm whales (below left).

Japanese—now take whale- and dolphin-watching tours in Japanese waters.

In Hong Kong, dolphin tours have already become popular. The tours are based on the resident pink Indo-Pacific hump-backed dolphins and finless porpoises that are seen in some of the most well-traveled waterways of the world. In Hong Kong, dolphin watching has alerted many people to the problems of conserving dolphins, which

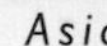

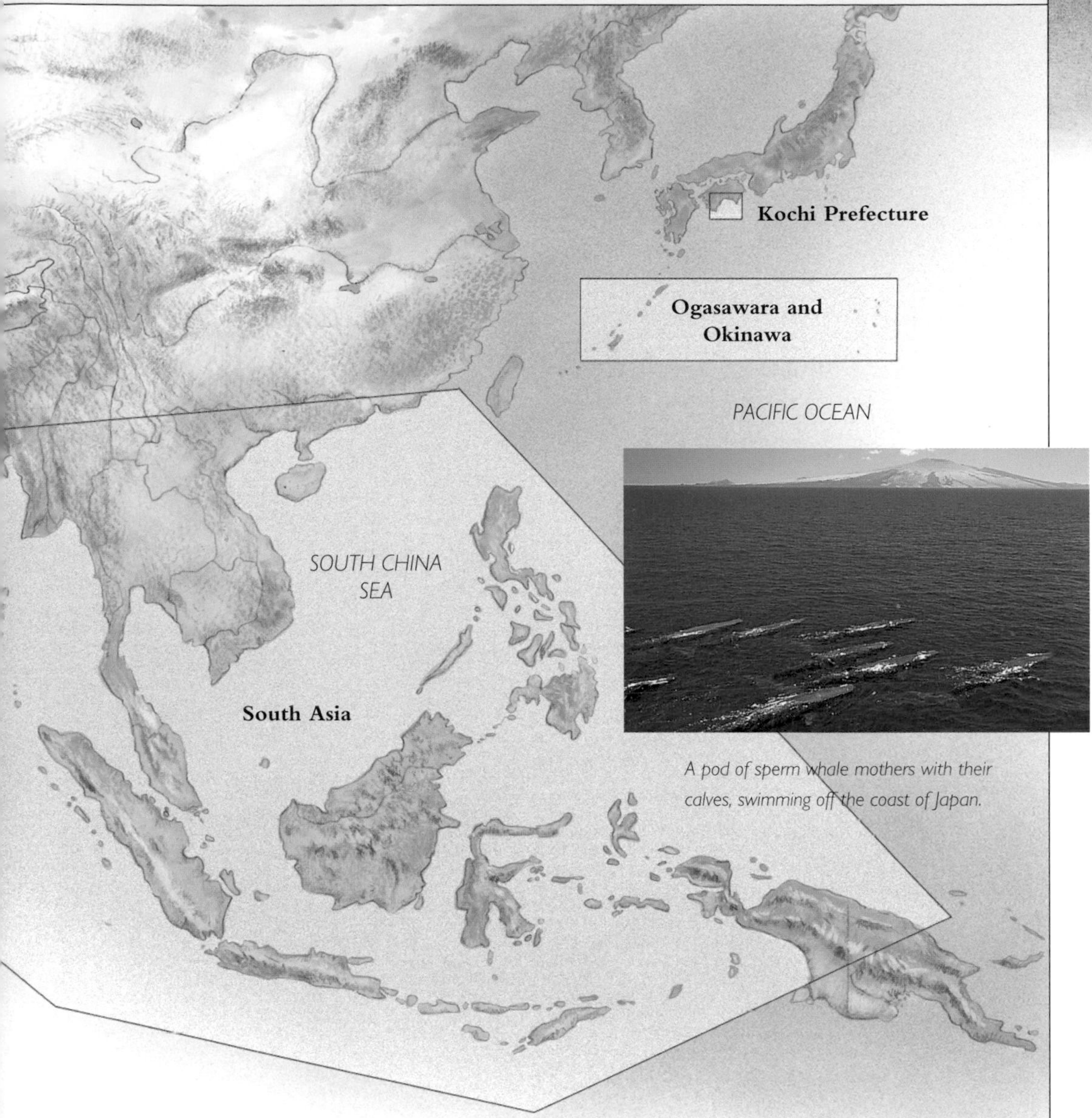

Kochi Prefecture

Ogasawara and Okinawa

PACIFIC OCEAN

SOUTH CHINA SEA

South Asia

A pod of sperm whale mothers with their calves, swimming off the coast of Japan.

are being displaced from local waters by industry. In Japan and China, along with other countries in Asia, the hope is that cetacean watching will expand and become even more important as an economic, educational, scientific, and conservation force. If this happens, there's a better chance that cetacean populations will increase and flourish.

In other parts of Asia, whale watching is newer and still developing. In Goa, India, small boats take holiday beachgoers to meet tropical dolphins just offshore. The same is true in Bali, Indonesia; off Phuket, Thailand; and off the east coast of Taiwan. Because of the great diversity of species offered, from sperm whales to rare dolphins, the Philippines has the potential to appeal to discerning and dedicated whale watchers and ecotourists. Educational and conservation programs have been established, and the Philippines may one day challenge even Japan for the title of hottest whale-watching ticket in Asia.

Whale watching aboard a Japanese fishing boat (above) in Ogata, Japan.

South Asia

Asia

Even more than in other parts of the world, tropical cetacean watching in South Asia can be extraordinarily diverse. Just a short boat ride from Queen's or Kowloon Piers, in Hong Kong, are wild dolphins, which is one of the last things you would imagine seeing in that environment. Close to Hong Kong's new airport, a dozen pinkish dolphins lift their backs out of the water to display the characteristic hump of their species. These are Indo-Pacific hump-backed dolphins—a resident population found in the inshore waters of eastern China.

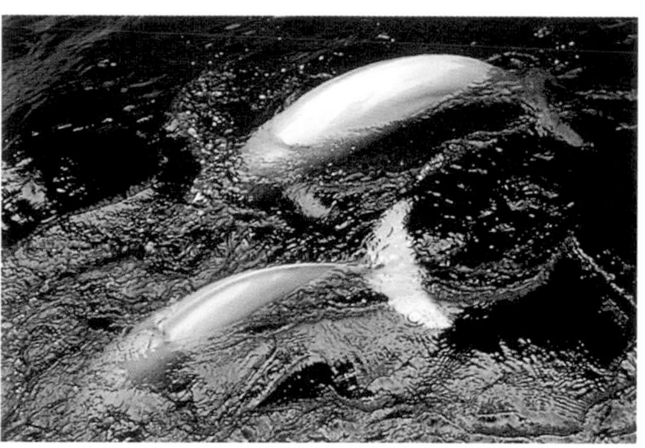

Tiny finless porpoises (left) near Hong Kong. Wooden boats on the beach in Goa, India (below right).

According to photo-identification studies, about 250 hump-backed dolphins use the North Lantau area of Hong Kong, living there year-round, feeding on a wide variety of fish—including gray mullet, white herring, shad, pilchards, and anchovies, as well as shrimp.

Along with the hump-backed dolphins are tiny finless porpoises. Looking like mini belugas, they butt the water with their round foreheads, poking around in the shallows. With neither a beak nor a dorsal fin, they are easy to distinguish from the hump-backed dolphin, with its long beak and prominent dorsal fin.

In the Tañon Strait of the Philippines, a wide variety of tropical whales and dolphins can be encountered. Dwarf sperm whales, a rare species anywhere else, can be seen swimming in family groups. Also watch for spotted, spinner, Risso's, and Fraser's dolphins, as well as pilot and melon-headed whales. Sperm and Bryde's whales are sometimes seen. Dolphins appear year-round, but the best months for spotting many species are April to June.

In Indonesia, sperm whales reside off Lembata Island in East Nusa Tenggara and off eastern Java, although tours are only occasionally available. From Bali, however, there are popular organized tours from Lovina Beach on the north side of the island where gregarious, acrobatic common and spinner dolphins can be seen.

In Goa, on the west coast of India, bottlenose and striped dolphins can be encountered just offshore. The small, wooden boats found along

Hong Kong's busy harbor (above). Melon-headed whales in Tañon Strait (left).

the beach offer impromptu tours of several hours. Thailand also offers dolphin watching as part of diving, marine-nature, and sea-canoe adventure trips out of Phuket. Dolphins are also sometimes advertised as part of trips to the Similan and Surin Islands in the Andaman Sea, but Thailand's potential is still largely undeveloped.

Most smaller cetaceans feed, socialize, and mate in the waters of South Asia year-round. Only baleen whales migrate to cooler waters to feed.

South Asia is one of the best areas to visit if you want to help save whales and dolphins. The survival of local whale and dolphin populations depends partly on the ability of local communities to manage cetacean tourism—to make a living from showing people "their" local wildlife.

TRAVELER'S NOTES

When to visit *Year-round, dolphins throughout region, sperm whales off Sri Lanka; Feb–Apr, blue whales off Sri Lanka; Apr–June, best for Philippines*
Weather *Hot, even at sea, but weather conditions vary across this vast region; main obstacles are prevailing winds that make whale watching in exposed areas difficult when the surf starts to build*
Types of tours *Half- and full-day tours, some extended multi-day expeditions; small boats, sailboats, canoes, outrigger boats, and motor cruisers; some land-based whale watching. Visitors arriving during storm and monsoon seasons should pay attention to local weather advisories*
Tours available *Hong Kong; India: Goa; Thailand: Phuket; Indonesia: Lovina Beach on Bali; Philippines: Tagbilaran on Bohol*
Information *Hong Kong Dolphinwatch, GPO Box 4102, Hong Kong, China, Ph. 852 2984 1414; Tourist Information Center, Jalan, Legian, Kuta, Denpasar Bali, Indonesia, Ph. 62 361 751551 or 62 361 751875*

Special Features

In the early 1980s, a three-year World Wide Fund for Nature (WWF) research expedition in the Indian Ocean identified a hotspot for whales and dolphins around Sri Lanka, south of India. Year-round populations of spinner and bottlenose dolphins were found, and there were sporadic sightings of striped, spotted, Risso's, Irrawaddy, and Indo-Pacific hump-backed dolphins. Most impressive of all are the large whales, including blue, sperm, and Bryde's whales, although the blue whales are present only from February to April.

Oceanic Society Expeditions in San Francisco was the first to offer trips in the 1980s. But the civil war in Sri Lanka forced cancellation of the program. Visitors to Trincomalee may be able to go a mile northeast to a military site called Fort Frederick and scan the Bay of Bengal. Within an hour, several cetacean species can often be spotted.

Japan: Ogasawara and Okinawa

Asia

In two tropical Japanese archipelagoes—the Kerama Islands off Okinawa and the Ogasawara (or Bonin) Islands—humpback whales visit every winter to sing, mate, and raise their calves. The Ogasawara Islands, 600 miles (1,000 km) south of Tokyo, are part of a volcanic offshore chain. At the southern end, Chichi-jima and Haha-jima, two inhabited islands, have long been popular with divers, underwater photographers, and nature tourists. Whale watching began here in 1988. Access is by a 29-hour ferry ride from Tokyo.

The humpback (left) is just one of a number of cetacean species seen off the Kerama and Ogasawara islands.

A typical whale-watch day in Chichi-jima begins with a trip up the hill for a talk on whales and a chance to scan for cetaceans from land. Often, long humpback flippers can be seen waving or slapping the surface. Until a few decades ago, from various Japanese ports, whales were spotted from strategic lookouts on land, alerting the whalers to leave port. These days scientists from the Ogasawara Whale-watching Association guide visitors and report sightings to fishing boat captains who take tourists out to find the whales. Besides humpbacks, other species commonly seen around Ogasawara are Bryde's, sperm, and short-finned pilot whales, along with bottlenose and spinner dolphins. There are also common, Pacific white-sided, spotted, rough-toothed, Risso's, striped, and Fraser's dolphins. Dolphin watching in this area is a popular, but separate, pursuit to whale watching, with operators specializing in watching or swimming with (mainly) bottlenose dolphins.

Access to the Kerama Islands is by jet airplane through Naha on Okinawa, then a short ferry ride to Zamami (the main whale-watch village) or Tokashiki. The Keramas are famous for diving opportunities, and many whale-watch operators in Zamami offer diving tours throughout most of the year, although some tours concentrate only on whales during the whale-watch season. The prime areas for diving are the relatively untouched coral reefs around the islands. A few

The coral seacoast (above) off Okinawa. A pod of spinner dolphins (left) leaping in the waters off the coast of Ogasawara Island.

of the local operators offer visitors the chance to dive in the morning and whale watch in the afternoon, or vice versa.

In the Kerama Islands, humpback whales, bottlenose dolphins, and the comparatively rare rough-toothed dolphins are commonly seen. Occasional sightings are made of false killer and short-finned pilot whales, along with common, spinner, and spotted dolphins.

Whale-watch clubs are popular in Japan. At both Ogasawara and Zamami, the local whale-watching associations send out newsletters, design T-shirts for sale, and manufacture buttons and bumper stickers. They also help manage the promotion and sales of whale-watching trips. These are two of the most active and popular whale-watch clubs in Japan. Each has hundreds of members from all over the country and abroad. Club members regularly receive news of their favorite whales, whale-watch schedules, invitations to special events, and special prices for whale watching.

Special Features

Japanese scientists aboard whale-watch boats in Ogasawara and the Keramas have compiled a photo-identification catalog of more than 600 individual humpback whales. A female humpback whale photographed in April 1990 and March 1991 in Ogasawara, turned up in August 1991 on the summer feeding grounds off British Columbia, some 4,900 miles (7,900 km) away. Those feeding grounds are commonly used by humpback whales from Hawaii, but not Japan. Yet a few humpbacks are known to migrate to British Columbia not only from Japan and Hawaii, but from Mexico as well. This indicates some exchange on the feeding grounds among the three main breeding areas (Hawaii, Mexico, and Japan) for North Pacific humpback whales.

Traveler's Notes

When to visit *Feb–Apr, humpback whales winter on the mating and calving grounds around Ogasawara and Okinawa and the Kerama Islands; year-round, various dolphins*
Weather *Warm to hot during the season, but often windy and cool at sea*
Types of tours *Half-day tours; inflatables, diving and fishing boats; some whale watching from ferries*
Tours available *Chichi-jima and Haha-jima in the Ogasawara Islands; Zamami and Tokashiki in the Kerama Islands; Naha on Okinawa*
Information *Ogasawara Tourism Association, Chichi-jima, Ogasawara-mura, Tokyo 100-21, Japan, Ph. 81 4998 2 2587; Zamami Village Office, 109 Zamami, Zamamison-aza, Okinawa-ken, 901-34, Japan, Ph. 81 98 987 2311*

AUSTRALIA *and* OCEANIA

Whale watchers in Australia and Oceania see resident Southern Hemisphere cetaceans, as well as those using the waters for migration, mating, and calving.

Whale watching throughout the waters of Australia and Oceania has mostly developed during the 1990s. Australia and New Zealand have led the way, aided by well-developed domestic travel industries that help support whale watching, as well as attracting visitors from around the world.

In Australia, humpback and southern right whale watching was mostly land-based until 1987, when boat-based tours operating out of Hervey Bay, Queensland, gained in popularity. Along with members of many communities near the eastern and southwestern coasts of Australia, watchers avidly follow the annual migrations of the humpbacks.

Australia also offers outstanding destinations for viewing migrating southern right whales. In Warrnambool, Victoria, since the early 1980s, the southern right whale nursery at Logan's Beach has attracted thousands of visitors every year. Some adventurous tourists trek to the head of the Great Australian Bight or the Bunda Cliffs, along the Eyre Highway, for some of the most spectacular cliffside whale watching in the world.

East Coast Australia
INDIAN OCEAN
Western Australia
Southern Australia
SOUTHERN OCEAN

Coastal cliffs (top) of South Australia. A southern right whale and dolphins (left) off Australia's south coast.

At Monkey Mia, in Western Australia, bottlenose dolphins have enjoyed a friendly relationship with humans for many years. Thousands of people visit every year, wading in the shallow water where dolphins come to interact with their land-based neighbors. Several other dolphin populations are found in inshore waters around Australia and these have awakened the keen interest of researchers and whale watchers alike.

New Zealand's whale watching began around the same time as Australia's, but has since taken off in different directions and with a flavor all its own. Whales spotted around New Zealand are largely toothed whale species that are resident rather than migratory. Sperm whale watching at Kaikoura, New Zealand's premier watching site, has helped create one of the world's most charming communities dedicated to whale watching. Elsewhere around New Zealand, rare dolphins lend a special magic to the watching—the Hector's dolphin is found only in New Zealand waters. Dusky dolphins, also seen in a number of other Southern Ocean locations, are still most frequently spotted here.

Although the whale-watching opportunities in the South Pacific islands of Oceania are less developed than those in Australia and New Zealand, nearly every year another island sets up watching opportunities. These are boosting tourism, which means that the cetaceans may be better looked after. Such tours are sometimes associated with research work or, occasionally, diving tours. Tonga has taken the lead with humpback tours to meet mothers and calves wintering near the islands, but other Pacific islands also have nascent dolphin-watching industries. These include Tahiti, Niue, Moorea, Fiji, New Caledonia, and Western Samoa.

Humpback mother and calf, Tonga, South Pacific Ocean.

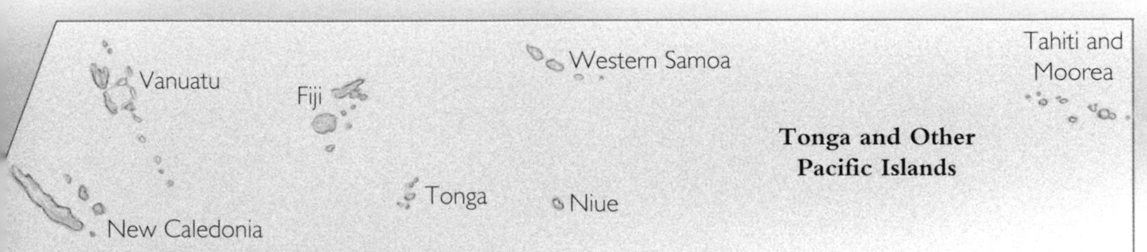

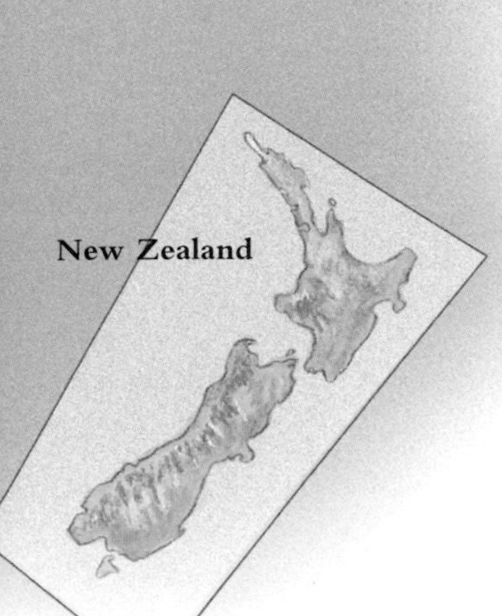

Dusky dolphins playing off Kaikoura, New Zealand's premier watching site.

East Coast Australia

Australia and Oceania

Huge humpbacks roll over and over in the wake of the boat, as if to show off the extensive whiteness of their bellies, flippers, and flukes. Their immense bodies are set off by cascades of froth and foam. It's morning in Hervey Bay, and the sun is rising over nearby Fraser Island, the world's largest sand island. Hervey Bay, the whale-watch capital of Australia, is 180 miles (290 km) north from Brisbane.

Between August and October, several hundred migrating humpback whales pass through the sandy strait between Fraser Island and the mainland. The first to arrive, from their winter grounds around the Whitsunday Islands, are the older juveniles, followed by the mature males and, finally, mothers and calves. These whales stop off in the warm, sheltered waters of Hervey Bay before moving on to their final summer destination, Antarctica, where they feed on fish and krill.

The humpbacks of the Southern Hemisphere are known to be whiter on the underside than their northern counterparts, although both are considered the same species. In recent years, an all-white humpback—an albino—has been sighted off eastern Australia.

Most of the whale-watch boats depart from Urangan Harbour, Hervey Bay, but others leave from Bundaberg, farther north, and other towns along the Queensland coast. The humpbacks, as well as various dolphins, can be seen in the waters between the Great Barrier Reef and the mainland. From Airlie Beach, tours depart to see humpback whales on their winter breeding grounds in the waters surrounding the Whitsunday Islands.

In New South Wales, south of Queensland, humpbacks pass Byron Bay at Cape Byron, Australia's most easterly point. Land-based whale watchers have assisted researchers here every year by counting the humpbacks passing below the cliffs. These whales come closest to shore and in the greatest numbers during June and July.

A humpback whale shows its pale ventral side as it swims upside down in Hervey Bay off the east coast of Australia.

Seven bottlenose dolphins surfing off the coast south of Wollongong (above). Cape Byron (left), Australia's most easterly point.

Some 50 miles (80 km) south of Sydney, at Wollongong, humpback tours have a split season. For the northward migration, the season is late May to mid-July; on the southward journey, the humpbacks pass from late September to November. Dolphin sightings include mainly bottlenose, as well as common and Risso's dolphins.

The town of Eden, about 300 miles (485 km) south of Sydney, on Twofold Bay, offers a combination of historical whaling interest and whale-watch tours. These tours can catch migrating humpbacks during their northerly migration in June and July and their return south in October to November. Because Twofold Bay is near the far southeastern corner of Australia, it is both the first and last land point the humpbacks pass on their journey to and from Antarctica. It is also possible to see bottlenose dolphins here and, sometimes, southern right and blue whales, as well as Australian fur seals.

Special Features

Visitors to Hervey Bay may want to spend an extra day or more exploring sandy Fraser Island, listed as a World Heritage site. It has tropical rain forest, heathland covered in wildflowers, and long, sandy beaches. Most of it is protected as a national park. Seventy miles (112 km) long and 14 miles (22 km) across at its widest point, Fraser Island has numerous lakes, hiking trails, and hundreds of native animals and birds. The forest trees include swamp mahoganies, forest red gums, and various eucalypts, including blackbutts and scribbly gums. Don't miss Rainbow Gorge and Woongoolver Creek, the Maneno shipwreck, the Cathedral Sandcliffs, and the wild horses. Along the high dunes on the west side of the island are excellent land-based lookouts for humpbacks, often seen playing close to the island along Platypus Bay. Remember to take your own food and water.

TRAVELER'S NOTES

When to visit *Humpback whales: Queensland, including Hervey Bay, Aug–Nov; New South Wales, including Wollongong, late May–mid-July, late Sept–Nov, and Eden, June–July, Oct–Nov. Dolphins: year-round*

Weather *Queensland coast, warm to hot on humpback breeding grounds; New South Wales, cool to cold on water*

Types of tours *Half- and full-day tours, some extended multi-day expeditions; inflatables, sailboats, diving boats, and large whale-watch boats; land-based whale watching also good*

Tours available *Queensland: Airlie Beach, Bundaberg, Hervey Bay, Tangalooma; New South Wales: Byron Bay, Coff's Harbour, Eden, Fairy Meadow, Wollongong*

Information *Queensland Tourist and Travel Corp., Level 36, Riverside Centre, 123 Eagle St., Brisbane, Queensland 4000, Australia, Ph. 61 7 3406 5400; Tourism New South Wales Travel Centre, 19 Castlereagh St., Sydney, New South Wales 2000, Australia, Ph. 61 2 132 077*

Southern Australia

Australia and Oceania

Southern Australia has some of the most outstanding land-based whale-watch sites in the world. Photographs taken from the cliffs and beaches are the equal of close-up photographs from boats—with the added advantage of a firm shooting platform. Forget about being seasick.

A pair of orcas spyhopping (left) off the coast of Southern Australia. Two common dolphins riding a wave at sunset (bottom right).

In South Australia, endangered southern right whales come in close to shore. Tours are rugged, multi-day excursions across the outback—a chance to see a wide variety of South Australia's native wildlife, as well as the spectacular coast around the Great Australian Bight.

Southern right whales can be seen all along the Bunda Cliffs, tracing an 80 mile (130 km) stretch of the Eyre Highway through Nullarbor National Park. Visitors can stay at the caravan park, the Nullarbor Hotel-Motel, or camp in the national park. For a camping permit, contact the National Parks and Wildlife Service in Ceduna.

The most reliable spot for whale watching is farther east, at Twin Rocks, at the head of the Great Australian Bight. Up to 70 whales have been seen at one time, some within 325 feet (100 m) of the shore. Twin Rocks is situated on Yalata Aboriginal land, 685 miles (1,100 km) by road from Adelaide along the Eyre Highway. All whale watchers must obtain permits at the Yalata or Nullarbor Roadhouses on the Eyre Highway, before attempting to cross Yalata lands.

More accessible to Adelaide, within an hour or two's drive, are various other southern right whale lookouts. In recent years, the most popular has been the Victor Harbor coastline, south of Adelaide, from the Bluff to Middleton Bay. Other possible sites include Waitpinga, Parsons Beach, and Goolwa.

Although the southern right whale is by far the most commonly seen whale, whale watchers should watch out for other cetacean species. At least 25 species have been recorded along Southern Australia, many of them from strandings, so beachcombers may come across

A southern right whale with her calf (above) off the coast from the Nullarbor National Park, South Australia. There is also excellent land-based whale watching (right) at Warrnambool, Victoria.

some as well, while looking for cetaceans surfacing and spouting offshore. Possibilities include orcas; bottlenose and common dolphins; humpback, blue, minke, pilot, false killer, and sperm whales; as well as various beaked whale species. This is one of the few places in the world where regular strandings of rare pygmy right whales occur.

Every year between May and late October, the city of Warrnambool, Victoria, attracts thousands of visitors who come to see the southern right whale nursery at Logan's Beach. These whales come in close to shore and can be spotted from various observation platforms. Logan's Beach is only 2½ miles (4 km) from Warrnambool, and 165 miles (265 km) from Melbourne.

Special Features

Visitors to Australia's southeastern coast can watch dolphins, although this site is not as popular as the world famous dolphin watching offered at Monkey Mia, in Western Australia (see p. 452). One accessible dolphin population in Victoria lives in Port Phillip Bay, which is one of Melbourne's busy holiday regions. More than 100 bottlenose dolphins living here have been photo-identified and studied since 1990 by the Dolphin Research Project, Inc. Like bottlenose dolphins everywhere, those found in Port Phillip Bay are typically friendly and curious. Boat tours to see the dolphins are also offered, especially around Point Nepean, and some years humpback, southern right, killer, and pilot whales, as well as orcas, come into the bay.

TRAVELER'S NOTES

When to visit *Year-round bottlenose dolphins at the Head of Bight, South Australia, and Port Phillip Bay, Victoria (summer best at south end of bay); May–Oct southern right whales at the Head of Bight and other bays along the South Australia coast; mid-June–Oct southern right whales at Head of Bight and Victor Harbor, SA, and Logan's Beach, Vic.*

Weather *Cool to cold on the water, but can be warm from sheltered lookouts*

Types of tours *Largely land-based whale watching, some organized as multi-day expeditions, but most are informal day trips; some half- and full-day boat tours, inflatables, and small boats out of Port Phillip Bay*

Tours available *South Australia: Ceduna, Victor Harbor; Victoria: Moorabbin, Logan's Beach*

Information *South Australian Travel Centre, 1 King William St., Adelaide, South Australia 5000, Australia, Ph. 61 8 212 1505; Tourism Victoria, 55 Swanston St., GPO Box 2219T, Melbourne, Victoria 3001, Australia, Ph. 61 3 653 9777*

Western Australia

Australia and Oceania

Since the 1960s, the dream of meeting dolphins in the shallows of a sandy beach has attracted people from around the world to Monkey Mia. Located at the southern end of Shark Bay, on the Indian Ocean, Monkey Mia is 505 miles (810 km) north of Perth, and is the most frequented cetacean-watching site in Western Australia, with 100,000 visitors a year.

Visitors commonly wade into the warm, shallow water while the dolphins approach, swimming up to nudge bathers' legs, and allowing themselves to be touched. Those swimming close to shore are a small group of six bottlenose dolphins—currently three adult females and their three calves. From time to time, the individual dolphins have changed, yet the number has stayed at about six, and their interaction with humans continues, most days, year after year.

Local rangers are on hand to supervise, provide information, and make sure that only a few people enter the water at a time. Visitors stand in the shallows and watch the dolphins swim up to them. In the distance, and from other points along the shore, many more dolphins belonging to the population living in the area can be seen.

Because of the accessibility of these dolphins and the clear-water viewing conditions, world researchers have taken the opportunity to study their behavior. Much of what we know about bottlenose dolphin social behavior comes from those studied at Monkey Mia, as well as another bottlenose group resident in the waters off Sarasota, Florida, in the United States.

A ranger keeps watch on proceedings as a bottlenose dolphin (above) greets tourists in the waters of Monkey Mia (right).

Visitors to Monkey Mia during the humpback whale migration, from July to September, can also take boat tours or watch whales from land. Whale-watch boats depart from Denham, 15½ miles (25 km) away, or from Carnarvon, 217 miles (350 km) away. The best land-based spot is Point Quobba, north of Carnarvon. You can drive or fly to Denham and Carnarvon from Perth.

Besides the Shark Bay area, Western Australia has thriving boat-based humpback whale

A southern right whale calf (above) learns survival skills in the shallow waters around Cape Arid National Park, Western Australia.

watching on the southwest coast, especially around Perth. One of the most popular ports is Hillary's Boat Harbour, a few miles north of Perth. Boats also leave from Fremantle, south of Perth. Most of the humpbacks come through between September and November, staying close to shore, with many traveling between Rottnest Island and the mainland—easily accessible to whale watchers on half-day trips. Tour boats show a 97 percent success ratio with an average of four whales seen per trip. For the most part, the boats don't venture far offshore. In recent years, particularly out of Geraldton, about 250 miles (400 km) north of Perth, the boat trips in search of humpback whales have occasionally found Bryde's, sei, and minke whales.

Special Features

The Albany area, 255 miles (410 km) south of Perth, is accessible by direct flight or road and provides another window on whales in Western Australia. Albany was the last whaling site in Australia. Since the Cheynes Beach Whaling Station closed in 1978, the whaling boat *Cheynes IV* has been on display. Also worth a visit is Albany Whale World, devoted to the region's whaling history. Fortunately, some whales still survive and on regular tours from August to November, you can meet endangered southern right whales. Many tours offer a full experience of the region with a visit to the old whaling station and sightseeing around King George Sound to see local seals, bottlenose dolphins, pelicans, and other birds.

TRAVELER'S NOTES

When to visit *Year-round bottlenose dolphins at Monkey Mia (Apr–Oct, dolphins approach swimmers most often, with less frequent sightings Nov-Mar); May–Oct southern right whales (Aug–Nov is prime for Albany area); Sept–Nov humpbacks in Perth area (July–Sept in northern part of Western Australia)*
Weather *Generally cool on the sea for boat-based whale watching; shore-based dolphin and whale watching can be warm or even hot in summer months, particularly at Monkey Mia*
Types of tours *Half- and full-day tours, some extended multi-day expeditions; inflatables, sailboats, and large boats; land-based whale watching*
Tours available *Perth, South Perth, Hillary's Harbour, Fremantle, Geraldton, Exmouth, Carnarvon, Albany, Denham, Monkey Mia (land-based watching)*
Information *Western Australia Tourism Commission, Floors 5 & 6, 16 Saint George's Terrace, Perth 6000, Western Australia, Australia, Ph. 61 8 9220 1700; Shark Bay Tourist Bureau, 71 Knight Terrace, Denham, Western Australia 6537, Australia, Ph. 61 8 99481 253*

New Zealand

Australia and Oceania

Few communities in the world have become so captivated and identified with whales and dolphins as Kaikoura, New Zealand. Since the late 1980s, Kaikoura—a small town at the foot of snow-capped peaks on a point jutting out into the sea, on the east coast of the South Island—has become an idyllic spot to spend a few days, go whale and dolphin watching, maybe see some seals, or take the time to go hiking.

New Zealand's Hector's dolphins (left), Banks Peninsula. Watching dusky dolphins (far right).

Sperm whale watching in Kaikoura is a year-round phenomenon. The main operation is run as a community trust by the local Maori people. Their boats boast a 97 percent success rate for sightings between April and July and about 95 percent for the rest of the year. Of course, on some days it is not possible to go out because of bad weather or rough seas, but when you are sitting in a friendly local cafe reading whale brochures, it is comforting to know that the whales will still be out there when the weather, with any luck, clears in the next day or two.

Along with sperm whale watching, Kaikoura offers specialized tours for dolphin watching, swimming with dolphins, and whale watching from a helicopter or seaplane. You can swim with pods of playful dusky dolphins in the morning and fly over them and the sperm whales by helicopter or seaplane in the afternoon. Don't worry: each type of whale watching has its own regulated code of contact, so the animals are not disturbed. Aircraft, for example, cannot swoop too low, as the sound might bother the whales.

There are also kayak tours and various land-based hiking and birding tours on offer. Best access to Kaikoura is through Christchurch airport followed by a few hours' drive north along the coast of the South Island.

The sperm whales living off the coast from Kaikoura are bachelor males (see also p. 307). Within the deep canyons located close to shore,

The snow-capped Kaikoura Range (above) provides a dramatic backdrop to New Zealand's most popular whale-watching area.

they hunt and catch squid to feed on. Besides the sperm whales, long-finned pilot whales sometimes come in to dive for squid, and occasionally orcas also swim through the area.

Tour operators use directional hydrophones to locate sperm whale clicks. They then head for the sounds and wait for the whales to surface. After about an hour watching the whales, the tour boats typically take a swing inshore to look for Hector's or dusky dolphins. And if they cannot be found, there is always a visit to the seal colonies, on or near the rocks.

Additional places where common, bottlenose, and other dolphin watching occurs, include South Island ports such as Picton and Te Anau. On the North Island, there are tours in the Bay of Islands, accessible through Paihia, and in the Bay of Plenty, accessible through Tauranga and Whakatane. Orcas and long-finned pilot whales are also sometimes seen in these areas.

Experienced whale watchers are always on the lookout for rare beaked whales around New Zealand—a good place to find them. Unfortunately, most beaked whale records are of strandings. New Zealand has some of the highest numbers of cetacean strandings in the world.

Special Features

Besides sperm whales, New Zealand offers the rare chance to see a small, attractive dolphin with a rounded dorsal fin—the Hector's dolphin. This dolphin is found only in waters around New Zealand. It belongs to the rare genus of *Cephalorhynchus* dolphins with just four members; two of the others are seen off South America, and one off South Africa. Even most cetacean scientists have never seen these dolphins at sea. Perhaps a handful of people worldwide have seen all four. Kaikoura is one place to see Hector's dolphins, but they are even more commonly found farther south, from Akaroa on the Banks Peninsula.

TRAVELER'S NOTES

When to visit *Year-round sperm whales, Hector's, common, and bottlenose dolphins; Oct–May dusky dolphins close to shore (esp. Kaikoura)*
Weather *Cool (summer) to cold (winter) on the sea, Kaikoura, South Island and southern North Island; cool (winter) to warm (summer) on the sea from Bay of Plenty to Bay of Islands, North Island*
Types of tours *Half- and full-day tours, extended multi-day expeditions; inflatables, sailboats, motorboats, large whale-watch boats; some whale watching from ferries; helicopter and fixed-wing aircraft*
Tours available *South Island: Kaikoura, Akaroa, Picton, and Te Anau; North Island: Paihia, Tauranga, and Whakatane*
Information *Canterbury Visitor Information Centre, PO Box 2600, Christchurch, New Zealand, Ph. 64 3 379 9629*

Tonga and Other Pacific Islands

Australia and Oceania

The Kingdom of Tonga, the "Friendly Islands," is located in the western South Pacific, 1,400 miles (2,250 km) northeast of New Zealand. Like most South Pacific nations, it is composed mainly of water. Of about 170 islands, only some 36 are inhabited. There are three main island groups: two are coral formations, while the third, Vava'u, is volcanic.

Humpback whales return in large numbers from the Antarctic to the warm seas around Vava'u to mate and calve during the austral winter. Access to the Vava'u group is through the airport north of Neiafu, on 'Uta Vava'u. During the whale-watch season, whales around Vava'u can be seen fighting over potential mates. Even before humpbacks are sighted, a hydrophone is often dropped below the surface of the water to eavesdrop on the singing males.

Whale-watch trips are offered out of the Bounty Bar in Neiafu. Besides humpbacks and occasional sperm whales, there are short-finned pilot whales and spinner and other tropical dolphins that might approach the boat. Whale watching and research are new here, so future trips may reveal more resident or migratory ceatceans.

Several hundred miles northwest of Tonga lies the much more extensive and populous Republic of Fiji, with 844 islands and islets, about 100 of which are inhabited. The larger islands, including the two main ones, are rugged and mountainous. The Great Sea Reef of coral stretches for 300 miles (500 km) along the western fringe of Fiji. Sailboat, kayak, and diving tours are available, offering sightings of tropical dolphins. In 1995, photo identification and behavioral research began with a small pod of spinner dolphins living near Tavarua and Namotu islands, better known as destinations for serious surfers. These small islands, west of Nadi at the southern edge of the reef that encloses the Mamanucas, are accessible by boat from Nadi, on Viti Levu. Researchers estimate that 60 dolphins live in the area and, according to islanders, dolphins have lived there as long as

A humpback surfaces in the waters off Tahiti (top). Spinner dolphins (above) are found in many parts of the Pacific Ocean.

anyone can remember. Tourists are invited to spend a day cruising on a boat specially designed for dolphin watching and research.

Cetaceans can also be seen in French Polynesia (Tahiti), New Caledonia, Niue, and Western Samoa. Exciting spinner dolphin tours, begun by an American scientist studying the spinner's behavior, depart from the Richard Gump South Pacific Biological Station on Cook's Bay, on the north side of Moorea, and take visitors outside the lagoon to meet the dolphins. In New Caledonia, dolphin tours are available out of Noumea, and humpback whales are sometimes seen in August and September. There is occasional humpback whale watching from Niue and Western Samoa, but tours are yet to become as popular as in Tonga.

Fiji, "the soft coral capital of the world," has year-round diving only 10–15 minutes by boat from most resorts. Fiji also has live-aboard dive boats, and resorts cater to low- and high-budget divers. Some of the interesting species to be seen include hundreds of hard and soft coral, sea fans, and sea sponges. You might meet the territorial clownfish, living in a symbiotic relationship with the poisonous sea anemone, and surgeonfish, trumpetfish, red lizard fish, batfish, and parrotfish. At the edges of the reefs are barracuda, jackfish, small reef sharks, stingrays, and large parrotfish. Large sharks and the aggressive gray reef shark are usually found away from the coast in deeper water. But remember: coral is alive and fragile—only travel with ecologically sound operators and follow the rules.

Special Features

No matter which island you visit, don't miss the coral reef diving. The greatest biological diversity in the tropical South Pacific is invariably underwater. If you can't scuba dive, try snorkeling.

The Vava'u group (above) comprises a part of some 170 islands making up Tonga.

TRAVELER'S NOTES

When to visit *July–Nov humpback whales in Tonga; year-round, tropical dolphins in all locations, but Apr–Oct best for weather*

Weather *Hot during dry season Apr–Oct; sun averages 6–8 hours a day, even in wet season*

Types of tours *Half- and full-day tours, some extended multi-day expeditions; inflatables, sailboats, kayaks, and diving boats*

Tours available *Tonga: Vava'u; Fiji: Nadi; French Polynesia: Moorea; New Caledonia: Noumea*

Information *Tourism Council for the South Pacific, 35 Loftus Street, PO Box 13119, Suva, Fiji Islands, Ph. 679 304 177; Whale Watch Vava'u Ltd., c/- Bounty Bar, Private Bag, Neiafu, Vava'u, Kingdom of Tonga, Ph. 676 70 576*

THE POLES

Against stark, frozen vistas, the poles provide a variety of spectacular sights for whale watchers, with an explosion of life throughout the ecosystem.

Before the long history of whaling began, the Arctic and Antarctic regions, in summer, held the greatest density of whales on Earth. Blue, fin, sei, minke, humpback, along with other great whales, gathered in huge numbers around the poles to feed on massive concentrations of krill and other plankton, fish, and squid. During the winter months, most whale species retreated, some migrating as far as the equator to give birth, mate, and raise their calves.

But whaling changed all that. Arctic whaling commenced in 1607 off Svalbard, north of Norway, and spread from there. The bowhead whale was the first Arctic casualty, with many other species following.

Despite its geographic position at the top of the continents of Europe, Asia, and North America, the Arctic has been only a little more accessible for tourism than Antarctica. Traveling around the Arctic is difficult and expensive. The first whale-watch trips, established in the early 1980s, were from North America, to the subarctic of northern Manitoba, Canada, where belugas and polar bears can be seen in and around the Churchill River. Since then, trips to see belugas and narwhals in northern Canada and Greenland have been organized. Since the end of the Cold War, former Russian icebreakers have been made available for extended

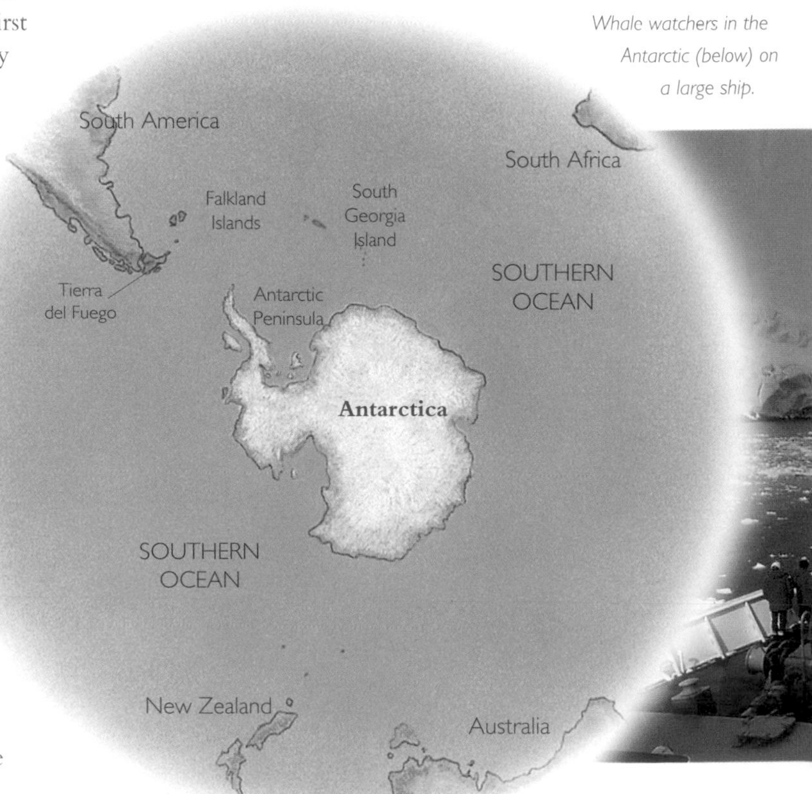

Whale watchers in the Antarctic (below) on a large ship.

Scanning the ice floes in Antarctica (left) for orcas. Belugas (below) gather to swim and molt in the freshwater shallows off the coast in the Canadian Arctic.

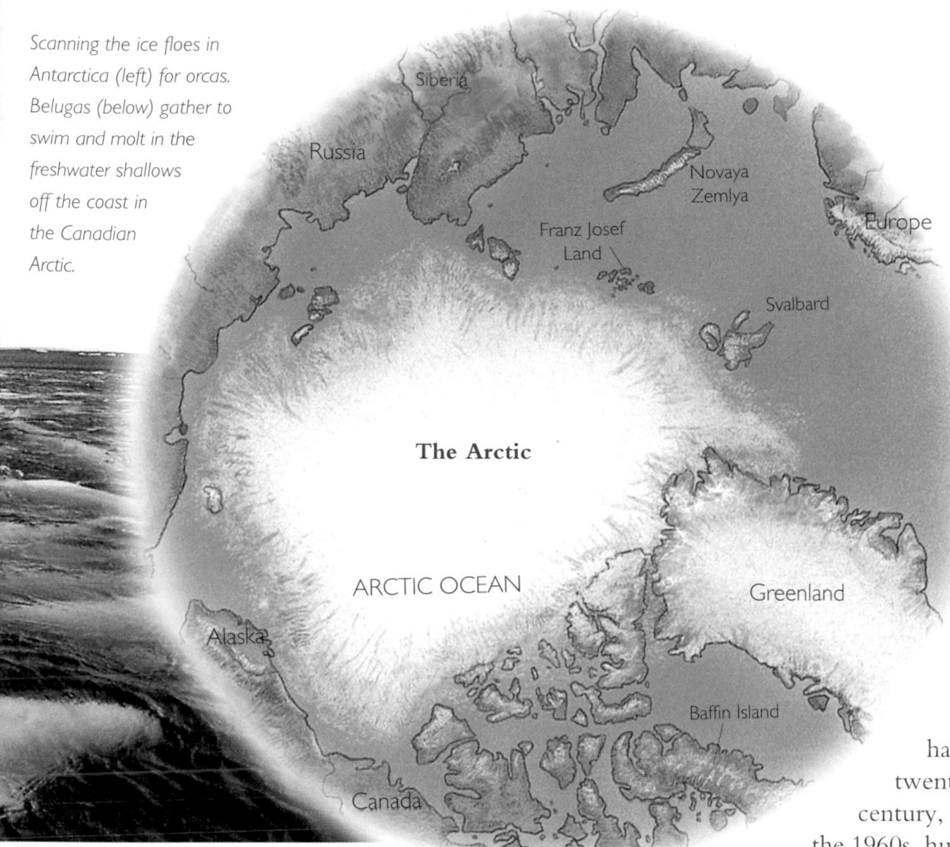

nature cruises to the far north of Canada, Greenland, Norway, and Russia. These boats stop in various ports during their northern journeys, often encountering bowheads, narwhals, and belugas—three cetacean species found only in Arctic regions.

For a long time, the Antarctic, in contrast, seemed to be relatively safe from the threat of whaling. But with the advent of exploding harpoons and long-range factory ships, modern whaling took its toll.

In the first half of the twentieth century, up until the 1960s, hundreds of thousands of whales died in the Antarctic, as one large whale species after another was hunted nearly to extinction. Today, the whales in this region are largely protected from whaling, and some species are slowly rebuilding their numbers. But it will take years before we know if endangered blue whales, for example, will survive, much less return to anything approaching their original numbers.

When the first cruise ship visited the Antarctic Peninsula in 1957, whale watching was unheard of. By the 1980s however, it had become a key feature of organized tours, along with viewing penguins, seals, and giant icebergs. Antarctic cruises offer half a dozen cetacean species seen only in the far south of the Southern Hemisphere, in addition to most of the large baleen whales and the ubiquitous orca.

The Arctic

The Poles

Arctic whales, including tusked narwhals, snow-white belugas, and massive bowhead whales, hold a mystery all their own. For many years, only scientists and adventurers could witness these arctic sea mammals in their icy, year-round habitat. However, now there are organized tours to meet them, mainly during the long summer days of the midnight sun.

True arctic whale watching is accessible through much of the Arctic. Many of these trips are cruises, mainly aboard icebreakers or specially strengthened ships, with itineraries spanning two or more areas, including Greenland, northern Canada, northern Alaska, Svalbard (the far northern island group off northern Norway), Siberia, and the Russian islands of Franz Josef Land and Novaya Zemlya. Such trips are not solely for whale watchers, but they include regular sightings of arctic whales, as well as (depending on location) minke, fin, and humpback whales and orcas. Gray whales can be seen in the eastern Russian and Alaskan Arctic. Closer to land or ice, you can sometimes see polar bears, walruses, seals, arctic foxes, and many bird species. Helicopters and inflatable Zodiac boats, which are carried on some ships, are also used to find and view whales and other wildlife up close.

Summer is the season various baleen whales come to the Arctic, or subarctic, to feed. At that time, some belugas move into arctic river mouths, while narwhals are seen offshore, segregated into all-male and nursery groups.

Besides cruises, it is possible to fly to remote arctic outposts in northern Canada, Svalbard, and Greenland to take excursions in small boats. One of the better areas is in northwestern Greenland, north of Disko Bay, where whale-watch safaris into Uummannaq Fiord and Baffin Bay depart from Uummannaq. The Uummannaq Tourist Service offers four- to five-hour tours, with hydrophones, and a virtual certainty in summer of seeing and

An impressive show of tusks by male narwhals in the cold waters surrounding the eastern Canadian Arctic (left).

Belugas in the shallows of Somerset Island, in the Canadian Arctic (above). Hudson Bay, near Churchill, Manitoba (right).

hearing whales. Fin whales are the most common, followed by minke whales, narwhals, and belugas, and occasionally sperm whales and orcas. Some of these species can be more easily seen in other parts of the world, but this is one of the few places to find the legendary narwhal, the animal whose tusks were once sold as unicorn horns. Imagine crossed tusks protruding from the water, and the dull thud of tooth against tooth as males joust. (For more information on Greenland, see pp. 432-3.)

Northern Canada also has whale-watch tours from sites around Pond Inlet and Somerset Island to see belugas, narwhals, and bowheads. These are rugged, multi-day tours offered by charter or through expedition tour companies. Some are led by Inuit or local people. There are even whale-watch expeditions by sea kayak.

Special Features

Perhaps the most accessible subarctic location is Churchill, on Hudson Bay, northern Manitoba, Canada. Churchill is accessible by jet or 40-hour passenger train from Winnipeg. Although considerably south of the Arctic Circle, belugas come in close to the mouth of the Churchill River, swimming some miles upriver from June through August. Churchill is also known as the "polar bear capital of Canada." Polar bears wander into the area from early July. By September, when the belugas leave the river mouth to head back to the open Arctic, the polar bears reach large numbers that peak in late October and early November. August is the best month for those who want the chance to see both belugas and polar bears. All tours can be booked in Churchill.

TRAVELER'S NOTES

When to visit *June–Aug for most of the Arctic; Aug best for belugas and polar bears in Churchill*

Weather *Cold on water throughout the Arctic, snow possible; Churchill, warm temperatures by day, often dipping to freezing at night*

Types of tours *Half- and full-day tours, some extended multi-day expeditions; inflatables, sailboats, and large whale-watch boats*

Tours available *Canada: Churchill; Greenland: Uummannaq; Norway: Sveagruva on Svalbard*

Information *Greenland Tourism a/s, Postbox 1552, DK-3900 Nuuk, Greenland, Ph. 299 22888; Churchill Nature Tours, PO Box 429, Erickson, Manitoba ROJ OPO, Canada, Ph. 1 204 636 2968; Marine Expeditions Inc., 30 Hazelton Avenue, Toronto, Ontario M5R 2E2, Canada, Ph. 1 416 964 9069; Noble Caledonia Ltd., 11 Charles St., Mayfair, London W1X 8LE, England Ph. 44 171 409 0376; Arcturus Expeditions Ltd., PO Box 850, Gartocharn, Alexandria, Dunbartonshire G83 8RL, Scotland, Ph. 44 1389 830 204*

Antarctica

The Poles

In many ways the ultimate whale-watch destination, Antarctica is a marine paradise for the nature lover. Most of the cold, deep water that fills the world's ocean basins comes from here. Massive upwellings around the continent create an environment ideal for plankton, which supports the largest and most massive aggregations of krill in the sea.

During the first half of the twentieth century, up until the 1960s, the seas around Antarctica were the scene of large-scale whale slaughter. Even today, several decades after factory whaling has stopped, blue, fin, humpback, and sei whales still exist in far fewer numbers, with the minke whale being the sole exception.

The only way for most people to get to Antarctica and watch whales is aboard a large cruise ship. These trips are not exclusively whale-watch tours but extended cruises that include sightings of birds, seals, icebergs, penguins, and cetaceans, as well as visits to Antarctic research stations. The cruises are offered by various companies based in the United States, Canada, Britain, Germany, Australia, and New Zealand. However, tour agencies worldwide will sell space on the ships. There are a few air tours to Antarctica, but these are not recommended for whale watching.

Besides South American departures, some cruises leave from various ports in Australia, New Zealand, and South Africa. However, for most visitors, the main part of the journey starts in southern South America, when they board a cruise ship in Ushuaia, Argentina, or nearby southern Chile. The journey from South American ports to Antarctica takes several days, during which the ship passes through three ocean biomes, or ecological zones (see p. 248).

An orca with calf (above), possibly on the lookout for penguins. Orcas are known to knock penguins off ice floes as they float by.

The first zone is along the inshore waters around Tierra del Fuego and the surrounding islands, as the ship winds its way south past Cape Horn. Here you might see Commerson's and Peale's dolphins, and with any luck, some of the rare Burmeister's or spectacled porpoises—all found only, or mainly, in this part of the

A humpback (above) around the Antarctic Peninsula. A meeting between a tour ship and a yacht in Lemaire Channel (left).

world—as well as two Southern Hemisphere residents, the dusky dolphin and the southern bottlenose whale. As you motor across the Drake Passage and south to Antarctica, reaching the high seas off the continental shelf, hourglass dolphins sometimes accompany the ship, and you might see long-finned pilot whales and southern right whale dolphins. Keep a lookout for fin, sei, and Cuvier's beaked whales, too. Finally, as the Antarctic Peninsula nears, minke and humpback whales, which migrate closer to the ice, are more commonly seen feeding in the rich patches of krill and fish. Moving through the last two zones are opportunistic orcas, feeding on fish and seals and even knocking penguins from ice floes at times. This is life on a larger canvas than almost anywhere else in the world.

Most trips visit the Antarctic Peninsula; only the more expensive, longer cruises venture to the main continental part of Antarctica, which is 97 percent covered with ice. However, if you can include the main part of the continent, you will see more wildlife and get a glimpse of life nearer the heart of this last unknown continent in an atmosphere that is eerie and majestic.

Special Features

Some cruises stop in the Falkland Islands either before heading south for Antarctica, or on the return journey. Watch for the orcas that often feed on gentoo penguins around Sea Lion Island. Other cruises visit the subantarctic island of South Georgia, site of a large former whaling station, as well as home to fur seals, elephant seals, breeding king and macaroni penguins, and albatrosses.

Traveler's Notes

When to visit *Late Nov–Mar: baleen whales—humpback, minke, fin—feed around Antarctica, along with orcas and hourglass dolphins. The window for sailing to Antarctica is only 3–4 months*
Weather *Cold, take winter gear even in Antarctic summer; cruise ships offer shelter from rain and cold, but dress warmly to see whales close up from deck or inflatable boats launched from the ship*
Types of tours *Extended multi-day expeditions*
Tours available *Through Abercrombie & Kent (USA), Adventure Associates (Australia), Aurora Expeditions (Australia), Hanseatic Tours GMBH (Germany), Marine Expeditions Inc. (Canada), Mountain Travel-Sobek (USA), Natural Habitat Adventures (USA), Ocean Adventures (UK), Orient Lines (USA), Quark Expeditions (USA), Society Expeditions (USA), Southern Heritage Expeditions (New Zealand), Special Expeditions (USA), Travel Dynamics (USA), Wild-Oceans/WildWings (UK), and Zegrahm Expeditions (USA). Some cruise ships carry inflatables for close viewing*
Information *Contact your travel agent*

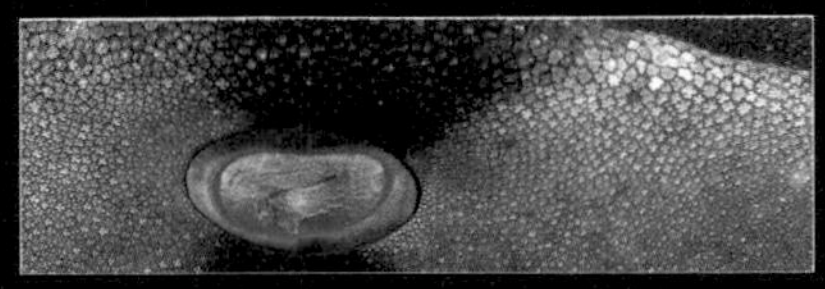

INDEX *and* GLOSSARY

Human life is limited, but knowledge is limitless.

The Preservation of Life,
CHUANG-TZU (4th century BC), Chinese writer

INDEX *and* GLOSSARY

In this combined index and glossary, **bold** page numbers indicate the main reference, and *italic* page numbers indicate illustrations and photographs.

I

J, K

L

M

S

CONTRIBUTORS

SHARKS AND RAYS

Kevin Deacon, a noted underwater photographer and marine naturalist, is also a PADI underwater instructor. He lives in Australia and is managing director of Dive 2000, which specializes in diving expeditions. His award-winning photographs appear regularly in books and magazines.

Peter Last, B.Sc. (Hons), Ph.D., trained as a marine biologist, but has since developed a major interest in the taxonomy, biogeography, and ecology of Indo-Pacific fishes. He has co-authored three comprehensive identification guides to fishes, including a recent review of the highly diverse shark and ray fauna found in Australian waters.

John E. McCosker, Ph.D., is Senior Scientist and Chair of Aquatic Biology at the California Academy of Sciences, San Francisco, U.S.A. He trained as an evolutionary biologist, and his research covers the evolution of marine fishes and the behavior of sea snakes and sharks. His published works include 170 articles and books.

Leighton Taylor, B.A. (Biology), M.S. (Zoology), Ph.D. (Marine Biology), is a Fellow of the California Academy of Sciences and a Research Associate of the Bishop Museum of the Waikiki Aquarium in Hawaii. Among his notable achievements during more than 30 years' research, he is credited with discovering the megamouth shark.

Timothy C. Tricas, B.S., M.S. (Biology), Ph.D. (Zoology), is Associate Professor of Biological Sciences at the Florida Institute of Technology, Melbourne, U.S.A. His research focuses on the sensory biology of sharks and rays, and he has also studied the feeding and mating behavior of these animals and coral reef fishes for more than 25 years.

Terence I. Walker, B.Sc., is currently working on a Ph.D. thesis. He is principal marine scientist at the Marine and Freshwater Resources Institute, Queenscliff, Australia, and has more than 25 years' experience in fisheries stock assessment, research, and management. He has published more than 100 scientific and management papers.

WHALES, DOLPHINS, AND PORPOISES

Mark Carwardine graduated in zoology from London University and worked as Conservation Officer with the World Wide Fund for Nature in Britain. He has also worked as a science writer with the United Nations Environment Programme (UNEP) in Nairobi, Kenya, and as a consultant to the World Conservation Union in Switzerland. Since 1986, Mark has been a freelance consultant, writer, lecturer, and broadcaster. He has written extensively for both children and adults.

Ewan Fordyce completed his doctorate in zoology at the University of Canterbury, New Zealand. He has been involved in the study of fossil cetacea from Antarctica, Australia, and New Zealand, and the recovery of scientific material from strandings. He is also interested in the taxonomy, anatomy, and evolution of fossil and living cetacea. He is Associate Professor, Department of Geology at the University of Otago, New Zealand, and a research associate of the Smithsonian Institution.

Peter Gill has been involved in the study of whales since 1983. He has an honors degree in zoology from Flinders University, Adelaide, Australia. Peter has undertaken extensive research in Antarctica, Australia, and New Caledonia, observing whales at close range, and also spent two years working for Greenpeace as a marine mammals researcher. He presently works in the Blue Mountains, Australia, as a freelance marine mammal researcher, photographer, lecturer, and writer.

Erich Hoyt has been going to sea since 1973 when, as a documentary filmmaker, he met orcas off the west coast of Canada. His has written books, and his articles on wildlife, conservation, and science have appeared in more than 150 magazines and newspapers. Erich has helped design exhibits at science museums in the United States. Since 1990, he has been a consultant for the Whale and Dolphin Conservation Society, writing and speaking on captive dolphins, whale watching, and marine-protected areas. He resides in Scotland.

CAPTIONS

Page 1: Great white shark from below, Australia.
Page 2: Pacific manta ray and diver off the west coast of Mexico.
Page 3: Humpback whale fluking, Hawaii.
Pages 4–5: Gray reef sharks at Bikini Atoll.
Pages 6–7: A Tunisian mosaic depicting cherubs playing with dolphins.
Pages 8–9: Common dolphins, Sea of Cortez, Mexico.
Pages 10–11: Silhouette of a manta ray, Ningaloo Reef, Western Australia.
Pages 12–13: Shark silhouetted at a cave entrance, Maui, Hawaii.
Page 14–15: Caribbean reef shark swimming over a reef in the Bahamas.
Pages 28–29: Manta ray, with remoras attached, encounters a snorkeler on the Great Barrier Reef.
Pages 50–51: Caribbean reef shark and diver, New Providence (Nassau), Bahamas.
Pages 66–67: Schooling hammerhead sharks at Cocos Island, Costa Rica.
Pages 90–91: Pacific manta ray with remora in sunshine, Pacific Ocean, west coast of Mexico.
Pages 108–109: Port Jackson shark.
Pages 175–175: Bluespotted ribbontail ray.
Pages 200–201: Snorkeler on a reef in Indonesia.
Pages 242–243: Humpback whales breaching.
Pages 246–247: Beluga whale.
Pages 256–257: Female humpback whale and her week-old calf swimming in the South Pacific Ocean near Tonga.
Pages 272–273: Humpback whales feeding on herring.
Pages 292–293: Breaching orca off Vancouver Island, Canada.
Pages 312–313: A minke whale swims upside down past a tourist boat, Husavik, Iceland.
Pages 324–325: A gray whale passes through kelp, Channel Islands, California.
Pages 338–339: Atlantic spotted dolphins swimming in the Bahamas.
Pages 390–391: Northern right whale displaying its flukes, Newfoundland.
Pages 464–465: Detail of eye and spiracle of a Port Jackson shark.

PICTURE CREDITS

t = top, b = bottom, l = left, r = right, c = center, i = inset APL = Australian Picture Library; ARL = Ardea London; Aus = Auscape International; BCA = B. & C. Alexander; BC = Bob Cranston, San Diego; BCL = Bruce Coleman Ltd; CSIRO = Commonwealth Scientific and Industrial Research Organisation (Fisheries), Australia; EV = Earthviews; FLPA = Frank Lane Picture Agency; HH = Hedgehog House, New Zealand; IPL = International Photo Library; IV = Innerspace Visions; JR = Jeffrey L. Rotman Photography; KA = Kelvin Aitken; MEPL = Mary Evans Picture Library; MC = Mark Carwardine; Minden = Minden Pictures; MMI = Marine Mammal Images; OEI = Ocean Earth Images; OSF = Oxford Scientific Films; PEP = Planet Earth Pictures; PM = Picture Media; RHPL = Robert Harding Picture Library; STO = Stock Photos P/L; TGC = The Granger Collection, New York; TIB = The Image Bank; TPL = photolibrary.com; TSA = Tom Stack and Associates; UGPA = Underwater Geographic Photo Agency; WO = Weldon Owen Pty Ltd

1 Marty Snyderman/PEP. **2** Mark Spencer. **3** c Doug Perrine/PEP. **4–5** James D. Watt/PEP. **6–7** Paris, Musée du Louvre/Lauros-Giraudon. **8–9** BC. **10–11** KA. **12–13** David B. Fleetham/TSA. **14–15** Howard Hall/OSF. **15i** Howard Hall/OSF. **16–17c** Staatl. Museum für Naturkunde Stuttgart. **16** b Ed Robinson/TSA. **17t** Ken Lucas/PEP; b Mike Brock/EV. **18t** Mike Turner/TPL; b Mark Conlin/IV. **19t** Ron and Valerie Taylor/IV; b Hulton-Deutsch/TPL. **20t** Michael Rose/FLPA; b Georgette Douwma/PEP. **21t** Nigel Marsh/UGPA; c Rudie Kuiter. **22** Neil McDaniel/Aus. **23t** Rudie Kuiter; c Rudie Kuiter/IV; b Rudie Kuiter/IV. **24t** Bruce Rasner/JR; b David B. Fleetham/Silvestris/FLPA. **25t** Doug Perrine/PEP; c Phillip Colla/IV. **26c** Tui De Roy/OSF. **27tl** Randy Morse/TSA; tr Kelvin Aitken/OEI. **28–29** Kevin Deacon/Aus. **29i** Kevin Deacon/Aus. **30t** Carl Bento/Australian Museum; br Le Monde à Vos Yeux/Gamma/PM. **31tr** Dr Samuel Gruber/IV; bl Ron and Valerie Taylor/ARL. **32t** Fitzwilliam Museum, University of Cambridge/Bridgeman Art Library; c David B. Fleetham/TSA, b Toby Adamson/Environmental Images. **33t** Stuart Bowey/Ad-Libitum; b P. Morris/ARL. **34t** Image Library, State Library of N.S.W.; b Mark Conlin/IV. **35t** Doug Perrine/Aus; c Ron and Valerie Taylor/IV. **36t** ZEFA/APL; b Dan Guravich/TPL. **37t** Alan Levenson/TPL; b Greg Vaughn/TSA. **38t** Kelvin Aitken/OEI; b David B. Fleetham/TSA. **39t** Jean-Paul Ferrero/Aus; b Doug Perrine/PEP. **40l** Tammy Peluso/TSA; r Rodney Fox/JR. **41t** Doug Perrine/IV; b Vandystadt/APL. **42** David B. Fleetham/OSF. **43t** Jeffrey L. Rotman; b Ron and Valerie Taylor/IV. **44t** C. S. Johnson; b C. S. Johnson. **45t** Rebecca Saunders; c Marty Snyderman/IV. **46c** Kevin Deacon/OEI; b Kevin Deacon/OEI. **47t**, b Kevin Deacon/OEI. **48t** Kevin Deacon/OEI; b Paul Steel/STO. **49t** Jean-Paul Ferrero/Aus; b Joe Sohm/STO. **50–51** Mark Spencer/Aus. **51i** Mark Spencer/Aus. **52t** Carl Roessler/IV; b Mike Bacon/TSA; **53t** Randy Morse/TSA; b Randy Morse/TSA. **54c** Kevin Deacon/OEI; b Kevin Deacon/Aus. **55t** Kevin Deacon/OEI; b Kevin Deacon/OEI. **56c** Kevin Deacon/OEI; b Kevin Deacon/OEI. **57t** Avi Klapfer/IV; b Kevin Deacon/OEI. **58t** Tom Campbell/IV; b Mark Conlin/IV. **59tl** F Jack Jackson/PEP; tr Kevin Deacon/OEI; b Rory McGuiness/Ron and Valerie Taylor. **60t**, b Kevin Deacon/OEI; c David B. Fleetham/TSA. **61** t Kevin Deacon/Aus; c Leo Collier/PEP. **62t** Kevin Deacon/OEI; b Ed Robinson/TSA **63t**, c Kevin Deacon/OEI; b Mark Spencer/Aus. **64t** David B. Fleetham/TSA; b Kevin Deacon/OEI. **65l** Kevin Deacon/OEI; r Marty Snyderman/IV. **66–67** Alex Kerstitch/PEP. **67i** Alex Kerstitch/PEP. **68** Norbert Wu. **70t** Doug Perrine/PEP; b Staatl. Museum für Naturkunde Stuttgart. **72** Flip Nicklin/Minden. **73** James D. Watt/EV. **74** Kevin Deacon. **77** Charles Glatzer/TIB. **78** Ken Lucas/PEP. **79** Ko Fujiwara/TPL. **80** TSA. **81t** Doug Perrine/PEP; r Tui De Roy/OSF. **82** Mark Conlin/IV. **83t** Doug Perrine/PEP; b D P Wilson/FLPA. **84** Mark I Jones/Aus. **85** Kevin Deacon/OEI. **87** Frans Lanting/Minden. **89t**, bl, br Doug Perrine/IV. **90–91** Becca Saunders. **91i** Becca Saunders. **92** Becca Saunders/Aus. **94t** John Cancalosi/Aus; b KA. **95t** George I. Bernard/OSF; b KA. **96t** Thor Carter/CSIRO; cr, b Thor Carter/CSIRO. **97t** Thor Carter/CSIRO; b Phillip Colla/IV. **98l** George Bingham/BCL; r Max Gibbs/OSF. **99t** David B. Fleetham/TSA; b Ocean Images Inc./TIB. **100t** Kevin Deacon/OEI; b KA. **101t** Rudie Kuiter; c Thor Carter/CSIRO; b KA. **102t**, b Thor Carter/CSIRO. **103t** Ron and Valerie Taylor; b Kathie Atkinson/Aus. **104t** Nigel Marsh/UGPA; b Michael S. Nolan/IV. **105** t Kurt Amsler/PEP; c Ed Robinson/EV. **106t** Ken Hoppen; b Marty Snyderman/PEP. **107** t Becca Saunders/Aus; b Doug Perrine/Aus. **108–109** Kelvin Aitken/OEI. **109i** Kelvin Aitken/OEI. **112t** Rudie Kuiter/IV. **113t** Kelvin Aitken/OEI; b David B. Fleetham/OSF. **114t** Saul Gonor/IV; b David B. Fleetham/IV. **115t** Monterey Bay Aquarium. **117t** Daniel Gotshall/PEP. **118t** Mark Spencer/Aus; c Georgette Douwma/PEP. **119t** Fred Bavendam/OSF; b Kelvin Aitken/OEI. **120t** Nigel Marsh/UGPA; b Kelvin Aitken/OEI. **121t** Kelvin Aitken/OEI; c Neville Coleman/UGPA; b Neville Coleman/UGPA. **122t** Fred Bavendam/OSF; b Cherie Vasas/Nature Travel and Marine Images/OEI. **123t** Kelvin Aitken/OEI; b Fred Bavendam/OSF. **124t** Kevin Deacon/OEI; b Ron and Valerie Taylor. **125t** Doug Perrine/IV; b Doug Perrine/IV. **126t** Nigel Marsh/UGPA; b Rod Salm/PEP. **127t** Kevin Deacon/Aus; b Kevin Deacon/OEI. **128t** Becca Saunders/Aus; b Kelvin Aitken/OEI. **130t** Bruce Rasner/JR; b Tom Haight/IV. **131t** Ferrari/Watt/IV. **132t** Bernie Tershy and Craig Strong/EV. **133t** Howard Hall/IV; b Tony Crabtree/OSF. **134t** Kelvin Aitken/TPL. **135t** David Hall/IV; b Darryl Torckler/TPL. **138t** Rudie Kuiter/IV; b Scott Michael/IV. **139t** Ken Lucas/PEP; b Mark Conlin/PEP. **140t** Doug Perrine/IV; b Doug Perrine/IV. **141t** Charles and Sandra Hood/BCL; b Charles and Sandra Hood/BCL. **142t** Kelvin Aitken/OEI; b Kelvin Aitken/OEI. **143t** David B. Fleetham/OSF. **144t** Mark Conlin/IV; bl Ken Lucas/PEP; br Marty Snyderman/PEP. **145t** Ken Bondy/IV. **146t** F. Jack Jackson/PEP; b Kurt Amsler/IV. **147t** David B. Fleetham/OSF; b David B. Fleetham/OSF. **148t** Doug Perrine/IV; b Doug Perrine/IV. **149t** David B. Fleetham/OSF; b Kelvin Aitken/OEI. **150t** Doug Perrine/Aus; b Flip Nicklin/Minden. **151t** Doug Perrine/IV; b Gary J Adkison/IV. **152** James D. Watt/EV. **153t** Tom Campbell/IV; b Neville Coleman/UGPA. **154t** Neville Coleman/UGPA; b Neville Coleman/UGPA. **155t** Kelvin Aitken/OEI; b Doug Perrine/IV. **156t** Brian Parker/TSA; b David B. Fleetham/TSA. **157t** Brian Parker/TSA; b David B. Fleetham/TSA. **158t** Doug Perrine/IV; b Jeffrey L. Rotman. **159t** Richard Herrmann/OSF; b Richard Herrmann/IV. **161t** Doug Perrine/IV; b Doug Perrine/IV. **162t** Pete Atkinson/PEP; b David B. Fleetham/OSF. **164t** Tui De Roy/Aus; b Jeffrey L. Rotman. **165t** Ron and Valerie Taylor; b Gary Adkison/IV. **166t** Doug Perrine/IV; b Doug Perrine/IV. **167t** Rudie Kuiter/IV; b Warren Williams/PEP. **168t** Chris Huss/IV. **169t** David B. Fleetham/OSF; b Gwen Lowe/IV. **170t** Verena Tunnicliffe/PEP. **172t** Norbert Wu/IV. **173b** David B. Fleetham/IV. **174–175** Kevin Deacon/OEI. **175i** Kevin Deacon/OEI. **178t** Rudie Kuiter/OSF. **179t** Mark Strickland/IV; b Ron and Valerie Taylor. **180t** Mike Bacon/IV; b Mike Bacon/IV. **181t** Randy Morse/TSA; b Phillip Colla/IV **182t** Robert Commer/EV; b Ken Lucas/PEP. **183t** Rudie Kuiter/IV. **184t** KA; bl Neville Coleman/UGPA; br Nigel Marsh/UGPA. **185t** Paul Kay/OSF. **186t** Scott Michael/IV. **187t** Randy Morse/TSA; b Norbert Wu/IV. **188t** Rudie Kuiter/OSF; bl Neville Coleman/UGPA; br Rudie Kuiter/OSF. **189t** Max Gibbs/OSF; b Patrice Ceisel/TSA. **190t** Georgette Douwma/PEP; c Doug Perrine/IV; cr Doug Perrine/Aus. **191t** Ben Cropp/Aus; b Nigel Marsh/UGPA. **192t** Jeffrey L. Rotman; b Kevin Deacon/OEI. **193t** Nigel Marsh/UGPA. **194t** Georgette Douwma/PEP; b Nigel Marsh/UGPA. **195t** Randy Morse/TSA; b Howard Hall/OSF. **196t** Rudie Kuiter/IV; b Pacific Stock/APL. **197t** Mark Conlin/IV; b Mike Turner/TPL. **198t** Robert Hessler/PEP. **200–201** David B. Fleetham/TSA. **201i** David B. Fleetham/TSA. **204–205** Jeffrey L. Rotman/BCL. **204b** Richard Herrmann/OSF. **205cr** Therisa Stack/BCL; b Randy Morse/BCL. **206–207** Ed Robinson/TSA. **206c** James D. Watt/IV; b Stan Osolinski/OSF. **207c** Pacific Stock/APL. **208–209** Jeff Foott/Aus. **208c** Howard Hall/OSF. **209c** Richard Ustinich/TIB; b Pieter Folkens/PEP. **210–211** Marty Snyderman/PEP. **210** b Mark Spencer/Aus. **211cl** Richard Herrmann/OSF; cr KA. **212–213** Jeff Hunter/TIB; **212c** Kurt Amsler/PEP; b Jeff Hunter/TIB. **213b** Gary Bell/APL. **214–241** Walter Iooss Jr/TIB. **214b** Jeffrey L. Rotman. **215c** Lane Photo/TIB; b Doug Perrine/IV. **216–217** Flip Nicklin/Minden. **216b** Flip Nicklin Minden/APL. **217c** Flip Nicklin Minden/APL. **218c** David B. Fleetham/IV; b William S. Paton/BCL. **219c** Charles and Sandra Hood/BCL. **220–221** Kevin Deacon/OEI. **220b** Kevin Deacon/OEI. **221c** Alex Double/PEP; b Kevin Deacon/OEI. **222–223** Graham Goldin/STO. **222cr** Ron and Valerie Taylor; c Georgette Douwma/PEP. **223** cl Ron and Valerie Taylor. **224–225** Kevin Deacon/OEI. **224c** Kevin Deacon/OEI; b Kevin Deacon/OEI. **225cl** Max Gibbs/OSF. **226–227** Jeff Hunter/TIB. **226c** KA; **227c** Steve Rosenberg Pacific Stock; b KA. **228–229** Lionel Isy-Schwart/TIB. **228b** Michael Cufer. **229c** Michael Cufer/OEI; b Michael Cufer. **230–231** KA. **230b** Dr Heinz Gert de Couet/Aus. **231c** Jean-Paul Ferrero/Aus; b Max Gibbs/OSF. **232–233** Kevin Deacon/OEI. **232bl** Kevin Deacon/OEI; br Kelvin Aitken/TPL. **233c** Kevin Deacon/OEI. **234–235** Kevin Deacon/OEI. **234b** Cherie Vasas. **235cl**, cr Kevin Deacon/OEI. **236–237** Manfred Gottschalk/TSA. **236c** KA; b Becca Sauders/Aus. **237c** Doug Perrine/IV. **238–239** Attila A Bicskos. **238b** Kevin Deacon/OEI. **239cl** Kevin Deacon/OEI; cr Kevin Deacon/Aus. **240–241** Neville Coleman/PEP. **240c** Kevin Deacon/OEI; b Kevin Deacon/OEI. **241cl** Kevin Deacon/OEI; cr Kevin Deacon/OEI. **242–243** Sanford/Agliolo/Stock. **244–245** Kevin

Schafer/HH. **246**t MC; bl James D. Watt/PEP; br Richard Coomber/PEP; bt David B. Fleetham/OSF; 247 t Doug Perrine/Aus. **248**c Colin Monteath/Aus. **248–249**c Becca Saunders/Aus. **249**r François Gohier/ARL; b Kenneth C. Balcomb III/EV. **250**c James D. Watt/PEP; bl Ian Beames/ARL. **251** b Andrea Florence/ARL. **252**c e.t. archive. **253**t François Gohier/ARL; c Michael S. Nolan/IV; b Bill Wood/PEP. **254**t Graham Robertson/Aus; c Doug Perrine/IV. **255**bl MC; br MC. **256–257** Jean-Marc La Roque/ARL. **258**t Roger-Viollet; b TGC. **259**t TGC; c Old Dartmouth Historical Society—New Bedford Whaling Museum. **260**t Ann Ronan at Image Select; b Image Library, State Library of N.S.W. **261**t MEPL; c MMI; bl MEPL; br Ian Cummings/BCA. **262**b BC. **263**t Brian Sytnyk/Stock; c Kelvin Aitken/OEI; b BC. **264**t Gleizes/Greenpeace; b Wendy Else/BCA. **265**t Harald Sund/TIB; c McTaggart/Greenpeace. **266**c Tony Arruza/TPL; b MC. **267**t Charlie Dass/TPL; b MC. **268**c Wei Dong Cheng/TIB; b Flip Nicklin/Minden. **269**t BCA. **270**b MC. **271**tl Beltra/Greenpeace; tr Geier/Greenpeace; b Steve Dawson/HH. **272–273** Michio Hoshino/Minden. **274**tl R. Ewan Fordyce; tr R. Ewan Fordyce. **275**l R. Ewan Fordyce; c R. Ewan Fordyce. **276**t Marty Snyderman/IV. **277**t Michael S. Nolan/IV; c D. Parer and E. Parer-Cook/Aus; b Richard Herrmann/OSF. **278**t Tony Martin/OSF; b Peter Gill. **279**t Doug Perrine/IV; b Tony Martin/OSF. **280**t Jeff Foott/TSA. **281**t Brandon D. Cole/IV; c Doug Perrine/IV. **282**b Flip Nicklin/Minden. **283**t R. Ewan Fordyce; b Doug Perrine/IV. **284**t Marilyn Kazmers/IV; b François Gohier/ARL. **285**t Doug Perrine/IV; c Brian Parker/TSA. **286**b Doug Perrine/IV; **287**t Ingrid Visser EV; b Kelvin Aitken/OEI. **288**t BC. **289**t Peter Gill; b Doug Perrine/IV. **291**t Jean-Paul Ferrero/ARL; c Howard Hall/PEP; b François Gohier/Aus. **292–293** BC. **294** t François Gohier/ARL; c Doug Perrine/IV; b Pieter Folkens/PEP. **295**t Andrea Florence/ARL. **296**t Doug Perrine/Aus. **296–297**t Flip Nicklin/Minden; b Doug Perrine/IV. **298**t Rod Scott; c IFAW/IV; b Doug Perrine/IV. **299**t Doug Perrine/PEP. **300**t D. Parer and E. Parer-Cook/Aus; b Doug Perrine/IV. **301**t François Gohier/ARL. **302**t Doc White/PEP; c Pieter Folkens/PEP. **303**t James D. Watt/PEP; c Clive Bromhall/OSF; b Doug Perrine/Aus. **304**c Daniel J. Cox/Liaison International/Wildlight Photo Agency; b Doug Perrine/Aus. **305**t Flip Nicklin/Minden; b Alain Ernoult/TIB. **306**c Doug Perrine/IV; b Howard Hall/OSF. **306–307**t Doug Perrine/PEP. **307**c Flip Nicklin/Minden. **308**l Richard Smyth/Aus; b Jen and Des Bartlett/OSF. **309**t Peter Gill; c Doug Perrine/IV. **310**c Jean-Paul Ferrero/ARL. **310–311**t John and Val Butler/Lochman Transparencies. **311**c The New Zealand Herald; b Jean-Paul Ferrero/Aus. **312–313** BCA. **314**t Diana McIntyre/MMI; b Howard Hall/OSF. **315**t Colin Monteath/Aus; b Jiri Lochman/Lochman Transparencies. **316**tl WO; tr WO; b Paddy Pallin. **317**t MC; b WO. **318**c Alisa Schulman/MMI. **18–319**t Steve R. Burnell, b John Eastcott/PEP. **319**tr Peter Gill. **320**t MC; b Colin Monteath/Aus. **321**t Thomas Kitchin/TSA; b Flip Nicklin/Minden. **322**t Kurt Amsler/PEP; c Ben Osborne/OSF. **323**t Michael S. Nolan/IV; r Mark Carwardine/IV. **324–325** BC. **326**t Chip Matheson/MMI. **327**t Hiroya Minakunchi/IV; b Barbara Todd/HH. **328**t Doug Perrine/PEP; c Godfrey Merlen/OSF; b MC. **331**t MC; c Phillip Colla/IV (#1188); b David B. Fleetham/OSF. **332**tl D. Parer and E. Parer-Cook/Aus; tr Thomas Kitchin/TSA; b MEPL. **334**c Doug Allan/OSF. **335**t Howard K. Suzuki/IV; c Robin W. Baird/MMI; b Doug Perrine/PEP. **336**t Diana McIntyre/MMI; c François Gohier/Aus; b Flip Nicklin/Minden. **337**t Jim Nahmens/MMI. **338–339** Doug Perrine/PEP. **340–341** as for pages 372–373 and 384–385. **342**t BC; b Katy Penland/MMI. **343**t François Gohier/ARL; b Lura Meyer/MMI. **344**t BC; b James D. Watt/IV. **345**t Greg Silber/EV. **346**t Kevin Deacon/OEI; c Ben Osborne/OSF. **347**t Tui De Roy/HH. **348**t Doug Perrine/Aus. **349**t Tui De Roy/HH; c MC. **350**t Doc White/PEP; c IPL. **351**t BC; b Mike Bacon/TSA. **352**t François Gohier/ARL; b Doug Perrine/Aus. **353**t Robert L. Pitman/EV. **354**t Whale Watch Azores/IV. **355**t Hal Whitehead/MMI; b Godfrey Merlen/OSF. **356**t Scott Benson/MMI. **357**t James D. Watt/IV. **360**t MC. **361**t Gregory Ochocki; b Flip Nicklin/Minden. **362**t Andrea Florence ARL; b Wyb Hoek/MMI. **363**t Thomas Jefferson/MMI. **364**t Ed Robinson/TSA; b Doug Perrine/IV. **365**t Doug Perrine/Aus; c Doug Perrine/Aus. **366**t Hal Whitehead/MMI; b Richard Sears/EV. **367**t Phillip Colla/IV (#44); b Marilyn Kazmers/IV. **368**t Steve Dawson HH; b Hiroya Minakuchi/IV. **369**t MC; b Paul Ensor/HH. **370**t Colin Monteath HH; b Colin Monteath/Aus. **371**t Robert L. Pitman/IV; c Steve Dawson/HH. **372**t Pete Oxford/PEP; b Robert L. Pitman/IV. **373**t Doug Perrine/IV. **374**t Robert L. Pitman/IV; b James D. Watt/PEP. **375**t Robert L. Pitman/IV; b Robert L. Pitman EV. **376**t Robert L. Pitman/IV; b James D. Watt/IV. **377**t Doug Perrine/PEP; c Flip Nicklin/Minden. **378**t Doug Perrine/Aus; b Doug Perrine/IV. **379**t François Gohier/ARL; c Robert L. Pitman/IV. **380**c Stephen Leatherwood EV. **381**t Dave B. Fleetham/TSA; b Doug Perrine/IV. **382**t BC; b Michael S. Nolan EV. **383**t Kim Westerskov/OSF; c François Gohier/ARL. **384**t Kelvin Aitken/OEI; b Doug Perrine/IV. **385**t Dennis Buurman/HH. **386**t Flip Nicklin/Minden, b Doug Allan/OSF. **387**t Jeff Foott/TSA; c Gary Milburn/TSA. **388**t Sharon Nogg/MMI; b Robin W. Baird/MMI. **389**t Kenneth C. Balcomb III/EV; b C. Faesi/MMI. **390–391** François Gohier/Aus. **392–393** as for pages 404–405. **394**t Mark Conlin/IV; b Doug Perrine/IV (Hawaii Whale Research Foundation NMES permit #633). **395**b Eric Sander Gamma/PM. **396**c Brandon D. Cole/IV; b Richard Sears/EV. **200–201**t Duncan Murrell/OSF. **397**c Nick Nicholson/TIB. **398**c Marilyn Kazmers/IV. **398–399**t Michael S. Nolan/IV. **399**c François Gohier/ARL. **400**c Tom Campbell/IV. **400–401**t BC. **401**c ACS-G Bakker/MMI. **402**c Tui De Roy/HH. **402–403**t Marilyn Kazmers/IV. **403**c MC. **404**cl Howard K. Suzuki/IV; cr Michael S. Nolan/IV. **404–405**t James D. Watt/PEP. **405**c Kjell Sandved/OSF. **406**t Mel Digiacomo/TIB; b Doug Perrine/IV. **407**c Doug Perrine/IV. **408**c David B. Fleetham/OSF. **408–409**t Monica Borobia/MMI. **409**c Ken Lucas/PEP. **410**c BCA. **410–411**t MC; b Godfrey Merlen/OSF. **411**c Joseph Devenney/TIB. **412**c MC. **412–413**t Steve Bunnell/TIB. **413**c MC; b MC. **414**c Doug Perrine/PEP. **414–415**t Marty Snyderman/PEP. **415**c Doug Perrine/PEP. **416**c Doug Perrine/Aus. **416–417**t MC. **417**c Doug Perrine/PEP; b MC. **418**t James D. Watt/EV; b Skeet McAuley/TIB. **419**c Frank Nowikowski South American Pictures. **420**c Carlos Angel Gamma/PM. **420–421**t Carlos Angel Gamma/PM. **421**c Luis Castaneda/TIB. **422**c Thomas Henningsen MMI. **422–423**t Andrea Florence ARL. **423**c Ann Ripp/TIB. **424**c Doug Perrine/PEP. **424–425**t MC. **425**c Doug Perrine/IV. **426**t Clive Collins; b Doug Perrine/IV. **427**t Adam Woolfitt/RHPL; c MC. **428**c MC. **428–429**t Michio Hoshino/Minden. **429**c BCA. **430**c Tui De Roy/Aus. **430–431**t D. Parer and E. Parer-Cook/Aus. **431**c MC. **432**c Tui De Roy/OSF. **432–433**t François Gohier/Aus. **433**c David Lomax/RHPL; b Charles Bishop/PEP. **434** b Dominic Harcourt-Webster/RHPL. **434–435**t Andrea Pistolesi/TIB. **435**c Doug Perrine/IV. **436**c Doug Perrine/Aus. **436–437**t MC. **437**c MC; b Michael Pasdzior/TIB. **438**c MC. **438–439**t A. E. Zuckerman/TSA. **439**c Jean-Paul Ferrero/Aus. **440**c Paul Slaughter/TIB; b David B. Fleetham/OSF. **441**tr Flip Nicklin/Minden; b MC. **442**c Kenneth C. Balcomb III/EV. **442–443**t P. & G. Bowater/TIB. **443**c David B. Fleetham/IV; b Rick Strange/TPL. **444**c Kyoichi Mori/OWA. **444–445**t TIB. **445**c Kyoichi Mori/OWA. **446**t M. P. Kahl/Aus; b Steve R. Burnell. **447**c Jean-Marc La Roque/Aus; b Flip Nicklin/Minden. **448**b Clive Bromhall/OSF. **448–449**t Tony Karacsonyi, Sydney. **449**c Jean-Paul Ferrero/Aus. **450**c Michel Nolan/TSA. **450–451**t Richard Smyth/Aus. **451**c Ken Stepnell/TPL; b François Gohier/ARL. **452**c Flip Nicklin/Minden. **452–453**t Richard Smyth/Aus. **453**c MC. **454**c Steve Dawson HH. **454–455**t Kim Westerskov/OSF. **455**c Dennis Buurman HH. **456**c Pete Atkinson/PEP. **456–457**t Pete Atkinson/PEP. **457**b Peter Hendrie/TIB. **458–459**c Flip Nicklin/Minden; b Harald Sund/TIB. **460**b Doug Allan/OSF. **460–461**t Doug Allan/OSF; **461**c Dominique Braud/TSA. **462**c Marc Webber/PEP. **462–463**t Colin Monteath HH. **463**c Ben Osborne/OSF. **464–465** Kelvin Aitken/OEI. **465**i Kelvin Aitken/OEI.

ILLUSTRATION CREDITS

Martin Camm 68, 69, 71, 72, 84 (non-aggressive behavior and line), 86, 86–87, 92, 93 (ref. material: 110–11 T. Tricas and J. McCosker, Proceedings of the Californian Academy of Sciences. 43 [14]: 221–38), 282, 288, 326, 329, 330, 333. **Clive Collins** 360, 361 (maps). **Marjorie Crosby-Fairall** Page trim for chapters 7 and 8 of Whales, Dolphins, and Porpoises. **Ray Grinaway** 269, 279, 323. **Gino Hasler** 73, 74, 75, 76, 77, 78, 80, 82, 251, 274, 280, 286, 296, 299, 301. **Ngaire Sales** Page trim for chapters 6, 7, and 8 of Sharks and Rays. **Roger Swainston** 112, 115, 116t 116b 117, 118, 129t, 129b, 130, 131, 132, 134, 136t, 136b, 137t, 137b, 143, 145, 146, 152, 157, 160t, 160b, 163t, 163b, 168, 170, 171l, 171r, 172, 173, 178, 1183, 185, 186, 193, 198, 199t, 199b (ref. material: 116t, 131 Ken Graham, N.S.W. Fisheries; 129t N.S.W. Fisheries; 178, 186, 198, 199t, 199b, CSIRO; 183 Museum of New Zealand Te Papa Tongarewa), 345–348, 353, 354, 356–359, 363, 373, 380, 385, 386. **Steve Trevaskis** 88. **Rod Westblade** 84 (aggressive behavior). **Kenn Backhaus** All map illustrations.